ALL THE MIRACLES OF THE BIBLE

THE "ALL" SERIES BY HERBERT LOCKYER . . .

All the Apostles of the Bible

All the Books and Chapters of the Bible

All the Children of the Bible

All the Divine Names and Titles in the Bible

All the Doctrines of the Bible

All the Holy Days and Holidays

All the Kings and Queens of the Bible

All the Men of the Bible

All the Messianic Prophecies of the Bible

All the Miracles of the Bible

All the Parables of the Bible

All the Prayers of the Bible

All the Promises of the Bible

All the Trades and Occupations of the Bible

All the Women of the Bible

More than 600,000 copies of the "All" series are now in print.

ALL THE MIRACLES OF THE BIBLE

The Supernatural in Scripture
Its Scope and Significance

by

HERBERT LOCKYER

Zondervan Books
Zondervan Publishing House
Grand Rapids, Michigan

ALL THE MIRACLES OF THE BIBLE
Copyright 1961 by Zondervan Publishing House
Grand Rapids, Michigan

Zondervan Books are published by
Zondervan Publishing House, 1415 Lake Drive, S.E.,
Grand Rapids, Michigan 49506

Library of Congress Catalog Card Number: 61-16752

ISBN 0-310-28100-8

Printed in the United States of America

88   89   90 / 32   31   30   29

Dedicated to
My Esteemed Cousin,
ARTHUR HEDLEY
Whose Triumph in Adversity
is a
Constant Miracle of Grace.

TABLE OF CONTENTS

ALL THE MIRACLES OF THE BIBLE

INTRODUCTION

Because of the greatness and magnificence of the Bible, there are many ways by which we can approach it, and in our quest for truth we should guard ourselves against becoming slaves of any one method of study.

What a prodigal variety of themes the Bible presents for our prayerful and patient meditation, some of which belong on an exceptional level, as Dr. A. T. Pierson reminds us! They stand out by themselves in a separate group. They remind us of mountain peaks which, however separate, are parts of one range, by their very altitude and solitariness attracting special notice.

Is such an observation not true of the miracles of the Bible, which go to make it the most fascinating, authentic record in the world? While the border line between the natural and supernatural may, in some manifestations, be so thin that a perfectly complete list of miracles would depend on one's definition of a miracle, we have a galaxy easily distinguishable as miraculous.

Among Scripture prominencies are three that deserve special treatment, namely, *the miracles, the parables*, and *the discourses*. In some cases these are closely related.

The miracles provide us with a special exhibition of super-natural power.

The parables contain divine illustrations of truth.

The discourses reveal the continuous development of truth.

Before entering the rewarding study of the individual miracles of the Bible, it may be found profitable to consider several features of miracles themselves.

1. The Definition of the Term "Miracle"

What is a miracle? A miracle has been defined as a work wrought by a divine power for a divine purpose by means beyond the reach of man. The general idea is that it is something wonderful or unusual—an event, experience, or discovery so singular and strange as to awaken in one the feeling of awe. Phenomena in nature and events in history are labelled "miracle." If a friend escapes death in a car accident, we are apt to say, "It was a miracle that he was not killed." The ordinary course of nature is referred to as a miracle. Augustus expresses the thought, "The daily miracle of God has grown cheap by repetition." But the nature of Christian miracles presents essential features the common use of the word ignores. Professor T. H. Huxley well expressed the need of a previous definition when he wrote, "The first step in this, as in all other discussions, is to come to a clear understanding as to the meaning of the term employed. Argumentation whether miracles are possible, and if possible, credible, is mere beating the air until the arguers have agreed what they mean by the word 'miracle.' "

Webster's definition of a miracle is clear and concise—"An event or effect in the physical world deviating from the known laws of nature, or transcending our knowledge of these laws; an extra-ordinary, anomalous, or abnormal event brought about by super-human agency."

Wm. Taylor defines a miracle as, "A work out of the usual sequence of secondary causes and effects which cannot be accounted for by the ordinary operation of those causes, and which is produced by the agency of God through the instrumentality of one who claims to be his representative, and in attestation of the message which he brings."

The Bible describes its miracles in its own way and from its own points of view. As W. D. Thomson says, "Being exclusively a religious book, the Bible does not set itself to define miracles from the standpoint of nature or science, but from the standpoint of the moral source, the moral power, the moral aim, and the moral effect which they represented. . . . In outlining its definition of these miracles, the Bible wisely selects its terms from a supreme and sole regard to religious and moral considerations; thus simply remaining silent as to all questions bearing on the relations of the miraculous to the internal arrangements, forces, and laws of nature."

The term "miracle" then, from the Biblical standpoint, is used to describe the wonderful phenomena accompanying the Jewish and Christian revelations, especially at critical moments. The Biblical conception of a miracle is that of some extraordinary work of deity transcending the ordinary powers of nature and wrought in connection with the ends of revelation.

Bible miracles often display the reversal of nature's course. They form an effect contrary to the established constitution and course of things. Many of the miracles are a sensible deviation from the known laws of nature, proving that God is not only the Maker of all these laws, but also their Sovereign, and consequently He is able to deal with them as He deems fit. Having created what we call "nature," He has the power to control and change it, suspend or direct its laws for a season, according to His holy will, which is ever good and just.

One of the difficulties voiced by modernism as to the possibility of miracles is that the laws of nature are self-existent and uncaused and that there cannot be any deviation from them. But if these laws were designed by a Supreme Will, surely this Will has the power to introduce or interpose a new agency into them? In Bible miracles, original laws are not suspended, violated, or modified in any way, but a *super*natural power outside of nature intervenes with a new effect. As David Hume, the Scottish philosopher, puts it, "A miracle is not a violation of the laws of nature but the introduction of a new agent." Disturbance entered the world by sin, as nature visibly attests, and God must needs miraculously interfere to nullify that disturbance. That is what He did in many of the miracles the Bible records.

But although God is beyond and above nature, He never violates any of its laws. Neither is nature, as Spinoza expresses it, "the strait jacket from which God cannot escape." If we deny Him the power to perform miracles, then He is no longer a God of freedom, a living God, above nature and independent of nature, as Trench reminds.

2. The Design of Miracles

An important aspect of Bible miracles is the fact that they are proper proofs of a divine revelation. It is questionable whether there can be an authentic revelation without miracles. They are not only proofs of a revelation but form a revelation in themselves. Of course, miracles guarantee the authenticity of a revelation. Bible miracles form an integral part of Holy Writ and testify to its divine inspiration and veracity. Apart from these miracles we have no other evidence of the supernatural working on man's behalf in time of crises.

Miracles, as an integral part of the Bible, provide evidence that it is God's divinely inspired Word. Without its miraculous content we could not accept it as a supernatural Book. No miracles—no striking proof of its divine authorship. Among other aspects of the design or purpose of the inclusion of so many miracles is the manifestation of the glory of God. How eloquently they speak of His sovereignty in every realm! He is Lord *in* and *of* all (John 11:4). Miracles are "both the official and authoritative seal of God."

Miracles are also the insignia of Christ's deity—"a constitutive element of the revelation of God in Christ"—and Messiahship (John 2:11; 11:4; Matthew 11:4-6; Acts 2:20; 10:38). In these displays of His inherent power, we have the exercise of His creative, punitive, and healing authority. And all of His miracles were in "accord with His miraculous origin, sinless nature and moral perfection." They provided God with a method of authenticating Christ's divine mission. He Himself regarded His miracles as evidence that He was from God —and *was* God (John 14:24). Later on, as we come to the study of New Testament miracles, we shall see how many of His miracles were the natural expression of His sympathy for a suffering humanity, as well as the confirmations of His divine commission and teachings.

While we have only samples out of the mass of miracles Jesus performed, those which we have reveal Him as being more than a prophet or a divine messenger in a delegated sense. The apostles could heal the sick and even raise the dead, but they never turned water into wine nor walked the waves. Many of Christ's miracles were "evidently unique" and were proofs of His Godhead and the *insignia* of His Godmanhood as found in Psalm 8 and Hebrews 2. His miracles prove beyond doubt that He had supreme command over nature and also over the soul and body of man. A further evidence of design in Bible miracles is the fact that they confirm the divine nature of Christianity and are evidences of the authority of the Gospel (Mark 16:20; Hebrews 2:4. See Exodus 4:1-5).

The fatal weakness of a religious leader like Mahomet, and one of which he was acutely conscious, was that he could show no miracles attesting the divinity of his mission. With the Bible, however, miracles prove doctrines and doctrines approve the miracles, and both are held together in a blessed unity in the person of Christ who performed the works and proclaimed the words. Christianity and Christendom can only be explained by accepting the miracles which introduced them. If Bible miracles "had been mere wonders, any one would have been a fit witness of their performance. But they were designed to manifest the supremacy of deity and to attract the witnesses to the kingdom of God."

In his chapter on "The Apologetic Worth of Miracles," Trench quotes the somewhat over-strong statement of Augustine that "miracles lead us to faith, and are mainly wrought for the sake of unbelievers." But, as Trench goes on to prove, a miracle of Christ would,. for example, produce different effects. "He raised a man from the dead; here was the same outward fact for all; but how diverse the effect!—some believed, and some went and told the Pharisees (John 11:45, 46). Heavenly voices were heard—and some said it thundered, so dull and inarticulate had those sounds become to them, while others knew that they were voices wherein was the witness of the Father to His own Son (John 12:28-30)." To all who believe, miracles occupy a prominent place in the array of proofs for the certainty of those things believed. In his excellent summary on "Miracles" in *The International Standard Bible Encyclopaedia*, H. Wace says:

> On the whole, it is perhaps increasingly realized that miracles, so far from being an excrescence on Christian faith, are indissolubly bound up with it, and that there is a complete unity in the manifestation of the divine nature, which is recorded in the Scripture.

Finally, Bible miracles were designed to symbolize the spiritual blessings that God is able and willing to bestow upon our needy hearts. The majority of miracles were acts of mercy and are conspicuous as emblems of redemption. By the genuineness of the visible miracle that of the invisible miracle is confirmed to us. As W. M. Taylor reminds us, the miracles Christ performed, for example, were parabolical illustrations of the great salvation which He preached. Miracles are parables of grace, and parables are miracles of power. Miracles, then, have a two-fold value, a physical and a spiritual. Thinking principally of Christ's miracles, His expulsion of demons symbolizes His power over the spirit world of evil; the healing of lepers illustrates the removal of sin's loathsome defilement; the raising of the dead demonstrates Christ's power to raise those who are dead in sin—and so on.

3. The Description of Miracles

In any phase of Bible study, the close examination of the words used is vastly important. While we employ the general term "miracle" to describe the manifestation of supernatural power, various terms are used of miracles, because no one term can possibly exhaust all the significance of a miracle. All the terms that are used emphasize the exercise of divine power.

Trench has the comment, "Each term embodies some essential quality of the same thing; and not from the contemplation, exclusively, of any one, but only of all these together with an adequate conception of that which we desire to understand be obtained." Among the most conspicuous terms describing what we call "miracles" are the following:

WONDERS—*Terata*

This word indicates the state of mind produced on the eyewitnesses by the sight of miracles. Astonishment was excited in them. The extraordinary character of the miracle was observed and kept in the memory. *Wonder* is the most frequent word used (Mark 2:12; 4:41; 6:51; 7:37. See Numbers 16:30; Acts 3:10, 11). To beholders, such a display of power was contrary to previous expectation—opposite to any law with which they were acquainted. Such miracles, however, were not to be regarded merely as "wonders," producing a momentary amazement. Attention had to be given to their purpose and to their inner spiritual appeal (Acts 14:8-15). As Godet expresses it:

> The miracles of Jesus are not mere prodigies (*terata*) intended to strike the imagination. There is a close relation between these marvellous facts and the person of Him who does them. They are visible emblems of what He is and what He comes to do, images which spring as rays from the abiding miracle of the manifestation of Christ.

SIGNS—*Semeion*

Here we have a word carrying with it a

particular reference to the significance of miracles as being seals by which God authenticated the miracle-worker himself. In *semeion*, the ethical purpose of the miracle is most prominent. A miracle was to be looked upon as a token and indication of the near presence and working of God and a proof of the genuineness of revelation. The miracles of Christ were signs and pledges of something more than beyond themselves (Isaiah 7:11; 38:7). As we have indicated, they were seals of power set to the person performing the miracle (Mark 6:30; Acts 14:3; Hebrews 2:4). They were legitimate acts whereby the miracle-worker could claim to be accepted as God's representative (I John 2:18; II Corinthians 12:12). The "signs" given to Saul, Eli, Gideon, and others are not to be thought of as *miracles* (I Samuel 10:1-19; Judges 7:9-15; Luke 2:12). *Sign* designates a proof or evidence furnished by one set of facts to the reality and genuineness of another" (II Corinthians 12:12).

POWERS—*Dunamis*

Miracles are also "powers" in that they manifest the mighty power of God which was inherent in Christ Himself, "the great power of God" (Acts 8:10), and who was made unto us—power. This word points to new and higher forces working in this lower world of ours (Hebrews 6:5). *Semeion* refers to the final cause of miracles; *dunamis*, to their efficient cause. The plural, "powers," is the same word translated "wonderful works" (Matthew 7:22); "mighty works" (Matthew 11:20; Mark 6:14; Luke 10:13); and "miracles" (Acts 2:22; 19:11; I Corinthians 12:10, 28; Galatians 3:5).

The three words considered are combined in one verse—"Jesus the Nazarene, a man set forth by God to you by works of power (*dunamesin*), and wonders (*terasin*), and signs (*semeiois*), which God wrought by Him in your midst" (Acts 2:22).

Other descriptive words of miracles are "works," as John frequently calls them (5:36; 7:21; 10:25, 32, etc.); "great things" (Luke 1:49); "glorious things" (Luke 13: 17); "strange things" (Luke 5:26); "wonderful things" (Matthew 21:15); "marvellous things" (Psalm 78:12); "marvellous works" (Psalm 105:5; Isaiah 29:14).

Combining all the terms used in the Old Testament and New Testament to describe the Biblical idea of miracles as manifesta-

tions of God's extraordinary work, they indicate powers transcending the ordinary powers of nature, wrought in connection with the ends of revelation.

4. The Doers of Miracles

In classifying the performers of Bible miracles, we find them to be divine, angelic, human, and satanic.

Miracles were performed directly by God.

Each Person in the Trinity exercised miraculous power. Acceptance of the omnipotence of God precludes any doubt about the miraculous (Job 40:2, 9; 42:2; Amos 4:13; 5:8; Colossians 1:16, 17, etc.). When a Spirit-inspired faith rests on declarations like—"I know that Thou canst do everything," or "With God, all things are possible," then miracles present no mental difficulty. There are many Scriptures presenting God as the direct agent in miracles (Exodus 8:19; Acts 14:3; 15:12; 19:11, etc.).

Miracles were performed by Christ.

The divine attribute of omnipotence is ascribed to Christ and was exercised by Him. He strides through the gospels as the Son of Man to whom *all* power was given (Matthew 10:1; 28:18; John 10:17, 18; 11:25; Colossians 2:10; Revelation 1:8, etc.). Christ's miraculous power was foretold (Isaiah 9:6; 35:5, 6; 42:7) and so was asked for by John the Baptist (Matthew 11:2-4). It was because of this that the people called Him "the Son of David" (Matthew 12:23; John 7:42). Christ never performed miracles simply to display His power, nor to astonish people. He always used His power to aid and relieve the needy.

A noticeable feature of the life of Christ was His refusal to employ on His own behalf the power He shared with God as the One co-equal with Him. His temptation in the wilderness is an illustration of this. His was a fixed determination never to use His powers to secure His own safety or aggrandizement, nor in order to beat down the resistance of unbelief. Delivering others from the crushing bondage of nature, He Himself was subject to its heaviest laws.

We never find Christ working a single miracle on His own behalf. He will turn water into wine, that nothing may mar the gladness of a marriage feast; but He asked the woman at the well to give Him a drink, and when He was dying He depended upon the bystanders to assuage His thirst. He will provide an ample meal for multitudes as they listened all day long to His soul-inspiring teaching, but would not convert the stones of the wilderness into bread to satisfy His own hunger. Though Himself "Wonderful" (Isaiah 9:6), and claiming to be "the Life" (John 14:6), and raising the dead, He appeared to be helpless in His encounter with death. Enriching others, He elected to remain impoverished.

Miracles were performed by the Holy Spirit.

Co-equal with the Father and with the Son, the Spirit shares the attribute of omnipotence (Genesis 1:2; 6:3; Acts 5:3, 4, etc.). Under this section we can place those miraculous gifts Christ manifested (Matthew 12:28). These gifts were foretold (Isaiah 35:4-6; Joel 2:28, 29); are enumerated (I Corinthians 12:4-10, 28; 14:1); were experienced on the Day of Pentecost (Acts 2:1-4); were communicated as the Gospel was preached (Acts 10:44-46), and by the laying on of hands (Acts 8:17, 18; 19:6); and were dispensed according to the sovereign will of the Spirit (I Corinthians 12:11).

These miraculous gifts of the Spirit were to be sought after (I Corinthians 12:31; 14:1); were not to be neglected, despised, or purchased (I Timothy 4:14; II Timothy 1:6; I Thessalonians 5:20; Acts 8:20); could be possessed without saving grace (Matthew 7:22, 23; I Corinthians 13:1, 2); and were to be thought of as temporary (I Corinthians 13:8).

Miracles were performed by angels.

With the Persons of the Trinity, almightiness is inherent in each, but the angels and men, power is delegated. The angels were created by God and exist to carry out His will and work. "Omnipotence has her servants everywhere," and multitudes of them comprise the angelic hosts. Scripture is replete with angelic agency in Bible miracles (II Samuel 24:16; Luke 1:11-13, 57-59; John 5:2-4; Acts 5:17-24, etc.).

Miracles were performed by the servants of God.

Human agents could not act directly. They had no reservoir of deity. They could only perform miracles as power was delegated to them by God. As our following studies will prove, honored servants like Moses, Aaron, Joshua, Samson, Samuel, Elijah, Elisha, Isaiah, Peter, Stephen, Philip, Paul, Barnabas, and other apostles and disciples (Luke 10:9, 17; Acts 2:23; 5:12) were only channels through whom miraculous power flowed.

Those who performed miracles had to disclaim any inherent power of their own (Acts 3:12) and had to possess faith in God's power to perform what was impossible from the human standpoint (Matthew 17:20; 21:21; John 14:21; Acts 3:16; 6:8). Further, many miracles occurred at the command, or at the prayer, of the person to whom they are attributed. The whole significance of our Lord's miracles is that they occur at His word and in obedience to Him. "What manner of man is this that even the winds and the waves obey Him" (Matthew 8:27).

Miracles were performed by evil agents.

In some mysterious way the Devil and those under his sway have had, and are to have, power to counterfeit the prerogative of deity, namely, the display of miraculous power. The Bible speaks of miracles performed through the power of the Devil (II Thessalonians 2:9; Revelation 16:14); by false christs and false prophets (Matthew 24:24; Revelation 13:13). These miracle-workers are exemplified by the Egyptian magicians (Exodus 7:11, 22; 8:7), by the Witch of Endor (I Samuel 28:7-14), by Simon Magus (Acts 8:9-11). Counterfeit miracles were designed to support false religions (Deuteronomy 13:1-3); are a mark of apostasy (II Thessalonians 2:3, 9); deceive the ungodly (II Thessalonians 2:10-12; Revelation 13:14; 19:20); and are not to be countenanced (Deuteronomy 13:3).

5. The Distribution of Miracles

Our enumeration of miracles proves what a very conspicuous feature of the Bible they are. Yet miracles are not abundant in *all* parts of the Bible. Many of them were performed in time of crises. The miracle of creation introduced the history of the world and of humanity. Bible miracles—not including prophecies and their fulfilment, which are also miracles—fall into great periods, centuries apart:

The establishment of the
Jewish nation   1400 B.C.
    Moses and Joshua are conspicuous
    as miracle-workers.
The crisis in struggle with
idolatry   850 B.C.

Elijah and Elisha are prominent in this era.

The Captivity, when idolatry was victorious   600 B.C.

Daniel and his friends were subjects of miracles.

The introduction of Christianity 1 A.D. The virgin birth of Christ was the initial miracle of the New Testament. Christ and His apostles were the miracle-workers.

The great tribulation

Great signs and wonders are to characterize this period.

While there is no record of miracles in the poetical books—Job, Psalms, Proverbs—yet these books are loaded with expressions of the miraculous acts of God on behalf of His people. All through Job, God's supreme power is exalted. Throughout the Psalms, the historic consciousness of a great and tenacious people is indissolubly bound up with the miraculous.

As for prophecy, it offers one of the greatest of miracles in that it reveals God as the Ruler of human life, history and destiny. From Abraham on, the destiny of the Jewish people was a foreshadowing of the Advent of the Messiah, who did not, like Buddha or Mahomet, create a new office but came to fulfil offices predicted by the prophets (Luke 24:27).

6. The Division of Miracles

Bible miracles fall into clearly-defined divisions or catalogs, and when classified, they reveal the prerogative of deity to exercise almightiness in any realm. The following divisions corroborate the divine affirmation that God doeth according to His will among the army of heaven and among the inhabitants of earth (Daniel 4:35).

Power over nature

Old Testament and New Testament miracles serve to exhibit that God is able to do as He deems best in His created world. None can stay His hand, saying, "What doest Thou?" He is supreme in the realm of inanimate objects.

Here are miracles that have to do with *water:*

The Red Sea, Jordan, Marah, Merabah, Rephidin, Jericho waters, swimming iron, Carmel, stilling storms, water into wine, walking on sea, Bethesda Pool.

Here are miracles that have to do with *fire:*

Pillar of fire, Shekinah fire, Carmel fire, fiery furnace.

Here are miracles that have to do with *oil:*

The Widow's cruse, oil in vessels.

Here are miracles that have to do with the *sun:*

Joshua, dials of Ahaz and Hezekiah, last days.

Here are miracles that have to do with *food:*

Manna, meal in barrel, feeding hundreds or thousands.

Here are miracles that have to do with *natural elements:*

Thunder, hail, rain, floods, earthquakes, withered trees, opened doors.

Then in the animate realm, as the Lord of life, God exhibits His ability to command living objects to do His will. Serpents, frogs, lice, flies, murrain, locusts, ravens, lions, fish, swine, and vipers all play a part in miracles.

Power over disease

The provision, prevention, and the permission of diseases are also related to Bible miracles. The range covers boils, leprosy, poisonous serpents, deadly pottage, withered hands, sicknesses, fevers, issue of blood, dropsy, blindness, deafness, dumbness, lameness, and infirmities.

Power over death

As the Lord of life, the keys of life and death dangle at His girdle. Among those divinely stricken were the multitudes at the flood, Nadab and Abihu, the Taberal burning, Kibroth, Hatawah, Korah, Uzzah, widow's son, Shunammite's son, Syrian army, Sennacherib's army, Philistines, Ananias and Sapphira, and Herod. Enoch and Elijah miraculously missed death. Resurrections include Elijah's bones, the three Christ raised from the dead, His own resurrection, and apostolic resurrection.

Power over demons

Although the Devil, the prince of demons, is mighty, he is not almighty as God is. He is only a dog on a leash and cannot go any further than divine permission, as the experiences of Job teach us. Thus, in the realms of evil spirits, God is able to exercise His omnipotence. Miracles in this connection cover the witch at Endor, demoniacs, lunacy, unclean spirits, etc.

Our study of Bible miracles will prove

that the Lord is triumphant over all human disorders, whether physical, mental or nervous; over all cosmic forces, on land or sea, organic and inorganic; over the spirit-world represented by the Devil, demons, and death. For a full synopsis of the realms associated with miracles, A. R. Habershon's *The Study of Miracles* is recommended.

7. The Disappearance of Miracles

The matter of the desistance of miracles calls for some attention. When did they cease to be performed? With the passing of the apostles, was the delegation of miraculous power withdrawn? There is record of miraculous cures in the Church after the first century, but miracles were not recorded under inspired guidance like the miracles of the apostolic age. In many cases, Church miracles are overlaid with legend.

Trench remarks that "few points present greater difficulties than the attempt to fix accurately the moment when these miraculous powers were withdrawn from the Church, and it entered into its permanent state, with only its present miracles of grace and the records of its past miracles of power; instead of actually possessing those miracles of power by whose aid it first asserted itself in the world."

Old Testament miracles established the supremacy of God as *God* over all the dead gods of idolatry. The miracles of Christ established His claims to deity and Messiahship. Apostolic miracles established the Church as a divine institution, and once firmly established was mainly left to ordinary providence. Fuller remarked, "Miracles are the swaddling clothes of the infant churches, not the garments of the full grown." In "the act of *becoming*," miracles were necessary, but when the Church had reached the stage in the mind of God of "actually being," then the props and strengthenings of the tender plant were safely removed from the hardier tree. "When that which is perfect is come, then that which is in part shall be done away" (I Corinthians 13:8-10). Faussett expresses it, "The edifice being erected, the scaffolding is taken down; perpetual miracle is contrary to God's ways."

In the place of miracles we have the practical results of Christianity—results far more observable now, over nineteen centuries after the coming of Christ, than they were at the first.

The cessation of miracles brings us to a consideration of what are known as *ecclesiastical miracles,* or miracles the Church alleges to have performed. Of these miracles Fausset says that they are ambiguous and legendary; that is, they resemble known products of human credulity and imposture. Many are childish and palpably framed for superstitious believers rather than as evidences capable of bearing critical scrutiny. Most of them are told long after their presumed occurrence.

Since its inception around the fourth or fifth century, the church of Rome has been notorious in pretences to miracles, which are still professed and indicate the chicanery and the corruption of Romanism. Images have nodded, smiled, frowned, or spoken on certain occasions. The blood of some saint has annually liquified. Wounds bleed every Friday. Shrine cures are widely advertised. These popish miracles, prevalent in popish countries, are as different from New Testament miracles as night is from day. Bible miracles are not doubtful, as the liquifaction of St. Januarius' blood, nor stories resolved into exaggeration. Neither are they gradual, but for the most part are instantaneous (Luke 18:43); not incomplete not merely temporary, but complete and lasting. Often Bible miracles were witnessed to at the cost of suffering and death.

The claim to miracles is not confined to the Roman church. There are fake "faith healers" abroad today who fatten themselves financially on the physical disorders of many earnest hearts who are clutching at any straw for healing. How heartless these so-called "faith healers" are in leaving behind them multitudes of deceived, disappointed, and unrelieved sufferers! Justice demands their exposure and punishment.

Before leaving this question of the cessation or continuance of miracles, it must be made clear that we are not asserting that God does not exert His supernatural power today when and where a miracle is necessary. As the omnipotent One, He does not change; and there are faithful, reliable Christians who, apart from Romish claims or attendance upon a "faith healer," have experienced that there is still nothing too hard for the Lord. What we do affirm, however, is that in this age of grace, the perpetual miracle is contrary to God's order.

For a further consideration of this matter, the reader is referred to Trench's excellent summary in his chapter on "Other Cycles of Miracles."

Discussing this aspect of miracles, Dr. A. E. Garvie concludes his article in Hasting's *Dictionary of the Bible* with this expressive paragraph:

At the beginning of the Christian Church the miracles had some value as evidence. Today the change Christ has wrought in human history is the most convincing proof of His claim; but we must not ignore the value the miracles had when they occurred, and their value to us still as works of Christ, showing as signs of His grace.

8. The Denial of Miracles

Deniers of the miraculous are like the poor—always with us. Matthew Arnold dismissed the subject of miracles with the airy dictum—"They do not happen." The three great aspects of our faith which Higher (or destructive) Criticism has attacked are: inspiration of Holy Writ, the necessity of the Christian dogma and the credibility of miracles. Agnosticism has always been sceptical in its attitude towards the fundamental truths as taught in the Bible. W. D. Thomson says that "The agnostic, *as an agnostic*, has neither a scientific system, nor a speculative theory, nor a religious creed," and then goes on to quote Frederick Harrison thus:

Agnosticism is not a religion, nor the shadow of a religion. It offers none of the rudiments or elements of religion. It is the mere disembodied spirit of a dead religion; and it has shown that religion is not to be found anywhere within its realm of abuse.

Sir Julian Huxley, prominent present-day biologist, an avowed agnostic and ardent apostle of evolution, rejects Bible miracles. Having concocted a new religion without revelation, Huxley, who has been referred to as "Darwin's bulldog," affirms that "there is no longer either need or room for supernatural beings capable of affecting the course of events in the evolutionary pattern of thought." In his address at the special convocation of Chicago University commemorating the centenary of Darwin's theory of evolution, Huxley threw overboard the initial miracle of the Bible, namely the creation of the universe and of man. Here is his recorded statement:

The earth was not created. It evolved. So did all the animals and plants that inhabit it, including our human selves, mind and souls as well as brain and body.

Then, sacrilegiously, this agnostic biologist went on to say that "evolutionary man can no longer take refuge from his loneliness by creeping for shelter into the arms of a divinized father figure whom he has himself created." Here is Huxley's rejection of the Bible's revelation of God. But He that sitteth in the heavens only laughs (Psalm 2).

Many scientists and teachers today affirm that the doctrine of evolution is conclusive against the possibility of such divine deviations from the usual order of things as miracles are. But evolutionists, with their unproven theories cannot explain the miracle of life, even if it did begin as a protoplasm, as they affirm.

The long history of the rejection of the miraculous requires more attention than we have space for. A full treatment of this phase of our study can be found in Trench's chapter on "The Assaults on the Miracles." Jewish leaders in our Lord's day, hostile to His teachings, set aside His miracles as being satanically inspired (Matthew 12:24; Mark 3:22-27; Luke 11:15-22). But Christ had no pact with the Devil. He was "the strong man" able to enter the Devil's house and spoil his goods.

Trench cites heathen philosophers like Celsus, Heirocles, Porphry, and Appollonius as deniers of miracles. Appollonius said of Christ, "Yet do we not account him who has done such things for a god, only for a man beloved, the gods: while the Christians, on the contrary, on the ground of a few insignificant wonder-works, proclaim their Jesus as God."

Coming to pantheistic and sceptical deniers of miracles, Trench quotes at length the arguments of Spinoza and Hume against the reality of Bible miracles. With the rise of rationalism, Paulus, Woolston, and Strauss were conspicuous in their rational explanation of miracles. The water was not changed into wine at Cana. A new supply of wine was brought in. There was no miracle of the loaves. Christ and His disciples gave their store, an act of liberality quickly followed by others until there was sufficient for all. He never healed lepers—only pronounced them clean. Lazarus never actually died, he only swooned—which is also the claim of the rationalist regarding the death of Christ.

The tragedy is that many so-called Christian preachers and teachers, modernistic in their outlook, apply the rationalistic treatment to the miracles. To them, there is a fit explanation for the miraculous element in the Bible. Its miracles were simply the conscious clothing of spiritual truth, allegories devised artificially. It is to be regretted that several theological colleges and schools, liberal or modernistic in theology, subtly deny the miracles of the Bible and thrust young men out into the ministry with a rejection of the supernatural. Bible miracles are purely fabulous and legendary and consist of a halo of fancy around a nucleus of fact.

We readily admit that Bible miracles in their relation to nature surpass our comprehension. Because we "see through a glass darkly," the manner in which the divine power affected them is hidden from our view. But we do not reject them on that account. We cannot adequately understand the mysterious and marvelous nature of the common modes of energy everywhere at work in nature.

Bible miracles are stated as facts, and by faith we accept them. If we reject the miracles, particularly those of Christ and His apostles, as being the imaginative concoctions of New Testament writers, then we attribute to these eyewitnesses of the supernatural a wholesale untrustworthiness, or a superstitious misrepresentation or fraud. Gospel miracles were wrought in the presence of enemies and so subjected to the severest scrutiny; but they emerge as being among those things most surely believed by the apostles.

The evidence of our faith would be seriously damaged if the miracles were set aside. In respect to New Testament miracles, we should lose the positive evidence we now possess of our Lord's saving power if the same did not constitute in themselves a revelation.

9. The Defense of Miracles

Job supplies us with a magnificent description of God's power—"Lo, He is strong" (9:19). The Hebrew word for "strong" signifies a conquering, prevailing strength, and suggests the superlative degree. "He is most strong," that is, God Almighty (Genesis 17:1). And because of His almightiness, He can do whatever is feasible. While there is a difference between authority and power, God possesses both.

Because He is the Creator of man, God has the sovereign right and authority over man. None can dispute with Him or seek a reason for His actions (Daniel 4:35; Psalm 75:7). As the supreme Monarch, all power is vested in Him (Isaiah 14:12; Romans 13:1). But what is the use of authority without power to enforce His claims? Allied to divine authority is divine power. The God of the Bible is the God of nature, the God of all miracles who upholds all things by the word of His power. To create something out of nothing, to transform sinners into saints, to command nature requires a power not of man. Omnipotence, then, is the proof of the miraculous (Exodus 7:3; Deuteronomy 4:34, 35).

Further, God's relation to nature, as contained in the Bible, is consistent with the working of miracles. Such a relationship, as W. D. Thomson elaborates on, is six-fold:

God created nature (Colossians 1:16).

Having created nature, He is above, and at the same time, in it as a constant source of energy and causation. Here the transcendence and the immanence of God are united by one tie by which nature exists in dependence upon Him as Creator.

God is the upholder of nature (Colossians 1:17).

The Bible not only exalts God above nature, it also brings Him into direct relation to nature, so that everything is filled by Him. He dwells in nature as the omnipresent, as well as the omnipotent, God. He is "the life of all that lives; the Spirit of all spirits. As He is all in all, so is all in Him."

God transcends nature (Psalm 90:2; 102:25-27).

Nature depends upon Him for its existence, yet He is Himself self-existent and independent.

God is immanent in nature (Ephesians 1:11).

God dwells in His created universe and is continually exercising His power as an efficient cause.

God's purpose in created nature (Ephesians 1:9-11).

God created nature, and continues sustaining it in existence, for purposes of holy love.

God's nature is a medium of his self-revelation to Man (Romans 1:19, 20).

Nature has been referred to as God's braille for a blind humanity. The Bible which reveals Him is of a supernatural character, and therefore miracles are natural to it.

Yet with all His infinite power, there are some things God cannot do. He cannot do that which stains the glory of His Godhead. He cannot deny Himself. He cannot sin or countenance sin or hypocrisy. He cannot contradict any of His glorious attributes.

Because of all God is in Himself, and all He possesses, He has unlimited freedom to accomplish what He deems best. He would not be the Lord God Almighty if He could not perform supernatural acts consistent with His own being and character.

PART ONE — OLD TESTAMENT MIRACLES

PART ONE — OLD TESTAMENT MIRACLES

A study of the kind before us in this volume necessitated considerable research in literature dealing with the miraculous content of the Bible. A surpassing feature of one's quest for works of profit is the fact that there is no theological treatise, at least known to the writer, dealing with *all* the miracles of the Bible. Somehow Old Testament miracles, which are as numerous, if not more so, than those found in the New Testament, are sadly neglected. Concentration appears to be on the miracles of the gospels, particularly those of Christ, as can be seen by referring to many of the books mentioned in our bibliography.

In several, we have scant references to some of the miracles performed by the prophets and the apostles, but a complete and comprehensive list is lacking. We trust we have succeeded in the somewhat arduous task of cataloging and briefly expounding *all* the specific miracles of the miracle Book, the Bible. As the reader will discover, we have not included theophanic appearances, visions, revelations of coming events, and prophecy, many of which breathe the air of the supernatural. Prophecy in itself is a wonderful miracle in that it reveals God as the Ruler of human life and history. It is to Dr. John Cumming that we are indebted for the thought that—

> *Prophecy* is a cartoon of the future, which events will fill up.
> *Miracles* are the fore-acts of the future, done on a small scale.
> *Parables* are fore-shadows of the future, projected on the sacred page. All three grow every day in radiance, in interest, in value. Soon the light of a Meridian Sun will overflow them all. May we be found ready.

It is somewhat profitable to compare and contrast Old Testament miracles with those of the New Testament. The Old Testament miracles were for the most part to destroy enemies, and the glorious declarations of Moses (Deuteronomy 4:32-35) regarding the presence of the miraculous in the life and history of Israel refutes the critical theory that the records of these miracles are unhistorical. The God of the Jew was, and is, the God manifest in miraculous acts of deliverance. New Testament miracles were acts of mercy, apart from the withered tree and demon-possessed swine, both symbolical lessons of warning to men. Christ's miracles declare Him to be the Saviour of the whole man.

Old Testament miracles attested God's presence as King of the theocracy. New Testament miracles attested the deity of Christ—God manifest in flesh—and also the divine authority vested in the apostles. Old Testament miracles, for the most part, were born with pangs and ardent intercession and with a seeming uncertainty as to the issue —those of Christ were always accompanied with the greatest ease and with certainty of issue. Moses had to plead and struggle with God over his sister's leprosy (Numbers 12:13-15), but Christ heals a leper by His touch and other lepers by remote control (Matthew 8:3; Luke 17:14). Elijah had to tarry long and send his servant up seven times for tokens of rain; he had to stretch himself thrice on the dead child and painfully win back life (I Kings 17:2-22; 18:42-44). Likewise Elisha, after much effort, restored another child to life (II Kings 4:31-35). By way of comparison, Christ, as the Lord of the living and the dead, raised the dead with great ease.

Old Testament performers of miracles prayed for results; Christ commanded them. In the Old Testament, miracles were accomplished in the name of the Lord; Christ's miracles were in His own, or His Father's name. His miracles were also freer and more gentle and brilliant than those of the Old Testament. Elisha fed 100 men with 20 loaves, but Christ fed 5,000 with 5 loaves. Many Old Testament miracles were performed by means—rods ministered in mighty acts; a tree was used to heal bitter nature; a mantle to divide waters, etc. But Christ accomplished His miracles simply by the agency of a word or by a touch. He needed no recognized instrument of power.

Further, Old Testament miracles wear a far severer aspect than those of the New Testament in keeping with the covenant of the law, and the covenant of grace. Then Old Testament miracles were eminently those of strength and power to impress a rude and heathen age. Christ's miracles were those of grace and love. The miracles of Moses so frequently inflicted death as the punishment of sin—in contrast the miracles of Jesus were, for the most part, miracles of mercy. In his first miracle Moses turned water into blood. In Christ's first miracle, He turned water into wine.

As to the profit of the study of Bible miracles, Ada R. Habershon says that such a theme is intensely practical, having a threefold effect:

It enlarges our views of God and His power.

It adjusts our views concerning man and his insignificance.

It stirs our wonder that He who is so mighty should deign to dwell with man, and in man, and should concern Himself with all the interests of His children. "As His majesty is, so also is His mercy."

I.

THE MIRACLE BOOK

(II Timothy 3:15-17; I Peter 1:10-12, 15; II Peter 1:21; Hebrews 4:12; Exodus 4:15; Revelation 22:19)

Usually theological treatises dealing with Bible miracles, either for or against, omit any reference to the Bible as a miracle in itself. It is not only a Book relating credited miracles—everything associated with the Bible is miraculous, as one writer at least, Ada R. Habershon, indicates in her illuminating volume, *The Study of Miracles.* Everything about the Bible is supernatural, and in spite of all destructive criticism has done to weaken its authority, it remains an ever-present miracle. And who but God could have conceived, and caused men to compose, such a perfect Book which Jerome called the "Divine Library."

Miracle of its inspiration

Although we may not be able to tell how God inspired holy men of old to write the Bible, nor how the Holy Spirit affected the writers He employed, it cannot be gainsaid that we have in the Bible the seal of divine authority. Biblical inspiration embraces not only the subject matter but also the very words in which it is expressed, down to the minutest detail, so that as originally written the Bible is wholly inspired (Matthew 5:18).

The divine inspiration of Scripture was the unvarying conviction of the Christian Church until the dominance of liberalism towards the close of the last century. Modernists, repudiating the infallibility of the Bible, have wrought havoc within Christendom, robbed many of the note of certainty in their faith, and destroyed the influence of the Church, as well as emptied her precincts. Modernistic preachers wield a blunted sword that fails to win the victories of those like Wesley, Whitefield, Spurgeon, and Moody, who believed the Bible to be the divinely inspired revelation of God.

Miracle of its antiquity

This sacred volume, which took some 1,500 years to complete, has been in existence in its completed form for almost two millenniums, and yet is as virile today as ever. Are there any books in the world over 1,000 years old read by people today? It has been said that of the 50,000 books printed over 300 years only 59 have been reprinted. After five years, an ordinary book is generally reckoned to be dead by the publishers; yet century after century the Bible has increased its circulation.

Miracle of its accuracy

Archaeology has proved to be an invaluable aid in confirming Bible records. Excavations carried on in all Bible lands by the pick and spade of the archaeologists have proved many of the deductions of the higher critics to be false and the Bible to be true. Eminent scholars, like Professor Sayce and Sir William Ramsey, humbly confessed their changed attitude toward the criticism of the Bible as the result of the discoveries of archaeology.

While the Bible does not set itself up as an up-to-date scientific treatise, and may not therefore carry the language specially for the benefit of the twentieth-century scientist, it is yet in accord with all true science.

Miracle of its harmony

The unity, making the 66 books of the Bible one book, is another striking evidence of its supernaturalness. On any given subject, harmony prevails throughout. Though written by some 40 writers over 1,500 years, its 66 books agree. There are 333 prophecies in the Old Testament about Jesus Christ, while the New Testament quotes 278 references word for word from the Old Testament, 100 partly word for word, and 124 incidents mentioned therein (Luke 24: 27).

Miracle of its preservation

We could fill volumes with the divine preservation of the Bible through the centuries. Nothing man or devil has done has been sufficient to destroy "the Word of the Lord enduring forever." It has been publicly burnt. It has carried the death penalty for its possession, but all efforts to exterminate it have failed. Now it is universally honored and read.

Miracle of its preparation

How all the books of the Bible came to be chosen and formed into the present canon is an aspect beyond our present task. What we do believe is that in the Bible as we now have it there are evidences of the superintendence of the Holy Spirit. While within the last quarter of a century we have had a flood of new versions, translations, and interpretations, God's providence has kept from harm and error the treasure of His written Word. Westcott and Hort, great scholars of their time, gave long and arduous research in old manuscripts. Here is their considered judgment:

With regard to the great bulk of the words of the New Testament, as of most other ancient writings, there is no variation or other ground of doubt; and, therefore, no room for textual criticism. . . . The amount of what can, in any sense, be called substantial variation, is but a small fraction of the residuary variation, and can hardly form more than a thousandth part of the entire text.

Out of every thousand words of the Greek Testament there is practically no question that nine hundred and ninety-nine were the actual words written by the apostles and evangelists. The Christian, therefore, can take the whole Bible in his hand and say without fear or hesitation that he holds the revealed Word of God handed down, without essential loss, from generation to generation throughout the centuries.

Miracle of its abiding power

Supernatural in its preparation and preservation, it is likewise supernatural in its power. No other book has influenced men and nations like the Bible. Miraculous in its working, it produces miracles in the hearts and lives of those who believe it, and we will never be able to explain how its truths give life to those who were dead in sin. Modernism and rationalism may try to weaken the Bible's power and authority, but it continues its triumphant ministry in a world of need and is still living, active, sharper than any two-edged sword (Hebrews 4:12 RV).

Miracle of its circulation

The Bible is still the world's "best-seller," even though it is thousands of years old. Even in this highly scientific age of ours, when multitudinous books, both good and bad, are pouring out of the presses, the Bible outstrips all in its circulation. It has been translated into well over 1,000 languages with a yearly production of over 30 million copies. It goes everywhere, into the snow igloos of the Eskimos, the bamboo huts of the tropics, the skin tents of the Bedouins, and the boat houses of the Chinese river people. What else can we say but, "All Hail, miracle Book!"

II.
THE MIRACLES OF THE BOOKS OF MOSES

1. The Miracle of Creation

(Genesis 1; Hebrews 11:3; See Psalm 104; Job 26:8; Proverbs 8)

Some of the greatest miracles ever performed form the opening of God's miraculous Book. What a stupendous, staggering display of divine power fills the opening pages of the Bible! Space does not allow us to deal with all that is associated with the Genesis account of creation. The whole wonderful record of creation is compressed in the majestic opening phrase of the Bible, "In the beginning God created the heaven and the earth" (1:1), just as the only authentic record in the world of man's beginning is found in the words, "The Lord God formed man of the dust of the earth, and breathed into his nostrils the breath of life, and man became a living soul" (Genesis 2:7). With saints of old, we too affirm that "through faith we understand that the worlds were framed by the Word of God" (Hebrews 11:3).

As to the Creators, the Bible declares that all three Persons of the Trinity were united in the work of creation. The psalmist brings Father, Son, and Spirit together in one verse in his description of creation. "By the *Word* (Christ) of the *Lord* (Jehovah—God) were the heavens made; and all the host of them by the *Breath* (Spirit) of His mouth" (33:6). Isaiah indicates God's share in creation (42:5-7); David speaks of Christ's part in creation (Psalm 102:25-27; Hebrews 1); Job gives us a glimpse of the Spirit's partnership in such a task (26:13).

Creation is both a monument of divine power and a mirror reflecting divine wisdom. Let us first of all look at the monument of power as revealed in the creation of the universe and of man.

The creation of the world

If a miracle is something above the comprehension of man, then the formation of the universe was a miracle, and one of the mightiest of miracles. Thomas Watson, the old Puritan expositor whom C. H. Spurgeon loved to read, wrote of creation as "the heathen man's Bible, the ploughman's primer, and the traveller's perspectus glass through which he receives a representation of the infinite excellencies what are in God. The creation is a large volume in which God's works are bound up; and this volume has three great leaves in it, heaven, earth, sea."

The Trinity fashioned the world out of nothing. There was no pre-existent matter to work with. In the building of the Temple, Solomon needed workmen and they required tools, but no tools were necessary when the world was created. In generation, there is some substance to work upon, but the glorious fabric of creation came out of the womb of nothing. God hung the world on nothing.

The Trinity made the universe with a word. They spoke and it was done. By Their word the heavens were made (Psalm 33:6). The disciples marvelled that Christ could with a word calm the sea, but it was a greater miracle to cause the seas of the world to appear with a word.

The Trinity fashioned everything good—that is, without defect or deformity (Genesis 1:31). Divine fingers created a perfect work (Psalm 8:3). It was not long, however, before the sin of man marred a beautiful earth. "Sin has eclipsed the beauty, soured the sweetness, and marred the harmony of the world," says Thomas Watson.

The Trinity beautified creation. Not only was the world created for man's profit, but for His pleasure. Thus the earth was decked with flowers, and the heavens studded with the jewels of the sun, moon and stars, so that all aspects of the universe might be admired. What lovers of beauty the Persons of the Trinity must be!

Here are a few scattered, expressive quotations setting forth the beneficent and beautiful aspects of creation:

"The sun for a light by day, and the ordinances of the moon and of the stars for a light by night."

"He bringeth out their host by number; He called them all by name; by the greatness of His might, and for that He is strong in power, not one of them is lacking."

"He maketh the outgoings of the morning and the evening to rejoice."

"He thundereth with the voice of His majesty; great things doeth He, which we cannot comprehend."

"He maketh the clouds His chariots; He walketh upon the wings of the wind."

"He giveth snow like wool; He scattereth the hoarfrost like ashes. He casteth forth His ice like morsels; who can stand before His cold."

"He calleth for the waters of the sea and poureth them out upon the face of the earth."

"He sendeth forth springs into the valleys; they run among the mountains" (Psalm 65:5; 104:3, 10; 147:16, 17; Job 37:5; Jeremiah 31:35; Isaiah 40:26; Amos 5:8).

All of these passages also indicate divine power at work in and behind nature.

Of the manifestation of miraculous power, Henry Thorne has this to say in his first volume on *Bible Readings in Genesis*:

If by the miraculous we understand the putting forth of divine power by methods and processes which are unusual and incomprehensible, so far as human beings are concerned, then the story of creation is the story of the miraculous. If the miracle of creation be credible, then it is not irrational to believe that other miracles may have been wrought. The multiplication of the loaves and fishes is a small matter when compared with the bringing into existence of countless acres of barley and wheat, and the innumerable occupants of oceans and trees. The blighting of a fig tree is a minor matter as compared with the marvels of creation as seen in the vegetable world. The miracle of creation is no lying miracle; it is a splendid reality. It is a miracle of mercy, for it is evidently wrought in anticipation of the Fall. It reflects the power, the wisdom, the greatness, the glory, and the goodness of the One by whom it was wrought.

Having considered creation as a monument of divine power, let us briefly dwell upon creation as a mirror reflecting divine wisdom. As "the only wise God," He was well able to curiously contrive the universe. No matter where we turn we have thought, design, and plan in all His created works. Is this not seen in marshalling and ordering everything in its proper place and sphere? "Lord, how manifold are thy works! *in wisdom hast thou made them all*" (Psalm 104:24).

Miracles of divine wisdom confront us on every hand. For example, take the statement, "Thou hast made summer and winter" (Psalm 74:17)! Dear old Watson, in his quaint yet telling fashion, has this comment when dealing with the wisdom of God, as seen in creation and redemption:

If the sun had been set lower, it would have burnt us; if higher, it would have not warmed us with its beams. God's wisdom is seen in appointing the seasons of the year. If it had been all summer, the heat would have scorched us; if all winter, the cold would have killed us.

The wisdom of God is seen in chequering the dark and light. If it had been all night, there had been no labour; if all day, there had been no rest.

Wisdom is seen in mixing the elements, as earth with the sea. If it had been all sea, we had wanted bread; if it had been all earth, we had wanted water. The wisdom of God is seen in preparing and ripening the fruits of the earth, in the wind and frost that prepare the fruits, and in the sun and rain that ripen the first-fruits. God's wisdom is seen in setting bounds to the sea, and so wisely contriving it that though the sea be higher than many parts of the earth, yet it should not overflow the earth.

Great and marvellous though the present universe is, its tragic dissolution is foretold (II Peter 3:10-12; Revelation 20:11; 21:1), as well as its coming transformation into the new heaven and the new earth. In this new and eternal world, however, one conspicuous part presently covering two-thirds of our earth will be missing—"there shall be *no more* sea" (Revelation 21:1).

The creation of man

If a miracle is a departure from the regular course of things, then the creation of man was a miracle. As it is evident that there must have been a first man, it is equally evident that that first man must have been brought into being by the working of a miracle. And, accepting the Almightiness of God as we do, we see no reason why He was not able to fashion Adam, in a moment of time, out of a few particles of dust (Genesis 1:26,27; 2:7).

Man is the most exquisite piece—God's masterpiece—in creation. Made with deliberation and counsel ("Let us make men"), he is a microcosm, or little world. The plural will be noted, "Let *us*," meaning that a solemn council of the Trinity was called, and God stamped His image on man and made him partaker of many divine qualities.

Self-evolution was unknown to the ancients and they, therefore, gave God all the glory of their creation. Job, for example, had no doubt as to how he came into being:

Thine hands took pains about me, and
fashioned me together round about . . .
Thou hast made me as the clay . . . Thou
hast clothed me with skin and flesh, and
hast fenced me with bones and sinews . . .
The Spirit of God hath made me, and the
breath of the Almighty hath given me life
(10:8-11; 12:10; 33:4).

David says, "I was curiously wrought"
(Psalm 139), and because our bodies were
made out of dust, and that dust out of
nothing, what room is there for pride? No
matter how beautiful we may be, the same
is only well-colored dust, and as dust must
return to dust. Into the body life came,
and He who gave life and sustains it can
recall it at will. "In whose hand is the soul
of every living thing, and the breath of all
mankind" (Job 12:10).

How unworthy and adverse is the theory
of evolution alongside of the noble account
of man's beginning! Julian Huxley, the high
priest among modern evolutionists, has no
time for the Genesis record of creation.
This "so-called revelation of Scripture," as
he calls it, is "simply an appeal to mythol-
ogy, and I do not concern myself with it."
To him, "God is one among several hypoth-
eses," and, therefore, not the Almighty
One able to create man as the Bible affirms. To Huxley, man gradually evolved,
passing through multitudinous stages until
he became an ape; then through the missing link, (which evolutionists cannot discover), man appeared. No wonder Huxley
speaks of men as "trivial microbes." But a
man equally as learned as Huxley, Sir J.
William Dawson of McGill University, said,
"Evolution as an hypothesis has no basis in
experience or in scientific fact." Professor
S. F. Wright of Oberlin College, in his
Other Side of Evolution, affirms that, "The
doctrine of evolution as it is now becoming
current in popular literature is one-tenth
bad science and nine-tenths bad philosophy." Dr. Etheridge, curator of the natural
history branch of the British Museum, has
this authoritative word: "In all this great
museum, there is not a particle of evidence
of the transmutation of species. Nine-tenths
of the talk of evolutionists is sheer non-
sense. Men adopt a theory and then strain
their facts to support it. *This museum is
full of proofs of the utter falsity of their
views.*"
The position of the evolutionist, whether
religious or otherwise, seems to be, "We
shall strain out as much of the gnat of the

supernatural as we can, and swallow as
much of the camel of evolution as we can,"
as Dr. Franklin Johnson expresses it in
Fallacies of the Higher Criticism.
As we conclude this section on the miracle of creation, a word or two may be in
order concerning the relationship between
the Bible and science. When the Bible is
rightly understood and honorably and hon-
estly compared with *true science*—not *theories*—it is found to be up-to-date and correct.
Lord Kelvin, who was no mean scientist,
said, "There is not a single ascertained fact
of science that conflicts with any statement
of the Bible."
There are no errors in the Bible, whether
scientific or otherwise. On the contrary,
there are many remarkable anticipations of
scientific discovery—namely, the fact that
the atmosphere has weight; that the blood
circulates; that minute dust particles give
the sky its hue; that animals breed true;
that man cannot govern himself; that science
cannot find out God. To quote from the
"Foreword" of Lt. Col. Merson Davies'
great book, *The Bible and Modern Science:*

The Bible waits at the head of the paths
of scientific progress to greet the dis-
coverer with its revelation of prior
knowledge. . . . The investigator climbs
upward through the twilight and finds
Scripture illuminating the summit of
his climb.

The Bible is not, and was never meant to
be, a scientific book; yet many of its statements invade the realm of science simply
because that it is the divine revelation from
Him, who knows the end from the beginning. Here are two illustrations describing
the correspondence between the order of
items in the Genesis story of creation and
the latest findings of science.
The order which geology claims as correct for the development of this earth is
exactly the order of Moses.
   (1) Chaos
   (2) Light
   (3) Firmament, or expanse
   (4) Dry land
   (5) Vegetation
   (6) Life in water, in air, on land
   (7) Man
In comparative anatomy, the question of
rank among the vertebrate animals is determined by the proportion of brain to
spinal column. These proportions work out
thus:

Fish,	2–1
Reptiles,	2½–1
Birds,	3–1
Mammals,	4–1
Man,	33–1

Thousands of years before comparative anatomy took rank among the sciences, the author of Genesis followed the correct order of classification in his story of creation. Let us never be afraid of science discrediting the Bible, which is "settled in Heaven" and will stand when man-conceived theories cease. Whence came the knowledge of Moses? "Not from the laboratory of the chemist, not from the observatory of the astronomer, not from the dens and caves and forests explored by the geologist; it came from Him in whom is all knowledge, and to whom the discoveries of scientists are as the small dust in the balance of the sun of what may be known."

2. The Miracle of Enoch's Translation

(Genesis 5:19-24; Hebrews 11:5. See Jude 14, 15)

If a miracle is something that cannot be accounted for by what we have seen and known, then the whole book of Genesis is a miracle. Enoch's translation, the Ark, the confusion of tongues, and other miracles prove this first book of the Bible to be of a supernatural character. Here is the only authentic book of origins or beginnings in the world; and science cannot account for its existence, for it cannot be denied that Genesis contains records which, though they agree with the most advanced science of the age, were written thousands of years before modern science had opened its eyes.

Coming to the brief yet blessed biography of Enoch, we discover that everything about his testimony and translation is miraculous. The first mention of this saint is in Genesis 5, a register of births and deaths and a chapter of remarkable longevity. If we add together the life-span of those who are named we have a period of 8,575 years. Enoch had the shortest life span, 365 years, and his son Methuselah lived 969 years— 31 years short of a millennium.

The testimony of Enoch

The unstained testimony of this patriarch was a miracle of grace. The Enoch we are considering, the son of Jared, must not be confused with a previous Enoch, Cain's eldest son (Genesis 4:17, 18).

(1) He walked with God.

Twice over we have the phrase, "he walked with God" (Genesis 5:22, 24). The repetition emphasizes how conspicuous this phase of his character was. Although Enoch begat sons and daughters, he did not find family ties and trials to be incompatible with a life of devotion to God. Family responsibilities never quenched the fire of his piety, and family joys were not permitted to detract from the goal of his consecrated life. It is somewhat interesting to note that it is only after the birth of Methuselah, when Enoch was 65 years of age, that the record says that he walked with God. The gift of a child possibly awakened in him a new love to God, as well as a deeper sense of his responsibility as a father.

Further, although Enoch lived in a contaminated age, he kept himself unspotted from the corrupt world surrounding him. Something of the wickedness of the antediluvian age in which he lived and which he witnessed can be gathered from his prophecy which Jude quotes. Even in his apostate time, Enoch demonstrated the hope of immortality. The repeated phrase, "he walked with God," affords one of those particular examples of the effects of God's grace and contains the principle of all that was excellent in Enoch's character.

It is only of Enoch and Noah that we read that they "walked with God" (Genesis 5:24; 6:9). "Others walked before God" (Genesis 17:1). Such a walk implies *agreement*, for how can two walk together except there be agreement in mind and will? (Amos 3:3); *familiarity*, for how can two walk together unless they open to each other their confidences? God and Enoch were friends and communicated to each other their secrets (John 14:21, 22); *affection*, for love is the essence of material intercourse. God and Enoch loved each other, and thus avoided any possible estrangement (Psalm 37:4).

Fausset suggests that the phrase, "walking with God," may have been a relic of the first Paradise, when man walked and talked with God in holy familiarity, and an anticipation of the second Paradise (Revelation 21:3; 22:3, 4).

(2) He pleased God.

Before his translation, Enoch had this testimony that "he pleased God." This added feature, which the LXX translates as "he walked with God," denotes, as Fausset reminds us, a steady continuance in well-doing, and a life spent in the immediate presence of, and in constant communion with, God. He was a fitting type of Christ of whom God said, "This is My well-beloved Son in Whom I am well pleased."

Enoch is spoken of as being the "seventh" from Adam. "Seven" is the number indicating divine completeness. Enoch typifies perfected humanity. Irenaeus says, "As angels fall to earth by transgression, so this man was raised to heaven by pleasing God."

Enoch's holy walk elicited little pleasure from those around him. His godliness found no acceptance with his godless contemporaries as the reference in Jude suggests (16, 18). So deep was the depravity of the antediluvians that Enoch's testimony and warning had no impact upon them, and the flood came and took them all away, except his grandson Noah and his family.

(3) He believed God.

Enoch knew that without faith it was impossible to please God; thus his faith was the mainspring of the life acceptable to God (Hebrews 11:5, 6). Charles Simeon has a suggestive footnote on "translated *by faith.*"

Though faith might have more immediate respect to some promise given him relative to his translation, yet we can scarcely conceive but that it had a further respect to the promised Messiah. And this idea is greatly strengthened by the account Jude gives us of his foretelling the very manner of the future Judgment (14, 15), for if he prophesied of Christ's *second* coming, doubtless he was not ignorant of His *first* advent.

(4) He prophesied for God.

Enoch was a seer, as well as a saint, and a seer because he was a saint. Enoch was one of the guardians of prophecy. The Arabs have a legend that it was Enoch who invented writing. The Jews affirm that he left many written books. Is not his solemn prophecy of the Lord coming "to execute judgment" one that needs to be declared from the housetops in our godless age? Somehow we are drifting away from the stern warning in the Bible concerning the coming judgment, and eternal hell of the wicked.

The translation of Enoch

Scarcely 50 years after the death of Adam, with whom Enoch must have conversed on the origin of creation, sin and death, Enoch was given an intimation of the life to come. Under the old dispensation, patriarchs looked for a better, even a heavenly, country (Genesis 49:18; Job 19:25; Hebrews 11:10, 13, 16), and confessed that they were strangers on the earth. Then, for Enoch, the miracle happened. Just as God transferred the prophet suddenly from one place to another (I Kings 18:12), and caught away Philip (Acts 8:39), so Enoch, alive and well, was caught up to heaven. Elijah, in his translation, caught a glimpse of the same glorious hope.

The language used to describe Enoch's miraculous translation is profitable to observe. First of all, we have the arrestive phrases—"He was not" and "He was not found" (Genesis 5:24; Hebrews 11:5), suggesting the thought that one day this godly man was missed and could not be found. Possibly, he was sought for by his friends who honored him (see II Kings 2:16), or by his enemies who hated him (see I Kings 18:10). Yet his sudden disappearance was only a nine-day wonder, as the rapture of the saints will be at Christ's return.

"God took him"—"God had translated him." These phrases imply Enoch's miraculous ascension (Genesis 5:24; Hebrews 11: 5). He was the first saint to hear the musical voice saying, "Arise up, my love, my fair one, and come away" (Song of Solomon 2:10). Up he went from a persecuting and ungodly world, which probably sought to destroy him because of his pungent warnings (Jude 14, 15). Enoch did not see death, meaning, he had no experience of it. He was not raised from the dead for he had never died. He was transplanted to another sphere. "*Translated* implies a sudden removal from mortality to immortality without death, such as shall pass over the living saints at Christ's coming (I Corinthians 15:51, 52), of whom Enoch is a type." And his translation was an appropriate testimony to the truth he announced in the face of a mocking, infidel world— *Behold, the Lord cometh!*

"Enoch," says Fausset, "is a specimen of transfiguration without death in instantaneous change, an earnest of those saints who shall be found living, and shall be transfigured in a moment into the likeness of

Christ's glorious body at His appearing." If we have Enoch's testimony, there is no doubt about one participation in his translation.

3. The Miracle of the Flood

(Genesis 7:9-12, 17-24; 8:2; Matthew 24:37-39; Hebrews 11:7; I Peter 3:20; II Peter 2:5)

The terrible catastrophe overtaking the antediluvians is a tragic reminder of what can happen when God unleashes the powers of nature, which He Himself created. Although liberal-minded theologians dismiss the account of the Flood as myth or fable, true Christians have no doubt as to its reality. Sir Leonard Woolley and Dr. Langdon, who both discredited the Genesis record of the Flood, went out and excavated in the regions of Ur and Kish in 1927 and found such unmistakable evidence of the Flood that in March 1929 they wrote to the London *Times,* "We were loath to believe that we had obtained confirmation of the Deluge of Genesis, but there is no doubt about it now."

The housing of thousands of birds and beasts and creeping things in the Ark God designed and commanded Noah to build, and the fearful deluge destroying all that had life outside the Ark, stands out as one of the most awesome miracles of the Bible. For an excellent summary in connection with archaeological discoveries in the Flood region, and traditions of the Flood, the reader is referred to Halley's *Pocket Bible Handbook.*

If our space permitted, there are so many interesting aspects of the Flood record we would have liked to develop. There are the predictions of the Flood by God over 120 years before its occurrence; the prophetic phase of the Flood as given by Christ in His Olivet Discourse; the necessity of the Flood because of universal corruption and violence; the extent of its coverage and destruction; the size, form and occupants of the Ark; and the noble example, patience, and the altar of Noah. But as this is a book dealing with Bible miracles, we must concentrate on the actual, heaven-commanded Flood itself—a miracle of nature if ever there was one.

While the physical causes of the Flood are clearly stated, behind the surging torrents of water bringing such terrible destruction, there is the direct action of Him who is spoken of as the Father of the rain (Job 5:10; 38:28). He it was who unleased the volume of water from below and above. "His hand drew the map of the earth's surface, shaping the coast line and giving to the oceans their boundaries," says Ada R. Habershon, "and His power extends over all the waters that are upon the earth as well as those in the clouds above."

God's power over all seas, rivers, springs, and streams is clearly taught in Scripture (Psalm 104:10; 107:22, 35; Job 12:15; Genesis 7:11). Thus when He punished the wickedness of the earth by means of the mighty Flood, He broke up the fountains of the deep, meaning that by some rapid change, the waters He had bounded at creation were let loose to fulfil His purpose. At the same time, the clouds poured down their extraordinary torrents of rain, as if the upper floodgates were thrown open to meet the ocean bursting its way up through the abysses of earth. Vast displacements of water produced terrible effects. Halley draws attention to the fact that "the map of the Armenian mountain country is almost like the crown of a vast island system surrounded by the Caspian, Black, Mediterranean, and Arabian Seas and Indian Ocean. A cataclysmic subsidence of the region would cause the waters to pour in from all these seas, that from the Indian Ocean bore the Ark swiftly northward." Since the seas are His, because He made them, they obeyed His bidding.

As to the destruction the Flood caused, the whole race—computed to be well over 1,000,000 people alive at that time—perished. Only four men and four women were spared because they did not go with the great sin drift. After more than 1,600 years of human history, the race was so utterly corrupt morally that it was not fit to live. The gruesome fact of the Flood is that there are limits even to the mercy of God, and that the laws of nature are so framed that they utter loud and sometimes awful portents against breaches of divine mercy and against those laws which are the expression of God's moral government.

To destroy all the human race with the exception of eight souls was indeed a terrible resolve, yet although the judgment was so devastating, it was strictly just. As the Judge of all earth, God is always just and right. So, as Charles Simeon reminds us, "Never, from the foundation of the world to this hour, if we except the sacrifice which Christ made of Himself upon the cross for the sins of men, was there such a demonstration of God's hatred of sin, as that which was given at the universal deluge. All flesh having corrupted their way, God determined to destroy from the face of the earth every living thing."

Amid such destruction, however, there was the manifestation of grace for we read that God shut Noah and his family in the Ark. "The assigning to Jehovah of this act of personal care for Noah is very remarkable." All Noah could do as the floods rose was to look through the one window in the top of the Ark. "While the windows of heaven were open (Genesis 7:11), Noah kept his window closed, but when the windows were closed the window of the Ark was opened (Genesis 8:2)" is Henry Thorne's suggestive comment. This brings us to the double, opposite effect of the miracle of the Flood. All who were in the Ark were saved from death; all who were outside the Ark were destroyed, proving that "grace is always superior to law, for even when law was reigning, it could come in and counteract the law; but when grace is reigning, law is powerless to upset it. When law, like a deluge, would overwhelm with judgment, grace provides an Ark which rides above the Flood."

After raining for nearly six weeks (Genesis 7:4, 12) and the waters covering the earth for another 110 days after the rain ceased—making 150 days in all (7:24), another miracle was necessary to make the earth dry again (8:14). The Bible, in a graphic paragraph, tells us how the Flood ceased:

God made a wind to pass over the earth, and the waters assuaged; the fountains also of the deep and the windows of heaven were stopped, and the rain from heaven was restrained; and the waters returned from off the earth continually: and after the end of the hundred and fifty days the waters were abated (Genesis 8:1-3).

The creative wind (Genesis 1:2) began to blow as the rain ceased, and it affected the course of the Ark. "Stormy wind fulfilling His word." God often called upon His winds to carry out His purpose of judgment or mercy. They said of Jesus, "What manner of Man is this that even the winds and the waves obey Him." Following upon the cessation of the Flood came God's covenant that never again would He destroy the human race in such a way. The brilliant and beautiful rainbow became a symbol of God's faithfulness (Revelation 4:3). The earth's next destruction will be by *fire* (II Peter 3:7). That rainbow was for those brought through the Flood, not for those who were dead when it appeared. Those who are dead in their sins have no covenant with God. Every time a Christian sees a rainbow his faith in a covenant-keeping God is intensified.

4. The Miracle of Babel

(Genesis 11:1, 5-9; Isaiah 13:1)

As we pass from miracle to miracle, we are amazed, not only at the display of the sovereignty of God in every sphere, but also at the sorrow sinners occasioned Him. "Poor God," as one has described Him. Disappointment came to Him after He did His best for men in the crises of history. After the wonderful creation, Adam and Eve failed Him. After Noah's miraculous deliverance from the Flood, he and his family failed Him. Now, at Babel, for the third time, man failed God, and for the third time God did not utterly destroy sinners, but "preserved a line which led to Calvary and universal redemption."

The story of the building of Babel is told with remarkable brevity. The Bible never wastes words. Hosts of nomads from the East settled in Babylonia (Genesis 10:10)—a decision altogether against the Divine purpose (Genesis 1:28; 9:1, 7, 9). The whole earth used only one language with few words, or one kind of words. What that language was we cannot tell. Some writers suggest that it was the Hebrew tongue. This much do we know, that the faculty of speech and the words of the first language were divinely created and given. Adam could not have invented the language he used in conversing with his Creator. Both Adam and Eve instinctively understood the divine language and gave to the animals expression of their habits and nature. It was this language God used in giving to Moses the revelation found in Genesis, and it was the same language used universally at Babel, some 100 years after the Flood (Genesis 10:25; 11:9).

At Babel, the native name for Babylon,

the people built a city and a tower. Babylon, among all the cities of the ancient world was noted for its high towers. Babel, meaning *confusion,* stands for "an impossible lofty structure, a visionary scheme, a turbulent assemblage and a scene of utter confusion, a place of uproar." Now we speak of a confusion of voices, sounds and noises as "a perfect babble." In the spirit of rebellion the people said, "Let us build ourselves a city with a tower." There is, of course, nothing wrong in building cities, a project that commenced with Cain (Genesis 4:17). The evil phase of such a project was the desire to have "a tower whose top reached the heavens," thereby making a name for the builders themselves. But God alone has the right "to make Himself a name" (Isaiah 63:12, 14; Jeremiah 32:20).

Fausset says that this proud ambition had a two-fold object:

(1) They wished to have some central beacon which might guide them on their return from their wanderings.

(2) They had a distinctly ambitious object, for by remaining as one nation they would be able to reduce to obedience all the tribes now perpetually wandering away from them, and so would "make them a name"—a sort of universal empire.

Having lost the inward spiritual bond of unity—love to God uniting them in love to one another—they endeavored to make up for it by an outward forced unity. Such a proud ambition was open rebellion against a false security and another sad instance of the perverseness of man, necessitating another miracle of judgment. The action of the builders proved that although the Flood destroyed sinners, it did not destroy sin. Doubtless the Devil, in prompting those builders, thought he could defeat God's purposes. But no Devil or man can succeed at that (Proverbs 21:30).

God interrupted the builders in the midst of their hopes and plans, even as He did when the rich farmer wanted to build larger barns. Human sin is no match for divine sovereignty, so the Trinity came down and made a babble of the one language. "Let *us* go down" (see Genesis 1:26; 11:7). In ten thousand ways the Trinity can render the plans of the wicked abortive (Proverbs 5:21; 11:21). The confusion of tongues was God's method of dispersing the race to its task of subduing the earth. In such a punishment there was a providence, for the dispersion was a means of deliverance.

The true origin of the diversity of languages and distinct dialects, of which there are now over 7,000, is here in the miracle before us. Rebellious men may say, "Our lips are our own: who is Lord over us" (Psalm 12:3), but the God who created speech has power over it. Having made man's mouth (Exodus 4:10-12), He can cause articulate men to be dumb (Ezekiel 3:26, 27; Luke 1:20, 64), or make the dumb to speak (Matthew 15:31). At Babel, God confounded the language men spoke and defeated thereby their attempt to create a central city to defeat the divine purpose. Because they could no longer understand one another's speech, they dispersed. "The divine means of counteracting men's ambitious and ever-recurring dreams of universal sovereignty is the law of diversity of speech."

Of this miracle of the confusion of tongues, Faussett remarks, "The cause of the division of languages lies in an operation wrought upon the human *mind,* by which the original unity of feeling, thought and will are broken up. . . . The confusion of tongues was not at random, but a systematic distribution of languages for the purpose of a systematic distribution of man is emigration" (Genesis 10:5, 20, 31).

Today, diversity of language keep nations apart and often prevents portions of the same kingdom from agreeing heartily together. Such diversity of speech places obstacles in the way of commercial intercourse, or has caused distant nations to consider each other as enemies. The variety of languages that are now spoken by men and the distinctiveness of their nationalities are standing monuments of the folly of resisting the purpose of God. Then think of the obstacle such diversity is to the spread of the Gospel! In order to speak to the heathen in their own tongues, missionaries have to spend years mastering the native language and idioms.

Although the primitive language has been lost and various tongues characterize the nations of the earth, the time is coming when there will be one "pure language" (Zephaniah 3:9). Then "His name will be one" (Zechariah 14:9). In heaven with one tongue, the redeemed sing praises unto Him through whose grace they find themselves in the Eternal City.

5. The Miracle of Plagued Pharaoh

(Genesis 12:10-20)

One of the distinguishing features of the Bible is its faithfulness and candor in portraying human life and character. It is never guilty of whitewashing any of its saints. It paints its picture, as it is said Oliver Cromwell wanted his portrait, "wart and all." Devil depths, as well as angel heights, are seen in the lives of some of the best of men—a feature encouraging to our hearts, for here are men of like passions as ourselves.

Abraham stands out as one of the greatest characters in Old Testament history. What a man of remarkable faith he was! Yet the Bible does not gloss over the fact that he was a man of failure as well. Abraham's response to the call of God was unique. His obedience was complete. "He went out not knowing whither he went" (Hebrews 11:8). All through his long pilgrimage of 175 years, his main direction was God-ward (Hebrews 11:10). Yet there were two or three sad relapses or retreats (Genesis 12:10-20; 20).

One of Abraham's backslidings is in the somewhat unnoticed miracle before us which was an acted parable of God's preventitive grace. The occasion of the heaven-sent plague upon Pharaoh's house was Abraham's act of disobedience. God had led the patriarch to Canaan, but he went into Egypt without divine guidance. Famine in Canaan was the cause of his departure from the path of obedience. He should have relied upon the promise, "In the days of famine thou shalt be satisfied" (Psalm 37:19). Famine was often a disciplinary testing of God's people in the land (Genesis 26:1; 42:5; Ruth 1:11; Psalm 105:16). The resort to Egypt (type of the world) typifies the tendency to substitute for lost spiritual power the fleshly resources of the world instead of seeking through confession and amendment the restoration of God's favor.

What a contrast the One greater than Abraham presents when He was without food in the wilderness. Christ would do nothing to dishonor His Father. Bread was a secondary consideration with Him. His meat was to do the will of His Father, or to live "by every word that proceedeth out of the mouth of God" (Matthew 4:4). Down in Egypt Abraham placed Sarah his wife in circumstances of great moral danger, and also exposed her to gravest danger as the mother of the promised seed. Sarah, a woman of remarkable beauty, was Abraham's half-sister. They had the same father, but not the same mother (Genesis 20:12). But when Abraham told Pharaoh that Sarah was his sister (Genesis 12:13, 19), he lied in that he implied that Sarah was wholly his sister and not his wife. Possibly it was because Abraham knew how ancient monarchs would employ any means, however cruel and violent, to secure a radiantly beautiful woman for their harems, that he acted as he did. Pharaoh, pleased with Sarah as a valuable acquisition and feeling he was acting lawfully, took her into his house and generously rewarded Abraham.

Just what the plagues were the Lord sent upon Pharaoh and his house as a warning to the monarch that he was not to touch Sarah, we are not told. Perhaps as the plagues fell, Sarah revealed her true relationship to Abraham. Plagues in Scripture are used for all diseases and inflictions of temporal sufferings by the immediate hand of God. A plague, then, can represent any sudden, severe and dangerous disease, or sickness, or pestilence that "walketh in darkness" (Psalm 91:6)—that is, a mysterious, sudden calamity in the night, in the absence of the light and heat of the sun. Doubtless, the alarming marked troubles or afflictions of whatever sort they were only lasted as long as Sarah was under Pharaoh's roof.

God had said to Abraham when He called him, "I will bless thee and make thee a blessing," but in Egypt Abraham was a curse. What a repulsive picture of contempt and abject cowardice he presents in placing his wife in the home of another man! No wonder the heathen prince hurried the man of God out of his land, as if he were chasing away a pestilence. Abraham had acted without praying; he feared man; he tampered with the truth; and he suffered the humiliation of an ungodly man's censure.

The silence of Abraham, when rebuked by Pharaoh and expelled from Egypt, seems to indicate his consciousness that "Pharaoh had acted more righteously than he had. Yet his repetition of the same offense (Genesis 20) proves that Abraham did not feel much self-reproach at what he had done." This fact is evident, that the God who plagued Pharaoh preserved the chastity of Sarah and graciously pardoned the sinning of Abraham. Grace brought him up out of Egypt (Genesis 13:1) and led him "to the place of the altar which he had made there at the first." Forgiven and restored, Abraham resumed his life as a pilgrim and a worshiper with his tent and altar, neither of which he had in Egypt.

6. The Miracle of the Smoking Furnace and Burning Lamp

(Genesis 15:17, 18)

After Abraham's successful war with Chedorlaomer, God entered into a covenant with His servant that his seed should be as innumerable as the stars. Up to this time Abraham had only received general promises of offspring and of the land being the possession of his seed. With the advancing years of Sarah and himself, it seemed as if hope of seed of their own was well-nigh impossible. But God vouchsafed Abraham a definite, specific revelation.

The senses of Abraham were divinely closed to all earthly impressions. A mysterious utterance came to him "in a vision." This was "the vision of the Almighty" (Numbers 24:4). Divine presence was granted to Abraham, and during this unusual experience Abraham received the encouraging word regarding God as his shield and exceeding great reward. Abraham became passive in the hands of the Almighty and believed Him regarding the countless host that would come from his loins.

A covenant was confirmed in ancient manner by cutting dead animals in two. Henry Thorne informs us that:

The three animals, each of three years old, may be a suggestion of the mystery of the doctrine of the Trinity. The two birds would fitly represent the two parties to the covenant, and as they were not to be divided, they were, perhaps, intended to represent the unity of purpose and of responsibility that existed between the parties. The animals were divided in the midst, and in each case the separate portions were placed on opposite sides to each other so as to form a narrow lane through which the covenanting parties might pass.

At night in a deep trance, with those accompaniments of terror so powerfully described in Job 4:12-16, when the creature cannot but feel that he is near the manifest presence of the Creator (Daniel 10:8), the full revelation of Abraham's posterity was given him by God. By the "horror of great darkness" is not meant any mental terror. God is the One who is able to clothe the heavens with blackness. What Abraham experienced was a bodily terror, caused by a deep gloom settling around him, equivalent to the effect of an eclipse of a setting sun, shutting out all mortal objects from his view.

When it was dark, between the pieces of slaughtered animals a smoking furnace and a burning lamp passed. Such figurative language is most suggestive. Orientals used in their houses a circular firepot around which they would sit for warmth. The one in the narrative before us was one wreathed in smoke out of which shot a torch of flame, or "a lamp of fire," as the margin puts it. Thus there was only one symbol that passed between the divided carcases. Fire is the symbol of deity and of divine holiness. "Our God is a consuming fire" (Deuteronomy 4:24; Hebrews 12:29). The God answering by fire is the covenant-keeping God. Divine presence and immutability were therefore manifested by the fiery furnace and the lighted lamp.

Doubtless a prophetic significance is attached to these symbols. The furnace can be made to represent the suffering associated with the bondage, the servitude and the cruelties when Israel was under the dominance of Pharaoh (Deuteronomy 4:20; Isaiah 48:10). As a furnace purifies gold (Proverbs 17:3), Israel's sufferings served a great moral purpose. The lamp, or torch, represents the light Israel enjoyed during the dark night of her captivity. He who was her Light brought her forth to the full realization of her privileges, as the Messianic race.

7. The Miracle of Sarah's Conception

(Genesis 17:15-19; 18:10-14; 21:1-8)

For a woman to give birth to a baby when she is 90 years old is nothing else but a miracle. It was one in the case of Sarah, for she was long past the natural age of conception when Isaac was born. The key to this wonderful miracle in the realm of natural generation is the Lord's own question to doubting Sarah, "Is anything too hard for the Lord?" (Genesis

18:14. See Luke 1:37; Jeremiah 32:17). The phrase she used, "After I am waxed old," actually means "to be worn out like an old garment."

Alas, the continual barrenness of Sarah caused her to stagger at the promise of God regarding an heir, and so she resorted to an unworthy method—a carnal policy—to fulfill the divine purpose. Impatient over God's apparent delay, she gave Hagar her handmaid to Abraham, and she bore him Ishmael. She was made to feel she had done wrong (16:5), and Hagar suffered because of it. The bitter fruit of unholy offspring survives in the religion of Mohammed.

As with Jesus, who came from the line of Isaac, the name of the child Sarah was to bear was given by God before his birth (Genesis 17:19; Matthew 1:21). "Isaac," meaning "laughter," perpetuated the laughter of his father and of his mother (17:17; 18:12) and was "a standing memorial that his birth was contrary to nature, and one of which the promise was provocation of ridicule in the sight even of his parents." Sarah gave utterance to her surprise and mingled emotions in her little poem:

> Who would have said unto Abraham,
> Sarah suckleth sons?
> For I have borne a son to his old age.

The fourfold repetition of Sarah's name in three verses (Genesis 21:1-3) is emphatic and impresses us with the fact that Sarah was, without doubt, the mother of this miraculously conceived child. Although Isaac's birth was a miracle, it is but fitting to observe that human life at that period was very much longer than today, so that a woman of 90 as Sarah was when Issac was born (she died at the age of 127) was not at all so aged as would appear in present times. When Isaac was born, Shem was about 560 years old. Sarah is one of the very few women of the Bible whose exact age is given (Genesis 17:17). We have the approximate age of Anna, the prophetess (Luke 2:36, 37). The daughter of Jairus was "about twelve years of age" (Luke 8). So even in Biblical times there was a tendency to suppress information as to the age of women.

In any consideration of Sarah, the prophetic touch must not be neglected. It was said of her that she should grow into nations and that kings of people should spring from her (Genesis 17:16). Then the offer-

ing up of her son by his own father foreshadowed the love of God to mankind in the sacrifice of His only begotten Son (Genesis 22:3-10; comp. with John 3:16).

As to the truth of the sacred narrative of Sarah's life, the veracity of it appears in the faithful record of her faults as well as her faith. Fausset reminds us that it was her motherly affection that so won Isaac that none but Rebekah could comfort him after his mother's death (Genesis 24:67). Sarah was 127 years old when she died at Hebron, 28 years before Abraham's death. She was buried in the cave of Machpelah which Abraham bought from Ephron the Hittite. Today her shrine is shown opposite Abraham's, with Isaac's and Rebekah's on one side, Jacob's and Leah's on the other.

8. The Miracle of the Blinded Sodomites

(Genesis 19:9-11)

The evil principle which the Bible has no hesitation in calling *sin*, which had already wrought terrible havoc in the world, is again conspicuous in the chapter before us. The trail of the serpent can be traced in the inhuman loathsomeness of the men of Sodom, in the incredible shame of Lot toward his daughters, and in their unnatural action toward their father. The prophet Ezekiel wrote of the iniquity of Sodom and of her pridefulness of bread and abundant idleness (16:49).

The identity of the three heavenly visitors who looked toward Sodom (Genesis 18:1) can be easily distinguished. One was the Lord Himself—a theophanic appearance —and the other two who arrived at Sodom were His angelic messengers (19:1). Lot's reception of the angels lacked the warmth Abraham had extended to them. In spite of the licentiousness of the people of Sodom, Lot pressed his hospitality upon the angels who were not as ready to accept it as they did when Abraham offered to entertain them. Lot's character had deteriorated. Living in Sodom had sapped those springs of spiritual power so prominent in Abraham.

An aggravation of the guilt of Sodom and Gomorrah is seen in the fact that they were the descendants of holy Noah (Genesis 6:9) and had become so utterly wicked less than one hundred years after his death. The sins of these guilty cities cover almost all the possibilities of human wickedness.

Pride, satiety, shamelessness, evil influences, adultery, filthy conversation, and fornication (Ezekiel 16:49; Isaiah 3:9; Jeremiah 23:14; II Peter 2:7; Jude 7), all cry out for divine punishment. With the development of cities, corruption became more marked. Sodom was so rich in horticultural beauties that it was deemed to be "as the garden of the Lord." But matching its beauty was its beastiality.

Evidently Lot, as he entertained the angels, believed their solemn message and endeavored to restrain the wicked Sodomites, whom he called his "brethren" as they sought to commit sodomy with the angels. Lot's low moral standard appears in his willingness to hand over his daughters to the lustful Sodomites. He wanted to commit one sin in order to prevent another. Prostitution, he felt, would not be as bad as sodomy, or homosexuality, as we now call it. The record shows that Lot offered no prayer for Sodom as Abraham had done. He manifested no desire for the salvation of the sinners in Sodom. Because of his compromise, the people of Sodom despised him, and he lost any influence he had with his own family (19:9-14).

Jude describes the Sodomites as those who defiled the flesh, despised dominion, and spoke evil of dignities (7, 8). The licentiousness and contempt of dominion are seen in the action of the Sodomites despising Lot's entreaty and charging the door of Lot's house to drag his visitors out. Judgment came upon them and, smitten with blindness, they wearied themselves to find the door—which brings us to the miracle God performed.

Our eyes are that perfect organ of vision "on which the light waves fall and are focused by the beautiful lens, refracted on to the retina and finally conveyed by the optic nerve to the brain." How great God is to have conceived all the intricacies of our visual organs. All the wonders of the eye, which even occulists cannot fully explain, are the product of divine wisdom and skill. Because God fashioned the human eye, it is not too difficult to believe the various miracles in the Bible affecting man's sight. Cures of blindness is one of our Lord's most frequent miracles. In the case of the Sodomites, God instantly deprived them of their sight, as He did in the case of the Syrians who came to take Elisha (II Kings 6:18, 20) and of Elymas the sorcerer (Acts 13:11).

The word used for "blindness" here (19:11) is only found once elsewhere (II Kings 6:18), and in both cases actual, permanent blindness is not meant, but a temporary derangement of optical powers. Ellicott comments:

> The word really means a disturbance of vision caused by the eye not being in its proper connection with the brain. And so the men of Sodom ever seemed just upon the point of reaching the door, and pressed on, and strove and quarrelled, but always failed, they knew not how, but as they always supposed by another's fault. It is a strange picture of men given over to unbelief and sin, and who "see not," because they reject the true light.

At the summit and base of Mount Madherah are blocks of stone, which the Arabs affirm are monuments of "a people who once dwelt there, to whom travelers came seeking hospitality; but the people did to them a horrible deed, wherefore the Almighty in anger rained down stones, and destroyed them off the face of the earth."

9. The Miracle of Sodom and Gomorrah

(Genesis 19:15-25, 28, 29; see Matthew 10:15; II Peter 2:6; Jude 7; Isaiah 1:10-13, 19; Ezekiel 16:49; Jeremiah 49:18)

The sins of Sodom and Gomorrah cried to the Lord for vengeance. Our Lord's description of the Sodomites implies a condition of indifference regarding their impending peril (Luke 17:28). Taken up with their "buying and selling, and planting and building," all they lived and labored for was submerged beneath a wave of divine judgment. The fire of destruction from the Lord destroyed not only all their property, but also their *persons,* "all the inhabitants" (19:25), as in the case of all the antediluvians.

The fact that the apostate and wicked Sodom and Gomorrah, Lot's residence (Isaiah 1:10; Revelation 11:8), were in the very midst of Canaan aggravated the guilt of the Canaanites, who in Joshua's time took no warning from their punishment to avoid their sins (Leviticus 18:24, 25; Joshua 10:40). These cesspools of wickedness were only 20 miles from the city of Melchizedek. The doom of these cities was foretold by God and is often referred to in Scripture; and it is a forerunner of the conditions of things on the earth as the time of Christ's return draws near. The terrible catastrophe overtaking the cities is confirmed by ancient historians and also by present day archaeologists and travelers. The desolate region of the Dead Sea, for example, still proclaims the truth to those who have ears to hear, that "sin shall not go unpunished." Jude speaks of the Sodomites as "suffering the vengeance of eternal fire" (7).

As to the miracle of judgment itself, the sacred record says that the Lord rained upon the cities brimstone and fire out of heaven (19:24). The repetition of the dread title "Jehovah," together with the fact that the burning brimstone came from heaven, add to the horror of the judgment. Some of the old commentators saw in the three-fold repetition of the name Jehovah an indication of the Holy Trinity, as though God, Christ, and the Spirit united in such deserved judgment. Although heaven used natural agencies in the destruction of the cities, "yet what was in itself a catastrophe of nature became miraculous by the circumstances which surrounded it." To quote Ellicott again,

> As far as the catastrophe itself, it was not a mere thunderstorm which set the earth, saturated with naphtha, on fire; but, in a region where earthquakes were common, there was apparently an outburst of volcanic violence, casting forth blazing bitumen and brimstone. This falling down upon the houses, and upon the soil charged with combustible matter, caused a conflagration so sudden and widespread that few or none could escape. Sulphur and nitre are still found as natural products on the shores of the Dead Sea.

Fire is mentioned as being among those elements fulfilling the divine command (Psalm 148:8). Fire falling from heaven is frequently found in the Bible. It came not only as a sign of judgment but also as a sign of acceptance (Leviticus 9:24). If, as some writers suggest, the fire destroying Sodom and Gomorrah burst forth from a subterranean source, it was yet directed by the Lord. Fire is a symbol of divine presence and judgment and is used by Jude to describe the place of eternal torment (Jude 7; Revelation 20:10).

Brimstone, a once common English name for sulphur signifies "burning stone" and refers to the inflammable character of the element. It was probably the first chemical element discovered and used by man.

Homer and the ancient Greeks used it as a fumigator and as a "pest averter." Gardeners today use it to preserve roots. The word "brimstone" is believed to be related to *bitumen,* a substance abounding in the Jordan Valley and around the Dead Sea. The earth tremors Ellicott mentions may have caused a combustion of sulphur or petroleum in the vicinity which spouted up and descended on the cities as if raining from the heavens. Bible references to brimstone are numerous.

M. G. Kyle, the renowned archaeologist, has in his *Explorations at Sodom,* this enlightening paragraph:

> Under Mount Usdom (Sodom) there is a stratum of salt 150 feet thick. Above this is a stratum of marl mingled with free sulphur. It is a burned out region of oil and asphalt. A great rupture in the strata occurred. At the proper time God kindled the gases. A great explosion took place. The salt and the sulphur were thrown into the heavens red hot, so it did literally rain fire and brimstone from heaven.

Thus, mineral found in quantities in the area of Sodom was the instrument used in the destruction of the cities of the plain (Genesis 19:24), for "divine miracle does not supercede the use of God's existing natural agents, but moves in connection with them." Yet we read that in spite of impending doom, Lot lingered. He still clung to his possessions and was loth to leave them. Delay, however, would be fatal. His only safety was in flight. The angels had to take him by the hand and drag him away from the immediate catastrophe. In mercy the Lord said, "Escape for thy life; look not behind thee, neither stay thou in all the plain." A total adandonment of Sodom in heart and will was demanded. Disobedience of such a divine command resulted in terrible punishment as the next miracle proves.

10. The Miracle of Lot's Wife

(Genesis 19:24-28; Luke 17:28-32)

The entreaty of the angels as they sought to deliver Lot's family should be emulated by those who are ambassadors of God in this Gospel age. Multitudes are "in danger of the judgment," and we should be persevering and importunate. An interesting phase of the angelic ministry was that they laid hold upon the hands of Lot and his wife and two daughters. Each felt the grip of an angelic hand. Both the hearts and the hands of the angels were employed in their mission of mercy.

Sodom and Gomorrah, with Adnak, Zeboim and Bela, were located in the Valley of Siddim in the Salt Sea, and were famous for their slime pits (Genesis 14:10). Ancient writers believed that Sodom and Gomorrah were buried beneath the salty deposit of the Dead Sea. Salt pits provided a source of great revenue, and vast sources of salt and slime or bitumen may have been one reason for the raids of Babylonian kings. There appears to be much evidence for the assertion that Sodom stood on the ground now covered by the Dead Sea, or Salt Sea. In the Bible, "salt" is used typically as that which prevents corruption, and the judgment of sin which hinders evil.

While Lot *lingered,* his wife *looked* back. God read the motive of her heart (19:26) and knew of her regret on having to leave the sinful pleasures of Sodom, so she looked back and stayed behind, and was thus guilty of an incurable rebellion. In Oriental countries it was the rule for the wife to walk behind her husband, which was one reason for her nearness to the eruption when it burst forth. She left Sodom as a city, but Sodom was very much in her heart. She was deeply attached to the life she was compelled to relinquish. Thus, as she followed her husband's footsteps, a partner of his flight, she glanced back and became a monument of God's displeasure (19:26). Had Lot *looked* as well as *lingered,* he too would have perished in like manner. Our Lord spoke of those who look back as not being fit for the kingdom of heaven. He also referred to the tragedy of Lot's wife as a spiritual lesson (Luke 17:28-32). This lover of Sodom is one of those suddenly struck down by death in some of the Bible miracles.

As to the miracle of the terrible end of Lot's wife, it is probable that she was struck by lightning and covered and stifled by sulphurous matter and vapors, transforming her into a pillar of salt, which is not to be taken metaphorically. Another explanation is that an earth-quake heaped up a mighty mass of the rock-salt found in a solid strata around the Dead Sea, and that Lot's wife was entangled in the convulsion and perished, leaving the hill of salt in which she was enclosed as her memorial. Entombed in this salt pillar, she became,

as the Apocrypha puts it, "a monument of an unbelieving soul" (Wisdom 10:7). Many pillars of salt at the south end of the Dead Sea have borne the name of "Lot's Wife." Travelers tell of local guides who affirm that if a finger or some other part of the pillar is broken off, it is immediately replaced by some miraculous process. As one guide expressed it, "You can slice off a piece from the pillar and it evaporates and the blemish heals up."

Toward the end of the first century Josephus, the Jewish historian, wrote:

> But Lot's wife continually turned back to view the city as she went from it, and being too nicely inquisitive what would become of it, although God had forbidden her so to do, was changed into a pillar of salt; for I have seen it, and it remains to this day.

Clement of Rome, also of the first century, and Irenaeus, of the second century, both attested that this pillar of salt was standing in their day. Dispute about the permanency of the pillar is trivial alongside the fact that this disobedient woman died a terrible death. Burnt and suffocated to death, her story remains as a solemn warning against disobedience of divine commands.

11. The Miracle of Closed Wombs

(Genesis 20:1-7, 17, 18)

How grateful we should be for the fidelity of Bible history! No matter how eminent the saint, his vices as well as his virtues are faithfully recorded. Abraham may be "the friend of God," but here we see him under another eclipse of faith, and although the father of the faithful, he yet received a just rebuke from a heathen monarch for a heinous transgression.

While there are those writers who see in Abraham's experience in Gerar a variation of a similar record of his lapse in Genesis 12, we believe the two narratives to be totally different. Abraham's false representation before Pharaoh some 20 years before is not to be confused with his want of faith before Abimelech, king of the Philistines (Genesis 26:1). In this second denial of Sarah as his wife, Abraham sinks to a depth of moral degradation contemptible in the extreme. In fact, his fall this time was deeper than the prior one, for he now had the divine promise that within a year Sarah would become the mother of a child miraculously given.

One would have thought that Abraham and his wife would have benefited from the rebuke of Pharaoh after the previous deceit and the exposure of Sarah to danger. Why did this honored, and otherwise godly pair, have recourse to further deceit at the very time when such abundant revelations were being made to them? Why did they become entangled again in the yoke of bondage? Ellicott offers the explanation:

Holy Scripture neither represents its heroes as perfect, nor does it raise them disproportionately above the level of their own times. Its distinguishing feature rather is that it ever insists upon a perpetual progress upwards, and urges man onward to be better and holier than those that went before. Abraham was not on the same high spiritual level as a Christian ought to be who has the perfect example of Christ as his pattern, and the gift of the Holy Ghost for his aid; and the fact that God rescued him and Sarah from all danger in Egypt may have seemed to him a warrant that in future difficulties he would have the same divine protection. Human conduct is ever strangely checkered, but we have a wholesome lesson in the fact, that it was Abraham's politic device which twice entangled him in actual danger.

Sarah, now 90 years of age and with a somewhat fading natural beauty, possibly renewed her physical appearance and appeal through the promise of a son. Thus when Abimelech saw her, he desired her. He was withheld, however, from sinning against another man's wife. God appeared to him in a dream and warned him that death from the malady he was evidently suffering from would be the result of retaining Sarah. So she was delivered through a dream—a supernatural intervention. The Bible reveals that the ungodly, as well as the godly, are influenced by dreams (Genesis 41:8; Daniel 2:3; Matthew 27:19).

As a Philistine king indulging in polygamy, Abimelech claimed the right of taking female relatives of any of his subjects or of travelers passing through his territory and adding them to his harem. His answer to God reveals that he did not feel he had violated any of his own rules of morality. When Abimelech discovered that Sarah was Abraham's wife he acknowledged his wrong, and was grateful that he had been prevented from disgracing Sarah. Was there not a touch of irony when dismissing Sarah he called Abraham her "brother" (20:16)? As such, Abraham should have been Sarah's protector instead of sacrificing her virtue and honor as he did. How Abraham must have blushed when satirically rebuked by Abimelech! He must have been ashamed to lift up his head. Doubtless deepest penitence was his for groundless fears and for an acted lie.

Abraham had dealt falsely with Abimelech and he might do so again (21:23), so he requested the patriarch that he would not do so again. Does this not teach us that our credit with others is largely in proportion to our trustworthiness? Abimelech made Abraham the recipient of costly gifts. When Pharaoh took Sarah and lavished gifts upon her, they were given back when, in displeasure, Pharaoh told Abraham "to go his way." Abimelech acted more generously, for he not only bestowed presents upon Abraham and Sarah but gave them permission to live where they pleased in his land.

After Abimelech had granted Abraham a liberal compensation for taking Sarah, Abraham interceded for the Philistine king whose malady in some way had so affected his whole household as to produce general barrenness. Whether the women of his harem were childless because of some disease of Abimelech's, or as a plague because of sins, we have no knowledge, nor is it clearly revealed. It may have been this fact that prompted Abimelech to take Sarah in the hope of having an issue. But what a catastrophe this would have been had it happened, since Sarah was to become the mother of the promised seed of Abraham. God, however, miraculously interposed to prevent Abimelech's desire.

Abraham prayed for Abimelech and his household and God answered prayer in healing the king of his sterility and in restoring fertility to his wives and concubines. The Creator, having fashioned the reproduction organs of male and female, is able to command and control them at His bidding, as the experience of Sarah herself so forcibly proves. Fertility or barrenness depend upon His will.

12. The Miracle of Hagar's Well

(Genesis 21:14-21)

No one can read a pathetic story like Hagar's without realizing what a hard taskmaster sin is. When men and women sin, they reap what they sow, for even in this life sin carries its own punishment. Sarah, to whom the covenant-keeping God revealed His plans concerning her, must have known that she erred when she gave Hagar the Egyptian into Abraham's bosom in the hope of having the promised seed by her. Hagar is never acknowledged as Abraham's wife. She was a legal concubine in his household during his sojourn in Egypt. As soon as this illicit device was executed, all concerned began to suffer for it. Hagar, knowing that she was to become a mother, began to despise her mistress Sarah, causing her to become indignant with Hagar. Abraham became embroiled in the quarrel and was accused by his wife of assisting Hagar in her insolence. Sarah developed a contemptuous attitude toward Hagar and treated her with excessive severity.

The atmosphere of that ancient home must have been unbearable. Domestic harmony was destroyed by those very means Sarah had adopted to increase her happiness. Hagar, rather than to endure unkind treatment, fled from the home, and returned to it only when commanded to do so by the angel of the Lord (16:3-9). During the next 18 years there must have been many occasions of vexation and dispute. With the absence of love between Sarah and Hagar, relationships must have been strained. At last Hagar and her son were expelled. Ishmael, who possibly disputed Isaac's title to the birthright, mocked him or derided his pretensions to inherit his father's substance.

The record of the expulsion of Hagar and Ishmael, although a sorrowful one, is simply and touchingly set forth. Abraham's provision for them as they faced the unknown was meager in comparison with his opulence. Their sudden dismissal meant lack of time to plan for the days ahead. But in the wilderness, a compassionate God was watching them, and mercy prevailed on their behalf (Genesis 16:7-13). Ishmael was Abraham's son and God overshadowed him and saved him from dying from thirst (Genesis 21:17-19). He became the founder of the great Arabian nation.

How heart-moving is the scene of mother and son wandering in the wilderness, using the waterskin sparingly in the hope of discovering a well. At last the water is spent and death appears imminent. Hagar crawls to a nearby shrub and casts herself under it because she cannot bear to watch Ishmael die. But the boy's mute prayer and Hagar's outcries of grief are heard and heaven comes to their relief and they are preserved from death. Encouraged by the angel's voice Hagar searches and finds a spring of living water. Abraham only gave her a "bottle of water" which was soon exhausted. God directed her to a neverfailing well of water. How prodigal He is in His provision!

The miracle here consisted not in the creation of a well for Hagar's use. It already existed. What happened was that God opened her eyes and enabled her to see, not a mirage so despairing to travelers, but the existence of real water. Often in great extremity God opens our eyes to see abundant help near at hand. Desperate prayer brings Him to our side (II Kings 6:17-20; Luke 24:16, 31). On her previous expulsion from Abraham's household, Hagar spoke of God as "a God of seeing," or "a God that permits Himself to be seen." The name of the well was called *Beer-lahai-roi* meaning, "The well of Him that liveth and seeth me." This well of the living-seeing God became a favorite dwelling-place of Isaac (Genesis 16:13, 14; 25:11).

That the record of Hagar and Ishmael is more than strictly historical is clear from Paul's allegorical application of it (Galatians 4). Hagar and Sarah represent two covenants, while Ishmael and Isaac provide the contrast between law and grace.

13. The Miracle of the Burning Bush

(Exodus 3:1-14; See Deuteronomy 33:16; Mark 12:26; Luke 20:37; Acts 7:30, 31)

In God's portrait gallery of saints, Moses has a niche all his own. He is conspicuous as a prophet and leader in the pre-Christian world. He is described as "Jehovah's slave" (Numbers 12:7; Deuteronomy 34:5, etc.); as "Jehovah's chosen" (Psalm 106:23); as "the man of God" (Psalm 90, title; I Chronicles 23:14). Details of his life and character are to be found, not only in the Pentateuch which he wrote, but in other Bible books (Acts 7:20-38; Hebrews 11:23-28, etc.). H. H. Halley computes that the story of Moses occupies one seventh of the whole Bible, or an amount two thirds the size of the entire New Testament. Moses lived for 120 years—40 years in Egypt, 40 years in Arabian exile, and 40 years as leader of Israel.

When the divine call to lead Israel out of Egyptian bondage came, Moses was keeping the flock of Jethro his father-in-law—occupied like others at a proper calling (Luke 2:8, 9). At the burning bush, Moses received two great revelations of God, both related to Israel His people:

(1) His preserving presence (Exodus 3:1-10)

(2) His eternal being (Exodus 3:14)

God's estimation of Moses is seen in the fact that no other mortal has been "the agent of so many and such stupendous manifestations of supernatural power. What remarkable miracles he performed, and what miraculous help was his! His high spiritual privilege, however, as in Paul's case, was accompanied by almost unbelievable suffering." Trials and tribulations followed him from Egypt to the border of Canaan. The strong attachment of Moses to the people of Israel, on whose behalf he received the vision at the burning bush, and for whom he performed many miracles, occasioned him the loss of everything dear to worldly ambition. In refusing to be known as the son of Pharaoh's daughter, Moses renounced honor, wealth, and pleasure (Hebrews 11:24-27).

So great were his cares and dangers when called to lead Israel at the age of 80, that nothing short of the fullest conviction that he was acting by divine authority could have led him to bear the weight of such a solemn charge. There were times when, in the bitterness of his soul, he entreated God to release him from his delegated obligation and conspicuous position (Numbers 11:14, 15). But assured of divine aid and armed with power to work miracles, Moses went out to become one of the greatest national leaders of all time.

The miracle of the burning bush assured Moses of divine presence in a very special way. Here was a double miracle—the bush burned but was not consumed, and amid the burning was Jehovah, impervious to fire, talking to Moses. The three Hebrew youths in the fiery furnace saw One like unto the Son of God amid the flames (Daniel 3:25). What excited the astonishment of Moses was not so much the burning bush but that God was in the bush. Though nothing was to be seen but an appearance as of material fire, the knowledge that God was

there rendered the fire awful and led Moses to hide his face.

The One addressing Moses out of the fire was the Second Person of the Trinity (3:2, 4), and the repetition of name marks extreme urgency (See Genesis 22:11; I Samuel 3:10; Acts 9:4). Here we have a theophanic appearance with fire, of which there are four mentioned in the Bible. (Exodus 3:2; 13:21; 19:18; II Thessalonians 1:8). There are other divine manifestations associated with fire. The flame in the bush does not represent "the flame of persecution of God's enemies without but the flame of the Divine Presence within."

As to the particular kind of bush God used as a medium of revelation, diversity of opinion prevails. No special shrub was created, but one very common to the region is meant. The LXX translates it "blackberry bush," which the monks of the convent of St. Catherine at Sina planted at the rear of the "Chapel of the Burning Bush" in token of the tradition that the burning bush was a blackberry bush. The *cassia* has also been suggested. But as neither of these grew in the region, it would seem as if a shrub, one of the various acacias so common to the part where Moses received the divine revelation is meant.

The command to Moses to remove his sandals was in keeping with a custom observed by the Egyptians before the time of Moses, of removing from their feet their sandals or shoes on entering a temple, palace, or even the private house of some great person. This custom prevails today among many Orientals. Here ordered by God, it was an indication for Moses to reverence the place His presence had hallowed. Jacob had a similar experience (Genesis 28:16, 17).

That the miracle of the burning bush typifies miracles of God's preserving grace is an aspect noted by several conservative expositors. For example, the bush can represent the status and condition:

(1) *Of the Israelites in Egypt and in history*

In spite of all their afflictions under Pharaoh, the Jews could not be destroyed (See II Corinthians 4:8-10). Groaning under the rigorous burden of their taskmasters, the Jews, like the bush, were never reduced to ashes. The flame was in the bush, not the bush in the flame. Israel was the lowly acacia, the thorn bush of the desert, yet God condescended to abide in the midst of her (Zechariah 2:5). Being in her, He protected her, not *from* suffering, but preserved her *in* and *through* "the flame of fire" of Egyptian persecution (Exodus 1:9-22), as He has all down the ages. The indestructible Jew is the miracle of history. In spite of all means to destroy God's ancient people, they have multiplied.

(2) *Of the Church in the world*

The Church of God, like Israel, has at all times suffered by persecution. Yet it has survived many a fiery trial and, in spite of all worldly powers confederated against it, is as great and powerful as ever. As the Creator of the Church, for "with His blood He bought her," the Master said that the gates of hell can never prevail against her. She has worn out many an anvil of antagonism. In all ages, the Church of Christ has been like a bush burning with fire. Conflict without and corruption within have not destroyed her. Indwelt by the invincible Lord, the Church continues by a power greater than her own.

(3) *Of the individual believer*

The illustration John Bunyan uses of the fire which men try to put out but fail is an apt one. Someone behind the fire keeps pouring oil on it and it maintains its glow. The fire of affliction surrounds many of the Lord's people. In every age and place, the godly suffer persecution (II Timothy 3:12) and it is no less a miracle that when many would "make shipwreck of faith and of a good conscience," the furnace, instead of destroying, purifies and refines (Romans 5: 3-5). Ever present (Matthew 28:20), the Lord preserves His own.

The flame of fire in the lowly desert bush can also typify the combination of deity and humanity in Christ who was the great "I Am" in revealing His power to Moses. M. G. Kyle gives us the interesting suggestion that the burning bush gave the world a needed revelation of God.

The prevailing idea of God in the regions round about was that God dwelt in darkness. The approach to God in Egyptian temples was through ever-deepening gloom. It was thought that God was very dangerous and apt to be a *destroyer*, so that a priest must always intervene. God as a gracious *Saviour* was the new idea revelation was bringing to the world. This was now first clearly announced, but was not to be fully revealed throughout the time of the long line of priests until the Great High Priest should come and make "a way of approach" that we may come "with boldness unto the throne of grace."

Moses in his farewell messages to the twelve tribes congratulated Joseph on "the good-will of Him who dwelt in the bush" (Deuteronomy 33:16). Are we not truly blessed if recipients of such a divine favor? To each of us, God is "a wall of fire" for protection (Zechariah 2:5). To those who spurn His grace and mercy He is "a consuming fire" for their destruction. For them, there is nothing but "a fire that never shall be quenched."

14. The Miracle of the Rod

(Exodus 4:1-5; 7:8-13. See II Timothy 3:8)

In spite of all the divine assurance received that all courage and power would be his as he faced Pharaoh with the demand to let Israel go, the faith of Moses was weak. When he urged that he was unfit for his mission God's reply was, "Not unfit, *since* I will be with thee. I will supply all thy defects, and make good all thy shortcomings." Moses, however, was not overwilling to believe that divine strength could be made perfect in his weakness. His distrust of himself is outstanding and, as Dr. Graham Scroggie reminds us, "When God called Moses, he offered five excuses in an attempt to evade his task. He pleaded:

(1) No fitness (Exodus 3:11).
(2) No message (3:13).
(3) No authority (4:1).
(4) No gift of speech (4:10).
(5) No inclination (4:13).

But God met him at every point, promising:

(1) His presence (3:12).
(2) His name and covenant (3:14-22).
(3) His power (4:2-9).
(4) His enabling (4:11, 12).
(5) His instruction (4:14-16).

As the chapter before us opens, we have Moses expressing a positive conviction that he would not be believed in by Pharaoh in his demand as God's spokesman for Israel's release (4:1). Such a commission to deliver his kinsmen from a dreadful slavery at the hand of the most powerful nation of the times was an appalling commission. "Let not those who halt and stumble over little difficulties of most ordinary lives think hardly of the faltering of Moses' faith before such a task" (Exodus 3:11-13; 4:1,

10-13). The divine encouragement was of a three-fold nature. "Thou shalt say . . . *I AM* hath sent me unto you" (Exodus 3:14). God also gave Aaron to Moses for a spokesman (4:14-16). Then there was the rod of power for working wonders (4:17).

The rod in Moses' hand was possibly the shepherd's crook he used when in the desert, or one which, as a shepherd of eighty years of age, he needed for support. What awe must have filled his heart as he witnessed the performance of a double miracle! God commanded an inanimate object (wood) to turn into an animate one (a serpent). Then the serpent was changed back into wood. This miracle was wrought three times—first, when Moses was alone, then before the elders of Israel, and afterwards before Pharaoh. The rod Aaron is referred to as having was the same one Moses used. Sometimes it is spoken of as belonging to Moses and sometimes to Aaron (4:17; 7:9).

The magicians of Egypt, whom Paul names as Jannes and Jambres (II Timothy 3:8), could, to all appearance, imitate the miracle at its commencement. Perhaps, as conjurors, they used some sleight of hand. But when the serpents became once more rigid like rods, we read, "Aaron's rod swallowed up their rods" (7:12). This was the first blow inflicted on the gods of Egypt. Trench has an illuminating comment on the jugglery of the Egyptian magicians:

> We contemplate their wonders as mere conjurors' tricks, dexterous sleights of hand, with which they imposed upon Pharaoh and his servants; making believe, and no more, that their rods also changed into serpents (7:11, 12), that they also changed water into blood (7:22). Rather was this a conflict not merely between the might of Egypt's king and the power of God; but *the gods* of Egypt, the spiritual powers of wickedness which underlay, and were the informing soul of, that dark and evil kingdom were in conflict with the God of Israel. In this conflict, it is true, their nothingness very soon was apparent; their resources quickly came to an end; but yet most truly the two unseen kingdoms of light and darkness did them in presence of Pharaoh as open battle, each seeking to win the king for itself, and to draw into its own element.

The *rod* is the emblem of divine power and authority (Exodus 4:2-4; Numbers 17; Psalm 2:9), and the *serpent* is the emblem of Satan's power. The miracle of the transformation of Moses' rod therefore symbolizes God's power over Satan. In the effort of the magicians, Satan sought to imitate the power of God. We read that "Moses fled" from the serpent. As he wrote *Exodus,* it was quite natural for him to recall and record his alarm over such a strange and unusual phenomenon. Faith, however, triumphed over instant recoil for in response to the divine command Moses became daring enough to stoop and lift the reptile by its tail—the reverse action to Egyptians handling poisonous snakes, who take hold of them by the neck so that they cannot bite. "To test the faith and courage of Moses, the command is given to lay hold of *this* serpent by the tail."

15. The Miracle of the Leprous Hand

(Exodus 4:6-12)

The three signs of identification, the rod, the leprous hand, and the water turned to blood, prove that God is patient with reasonable doubt. Moses' plea of inability as a leader was met at every point by divine encouragement. Then these signs were intended to prepare and commission Moses to deliver Israel from Egyptian bondage, and to show that God would employ miracles to speak to men. "The words of God's signs," says the Psalmist (105:27). Israel had to be convinced of Moses' leadership, and Pharaoh had to be convinced that Israel must leave Egypt. Thus, the three signs are related.

The rod turned into a serpent emphasized that divine power was available to accomplish the divine plan. Here we see how God can make a feeble instrument into a power to chastise and to destroy. All power is His over Satan and his strength and schemes.

The hand turned leprous speaks of divine power to cleanse from sin—a disease more loathsome and incurable than leprosy. The mission of Moses was to punish and to save. Power can be ours not only over Satan, but over the sin he introduced.

The water turned into blood suggests a divine power waiting to judge with death all those who finally despise divine grace. Here we have typified the conversion of the peace and prosperity Egypt experienced at that time into calamity, suffering and bloodshed. Blood poured out symbolizes divine wrath.

Those who were not fully impressed with

the first miracle of the wonder-working rod, since Egyptian serpent charmers could imitate this miracle, might be more impressed with the miracle of the leprous hand. The third miracle was intended to persuade the greater number. The turning of the water into blood was not required, for the first two miracles were believed. The third sign became the first plague of judgment upon Pharaoh. All three signs were not given merely to encourage Moses, but were to be his credentials in the sight of Aaron (4:28); of Israel (4:30), and ultimately Pharaoh (7:9, 10).

In the sign of the hand there was a double miracle. Quickly, a healthy hand became leprous, and just as instantaneously, a diseased hand was made whole. As a sign of power or judgment, leprosy was on several occasions sent by God, as further miracles will show. This particular sign was not shown to Pharaoh, since it typifies power over sin for the people of God. The worst form of this foul disease is implied by the word used here and was the kind the Greeks named "the white disease" (4:6) because the skin of the sufferer became glossy white, and his hair became as "white as wool." Israelites were called "the lepers," probably from the momentary act of Moses exhibiting a leprous hand.

The narrative before us ends with Moses still reluctant to go out on God's promised power. He protested that he was not gifted with facility of speech. He had difficulty in expressing words. "Slow of speech" is said by some writers to suggest a natural stammer. It was thus that his more eloquent brother, Aaron, became his spokesman and together they went forward to their mission with heaven-given signs of identification.

16. The Miracle and Miracles of Moses

(Hebrews 11:23-28; Exodus 4:29-31; Psalm 105:26, 27)

Before we examine separately the many miracles Moses performed, it is necessary to briefly survey the miraculous element in the life and labors of this conspicuous Old Testament saint who became the deliverer, lawgiver, prophet, prince, and writer. The history of Moses proves that the air of the supernatural surrounded him. Whether we think of his deliverance from death while yet an infant, his discovery and adoption by Pharaoh's daughter, his miraculous sustenance on Mount Sinai for almost seven weeks, his revelations of, and from, God, his transfigured countenance after an audience with the Almighty, his burial by God, his appearance on the Mount of Transfiguration—everything about Moses indicates a supernatural supervision.

Because he was outstanding among Old Testament prophets and intimately associated with the development of Israel as a nation, we agree with the sentiment that "the existence and character of the Hebrew race require such a person as Moses to account for them. In the New Testament, Jesus and the apostles thought of Moses as something more than the representative of the old dispensation. To them he was an historical personage of such unique prominence in Israel's history that his whole career appeared to them to afford parallels to spiritual factors in the New Covenant (John 3:14; II Corinthians 3:7-18, etc.). Our Lord, Jews, and Christians held Moses to be the writer of the Pentateuch (Genesis to Deuteronomy). See Luke 2:22; 16:29; 24:27, etc. Without doubt, he stands out as one of the greatest and most divinely honored men of all times.

As to the miracles Moses wrought during a period of forty years, often as judgments on those who witnessed the display of divine power, nothing short of the fullest conviction that Moses' miracles were wrought by God could have induced the Jews to obey the burdensome laws he imposed. The people would not have accepted him as God's representative had he not had credentials to produce. Power of working miracles is given to men, as we have already indicated, primarily and mainly for their credential value, to accredit them as God's sent-ones. Ellicott comments:

There had been no appearance of Jehovah to any one for above four hundred years, and the people might have thought that the age of miracles was past. Miracles cluster around certain crises in God's dealings with man, ceasing altogether between one crisis and another. They were suspended for above 500 years between the time of Daniel and the appearance of the angel to Zacharias.

As to the reality of Moses' miracles, Leslie in *Short Method With the Deists*, observes these four notes of truth in the Law-Giver's works:

(1) They were such as men's sense can clearly judge of.

(2) They were publicly wrought; two nations, Israel and Egypt, were affected by them, and above two million Israelites for forty years witnessed them.

(3) Public monuments and, what is more convincing, outward observances continually were retained in commemoration of the facts.

(4) These monuments and observances were set up at the time the events took place, and continued without interruption afterwards (Deuteronomy 8:4; Exodus 20:18; 40:38; Joshua 3:16; Numbers 16:21, etc.).

In an approach to a survey of the miracle-plagues upon Egypt, there are one or two aspects worthy of note. First of all, the number of them (ten) has an interesting association. *Ten* is one of the perfect numbers of Scripture and is significant of *completeness*—the whole cycle is complete, nothing wanting. God said that He would execute judgment against *all* the gods of Egypt (Exodus 15:11; Numbers 32:4), and, as succeeding studies will show, each plague was directed against a particular heathen deity. Thus, in the ten plagues, we have the full flood of God's wrath and judgment upon Egyptian idolatry—the completion of God's visitation upon a God-opposed world power, from whom Israel was being weaned. These plagues were not meant to reduce Pharaoh's resistance merely; they were designed to destroy idolatry.

Another noticeable feature of these ten miracle-plagues is the way they harmonize with nature, as we might expect, since the God of revelation and of judgment is the God of nature. As with Christ's miracles and parables, so with the Egyptian plagues there is "the principle of the law of continuity of the human with the divine," for these plagues have "a demonstrable connection with Egyptian phenomena, in most cases not reversing, but developing, nature's forces for a foretold particular end and at a defined time." As all theophanies and miraculous doings are embodied in natural events, the miraculous working of God is associated with natural phenomena.

Then there is the matter of difference between the miracles of Moses and those of the New Testament. Many contrasts and comparisons characterize the miracles of Old and New Testaments. Christ's miracles were always accomplished with the highest ease—He speaks, and it is done. Moses speaks hastily and acts unbelievingly (Numbers 20:11). Elijah and Elisha had to pray long and put forth much effort in their miracle ministry (I Kings 18:42-44; II Kings 4:31-35). Where the miracles are similar in kind, like the feeding of the hungry, Christ's are larger, freer, and more glorious. Further, Old Testament miracles often wear a far severer aspect than those of the New. The miracles of Moses were more or less miracles of the law, teaching the awful holiness of God and His hatred of sin. In the main, Christ's miracles were works of grace and mercy and were related, for the most part, to the human body, just as His parables were for the human soul. Old Testament miracles were of an external nature, and were performed to display divine power. New Testament miracles, less startling than the Old, carry a far deeper inward, spiritual significance.

Mention must also be made of the fact that the miracle-plagues are essentially Egyptian, each of them "suiting the place, the time, and the circumstances under which they are stated to have been wrought." Plagues, not necessarily divine visitations, are frequently cited in the Bible. The characteristic feature of the Egyptian plagues we are now to consider was the suddenness, intensity, and complete devastation so much beyond all precedent as to impress the recipients and onlookers as being unusual manifestations of divine power. In their systematic severity, the plagues stand out as *miracles of power*.

17. The Miracle of the Nile

(Exodus 4:9; 7:14-24; Psalm 78:44; Psalm 105:29)

The ten miracles Moses wrought in Egypt reveal a conflict between "the divine and the diabolical," as Dr. Graham Scroggie puts it. But these contrasting powers are not commensurate in their bid for the souls of men. "The struggle was protracted and the battle swayed to and fro, but the devil was defeated by the Deliverer." These miracles likewise proved God's power over Egypt's deified powers of nature. Thus the first stroke affected the very source of the nation's life and wealth—the Nile River.

What a striking contrast there is between Egypt's first plague of water changing to blood, and Christ's first miracle of water becoming wine. The former is *gruesome*—the latter, *gladsome*. Both Trench and Habershon draw attention to the impressive contrast. The first miracle of Moses had its fitness, for the law, which came by Moses, was a ministration of death, working wrath (II Corinthians 3:6-9). So water turned into blood was a symbol of death. Christ's first miracle has an inner, unpolitical meaning. Turning water into wine symbolized a ministration of life, for Jesus came as the True Vine making glad the heart of man (Psalm 104:15). Thus, His initial miracle was a symbol of joy. C. H. Spurgeon's comment on the two miracles is suggestive:

> When He turned all the waters of Egypt into blood so that they loathed to drink of the river, it was a sure proof that God was there; but to my soul it was a more assuring proof when He turned my water into wine, and made my ordinary life to become like the life of those in Heaven by His sovereign grace.

As the wonder-working rod was stretched out over the Nile, all the water was turned into blood, even the water in carrying vessels, pools, and ponds. Streams were polluted and the fish died, and the land was filled with corruption (7:20, 21). This plague inflicted by Aaron occurred during the morning, probably when Pharaoh and his courtiers went to the river to bathe, or to worship it, since the Nile was one of the great gods of the Egyptians. *Hapi* was the name of this Nile god.

The Nile was also the center of Egypt's national life as well as its religious life. Egypt was the product of the Nile, "the very soil being all brought down by it, and its irrigation being constantly dependent upon it." This idol river also abounded with fish of various kinds which provided the Egyptians with further idols to worship. At least three species of the Nile fish were sacred—*the oxyrhineus, the lepidotus, the phagrus*, or *eel*. Thus the plague produced a double severe punishment. In one stroke, the Egyptians were deprived of their water and fish supply. Because the water was singularly delicious and wholesome, emphasis is added to the words of Moses that the people should "loathe to drink of the water of the river" (7:17-19). The draught was too nauseous.

Those who seek to explain the miraculous in Scripture from a rationalistic point of view draw attention to the natural phenomena that the Nile rises in June when its waters become discolored from fragments of vegetable matter or reddened by enormous quantities of minute organisms. By August, when the river is at its height, the water has a dull red color resembling blood and emits offensive odors. It is easy, therefore, to see how this could be treated as a miracle.

But the dreadful severity of this plague constituted its "wonder." As Ellicott remarks, "The natural discoloration of the Nile, whether by red earth or organisms, has no pernicious effect at all upon the fish, nor is the water rendered by these discolorations at all unfit for use." While the Nile often had a natural offensive color, the people paid no attention to it. The Bible says that the river was "turned to blood," and that its water was loathsome to drink, and that the bodies of putrid fish caused a disgust and horror that were unspeakable. The suddenness of the change, as well as the dreadful severity of the stroke, reveals God's absolute right to do what He will with creations and creatures of His own handiwork.

In an endeavor to nullify the supernaturalness of the plague, the magicians tried to imitate the miracle. By some device of magic, as seen in the East today, they gave a very poor imitation of the work of Moses and Aaron who had turned *all* the waters —canals, lakes, and reservoirs—into blood. The magicians could not act on this large scale but could affect a small quantity of water near at hand (7:24). They took advantage of the materials the "wonder" had provided. Their supposed miracle was subjected to no test, and was perhaps not even done in the presence of any hostile witness. It would seem, however, as if the act of the magicians led Pharaoh to harden his heart and refuse the request of Moses and Aaron to let the Israelites go. The king paid no attention to such a matter. Doubtless care was taken to keep him supplied with the well water for his ablutions. Having more generous liquids in his store, he could do without drinking water for a while. Not only was he proud, impious, and obstinate but also idolatrous. He professed not to know who Jehovah was (5:2). Here Moses is commanded to give Pharaoh both His name and title—*Jehovah, the God of the Hebrews* (7:16).

One expositor suggests that the punishment of this plague was retaliatory. The

Egyptians had made the Nile the means of destroying Hebrew infants (1:22), so that Hebrew parents loathed to drink of it, as though it had been stained with the blood of their children; so is it now made by means of blood undrinkable for the Egyptians.

18. The Miracle of the Frogs

(Exodus 8:1-6; Psalm 78:45; 105:30)

The plague of frogs, like the first plague, was threatened beforehand. Some of the succeeding plagues fell without warning. Mercy was mixed with judgment. God gave the Egyptians time to repent and escape from more severe plagues. When they failed to heed the warning of Moses and Aaron, the brothers used the wonder-working rod again, and God summoned His armies of frogs to cover the land. He created them by myriads and of different ages and sizes to execute His vengeance upon an idolatrous nation.

Plagues of frogs were common to Egypt. In September after the overflow of the Nile, as the waters receded, frogs would multiply in the putrid marshes. These amphibian reptiles are several times mentioned in Scripture, and always, except in the book of Revelation, in connection with Egypt. Two species of frogs are to be distinguished—those living in the waters and those living on the land. The miracle of this plague, worse than the previous one, consisted in the sudden appearance of both kinds of frogs in great abundance and in their death at a given time. In a moment the land was full of them, and the God who called them into being in an instant deprived them of life without a word (8:13,14; Psalm 78:45). The frogs did not return into the river or marshes; they died where they were in countless thousands so that they had to be gathered into heaps, and the land *stank*. In the first plague the *waters* stank (7:21); in this one the *land* stank (8:14). In the first plague we are not told that Pharaoh personally suffered, but under this second divine affliction, king and people alike suffered (8:4-8); court, as well as the cottage, were filled with the stench of dead frogs. Penetrating every place, filling beds and covering food and defiling the water, the frogs must have made life intolerable. Such a terrible infliction had a double effect.

First of all, it was a severe trial to the religious feelings of the Egyptians and tended to bring their religion into contempt. This plague was directed against the female deity with a frog's head known as *Heka* or *Heqt*, worshiped as the wife of Chnum, god of cataracts or of inundation. This was a very old form of nature worship in Egypt, the frog—resembling our toad—being made the symbol of fecundity and regeneration. An Egyptian cuneiform represents *Seti*, father of Rameses II, offering wine to an enshrined frog with the inscription, "The sovereign lady of both worlds." Therefore, with the frogs held sacred as an emblem of *Osiris*, the plague affords an instance in which God punishes men by means of the very things they improperly regard. What a terrible blow to the idolatrous faith of a people who held in high honor and worshiped the "frog." Frogs have been found fully preserved and embalmed in the tomb at Thebes.

Secondly, the Egyptians worshiped cleanliness and set much value upon it. Ablutions were frequent and great care was taken to avoid contact with anything foul or unclean. Priests were required to dress in linen, Herodotus tells us, and to wash their entire bodies twice every day. The polluting presence of frogs in washing water, and in ovens, kneading troughs, and beds must have been horrible to the senses —nauseous and revolting to those loathing anything foul. As Ellicott comments:

> The frogs were hideous to the eye, grating to the ear, repulsive to the touch. Their constant presence everywhere rendered them a continual torment. If other later plagues were more injurious, the plague of frogs was perhaps of all the most loathsome.

Once again, the Egyptian magicians tried to imitate the plague. As frogs were naturally plentiful, they could have produced some, but they had no power to imitate God in creating frogs. Neither had they power to bring sudden death to multitudes of frogs. "They would have shown their own power and the power of their gods far more satisfactorily had they succeeded in taking the frogs away." By their magic art or sleight of hand, these magicians only increased the general misery of the people by adding to the number of frogs, after the land was swarming with them. What a poor and miserable imitation of a truly miraculous act!

The effect of the miracle upon Pharaoh is instructive. The haughty spirit of the monarch was slightly broken. In the first plague, he retired, sullen and hardened, into his house (7:23), but in this judgment he appealed to Moses and Aaron to remove the frogs, and in doing so revealed the first sign of yielding. Personal suffering from the loathsome frogs led Pharaoh to make a concession. He now acknowledged the power of God and also the effectual, fervent prayer of the righteous—"Intreat the Lord, that *He* may take the frogs from me, and from my people." But when Pharaoh "saw that there was a respite, he hardened his heart" and went back on his promise to let the people of Israel go (8:8, 15). Stifling an inner conviction, he manifested a callous attitude, thereby adding to his guilt.

19. The Miracle of the Lice

(Exodus 8:16-19; Psalm 105:31)

In a warm country and to a cleanly people like the Egyptians, this third infliction of divine judgment must have produced most irritating pain and distress. Whether the lice in question were mosquitoes, sandflies, ticks, or fleas is a doubtful point. This we do know, that having created various insects, God can command them to execute judgment upon an idolatrous nation. Thus the dust all over the land was instantly changed into lice and the magicians knew at once that none but God could have worked such a miracle (8:18). In the previous miracle we have life *multiplied* (the frogs swarmed out of the waters, their natural element), but in the miracle before us we have life *created* out of the dust of the ground.

As Aaron stretched forth the wonder-working rod, land-dust became energetic with life, and man and beast were covered with freshly-created, loathsome, disgusting insects. These millions of aggravating ticks or fleas were not those the whole mass of dead frogs could breed, but a newly created vast swarm—an instance of spontaneous generation that biologists call "biogenesis." The louse is so prolific that in six weeks the parent female may see 5000 of its own descendants. Scientists are struggling to produce *life*, but they never will. This is the prerogative of Him, who is the Author and Giver of life. The magicians by juggery or by Satanic power could *imitate* life but not

create life. The noisome, nauseous insects plaguing the people came into being as the result of a definite creative act and as a scourge of indolence. The only living creature that the Bible says is fashioned out of dust is *man*. What a singular conjunction! We wonder whether it was this fact that compelled the magicians to confess, "This is the finger of God"?

This third plague came without warning. In a moment, the excessive quantity of dust, common to the land, became a plague of lice bringing with it God's judgment on Pharaoh for hardening his heart and breaking his promise to Moses and Aaron (8:15). The monarch was not given any time or option of avoiding the plague by submission to God's will. The plague also struck another blow at Egypt's idolatry. The dust of the earth was worshiped in Egyptian pantheism as *Seb*, the earth god, or father of the gods. Further, personal cleanliness formed an integral part of Egyptian religious life, and bodies covered with lice must have been a shock to pride. Herodotus tells us that no person was allowed under any consideration to enter any temple with vermin upon them, and that their priests had to shave every three days. Priests and people were accustomed to continual ablutions in their persons and garments. Lice-covered bodies must have been a terrible blow to the religion and regulations of the people. Although this dreadful plague (the removal of which is not recorded) caused no great calamity, it was enough to warn the Egyptians and give hope to Israel.

The utter inability of the magicians to imitate this plague deserves fuller notice. The phrase "did so" (8:18) means they *tried* to do so, but failed to produce a counterfeit of the miracle. "They took moist earth, and dried it, and pulverized it, and tried the effect of their magic charms upon it, but failed to produce lice, as Aaron had done." Their powerlessness was evident. All their resources failed to produce life. Humbled, they confessed their failure to Pharaoh in a brief but pregnant sentence: "This is the finger of God." Then they retired from the contest vanquished, and we hear no more of these boastful imitators who had been forced to admit the manifestation of the supernatural.

The acknowledgment of the supremacy of God by his magicians failed to impress Pharaoh, for his heart remained hard. Perhaps this plague did not impress him as the frogs had done. Herodotus suggests that the monarch was not affected very much by the visitation of lice, since he would possess mosquito curtains, and could inhabit the loftier regions of his palace, which would be above the height whereto the mosquito ascends.

Cleanliness may be next to godliness— but sometimes it is a long way off from it. The Egyptians were clean but far from godly. All who are godly should be clean. Did not Jesus speak about those who were fastidious about external cleanliness yet full of all that was putrid within? For another creation of God, see Psalm 51:10.

20. The Miracle of the Flies

(Exodus 8:20-31; Psalm 78:45; 105:31)

As we approach a consideration of this fourth plague, it will be noted that the word "flies" is in italics, indicating that there is no certainty as to the identity of the devouring insect mentioned. Although the word is given seven times in the narrative, it is not found in the original. The number and variety of insects are legion in Bible lands. It is generally held that a kind of beetle, injurious both to the persons and property of men, is meant. These "bloodsuckers" were also destructive in field crops (Psalm 78:45 represents the insect as "devouring," which is true of beetles but not flies). Whatever the insect is of little matter alongside of the effect produced and the result, for here was a plague which, if less disgusting than some others, was far more injurious.

As the result of the first plague, the *river stank;* under the second plague the *land stank;* under this terrible visitation the land was *corrupted* or *destroyed* "early in the morning" when Egyptian kings went to the Nile both to worship it and wash in it. What a full day of destruction the beetles must have had, in a plague exceeding in severity the former ones! All Egyptians, along with their possessions and properties, came under the blight. The rationalistic and liberal explanation of the plague is a denial of its supernatural element. Many insects came to maturity after the waters of the Nile inundation and the pools in which the larvae had lived dried up. The decomposing bodies of the frogs would produce pestilential effects. Bacteriological research shows that some insects are a serious factor in the spread of disease.

While there is no doubt that the swarms of flies were aggravated by the effects from the dead and decaying frogs, the language used in the record of the plague clearly implies the creation of God of new swarms of flies. "I will send" (8:21). Such a miracle consisted not only in the flies overwhelming and destroying the land, but in their appearing at the moment of command and disappearing just as rapidly (8:30, 31). The latter action seems not to have happened with the frogs or with the lice.

The result of the plague was most disastrous. Many of the inhabitants were destroyed, probably stung to death by the venomous insects. Pharaoh suffered with his subjects, or rather, *more* than his subjects for it was upon him that the flies inflicted their painful bites. "I will send swarms of flies upon *thee*" (8:21). Then it was "his palaces" that bore the brunt of the plague, for the flies or beetles destroyed his costly and magnificent furniture and ravaged his fertile fields (8:24). It was, therefore, because of his personal experience of this devastating plague that he gave way before it almost at once and immediately called for Moses (8:25).

This fourth plague was a further judgment of God upon Egypt's idolatry. Because the Egyptians believed them to be the symbol of creative and reproductive power, beetles were deemed sacred and were seldom destroyed. They were emblematic of *The Sacred Scarabacus*, as *Shu*, son of Ra, the sun god, or as *Iris*, queen of heaven. In his form as *Khejra*, Ra was worshiped as the creator. *Beelzebub* (II Kings 1:2) signifies "god of flies," and it was his function to send flies and drive them away, especially from the sacrifices. Milton in *Paradise Lost* makes Beelzebub, the fly-lord, a fallen angel next to Satan himself in power and crime. On this occasion, however, the lifeless god proved to be impotent, and the judgment must have produced dismay and terror among the Egyptians. In view of Pharaoh, priests, and people, God exhibited worthlessness of their numerous deities.

There is a marked aspect of this plague we cannot ignore, namely, the providential separation of Israel from Egypt. "I will put a division (Hebrew, *a redemption*) between my people and thy people" (8:23). Such an immunity makes the miracle more evident and was another step toward establishing the claims of God that He was the God of all the earth and that He had taken Israel under His especial care. Goshen, given to the Israelites by a previous Pharaoh (Genesis 45:10; 46:28, 34) was severed from the rest of the land and spared the effect of the plague. This new feature must have made a deep impression on king and people. It certainly added to the greatness of the miracle. God commanded His destroying hosts not to harm one of His own.

The influence of the miracle upon Pharaoh himself is likewise impressive. Although he finally hardened his heart again, he was greatly impressed with the plague and partially relented. Awed by the severity of this dire calamity, he called for Moses and Aaron and told them to go and sacrifice to their God "in the *land*" (8:25). The last little clause robs Pharaoh's permission of its reality. Three days' journey into the wilderness had been demanded (3:18; 5:3), and nothing less could be accepted by Moses. Thus Pharaoh's unworthy compromise was firmly rejected with the warning that further trifling with the unanswered claims of Jehovah would be sorely and severely dealt with (8:29).

Moses explained to Pharaoh why remaining "in the land" to sacrifice would be impossible. Sheep and cows were deemed sacred by the Egyptians and in the use of them for a sacrifice to God, the Israelites would have to "sacrifice the abomination of the Egyptians." Moses knew that to offer these animals in the sight of Egyptians, who abominated killing cattle, would result in a riot or a civil war, and so refused it, with the warning to Pharaoh to deal deceitfully no more. Even kings must be rebuked when they openly break the moral law (I Samuel 13:13; Matthew 14:4, etc.). Because Pharaoh had promised unconditionally to let Israel go if the frogs were removed (8:8), then flagrantly broken his word, Moses was justified in rebuking the monarch's deceit.

The world around would prescribe limits to the service we should pay God, but no matter what opposition may face us, ours must be the courage and determination to serve Him to the limit of His requirements. Satan is crafty enough to prevent any definite breach between the Church and the world.

21. The Miracle of Murrain of Beasts

(Exodus 9:1-7; Psalm 78:50)

That God created all things by the will of His mind and the work of His hands is proven in this fifth announced plague, exposing as it did the Egyptians adoration of animals. As we examine this miracle, we note how the severity of judgment increases and the command of God for the complete and final release of His people becomes more peremptory.

The word *murrain* means "death" of "mortality," which was especially and directly inflicted by "the hand of the Lord" upon cattle. Those who reject the miraculous in Scripture explain this plague as being a natural result of contagion caused by the beetle plague. Scripture, however, describes the plague as being produced by "the hand of the Lord" (9:3), and says that "the Lord did that thing" (9:6). Having made all creatures, God is able to do as He wishes with them. Here He strikes the beasts with a pestilence (Psalm 78:50), and because it was a miracle, it came at an appointed time and exempted the Israelites. The disease of "rinderpest" was a distressing disorder affecting horses, camels, oxen, and sheep, thereby crippling resources for trade and commerce.

"All the cattle of Egypt died" means "all the cattle which is in the field," that is, the open air at that time. Evidently those confined to stables and shade were not smitten (9:3, 6). "All cattle" signifies cattle of every kind. Cattle were affected by the next plague, too (9:10). *Murrain* was not uncommon in Egypt, but God took care that this plague should not be ascribed to natural causes by marking its miraculous character:

(1) By appointing a set time (9:5)— "on the morrow." Here again judgment is tempered with mercy. This delay enabled any Egyptians believing Moses to save their precious cattle by housing them.

(2) By exempting the cattle of Israel (9:6). Again God separated His own. Israel's separation of their cattle from the deadly contagion was a step in their preparations for their departure from Egypt. This second preservation of Israel from judgment was a matter of surprise and enquiry on Pharaoh's part (9:7). The rationalist affirms that the direction of the wind or other natural courses prevented the "murrain" from reaching Israelite territory. But we believe that the God who smote Egyptian cattle was also responsible for the immunity Goshen enjoyed.

(3) By making the disease fatal to *all* Egyptian cattle left "in the field" and aiming

the judgment at animal worship. *Apis*, the sacred bull, was one of the chief gods of Egypt. The bull was so venerated that on a certain occasion the whole nation went into mourning on the death of one. This plague, then, must have been a sad and terrible blow to the religious faith and feelings of the people.

The effect of the miracle upon Pharaoh was slight. He was less impressed by this plague than the previous one and gave no sign of submission. There was no softening of heart or exercise of conscience. "Loss of property would not much distress an absolute monarch, who could easily exact the value of what he had lost from his subjects." Pharaoh's heart remained hard. How impressive is the longsuffering of God in sparing the king, whom He could have smitten with sudden death after his first refusal to let Israel go.

God has no pleasure in the judgment and death of the wicked. The sinner should see in Pharaoh a striking portrait of himself. After rejecting overtures of mercy he was given over to a reprobate mind and, joined to his idols, was left alone.

22. The Miracle of Boils and Blains

(Exodus 9:8-11; II Timothy 3:9)

It was six months since the first plague. There had been a plague a month, increasing in severity; and now, once again, God reveals His omnipotence by turning ashes into boils, which afflicted magicians, men, and cattle. The "murrain" of the former plague was upon beasts only. Now "*all* the Egyptians" suffered throughout "*all* the land of Egypt." It was not announced beforehand to the people, nor were they allowed the opportunity of escaping it.

This further judgment plague was a severe one, inflicting for the first time acute suffering on the bodies of men, causing them to realize that God was able to smite with a terrible disease—and if with a disease, why not with death? The *boils* in question were burning carbuncles, a severe cutaneous disorder accompanied by pustules or ulcers. Doubtless the smitten Egyptians suffered unequally. Some would be like Job, covered with "sore boils from the sole of his foot (as the magicians were, seeing they could not stand) unto his crown" (2:7).

While diseases of this character were not uncommon in Egypt (Deuteronomy 28:27),

they were not as severe as this one and do not attack indifferently man and beast. A lump of figs could cure Hezekiah's boil but this was no relief for the smitten Egyptians. The miraculous character of this plague is shown—

(1) By its being announced beforehand
(2) By its severity—a visitation of a divine order
(3) By its universality—not limited to a special class or sphere
(4) By its extension to animals
(5) By the preservation of Goshen and the Israelites from the painful ulcerous sores.

The ashes of the furnace which Moses sprinkled toward the heavens and God turned into the boils provide an interesting aspect. One expositor suggests that the furnace in question was the one where human victims to an Egyptian god were burnt alive and that Pharaoh possibly was standing before the furnace. Moses in the sight of the king cast ashes heavenward, presenting it, as it were, to God in evidence of His people's wrong. This fact is evident that if the living sacrifices offered by the Egyptians were meant to avert the plagues, the ashes, instead of doing so, brought a fresh one. Ashes were changed into germs bringing a sore affliction and became to the Egyptians a whip wherewith God scourged them. Archaeologist Kyle says that "the ashes were used, probably in the same way and to the same end as the clay was used in opening the eyes of the blind man (John 9:6), namely, to attract attention and to fasten the mind of the observer upon what the Lord was doing."

The sprinkling of ashes is a very ancient custom, being still practiced in certain parts of the East. As employed by Moses, such a significant action was not only the invocation of divine judgment upon the Egyptians because of their oppression of Israel, but also another evidence of divine displeasure over Egyptian idolatry. Flung to heaven, the ashes were a challenge to *Neit*, the great mother queen of highest heaven. The scattered ashes to the wind may also have been an acted protest and stern rebuke against *Sutech*, or *Tyhon*, the evil genius, warning the idolaters that worse plagues would overtake them if they failed to recognize the God of heaven (9:15).

As for the effect of the plague upon Pharaoh, his obdurate heart remained untouched. The mercy of God allowed him another chance to repent. Now "the judicial punitive hardening of Pharaoh's heart by God Himself begins." "The Lord hardened the heart of Pharaoh." Twice he had hardened his own heart, meaning he had crushed inclinations to yield to the manifest tokens of God's power; now God gives the king over to a reprobate mind (Romans 1:28). In leaving him to his own determination not to yield to divine influences, God hardened his heart finally. As for Pharaoh's magicians, the plague was made to fall with special violence upon them for "they could not stand before Moses because of the boils" (9:11). Any effort on their part to withstand Moses this time was completely foiled (II Timothy 3:8). They specially smarted under the severity of this divine infliction, and appear no more. Because God is supreme in any realm, why should we charge our souls with care? Weapons formed against us by adversaries cannot prosper. Living in the Goshen of divine acceptance, we have the assurance of divine preservation from the deserved judgment of the ungodly.

23. The Miracle of the Hail Storm

(Exodus 9:13-25; Psalm 78:47, 48; 105:32, 33)

A marked feature of this seventh announced plague is the great circumstantiality of detail given it in the record of it. The plagues as a whole fall into triads, or groups of three. This first plague or miracle of the last group presents several new features which we enumerate in the following way:

(1) The miracle is introduced with an unusually long and solemn message, and one full of marvels. In it, the divine purpose in raising Pharaoh up and his resistance of Divine judgment is set forth (Romans 9: 17). Pharaoh was warned that God was about to "send *all* His plagues *upon his heart,*" and that in his person he would be a monument of God's power throughout all generations (9:16). How amazed we are at the pride and obduracy of Pharaoh's heart! Judgments or mercies had little effect upon him.

(2) The miracle of hail is the first among the plagues to attack human life, which it did on a large scale, causing all those exposed to it to perish (9:19). The loss of men and cattle must have been tremendous.

(3) The miracle was more destructive than any previous plague. In the plagues, a certain progression can be seen. The earlier ones, for example, caused more annoyance than injury. Then there were those resulting in loss of property. Attacks upon men's bodies to hurt, not kill, followed. Now life itself is attacked. Not only were plants, trees, and harvests destroyed, but men and cattle perished. The elements of nature were combined and commanded by God to descend with terrific force upon the land and its people. Pharaoh was warned by Moses to bring all men and cattle out of the field on pain of their destruction. Never since her formation as a kingdom had Egypt experienced storms and hurricanes like it (9:18, 24).

(4) The miracle was accompanied with terrible demonstrations. Here the God who fashioned all the forces of nature unleashes some of them, thereby displaying His supremacy. As the Author of what we call the laws of nature, God is able to restrain them, prescribe their proportion, and appoint the place where they should operate (Psalm 104:10; II Chronicles 7:13; Amos 4:7, 8). The release of these forces also astonished and alarmed the Egyptians because hail, thunder, lightning, and rain were very seldom experienced in the land. In order we have:

HAIL. While hail was not unknown in Egypt, its appearance was most rare. The hailstones must have been of an enormous size and weight to kill men and cattle. The hail broke off all the small boughs and twigs, thereby destroying the prospect of fruit. "Hail is used as the ammunition of God's artillery" (Job 38:22). God knows how to govern the storms we cannot see.

THUNDER. Thunderstorms were uncommon, and when they did occur, they were for the most part mild and harmless. Thunder is also part of God's ammunition in battle (I Samuel 7:9, 10).

RAIN. Job gives us an accurate account of the history of the rain's formation and ascribes power to God, who is the rain's Father, the right to use it as He deems fit (5:10; 38:27, 28; Psalm 135:7). He can send it in blessing or judgment (Deuteronomy 11:14; Genesis 7; Jeremiah 14:22). Thunderstorms are accompanied by a deluge of rain.

FIRE. By fire mingled with hail and running along the ground, we can understand electrical storms, excessive lightnings involving great peril to life and property (Ezekiel 1:4). What a manifestation of divine mercy it is that lightning is accompanied by rain to soften its rage and prevent greater damage (Job 38:25). Such a combination of forces, as well as their intensity, must have been awe-inspiring, as well as destructive.

(5) The miracle had a double effect. It tested the degree of faith to which the Egyptians had attained, by means of a revelation of the way whereby they could escape destruction and death. We here have an illustration of salvation by faith, for many of the Egyptians feared God's word and obeyed, while the rest suffered for their disregard. It was thus with those who witnessed God's power in the Early Church—"Some believed the things which were spoken, and some believed not" (Acts 28: 24). When they received leave to go, Israel knew they had sympathizers among Pharaoh's servants.

(6) The miracle reveals how God delights in mercy. A merciful warning was given to those who believed to save their cattle (9:19). How God delights in mercy, even although judgment is His strange work! The total extinction of all crops in the country, except Goshen, would have been the result of the plague had not the wheat and the rye, then in germ, not been preserved (9:32). Because of grace, Pharaoh was not destroyed at once (9:19) but was urged to bring all his people and cattle under cover and thus escape death. Further, mercy is seen in the preservation of God's own in Goshen (see Isaiah 32:18, 19). No plague came nigh their dwelling (Psalm 91).

(7) The miracle, announced in the morning, was directed against Shu, god of the atmosphere, and the two gods, *Iris* and *Osiris*. How utterly helpless these atmospheric gods were to help the land and its people when smitten by atmospheric forces! The time element (9:31, 32) helps to show that the ten plagues were spread over three to four months, and that the seventh plague is accurately dated in the season of the year.

(8) The miracle humbled the haughty monarch, but not sufficiently. For the first time Pharaoh recognizes Jehovah as God. "Jehovah is righteous and I and my people are wicked" (9:27). Terror, not faith, constrained him to justify God in the infliction. Alas, on the removal of the judgment, both Pharaoh and his unbelieving servants hardened their hearts (9:34)! They "sinned yet more."

The question may be asked, why these awful judgments, increasing in severity as they succeed each other, were sent? The answer is given — Jehovah's *power* must be shown and Jehovah's *name* declared throughout the earth (9:16). The intensification of the effect of the various plagues beyond all precedent were designed to impress everyone as being a special manifestation of the might of Him who is high over all. How tragic is it when sinners refuse to humble themselves before God, even although warned of their peril! If only they would consider the guilt, folly, and danger of delaying true repentance before God, He would not give them up to judicial hardness and a reprobate mind.

24. The Miracle of the Locusts

(Exodus 10:1-20; Psalm 78:46; 105:34, 35)

This eighth plague offers another striking evidence of the fact that in the use God makes of miracles, He guides, quickens, and intensifies the powers of nature, rather than working contrary to them. In the threatened mighty swarm of locusts, so numerous that the face of the ground could not be seen, God was about to show how He could command even locusts to carry out His purpose. Pressure upon Egypt to tremble under God's mighty hand would be heavier than before, and either the haughty spirit of Pharaoh would be broken or he must perish by judgment.

In the miracle-plague of locusts, as in plagues three and four, God rallies insect life to chastise the presumption of His enemies. After the desolation caused by the hailstones of the previous plague, the locusts speedily effected the completion of ruin to all crops. As to the design of such a devastating plague, Ellicott has this comment:

> The accumulation of plague after plague, which the obduracy of Pharaoh and his subjects brought about, was of vast importance in presenting Israel, and even to the surrounding nations, a manifestation of the tremendous power of God, calculated to impress them as nothing else would have done.

A locust plague at any time was a terrible invasion. These insects, some three inches in length, and having two pairs of wings, always appear in vast clouds and repose at night on the earth. If squashed under foot, they emit an unbearable smell. Their numbers and destructive powers aptly fit them to devastate all kinds of property. They are likened unto horses prepared for battle (Joel 2:1-11; Revelation 9:7, 9). Where they alight, they devour every green thing. They enter windows (like a thief, as Joel expresses it), devouring food, the leather of the water vessels, and even wood. They are usually borne in by an east wind and carried away on a west wind. Their lightness and fragility render them helpless before a wind.

We cannot dismiss the plague by saying that atmospheric conditions alone were responsible for the swarm of locusts. The description proves that this was no ordinary plague. While Egypt had been plagued by locusts before, this plague was without precedence. God had the locusts in reserve ready for invasion. He fixed the time of their arrival and controlled the winds guiding their movements. By lifting his wonderworking rod, Moses gave the signal for the locusts to begin their destructive mission. Then, because the wind fulfils God's will (Psalm 104:3; 148:8; Job 36:26-33), both the natural east wind (which blew for 24 hours) and the west wind carry out His work of judgment. Thus the plague attacked what Egypt prized so much, namely, their land (which among other titles was called "the land of the sycamore"). Vegetation was then at its full around the middle of March.

Such a plague, which the Bible uses to represent great and terrible armies and teachers who corrupt the Gospel (Revelation 9:3), was another judgment upon Egyptian idolatry. The god, *Serajia*, was reckoned to be the protector of the land from locusts. How the religious belief of the people must have been shattered as they saw how helpless their deity was against God's invading host!

Because of the threat of this plague, Pharaoh's officials begged him to yield to the request of Moses. The magicians had retired from the scene when they saw the finger of God. Many of the people feared the Lord as the result of the hailstorm. Now the officers of the court, those closest to the king, believed that the words of Moses about the locusts would come true and urged Pharaoh to let Israel go, lest Egypt be destroyed. Pharaoh yielded to such a plea; but when he heard that Moses demanded all of Israel and her possessions to go, he refused peremptorily and charged Moses with evil intentions. Leaving Pharaoh's presence, Moses stretched out his hand over Egypt and judgment fell.

The desperate situation the miracle created quickly brought Pharaoh to an acknowledgment of God (10:16), and elicited from him the greatest profession of repentance yet manifested. Hastily calling for Moses and Aaron, the king said that he had sinned against the Lord and against His servants, and begged forgiveness and the removal of the plague. Pharaoh's repentance, however, was shortlived. God had made the wind His messengers in bringing the locusts, then, with Pharaoh's repentances, He caused the wind to show mercy in the removal of the locusts. But with their removal, Pharaoh's heart became more hardened necessitating still further and even more glorious displays of Jehovah's power and name.

A plague of locusts as a mark of divine displeasure is to overtake Israel in apostasy from God and truth in the last days (Revelation 9:1-11). Charles Simeon, the unique expositor of over a century ago, provides us with the following application:

> If we look inward, and see how *we* have withstood the commands of God, and how little effect either His judgments or His mercies have produced on us, we should find little occasion to exult over Pharaoh.

25. The Miracle of the Darkness

(Exodus 10:21-29; Psalm 105:28)

The plagues upon Egypt deepen in intensity and affect property as well as persons. As to this ninth plague, can we conceive of a judgment more appalling than this one of darkness which God is visiting "one of the sunniest lands of the world" with? In order that the terrible character of this, the severest of any of the judgments which had yet fallen upon Egypt, be understood, it must be remembered that the worship of the *sun* was common in Egypt and in Eastern lands generally.

One of the principal cities, called *On*, meaning "house of the sun," was the seat of the idolatrous form of sun-worship. The plague of darkness, therefore, robbed the Egyptians of their supreme god, *Ra*, the sun god, and proved Jehovah to be the God of gods. *Ra* was among the principal objects of heathen worship in the delta, where the cities of Heliopolis and Pithom were dedicated to him.

Darkness was a creation of *Set*—the evil principle, the destroyer of O.iris—and of *Apophis*, the great serpent, the impeder of souls in the lower world.

It must have been a crushing blow to the religion of Egypt when darkness covered it. Had *Ra* died? Had *Set* triumphed over his brother, or had *Apophis* encircled the world with his dark folds and plunged it into eternal night?

Although God used a natural occurrence to accomplish His purpose, we must not dismiss the supernatural aspect of the plague. Egypt had what was known as "the khamsin period." *Khamsin* was a wind of the desert when, in consequence of a west, electrical wind, dense masses of fine sand from the desert would intercept the rays of the sun and create a darkness that could be "felt." The word used in the narrative for darkness is the same word in the original to be found in Genesis 1:2. Such a preternatural continuance of absolutely impenetrable "blackness of darkness" must have caused feelings of intense alarm and horror. The dreadful horror of this monster from the desert can hardly be exaggerated. For the Egyptians, coming as it did without any warning and as a God-sent plague, it must have produced wide-spread consternation. The plague was most sensibly and painfully felt by the Egyptians, for "they saw not one another" (10:21, 23).

Beyond all astronomical and atmospheric changes responsible for "darkness" is the fact that the God who said, "Let there be light," can also command darkness to cover any part of the earth. Goshen was not robbed of light. In many parts of the Bible, "darkness" is presented as one of God's agents (Joshua 24:7; Exodus 20:21; Isaiah 50:3-6). He who can create darkness can also hide in it (Matthew 27:45). Here, in the plague we are considering, the thick darkness was absolute, equal to that of the darkest night, making impossible free movement (10:23).

God in His mercy graciously limited the appalling darkness to three days. If such a scene of horror had been prolonged, it would have resulted in either death or insanity. Relief, however, was vouchsafed to Israel in Goshen, all of whom had light in their dwellings (10:23). Sometimes the darkening sand-cloud travels in a narrow stream so that part of the land is light while the rest is dark. But Israel's preservation from such dense darkness was of no ordinary character. Just as the darkness was a visitation hitherto unknown, so the separation of Israel from visitation was divinely ordered.

This particular plague is highly instructive in that it serves to prove that there is a difference between the Lord's people and others. "The Lord doth put a difference between the Egyptians and Israel" (11:7). In such an act God reveals His sovereignty and grace, for the two nations, Israel and Egypt, typify the friends and the enemies of God. So the cloud which brought darkness to one, reserved light for the other; and, as we are to find, the sea was a passage to one and a grave to the other.

When the land was plunged into an eternal light, Pharaoh called for Moses and permitted all the Israelite families to depart —a concession marred by the proviso, "Only let your flocks and herds be stayed" (10:24). Pharaoh wanted to retain the cattle for the return of the people. Moses rejected the proffered compromise. Not only would he take every beast, but Pharaoh himself must provide the Israelites with cattle for their burnt offerings. Not one hoof would be left behind because the cattle Israel had was theirs, and not Pharaoh's. Also, *all* the cattle, to the very last head, were God's, who had commanded *all* the people and *all* their possessions to leave Egypt for the wilderness, there to serve Him (Exodus 3:12).

Pharaoh's rejection of Moses' demand was rude, fierce, and uncourteous. Unable to cause Moses to bend, Pharaoh dismissed him with the threat of death if he should appear in his presence again. As an Egyptian monarch, Pharaoh had the power of life or death. The question arises, why hadn't Pharaoh killed Moses before this? Why did he allow Moses to come and go with such freedom, defying him and his people as he did in his own palace? Pharaoh knew that Moses had been known as the son of a previous Pharaoh's daughter, and that he would still have many friends in Egypt (11:3). But is it not more likely that Pharaoh instinctively knew that Moses was God's representative and that as His prophet he dare not harm him? This we do know, that in driving Moses from his presence the infuriated monarch sealed his own doom. The calm and dignified reply of Moses was a warning that the terrible contest was drawing to a close, "Thou hast spoken well: I will see thy face again no more" (10:29). The plague of darkness provides us with a lesson for all times. The second step in the spiritual life is not revealed until the first step is taken (John 7:17). Egypt must be left (Exodus 10:26); that is the first step, before the nature of spiritual worship can be learned.

26. The Miracle of the Death of the Firstborn

(Exodus 11; 12:29-33; Psalm 78:51;
105:36; 135:8; 136:10;
Hebrews 11:28)

The opening parenthetic passage (11:1-3) refers back to the revelation given to Moses before his interviews with Pharaoh began (3:22); then there follows the divine announcement by the mouth of Moses of the last plague, the coming destruction of the firstborn in Egypt. The conditions governing the institution and observance of the Passover are given in chapter twelve, verses one to twenty-eight. Thereafter, the plague of death, a plague resulting in a nation with drawn blinds, is visited upon Egypt.

In the introduction of his study of the tenth plague, Walter Scott, commenting upon the peculiar air of solemnity associated with this miracle, not merely in the terrible nature of the judgment, but also in its attendant circumstances, says:

> One feels treading on holy ground. This midnight visitation of sharp and sudden judgment, death upon the firstborn—the pride, the glory, the strength of Egypt—sent a bitter wail of anguish throughout the whole land. From it none could escape; it could not be foreseen nor averted in any wise. It embraced in its range the monarch on the throne to the maid-slave at the mill. The prince, people, cattle, and beasts all came in as sharers of this severe judgment.
> . . . Not a household but was visited in judgment. Such a cry never before was heard in Egypt, and never will—although that land is yet to be visited by judgments which will desolate it and its people, oppressed even as they oppressed Israel (Isaiah 19).

Because of the lapse of several days since the termination of the last plague, the people wrapped themselves in a false security, but at midnight—at the weirdest hour, at the most silent time, in the deepest darkness, sudden calamity fell upon them. While such national mourning had been prophesied (11:6), the particular night had not been pronounced. This plague stands alone in that it not only brought death into Egyptian homes but ensured Israel's release from bondage. The combination of public calamity, private grief, and shocked religious fanaticism are to be found in "the great cry in Egypt" (12:30).

There seems to be a diversity of views as to the exact nature of this last crushing disaster—an April day which was both a birthday and doomsday in many a home. Rationalism explains the plague as a natural occurrence. "Malignant epidemics have at all times been the scourge of Bible lands: and it is worthy of note that many authorities state that pestilence is often worst at the time of the *Khamsin* wind." Although this plague had been foretold as the "pestilence" (9:15), and "the *pestis major* or verulent bubonic plague corresponds most nearly in its natural phenomena to this plague," we believe this dreadful visitation was ordered of God.

Life and death are in God's hands. He gives life, sustains life, and recalls it as He deems fit (Job 12:10). Death, then, comes at His bidding, whether through a lingering disease or instantaneously and dramatically (I Samuel 25:38; II Kings 19:35; II Chronicles 13:20; Acts 5:5, 10; 12:23). "He killeth and maketh alive" (I Samuel 2:6). The death stroke on the firstborn was the crowning judgment and was *altogether* supernatural. The other plagues may have been the intensification of existing scourges, but this plague was not without request for a parting blessing—"Bless me also" (12:32). Having a nation of drawn blinds, Pharaoh's humiliation reached its extreme point. As Ellicott summarizes Pharaoh's reaction to the divine stroke:

> He is reduced by the terrible calamity of the last plague not only to grant all the demands made of him freely, and without restriction, but to crave a blessing from those whom he had despised, rebuked (5: 4), thwarted, and finally driven from his presence under the threat of death (10:28). Those with whom were the issues of life and death must, he felt, have the power to bless or curse effectually.

A brief word will suffice concerning the separation of Israel from judgment of the destroying angel. Why was he instructed to discern between the Israelites and the Egyptians? The Israelites had also sinned and come short of God's glory and, as sinners, deserved death as well as the Egyptians.

"The soul that sinneth, it shall die," and in the awful judgment of death all were equally involved, and there should have been no exception. Proud Egyptians and oppressed Hebrews were before God a part of a ruined humanity. But the sword of judgment did not fall upon Goshen. Why? The God who bore the sword on that dark midnight hour, and brought death to every unsprinkled house had appointed a righteous ground and means of deliverance. The lamb slain *instead* of the Israelite was an impressive reminder that the only way of escape from wrath is by another bearing the judgment. Thus the glorious truth of substitution emerges from this miracle (I Corinthians 5:7). The blood shed and sprinkled ensured deliverance from death (Hebrews 12:24; I Peter 1:2). How the whole Jewish nation must have been struck with wonder at this astonishing display of God's mercy toward them because of the slain lamb! We, too, are absolutely saved from eternal death because of the value of God's Lamb sacrificed for our sins.

Can we not take comfort from the thought that, whoever and whatever may menace us as those redeemed and sheltered by the blood, that the Redeemer Himself is our Protector? While He is for us, none can be effectually against us. No weapon formed against us can prosper (Isaiah 54:17). Sprinkled with the precious blood of Christ, we too, are untouchable (Hebrews 11:28).

27. The Miracle of the Cloud and Fire

(Exodus 13:21, 22; 40:34-38; Psalm 78:14; 105:39; Nehemiah 9:12, 19; I Corinthians 10:1, 2)

After a sojourn in Egypt lasting 430 years, Israel was dismissed by Pharaoh and departed from their Egyptian bondage some two millions in number. We are told that "a mixed multitude went up also with Israel" (12:38), but what the exact component elements of this mixed company were, we are not told. Possibly there were Egyptions who, impressed with the miracle-plagues, embraced Judaism. Then there may have been some foreigners, captives from other countries, and who, like the Israelites and believing Egyptians, were eager to escape from their masters. This mixed multitude became a snare to Israel (Numbers 11:4).

Directions as to the Passover, the sancti-

fication of the first-born, and the law of redemption were set before the marching host by their deliverer and leader, Moses. At the outset of the long journey, however, it was made clear to Israel that God was to be their Guide. As they left Egypt, God did not lead the people through the land of the Philistines, although that was the nearest way to the Red Sea (13:17). God led the people about, meaning, He took a circuitous route (13:18). Why this long way round? The divine answer to this question is stated, "The people would probably have repented when they saw war, and would have returned to Egypt." After four centuries of slavery, the Israelites were in no position to fight a war-like people like the Philistines, so their course was deflected by God as Moses led the host in military order.

Encamping at Etham, at the edge of the wilderness, an incident of a miraculous and abnormal character occurred — "The Lord went before them" (13:21), constituting Himself, thereby, the Generalissimo of the orderly army of two million souls as they commenced their march through the "great and terrible wilderness." Here they were without arms, without stores either of clothing or provisions, without knowledge of where bread and water for their sustenance was coming from. But God in His goodness came to them in a pillar of cloud by day and of fire by night to protect them until they came to the promised land. God did not tell His people to "go" to Canaan, but "come." He was to be the Guide and traveling Companion through the unknown journey.

As the Creator of all solar light, He can use all kinds of light to manifest His presence, and "the pillar" was the miraculous, visible manifestation of the divine presence, but His glory was veiled. This "pillar," which cannot be rationalistically explained, had the appearance of smoke by day and would shelter the people from the heat of the sun (Psalm 105:39; Isaiah 4:5), and the appearance of fire by night. So the people had no darkness at all. Thus it guarded as well as guided them. Fire also symbolized God's purity and glory (24:17), as well as His consuming wrath against transgressors (Leviticus 10:2; Numbers 16:35). While "the pillar" gave protection, guidance, and light to the Israelites, it also interposed between them and the pursuing Egyptians, to whom "the pillar" was "a cloud and darkness."

Further, this "pillar" was both a signal

and a guide. When it moved, the people moved; when it stopped, they encamped (40:36-38); where it went, they followed. The double ministry of the "pillar" bore some resemblance to the fire and smoke signals generals used at the head of their armies. When the congregation was at rest, the cloud abode on the Tabernacle over the mercy seat (13:21, 22; 14:19, 24). When God wished to communicate His will and word to Moses, the cloud descended to the door of the tent of meeting (33:9-11; 34:5; Numbers 11:25; 12:5; Deuteronomy 31:15). At all times, the cloud was the manifestation of divine favor as well as divine presence. Later the Jews named it *the Shekina* (29:42, 43).

This symbol of God's presence, protection, and provision remained with the people all through the wilderness up until the death of Moses their leader. It probably disappeared at Abel-shittum (Numbers 9:16; 10:34; 33:49; Exodus 40:38). The Lord "took it not away." Although His people proved to be "rebellious and stiff-necked," with every fresh trial calling forth a murmering, discontented spirit, God revealed inexhaustible patience, unbounded kindness, and matchless grace in that He bore with their manners during the forty years in the wilderness (Nehemiah 9:16-19).

Reaching the land of promise, the people no longer required "the cloud." It had served its purpose and so it disappeared. Now the people must walk by faith and not by sight. It was not from want of faith, or from failure on the part of Israel, that in the days of Joshua the cloud was no longer their guide. As with other miraculous signs, it was no longer needed. The cloud overshadowing Israel is a emblem of a richer mercy (Isaiah 4:5, 6). The Church of Jesus Christ has His promised presence and provision until her completion at His return for her. "Lo, I am with you always." Through the trackless desert of this world, He is ever near who said, "I will never leave thee, nor forsake thee" (Hebrews 13:5).

28. The Miracle of the Red Sea

(Exodus 14:21-31; Psalm 78:53; 106:7-12, 22; Hebrews 14:29)

The successive blows that fell upon Egypt were meant as divine judgment upon its wisdom and idolatry. Its gods, one after another, instead of coming to the help of the distressed worshipers, became plagues which were a source of misery to king and people alike. Now the contest is almost over and Egypt's power is to be crushed. By one grand act, namely, the magnificent action at the Red Sea, God accomplished in glory the deliverance of His own people and sunk the chivalry and power of their enemies as lead in the depths of the sea.

When Israel knew that Pharaoh and his host were pursuing them and that, with the Red Sea facing them, there was no avenue of escape, we read that they were sore afraid and cried unto the Lord and said that it might have been as well to die in Egypt as perish in the waters of the Red Sea. To all appearances the doom of the two million Israelites was settled, since the only way of escape was the valley through which they had passed. But "man's extremity is God's opportunity." The fact that God had brought His people thus far should have been enough for their faith. With Israel covered by the blood of the lamb and protected by the cloud, the dispute now was not between Pharaoh and Israel, but between God and Pharaoh. Because he had driven the Israelites to the edge of the sea, perhaps Pharaoh anticipated that God had forsaken His people and that his gods would yet triumph. Were the people not entangled in the land and shut in within the wilderness? They certainly were, but all were to realize that salvation is of God.

In one way, the fear of Israel was legitimate. The 600,000 males, by leaving Egypt, threw the whole course of commerce and business into disorder, and Pharaoh wanted them back. So with 600 chosen chariots, with chariot horses and a division of the royal guard, Israel was pursued. Why should Israel be afraid of a force their number? The answer is that although Pharaoh's host was fewer than the 600,000 Israelite males, the token Egyptian army behind them was well-trained and accustomed to war. The Israelites, however, were mostly unarmed, untrained, and ignorant of warfare. Thus unmatched, Israel cried unto the Lord and were assured He was about to help them since they could not help themselves. All the proud, haughty, threatening Egyptians would soon be pale corpses strewn along the shore of the Red Sea.

The command came to "Go forward," and the people struck their tents and followed Moses to the edge of the sea. This believing leader stretched his rod over the sea and the water divided, leaving a dry space for Israel to pass over. The parted waters came together and drowned the Egyptians, with God getting Himself honor upon Pharaoh and all his host (14:17, 18). Is not honor due to Moses for his unquestioned compliance to the divine command?

Those who reject the miraculous in Scripture either dismiss the miracle of the Red Sea as the product of "mythological fancy or of legendary accretion," or explain it as a natural occurrence. One theory is that at that particular time the water receded at the point where Moses stood, leaving very shallow or dry places, and that therefore the Israelites could easily pass over before the waters returned. So a miracle was not necessary. But there were no tides in the Red Sea with regular ebb and flow. An Egyptian tradition states that Moses waited for the ebb tide in order to lead the Israelites across the sea.

Speculation as to divine agency in this event is useless. Everything connected with it was supernatural. As *The International Standard Bible Encyclopaedia* puts it:

It was by a miracle of prophecy that Moses was emboldened to get his host into position to avail themselves of the temporary opportunity at exactly the right time. The opening of the sea may have been a foreordained event in the course of nature which God only forenew, in which case the direct divine agency was limited to those influences upon the human actors that led them to place themselves where they could take advantage of the natural opportunity. . . . The disturbance of the waters was beyond the powers of human agency to produce.

Let us examine the various elements contributing to this most stupendous display of God's power. Trench reminds us that in remarkable words the author of Wisdom of Solomon (19:6) describes how, at the passage of the Red Sea, all nature was in its kind molded and fashioned anew, that it might serve God's purposes for the deliverance of His people and the punishment of His enemies. Because of this double result of the miracle, it is justly called "great." Pharaoh had destroyed the male children of the Israelites in the River Nile; now God, through Moses who was saved from the Nile, is about to visit this iniquity on Pharaoh and his hosts in the Red Sea.

First of all, we have "the Angel of God" who went before the camp of Israel (14:19,

20). Who was He and what part did He play? The *Jehovah* of 13:21 here became "the Angel of God," as "the Angel of Jehovah" in the burning bush (3:2) becomes "God" (3:4) and "Jehovah" (3:7). If this is a theophanic appearance of our Lord, He is to be distinguished from the cloud, the movements of which He antedated and directed. He it was who delayed and troubled the Egyptians by involving them in "cloud and darkness," and who encouraged and aided the Israelites by affording them abundant light through the cloud to further their progress.

Winds played an important part in the performance of this spectacular miracle. He who "walketh upon the wings of the wind" (Psalm 104:3) knew how to cause His wind to blow and thrust the waters back to form a road for His people to cross over. All night a strong east wind blew, and then wind from the opposite direction drove the waters back into their place (14:21, 26). Moses, in his song describing the miracle, spoke of the wind as "the blast of God's nostrils" (15:8), and said, "Thou didst blow with Thy wind, and the sea covered them" (15:10). Three times the wind is mentioned as the means God employed in opening water. God's "strong east wind," then, opened in the sea a sure retreat for all the Israelites, but resumed its wonted state and overwhelmed the Egyptians, thus affording a road for Israel but a grave for Egypt. The sea, being His because He made it, was controlled by its Creator.

The waters, as a wall on both sides of the Israelites (14:22, 15:8), provides expressive imagery. Think of the sea which, at its deepest soundings is 6,000 feet and miles broad at its narrowest parts, dividing in two, and leaving its bed firm and dry and forming perpendicular walls of great height! What a mighty act of omnipotence! God's power to make things stand upright or fall, contrary to nature, is exemplified by the waters of the Red Sea which stood in a heap, and later the walls which fell flat. Both actions were easy to the omnipotent One (15:8; Joshua 3:16; 6:20). We recognize that rhetorical use is made of the word "wall" in Scripture (Proverbs 18:11; Isaiah 26:1; Naham 3:8), but in the miracle before us the water on either side of the channel served the purpose of a wall for protection. There was no chance for Pharaoh to intercept the Israelites by a flank movement. Kalisch has given us the poetic phrase "the water gave up its nature, formed with its waves a strong wall, and instead of streaming like a fluid, congealed into a hard substance." The east wind, freeing the channel from water and blowing at the precise time that Moses reached the place of crossing, points to a supernatural agency at work. In like manner, the timing of the return of the piled up waters saving Israel and destroying Egypt must have been a direct act of God.

Another aspect of God's power over all kinds of inanimate objects, proving that it pervades all particles of matter, is seen in the chariot wheels of the Egyptian host being shaken off (14:25 margin). Not only did the wheels become "entangled," implying their sinking in the soft ooze, but the wheels parted from the axles. Convinced that God was indeed fighting for Israel, the Egyptians turned and fled (14:25). Amid the confusion and chaos of obstructed chariots and frightened horses, there came the final catastrophe. At the divine command, Moses stretched his hand over the sea and the parted water flowed inwards, drowning the Egyptians (14:26-28). Thus the forces of nature, controlled by God, destroyed a mighty host.

As Pharaoh was with his host, it is evident that he perished with it. "Egyptian monarchs of the Rameside period almost always led their armies out to battle, and when they did so, uniformly rode with a single attendant, who acted as charioteer, in a two-horse chariot." The exact indentification of the Pharaoh who perished is another matter. It is thought that the Exodus from Egypt occurred during the reign of Thothmes III, who was the fourth king of the 18th dynasty and who is not recorded as being buried with his ancestors. Tombs have been found in Egypt for every Pharaoh of his dynasty, but not for the Pharaoh Moses challenged. Does not this singular fact indicate that his tomb was in the Red Sea where he drowned with his army. It would have been a blot on his monumental history, if such a tragic end had been recorded.

The objection raised as to how two million people could cross the Red Sea in a single night can be quickly answered. They were in the hands of a mighty God who interposed for them and who was well able to provide His people with all necessary speed and agility for their flight which, cov-

ering some two months, is clearly marked—
To the Red Sea (12:37–14:14);
Through the Red Sea (14:15–15:21);
From the Red Sea (15:22–19:2);
The Exodus from Egypt is among the miraculous events to be repeated in the last days (Comp. 14:15 with Isaiah 11:15, 16; Zechariah 10:10, 11).

We cannot conclude our study of Israel's grand deliverance without a reference to the hallelujah chorus of rejoicing which such a miracle inspired. Although Moses, with his native modesty, does not say that he wrote the magnificent ode, known as *The Song of Moses*, there is no doubt as to its being his production. Simeon spoke of it as, "The most ancient composition of its kind, that is extant in the world." Summarizing the miraculous visitations he had witnessed, Moses shows that God was "exalted far above all other gods" (7:5; 14:4, 18). The gods of Egypt were nonentities, but God was unapproachable in His—

(1) *Holiness:* "Glorious in holiness" (15:11). Of holiness, heathen gods were destitute. Much evil was associated with the worship of them.

(2) *Awefulness:* "Fearful in praises." As the Almighty One, God was the proper object of profoundest awe, even to those who approach Him with praise and thanksgiving. Any awe or reverence heathen gods received was without foundation.

(3) *Supernaturalness:* "Doeth Wonders." Using and overruling nature, God caused all men to marvel at His almightiness. The ability of Egypt's gods to work wonders was nil. "Among the gods there is none like unto Thee, O Lord; there is none that can do as thou doest" (Psalm 86:8).

Halley had this comment: "In God's mind, His deliverace of Israel out of Egypt was so similar to His deliverance of the Church out of the world at the time of the end, that He calls the triumphant songs of the Redeemed, *The Song of Moses and the Lamb*" (Revelation 15:3). Moses in the baptism of the Red Sea shook off the powers and principalities of Egypt, and Christ, in the baptism of Calvary, made possible a perfect deliverance for a sin-bound race. Through the red blood of the Saviour, a new and living way has been opened for us. The Red Sea typifies the redeemed baptized into Christ, who became the Leader and Com-

mander of His people. The believer's "Red
Sea" is Romans 4:24, 25, and his celebration
of deliverance is Romans 5:1-11 and I Corinthians 10:1, 2. No matter what obstacles
may confront, let us obey the command to
"God forward."

29. The Miracle Journey

(Deuteronomy 8:4; 29:5; Nehemiah
9:21; read Numbers)

The wilderness pilgrimage of Israel from
the Red Sea to Jordan presents a series of
miracles. From the beginning to the end of
their forty-year journey, the Israelites were
the recipients of God's miraculous provision
and protection. In the renewed commission,
God promised He would do marvels for His
people such as the earth had not witnessed
(Exodus 34:10). "According to the days of
thy coming out of the land of Egypt will I
show unto him marvellous things" (Micah
7:15).

First of all, there was the stupendous marvel of transporting and transplanting a whole
great nation from one land to another, main-
taining it in the interim of forty years in a
desert. How truly did God bear the people
as on eagles' wings from Egypt to Himself
in the wilderness! (Exodus 19:4). During
the period of the first thirty-eight years, the
first generation died out and a strong race
of desert warriors, as hardy as Arabs today, succeeded it (Deuteronomy 2:14). In
bravery, courage, fiber and quality of life
those that Joshua led across the Jordan were
far removed from the motley crowd that left
Egypt.

The book of Numbers, so named because
it contains an account of the numberings of
the people of Israel (the first of which took
place at the commencement of the second
year after their departure from Egypt, and
the second, in the plains of Moab at the
conclusion of their journey in the wilderness), abounds with evidences of God's miraculous help on the part of His people. The
Levites were separated from the mass of
the people and numbered by themselves.
The total number of men fit for war, from
twenty years old, were 603,550 (1:46);
this gives an addition of 3,550 to the number who left Egypt (Exodus 12:37). In the
plains of Moab at the end of the journey
there were none in the original census embraced in the second numbering, save Caleb
and Joshua. All the rest perished in the

wilderness as God said they would because
of their murmurings and rebellion.

The book of Numbers abounds with the
most signal displays of God's judgments
against sin, not only toward the heathen,
but toward His chosen people (11:1-35).
The earth became both their executioner
and their grave. Yet the book no less wonderfully displays the faithfulness of God in
the fulfilment of His promise to Abraham
that his seed should be as the stars of
heaven. At the close of the wilderness journey, the number of the people was found
to be scarcely less than when they went
into the wilderness. Of the men there were
601,730.

Then there was the miracle of provision
for some two million souls. The supply of
food, drink, and raiment for such a vast
host was supernatural, as the following
study of the wilderness miracles clearly
proves. Many of these miracles, grouped together according to their setting, typify
God's complete provision for His people—
guidance, shelter, food, water, etc. (Exodus 14-17). To support such a large nation
in a wilderness required continuous, miraculous provision and, apart from the land of
God, we have no explanation of the unfailing maintenance of the people for such a
long period.

The organization of such a vast camp was
marvelous and was carried out under divine instructions with military precision, the
twelve tribes arranged thus:

On the east—Judah, Issachar, and Zebu-
lon

On the south—Reuben, Simeon, and Gad
On the west—Ephraim, Manasseh, and
Benjamin

On the north—Dan, Asher, and Naphtali.

Although the wilderness was a period of
apostasy (Ezekiel 20:16; Amos 5:25; Hosea 9:10), yet God was unfailing in His
bountiful provision. The failure of their
clothing to wax old meant that God supplied their wants, partly by ordinary and
occasional miraculous means (Deuteronomy
8:4; 29:5; Nehemiah 9:21). Ellicott says
that old Jewish writers affirm that the raiment grew with their growth, from childhood to manhood. "We cannot say that
anything miraculous is certainly intended,
though it is not impossible," comments Ellicott. "It may mean that God in His providence directed the people to clothe themselves in a manner suitable for their journey and their mode of life, just as He

taught them how to make and clothe His own tabernacle with various fabrics and coverings of skins." They never lacked new and untattered garments, or shoes to prevent foot swelling. Health was preserved throughout the journey. In spite of the long pilgrimage, the people walked and did not faint (Isaiah 40:31).

What a recital of divine tenderness and care the sacred historian describes! Not one of the mighty host lacked anything. The wilderness was part of the divine discipline but not the wanderings. Had the people confided in God, even days would have sufficed to have completed the journey from the Red Sea to Canaan, but it took over thirty-eight years (Deuteronomy 1:2). Yet all through the wasted years there was the exhibition of divine and unwearied patience with the murmuring host.

A few of the grave events in the wilderness are types or figures written for our admonition. Paul groups several together in moral order in warning the lax Corinthians against trusting in ordinances instead of Christ (I Corinthians 10:1-12). As to the purpose of the wilderness miracles, H. H. Halley says that they were of a three-fold nature:

(1) To preserve the nation. In God's plan, a Messianic nation had been devised to pave the way for the coming Messiah. God seemed to have thought that it was necessary to maintain the nation at all costs.

(2) To build into the nation, which had been nurtured in Egyptian idolatary, faith in Jehovah as the one true God.

(3) For the effect on surrounding nations, especially the Canaanites. Certainly it must have been known that this vast multitude of people were making their way toward Canaan in the belief that their God had given it them. The report of the miracles went ahead, and weakened the morale of the nations that were to be ousted.

30. The Miracle of Marah's Healing Waters

(Exodus 15:22-27; Numbers 33:8)

After a journey of three days from the Red Sea on the Arabian side, Israel reached the first camp and also the first trial. Early in their pilgrimage, the people were made to experience the hardship of the wilderness in lack of water and food which made necessary the manifestation of the miraculous on their behalf. Says Scofield, "These bitter waters were in the very path of the Lord's leading, and stand for the trials of God's people, which are educatory and not punitive."

Marah means "bitterness," indicating the bitter taste of the waters in those parts. The extreme bitterness of the springs is testified to by travelers. The word appears in *Mara*, the name Naomi asked to be called by (Ruth 1:20). In the light of her bitter experiences and her present pitiable plight, the old name *Naomi*, meaning pleasant and charming, became peculiarly inappropriate. She could not bear the contradiction between her name and disposition.

Suffering from lack of water (15:22), the people came to Moses and murmured. Moses prayed about the lack of drinking water and the Lord showed him a tree which had a sweetening virtue. "God seems to have made use of nature, as far as nature could go, and then to have superadded His own omnipotent energy in order to produce the desired effect." Evidently this once-bitter fountain has retained its sweetness, for as Faussett remarks, "the beneficial effect of the tree cast into the bitter water by God's direction is probably the cause why this fountain is less bitter than others in the neighborhood." At the next stop—Elim— the people found an abundance of shade and refreshment (15:27).

Ada R. Habershon reminds us that on two occasions a great chemical change was wrought on the water that was bitter—at Marah, then at Jericho where the waters were healed by salt from a new cruse (II Kings 2:21). Although use was made of a tree and salt, God alone was able to heal. God revealed Himself as Jehovah Rophi— "The Lord that healeth thee" (15:25,26).

The miracle at Marah affords a fitting type of all Christ is able to accomplish. Those bitter waters were healed by Him who came to bear the curse. Christ is the Branch who can sweeten the earth's waters. His cross is spiritually the tree which, when cast into the most bitter waters, sweetens and heals them (Galatians 3:13). "The cross became sweet to Christ as the expression of the Father's will (John 18:11). When our 'Marahs' are so taken, we cast the 'tree' into the 'waters' " (Romans 5:3, 4; Philippians 3:8; Acts 20:24).

31. The Miracle of the Manna

(Exodus 16:1-5, 14; Numbers
11:1-9; Nehemiah 9:15, 20; Joshua 5:12;
Psalm 78:20, 22-25; 105:40. See John
6:22-59)

The continued murmuring of the Israelites
after all the marvelous displays of divine
power on their behalf is a striking evidence
of their mistrust and ingratitude. In Egypt
the people, although slaves, were according
to Egyptian custom well fed (Numbers
11:5). Now, out in the wilderness, although
there was no real danger of starvation, they
murmured for food and yearned for the
flesh pots of Egypt. The Lord said He
would rain bread from heaven and thereby
prove the people to see whether they walk
in His law or not (16:4).

This was the third murmuring of Israel.
The first was at Pihaharoth, on the appearance of Pharaoh's host (14:11, 12); the
second was at Marah because of the acid-
like water they found (15:24); this third
murmuring was in the wilderness of Sin because of the lack of food.

The manna, celestially supplied, appeared
in white flakes, or small, round grains or
seeds and resembled "hoar-frost." It fell
with the dew (Numbers 11:9) and was
seen when the dew disappeared (Exodus
16:14), and had the taste of honey-wafers
(16:31). Josephus speaks of it as "one of
the sweet spices." Such heavenly food
(Psalm 105:40) is poetically described as
angels' food—bread of the mighty—from
heaven because of its divine origin (Psalm
78:24, 25).

This divine supply for daily needs lasted
for forty years and ceased the day after the
people ate the produce of Canaan—the land
of milk and honey (Joshua 5:10-12). Once
the need of it was over, it suddenly ceased
to fall. God never wastes His power. It is
in like manner that Christ is the heavenly
Manna His people feed upon until they
reach their promised rest (Matthew 28:19).

The manna was also the first food to be
rationed by measure. Daily portions of the
food had to be gathered every morning. If
any was kept over from the previous day
it bred worms and stank. On the sixth day
a double amount was gathered, the Sabbath portion being miraculously preserved.
The substance, when ground, could be
stewed or baked (16:23; Numbers 11:8).
Rabbinical literature says that it could be
adapted to the taste of each individual who

could, by wishing, taste in the manna anything he desired.

Although an important article of diet, the
manna was by no means the sole one. Many
references prove that the people had other
food besides the manna. There was cattle
for consumption as well as for sacrifices (17:
3; 24:5); flour (Numbers 7:13, 19); food
in general (Deuteronomy 2:6; Joshua 1:11).
The Israelites did not deem the manna as
being substantial for they grew weary of
eating it and came to loathe it.

As to the significance of the term *manna*,
some writers suggest that the word is from
the Egyptian *mennu*, meaning "food." Our
English term is *menu*. One explanation of
the source of the name is found in the question, "What is it?" (16:15), or *manhu* which
also means "It is manna." Not having seen
the miraculous substance before, the people
asked, "What is it?" or "The what-is-it?"
Other scholars say the word means, "This is
a gift," which, of course, it was from God.

Although efforts have been made to identify the manna with existing Arabian lich-
ens, or honey-like gums or spices, no substance can be found anywhere in the world
to satisfy the requirements of Scripture
references to it—all of which speak of it
as being miraculously supplied. It was not
a natural product miraculously augmented
to feed well-nigh two million people. The
inescapable conclusion is that the manna
was a hitherto unknown food supplied in a
miraculous way. All allusions to it suggest
the supernatural (Nehemiah 9:30; Psalm
78:24; 105:40). None can explain how the
manna came down from heaven just as no
one can explain how the Lord of glory came
down from heaven.

A golden pot with an omer of manna was
laid up before God in the Tabernacle (16:
33; Hebrews 9:4). Christ frequently referred to the manna, or bread from heaven,
as being typical of Himself (John 6:31-63).
Paul speaks of it as the believer's spiritual
food (I Corinthians 10:3). John uses the
manna as a type of the overcomer's reward
and of his future spiritual sustenance (Revelation 2:17). Bishop Jewell once wrote,
"The Scriptures are manna given as from
heaven to feed us in the desert of this
world." Faith can sing of Jesus as our
Manna:

Thou bruised and broken Bread,
   My life-long wants supply;
As living souls are fed,
   O feed me, or I die.

32. The Miracle of the Quails

(Exodus 16:8, 11-13; Numbers 11:31-34; Psalm 78:26-30; 105:39-42).

In response to the murmurings of the people, God said that He would give them not only bread to the full to be gathered in the morning light, but flesh to eat in the evening—an allusion to the movement of quails which came up "at even" and covered the camp (16:12, 13). The glory of God was manifested in such a gift of food which was a transient gift, not as in the case of the manna which continued throughout the wilderness journey. The quails did not continue to fall as the manna but were twice miraculously supplied (16:13; Numbers 11:31, 32).

The common quail, closely related to our partridge which is somewhat larger, is still very abundant in the East. In migration, after a long flight over the Red Sea, the flocks, exhausted, drop to the ground as soon as they reach the coast and are easy to catch and kill. Being fat or plump after wintering in the south, they make good eating. Their flesh is said to be juicy and delicious to eat. If eaten too frequently, they prove to be unwholesome. Quails are like the brown and tan of earth and have pencilled markings. Using sticks to kill the confused thousands falling over and around the camp, the Israelites spread the small bodies on the ground to dry.

While nature and natural history can account for myriads of these birds, the weight of which, Pliny said, was sufficient to sink a ship if it were sighted and settled on, the miraculous cannot be dispensed with. While it is true that in many Old Testament miracles God is represented as having used natural phenomena and substances for special purposes, (not creating special substances for miracles but using materials already existing), the miracle of the quails consisted in their vast quantity at the needed time. The Bible says that there went forth a wind (east wind) from the Lord and brought the quails from the sea and let them fall by the camp (Numbers 11:31; Psalm 78:26, 27). It was God who, by His command, caused the quails to fly so low that they were very easily caught (Numbers 11:31, 32). They came at His bidding and landed in the place where He directed. The most insignificant bird cannot fall to the ground without Him (Matthew 10:29; Luke 12:6, 7).

Before the flesh of the quails was consumed, God's wrath smote the people for their gluttony. As they devoured the quails so greedily, the quails suddenly changed into deadly poison. Faussett comments, "Eating birds' flesh continually, after long abstinence from flesh, a whole month greedily, in a hot climate predisposed them by surfeit to sickness; God miraculously intensified this into a plague and the place became *Kibroth Hattaavah*, "the graves of lust." The mixed multitude, made up largely of the children of Hebrew mothers by Egyptian fathers were evidently responsible for the craving for the flesh pots of Egypt (Numbers 11:4). One solemn lesson to be learned from this incident is that God gave the people their request but sent leanness into the soul (Psalm 78:29; 106:15). Habershon says, "God hears and puts forth His power to work a wonder in their midst, namely, causing the birds to do what He wanted them to; but it proves no blessing, for it brings judgment and death upon them. There are some who teach that if we have faith enough we could get anything for which we choose to ask; but is not this a warning that we should first find out whether the desire is in accordance with God's will?"

33. The Miracles of the Smitten Rock

(Exodus 17:1-9; Numbers 33:12, 13; Nehemiah 9:20; Psalm 78:16, 17; 105:41)

After a journey of some fifty miles from the Wilderness of Sin, the Israelites came to Rephidim, a name meaning "resting places," a somewhat appropriate designation of this usually fertile spot. Occasionally, however, the brook dried up and by the time Israel reached Rephidim there was a scanty supply of water. Any extra the people had brought with them from the twelve wells at Elim must have been exhausted, and there was pressing need to replenish their waterskins. After a long march, weary and faint and suffering from thirst, the people were disappointed to find no water for themselves, their children, and their cattle (17:3). To their distress, the streams were dry and water had to be miraculously provided.

At Marah the people murmured because of the bitter taste of the water there; now they murmured because of the conspicuous lack of water, and under the circumstances we cannot be surprised at their chiding of Moses. "Nothing but a very lively faith, or an utter resignation to the will of God," says Faussett, "could have made a people patient and submissive in such an extremity." Alas, Israel quickly forgot the past wonders of God on their behalf! Thus it was not in faith, but wrath, the people cried to Moses, "Give us water!" To them, the future was foreboding. Had they been brought out of Egypt to perish in the wilderness from agonizing thirst?

Desperate, the Israelites were almost ready to stone their leader, Moses, to death. But he turned to God, and received the assurance of divine help. Moses was told to take the elders and his wonder rod and smite a rock in Horeb. The presence of the elders as witnesses indicated that "each miracle had an educational value (Deuteronomy 8:1-3) and was designed to call forth, exercise, and so strengthen the faith of the people." The rock in question could not have been the traditional "Rock of Moses" in Seil Leja, since this rock is a long day's journey from Rephidim where the miracle was performed.

Moses renamed this stopping place *Massah,* meaning "temptation," a reference to the question, "Wherefore did ye tempt the Lord?" (17:2). The same root is found in "trial" (Job 9:23) and in "temptation" (Deuteronomy 4:34; 7:19; Psalm 95:8). The second name Moses gave to Rephidim was *Meribah,* meaning "chiding," "strife," or "quarrel," and refers to the chiding of Moses by the people (17:2) who were guilty of doubting God and contending with Moses.

There was nothing miraculous in the actual smiting of the rock. But the water was God-produced. Moses, as God's representative, took his rod and smote the rock. He had nothing to do with the outflow of water. This came from Him who holds the waters in the hollow of His hand. (Isaiah 40:12). While it is true that Christ was "smitten of God" (Isaiah 53:4), yet it was cruel men who killed "the Prince of life" (Acts 3:15; 2:23). Man, however, had nothing to do with the marvelous results of His death. The Holy Spirit, like rivers of water (John 7:37-39), flowed down from the ascended Lord who, as the Rock, had been smitten (Acts 2:23).

Paul applies the smitten rock to Christ as the Source of living water, and in this identification implies the pre-existence of Christ and of His care for the nation from which He sprang. This Rock followed Israel in their journeyings, or rather He whom the rock typifies accompanied and supplied all their needs (I Corinthians 10:4-6). The comment of Dr. C. I. Scofield on Exodus 17:6 provides an impressive outline for preachers. Habershon shows how many typical miracles occur in pairs. Here, for example, we have in the wilderness provision, manna from heaven and water out of the rock, which severally typifies Christ as the Bread (John 6) and the Holy Spirit as the Water.

While a similar miracle was performed at Kadesh, probably in the first month of the fortieth year of the wilderness wanderings, it is not to be confused with what transpired at Rephidim (Numbers 20:1-13; Deuteronomy 8:15; 33:8; Psalm 81:7; 106:32, 33). It would seem as if the miraculous supply of water given at Rephidim had been suddenly withdrawn in order to test the faith of the Israelites. Again they murmured and wished that they had died with those who had perished in the plague which followed the rebellion of Korah.

The Lord appeared to Moses and Aaron and the rod was taken, but should not have been used as it was. Moses erred in that he smote the rock instead of speaking to it as God had commanded. The water was twice divinely given for Israel's need—the first time the rock was smitten in obedience to the divine word; the second time, smiting was an act of disobedience on Moses' part. God told Moses to *speak* to the rock not *smite* it. The murmurings of the Israelites caused Moses, the meekest of men, to lose his temper and to arrogate to himself the honor due only to God. "Must *we* fetch water out of the rock?" Water came, but not by Moses' power. Here is a case of God using a disobedient servant, simply because he was the best available for the accomplishment of the divine purpose. For speaking thus—"unadvisedly with his lips" (Psalm 106:33)—Moses was inflicted with the punishment of exclusion from the land of Canaan. The addition of *Kadesh* to Meribah distinguishes this latter miracle from the earlier one.

34. The Miracle Victory Over Amalek

(Exodus 17:8-16; Numbers 13:29; 14: 25; Deuteronomy 25:17-19; Psalm 83:7).

Amalek was the first to attack Israel in the wilderness journey from Egypt to Palestine. Later the Amalekites attacked again at Kadesh, an attack for which Moses ordered their extinction (Numbers 31:1-3). But they recovered and later oppressed Israel. As we shall see in a further study, the Amalekites were defeated by Gideon. Gradually they became incorporated with the Arabians. Amalek, grandson of Esau (Genesis 36:12), who was born after the flesh (Galatians 4:22-29), was the progenitor of the Amalekites, Israel's persistent enemy. Balaam speaks of them as "the first of the nations" (Numbers 24:20).

The occasion of the attack at Rephidim was not only Amalek's resentment over Israel's entrance into their fertile territory. Naturally, they wished to preserve themselves against invaders into their region. At Rephidim there was no water to drink and God miraculously caused it to gush from a rock. The heinousness of Amalek's sin in God's sight was in their effort to deprive His people of life which He had supplied by miracle. The signs and wonders on Israel's behalf had shown them to be God's people. Thus, when Amalek attacked Israel, the battle was not against Israel but against God. It is this fact that accounts for the severity of the doom of the Amalekites, which although delayed, was finally executed (I Chronicles 4:43).

To this audacity, Amalek added a cruel pitilessness in attacking the rear of an almost unarmed host at a time when it was "faint and weary." By guerilla warfare, there was a deliberate effort to defeat God's purpose at the very outset when Israel was most feeble, having recently come out of bondage (Deuteronomy 25: 17, 18). No wonder God caused Israel to be victorious! On so many occasions, Israel proved that the battle was not theirs but God's. The numerical and material strength of contending hosts counted for nothing. God gave the victory.

Another motive behind the attack of Amalek was the lack of any fear of God (Exodus 17:16, margin; Deuteronomy 25: 17-19). "Because the hand of Amalek is against the throne of Jehovah, therefore Jehovah will have war with Amalek from generation to generation." When the Bible speaks of sin, it presents the great evil of it to be that it dishonors God. It is because of this that destruction overtook the Amalekites (17:16) and others.

Unfit for battle themselves, Moses and Aaron and Hur, each of whom was around 80 years of age, retreated from the actual conflict to spend the time in intercessory prayer, and thus best help in the conflict. In order to teach the lesson of the power of prayer, God made the fortunes of the fight to vary according to the motion of Moses' hands. When they were up, Israel prevailed, and when they were down, Amalek prevailed. Victory was entirely regulated by what went on at the top of the hill. The good generalship of Joshua—first mentioned here—was useless aside from the uplifted arms of Moses, which indicated the recognition of God's part in the conflict. In this miraculous victory, the power of intercession is symbolized. Israel's defeat of Amalek illustrates the feebleness of a fighting arm apart from the power of intercession.

There followed the altar with its sacrificial offerings—an acknowledgment of the divine mercy and power in giving Israel the victory. Moses called the name of the altar *Jehovah nissi*, "The Lord is my banner" (17:15). The Banner under whose protection worshiping Israel fought and conquered was God himself. Several expositors suggest the spiritual application of the incident at Rephidim, where the conflict with Amalek sets forth the resources of man under the law rather than those of the believer under grace. The man under the law could fight and pray (17:9-12). Under grace, the Holy Spirit gains the victory over the flesh in the believer's behalf (Romans 8:1-4; Galatians 5:1, 17), but this victory is only as the believer walks in the Spirit. When action is in independence or disobedience, Amalek gains an easy victory (Numbers 14:42-45).

35. The Miracles at Sinai

(Exodus 19:16-25; Deuteronomy 4:5; 5:7-22; 9:8-11; Psalm 68:8; Hebrews 12:18-21)

Leaving Rephidim, the Israelites came to the desert of Sinai and camped before the mount (19:1, 2). It was in this plain, some two miles long and half a mile wide, that Israel abode for about a year. The particular peak in the Sinaitic mountains of the peninsula between the gulfs of Akabah and Suez, where Moses received the Law and instructions as to the Tabernacle, has never been identified beyond question. In the Old Testament *Sinai* (meaning "to shine") and *Horeb* (meaning "to waste") appear to be used interchangeably. *Sinai* is mentioned as a desert and a mountain 35 times. In 17 passages the same desert and mountain are called *Horeb*.

Some authorities suggest that *Sinai* refers to the entire chain of mountains and *Horeb* to a single peak. Volumes have been written to prove that this or that peak is the original "Mountain of the Law" where Moses received the Ten Commandments. The majority, however, incline to the belief that the ancient Horeb or Sinai was the peak now known by the Arabs as *Jebel Musa*, "Mountain of Moses." This peak is more than 6,000 feet high and near the top is a chapel dedicated to Elijah who heard the "still small voice" there (I Kings 19). The traditional Mount Sinai is an isolated mass of rock rising abruptly from the plain in awful grandeur. Scripture calls it "the mount" and "the mount of God" (3:1; 4:27; 19:2, 11).

When we read, "The Lord came from Sinai" (Deuteronomy 33: 1, 2), the passage must not be taken literally. In a symbolic way Moses implied that Sinai was the mount of revelation, the starting point where God manifested Himself to Israel and came to abide in the midst of His people. All of the miraculous phenomena associated with Sinai were intended to impress Israel with God's unapproachable majesty and holiness. So awful a manifestation has never been made at any other place or time, nor will be until the end-time period of human history.

Supernatural manifestations were loud thunder, fierce flashes of lightning, a fire leaping from the mountain to the sky, dense volumes of smoke producing an awful and weird darkness, a trembling of the mountain as by a continuous earthquake, a sound like the blare of a trumpet loud and prolonged, and then finally a clear penetrating. These impressive evidences of God's presence and power must have created a profound hush over the camp.

Fire is expressive of divine holiness, and also of divine hatred of sin. Because the mountain burned with fire, the smoke was real.

Thick cloud, or denseness of a cloud, proves that although God is light, clouds and darkness are also round about Him (Psalm 97:2). He dwells in "thick darkness" (II Chronicles 6:1). He who commands light can also command darkness to cover the earth (Exodus 10:22; 20:21). We now need not fear Sinai's blackness, because Christ endured the darkness of the cross for us.

Lightning is also another display of divine power. Today if a person is struck by lightning, the verdict is, "killed by the visitation of God."

Thunder is called the praise of God (Job 37:5 RV; Psalm 29).

Earthquake cannot take place without divine permission. When God commands the earth to open, it does so at the spot He indicates and in no other (Psalm 104:32) During the earthquake at Sinai, Moses was safe in the cleft of the rock (Exodus 33: 22).

The voice of a trumpet. This trumpet was supernaturally blown and called attention to the solemn proclamation about to be made. "The trump of God" is associated with Christ's return for His true Church (I Thessalonians 4:16). The great events to take place in the Great Tribulation are to be heralded by angels using trumpets (Revelation 8:7, 8, 10, 12; 9:1, 14).

Called to the summit of the mount to receive the Ten Commandments, Moses witnessed further displays of God's power. God spoke out the words of the law, which was kept for centuries in the ark but was lost during the Captivity. If some archaeologist should yet discover the two tables of stone, what a sensational and priceless relic they would be! The first two tables were fashioned by God (32:16); the second set was hewn by Moses. But in both cases, the commandments were written "by the finger of God" (24:12; 31:18; 32:16). The tablets of stone were inscribed by some supernatural process, the exact nature of which is not revealed. Christ referred to the Holy Spirit as "the finger of God" (Luke 11:20).

Moses was in the mount for forty days and forty nights and during this long period was divinely sustained, for he was without food or water (Exodus 24:18; 34:28; Deuteronomy 9:9). Perhaps manna fell around and provided sufficient sustenance.

Other miraculous fasts are recorded—those of Elijah (I Kings 19:8) and of our Lord in the wilderness of temptation (Matthew 4:2). Moses fasted for a similar period because of the idolatry of Israel (Deuteronomy 9:18, 25).

While Moses was absent from the plain and hidden from the view of the people by the thick cloud surrounding him on the mount, there took place the pitiful and inexplicable apostasy of Israel almost immediately after God had thundered from the mount—"Thou shalt have no other gods beside Me." The fashioning of the golden calf indicates that in spite of all the mighty works on their behalf, the Israelites were still under the spell of Egyptian idolatary. Out of Egypt as a place, they still had a good deal of Egypt in their hearts.

Aaron was evidently unable to control the multitude, and Moses, after his descent from the mount, called for immediate and severe discipline in such a crisis. The punishment was swift and terrible, for the people were made to drink the dust of the destroyed idol and many of them perished. "The Lord plagued the people" (32:35). Just what the nature this divine visitation was, we are not told. Sufferings of various kinds overtook those who transgressed in worshiping the golden calf. Moses felt the sin of the people so deeply that he pled with God to blot him out of His book.

Although Israel had flagrantly broken the divine covenant, God consented to renew it on terms strictly just and purely optional. Hitherto, He had promised to go up with His people (23:20-23), in the person of the angel in whom was His Name. Now, to mark His displeasure over their idolatry, He withdrew that particular promise and substituted for the divine presence the guidance of a mere angel (33:1-3).

Moses is summoned once more to the top of Sinai, to receive a second proclamation of the law, and the renewal of the divine covenant (34:10-28), and was again the recipient of the supernatural. The patriarch was hid in the cleft of the rock and covered with the divine hand. He craved for a beatific vision and was privileged to see more of God (His back parts) than any other man will behold until heaven is reached. The revelation of God's ineffable goodness was miraculously flashed into Moses' inmost soul and he communed with God "as a man speaketh unto his friend." From the overpowering sight of the glory of the godhead, Moses was miraculously protected and shrouded. All he was able to behold was a sort of afterglow the divine glory left behind.

The effect of so brilliant a vision was the reflection of the divine glory upon the countenance of Moses, which he was forced ordinarily to conceal from the people by means of a veil (34:29-35). Having desired to see the glory of God, he came down from the mount with a glory face. He had been changed into the same image (II Corinthians 3:7-18). Doubtless such a transformation of countenance supported the authority of Moses among a people of materialistic leanings like the Israelites.

Ellicott remarks that some commentators suggest that "the radiance Moses received was a part of man's original heritage, a feature of that 'image of God' wherein he was created (Genesis 1:27). The gift was forfeited by the Fall, and will not be restored generally until the consummation of all things. But meanwhile, from time to time, it pleases God to restore to certain of His saints the physical glory, which is the symbol of internal purity and holiness, as to Moses on Mount Sinai; to Moses and Elijah on the Mount of Transfiguration (Luke 9:31); and to Stephen when he pleaded before the Sanhedrin (Acts 6:15). A glory of this kind, but of surpassing brilliance belonged to the human nature of our blessed Lord, who concealed it ordinarily, but allowed it to appear temporarily at the Transfiguration and permanently after His Ascension" (Revelation 1:16; 10:1; 21:23; 22:5).

For the allegorical application of Sinai, one has to turn to the teaching of Paul. Exodus 19 should be read in the light of Romans 3:19-26; 7:7-24; Galatians 4:1-3, 25. At Sinai Israel learned these lessons that the Church should also learn, namely:

(1) The holiness of Jehovah through His Word

(2) The goodness of God through the provision of priesthood and sacrifice

(3) Man's own sinfulness and weakness through failure.

As to the establishment of the Tabernacle in the camp of the people, everything about this meeting place was supernatural. Its plan, down to the minutest detail, and the equipment of men to develop the plan were of God (36:1-7). Everything concerning the Tabernacle was executed "as the Lord had commanded."

36. The Miracle of Judgment Upon Nadab and Abihu

(Leviticus 10:1-7; Numbers 3:1-4; 26:61; I Chronicles 24:2)

What sad disappointment the best of men occasion God! As soon as the Israelites witnessed the divine manifestation of God's acceptance of the ritual connected with the institution of the priesthood, the whole worshiping congregation was to see a most daring act of sacrilege committed by two of the five newly-installed priests and also the awful punishment such offenders deserved. The two eldest sons of Aaron, Nadab and Abihu, who are mentioned twelve times in the Old Testament, always in conjunction, received the high distinction of accompanying Aaron, their father, and Moses to the summit of the hallowed mount (Exodus 24:1). They had been consecrated to God's service and a miracle attended their consecration (Leviticus 9:24). But priests were beset by the same infirmities overtaking the laity.

Ellicott says that the sin of Nadab and Abihu was of a complicated character and involved and consisted of several acts of transgression.

(1) They both offered unauthorized fire. Their vessels had to be filled with holy fire from the altar, which was always burned to be used in burning incense (9:24; 16:12; Revelation 8:5). Instead they used common fire—fire of their own creation. Here we have a striking illustration of the use of carnal means to kindle the fire of devotion and promise.

(2) Each took *his own* censer and not the sacred utensil of the sanctuary. If we worship God, we must worship Him in His way (John 4:24). Nadab and Abihu typify the "will worship" which Paul warns against, which often has a "show of wisdom and humility" (Colossians 2:23).

(3) They presumptuously encroached upon the functions of the high priest who alone burnt incense in a censer (16:12, 13; Numbers 16:46, 47). The ordinary priests only burnt it on the golden altar in the holy place (Exodus 30: 7, 8). Korah and his company were an exception since it was ordered by Moses for a special purpose (Numbers 16:6-25). The sin of Nadab and Abihu was the daring assumption of mere nature, aided by religious ordinances and ecclesiastical position to enter the Lord's presence.

(4) They offered the incense at an unauthorized time, since it was apart from the morning and evening sacrifice. They performed their duty in an irregular manner. Worship is only acceptable to God when offered as He has directed (Exodus 30:9).

As to the root of such a sin meriting terrible punishment, tradition says that Nadab and Abihu became intoxicated through drinking too freely of the drink offering and that trying to perform their service in such a bemuddled state of mind, they were not able to distinguish between the legal and illegal. To prevent the like evil recurring, the use of wine was forbidden to the priests when about to officiate in the Tabernacle services. This prohibition coming so directly after the sin of Nadab and Abihu, if the cause was indeed intemperance, is an undesigned coincidence and mark of genuineness. The true source of exhilaration to a spiritual priest is not wine, but the Holy Spirit (Acts 2:15-18; Ephesians 5:18). The present application of this truth is emphasized in Luke 1:15 and I Timothy 3:3.

The swift judgment overtaking the two priests was solemn as well as supernatural. Fire from the Lord devoured them and they died before the Lord (10:2). Yet somehow by the act of God their bodies were not charred, neither were their priestly garments burnt, since they were buried in them (10:5). Fire, symbol of divine acceptance (9:24) was also the sign of divine accusation. By fire, Nadab and Abihu had sinned, and by fire they died. The divine fire which issued forth to consume the sacrifices as a token of acceptance, now descended as the avenger of sin to consume the sacrificers, just as the same Gospel is to one a savor of life unto life, and to another a savor of death unto death (II Corinthians 2:16).

The offenders died supernaturally in the court of the sanctuary, that is, on the very spot where they had sinned (10:2), and in their death God was sanctified (10:3). "He had sanctified to Himself Aaron and his sons by the holy unction (8, 10, 12), that they might sanctify Him in strict performance of their sacred duties as mediators between God and man. Having failed to do this, God sanctified Himself in them by awful punishment inflicted upon them for their trangression."

Also by His righteous judgment, God glorified Himself before all the people. Death for such sin vindicated His holy law and reminded the people that they could not violate that law with impunity. A further token of divine judgment was the prohibition of any mourning for the two priests smitten by sudden death. "Uncover not your heads, neither rend your clothes" (10:6). Aaron, their honored father, must have been overwhelmed by the sin and punishment of his two sons, but the only token of his anguish was his forbearing to eat that sad day the flesh of the people's sin offering (10: 12-20). All other manifestations of mourning were prohibited (see Luke 9:60 for the application to our spiritual priesthood). Under such a crushing stroke, "Aaron held his peace." Grace raised him from his natural impulsiveness and enabled him to be submissive to the will of God.

37. The Miracle at Taberah

(Numbers 11:1-3; Deuteronomy 9:22;
Psalm 78:21)

While this unidentified stop on the journey is thought to have been Kibroth-Hattaavah (11:35), the first camp after the departure from Sinai, it is obvious that there must have been an encampment at Taberah (11:3). Probably the two names belonged to the same camp.

At Taberah, there were those among the Israelites who complained, or who "murmured sinfully before the Lord" (11:1 LXX). What they groused about it is not stated. Because we go on to read about the dissatisfaction of the sweet bread of heaven and the provision of quails, the discontent of the people may have been in this direction. This we do know, that the murmurers were consumed by fire at the outer edge of the camp for their sin.

Taberah, meaning "a burning," is related to the word "burnt" (11:1). Scripture does not tell us the extent of the fire, or the objects destroyed. Fire, symbol of divine judgment upon sin, broke out in the extremity of the camp, and was arrested in its destructive progress by the supplication of Moses. Doubtless, the murmurers and their possessions perished in the divine con-

flagration. While such a dreadful death by fire may show the great severity of divine judgment for murmuring, we must not forget that the complaint was against God's power and provision. Divine judgment after the giving of the law was more severe than that inflicted before it (see Exodus 14: 11-14; 15:24, 25; 16:2-8; 17:3-7). Ellicott, in this connection, says that "The writer of the Epistle to the Hebrews argues from the just recompense of reward which every transgression and disobedience received under the Law, the impossibility of the escape of those who neglect the great salvation of the Gospel" (See Hebrews 2:3; 10:28, 29; 12:25).

If the murmuring at Taberah was against the miraculous provision of God for the physical needs of the people, is it not typical of man's natural repugnance to the spiritual food God has provided in the Gospel, and of his restless cravings after worldly pleasures? It is for us to give heed to the apostolic warning against any phase of murmuring (I Corinthians 10:10).

38. The Miracle of Miriam's Leprosy

(Numbers 12; 20:1; Leviticus 13:46;
Deuteronomy 24:8, 9)

At Hazeroth, where Israel abode for awhile after leaving Kibroth-Hattaavah, there was a further display of God's power. Among the benefits conferred on Israel was the joint leadership of Moses, Aaron, and Miriam during the Exodus (Micah 6:4). But the privileged position of this family did not excuse them from punishment when they sinned. Moses, one of the greatest of God's prophets, was excluded from Canaan for having once spoken unadvisedly with his lips. Aaron suffered similar judgment (Numbers 20:12, 24). Miriam, although chosen as a leader of, and pattern to, Israel's women, was yet smitten of God with leprosy because of her jealousy. What a disgrace for the first woman ever to be spoken of as "a prophetess" (Exodus 15: 20)!

Miriam was the eldest child of Amram and Jochebed and at least 12 years older than Moses and 9 years older than Aaron. Miriam was the one who, when Pharaoh's daughter saw the babe in his bulrush ark, brought her own mother, Jochebed, to the princess as a nurse for the child (Exodus 2:7, 8). Now she appears to be the leader in the insurrection against the authority of Moses. Her name comes first suggesting she was the one who uttered the complaint. "Spake" (12:1) being in the feminine gender, bears this out, as does the fact that judgment fell upon her and not upon Aaron, although he was associated with his sister in the outburst against Moses. Being rather pliable, Aaron yielded to Miriam's suggestions, just as he did when the Israelites desired the golden calf.

How careful we should be in our treatment of those upon whom the hand of the Lord evidently rests! Miriam voiced the jealous feelings of Aaron and herself in a two-fold direction. First of all, there was criticism of Moses' wife—the Ethiopian, or colored, woman, he had married. While there is no hint of it in the Bible, it would seem, however, as if Zipporah were dead, and Moses had married one of the African Cushites who had accompanied the Israelites out of Egypt, or one who dwelt around Sinai. Such a marriage was not prohibited by the law, as marriage with Canaanites was (Exodus 34:16). Miriam was likely jealous because the Ethiopian woman had supplanted the influence she had had over Moses since the death of Zipporah. Feminine jealousy and ambition were the drawbacks to Miriam's otherwise commanding character. She it was who had led the praises of Israel after the triumph of the Red Sea (Exodus 15).

The sad story before us seems to suggest that jealousy over the superior position of Moses was the real cause of the strife. Had not God spoken to him as His friend? Surely Miriam and Aaron as joint leaders had every right to the same divine approval. God's reply to the curt, sour question, "Hath the Lord indeed spoken only by Moses?" implies that although Miriam was a prophetess receiving prophetical revelations, she did not receive them "mouth to mouth" and immediately as Moses who "beheld the similitude of the Lord." Miriam and others saw only in a "vision" or a "dream." Calvin remarks:

> Such is the depravity of human nature that Miriam and Aaron not only abuse the gifts of God towards the brother whom they despise, but by an ungodly and sacrilegious glorification extol the gifts themselves in such a manner as to hide the Author of the gifts.

God commanded the three to go out of the Tabernacle (12:4) and listen to His defense of Moses, who was faithful in the discharge of divine obligations. In His wrath, God withdrew the cloud from the Tabernacle, which was a visible token of His displeasure with Miriam and Aaron. Ellicott reminds us that, "The *lifting up* of the cloud was the signal for the breaking up of the camp and the resumption of the march; the *withdrawal* of the cloud was the token of the withdrawal of the divine presence and direction."

Upon the proud and jealous prophetess, the most humiliating of diseases fell. Leprosy, white as snow, afflicted Miriam who, as the instigator of the strife, alone suffers punishment and is smitten by the immediate hand of God. As a mark of power or judgment, leprosy was on several occasions sent by God, and He who caused the loathsome disease was alone able to cure it. God was able to send leprosy instantaneously and just as instantaneously remove it, as when Moses' hand was made leprous. In Miriam's case, in answer to the prayers of Moses and Aaron, she was quickly healed, though her defilement remained seven days.

Sin in the camp delays the progress of God's cause. For seven days the whole of Israel had to wait at Hazeroth. This was the period of purification prescribed by the Levitical law (Leviticus 14). "It was thus that Miriam who had placed herself on the level with the divinely-appointed head and ruler of her nation was to be excluded for seven days from any part or lot in the privileges which were enjoyed by the humblest member of the congregation." Miriam died at Kadesh in the first month of the 40th year of the wilderness journey (Numbers 20:1).

39. The Miracle of Judgment Against Rebellion

(Numbers 16; 26:9-11; Psalm 106:17)

The rebellion before us in Numbers 16 is the one solitary event which is recorded of the protracted 38 years' wandering, uncircumcision, and shame. The time and place of its occurrence cannot be positively stated. Probably it took place during one of the early years of the wilderness wanderings, either during Israel's abode at Kadesh, or shortly after their departure.

Korah is not to be confused with others of the same name (see author's *All the Men of the Bible*). The name occurs some

20 times in the Bible. The Korah before us was the only one of note among the Levites taking part in the rebellion and was the principal instigator in the affair costing his life and the lives of others. Associated with Korah in the insurrection were Dathan, Abiram, On, and 250 princes of the congregation, all of whom chided Moses for taking too much upon himself.

It is interesting to note how genealogies sometimes throw light on character. Thus we may trace the cause of Korah's rebellion, by observing.

(1) He was of the family of Kohath (Exodus 6:21, 24), which was most nearly related to Aaron and therefore most likely to aspire to his office.

(2) He was the son of Izhar, the second son of Kohath (Numbers 16:1), but that Ussiel, the fourth son of Kohath (Numbers 3:27, 30), had been preferred before him, and made prince and ruler of the Kohathites.

As to Dathan, looking to his genealogy, we can also account for his part in the rebellion against Moses. He was the descendant of Reuben, Jacob's first-born son, and therefore might seem on worldly principles to have a right to supreme command rather than Moses, the grandson of Levi, the third in descent from Jacob (Genesis 49:3, Numbers 16:1). Says old Bishop Hall:

> The Reubenites had the right of the natural primogeniture, yet do they vainly challenge pre-eminence where God had subjected them. But the man that will be lifting up himself in the pride of his heart from under the foot of God, is justly trodden in the dust.

The Bible presents various forms of sin in the wicked, and the sin of the rebels was contempt for God's minister (16:5); and they were punished for usurping the office of the priests. These rebels reasoned without reason. True, the Lord had declared the whole congregation of Israel, "a kingdom of priests" (Exodus 19:6), and the rebels argued that since the whole congregation was holy, there had been a usurping of authority on the part of Moses and Aaron who, it was affirmed, had taken too much upon themselves. They lost sight of the fact that Moses and Aaron were God's appointed representatives and had the precedence in drawing right to Him and of ministering in holy things. "Despising dominion and speaking evil of dignities" was

the sin of the rebels and they "perished by gainsaying," meaning, speaking against Moses—a warning to all self-sufficient despisers of authority.

Then there came the test of the censers (16:6), the use of which was the peculiar prerogative and the holiest function of the priesthood, and consequent vindication of Moses and Aaron and the punishment of the rebels. Korah, the ringleader of the rebellion, perished in the divine fire along with 250 princes who offered incense with him (16:27, 35) "They were punished by the same element as that by which they had sinned." Dathan and Abiram and their families and households were swallowed up in the opened earth and died a terrible death. All reasoning on the part of Moses was of no avail. The rebels stood their ground, defied Moses to do the worst, and they perished under the stroke of God's judgment. The supernatural control of the destructive forces of nature seen in the earth suddenly opening and in the fire from the Lord witness to His supremacy in every realm. God formed the chasm and confined destruction to Dathan and Abiram and their families. Fire enveloped only Korah and the 250 princes. This was why Moses spoke of the earth opening her mouth as a "new thing," *create a creation*, do something hitherto unknown (16:30, margin). All God's miracles are displays of creative power.

The sons of Korah did not perish with their father (26:11). When these sons came to sing their song of faith (Psalm 46 RV title), they must have remembered the terrible judgment that overtook their father and his fellow-conspirators. What happened became a sign unto them (26:10). The effect of the solemn warning on the survivors of Korah was that the family subsequently attained high distinction. Samuel came of this family (I Chronicles 6:22-28). The sons of Korah, as the Korahites, had the chief place assigned to them by David in keeping the doors of the Tabernacle and conducting the psalmody of the congregation (I Chronicles 6:32-37; 9:19, 33). Eleven psalms are inscribed with their name (44, 45, 46, 47, 48, 49, 84, 85, 87 and 88. See II Chronicles 20:19). These psalms indicate the firm faith of the Korahites in God. And they are remarkable for their depth of spiritual thought and their fervent glow of sanctified feeling. They are free from anything sad or harsh.

The apostle Jude, going back to Korah's rebellion, warns Christians against the same profanation of divine ordinances (verse 11; Numbers 16:40). Here is a type of Christendom's future apostasy and terrible doom. Fausset says:

Korah's sin answers to that of sacerdotalist ministers who, not content with the honour of the ministry (*nowhere in the N.T. are Christian ministers called* "sacrificing" or "sacerdotal priests," *Hiereis,* a term belonging in the strict and highest sense to Jesus Christ; restricted to Him and the Aaronic and pagan priests, and spiritually applied to all Christians (Matthew 8:4; Acts 14: 13; Hebrews 5:6; I Peter 2:5, 9; Revelation 1:6; 5:10; 20;6), usurp Christ's sacrificing and mediatorial priesthood; also to that of all men who think to be saved by their own doings instead of by His mediatorial work for us (Acts 4:12).

The day after the death of Korah, Dathan, Abiram, and the 250 princes of the assembly, there was a more widespread outbreak of rebellion against Moses and Aaron (16:41-50). What a striking illustration of the depravity of the human heart is afforded by the same spirit of rebellion which had been so signally punished on the preceding day! But quickly divine wrath was manifested and a plague struck the congregation, some 14,700 perishing that day. How dreadful is God's power! Aaron standing between the living and the dead until the plague stayed is strikingly typical of Christ, the Daysman between, "Who gave Himself for us an offering and a sacrifice to God for a sweet-smelling savor" (Ephesians 5:2).

40. The Miracle of Aaron's Rod

(Numbers 17; Hebrews 9:4)

The miraculous shooting forth of Aaron's dry rod was God's witness to the proof of the establishment of the priesthood in Aaron's person and in his posterity. Here was the witness to Israel that the recent rejection of Aaron's position and privilege was of the flesh.

The twelve tribes of Israel were represented by the twelve rods (the rod being the emblem of authority Exodus 4:2; Psalm 2:9; 110:2; Revelation 2:27), inscribed with their respective names. The prophet Ezekiel received a similar injunction to write on two rods (37:16). Although not the natural head of his father's house of Levi, yet as the divinely appointed head, Aaron wrote his name upon the rod of Levi. Out of the twelve rods, Aaron's was the only one that budded, blossomed, and yielded almonds, proving thereby the exclusive right of the tribe of Levi to the duties and privileges of the priesthood. Such a miracle prevented any future rivalry for the priesthood.

As the twelve rods lay in the Tabernacle of witness during the night, unseen by man, life came into the dead branch. The budding of the dry rod was entirely miraculous, for no human power can cause life to return and flower and fruit to appear. As a constant reminder of judgment upon rebellion and a perpetual evidence of Aaron's priesthood, the resurrected rod was kept in the sacred ark (17:10; Hebrews 9:4).

Alas, while Israel had witnessed so many displays of supernatural power both in grace and judgment and had experienced emotions of awe and of anxious apprehension, the hearts of the people were not deeply moved! In spite of divine assurances of protection if they were obedient to God, the children of Israel felt they were doomed to perish. "Shall *we* be consumed with dying?" (17:12, 13)

The budding of Aaron's rod is a type of Christ in resurrection, owned of God as High Priest forever more. "All authors of religion have died, Christ among them," says Scofield, "but only Christ was raised from the dead and exalted to be a high priest (Hebrews 4:14; 5:4-10)." Such a priesthood is typically set forth in Numbers 18 where Aaron bears the iniquity of the sanctuary. Christ made reconciliation for sin and secures the acceptance of the imperfect service of His people.

Aaron died when he was 123 years of age. Moses stripped him of his priestly robes and adorned Eleazar his son with them. Like Moses, Aaron was denied the privilege of entering Canaan because of rebellion at Meribah (20:10, 12, 24). On the summit of Mount Hor, Aaron died by the hand of God and found a grave there (Numbers 20:22-29). Christ represents an unchangeable priesthood (Hebrews 7:23, 24).

41. The Miracle of the Brazen Serpent

(Numbers 21:4-9; II Kings 18:4; John 3:14; I Corinthians 10:9)

The record of the miracle of the brazen serpent begins with a brief account of another miracle at Hormah. King Arad the Canaanite fought against the Israelites on the journey and took many of them prisoners. Israel vowed a vow of the utter destruction of the Canaanite cities if God would fight for them, which He did (Numbers 21:1-3). Victory was of the Lord.

Continuing their journey, the Israelites became discouraged, not only because of the hardships and dangers endured but also because they were turning their backs upon Canaan instead of marching by a direct course into the land. Being "discouraged" is not generally looked upon as sin, but discouragement very soon brings the soul into an attitude of doubt and rebellion, so that it is an easy prey to Satan, "the old serpent."

Discouraged, the people spoke against God and against Moses who was chided for the lack of bread and water. Loathing for the miraculous food, supplied so many years was also expressed. Serpents were sent as a punishment because of the murmuring of the people (Deuteronomy 8:15; 32:24; Numbers 21:4-9). As to the destructive serpents, or *the seraphim*, that is, "the burning ones" (Isaiah 14:29; 30:6), the language used denotes that God caused a quantity of a particular kind of serpent to suddenly appear. These were called "fiery serpents" either because of the bright fiery red upon their heads, or the sparkling gleam of the sun's rays from the polished and, as it were, blazing sunbeams on the scales, or because of the burning sensations produced by the deadly poison of venomous serpents when introduced into the blood.

This plague of serpents proved to be disastrous for "much of the people of Israel" died (21:7; I Corinthians 10:9). Every bite was fatal till the divinely appointed remedy was used. Conscious that such a severe judgment fell upon them because of their sin, the people sought out Moses and confessed that they had sinned against him and against the Lord. Again, as the intercessor, Moses prayed for the people, and was instructed to make a serpent of brass, place it upon a pole, and to tell the serpent-bitten among them that if they looked upon the brazen serpent they would be healed and live. The word used for the divinely-ordered pole (21:8) is the same which occurs in Jehovah-*nissi*, "The Lord is my standard or banner" (Exodus 17:15).

Such a miracle led Israel to adopt the serpent on the pole as an object of worship. Preserved and taken into Canaan, it became known as *Nehushtan,* a noun meaning "the great brass," and incense was burned to it because of its original use in the typical miracle. Hezekiah destroyed the serpent image as a prescient protest against relic worship (II Kings 18:4). The cross of Christ, which the serpent on the pole foreshadowed, has also been perverted into an idol. An empty cross has become a crucifix and venerated and bowed before.

In His evening conversation with Nicodemus, Jesus used the serpent lifted up on a standard as a fitting type of the death before Him (John 3:14; 12:32, 33). For a full treatment of the typical significance of the destructive serpents and the divinely appointed remedy the reader is referred to excellent outlines suggested by Fausset's or Fairbairn's Encyclopedia. Apocryphal literature says:

> The Israelites were troubled for a small season that they might be admonished having *a sign of salvation* . . . for he that turned himself towards it was not saved by the thing that he saw, but by Thee that art the Saviour of all (Wisdom 16:5-12).

Is this not the reason why, on our expressive Gospel hymns, sinners are exhorted to look in faith to Him who died upon the tree?

The Egyptians, among whom the Israelites had lived, associated the serpent with the healing art. Among the ancient Greeks, the serpent was the symbol of renovation and was believed to have the power of revealing medicinal herbs. The traditional emblem of the medical profession of our time consists of a serpent coiled round a pole or rod.

42. The Miracle of the Well

(Numbers 21:13-18)

Leaving Zared and coming to Arnon, the Israelites were reminded of the miracle of the Red Sea, the record of which is not only written in the Bible but in "The Book of the Wars of the Lord," about which nothing is known (21:14). *Beer,* meaning "a dug well," is the name of the station in the journey from Arnon to Jordan. Moses, the historian, gives us a poetical extract commemorating the digging of a well at this spot by the princes and nobles of the people. Perhaps we can identify this place with *Beer-elim,* meaning "the well of mighty men" (Isaiah 15:8).

God instructed Moses to tell the people that He would give them water, since He is able to provide wells in the desert (Psalm 78:15, 16). It is just as easy for Him to make water rise up from the depths as it is to make it gush out from a rock. The well was dug at the direction of Moses, who was shown by God the spot to dig. Tradition says that this was the last appearance of the water that "followed" the people before their entrance into Canaan (I Corinthians 10:4). In the strength gathered from the well water, Israel journeyed on to Jahaz where they fought with Sihon, king of the Amorites, defeated him, and possessed his land from Arnon unto Jabbok (21:19-30). After this God-given victory, another followed. Og, king of Bashan, was encountered at Edrei. Moses was given the assurance of a divine deliverance, none was left alive of the people of Og, and Israel possessed his land (21:33-35).

In magnifying the divine bounty to the children of Israel, Moses mentions, among many other things, the wells they dug (Deuteronomy 6:11). In hot climates where water is so scarce, a well or fountain of living or running water is a possession of inestimable value. Peter speaks of false teachers as "wells without water" (II Peter 2:17).

"Spring up, O Well!" What a song to sing to the Holy Spirit who is the Well of Living Water within the believer (John 4:14; 7:37-39)! Did we sing this song to Him? Is He constantly rising for our spiritual refreshment?

43. The Miracle of Balaam's Ass

(Numbers 22:20-35. Read Numbers 22-24; II Peter 2:15, 16; Jude 11; Revelation 2:14)

The arrestive narrative concerning Balaam (Numbers 11-24) is connected with the arrival of Israel in the plains of Moab and with their relationship to Moab and Ammon. Balak, king of the Moabites, sent messengers to Balaam, the soothsayer at Pethor, near the Euphrates, requesting him to come and curse the invading Israelites. At first Balaam refused, because God told him the Israelites were His chosen people.

But Balak sent more honorable messengers to Balaam and repeated the request with offers of larger rewards. This time God told Balaam to go but to do only what he was instructed to do. Then followed the incident of the angel and ass we are principally concerned with in this study.

Commenting on God's directions to Balaam, Scofield has the note:

In verse 12 the *directive* will of Jehovah is made known to Balaam; in verse 20, Jehovah's *permissive* will. The prophet is now free to go, but knows the true mind of the Lord about it. The matter is wholly one between Jehovah and His servant. The permission of verse 20 really constitutes a testing of Balaam. He chose the path of self-will and self-advantage, and Jehovah could not but gravely disapprove. The whole scene, verses 22-35, prepared Balaam for what was to follow.

God, who spoke through a serpent (Genesis 3), now rebukes Balaam through a speaking ass. These instances are unique in the Bible so far as dumb creatures being given the power of speech. An interesting feature to note is that Balaam did not show the least surprise when his faithful female ass suddenly starts speaking. Another feature is that the ass could see the angel with sword in hand while Balaam could not.

Actually, we have in this literal narrative of a real transaction a combination of miracles. The eyes of Balaam were holden so that he could not see the obstructing angel; then they were opened by the Lord (22:31) so that he could see the angel standing in the way with his drawn sword. As for the ass, God gives it both vision and vocal power, for it "saw the angel" (22:25, 27) and then its mouth was divinely opened to speak (22:28). Infidels and modernists may laugh at these miracles in their effort to confine God to natural law and scorn any promise that He can intervene in the natural course of events so as to perform a miracle, to fulfil prophecy, or to answer prayer. But true faith realizes that the giving of articulation to an animal is to God no more than the making of the blind to see, or the deaf to hear (I Corinthians 1:27). In this instance, God chose one of the foolish things of His world to confound the mighty. The more vile the means were, the better to confound the unrighteous Balaam.

As to the miracle of an ass speaking, we do not for one moment accept the theory that "by influencing the soul of Balaam, God caused him to interpret correctly the inarticulate sounds of the animal." Whether the ass understood the message it uttered is another matter. Possibly not, just as parrots or budgerigars utter words or phrases without understanding. The adequate cause of a female ass speaking with a man's voice is given—"The Lord opened the mouth of the ass"—and when God opens the mouth, an ass can speak as well as a man.

Personally, we believe with Fairbairn's observation that "the plain historical statement need give no trouble to those who believe that the serpent spoke with Eve: if one creature was made to speak as the instrument of Satan, another might well do the same as an instrument of the great Angel of the Covenant. . . . An ass was chosen, in the sovereignty of God, to rebuke the covetous eagerness of Balaam for reward, human reason and speech being miraculously conferred on her for the occasion." Think of it—a dumb beast rebuking an inspired prophet! How the brute's instinctive obedience stands in contrast to the gifted seer's self-willed disobedience!

Such a miracle was necessary to convince Balaam that the mouth and tongue should be under God's direction, and that the same divine power which caused the ass to speak contrary to its nature could make Balaam in like manner utter blessings contrary to his own inclination. As to a study of Balaam, who is the personification of self-deceit, the reader is asked to consult the author's volume on *All the Men of the Bible*. Suffice it to say that his history affords an illustration of the importance of comparing Scripture with Scripture. For a complete view of his character, we must compare what the Old Testament has to say of Balaam with Peter, who tells us of the motive that influenced him (II Peter 2: 13); with Jude, who informs us of the deep hold covetousness had upon Balaam (Jude 11); and with John, who particularly draws our attention to a very remarkable fact concerning Balaam, namely, that it was at his instigation Balak threw that temptation in the way of the Israelites which caused the destruction of 23,000 of them in one day (Numbers 25: 1-9; Revelation 2:14; I Corinthians 10:8). The total number of deaths in the plague was 24,000.

44. The Miracle of the Midianite Vexation

(Numbers 25 and 31)

The Midianites were descendants of the fourth son of Abraham and Keturah (Genesis 25:2) and controlled the rich pasture land around Sinai. Joseph was sold to the Midianites. Moses' wife, Zipporah, was a Midianite. At first, the Midianites were friendly to Israel, but later they seduced the people to idolatry and became hostile toward Israel. As descendants of Abraham, they should have feared and obeyed his God and remained kind to the Israelites, since they were of their own kindred. Moses was ordered to vex and smite the Midianites and the special judgments of God were directed against their sins of apostasy and of seduction (Psalm 106:28, 29).

While Israel defeated the Midianites under the leadership of Moses (Numbers 31), complete victory was reserved for Gideon who miraculously defeated them as we shall later see (Judges 6 and 7; Isaiah 9:4; 10:26; Psalm 83:9). By God's command, 1,000 warriors of every tribe of Israel, 12,000 in all conquered the first kings of Midian because of their seduction of Israel. Every male child was slain, and also every woman who had lain carnally with a man. Cities and castles were burnt (31: 17) and the prey divided among the Israelites.

When we consider the smallness of the number of the Israelitish warriors and the victory they achieved over superior hosts (although probably attacked by Israel in an unprepared and defenseless state), the fact that not one single Israelitish warrior perished (31:49) proves that God vouchsafed to grant His people miraculous aid and protection.

A word might be in order at this point regarding the plague that destroyed the remnant of the generation which had come out of Egypt (26:1-4; 32:11) and other plagues afflicting the people. In several cases, the exact nature of the plague is not given. It may have been any sudden, severe, or dangerous form of sickness and disease, or death (Numbers 11:33; 16:47; 25:9; Ezekiel 6:12). In some cases a few were smitten that many might be warned. The meaning of the word *pestilence* is "that which snatches away." Usually *plague* or *pestilence* represent a stroke from the hand of God. Such punitive phenomena suggest the peculiar working of God because of their severity, suddenness, and often their mystery. Blessed are those who enjoy the safety of all who dwell under the shadow of the Almighty (Psalm 91: 3, 6)!

45. The Miracle of Moses' Death

(Deuteronomy 34; Jude 9)

After the minute summary of the journeys of Israel from Egypt to Jordan and the revelation of divine instructions for entrance into, and life with, the land of promise, there came the blessing of the tribes by Moses (Numbers 32 - 36; Deuteronomy 1 - 33). Before his death, Moses appointed Joshua to succeed him (31:14, 23). Then follows the record of Moses' miraculous vision and death (Deuteronomy 34).

To no other mortal has there been granted the high privilege of being the agent of so many and such stupendous displays of supernatural power. Moses lived in the atmosphere of the miraculous and his end accorded with his life. First of all, there was the extraordinary intensification of Moses' powers of vision. Like Christ's view of the world kingdom (Luke 4:5), Moses saw the vast land Israel was to possess. Because of his hard, unsympathetic spirit at the rock, which God called rebellion (Numbers 20:8-13; 27:14), Moses *saw* the land but was not allowed to enter it. Earnestly he had longed to go over the border, but meekly he submitted to the divine prohibition (Deuteronomy 3:24-27; 34:4). Yet there on Mount Nebo at the age of 120, when "his eye not dim, nor his natural force abated" (Deuteronomy 34:7), Moses (whose name occurs some 805 times in Scripture) viewed the landscape of Canaan. "The Lord shewed him all the land of Gilead . . . unto the utmost sea." How thrilled he must have been by such a glorious vision!

Then there came the miracle of Moses' death and burial. How the greatest prophet in Israel died (Deuteronomy 34:10), we are not told. All we know is that his death "was according to the word of the Lord"

(34:5), a phrase which literally means, *upon the mouth of the Lord* or, as the rabbis expressed it, "by a kiss of the Lord" (see Song of Solomon 1:2). "For many years it had been the habit of Moses to do everything at the mouth of the Lord," says Ellicott. "Only one fatal mistake mars the record of obedience. It was but one last act of obedience to lie down and die at the word of Jehovah in calm silence so sublime." We then read that "God buried him" (34:6), the only one of the human race to have had this honor. Jesus was buried by His friends—Moses had God as his undertaker. Probably he was translated soon after; for he afterwards appeared with the translated Elijah and Jesus at the Transfiguration (Matthew 17:1-10). His sepulcher therefore could not be found. Israel mourned for Moses thirty days. A reason for God's mercy awaiting Israel is His remembrance of Moses (Isaiah 63:11).

Jude has a mystic word about Satan contending with Michael, the archangel, for the body of Moses (verse 9). Josephus affirmed that Satan fought against the resurrection of Moses on the ground of his sin (Zechariah 3:2). When this contest took place, we are not told. But Satan's struggle for the body of Moses was not successful, for he appeared in bodily form on the Mount of Transfiguration. Had he been a disembodied spirit, he would not have been seen by men. The answer to the strange question, "Why did Satan want the body of Moses?" has been answered in many ways. For example:

(1) To make it an object of idolatry. Perhaps Satan, who had the power of death (Hebrews 2:14)—which does not mean that he can at his pleasure inflict death on any one, but that he was the instrument of first bringing death into the world (John 8:44)—knew that the Israelites would be likely to worship such an honored body. What a snare that would have been.

(2) Further, Satan wanted to keep Moses' body as his own, as that of a murderer because he had killed the Egyptian (Exodus 2:12). God, however, guarded the precious dust and glorified it. On the mount, the thunders of Sinai gave way to the "still small voice" of Jesus only (Matthew 17:1-8).

III.

THE MIRACLES OF THE HISTORICAL BOOKS

1. The Miracle at Jordan

(Joshua 3:7-17; 4; Psalm 114:3)

That God buries His workman but carries on His work is forcibly illustrated in Joshua's succession to Moses (1:2). As a youth, Joshua had endured the slave labor amidst the Egyptian brickkilns, and early in life his solid, sterling qualities were revealed to Moses by the Holy Spirit. Joshua learned to rule by obeying first; then came to rule for God. He learned to command in after life by obeying when a youth.

As Moses' "minister," Joshua accompanied his predecessor to the Mount of God. He was Moses' confidential agent and personal attendant while he lived, and was the curator of that which Moses had written. Along with Caleb, he brought back a good report of Canaan and both of them encouraged Israel not to fear the inhabitants because the Lord was with Israel. The people would have stoned Joshua and Caleb, but they were miraculously preserved. The other ten spies were smitten with a plague and died.

By divine direction, Moses solemnly invested Joshua as his successor and he was duly inaugurated to the office to which he had previously been called (Deuteronomy 31:14-28). God set His seal upon Joshua's election by manifesting His presence in the divine pillar of cloud (Numbers 11:25; 12:5). The people came to honor Joshua as they had Moses, and under his leadership Israel came nearest to realizing the ideal of the people of God (Joshua 11:15; 24:24).

Joshua had witnessed the miraculous preservation of his people in Egypt and was with Moses in the wilderness and cognizant of Israel's supernatural provision. Now he himself was to become the channel through whom God was to continue the display of His power on Israel's behalf; and the effect of the miracles under Joshua kept all his generation faithful to God, so real and convincing were they, as we are now to see (24:31; Judges 2:7).

After the record of Joshua's commission and his assumption of command, we come to the initial miracle in the conquest of Canaan at Jordan. For such a special conquest, he received the promise of divine help and companionship (1:3, 5). The march from Shittim to Jordan was the first march of Israel under Joshua who, giving preliminary orders to priests and people, was encouraged by their obedience to his commands. The people used the same words God had given Joshua—"Be strong and of a good courage" (1:9; 18).

Then came the miracle. As soon as the feet of the priests rested in the overflow, the river was driven back—it recoiled and stood up as one heap. As far as the eye could see, the river bed was dry. The priests stood in the dry bed till all Israel crossed over. Instead of flowing outward as water generally does, God made the water to stand—something it cannot do of itself (3:13, 16; Psalm 114:3). Such a miracle was all the more stupendous because that was the time of the year the Jordan overflowed its banks as a consequence of the April rainy season and the melting of Hermon's snows (3:15, 16; 4:18, 19; 5:10, 12). Jordan was several times the scene of God's power. It was thrice divided miraculously.

Having been present when Israel miraculously crossed the Red Sea, Joshua now participates in another supernatural dividing of waters. This initial miracle proved that God was with Joshua as He had been with Moses. It established him as the divinely elected leader of Israel. It was a day that magnified him (1:5; 3:7). The people were also encouraged, but the morale of the Canaanites was considerably weakened (5:1).

"The drying up of the Red Sea and the Jordan form a beautiful type. In the Psalms they are mentioned together (Psalm 114:3, 5). Through the death of their Lord, His people are—

(1) Separated from the bondage of Egypt and delivered from their enemies—"delivered from the power of darkness."

(2) Led into the promised inheritance

81

which is theirs in union with Him in resurrection—"translated into the kingdom of His dear Son" (Colossians 1:13).

Two cairns were set up, one on either side of the river, to mark the place where the Israelites crossed. Every tribe was represented by a stone on either side of Jordan (4:3, 8, 9). The two cairns thus represented a complete Israel in the wilderness and a complete Israel in the promised land. "Thou shalt remember all the way the Lord thy God led thee." "By the grace of God I am what I am." The stones in Jordan stand, typically, for Psalm 22:1-18 (see Psalm 42:7; 88:7; John 12:31-33).

The command to the priests to come up out of Jordan (4:16) is a significant event, so marked as to receive a separate notice. Ellicott says, "We are not suffered to forget by what means Jordan was driven back and held in check," and the check was not meant to be perpetual. We are reminded that the suspension of the power of death has its limits. When the day of grace is over the waters will "return unto their place and flow over all the banks as before" (See Isaiah 28:16-20). Some 1300 years after Israel crossed Jordan, Jesus was baptized in its waters. Thus, "what was never a great Jewish river has become a very great Christian one." For the Christian, Jordan typifies death with Christ (Romans 6:6-11; Ephesians 2:5, 6; Colossians 3:1-3).

2. The Miracle Appearance

(Joshua 5:13-15; Acts 7:33; Hebrews 2:10)

Before Israel could be victorious in Canaan, "the reproach of Egypt" had to be removed. So there took place the mass circumcision of all the males born in the wilderness years of wandering. The people had "turned back in their hearts to Egypt" (Acts 7:39; Numbers 14:4) and bore the reproach of their apostasy all those lost years. The sign of the covenant—circumcision—had been omitted, as though they were no longer God's people. The miracle at Jordan, however, was the practical proof of Israel's restoration to divine favor, and therefore the covenant relationship had to be restored. The Passover could then be observed again, for the law was that "no uncircumcised person shall eat thereof" (Exodus 12:48).

As the people entered Canaan, the miraculous manna ceased (5: 11, 12). Fresh produce was brought into the camp the day after their heavenly sustenance was withdrawn. To inaugurate Joshua for his second great enterprise (namely, the conquest of Canaan), a divine manifestation, the character of which should be carefully noted, was granted unto Joshua, who had looked upon himself as the captain of the Lord's host. Now reverently, he pays homage to Him to whom the office rightly belonged. This vision has the atmosphere of supernaturalness. Here is a theophanic appearance of the Son of God, as the Captain of the Lord's host, identifying Him with the Jehovah of Exodus (3:5), where He appeared to Moses in a flame of fire out of the midst of a bush. Now, as Joshua commences the greatest task of his life, the Captain, the Prince-Leader, appears to lead the people into Canaan (See Hebrews 2:10). Joshua's eyes were miraculously opened to discern the identity of the Man with the drawn sword—the sign of victory.

The equality of the two visions (Exodus 3:5; Joshua 5:13-15) is proved by the use of the same command on both occasions. "Loose thy shoe from off thy foot; for the place whereon thou standest is holy ground." Immediately Joshua complied, and with due reverence recognized in the Captain the One to whom he must be subservient. No longer is the Lord the One suffering with and in His people. Here He stands ready to lead them into the Promised Land. Israel is now to look upon Him, not as an ally or an adversary, but as the Commander-in-Chief.

As we shall see, wars of Israel in Canaan are spoken of as "the wars of the Lord." The conquest of the land was not only an enterprise of Israel under the expert military leadership of Joshua. Such a conquest was a divine conquest in which human instruments were employed. Joshua was to be entirely subordinate to the heavenly Captain, who was about to fight, not for Israel or against Israel's foes but for His own right hand, with Israel as His ally. The task ahead was not one in which Israel was to ask for divine guidance and assistance. It was to be the Captain's task, hence His drawn sword. Joshua and Israel were to be part of His host in the subjugation of the Canaanites.

3. The Miracle of Jericho

(Joshua 6. See Joshua 2)

Here we have the first order of the Captain of the host of the Lord, namely, the surrounding of Jericho. This city of palms (Deuteronomy 34:3) was strategically the key of the land, being situated at the entrance of the two passes through the hills, one leading to Jerusalem, the other to Ai and Bethel. Thus Jericho was the first object of attack by Israel, and its miraculous overthrow was a fitting prelude to the victorious occupation of Canaan, in which the people were to become so dependent upon the drawn sword of the Captain (see Deuteronomy 20:1-4).

Modernists have tried to explain the miracle at Jericho as a natural phenomenon. The region, they say, was subject to earth tremors and one of them happened while the priests walked around the city walls. But trumpet blasts and shouts of the multitude were not able to cause destructive vibration sufficient to totter the poorly constructed walls. As Chrysostom put it: "Trumpets, though one were to sound for ten thousand years, cannot throw down walls; but *faith* can do all these things."

It is an undeniable fact that at the blowing of the rams' horns the walls fell flat, except the one part where Rahab lived. Archaeology confirms the Biblical record. Even though some volcanic agency was employed (Psalm 114), the fall of the walls was no less miraculous. No military skill or prowess of Joshua was allowed to be employed. The orders of the divine Captain were explicit. All the armed host of Israel had to march round the walls for six successive days. On the seventh day they were to compass the city in marching order for seven successive times, with the priests bearing the ark of the Lord—the peculiar symbol of His presence. The trumpets were to blast in token of His power. (See I Thessalonians 4:16). "The seven day's march round Jericho in absolute silence was well calculated to impress on the inhabitants the lesson of 'the forbearance of God.'" As the march ended and the last loud blast of the trumpets was heard, a mighty shout of the people rent the air, the walls fell prostrate, and Israel entered the city.

Jericho was taken by the Lord and thus Israel was inspired at the beginning of the conquest of powerful peoples. The miracle was wrought independently of any conflict on Israel's part, and it indicated that the occupation of the whole land was to be God's gift, and that it was a *fief* held unto Him at His pleasure. Other signs of His power shown at Jericho in later times were the healing of the waters by Elisha and the restoration of the sight of Bartimaeus.

After the calamity, Jericho became a city of the curse. The reason for the pronouncement of a curse upon whoever should rebuild it (6:17, 26) was that, as Professor Stanley observes, "it was a place of such strength that it was not to be left to be occupied by any hostile force that might take possession of it." The first to fall under the curse was Hiel the Bethelite in the reign of Ahab (I Kings 16:34). Such a curse appears to have been finally removed by the intercession of Elisha, at the request of the inhabitants (II Kings 2:18-22).

According to promise, the house of Rahab was spared. The onetime harlot staked her life upon divine promises, so she perished not with those who believed not (Hebrews 11:31). She was unafraid of the wrath of the king and thus proved her faith by her works (Joshua 2:21). Through her faith protection came, not only to her, but to her whole household. This Canaanite, who cast her lot with God's people, married Salmon, an Israelite, and became the ancestress of David and thereby of Christ (Matthew 1:5). A Gentile, and of the accursed race of Canaan, Rahab became an earnest of the admission of the Gentile world into the Church of God.

We cannot leave the miracle at Jericho without observing the miracle of grace which the writer of the Epistle of Hebrews must have had in mind when he rehearsed the heroes of faith in Israel. He speaks of the people passing, by faith, through the Red Sea as by dry land, with the pursuing Egyptians being drowned (Hebrews 11:29). But the next verse skips forty years and says, "By faith the walls of Jericho fell down" (Hebrews 11:30). Not a word about the wilderness wanderings. The God of grace had blotted them out. "Their sins and iniquities will I remember no more" (Hebrews 10:17).

For ourselves, the lesson of Jericho's destruction by no human means is that "the weapons of our warfare are not carnal, but mighty through God to be pulling down strongholds"—no matter how strong they may be.

4. The Miracle at Ai

(Joshua 7 and 8)

There may be those who question the performance of a miracle at Ai. Yet the whole tenor of the record suggests the miraculous. It was the Lord who permitted Israel's defeat and who, turning Himself from the fierceness of His anger (7:26), gave the king of Ai into the hand of Joshua (8:1), and who told Joshua to stretch out his spear (8:18). The Captain of the host, Jehovah, knew all about the secret of Achan (7:10, 11) and overruled in his exposure and judgment. There was, of course, nothing supernatural about the death of Achan and his family, as there was in the case of Korah and company.

Ai, a royal Canaanite city, was evidently a small one leading Joshua to feel that two or three thousand men would be sufficient to take a city of such limited dimensions and slender defenses (7:3). But Joshua's confidence was misplaced and Israel was repulsed in the attack upon Ai, not as the result of Joshua's misjudgment but because of the sin committed by Achan, which, in righteous judgment, was made the occasion of spreading fear and confusion among the Israelites.

The sin of Achan was covetousness. When Jericho was cursed, with all that was in it, Achan alone, in defiance of the curse saw, coveted, took, and hid "a Babylonish garment and two hundred shekels of silver, and a wedge of gold, fifty shekels" (7:21). Says Fausset, "The spoil of Jericho was the first-fruits of Canaan, sacred to Jehovah; Achan's sacrilegious covetousness in appropriating it needed to be checked at the outset, lest the sin spreading should mar the end for which Canaan was given to Israel."

The repulse of Israel's attempt to take Ai, and the taking of lots under Jehovah's direction led to Achan's sin as the cause of Israel's defeat (see Ecclesiastes 9:18). Once the sin was expiated, the city was captured and destroyed by a ruse (7:2-5; 8). The death of Achan turned away the angel of the Lord and the door of entrance to the promised land was thrown open. Such swift judgment is proof that He is no respecter of persons. Achan, although an Israelite, perished, and his name, meaning "he that troubleth," became an epitome of his history which tragically displays the folly and guilt of covetousnes. Ai was burnt by fire (8:19),

just as Jericho and Hazor were (6:24; 11:11).

The question has been raised whether Achan alone perished, or all his family and cattle with him. Some writers affirm that the children of Achan could not justly suffer with him because of the law (Deuteronomy 24:16) unless they had been accomplices in his guilt, of which there is no evidence. Had his family been stoned, the heap of stones would have included them also; whereas it is, "They raised over *him* a great heap of stones." But the tenor of the record indicates that all the family were destroyed together. "That man perished not alone in his iniquity" (Joshua 22:20). Warning had "been given that the man who took the accursed thing would be an accursed thing like it, if he brought it into his house (Deuteronomy 7:26), and would make the camp of Israel a curse also (6:18), and thus Achan's whole house was destroyed as though it had become a part of Jericho (see I Chronicles 2:7).

The severity of judgment the Lord permitted need not concern the mind when it is remembered that Israel, under Him, "entered Canaan to take possession of land desecrated by its previous tenants, not as mere selfish spoil, but for God's glory." Thus the people were reminded that the God who made has the power to destroy a whole family or nation for the guilt of one (II Kings 23:25-27). No mercy to Achan's crime was possible. It would have been injustice to all mankind. Grace prevailed, however, for "the valley of Achar" became "a door of hope" (I Chronicles 2:7; Isaiah 65:10; Hosea 2:15). For our edification, the sin of Achan and its results teach the wonderful truth of the oneness of the people of God. "*Israel* hath sinned" (7:11). What a solemnizing thought it is that the whole cause of Christ can be injured by the sin, neglect, or unspirituality of one believer!

5. The Miracle at Gibeon

(Joshua 10:1-11)

Again the divine Captain is found issuing a distinct command for the attack upon Gibeon, even as He did for all the important steps in the conquest of Canaan, and He was the One who gave Israel the victory over the Gibeonites (10:8-11). The general preparation of the Canaanites for the last struggle with Joshua found Gibeon, a city of considerable size, "like one of the royal cities, greater than Ai," making a league of peace with Joshua. Having neglected to consult his heavenly Captain, Joshua made the treaty without inquiring of the Lord (9:14).

Disguised as ambassadors in old clothes and with worn-out waterskins and moldy bread, the Gibeonites appeared to have come from a very far country to make a league with victorious Israel. Having had no experience of worn garments and stale provisions (Deuteronomy 29:5, 6), the Israelites, seeing the impoverished garb of the Gibeonites, fell for the ruse and secured their safety by deceit. When Joshua saw that he had been taken in, he reduced the Gibeonites to servitude. Having given his word, honorable Joshua kept his oath (Psalm 15:4; Ecclesiastes 5:2; see II Samuel 21:2-6).

Adoni-zedec, king of Jerusalem, hearing of Joshua's victory at Jericho and at Ai, and of Gibeon's league with Joshua, became afraid and formed an alliance. Hoham, king of Hebron, Piram, king of Jarmuth, Japhia, king of Lachish, and Debir, king of Eglon, joined with Adoni-zedec and marched against Gibeon. The Gibeonites, fearful that these five kings of the Amorites would seek to destroy them for the league made with Joshua, urged Israel's leader to come quickly to their aid—which he did.

A divine victory ensued, for the Lord gave the Amorites into the hand of Joshua, so much so that not a man of them was able to stand before him. The Lord, we read, discomforted them and slew them with a great slaughter. Those who fled died by the enormous hailstones the Lord cast down from the heavens. The prophecy made to Job is here realized. "Hast thou seen the treasures of the hail, which I have reserved against the day of battle and war?" (38:22, 23). How impressive is the employment of the artillery of heaven against His enemies! More of the Amorites died by hailstones than by the sword. When necessary, the Lord is able to work a miracle on the part of His beseiged people.

6. The Miracle of the Sun Standing Still

(Joshua 10:12-15; Isaiah 28:21)

We now come to the greatest miracle in the book of Joshua, the record of which, although a poetical quotation from the book of Joshua, nevertheless bears the stamp of divine inspiration. On the day the Lord delivered the Amorites into the hands of Israel, Joshua called upon the sun and the moon to stand still. Unless this had been a miracle on a stupendous scale, the statement about there never being a day like that before or after the miracle would be utterly meaningless (see Isaiah 30:26).

After the hailstone victory, Joshua at Bethron was to witness a miracle without parallel. In his book, there is no lavishing of miracles as in other parts of Scripture. But although there is an economy of miracles here, nevertheless there is this one proving that the Lord is supreme. Having created the sun and the moon, He is able to arrest and control their movements. Here is a miracle wrought in perfect conformity with the plans of Him who subordinates the firmest physical laws to the purpose of His moral administration, and who asserts that heaven and earth shall pass away, but that His Word endureth forever.

Those who object to the miraculous fail to realize that the universe is in the hand of Him who created it, and that He can stop the motion of any part or of the whole, with less trouble than a man can stop his watch. As the Almighty God, He can safely and effectually govern His own works. *The Bible Students Companion* has this pertinent comment on the miracle of Gibeon:

Surely God is infinitely wiser than the conductor of a ship, or of a railway train. They do not stop suddenly, but gradually, and therefore safely. A prudent and cautious engineer knows how to act—he would by turning off the steam, and the use of brakes, assert its course gradually to insure safety. So the Almighty God acted with infinite wisdom in working this miracle, and had respect to the welfare of His creatures by *gradual operation*, and not so by suddenly arresting the diurnal rotation of the earth.

To the believer in divine sovereignty, there is no problem here. The word used for the sun's standing is peculiar. It means *dumb* or *silent*, indicating that Joshua commanded the suspension of the motion of the earth around its axis, and that of the moon around the earth. The objection raised that if the earth had stopped in its orbit, it would have fallen into the sun, vanishes when we remember that He hung the earth on nothing and is able to control its movements. We may know the law and rate of the earth's motion, but we do not fully understand what the *cause* of the motion is, and therefore it is impossible to state what must be done in order to arrest the motion for a time.

The miracle was the act of an Omnipotent Being and, as a writer of the past century expressed it in dealing with Habbakuk's record of the unusual event:

> The prophet, according to his lofty manner, celebrates this event, and points out, in very poetical diction, the design of so surprising a miracle—"The sun and the moon stood still in their habitation: in thy light, (the long continued and miraculous light) thy arrows, edged with destruction, walked on their awful errand," in the clear shining of the day, protracted for this very purpose, thy glittering spear, launched by thy people, but guided by thy hand sprang to its prey (Habbakuk 3:11).

We read that the sun "hasted not to go down *about* a whole day" (10:13). In II Kings 20:11 we read that Hezekiah's sun dial registered a return of 10 degrees, about 40 minutes, which gives us the whole day added to time, and a day outstanding astronomers account for. The miracle at Gibeon appeared to be *local*, not universal. "Stand . . . upon *Gibeon*."

At the end of the miraculous day's operations, Joshua returned to Makkedah to dispose of the five escaped confederate kings, who were found hiding in a cave (10:16-30). These Northern kings were brought out and slain, and their bodies were hung on trees—a token of disgrace after death. Upon the cross of the true Joshua, or Jesus, the enemies of the Israel of God are exhibited. "He made a show of them openly, triumphing over them in it" (Colossians 2:15). With the conquest of Canaan over, after seven years of conflict, the land rested from war (11:23). God had commanded the utter extermination of the Canaanites, and the Israelites were simply His executioners who, without personal blood-thirstiness, exhibited His hatred of idolatry, learning themselves to hate it.

In his last counsels, Joshua acknowledged God's goodness and in his final commands recited His miraculous works on the part of Israel. Reviewing the life and labors of Joshua, we note that before attacking the enemies of God and Israel, he solemnly renewed the dedication of himself and his

people to God by the observance of circumcision and the Passover (Joshua 5). His manifest courage was supported by prayer, and God signally blessed it. The arrest of the journey of the sun and moon in response to prayer provide a remarkable illustration of James 5:16. "The good man's prayer is among the reasons by which the Omnipotent is moved in the administration of the universe."

Many commentators have dealt with the typical significance of Joshua and his work. He bore the name of *Jesus* (Acts 7:45; Hebrews 4:8). Moses, representing the law, could not bring Israel into Canaan— *that* was reserved for Joshua. So Jesus perfects what the law could not do, and brings His people into the heavenly inheritance (Acts 13:39; Hebrews 4; 7:19-25).

7. Miracles in the Book of Judges

(Judges 2:16-19; Nehemiah 9:27; Acts 13:20)

While the miraculous is not so spectacular in this second historical book of the Old Testament as in some previous books, nevertheless it is conspicuous in divine contacts with Israel, as well as in the lives of some of the judges. The people served the Lord all the days of Joshua and all the days of the elders who outlived him (2:7). Gradually, however, the people forgot the great work of the Lord and did evil in His sight. "The gradual tendency to deteriorate after the removal of a good ruler is but too common" (Acts 20:29; Philippians 2:12).

The book of Judges deals with events intermediate between the death of Joshua and the establishment of regal government and gives the history of fourteen of those extraordinary deliverers raised up from time to time in answer to the cries of God's people and their tears. The condition of the nation was deplorable, and these judges were appointed to govern Israel and to deliver her from the oppression of her enemies. These judges vindicated the sovereignty and grace of Jehovah. They were His viceregents carrying out part of that particular providence which distinguished Israel's God from heathen idols around. Not one of the judges, however, had anything whereof to glory in the flesh. All of them owed their position and power to the Lord (2:18). The function of the priesthood being in abeyance after the time of Joshua, the discipline and deliverance of the judges was just what the people needed. The provision of these judges was an act of Jehovah's "righteousness" or faithfulness to His covenant, consequent upon the nation's willingness to turn to Him in penitence (5: 11; Isaiah 45:8).

Indications of the supernatural are scattered throughout the book. It was the Lord who drove out the Canaanites (1:19), who "raised up"—this phrase is the keynote of the book—the judges (2:16, 18) as need required, and who caused His Spirit to equip them (3:10; 6:34; 11:29; 13:25). It was the Lord who in anger delivered His apostate people to their enemies (2:14, 20; 6:1, 2), and then emancipated them from bondage (4:14, 15, 23). It was God who summoned natural forces to assist His beleaguered people (5:4, 5, 20, 31). Yet, in spite of all supernatural aid, Israel failed to drive out all the Canaanites from the land because of their persistent apostasy (3:7).

8. The Miracles Under Othniel

(Judges 1:12-15; 3:9-11)

Intermarriage with the Canaanites and the countenance of their idolatry brought Israel under bondage to the king of Mesopotamia (3:5-8). When they cried unto the Lord in their distress (Nehemiah 9: 27; Psalm 107:13), He raised them up their first "savior," Othniel, the son of Kenaz. The Jews placed him highest among the judges and applied to him the words of Solomon: "Thou art all fair; there is no spot in thee" (Song of Solomon 4:7), because he alone of all the judges is represented as irreproachable.

"The Spirit of the Lord came upon him" (3:10) is a phrase indicating the supernatural aspect of Othniel's deliverance of Israel and his peaceful judgeship of the people for forty years. The phrase "came upon" actually means "clothed him" (6: 34; I Chronicles 12:18). For forty years Othniel was girded by the Spirit with all necessary courage, strength, and wisdom.

9. The Miracles Under Gideon

(Judges 6-8)

Gideon, a judge of great heroism and signally honored of the Lord, was another who experienced the supernatural in his ministry. Having lapsed into apostasy again, Israel was punished by further oppression. Midian prevailed against the Israelites and forced them to hide in mountain caves and dens (6:1, 2). When Israel would plough and sow their fields, Midian would come and reap or take away "the pastures of God" (Psalm 83:12). Thus Midian left Israel greatly impoverished. When they turned to God for deliverance, He answered the cry of the people by sending them a prophet who is here left nameless (6:7, 8), although there is a Jewish legend to the effect that he was Phinehas, the son of Eleazer. The prophet's message was one of needful rebuke, as well as assurance that divine deliverance from oppression was at hand.

An angel of the Lord supernaturally appeared sitting under an oak beside the altar in Ophrah and called Gideon from his threshing to accept the commission as Israel's deliverer. A word may be necessary regarding these supernatural or theophanic appearances of which there are four in the book (2:1-5; 3:10; 6:11, 34; 10:10-16; 13:3-25). Since the angel spoke to Gideon as the Lord, it has been suggested that he was no created angel but "the Angel of the Covenant," the One Joshua saw as "the Captain of the Lord's host." Further combined in the experiences of some of the judges was the special manifestation of this "Angel of God," and the corresponding mission of the Spirit of God (3:10; 6:11, 34). Under these divinely called and equipped saviors, there was an infusion of grace, giving a new impulse to the life of the nation. Alas, however, on each occasion the fresh impetus soon faded, indicating the sinking of strength residing in Israel. Thus in the closing years of Gideon's administration, his sun which rose so fair went down in a dark background of worldliness and apostasy (8:24-27).

The miracle of the rock-fire (6:19-24)

Gideon, also known as Jerubbaal (6:32), in addressing the Angel as Lord, asked why such a miracle-working One had allowed His people to become so impoverished. Assured by the Lord that he had been chosen to save Israel from Midian, Gideon asked for a *sign*, some clear proof that the angelic appearance was no mere vision but that the message he heard was really from God. Gideon went into his house and prepared a meal for the Angel under the oak. The Angel commanded Gideon to lay the meal of flesh and unleavened cakes upon the rock and then pour broth upon it. Obeying, Gideon witnessed a miracle, for the Angel took a staff, touched the offered meal, and fire came out of the rock and consumed it. Immediately the miracle-worker vanished out of Gideon's sight. He had seen the Angel of God face to face but did not die. "The belief that death or misfortune would be the result of looking on any Divine Being was universal among the Jews" (13:22; Genesis 16:13; Exodus 33:20, etc.).

Gideon, receiving a divine benediction, built an altar at the scene of the desired and demonstrated sign and called the place *Jehovah-shalom*, "The Lord is peace." The God who was able to bring water out of a rock can also produce fire—the common sign of His presence and of His acceptance of an offering—out of a rock (II Samuel 22:13).

The fire out of the rock consuming the flesh has a spiritual significance. Fire is a symbol of the Holy Spirit (Acts 2)—the Rock, a type of Christ, smitten of God. After Calvary, then came Pentecost. Fire came out of the Rock, and the mission of the Fire is to consume the flesh (Romans 8:1-13).

The miracle of the fleece (6:36-40)

The same night of the angelic appearance, God commanded Gideon to take a young bullock from his father's flock and, destroying his altar to Baal, to build another altar and offer a sacrifice upon it to Him. At night, Gideon carried out the task. In the morning, when Joash came to know of the daring action of his son against this idolatrous worship, in a cunning way he told those who sought the life of his son Gideon for his destruction of the Baal-altar, to let Baal plead for himself. It was on this day that Joash changed his son's name from *Gideon* to *Jerubbaal*, the latter name meaning "the antagonist of Baal." Gideon, true to his name which signifies "the hewer," was not afraid to stand almost alone among a cringing and apostate people as a true worshiper of Jehovah.

The Midianites with other foes of Israel gathered together and pitched in the valley of Jezreel, but "the hewer" was ready for the conflict. The Spirit of the Lord clothed Gideon with His own invincible power, and blowing a trumpet, Gideon rallied his own clan, the Abi-ezrites, to his support. Other tribes also responded to the call and challenge. Gideon was only too conscious of the fact that by human strength alone he was utterly helpless to repel the countless hosts of those eager to spoil Israel. Gideon needed fresh encouragement and confidence for the battle ahead and so asked for a double, divine sign.

Gideon, as a man of the fields, had no doubt about God's power over the dew and so requested that it might be directed and restricted in its descent, as a sign of God's presence and favor (Proverbs 3:20; Hosea 14:5). Dew on the fleece—the wool of one sheep (Job 31:20)—was a purely natural occurrence. "He shall come down like the rain into a fleece of wool" (Psalm 72:6 Prayer Book Version). But dew on the fleece only, with the surrounding ground dry, was an evidence of supernatural power, just as dry fleece but dew-laden ground was. The performance of this double miracle assured Gideon that he would be victorious as he led his army against the Midianites and that he had the direction and support of God.

Many commentators point out that the dew is not only a mark of divine blessing and a symbol of His reviving grace but prophetic of His dealings with Israel as a nation. "Israel heretofore was the dry fleece, while the nations around were flourishing," says Fausset. "Now she is to become filled with the Lord's vigor, whilst the nations around lose it. The fleece becoming afterwards dry whilst the ground around was wet symbolizes Israel's rejection of the Gospel whilst the Gentile world is receiving the gracious dew. Afterwards Israel in its turn shall be as the dew to the Gentile world" (Micah 5:7).

Ambrose saw in the fleece full of dew the Hebrew nation hiding the mystery of Christ within itself, and in the dry fleece that mystery extended to all the world but leaving the Hebrew nation dry. Ewald's comparison of the fleece to Gideon's character, cool amid the general passion, dry amid the general damp of fear, is suggestive.

The miracle of Midian's defeat (Judges 7; Deuteronomy 28:7, 28, 29).

God told Gideon that the army of 32,-000 which he had was too large for Him to achieve a victory in His way. Not wanting Israel to vaunt themselves against Him, He commanded Gideon to reduce his fighting host. One of the greatest dangers to which our poor, vain human nature is exposed is self-conceit. Often God pursues precisely the same course with us that He did with Gideon's army. He weakens our strength until we are reduced to absolute powerlessness and then He gives us the victory. His strength is made perfect in weakness (II Corinthians 12:9).

Gideon called upon all who were fearful and afraid to return to Mount Gilead, and 22,000 took advantage of the proffered liberty. These cowards felt they had no chance against the mighty Midianite host. With only 10,000 men left, God said, "The people are yet too many" (7:4). Here was a fresh trial of Gideon's faith. He had to learn that God is not necessarily on the side of big battalions. In this case, small numbers were essential for the method of victory God had in mind for Israel. Thus He removed the last ground for boasting from the people.

The final test came at the brook when the 10,000 were told to drink. To us it may seem a matter of small difference whether the men drank the water bowing down with face in the water or lapping up the water with the hand. Yet it was this difference that settled the question for Gideon as to the fitness or unfitness of those who were to conquer the Midianites. Often little things are a test of character such as the way we walk and the familiar actions of everyday life.

Out of the 10,000, there were 9,700 who who knelt and drank—the natural instinct of the thirsty—and who were rejected (Deuteronomy 20:8). An old Jewish writer says that those who went down on their knees to drink were secret idolaters, who had "bowed the knee to Baal" (I Kings 19:18). The other 300 only lapped the water with their tongues and these were chosen to fight against Midian. Lapping indicated a specific quality. Here were the men with nimbleness and alacrity and ability to move quickly in the attack of the enemy. Because this was to be a God-given victory, any thought of it being of man and not of God was demonstrated in the reduction of the army to 300 whose energy was shown by the way they drank the water (Psalm 110: 7). There were the men who were ready.

The God-arranged dream of the Midianite (7:13-16) is full of instruction. It consisted of a cake of barley overturning the tent. Barley bread was the poor man's bread. The Midianites called Gideon and his band "eaters of barley bread." Thus it

was a symbol of despised Israel. The "tent" symbolizes Midian's nomad life of freedom and power. But as the "bread" tumbled the "tent," so Israel was about to defeat Midian.

At midnight Gideon divided his 300 men into three attacking columns, and they were to follow him in the blowing of trumpets and the breaking of pitchers, so that their hidden lamps could shine forth suddenly in the face of the foe (see II Corinthians 4:6, 7 for a type of the Gospel light in earthen vessels). Attacking the Midianites, the 300 had to shout the war cry, "The sword of the Lord, and of Gideon!" (7:18, 20). The 300 had to stand still as if each trumpet holder seemed to have a company behind at his back. The foe not only fell to Gideon but in the terror of the moment and darkness of the night when they were unable to distinguish friend from foe, the Midianites slew each other. Out of a force of 135,000 (8:10), Midian lost 120,000 in that God-given victory of Israel (Deuteronomy 32:30).

It was a day of God's right hand (Psalm 83:9; Isaiah 9:4; 10:26; Habbakuk 3:7). The numerical strength of Midian counted for nothing. God gave Israel's 300 the victory over the multitudes that were like grasshoppers in the valley (7:12). By the simple stratagem of empty pitchers (7:16-25), Midian was defeated. "The glory of God's omnipotency," says Bishop Hall, "being manifested by the improbability of the means which He employed." In the mopping up process, two Midianite princes, Oreb and Zeeb, were captured and slain. Faint yet pursuing, Gideon's 300 valiant men captured Zebah and Zalmuna, kings of Midian, and their 15,000 men and slew them. Thus, as the sacred record expresses it: "Thus was Midian subdued before the children of Israel, so that they lifted up their heads no more: and the country was in quietness forty years in the days of Gideon" (8:28).

Leon Uris, in his glorious, heart-breaking, triumphant story of the birth of a new nation, *Exodus*, depicts one of his characters, Malcolm, standing by Gideon's supposed grave and reading in Hebrew the record of Gideon's victory. Closing his Bible and thinking of his struggle with the Arabs, Leon Uris makes Malcolm say,

Gideon was a smart man. He knew the Midianites were an ignorant and a superstitious people. Gideon knew he could play on their primitive fears and that they could be frightened by noise and by the night. Gideon knew it . . . and so do we.

Victory that day, however, came not because of any intuition or ability Gideon had. The whole campaign was God-planned and the victory, God-provided.

10. The Miracles During Samson's Judgeship

(Judges 13 - 16; Hebrews 11:32)

The period between Gideon and Samson was one of sin, servitude, sorrow, and salvation by God as Israel in despair cried to Him for emancipation from Gentile domination. The people were forever sinning and repenting, sinning and repenting, or as the hymn expresses it, "Forever wandering and coming back again." God sent an evil spirit between Abimelech, Gideon's son, and the men of Shechem (9:23), and bloodshed followed. God requited the wickedness of Abimelech (9:56). He murdered his brothers "on one stone," and in turn was killed by a stone flung on his own head. The anger of the Lord became hot against Israel (10:7), so much so that He permitted the people to be vexed and oppressed by heathen kings for eighteen years (10:8). As the people cried and repented, God became grieved for their misery (10:16). Fresh apostasy, however, engulfed Israel, resulting in God delivering them into the hands of the Philistines for forty years (13:1). Samson's birth found Philistine power in the ascendency.

The miracle of the announcing angel

The angelic Announcer who appeared to Manoah and his wife was no ordinary angel, but a Supernatural Being. Manoah said to his wife, "We have seen God" (13: 22). They witnessed His manifestation in human form (Exodus 33:20). Manoah's wife, who is identified as *Zelelponi,* spoke of Him as "A man of God, and his countenance was like the countenance of an angel of God, very terrible" (13:6). She was awe-struck by the majesty of His appearance (see Genesis 18:2; Luke 1:11-28). Manoah and his wife desired to know His name so that they might honor Him. His reply was, "It is secret" (13:18 margin, *wonderful,* same word that is used for "wonderously" in 13:19). "Thou shalt call His name Wonderful" (Isaiah 9:6). His

name is a secret known to His children (see Genesis 32:29; Psalm 25:14; Revelation 2:17; 3:12).

Manoah offered a burnt offering on a rock as a token of gratitude for the announcement of the Angel, and according to His name, "He did wondrously" in that He made a flame to arise and consume the offering, and then ascended in the flame (13:19, 20; Judges 6:21). Descending fire on a sacrifice was God's way of showing His acceptance. With deep spiritual instinct, Manoah's wife could say, "If God were pleased to kill us, He would not have received a burnt offering at our hands, neither would He have showed us all these things, nor at this time have told us such things."

What was the revelation the Angel made to this godly pair? (For they *were* God-fearing. Manoah, for example, means *rest,* and he was a man of rest, faith, piety, and hospitable. His wife and he expressed the yearning "at that time" for rest from their troubled days.) The Angel appeared first of all to Manoah's wife and announced to her that she would conceive and bear a son who would be ordained to a life of Nazaritism. She was barren and bore not, suggesting inability, for some reason or the other, to have children (Genesis 11:30). But Omnipotence is able to make the barren to rejoice. So the God who fashioned this childless wife was about to open her womb. Thus, as a child of promise, Samson was in a peculiar sense a gift of God, born to do a special work. An overruling providence would govern his acts and the source of his strength would be supernatural (14: 4; 16:30).

The divine enforcement of the Nazarite vow, and of the share of Samson's parents in that vow for the time of conception, is worthy of note. The vow consisted in abstention from wine and strong drink and any unclean food, and in uncut hair (Numbers 6:2-5). Such a vow doubtless impressed Manoah and his wife, as well as Israel, with the special character of the one to be born. The one to come was to be the divinely elected instrument in the deliverance of Israel from their long, degrading servitude. God meant him to be His representative man and a light to Israel. Manoah's wife conceived and bare a son who was named Samson, meaning "strength of the sun," and the supernatural element is seen in his birth and qualifications. As the child grew, the Lord blessed him and the Holy Spirit came upon him. There would be less juvenile delinquency in the world if only parents would emulate the example of Manoah and his wife in seeking God's direction on how to rear their children.

It is clearly evident that the humiliated and depressed condition of Israel found a fresh starting point in Samson's existence and peculiar task. He was born a champion and was divinely raised up to meet an existing emergency. In him, self-denial should have reached its highest significance. He should have been a living embodiment of Israel's calling as a consecrated people and of their power and prestige because of their vow of consecration. Alas, however, Samson's record became one of degeneracy and vicious self-indulgence! Although he judged Israel for twenty years (15:20), his remarkable career was fitful. Samson took advantage of his special endowment, thinking his supernatural gift enabled him to accomplish extraordinary deeds in a lower sphere. He yielded to fleshy sins and personal gratification. Yet in spite of his carnality, God continued to give him the gift of supernatural strength. Let us now consider some of the exploits in the life of Samson, to whom is given more space than that of any other judge, not because he was the best of them, but because of all the judges, Samson was the only Nazarite.

The miracle of the slain lion (14:5-10)

While Samson displayed a greater personal prowess than any of the other judges, he had a less noble character than many of them. As we examine his extraordinary feats, it must be borne in mind that Samson was no natural giant like Goliath whom David slew. He was an ordinary man who, at times, was seized upon by the supernatural impulse of the mighty Spirit of God. By his own natural strength, Samson could never have accomplished the terrific displays of miraculous power which burst upon the awe-stricken Philistines like a volcano.

It was at Timnath that Samson met the young lion. It was also at Timnath that Samson took to wife a Canaanitish woman—against the Mosaic law and much to the sorrow of his godly parents (Exodus 34:16; Genesis 34:4-12; II Corinthians 6: 14), for they knew not that God would overrule the course of events for the fur-

therance of His designs (14:6). Samson met the roaring, charging lion, and by mere hand tore it to pieces. Such a feat was the result of the Spirit of the Lord dominating and pervading Samson. There are seven references to "the Spirit of the Lord" in the book of Judges, four of which occur in connection with Samson (13:25; 14:6, 19; 16:20—by implication).

Samson was silent about his slaughter of the lion until enticed to reveal the deed to the men at his feast. By the slaughter of the 30 men of Ashkelon, God gave to him a proof and pledge of the might He would place at his disposal against the godless Philistines. What happened at Ashkelon, when without any weapon of any kind except the empowerment of the Spirit (14: 19), Samson slew 30 men courted the open hostility of the Philistines.

The miracle of the foxes (15:1-6)

Angered because his former wife was given to another, Samson had fresh ground with the Philistines and retaliated by catching 300 foxes, or jackals, setting them free among the fields of corn in pairs with burning torches tied between their tails. How Samson accomplished the colossal task of catching such a great number of foxes, at once and without traps of any kind, we are not told. This was another display of superhuman strength and wisdom. Widespread damage was caused among the standing corn of the Philistines, who showed that they too could play with fire because they retaliated by burning Samson's wife with her father. This act of vengeance only provoked Samson to achieve still greater destruction. The Philistines were to experience that they had erred in venting their fierce spleen on the man whose family and whose conduct had led to all their troubles.

The miracle of the hip and thigh slaughter (15:7, 8)

Revenge for the burning of Samson's wife and her father quickly came. The Philistines, roused to great indignation, had avenged themselves; now Samson retaliates by smiting them hip and thigh with great slaughter. No single, ordinary man without weapons could have accomplished such a great slaughter. If the task was carried out alone, then Samson must have had another infusion of supernatural power. A German expression has it, "A blow strikes a fugitive on the *hip,* and that would be enough; another blow on the *thigh* ends him."

After his revenge upon the Philistines, Samson retired to the top of the rock Etam.

The miracle of escape from bonds (15: 9-14)

The Philistines, stung into action over the slaughter of so many of their number, gathered together in hostile array to take vengeance on Samson for the tragic depletion of their number. They came to Etam, Samson's hiding place. The people of Judah, instead of rallying under Samson as the judge especially raised up to rescue them from Philistine bondage, agreed to deliver him into the hands of his enemies. Samson, believing that another opportunity of humiliating the Philistines would be his, allowed himself to be taken and led away bound to Lehi.

How the Philistines shouted with joy at seeing Samson bound with new cords! They cheered as they met him, but their "hurrahs" soon changed to moans. Now that he was their bound prisoner, they felt that he was powerless and utterly unable to inflict any further harm. But as the Philistines shouted, the Spirit of the Lord came upon Samson, and the strong cords binding him were loosed, or *melted,* or *flowed off.* This was no escapist trick such as Houdini could perform. Freedom from bounds became Samson's through a supernatural endowment of strength.

The miracle of the new jawbone (15:15-20)

Freed, Samson found a new or moist jawbone, meaning, the jawbone of an animal recently dead and before the bone had become brittle, and with it he slew 1,000 Philistines. He was able to fight with his fists as well as with his wits, yet nothing except superhuman power could enable one man to slay 1,000 at once. Ellicott has a most suggestive comment on this miracle.

If Goliath was able single-handed to strike terror into the whole army of Israel, Samson with his long locks and colossal strength would be still more likely to strike a terror into the Philistines, and all the more because a supernatural awe was doubtless attached to his name and person. The very fact that, though armed only with this wretched weapon of offense, he yet dared to rush upon the Philistines would make them fly in wilder panic (Joshua 23:10; Deuteronomy 32:30).

Elated over such a victory, Samson boasted of his great achievement in a sort of punning couplet (15:16), which Dr. Moore translates:

"With the bone of an ass, I ass-ailed my ass-ailants." A literal translation of the Hebrew of Sampson's couplet would be:

"With the jaw of an ass, a (m)ass two (m)asses,
With the jaw of ass I smote an ox-load of men."

Samson reverently gave God the glory for such a victory (15:18). Such a mighty task, however, was exhausting and Samson was overcome with thirst. Water out of the jaw has nothing to do with the jawbone Samson had thrown away. Actually the phrase here reads, "water from the (fountain called the) 'socket,' which is in Lehi." Samson called the place of his story *Ramath-lehi* meaning "the lifting up, or casting away of the jawbone." The place at which God provided the refreshing, reviving fountain was named *En-hakkore,* "the well of him that cried." It was in a similar manner that God satisfied Hagar's thirst (Genesis 21:19). John Milton wrote of this incident in the lines:

God, who caused a fountain at thy prayer
From the dry ground to spring thy thirst
    to allay.

The miracle at Gaza (16:1-13)

How, or why, Samson went to Gaza, the chief town of the Philistines in the very heart of their country, we are not told. The narrative here is brief and detached. At Gaza, he yielded to the solicitations of a harlot and spent the night with her. The Philistines, coming to know of Samson's presence in their city, surrounded the house but made no immediate attack. Possibly thinking that they had cornered him, they seem to have retired to rest (Acts 9:23, 24). At midnight, Samson arose and, again divinely empowered, uprooted the doors of the gate of the city with their posts and bars and, slinging them over his shoulders, carried them to the top of a hill—a distance of about a quarter of a mile. This was not a mere weight-lifting accomplishment. In spite of his lapse into carnality at Gaza, God mercifully continued His enduement of Samson.

The miracle of the hair (16:4-22)

Still following the same path of vicious self-indulgence, Samson became enamored of another harlot, Delilah, in the valley of Sorek. The Philistines, among whom Delilah plied her wares, knowing of Samson's weakness for women, solicited Delilah's aid in the enticement of their dreaded foe. In open violence they were helpless. "Friendships which are begun in wickedness cannot stand," says Bishop Hall. For a time Samson made sport of his paramour's enticements to wrest from him the secret of his unusual strength. Three times Samson deceived the Philistine woman, but at last he yielded to entreaties and explained that he was a Nazarite and that his hair, which had never been cut, was the secret of his remarkable power. Samson, weak in resistance, told her all that was in his heart, and that if shaven, he would become like any other man (16:18).

Such a fatal disclosure resulted in his death. Samson knew that to part with his hair would be to cast away the symbol of his consecration and formally to break his vow to God. Delilah lulled him into a profound sleep and stripped him of his locks. When he awoke at the cry, "The Philistines be upon thee," Samson went out as at other times, but found that he had lost, not merely supernatural strength, but the Giver of it. "The Spirit of the Lord departed from him" (16:20). Paying their bribe to Delilah, the Philistines quickly seized Samson, bound him with chains, put out his eyes, and made him grind in the prison as a slave.

"Eyeless in Gaza, at the mill with slaves."

The association of power with hair is interesting to note. Actually, there was no miraculous power resident in the long hair of Samson. The power was in what it represented, namely, the Nazarite dedication of his life to God's service. Yet hair, like the blood as a seat of life, was observed among the Semites. Absalom's luxuriant hair is mentioned as a sign of beauty. It was also a mark of effeminacy. Hair represents what is least valuable (Matthew 10:30).

The miracle at Dagon's temple (16:23-31)

Is there not something poignant about the phrase, "Howbeit the hair of his head began to grow again after he was shaven" (16:22)? With such a growth, Samson's strength returned. Alas, although his hair returned, his sight did not! In the depth of his humiliation, his Nazarite heart returned unto him. Samson appears repentant of his unfaithfulness and degradation of God's name and honor. Although he is not found praying until the bitter end of his life, nevertheless repentant prayer restored his power.

The Philistine lords were merry over Samson's sad plight and gathered themselves together to offer a great sacrifice unto Dagon their god for a joyous celebration. They sang in rustic rhythm:

> Our god has given us into our hand
> The foe of our land,
> Whom even our most powerful band
> Was never able to withstand (16:24).

Not content with this sacrificial, singing feast, the Philistines called for Samson to play the fool and by his pranks to entertain the assembled multitude of about 3,000. Josephus says that Samson was sent for that the Philistines "might insult him over their wine."

The prayer of Samson, even though he used three names of God—*Adonai, Jehovah, Elohim*, reveals a somewhat low level of spiritual enlightenment as well as of moral purity. He is concerned, not about the divine cause to which his Nazarite vows had dedicated him, but only for revenge on the Philistines for blinding him. If Samson could have triumphed over his foes without the sacrifice of his own life then, as one has expressed it, "he would have borne about in the blindness of his eyes a mark of his unfaithfulness as the servant of God." But he prayed to die with the Philistines.

Beseeching the lad who acted as his guide to lead him to the two middle pillars supporting the cloistered structure, Samson bowed himself with all his might and, slipping the pillars off their pedestals, brought death to himself and to the 3,000 men and women assembled for the occasion. "The dead which he slew at his death were more than they which he slew in his life" (16:30). Samson was the only judge to die in captivity, and dying thus, he left Israel in servitude to the Philistines (see Colossians 2:15; Matthew 27:50-54 for the typical significance of Samson's death-victory). John Milton in *Samson Agonistes* gives us the following description of Samson's heroic death:

> Straining all his nerves he bow'd
> As with the force of winds and waters
>   pent,
> When mountains tremble, and two massy
>   pillars
> With horrible convulsion to and fro,
> He tugg'd, he shook, till down they came
>   and drew
> The whole roof after them, with burst of
>   thunder,

Upon the heads of all who sat beneath—
Lords, ladies, captains, counsellors, and
  priests,
Their choice nobility and flower . . .

*   *   *   *   *

Samson with these unmix'd, inevitably
Pull'd down the same destruction on himself.

Samson wrought all of his great feats by
faith, the true secret of might (Hebrews
11:32; Matthew 21:21). The question may
arise why Samson, the fornicator, should be
mentioned among the heroes of faith. God
made use of him, as He did of others whose
characters were not highly commendable,
"to the degree in which they were conscious of His presence and power, and were
responsive to them, it can be said that they
were actuated 'by faith.' "

Fausset, commenting on the lesson of
his fitful and remarkable career, says that
Israel saw in Samson "a memorable example, and how much more important it
was to have the heart of the nation set right
with God, than to have a giant's strength
in his arms; how, if truly exalted, it could
only be by returning to righteousness." Endowment with the Spirit of God, Samson
was prodigal of his strength and careless of
his personal endowment. He failed to realize that physical endowments are no less
than spiritual gifts from God, and that to
retain them one must be obedient.

11. The Miracles in Samuel's History

(I Samuel 1:20; 2; Psalm 99:6;
Jeremiah 15:1)

The history of the judges after Samson
is one of moral declension. The record of
Micah and the Danites (17 and 18) is one
of idolatry and reveals how widespread in
Israel was infidelity. Then the incident of
a Levite and the Benjamites seethes with
revenge and shows how deeply the people
were sunk in immorality (19-21). Some
ancient editions of the Hebrew Scriptures
join Ruth on to Judges, and what a contrast this beautiful idyll presents. In Judges
we have impurity and war; in Ruth, purity
and peace. Ruth is like "a pure lily in a
miasmal pool."

Although Eli was the successor to Samson as judge, he was not the recipient of
any supernatural gift nor the channel of
any miraculous display. How he came to
be appointed judge we are not told. We
know nothing of the first 58 years of his

life and the last 40 do him no credit. He
was by no means a Nazarite. He had one
strong element in his character, namely
weakness. God could not have been pleased
with Eli since "the word of the Lord was
rare in those days, and there was no open
vision" (I Samuel 3:1).

While Samson wrought no permanent deliverance for Israel, yet he paved the way
for Samuel, Saul, and David. It was Samuel who *completed* Israel's deliverance from
the Philistines which Samson had *commenced*. Samson, the physically strong Nazarite, was the forerunner of Samuel, the
last and greatest of the judges and the first
of the prophets, the spiritual hero Nazarite. He was "the Nazarite of higher mould,
who should revive the cause of heaven in
its proper seat, and by strengthening the
people in their God should lead them on to
victory and peace." Of Samson we read that
God through him *began* to deliver Israel
(Judges 13:5). It was Samuel's task to
consummate that deliverance from the Philistines and to open up for Israel a new
national era of progress and order under
the rule of the kings whom the people
desired.

The miracle of Samuel's birth

Samuel was a divine gift to Hannah, who
had asked God for him. Hence the significance of his name—"Asked of God." Samuel was born in answer to prayer. Hannah,
of whom Dean Stanley said, "She was herself almost a prophetess and Nazarite" (1:
15; 2:1), was sorely grieved over her barren womb, her barrenness being supernaturally arranged—"The Lord had shut up
her womb" (1:5, 6). Peninnah, the other
wife of Hannah's husband, Elkanah, had
sons and daughters, a circumstance responsible for Hannah's broken heart. Although
it is said that Elkanah gave Hannah a
double portion as an expression of his deep
love for her, Peninnah, the other wife,
treated Hannah differently. She annually
provoked Hannah sorely and caused her
to fret over her childless condition. How
such a situation reveals the influence of the
sin of polygamy to poison the whole life
of a family!

During one of the yearly visits to the
house of the Lord, Hannah, bitter of soul,
prayed and wept and vowed a vow. If
God would remove her barrenness and give
her a son, then she would undertake two
solemn promises. First, she pledged the son
she asked for to the service of the divine

Giver all the days of his life. But He who heard the prayer of the distressed heart had still higher work for her yet unborn son. The second promise was that she would undertake to set him apart as a Nazarite and, as we know, Samuel became a perpetual Nazarite. The mighty God heard Hannah. "The Lord remembered her" (1:19) and opened her womb and she conceived and bare a son who, as soon as he was weaned, was taken to the house of the Lord and left there. For the loan of her son, God rewarded Hannah with another three sons and two daughters (2:21). Her song of praise is "the first hymn, properly so called —the direct model of the first Christian hymn of the Magnificat, the first outpouring of the individual as distinct from national devotion" (I Samuel 2).

Out of Hannah's sorrow there came a lovely song, a song divinely inspired, for its beautiful thoughts were first planted in her heart by the Holy Spirit who then gave her lips the grace and power to utter them in such sublime language. Hannah's song became one of the loved songs of the people and was handed down from father to son, from generation to generation in the very words which first fell from the lips of that godly, happy mother of the child-prophet in a home in which it was not easy to live.

A word is necessary regarding Eli mistaking the moving lips of Hannah as she silently prayed as the action of a drunken woman. With reverence and humility, she answered the accusation of the high priest, who quickly atoned for his unworthy suspicion.

The miracle of Samuel's call (I Samuel 3)

Have you noticed one or two miniature but precious miracles in connection with the call of the child-prophet of Israel? At Shiloh, where Samuel ministered before the Lord, wearing an ephod of blue and the coat which his mother brought him at each of her yearly visits, he grew and was in favor with the Lord and also men (2:26). The atmosphere in which he lived was a pure and holy one. Samuel slept within the Tabernacle, put out the lights, and opened the doors. Doubtless his routine of service was interrupted by sad thoughts respecting the evil practices of the sons of Eli, from whom Samuel kept apart. "Hophni and Phinehas, *the grown men,* prostituted the holy work to their own vile worldly ends: *the child* ministered before the Lord in his

little white robe, amid the stillness and silence and the awful mystery of the divine presence and protection."

We can imagine how eagerly Samuel anticipated the happy visits of his parents and brothers and sisters. Although Samuel was denied the constant care and training of his own parents, Eli gave to him the necessary education for his later life of stirring public work. Eli could no nothing with his own headstrong sons, but here was a boy to whom he could teach the story of his ancestors. Here was a lad Eli loved, and Samuel was an apt pupil of the old, sorrow-stricken high priest.

Before master and pupil there hung the dark curtains of the sanctuary, which separated them from the golden throne of God, on which His glory was pleased to rest, and it was here that the miraculous took place. In those days, there was no "open vision" (3:1), that is, direct, divine manifestations —no inspired voice to utter the word and will of God to His chosen people. Thus it happened one still night that, as Samuel slept, the Lord called him. Asked of God, given to God, he is now called of God. Three times over the call came (3:4, 6, 10).

Eli was partially blind and could not see very well; but his hearing appears to be unimpaired. Yet, although he was close to Samuel, he did not hear the divine voice. Neither did Samuel detect the Speaker, for on the first two calls, he arose and, with all obedience and respect for Eli, said, "Here am I, for thou calledst me" (3:5, 6). Now the accent of that Voice must have been like Eli's for Samuel to say as he did, "Eli, thou didst call me." The awesome Voice of the Lord in the sanctuary might have frightened the boy, so with all tender considerations, the God who made the voice with all its variety of tone and expression, ventriloquist-like assumed the peculiar accent of Eli.

As yet, "Samuel did not know the Lord, neither was the word of the Lord yet revealed unto him" (3:7), meaning, he had not had any direct, divine call (see Acts 19:2). With the second call, old Eli perceived that the Lord had twice called the child. Perhaps the half-blind master asked the somewhat perplexed young pupil where the Voice came from and he told Eli that it came from his chamber, and Eli knew that in the same direction, behind the veil, was the ark as the seat of God from which in old time His voice was heard. Comforting young Samuel, Eli said, "Go lie down: and it shall be, if He call thee, that thou shalt say, Speak, Lord, for thy servant heareth."

After he returned to rest, the Voice called Samuel the third time (Job 33:14), but there is this addition of the supernatural. "The Lord came, *and stood*, and called as at other times." How did the Lord come? In what form did He stand before the boy's couch? In the past, when the Lord was pleased to assume some form, the form is specified as, for example, when He appeared to Joshua as the Captain with a drawn sword. Being near the ark, it may have been God's "visible glory," the *Shekinah*, which Samuel beheld, as Moses did on Mount Sinai. From that dazzling glory came the Voice to which Samuel responded, "Speak, for thy servant heareth."

The repeated name, "Samuel, Samuel," is profitable to ponder. Usually when we call anyone by name and repeat the name, it is because we are deeply in earnest, or because what we have to say is urgent. Repetition is sometimes the language of passion, or the accents of grief and despair —"Absalom, Absalom." Thus it was with Samuel as the Voice, somewhat peremptory, summoned the young servant to receive an important message, a message of doom. What a message of fearful judgment for young ears to hear! (3:11-14).

With delicate consideration for Eli's feelings, Samuel lay until the morning, shrinking from telling his master God's solemn revelation. It was only at Eli's solicitation that Samuel told him "every whit." The gentleness of the holy lad only intensified the awfulness of the doom announced through him to the old, weak, and vacillant priest. Accepting the deserved judgment of God, Eli said, "It is the Lord: let him do what seemeth him good." Josephus tells us that Samuel was twelve years old when God called him, and it was through the unstained lips of this innocent child that Eli heard of the doom of his house.

The fame of Samuel, "the boy-friend of the Eternal," was established. Quickly he was recognized and revered as the prophet of the Lord who was to receive further supernatural revelations (3:21). Later on we read that "the Lord told Samuel in his ear" His secret about Saul (9:15). What a delightful aspect of God this is, whispering in the ears of a man! Actually, it reads, "The Lord uncovered the ear of Samuel,"

meaning, He gently brushed aside the Nazarite locks covering his ear and communicated His thought to Samuel. If God has Samuel's ear, Samuel had God's ear, for the prophet rehearsed the words of the people "in the ears of the Lord" (8:21). Alone in His sacred presence, Samuel poured out his heart to his God-Friend. What privileged communion and companionship these precious touches reveal! Are our ears turned to the accent of the Divine Voice?

The miracle of Dagon's fall (I Samuel 5: 1-5)

The destruction of *Dagon*, the heathen deity of the Philistines, proves God's power over all kinds of inanimate objects and shows that the supernatural can pervade all particles of matter. The tragic circumstances of Israel leading up to such a miracle can be briefly stated. There had been the miraculous and calamitous defeat of Israel, just as Samuel had prophesied (I Samuel 4). Thirty thousand footmen were slain, along with the iniquitous sons of Eli, Hophni and Phinehas, also as Samuel had predicted (2:34). News of Israel's defeat and the taking of the ark was too much for old Eli, now 98 years of age. Such a message broke his heart, and falling off his seat, he died of a broken neck. During the debacle, the widow of Phinehas, the evil warrior priest, gave birth to a son whom she named *I-chabod*, meaning "The glory is departed from Israel" (4:21, 22).

Flushed with pride and pleasure over their successful victory, the Philistines brought the much-prized ark of God from the battlefield to Ashdod and placed it in the temple of their popular god, *Dagon*. As Ellicott comments, "*This* was their vengeance for the slaughter of the 3,000 Philistine worshipers in the temple of the same deity at Gaza, not many years before, by the blind Hebrew champion, Samson." The insulted Dagon and all the murdered worshipers felt avenged by this humiliation of the "God of Abraham"—the golden ark, symbol of His glory, now in a heathen shrine at the feet of *Dagon*. The ecstasy of the Philistines, however, was short-lived for, as John Milton expressed it:

> This only hope relieves me, that the strife
> With me hath end, all the contest now
> 'Twixt God and Dagon; Dagon hath presumed,
> Me overthrown, to enter lists with God.
> His deity comparing and preferring
> Before the God of Abraham. He, be sure,

Will not connive or linger thus provoked.
But will arise, and His great name assert.

What was the appearance of *Dagon,* the chief national deity of the Philistines? The idol had a carved human-like head and hands, and the body of a fish. To the tail, the fish part, women's feet were joined. The upper part has perished but some of the four gigantic slabs representing the bottom part can be seen in the British Museum in London. The name *Dagon* is from "dagan," meaning "corn," and indicates the nature worship of the Philistines. "The divine principle supposed to produce the seeds of all things from moisture."

Dag means a "fish," and represented the sea from which the Philistines derived so much of their wealth and power. Says Keil, "This deity was a personification of the generative and vivifying principle of nature, for which the fish, with its innumerable multiplication, was specially adapted, and set forth the idea of the Giver of all earthly good."

On, or aon, means "idol." This symbolic form then, was compounded of human intellect (the top part of the idol) and of the properties of the sea (the bottom part). The idol thus signified both the commercial and maritime power of the Philistines.

This travesty of a god was soon to experience the power of the true God, from whom all earthly blessings flow. In the time of its seeming weakness, the ark showed itself stronger than the heathen god. Why? Because the ark represented the power and glory of the Lord, and His glory He will never surrender to another. Thus it came to pass that this grotesque image, on the day after the triumphant placing of the ark of the Lord in the idol shrine, was found prostrate on the temple floor before the desecrated yet sacred coffer of the Israelites.

The Philistines, thinking some accident had occurred, raised the idol to its place. But the next day the exultant Philistines were shocked to find that their idol had not only fallen again, but this time was broken in pieces. Only the stump remained, that is, the bottom fishy part (5:4). Disturbed, the Philistines knew that such a catastrophe was no accident, for the shattered remains had been contemptuously scattered over the threshold of the temple which the feet of priest and worshipers passed over into their sacred house. This cutting off of

Dagon's head and hands, and their lying on the threshold, prefigures the ultimate cutting off of all idols in the great day of the Lord (Isaiah 2:11-22). Our Lord, allowing Himself to be taken, went down into death, into the domain of him who had the power of death; but though His heel was bruised, He crushed the serpent's head. Even in His humiliating death, He showed Himself stronger than His foes. "Death could not hold his prey."

The miracle of the emerods (5:6-12; 6:17, 18; Deuteronomy 28:27; Psalm 78:66)

Still further judgment awaited the Philistines for the desecration of the ark of the covenant. The hand of the Lord was heavy upon them and He smote them with emerods, which proved His supremacy in the physical realm. None were spared this painful and distressing sickness; small and great alike suffered (5:9). *Emerods* or hemorrhoids, or tumorous veins causing bleeding piles, attacked the lower part, or "secret parts" of the abdomen.

Apart from those smitten with emerods, deadly destruction overtook others—a destruction "the hand of God" brought about. So great was the divine affliction that a great cry went up to heaven. The Philistines were forced to realize that God's hand was sore upon them and upon their god because of their treatment of the ark, and cried, "What shall we do with the ark of the God of Israel?" Making up their minds to get rid of this deadly trophy of their victory over Israel, the Philistines carried it about until at last they decided to return it to its own place (5:11).

The priests and diviners told the Philistines that they should place in the sacred historical treasure of Israel, as a trespass offering "five gold emerods and five gold mice, according to the number of the lords of the Philistines (6:17, 18). The LXX Greek Version of the Old Testament adds to the plague of emerods (5:6) "mice were produced in the land, and there arose a great and deadly confusion in the city." Hence the inclusion of mice with emerods as an expiatory offering (6:5).

The miracle of the two cows (6:6-17)

Once again the miraculous power of God is seen both in incidental and obvious ways. The Philistines, somewhat lax in their surrender of the ark, were reminded of the plagues upon Pharaoh because of his unwillingness to let Israel leave Egypt. Smitten already with one plague (emerods), did they want to experience the severity of ten plagues? In response to the divine command, the Philistines made a new cart to convey the ark to Beth-shemesh, a city given to the priests (Joshua 21:16). "This was so ordered in reverence to the ark, and was a right and true feeling" (Numbers 19:2; II Samuel 6:2). The provision of the new cart, however, was a distince act of rebellion against the command of the Lord, who had ordered the Levites to carry the ark on their shoulders (Numbers 4:15; 7:9).

The Philistines had now come to treat the ark with reverent awe, since because of their treatment of it, great evil had befallen them. The priests, however, not certain whether the plague of emerods had been sent by God or was an ordinary course of nature, suggested a strange experiment to satisfy the minds of those of the people. If the cows contrary to their expectation, kept on the road to Beth-shemesh, this would be a sign that they were being led and guided by a divine power and that the ark was a dangerous possession, well rid of. But if the animals, as was expected, left to themselves, returned to their own stalls, then the ark could be safely returned and their recent sufferings came as the result of natural causes.

The God who made the beasts of the field is able to command and control their movements, so the milk cows did not follow their own instincts and turn round and return to their calves shut up in the stall. A divine power drove the cows on and the dumb beasts continued their strange journey with their golden burden. The narrative tells the story of the divine interference of the "glorious arm" with exquisite simplicity and truth. What else could the Philistine princes do but follow, awe-struck, at a distance. What a convincing evidence of the supernatural is here presented!

The miracle at Beth-shemesh (6:19-21)

At last Beth-shemesh was reached. When the Ekronites refused to keep the ark, the wisdom of God arranged that it should be the priests and Levites who should receive the ark with all honor and to offer sacrifice before it. The people crowding in from all quarters and staring at the ark with profane curiosity were instantly smitten by the Lord.

Where it is said that "they had looked into the ark of the Lord" (6:19), it should be rendered "they looked at the ark." A foolish, irreverent staring, dishonoring the holiness of the sacred mercyseat, is implied. It is probable that the chief men of Beth-shemesh, drunk with wine because of the ark's joyful return, lost all sense of reverence, tried to look not only *at* the ark but *into* it. Perhaps they wanted to see if the Philistines had violated the secrets of the holy chest. No matter what prompted the men to gaze at or into the ark, "no profane eye in Israel had ever peered into it, since the golden cover—on which the glory of the Eternal loved to rest—had sealed up the sacred treasures in the wilderness."

The Lord's hand smote the profaners with a great slaughter. He is depicted as the One with the right and power to kill or make alive. There is some question as to the accuracy of the numbers mentioned as being slain—50,070. This large number is inconceivable since Beth-shemesh was only a small village with a population around 1,400. Scholars affirm a corruption of the Hebrew text at this point (6:19). The Arabic and Syriac Versions give the number of the stricken with sudden death as 5,070. Josephus omits the 5,000 and gives us 70, which is probably the correct number. For these men of Beth-shemesh, the throne of grace became a throne of judgment.

The rest of the people, lamenting and overwhelmed by the power and awesomeness of God, cried, "Who is able to stand before this holy God?" (6:20). They were forced to connect the invisible King with the golden ark. Solemnized by the fatal stroke overtaking their brethren, they felt that they were just as worthy of divine judgment and cried, "To whom shall He go up from us?" In the awful punishment of the men of Beth-shemesh for their irreverence and presumption, the law is represented as "a ministration of death." In the inquiry of those who were spared, "Who is able to stand before this holy Lord God?" a question was asked which the Gospel only can fully answer (Romans 3:21-26; II Corinthians 5:21).

The miracle at Eben-ezer (7:1-17)

In the chapter before us, with its record of the revival of Israel, we have another striking instance of God unleasing the powers of nature for the deliverance of His distressed people. Samuel appears on the scene again. During the twenty years (7:2) while the ark was away from Israel and the people were in servitude to the Philistines, we have little record of the prophet-judge. Now it is a time of crisis and Samuel emerges to interpose. During those twenty years, the prophet must have found the period wearisome. Yet through those long years he was not inactive. He labored incessantly "to make up the old worship of the Eternal and the pure life loved by God among His people."

In spite of the crushing blow inflicted at Aphek (chapter 4), the national life of the Hebrew people was by no means exterminated. Here we have its revival under happier auspices. "*All* the house of Israel lamented after the Lord" (7:2). Loathing their idolatry and sick of crime and folly, the people were exhorted by Samuel to put away all their strange gods —those favorite heathen deities they had countenanced. This was an hour of decision and Samuel, the wise and patriotic states-man prophet, knew that Israel's moment of deliverance and national restoration had come. So at Mizpeh the people met in sol-emn assembly and offered libations and prayer with confession and fasting. Sam-uel, assuming that function of the judge which involved military command and civil magistracy, offered a burnt offering and prayer, as the Philistines were again ter-rifying the people.

Samuel's life was one of prayer and inter-cession. He was born as the result of prayer, and prayer became the atmosphere of his life. His characteristic spiritual service was unceasing, crying to God at times "all night" (15:11) in intercessory prayer—a type of Christ who "continued all night in prayer" (Luke 6:12). At critical hours, as here at Mizpeh, Samuel was on his knees (7:5, 8, 9; 12:18, 19, 23; 15:11). Long after, he was extolled as a man of prayer (Psalm 99:6; Jeremiah 15:1). He knew that prayer was able to release heavenly forces. In response to Samuel's prayers and offering, God answered with a mighty thunderstorm and His people were deliv-ered from the Philistines without the use of any earthly weapons. Again "the Angel of His presence" with His glorious arm saved His people.

The terrible thunderstorm bursting over the Philistine hosts, accompanied, Josephus tells us, by the horrors of an earthquake, offers another striking instance of divine judgment by lightning. God gave its flash

charge to strike the mark and the Philis-tines were routed and smitten by the in-visible army fighting for Israel. At the scene of carnage Samuel took a stone and named it Eben-ezer, *the stone of help.* This was the name of the place where Israel was disastrously beaten and the ark taken (4:1; 5:1). Here the name become the memorial of an equally glorious, God-given victory over the Philistines. From this time of their defeat on, the hand of the Lord was against them all the days of Samuel (7:13).

For another twenty years Samuel, the circuit judge, exercised the chief authority in Israel. His fixed abode was at Ramah, his father's city, where he built an altar unto the Lord and where probably the prophet guarded the sacred vessels and furniture saved from the destruction at Shi-loh. It was at Ramah that he died and was buried. The ark was in safe keeping in "the city of woods," Kirjath-jearim.

The miracle of the lost asses (9:3-21; 10:2)

The record following Israel's deliverance makes sad reading. Samuel, now an old man, in spite of the awful warning in Eli's case of the danger of not correcting way-ward children, made his own evil sons, Joel and Abiah, to be judges over Israel. Lacking the ability and integrity of their honored father, they went after lucre, took bribes, and perverted judgment (8:1-3). This is the only recorded blemish in an otherwise holy life. Of Samuel it can be truly said that he "wore the white flower of a blameless life." He was a miracle of grace (12:1-5). It was the shameful con-duct of Samuel's sons that precipitated the change to a monarchy, and the appointment of a king-judge to succeed Samuel. Dis-gusted over the bad life and living of Joel and Abiah, the people clamored for a king like the surrounding heathen nations had, and again in the hour of national crisis, Samuel's one unfailing resort was the throne of grace. "Samuel prayed unto the Lord."

In answer to believing prayer, God re-vealed to Samuel the inner significance of the people's request and the kind of king they were to have. Such revelations are an aspect of the supernatural. God revealed that He, the invisible King, and not the visible prophet, was the One the people were rejecting. As the result of his reve-lation from God, Samuel told the people the power and personality of the autocratic

king they were to have as they passed from
a theocracy to a monarchy. Then the ninth
chapter begins with a brief account of the
family of Saul and something of his unique
personality (9:1, 2).

We thus come to the story of the lost
asses—an incident we believe, suggestive
of the supernatural power of the Creator,
since those straying asses were used by
Him to bring Samuel and Saul together.
The God who spoke through an ass and
provided an ass for His Son to ride on is
able to use such an animal for His own
purpose. Saul, the son of Kish, left the farm
and traveled far in search of the asses. Concerned lest his father should be troubled
over his long absence, Saul wanted to return without the asses, but Saul's servant,
knowing of Samuel's reputation as a seer,
persuaded his master to seek out the man
of God.

Once again we have a reminder of the
blessed intimacy existing between God and
Samuel. "The Lord told Samuel in his ear
the day before" all about the coming and
choice of Saul and about the safety of his
asses (9:15, 20; 10:2, 16). It was God
who told Samuel that the asses were in the
keeping of two men by Rachel's tomb.
"Thine asses . . . are found." Actually they
were never lost, for God's eye was not
only on the sparrows, but also on those
asses, and it was He who protected them
and saw that they were returned safe and
sound to Saul, now anointed king of Israel
by Samuel. Although it is characteristic of
asses to keep together, even if they run
away, a higher Hand kept those of Kish together during the three days of their ab-
scence from the farm. The intimation
regarding the three men Saul was to meet,
carrying sufficient provision for Saul and
his servant, and the revelation of the "signs"
to be given Saul (10:7), are further evidence of God's overruling providence. His
miraculous power is seen in the transformation of Saul who was "turned into
another man" (10:6, 9). Such divine communications of divine thoughts to Samuel
come within the realm of the supernatural.

The miracle at Gilgal (12:16-25)

Reminders of the miraculous are interwoven in the record of Saul's defeat of
the Ammonites. "The Spirit came upon
Saul" (11:6). "The fear of the Lord fell
upon the people" (11:7). "The Lord
wrought salvation in Israel" (11:13). Saul,
by his prompt action in the siege of Jabesh-

Gilead by the Ammonites, and in his defeat of them, proved himself worthy of
kingship and of the universal acknowledgement of his sovereignty.

In the chapter before us, we have a rehearsal of the mighty acts of the Lord on
the part of His people and the assurance
of the further manifestations on their behalf if only they would obey His commandments. Then we come to the dreadful sign
of heaven's displeasure for wishing for an
earthly king, a desire which but crowned
a long course of rebellion against the Supreme Sovereign. God's supremacy in the
realm of nature is seen in the terrible
storm of thunder and rain which came during the wheat harvest between May and
June when thunder and rain are seldom
experienced. This unusual phenomena,
which came in direct answer to Samuel's
prayer, smote the people with great fear,
and repenting, they besought Samuel to
intercede on their behalf. The thunderstorm declared Samuel's integrity and also
the people's sin. Promise of divine protection and favor were given, if the people
would fear and serve the Lord, whose
power they had just witnessed. If they
failed to obey Him, there was added the
warning that He would destroy both them
and their desired king.

Here again, we have illustrated the question of Job, "The thunder of His power
who can understand?" Ovid, the Latin philosopher, said, "When the thunderbolts
strike one man, it is not one man only
whom they fill with terror." Although that
thunderstorm at Gilgal killed no one, it
yet struck terror into the hearts of the
people who "greatly feared the Lord and
Samuel."

The miracle of the Witch at Endor
(I Samuel 28)

As there is little of the miraculous in
the life of Saul, we can very briefly scan
the chapter dealing with his failures and
fears. Because of his impatience over Samuel's apparent delay, Saul assumed the
priestly functions of the prophet and was
strongly rebuked for his foolishness and disobedience and told of his rejection as king
(chapter 13). The Lord graciously saved
Israel, in spite of Saul's behavior, from
the Philistines. God gave the unworthy
king to fight over all Israel's enemies and
subdue them on every side (14:47).

In the matter of Amalek, Saul again
yielded to disobedience and the reproach

of Samuel and the account of the last meeting between Saul and Samuel makes sad reading! (15:34). God's Spirit departed from Saul and an evil spirit terrified him (16:14), meaning that he developed a confused, turbulent state of mind, one which David alone, the newly anointed successor to Saul, could soothe with his sweet-toned harp (16:16-23). It is beyond the scope of our particular study to deal fully with the intervening events—Saul's jealousy of David because of his victory over Goliath; his determination to kill the much-loved David; his murder of the priests at Nob for their protection of David; and his evident change of heart toward David. What we are to dwell upon is the last glimpse we have of Israel's rejected king when the Philistines invaded Israel and somehow Saul sensed his tragic end was near.

The tragic chapter we are considering opens with the repeated announcement of Samuel's death and burial (25:1; 28:3), and introduces the strange yet supernatural experience of Saul. In his early zeal for God and pure worship, he had put away all familiar spirits and wizards out of the land. Now, in desperation, he seeks to invoke the aid of the dealers in occult and forbidden arts. Saul, in his fear, had inquired of the Lord what he should do, but "the Lord answered him not" in any of the accustomed ways. To this rejected man, the heavens were as brass. Thus, left to himself, he turned to superstition to aid him in his hour of dire need.

At Endor, a witch, or medium, was found, who apparently had escaped the general pursuits of those with familiar spirits in the early days of Saul. Coming in darkness and disguise to the witch's abode, Saul besought the witch by her occult power to bring back the departed spirit of Samuel. As the departed spirits of the faithful never revisit this world, the question is, what really happened when, exercising her wizardry, the witch, to her own consternation, produced Samuel, from whose lips Saul was to hear his doom? Was the apparition real or fraudulent? Although the straight simplicity of the narrative implies a miracle, let us think of a few explanations which scholars suggest.

The witch, although the Bible does not speak of her thus, was the equivalent of a spiritualistic medium—"mistress of a spirit by which the dead are conjured up."

She claimed to have power to convey messages from the dead to the living. It is a mark of these last days that an ever-increasing number of people meddle with spiritism and crave after miraculous evidences of the presence of the spirits of the dead. But the spirits of the faithful departed are not allowed to return to earth except by divine power and permission.

There are those who affirm that the alleged visit of Samuel was an imposition by the woman on the credulity of Saul, and they contend that there was no real appearance. Others say that the witch had power to raise the dead by Satanic agency. The orthodox view is that, by the command of God and not by the agency of the woman at all (but rather greatly to her dismay and discomfiture), Samuel really appeared. It is unthinkable that the spirit of the holy prophet could have been under the control of a wicked and presumptuous woman. God permitted Samuel, described as having the appearance of an old man covered with a mantle, to be seen by the woman (28:14).

The argument may be raised, how could a spirit bear the semblance of an old man and be clothed with a material robe? Bishop Wordsworth's comment is, "God designed that the spirit of Samuel should be recognized by human eyes, and how could this have been done but by means of such objects as are visible to human sense? Our Lord speaks of the *tongue* of the disembodied spirit of the rich man in Luke 16 in order to give us an idea of his sufferings; and at the Transfiguration He presented the form of Moses in such a garb to the three disciples as might enable them to recognize him as Moses."

Saul never saw Samuel, but recognized him from the description the witch gave and also by his voice. To quote Wordsworth again, "Samuel saw through Saul's disguise, which had deceived her whom Saul came to consult, as he spoke to Saul as Saul. So Abijah the prophet, though blind by age, saw through the disguise of the wife of Jeroboam" (I Kings 14:2, 6). Josephus suggests that Samuel most likely revealed the presence of Saul to the witch. Some word spoken by Samuel may have betrayed the king's identity to the woman. Her instant recognition of Samuel proves that the witch was not in a state of clairvoyance practicing mere juggery.

As Samuel appeared, Saul entered into conversation with him. This was no ventriloquist trick, when a thin, weak voice was made to appear as if a spirit was speaking through it (Isaiah 8:19; 29:4). In grave and measured tones, Samuel repeated the sentence of death against Saul for his disobedience of God's will and word and pronounced his death, that of his sons, and that of the suffering awaiting Israel because of its sin. When Saul heard of his fate he was sore distressed. But as W. M. Taylor says, "Although there was the wild wail of dark misery, the deep pathos and a wierd awesomeness in such a despairing cry," there was no confession of sin, no beseeching of mercy—nothing but the overmastering ambition to preserve himself.

The next day the Philistines beheaded Saul and his sons and exposed their headless bodies on the walls of Beth-shan. The army of Israel was utterly defeated and its camp ransacked, which terribly augmented the horrors and disasters of the rout of Saul's army.

How tragic it is when God departs from a man and becomes his enemy! Saul, knowing of the divine desertion, should have been more afraid to increase God's displeasure by breaking His law in connection with the consultation of the dead, as if they were less under His control than the living. But "abject superstition never reasons."

12. The Miracles in David's Career

(II Samuel 22; Psalm 78:70-72; 72:18, 19)

Tempted as we are to present a biographical study of "the most gifted and versatile personage in Israelitish history," we must again refer the reader to our presentation of David in *All the Men of the Bible*. This prodigal of the Old Testament, while a sinner like other men, is conspicuous as a shepherd, musician, poet, soldier, and king. The youngest of Jesse's eight sons, David was bright-eyed, ruddy, courageous, swift of foot, and contemplative (I Samuel 16:12, 18; 17:42). As a shepherd boy, he was acquainted with the solitude of nature and knew what it was to make his home in the gloomy caverns and desert wilds. Such pastoral country kindled within David's heart a love for God's created world which is reflected in many of his psalms (Psalm 19:1-6; 23, etc.)

God gifted David as a musician, and he became "The Hebrew Orpheus in whose music birds and mountains joined." When called and anointed to succeed Saul as king, his greatest gift was that of the Spirit (I Samuel 16:13), who inspired David to write his psalms (II Samuel 23:1-3) and who empowered him to accomplish great victories. His spiritual endowments corresponded to the high place and call David received when between 16 and 17 years of age. He was the king of God's providing, whose sovereignty is seen both in the rejection of Saul and in the choice of David. It was because of *this choice* that David became "the man after God's own heart," not his personal character and conduct. As the psalmist, he refers to this choice in Psalm 78:70-72. David never forgot his exaltation from a humble station to kingship (Psalm 89:19).

The miracle of the lion and the bear (I Samuel 17:34-37)

Always a child of nature, David was awed by the reflection of God's power in His universe. Tending his father's sheep, he had long hours of solitude and used them to think God's thoughts after him, as many of his noble psalms reflect (e.g., Psalm 8). David felt he was never away from God's all-seeing eye (Psalm 139). He was full of the spirit of faith in God and could thus say, "I am a wonder *sign*, or *miracle*) to many" (Psalm 71:7). God gave him victory whithersoever he went (I Samuel 18:7, 14).

Defending his ability and courage to go out alone against the challenging and taunting Goliath, David said to King Saul:

Thy servant *kept* [Saul *lost* his father's asses] his father's sheep and there came a lion, and a bear, and took a lamb out of the flock: and I went out after him, and smote him, and delivered it out of his mouth: and when he arose against me, I caught him by his beard, and smote him, and slew him. Thy servant slew both the lion and the bear: and this uncircumcised Philistine shall be as one of them, seeing he hath defied the armies of the living God.

Here in this colloquy between king and shepherd lad, we are not told exactly how David slew both the lion and the bear. The narrative implies that it was by his bare, strong hands that he slew these attacking beasts. Thrilled as he must have been by the record of Samson's rendering of the lion, David, in the moment of crisis, knew that the same God would endow him with all necessary nerve and strength for such an exploit. The future king was under God's eye, and he was thus able to testify of God's power and providence. If lions and bears held no fear for him, why should he be afraid of an idolater like Goliath? *Another* had helped David when he did his brave duty preserving his father's sheep and he knew that the same invincible Guardian would give him courage and power in a more dangerous encounter.

The miracle of Goliath's defeat (I Samuel 17)

There is no need to elaborate upon the account of David's brave encounter with the giant Goliath, a story that thrilled our young hearts whenever it was told—and still does! Goliath of Gath, perhaps a descendant of those giants "the sons of Anak," which the spies reported of to Moses (Numbers 13:32, 33), was the champion of the Philistine army which Saul encountered at Ephes-Dammim. The Israelites set the battle in array against the Philistines in the valley of Elah, but when Saul and his men saw the mighty giant, some 9½ feet high, they were dismayed and greatly afraid as they heard his challenge and defiance.

At this moment, when all Israel was stricken with fear at the strength of the foe, David, the agile youth, visits the camp. Looked upon as too young to go to battle, he was sent with provisions from home and to find out whether all his brothers were alive and well. Arriving at the camp, David heard Goliath's defiant challenge repeated on the fortieth day of the conflict and for the fortieth time. In spite of the uncharitable accusation of one of his brothers and the scorn heaped upon him by Goliath, David, recounting God's supernatural help in times past, courageously challenged the giant to combat.

After trying, then declining, Saul's armor, David took his sling and five smooth stones and, in spite of the contempt hurled at him by Goliath, confessed his trust in God and boasted in Him and went forth with the assurance of a God-given victory. David, with a zeal for the name and honor of God, knew that the battle would be His, and that all assembled would come to know that He saved not with sword and spear. There was no faltering in David's

step; his heart was strong with a heroic confidence born of his faith in God's almightiness.

In a moment, the miracle happened. With one small stone, the imposing giant was felled. David used Goliath's own sword to cut off his head and returned to Israel's camp with such a grim trophy of a divine victory. We know that as a shepherd boy, David had spent long hours of his pastoral care, practicing slinging until he acquired marvelous accuracy of aim. But was there not something more, nay, SOMEONE, behind that single, smooth stone? It was faith in the power and faithfulness of God, rather than in the skill and prowess of his own arm, that enabled David to put the embattled host of the Philistines to rout. The giant adversary fell under the God-empowered shepherd of Bethlehem and as a result of the God-directed stone.

Goliath, being almost twice David's height, was away up beyond the level of David's vision, but such a disparity made no difference to the shepherd lad who with deadly accuracy had brought down many a bird on the wing. But have you ever asked yourself this question: if David was so confident that God was to use him for the death of Goliath, and that one stone would be sufficient to kill him, why did he take *five* stones from the brook? Apart from all fanciful interpretations of the five stones, Scripture itself supplies the answer. Goliath the giant had four giant sons (II Samuel 21:15-22); so David, in faith, only took *five* stones from the brook, as if to suggest, "If, after I fell Goliath with the first stone, his four massive sons step into the breach, I'll fell them one by one with the remaining four stones." But only one stone with God behind it was necessary for victory over the Philistines that day.

As many of the experiences and exploits of David are reflected in his magnificent psalms, Psalm 144 celebrates his conquest of Goliath. In this great psalm, he gives God all the glory for teaching his fingers to fight. It was God who delivered His young servant from the imposing, hurtful sword of Goliath. Psalm 45:6-8 can also relate to the never-to-be-forgotten victory God gave to David, to whom many honors came because of his intense faith in the all-powerful, invisible King. Alas, however, such a glorious victory only fostered Saul's jealousy toward David, even though he became his son-in-law!

The miracle of the new cart (II Samuel 6)

David himself is the hero of this Second Book of Samuel. Both Samuel and Saul had passed on, and David is on Israel's throne from which he reigned and ruled for forty years. He was a just ruler, executing justice and righteousness unto all his people (II Samuel 8:15). Having a profound reverence for the ark, the visible symbol of God's presence and of His covenant with His people, David endeavored to restore it to its rightful place in the sanctuary.

The ark, however, was desecrated when placed upon a "new cart"—an imitation of the Philistines who were ignorant of God's law (I Samuel 6:19). God had declared that the Levites should carry the ark on their *shoulders* (Numbers 4:15; 7:9; 10:21). By placing the ark on a "new cart," the people were guilty of a distinct act of rebellion against the divine commandment. As the oxen drew the cart along, they fell. Uzzah put out his hand to prevent the ark from falling off the cart and was smitten by God with sudden death. Jewish tradition has it that Uzzah's arm was torn from his shoulder because of his error of rashness. "The Lord killeth and maketh alive" (I Samuel 2:6). Life and death are in His hands, and often sudden death is a token of divine judgment. David was troubled and afraid because of God's action, and he took the ark into the house of Obed-edom, who got the blessing David might have had. When the ark brought such sore punishment, everyone wanted to be rid of it. Obed-edom's entertainment of it was rewarded by God.

There is a wrong way of doing a right thing, and when men wilfully trifle with holy things, judgment falls (Leviticus 10:12; I Samuel 6:19; 13:12-14; II Chronicles 26:19). Anything introduced into the worship of God contrary to his requirements is deserving of His judgments. Three months later, David renewed his purpose and brought the ark—this time upon men's shoulders—with pomp, joy, music and dancing into the new tent which David had prepared for it (II Samuel 6:15; II Chronicles 1:3, 4). This greatest day in the king's history marked a turning-point in Israel's history. The only incident marring the glory of the hour was the taunt of David's wife, Michal. As the result of her utter lack of sympathy over David's joy,

Michal and he parted forever (II Samuel 6). The event of bringing the ark to Jerusalem is celebrated by David in Psalm 24.

The miracle of famine and pestilence (II Samuel 21:1-6; 24:15-17)

After David had come to know about Mephibosheth and had made gracious provision for Saul's lame son, a severe famine overtook the land. It continued for three years and was alarming enough to lead David to ask God for the cause of such a disastrous famine. As the man after God's own heart, he turned to the true Source for an explanation of such an unusual affliction. The answer was immediately forthcoming, "For the blood-guilty house of Saul." "Saul's sin consisted in the violation of the solemn oath, in the Lord's name, by which the nation of Israel was bound to the Gibeonites." He who giveth us our food in due season is able to withhold it as a token of His judgment upon sin and sinners.

Another calamity overtaking David in his more mature years, one that befell him at the zenith of his power, was the dread pestilence because of his sin of numbering the people (II Samuel 24:1). "Go number Israel and Judah," David commanded Joab. Behind the request for the census was a carnal, self-reliant spirit because of the plenitude of the resource of a self-ordered government. David was now at the head of one of the most conspicuous world powers of that time. He had an army of 28,000 soldiers and a personal bodyguard of 600 hired mercenaries. David had also instituted courts of justice and developed commerce and agriculture (I Chronicles 27:25). David, however, persisted in his census not with a view of levying taxes, but in order to ascertain the number of fighting men he actually had. It was a temptation to depend upon the arm of flesh, rather than upon God as he did when with a small stone he slew Goliath. Prosperity and power affected David's humble dependence upon God.

The royal conscription David ordered was not only displeasing to God, but unpopular with some of the people (24:3). Evidently there were those in sympathy with the king's edict, for "the anger of the Lord was kindled, not only against David, but 'against Israel'" (24:1). In one passage we read that the Lord moved David to take the step in question, and in another (I Chronicles 21:1) such a step is ascribed to Satan. Fairbairn's explanation of this apparent contradiction is most satisfactory:

> The purpose, in its sinful character and tendency, was really of Satan, since God tempted no man to evil; but Satan could only act a subordinate and instrumental part; and that the evil took this precise form rather than any other, was not of Satan, but of God; the ends of the divine government required that it should take this particular direction. So that the action might indifferently be ascribed to Satan or to God, according to the point of view from which it was contemplated.

As soon as Joab, who tried to divert David from his purpose, had rendered the sum of the people, the king's heart became repentant. But conviction of sin and repentance did not cancel deserved judgment. The prophet Gad brought to David from God the choice of three fearful calamities—seven years' famine, three months' pursuit before enemies, or three days' pestilence in the land. All three were realms in which God was able to manifest His supernatural power. Any of these chastisements was sufficient to lay in dust confidence in fancied greatness and to produce the feeling of feebleness and danger.

David intreated to be left in the Lord's hands, rather than be allowed to fall into the hands of men. God permitted a grievous pestilence to overtake the people, and no fewer than 70,000 perished. As the fatal plague spread, David besought the Lord to take his life, so that others less guilty might be spared. His shepherd-heart was moved as David prayed, "These *sheep*, what have they done?" God heard the cry of the repentant soul, and at the threshing floor of Araunah the Jebusite, the Angel of Death was arrested in his course. As a memorial of the transaction, David reared an altar and offered burnt sacrifices to the Lord which were consumed in a supernatural way—by fire from heaven (I Chronicles 21:26). David then bought the ground for the site of the future temple (I Chronicles 22:1; II Chronicles 3:1), for there the Lord not only pardoned the transgressors, but gave the more peculiar token of His presence to accept the worship of His people.

David's life was lived in the realm of the miraculous. "He sent from above, He took me; He drew me out of many waters" (II Samuel 22:17). Nine different attempts were made on his life, but divine presence and preservation overshadowed him during the years of his wanderings as a fugitive. Bitter experiences were his, but they gave birth to some of the finest of his lyrics. Persecutions resulted in psalms. "It was the cross which first brought David's poetical gift into full development." Viewing his life, he could write, "Blessed be the Lord God, the God of Israel, who only doeth wondrous things" (Psalm 72:18). By God's power, David conquered all his visible enemies and founded a dynasty. Alas, however, he failed to conquer himself and committed the double crime of adultery and murder, greatly blemishing thereby an otherwise noble and successive career! Yet the miracle of grace prevailed on his behalf, as the penitential psalms, 32 and 51, reveal.

13. The Miracles in Solomon's Reign

(I Kings 3:1-15; 4:29, 30; Matthew 6:29)

The history making up the two books of Kings is actually one book. The artificial division of the continuous history of Israel has no existence in the old Hebrew canon, but was borrowed from the LXX Version and possibly conceived merely for convenience of use or reference. Both books have a perfect unity of idea and authorship. The whole style and narrative of these two books is of an official and analytical character; dates and epochs are marked and authorities are quoted. The period covered by these two books is some 430 years of Israelite history.

The writer of I and II Kings emphasizes the idea of divine government over the people of covenant and traces their sins and their repentance—God's punishments and His forgiveness. He sets forth for believers in all ages the spiritual lessons taught by the "voice of God in history." It is not within the province of our present study to dwell upon the reigns of all the kings or of the relations of Israel as a nation to surrounding empires. Such a fascinating theme has been fully covered in the writer's *All the Kings and Queens of the Bible*.

As we approach the subject of the miraculous in Solomon's life, we have as the background of such a theme the effort of Adonijah to usurp the kingdom; the renewal of the oath David made to Bathsheba that Solomon, their son, would be David's successor; Solomon's anointing by Zadok the priest; the death of David; and the accession of Solomon, whose reign was to be one of colossal greatness.

In spite of all his glory and magnificence as the third and last king over the United Kingdom, Solomon never performed a miracle. He was the recipient of the supernatural but never a channel of it. At Gibeon the Lord appeared to Solomon in a dream by night (3:5, 15) and he received a direct communication from the Lord which was in striking contrast with the indirect knowledge of God's will to David through the prophets, Nathan and Gad (II Samuel 7: 2-17; 12:1-14; 24:11-14). The revelation of God's purpose through dreams is of a lower type than the waking vision. God said to Solomon, "Ask what I shall give thee?" To how many of us could God safely put such a question? (See John 15:7; I John 3:21, 22).

All Solomon asked for, in a prayer of singular beauty and humility, was wisdom from above—wisdom to follow God and wisdom to discern and do true justice between man and man. Such wisdom is supernatural and not acquired as the result of human teaching and experience. It was not a touch of genius, but a direct gift from God, with whom is all wisdom (3:28; James 1:5). God promised to add secondary blessings, which He did, and Solomon became the wisest of the sons of men of his or any succeeding day, and also the wealthiest and highest of all the monarchs of his time (I Kings 3:12, 13).

When God bestows such a supernatural gift upon a man, He tests him publicly, and thus, beside trying the man, manifests to all the man of His choice. Proof of Solomon's gift of unusual wisdom from God quickly came (3:16-28; 4:29-34; 10:3; II Kings 2:15). It must not be forgotten that God's continued bounty was conditioned by the recipient's obedience (3:14). One may ask why God established Solomon and endowed him with such remarkable wisdom and glory. The answer is to be found in the words, "That Thy way may be known upon *earth*, and *Thy* salvation *among all nations*" (Psalm 67).

The second supernatural appearance was also at Gibeon at the dedication of the magnificent Temple Solomon had built. "The glory of the Lord had filled the house of the Lord" (8:10, 11; 9:2). The bright Shekinah of the divine presence, at once cloud and fire, hallowed the consecration of the sanctuary and became a sign of its divine acceptance (see II Chronicles 5:11-14). So awe-inspiring was the glorious cloud of mystery that the priests could not stand to minister. They shrank from such glory of the Lord, whom none could see and live (Exodus 40:35; Isaiah 6:5).

When Solomon made an end of praying, fire came down from heaven and consumed the sacrifices—a manifestation distinct altogether from the appearance of the divine glory (II Chronicles 7:1). Was not this miraculous display of divine acceptance a preview to Israel of the glory yet to come in the Millennium, when One greater than Solomon will take the kingdom and reign in infinite might and wisdom and glory? The remarkable address Solomon gave at the Temple's dedication and the simple, sincere prayer he offered on bended knees and hands uplifted to heaven for a benediction upon the people (8:1-60), are evidences of the heavenly wisdom so abundantly bestowed upon the king, whose 40 years' reign ended in unrestrained polygamy and flagrant irreligion. No wonder Jesus, perhaps with a little cynicism, said that a common lily of the field had more unstained glory than Solomon's ever did.

14. The Miracles of Judgment Upon Jeroboam

(I Kings 13:1-7, 23-32; 14:1-6; II Chronicles 13:20)

The rupture of the United Kingdom of Israel goes back to Solomon's adultery and idolatry (I Kings 11). Toward the end of Solomon's reign, Ahijah, the prophet of Shiloh, met Jeroboam, the rebel, and intimated to him that God was about to rend the kingdom and that he should have *ten* tribes. Ahijah vividly symbolized the division by tearing the new four cornered garment into *twelve* pieces and giving Jeroboam *ten* of them.

What a great opportunity Jeroboam had of becoming a God-honored king! He was told that if he hearkened unto God and obeyed His statutes that God would be with him and build him a sure house as He did for David and would give him Israel (11:38). What more could a man desire than that! Yet his apostasy was wilful, designed, and persistent. He abandoned all prospects of a glorious heritage by his sinning and by causing Israel to sin. Twenty-five times his name carries the dreadful brand, *who made Israel to sin*. Jeroboam is conspicuous as a noted idolater and as one who gave his character to the after history of the kingdom.

Jeroboam violated God's commandment which had appointed to the Twelve Tribes *one temple, one priesthood,* and *one altar* at Jerusalem (Deuteronomy 12:5). He instituted:

New centers of worship in Bethel and Dan (12:29)

New altar of sacrifice (12:25)

New objects of worship, the golden calves (12:28)

New order of priesthood, non-Levitical (12:31)

New annual feast (12:32, 33)

Such deliberate disobedience was deserving of punishment and it came in a miraculous way. "God's fiats are irrevocable because with Him there is no changeableness, neither shadow of turning." Jeroboam stood at the altar to burn incense, but a prophet out of Judah pronounced two miraculous judgments. There was the supernatural prediction about the shattering of the false altar fulfilled by Josiah (II Kings 23:17, 20). Such a prediction angered Jeroboam and, putting out his hand to hold the altar in defiance of the prophet, he found it suddenly paralyzed.

The withered hand

This supernatural visitation should have warned Jeroboam of the failure of his strength and policy when opposed to the law and the judgment of God. By that blasted hand, God sought to bring Jeroboam back from his evil ways (13:33) and presumptuous sins. Jeroboam's arm was so dried up that he could not pull it back again. This sudden affliction proves that the God who made the body can suspend the use of any of its members when He deems fit. Jeroboam failed to worship God in His prescribed way and so was stricken with sudden paralysis. How we should bless Him that we live in an age of grace, and that He does not deal with us in supernatural judgment when we add our own inventions to His worship!

But the God who caused the arm to wither was able to restore it to its usual form and strength. In answer to the prophet's intercession, the king's arm was restored to what it was before—which sign of divine grace should have led to repentance (13:1-4). Alas, however, Jeroboam still persisted in his sinful ways, even with the manifest seal of heaven's displeasure upon them and the earnest protest of the more godly of his people!

The devouring lion (13:11-32)

Ada R. Habershon says that, "It is most instructive to link together all those miraculous instances of God's control over the king of beasts." They are never permitted to destroy God's faithful and obedient servants. But they are used as instruments of judgment upon the disobedient as we are now to see. When God calls the lions, they always obey. The prophet who foretold the destruction of the false altar was divinely charged that he should eat no bread, nor drink any water, nor retrace his step until the prophecy was fulfilled.

Refusing the king's invitation to return with him to the palace, the prophet succumbed to the old prophet of Bethel who, by means of a lie, caused him to disobey. The old prophet who, like Balaam, was guilty of base subterfuge and deceit, said that "an angel" had spoken unto him, which was a gross lie, for the advice he gave was contrary to God's command. The prophet accepted the hospitality of the worldly prophet but, leaving the house, was overcome and devoured by a lion. The double miracle here is that the man was eaten by a lion but that his ass was untouched— an evidence of God's control over the beasts of the earth. Even with this display of miraculous power, Jeroboam continued in his evil ways (13:33, 34). Such a strange, supernatural circumstance failed to wean him from the heinousness of his sin.

Ahijah's revelation (14:1-18)

Another evidence of the supernatural is seen in the revelation of the identity of Jeroboam's wife which God gave to Ahijah. The king tried to deceive the prophet by a cowardly ruse. His son Abijah fell sick, and Jeroboam told his wife to disguise herself and seek from the blind prophet information of the child's welfare. Doubtless, because of his dimness of vision, Ahijah would have been deceived, but the Lord revealed to His honored servant the trick of Jeroboam so that when the prophet heard the sound of the woman's feet he said, "Come in, thou wife of Jeroboam." What a shock that must have been!

The distressed mother heard of the fate of her son and took back to Jeroboam the announcement of the doom that his house would be cast off forever like dung and would not be buried. But such a stern message of woe had little effect upon the high-minded rebel. He had passed the line of repentance. As soon as his wife returned and crossed the threshold of their home, the God who has the prerogative of life and death withdrew the breath of their child before he was polluted by his father's sin.

Stricken with sudden death (II Chronicles 13:20).

Heavy disasters and ominous defeats befell Jeroboam during his lifetime. The Lord was against him (14:1-18; II Chronicles 13:1, 2), and his death was likewise a divine judicial visitation. He was stricken with a languishing disease from which he could not recover. The circumstances of his sudden death were such that men recognized in them "the finger of God" (I Samuel 25:38). After a reign of 22 years, the only commemoration the Bible gives him is "Jeroboam the son of Nebat, who made Israel to sin." This eternal brand indicated that in rejecting God's will, he was no longer king by the will of God, but a rebellious usurper. "The name of the wicked shall rot" (Proverbs 10:7). Thus his prophesied, terrible end was deserved. Jeroboam is a striking illustration of the solemn truth that:

The moving Finger writes, and having writ,
Moves on; nor all thy piety nor wit
Shall lure it back to cancel half a line,
Nor all thy tears wash out a word of it.

15. The Miracles of Elijah

(I Kings 17 - 19; Romans 11:1 - 5; James 5:17, 18)

See also I Kings 21:17-29; II Kings 1 - 2:14; 9:36; 10:16, 17; II Chronicles 21: 12-15; Malachi 4:5; Matthew 11:14; 16:14; 17:3-12; Mark 6:15; 9:4-13; Luke 1:17; 4:25, 26; 9:8, 19, 28-31; John 1:21, 25)

While miracles, declarations of supernatural power, revelations, and prophecies are scattered over almost all the pages of the Bible, we again draw attention to the fact that the majority of miracles are found in groups. As we have already seen, there are those related to Moses and Joshua when the Israelites were becoming a nation;

those connected with Elijah and Elisha as a protest against prevailing idolatry; those of Christ and His apostles associated with the consummation of the law and the commencement of the Gospel; those related to the last days as described in the book of Revelation. All of these miracles, particularly prominent in times of historical crisis, reveal a moral and spiritual end, namely, to manifest the sovereignty and power of God.

In approaching a study of the miracles of the two greatest of the non-literary prophets, we consider what Dr. Graham Scroggie says of them: "Their chief value is not in any lessons which any of them may be said to teach, but in the witness of them to the activity and action of Jehovah, alike in judgment and in mercy, among and on behalf of His people." Attention is drawn to the number of miracles each of the prophets performed. Dr. Scroggie gives Elijah eleven and Elisha eleven, with three of Elijah's as judgment-miracles and the others as mercy-miracles. On the other hand, Bullinger interprets Elisha's request for a double portion of Elijah's spirit (II Kings 2:9, 15) in the fact that Elijah wrought eight miracles and Elisha sixteen, all of which were parables in action. Closely following the narrative, we have endeavored to indicate the full total of the miraculous in the respective ministries of Elijah and Elisha.

As to comparisons and contrasts between these two great prophets, much need not be said at this point, since we have already dealt with this most interesting matter in *All the Men of the Bible*. Suffice it to say that both Elijah and Elisha stood alone in the kingdom of Israel. They were alike in the general nature and aspect of their work, though each had his own characteristic peculiarities, and each was suited to his proper time and sphere—so that here also wisdom was justified of her children. The contrast between the spirit of master and disciple should not be over-emphasized though, for Elisha could be as stern as Elijah (II Kings 2:23; 5:27). Perhaps the severer side of Elisha's character appears in his fuller, rather than in his private, life. Generally speaking, the ministry of Elijah typifies that of John the Baptist, while Elijah's miracles of mercy prefigure Christ's beneficent ministry.

Elijah, whose name occurs about 100 times in the Bible, is a rugged figure among the prophets who first steps across the threshold of history when Ahab was on the throne and is last seen in the reign of Ahaziah. His name, meaning "Jehovah is God," embodies his whole mission and message. The significance of his name was not only the motto of his life, but expresses the one grand object of his miraculous ministry, namely, to awaken Israel to the conviction that Jehovah *alone* is God. Old Testament prophets had two important duties to perform:

(1) To extirpate the worship of heathen gods in Israel;

(2) To raise the true religion of Jehovah to ethical purity. Elijah gave himself to the first task with great zeal. The second task was left to his successors.

The time had come then, in the history of God's chosen people when, as Professor Milligan expresses it, "either Israel must forever forfeit its place among the nations, and in the religious history of the world, or the Almighty must interpose and show Himself as He is, the only living and true God, the God of holiness and righteousness." That God chose to reveal Himself is evident from the mission of "Elijah the Tishbite," the ardent reformer, who suddenly appeared to combat the fierce spirit of Asiatic heathenism.

The Bible does not give us very much information as to his personal appearance. He is described as "an hairy man and girt with a girdle of leather about his loins" (II Kings 1:8). Tradition says he was a man of short stature and rugged countenance with the long flowing hair of a Nazarite. As a Gileadite, or *Highlander* of Palestine, the whole manner of Elijah speaks of the unconventional manners and the free life of a man brought up amid such surroundings. The sudden appearance of this man, with the impetuosity, the seasons of high daring and again those of depression, all so characteristic of a mountainous race, startled the court of Ahab who revelled in ease and luxury. With such a background and setting, we now come to examine Elijah's miracles in particular.

The miracle of the long drought (I Kings 17:1; James 5:17)

As the miraculous element is prominent in the life and labors of Elijah, we must accept his conception of God as the Almighty One, whose power is supreme in every realm. Drought was one of the recognized punishments for apostasy (Deuteronomy 11:16, 17). Declaring to Ahab that he had come to him in the name of Jehovah, the God of Israel, Elijah declared at once that God demanded the recognition of His true place in the life of the nation and would by no means give His place to another.

From New Testament references, we learn that the famine lasted three and one-half years—long enough to have brought terrible sufferings on the nation (Luke 4:25; James 5:17). Elijah himself was miraculously preserved during this long period, which was fixed, not by Elijah, but by Jehovah, and was ended by Him when the chastisement was deemed to be sufficient. "The shutting up of heaven at the prophet's word was Jehovah's vindication of His sole Godhead," says Fausset, "for Baal (though professedly *the god of the sky*) and his prophets could not open heaven and give showers (Jeremiah 14:22). The so-called god of nature shall be shown to have no power over nature: Jehovah is its sole Lord."

The assumed position of a Levitical priest (Deuteronomy 10:8) is worthy of note (17:1). "Jehovah God . . . before whom I stand." Whether Elijah had any Levitical connections or not, we are not told. What is inferred is that of the priestly position which the prophet deemed necessary to assume in the kingdom of Israel, on account of the dislocated, idolatrous state of the people. During the reign of Ahab, "there was neither king nor priest to do the part assigned them by the theocracy, thus the prophetic agency required to rise with the occasion, and, as under a special commission from God, had both to make known His will, and to do before Him priestly service."

The miracle of the ravens (17:2-7)

After uttering such a solemn judgment that the genial influences of rain and dew were to be withheld for years, it was necessary that a hiding place should be provided for Elijah so that he could escape the resentment of Ahab and the persecuting zeal of Jezebel. In quietness, Elijah was to learn the effect of his first public act and prepare himself for further exacting service. It was here at the brook *Cherith* that Elijah was to experience that God's care ever surrounds those who do His will. While at the brook, he was provided with a safe retreat and drinking water. But the prophet also needed food which God provided by means of the ravens, proving thereby that God cared for His servant when ordinary supplies failed.

The supplies of bread and flesh every morning and evening, ministered at God's command by ravens, have been questioned by those rationalistic minds who have no room for the miraculous in their thinking. There are critics who try to abandon a seemingly strange miracle for a gross improbability. The word for *ravens* might mean "Arabs" or merchants, or inhabitants of the city Orbi or the rock Oreb. But how could such regular sustenance in a time of intense drought by human hands be conveyed to the persecuted prophet in the face of the jealous vigilance of Ahab?

Is it not idle to try to explain away one miracle in a life and epoch teeming with miracles? The narrative plainly expresses a supernatural employment of the ravens for the purpose of sustaining Elijah. Although carnivorous birds themselves, ravens lose their ravenous nature when commanded to fulfill the will of their Creator, who is able to make the most unlikely instruments minister to His saints. Our Lord's reference to ravens is instructive (Luke 12:24). God "commanded the ravens to feed" Elijah (17:4), and all things are possible when He speaks. God's omnipotence is a most satisfying and easier explanation than all rationalistic or modernistic inventions. Elijah was miraculously fed on further occasions as we shall discover (17:9; 19: 5, 6). The ravens were commanded to feed Elijah *there*, right where he was by the brook. Anywhere but in God's appointed place he would have perished.

The miracle of the meal and oil (17: 8-16)

When the drought became more acute and the supply of water ceased, Elijah knew that his great God would preserve him, even though the brook dried up. Although safer with a poor widow in Zarephath, the most unlikely place to find a prophet since it was the native place of his deadliest enemy, Jezebel, Elijah was to learn there those lessons that would fit him for the tremendous task of defending Israel's religion against the assumptions of the crown. Experiencing fellowship with the race he had come to save in its suffering, the prophet was to become the chosen champion of the God of Israel against the formidable worship of Baal.

Elijah is commanded by God to go to Zarephath, and in confidence of faith he obeyed, assured that God's word would not fail. The prophet was constantly directed by God which, in itself, is another sign of the supernatural. As he approached the gates of the city, he met the widow to whom he had been sent (17:10; Luke 4:25, 26) and asked her to bring him water to drink. As the drought had not been so keenly felt near the mountain ranges of Lebanon, the widow was able and ready to provide Elijah with water. But as she turned to meet the prophet's request, he asked her for a morsel of bread which, because of the famine, was almost gone. She had just enough meal and olive oil for her last baking and thereafter expected death for herself and son. "The Lord God of gods, He knoweth" (Joshua 22:22), and because of His omniscience, He knew of the widow's extremity and heard the scraping of the bottom of the meal barrel.

Elijah assured the widow that her meal and oil would not fail until the famine ceased and commanded her to first feed him out of her scanty store. As God had met the prophet's need at Cherith, Elijah could comfort the widow with the word that God would provide for her needs and his. So the widow gave her all, as her New Testament counterpart (Luke 21:2), without asking where the next meal would come from, and found that in making God's will her *first* concern, He made her need *His* first concern. All necessary food was supplied until the Lord sent rain upon the earth. Blessed by believing, she strengthened Elijah's faith in God's ability to fulfil His word, when all seemed hopeless to human vision. Perhaps such a display of divine guardianship made the widow a true worshiper of Jehovah. Anyhow, we have here an illustration of the principle of God's daily care for His people as well as a miracle of His power.

As to the miracle itself, Ellicott suggests that it was doubly miraculous. In the first place, we see that God's higher laws of miracle, like the ordinary laws of His providence, admit within their scope the supply of homely and trivial needs. Then there is the miracle of multiplication. *Both* the meal and the oil were multiplied, doing rapidly and directly what, under ordinary laws, has to be done slowly and by indirect process.

All the time Elijah remained at Zarephath, his daily prayer of faith was answered by a daily miracle of God's providence in the unfailing supply of meal and oil. His trust in God was correspondingly strengthened and he himself prepared for stronger confidence in God's sovereignty and for the greater act of faith at Carmel.

The miracle of resurrection (17:17-24)

The widow's son, who shared in the daily miracle of food supply, fell sick unto death, and the grief-stricken mother turned upon the prophet with the appeal, "Thou art come unto me to bring my sin to remembrance and to slay my son." She recognized in Elijah a man of God—one having close intercourse with the God of righteousness and whose very presence made her conscious of her sinful condition. She felt that the death of her son was a divine judgment. Elijah, touched by the pained cry of the mother in her great grief, took the body of the dead boy up to his chamber and prayed that the child's soul come unto him again." In that upper room, believing prayer won its victory and had its reward, for the child revived. Like the Great Prophet of the New Testament, Elijah brought gladness to the heart of a bereaved mother by restoring her son to life (17: 23; Luke 7:11). Legend has it that the raised lad became a servant of Elijah and later on of the prophet Jonah. As for the glad mother herself, she now knew in a manner she had not known before that Elijah was the spokesman of God (17:24).

The miracle at Carmel (18:1-39)

After the years of the domestic and peaceful simplicity of his quiet refuge at Zarephath, Elijah is called to Carmel, there to experience the struggle and victory of a great warrior of God. What a great, dramatic chapter this is! Never did combatants seem more unequally matched. On the one side was Elijah, God's sole representative, in his startling costume and dignified mien, who ventured openly to espouse the cause of the God he trusted. On the other side, in the interests of the heathen god, Baal, were his 450 prophets and 400 prophets of Asherah—still fed by the royal bounty in spite of the grievous famine, eating at Jezebel's table under the queen's special patronage. Carmel represents a challenge of God's sovereignty as *God*. Suddenly crashing like a thunderbolt into the midst of Ahab's court, denouncing idolatry and predicting judgment,

then challenging Ahab to a contest on Carmel between God and Baal, Elijah provides us with one of the most spectacular records in the Bible—a record which found fitting modern expression in Mendelssohn's *Elijah*.

The place chosen to vindicate "the deity who was character against the deity who was not" was peculiarly suitable. "Throughout the Old Testament, Carmel appears either as a symbol or as a sanctuary." Elijah found it as the chief site of Baal worship, but it had been used for the worship of Jehovah, and it was the ruins of the old-time altar which Elijah restored. As the prophets of Baal gather at Carmel, Elijah calls for a decision in a somewhat impatient tone in which his patriotism, as well as his faith in God, blazed out against the people's madness. Ignoring Ahab, Elijah appealed directly to the people— "How long halt ye between two opinions? If the Lord be God, follow Him: but if Baal, then follow him."

Then came the decisive test, an appeal to God and to Baal to answer by fire. Baal's worshipers made the first appeal, offering their dressed sacrifice and crying, "O Baal, hear us." But there was no answer. Though Satan brought fire from heaven, it was only with God's permission (Job 1:16). Breathless expectation prevailed, not only among Baal's devotees but also among all Israel who were spectators of the contest. Elijah stood apart in scornful silence, but as the sun-god failed to manifest his power, the prophet mocked them. Then the people became frantic, leaping upon the altar and cutting themselves as they were taunted by Elijah's "savage humor" and "biting sarcasm."

By sunset, no answering fire had descended, and Baal was publicly defeated. Then the exhausted, blood-smeared prophets gave place to the lonely, confident prophet of God, who prepared to offer an evening sacrifice upon an altar of twelve stones, representing the twelve tribes of Israel. To make any vestige of fraud impossible, barrels were filled with water and it was poured upon the sacrifice three times. Then came Elijah's beautiful, quiet, solemn prayer, so opposite to the wild shrieks of Baal's prophets. The God who answered by fire was to be *the God*, and "the fire of the Lord fell," and the people fell on their faces and confessed that *Jehovah* was God. The humiliated priests hurried down the side of Carmel but swift and terrible judgment overtook them for all of them were slaughtered, for theirs had been high treason against God, the King of the national theocracy (Deuteronomy 13:9-11, 15; 18:20).

Elijah's action in commanding fire from heaven was not dictated by any revengeful feeling, but by a desire to convince a wicked king and an idolatrous people that the Lord was the true God, and that He alone ought to be worshiped and sought in time of trouble. In this day of grace, God does not send upon those who reject Him a judgment of fire. The zeal of John and James for fire from heaven was without knowledge, passionate and persecuting, though to them it seemed to spring from a just regard for their Lord (Luke 9:50).

The miracle of the rain (18:1, 2; 41-46)

The God who answered by fire now answers by rain, proving thereby His sovereignty in the realm of nature. The formation and function of rain is ascribed to God's power and direct control (Job 36: 27, 28 RV; Amos 4:7; 5:8; Jeremiah 14: 22). Because He it is who sends the rain, He is to be feared (Jeremiah 5:24). When there were disobedience and apostasy, rain was withheld (Deuteronomy 11:17), but on repentance and return to God, plenteous rain was given (Ezekiel 34:26, 27; Zechariah 10:1). The seriousness of the drought and its resulting famine is indicated by the search for green grass to keep the king's horses and mules alive (18:5, 6).

On his way from Zarephath to show himself to Ahab, Elijah received the divine announcement that the drought, which had lasted for "three years and six months," would end (Luke 4:25; James 5:17). "I will send rain upon the earth" (18:1). Therefore it was with great assurance that Elijah went on to meet Ahab, and after the crucial test and triumph at Carmel declared to the king that there was to be "a sound of abundance of rain" (18:41). As a rebuke to Ahab's shallow nature, Elijah scornfully told him to leave the place of carnage and return to his palace and eat and drink. Thus "the king goes to revel, the prophet to pray." The purpose of the drought was fulfilled, and the removal of the penalty was a sign of God's acceptance of the people's repentance and professed allegiance. Jehovah was once more publicly acknowledged as the one living and true God.

"The heavens heard the earth and forthwith began to temper their fiery glow." Elijah ascends Carmel to pray and to look for the refreshing shower (18:42). His posture is somewhat peculiar for he "put his face between his knees"—distinct from the accustomed attitudes of standing and kneeling. Confident of the returning rain, Elijah was caught up by the vehement excitement of what was to happen. The Bible makes it clear that the rain's withdrawal and then release years later were miracles related to prayer—God's reward for fervent prayers. What He had promised (18:1), Elijah must pray for. But let it not be forgotten that He who does great things in answer to prayer stoops to reveal His power in the small details of everyday life.

The seeming delay to Elijah's prayer, seen in his servant having to go seven times to scan the horizon for any sign of the promised rain, only added to the prophet's intensity and perseverance in supplication (James 5:7). Says Ellicott, "The contrast is remarkable between the immediate answer to his earlier prayer (18:36, 37), and the long delay here. The one was for the sake of the peole; the other for some lesson—perhaps of humility and patience—to Elijah himself. He had to learn how to wait, as well as pray." When the answer did come, it came speedily. The little cloud, no bigger than a man's hand, was soon a storm blackening the whole heavens, borne by a hurricane from the west. How true it is that "more things are wrought by prayer than this world dreams of."

The miracle of transportation (18:46)

One is somewhat intrigued by a miniature incidental miracle in the life of Elijah. The sudden appearance at critical moments and swift withdrawals, so characteristic of his ministry, add much to the romance of his story and to the fascination of his personality. Without doubt, the prophet's locomotion was of God. He is introduced to us with suddenness, and his appearances and disappearances seem abrupt, mirroring, perhaps, the somewhat abruptness of his character. "No attachments could localize Elijah," says Dr. Scroggie, "so we find him swiftly moving over great distances; suddenly appearing; suddenly disappearing."

Space was no hindrance to the prophet, or rather to the God he so faithfully served.

Omnipotence can instantaneously transfer things or persons from one place to another (John 6:21). It was thus that He carried both Elijah and Philip whither He would (18:12; Acts 8:39). It is believed that the Spirit carried Elijah away to some unknown region after he met Obadiah (18: 10, 12). "He came like a whirlwind, he burned like a fire, and in fire and whirlwind he disappeared." As soon as the rain came, Elijah was at the head of the people, bringing the king, conquered if not repentant, home in triumph. Ahab was in haste to reach his palace lest the torrential rain should make the Jezreel plain impassable with mud.

Elijah, with God-given alacrity and strength—a strength above nature ("the hand of the Lord" was upon him)—ran, like a courier, before Ahab's chariot amid torrents of rain, a distance of some fifteen miles. But he went no further than the city. He shrank from the contamination of the court and its luxuries. This noble-hearted prophet, rejoicing in his God-given triumphs, knew he would be safe and honored at Jezreel.

The miracle of the angelic meal (19:1-18)

Reaching his palace after the calamity at Carmel, King Ahab was not long in recounting to his unqueenly queen, Jezebel, the fate of her pampered priests. Enraged over the exposure of Baal's utter futility, she sent a messenger to Elijah, threatening to slay him on the morrow (19:2). Receiving such an ominous threat, the champion lost heart and his courage sank at the tidings. He sought safety in instant flight and never halted until he came into the southern wilderness. Under the scanty shade of a desert broom bush, he rested and prayed that he might share the common fate of mankind in death. A bad woman like Jezebel should not have made Elijah do a cowardly act. He could face 850 men (18: 19), but the threat of a godless woman caused him to flee (19:1-4).

The events at Carmel had been a great strain, mentally and physically, and the lion-hearted prophet gave way, quite naturally, to feelings of despair and despondency. Mighty forces had operated through his hand. Elijah had stood out alone against a deeply-rooted Baalism but the throne of iniquity seemed to be invincible and his struggle against idolatry a hopeless one. So he felt his task was lost as well as ended.

Now he wanted to be left to die the death of the righteous. Elijah virtually sighed and said:

So much I feel my genial spirits droop,
My hopes are flat, nature within me seems
In all her functions weary of herself.
My race of glory run, and race of shame,
And I shall shortly be with them at rest.

Elijah, however, was to realize that his work was by no means done, and so the miraculous prevailed on his behalf. Actually, we have a combination of beneficent miracles in the restoration of God's tired, discouraged servant, which suggest His care for his needs. First of all, God gave His beloved prophet sleep—and what a boon this gift is to careworn minds and bodies! How the shadows disappear with a good sleep! "Tired nature's kind restorer, balmy sleep."

Aroused by an angel, Elijah found a meal prepared for him. Sleep and food are two essentials. Fed by ravens at Cherith, he now finds himself with an angel as his host. Here we have "a miraculous ministration of some unearthly food." It must have been good, for after partaking of that angel-provided meal, Elijah forgot his distress in another sleep.

The second time, the angel aroused Elijah and bade him eat and drink against the journey ahead. The great God who provided for Samson's thirst again supplies Elijah with a meal so wonderfully nourishing that he existed on the strength of it for forty days (19:8). While in Horeb during this period, the prophet's spirit was divinely calmed and he was ready to receive the spiritual lessons awaiting him. No merely natural supply of food could have sustained the physical frame of Elijah for so long. Whatever natural food the angel may have used was supernaturally strengthened. As he lived "in the strength" of divinely provided food, he came to learn that "man does not live by bread alone, but by every word that proceedeth out of the mouth of God" (Deuteronomy 8:3). Total abstinence from both food and drink lead to death by starvation in eight days or more, depending on the original physical conditions of the individual. Habershon observes:

The fact that God could sustain Moses and Elijah for days without food does not lead us to expect that if we starve ourselves we shall be strong and healthy. His law is that life must be sustained by food, and this applies to the physical, mental, and spiritual parts of our being.

The miracle of divine manifestation (19: 9-18)

Borne to Horeb (Sinai), possibly by the Spirit of God, Elijah with undecayed freshness, holds a face-to-face communion with heaven. Taking up his abode in a cave, he was made the recipient of a supernatural manifestation. The word of the Lord rang out in the silence of the cave. "What doest thou here, Elijah?" (19:9). The severe and stormy mood of the prophet had passed away, and in a tender and more subdued frame of mind he told the Lord how zealous he had been for His interests and that he alone was left to raise a voice against the wide-spread idolatry of his time. Then the Lord told him to stand before Him on the mount as He passed by and demonstrated His power in mountain destroying winds, earthquake, and fire which were associated with two former manifestations at Horeb, to Moses and to Israel (Exodus 19:16-18; 34:5-8). These signs of visible, miraculous power formed the natural clothing for the terrors of the law, which is the will of God visibly enforced.

Elijah's temperament cried out for visible manifestations of divine power and vengeance, but in the "still small voice" he was taught the higher lesson of the subtler power of spiritual influence, penetrating to the inmost soul, the terrors of external power cannot reach. "Not by might, nor by power, but by my Spirit, saith the Lord of hosts" (Zechariah 4:6). The terrible manifestations of power, more terrifying than Elijah had yet known, with God unleashing the grand forces of nature, came before him in rapid succession, perhaps in the same cleft of the rock in which Moses hid as the Lord passed by. But after hearing "a sound of gentle stillness," over-awed by the divine presence, the prophet drew his rough mantle over his face, realizing that the God whose glory he had just witnessed was also a God full of compassion and waiting to be "gracious to a repentant Israel."

"Those astounding phenomena prepared the way for Jehovah to savingly reveal Himself," says Fausset. "This is God's immediate revelation to the heart. Miracles sound the great bell of nature to call attention; but the Spirit is God's voice to the soul. Sternness hardens; love alone melts."

After such a supernatural revelation, Elijah received a new commission and returned to the work of reformation not yet complete, in which Hazeel, Jehu, and Elisha were to share. Elijah was also given to understand that he had not been alone in his stand against idolatry. There were 7,000 who had not bowed the knee to Baal nor kissed his image. If this great number had been less secret in their witness and identified themselves with Elijah when he stood alone at Carmel, the prophet might not have been so despondent over Jezebel's threat of death.

The miracle of fire from heaven (II Kings 1:9-15)

Before we meet Elijah again, brief mention can be made of touches of the supernatural in the continued history of Israel. In the battle between Ahab and Ben-hadad, an unknown prophet came to Ahab with the divine announcement that drunken Benhadad would be divinely defeated (I Kings 20:13). The king of Syria, thinking that God was only the God of the hills, came to experience that He was also the God of the valleys (I Kings 20:28).

Then there was the prophecy, supernaturally imparted, by one of the sons of those prophets who looked up to Elijah with awe and some terror, and to Elisha with affection and respect, about the disobedient being slain by a lion (I Kings 20: 35, 36). Elijah now appears in the vineyard of Naboth where he had been sent by God. After a period of silence, he emerges to the higher moral duty of rebuke and crime and avenging innocent blood. Ahab, denounced by Elijah for his foul crime, humbled himself but yet heard his doom and that of his evil wife (21:17, 29; 22:37, 38; II Kings 9:8, 36).

We then have the prophet Micaiah's imprisonment for his courage to witness as God's spokesman against Ahab, who disguised himself as he went out to battle— as if any disguise could deceive God and deter judgment overtaking him. A young man, whom Josephus identifies as *Naaman* drew a bow at a venture and smote Ahab in an unprotected part of his body. Who but God could have been behind the bow, directing its arrow to that vital spot resulting in Ahab's predicted death?

After the death of Ahab, Elijah was commanded by the angel of the Lord to meet the messengers of the new king of Samaria and pronounced his fate for neglecting God and consulting Baalzebub (II Kings 1:1-8). Ahaziah asked for Elijah's description and was told that he was "an hairy man and girt with a girdle of leather about his loins." *Hairy* may refer to a hairy mantle, sign of the prophetic office, or to the uncut hair, symbol of the Nazarite vow. The leather girdle, such as only the poorest would wear, spoke of Elijah's contempt for earthly display, and of sorrow for national sins and their consequences.

When Ahaziah met Elijah, he called upon him as a man of God to come down from the hill and meet him. Perhaps the king felt his power to be irresistible, even in the presence of a man of God. Thus, "the true God was insulted in the person of His prophet." Elijah's proof that he was God's man was his power to call fire down from heaven to consume Ahaziah's 50 soldiers. By this manifest miracle, God vindicated His own cause and also the claims of His servant. Another 50 soldiers came to present the king's command for Elijah to come down quickly, and again fire from heaven, called this time "the fire of God" (1:12), consumed the 50 men, thereby emphasizing that authority to command properly belonged to the prophet, and that God was ever at hand to protect His prophets. On the third appeal Elijah descended the hill and came to the king.

To our Christian way of thinking, the judgment-miracles, like the above burning to death of one hundred men, appear to be harsh and intemperate and out of all proportion to the sin they were guilty of. Was Elijah "the merciless wielder of the power committed to him?" It must not be forgotten that it was God who sanctioned the procedure of Elijah by sending fire from heaven; therefore, it is useless to charge the prophet with unfeeling severity, since he was only the agent of divine judgment. In his volume on *Elijah and Elisha*, R. S. Macintyre says, "We may be assured that the swift and terrible judgment upon the two companies of soldiers roused very different feelings in Israel from what a similar occurrence would awaken in our own time, and that the effect of it would be on the side of righteousness, by the quickening of the moral feelings of the people. In the fact that the fate of the soldiers was bound up with that of their leaders, we have an instance of that solemn law of corporate responsibility which is seen at work in so many cases both in Scripture and life"

(Genesis 19:24, 25; Joshua 6:21-25; 7:24; I Samuel 15:3).

After the most extraordinary visitations of divine power and threatenings of coming judgments still more appalling, the Israelite court continued wedded as much as ever to its idolatry, practically defying God to His face. How merciful, patient, and forbearing He had been with His people! Severity of judgment by fire, then, was due to the greatness of the guilt of Israel's king and of his subjects who strove against God in the person of His prophet. Hardening themselves in their idolatary made them guilty of high treason against God, a sin which incurred the penalty of death under the theocracy. Viewing the judgment-miracles as a whole, what else can we say but, "Shall not the Judge of all the earth do right?"

The miracle at Jordan (2:1-8)

The selfless, dynamic ministry of Elijah attracted the youth of his time, begetting within many of them boldness in witness (I Kings 20:35, 36; Micaiah, in chapter 22). Many of these young men were formed into "the school of the prophets" or "sons of strength," as 50 of them are expressly called. The headquarters of such prophetic teaching was at Bethel, one of the two centers of idolatry (II Kings 2:3, 16). Elijah, the acknowledged head of the prophetic schools, received divine intimation of his approaching end and under divine guidance, visited Gilgal, Bethel, Jericho, and Jordan successively. Doubtless the renowned prophet gave parting counsels to the prophetic students in these places, who also had received the divine announcement of their leader's immediate translation.

References to Elisha at this juncture are somewhat impressive. With Elijah, he started out from Gilgal and they went both together to Bethel, Jericho, and Jordan. Elijah urged Elisha to tarry behind, but three times over Elisha replied, "As the Lord liveth, and as thy soul liveth, I will not leave thee" (2:2, 4, 6). Elijah desired to meet his end alone, but Elisha bound himself by an oath not to leave his master.

How good of God it was to give Elisha to Elijah as an intimate companion in the closing period of his work. His life and lot had been a very lonely one and he needed companionship; so God gave him Elisha, just as He gave young Timothy to the aged Paul. Elisha, ever submissive to Elijah his master, became his counterpart and successor and made up to him what was lacking in his rugged character.

When they reached Jordan, Elijah, in the sight of fifty of the sons of the prophets and also of Elisha, took his hairy mantle and smote the waters, a symbolic action like that of Moses stretching out his rod over the sea. Such an action was the outward and visible sign of the invisible and spiritual force of faith. The waters, originally created by God, obeyed their Creator and parted, and Elijah and Elisha passed over toward the wilderness on the east. As we shall presently see, this same miracle was repeated by Elisha as a sign of heaven's authentication as Elijah's successor. As the last miracle performed by Elijah, it was a manifest token to the sons of the prophets witnessing it that their revered leader was indeed a true prophet of God.

The miracle of translation (2:9-11)

Once over Jordan, Elijah was desirous of bestowing a departing, spiritual benediction upon his spiritual son (Genesis 27:4). "Ask what I shall do for thee, before I be taken up from thee." All Elisha asked for was a double portion of Elijah's spirit, which was a hard thing to request, since the granting of such a petition was not in Elijah's own power, but in God's only. He replied that if he was a witness to Elijah's translation, then Elisha would be blessed with the boon he asked for.

By the "double portion" we are not to understand a gift of the miraculous or a gift of the spirit of prophecy twice as large as Elijah himself possessed. No superlative endowment is meant. The expression "double portion" is used in connection with the firstborn son, who by the law inherited two parts of his father's property (Deuteronomy 21:7). Elisha asked, then, to be treated as the first born among "the sons of the prophets," and so to receive twice as great a share of "the spirit and power" of his master as any of the rest. In effect Elisha asked, "Let me be the firstborn among thy spiritual sons."

How dramatic was the miraculous removal of Elijah! Suddenly, while Elijah and Elisha were in holy concourse, there appeared "a chariot of fire and horses of fire, and parted them both asunder." The might of the Lord separated them, and a flaming war-host surrounded Elijah and he was taken up to heaven, not in a fiery chariot, but by a whirlwind. God answered Job out of the whirlwind, and Ezekiel describes the

Almighty's whirlwind as a great fiery cloud (Job 38:1; Nehemiah 1:3; Ezekiel 1:4). Amid a grand display of His power in and through the forces of nature, God took Elijah to be with Himself. Ancient Jews recognized the presence and power of God in the terrific phenomena of nature (Psalm 18:6-15; 104:3).

Elisha saw the horses and chariot of fire which he later on prayed that his own servant might see (6:17); and these were signs for those who received Elijah's testimony and trod in his footsteps, signs of heaven's acceptance of his life and labor. These miraculous manifestations were also signs to those who rejected his divinely attested witness, a precursor of the coming whirlwind of wrath and fiery indignation. Elisha, realizing his master had gone, cried in his distress, "My father, my father." He had lost one who had been as a father to him, and Israel had lost her chief strength. Elijah had been to the nation as "a chariot, and the horseman thereof." The Targum paraphrase has it, "My master, my master, who was better to Israel than chariots with horsemen by his prayers."

The actual, visible translation of Elijah is often compared to Christ's Ascension, but such a comparison is scarcely warranted. Christ passed through death, and His body was buried in a grave. Elijah, on the other hand, like Enoch before him, did not die. Elijah went up bodily into heaven and was transfigured, as he was translated in the glorified body he appeared with on the Mount of Transfiguration (Matthew 17:3). What a glorious consummation Elijah had to a career of trial and conflict! The same Spirit who had enabled him to run very swiftly and who transferred him suddenly from place to place now suddenly translates him from earth to heaven in the twinkling of an eye.

How unsearchable is God's providence! Elijah was taken up to heaven without dying, but John the Baptist, who came in the spirit of Elijah and was more than a prophet, was sacrificed to the revenge of an adulteress and died a tragic death (Matthew 11:11; 14:8-11).

The miracle of Transfiguration (Luke 9: 28-35)

After many generations, Elijah reappears to mortal view and was instantly recognized by Peter, although he had never seen the prophet in the flesh. Along with Moses, Elijah talked with Jesus of His death. "The subject of that blessed discourse on the holy mount was His death as God's sent One. This was the grand center to which the law (represented by Moses) and the prophets (represented by Elijah) converge. The law given by Moses found its most outstanding champion in Elijah, and their conversation with Christ was related to the harmony of their work and the common purpose of their ministries." For evidences of Elijah's influence even in New Testament times, see Matthew 27:47; Luke 1:17; Romans 11:2-5; James 5:17, 18.

As to the typical significance of the joint, miraculous reappearance of Moses and Elijah—the former typifies the dead in Christ who are to rise first when He returns; and the latter prefigures that portion of the true Church caught up to meet the Lord in the air without dying.

16. The Miracles of Elisha

(II Kings 2:19 - 5:27; Luke 4:27)

For the call of Elisha, we go back to Elijah's deep experience in the cave at Horeb. The Lord had prophesied that Elisha would slay His enemies (I Kings 19:17). Then suddenly and mysteriously Elijah appeared to Elisha while he was plowing with his oxen, and casting his rough hair mantle upon him, called him to follow him in the rest of his wanderings. The mantle, characteristic of an ascetic recluse, was part of the form of adoption of a child, the spiritual significance of which Elisha quickly realized (II Kings 2:13, 14). As soon as Elijah gave the call, he passed on, leaving the matter of obedience to the free act of Elisha himself. After the farewell feast, Elisha rose up and followed Elijah.

In approaching a study of the miracles of Elisha, we cannot fail to notice that they were revered to the miracles of the Exodus, when God redeemed His people from captivity. Under Elisha we see Israel being handed over to bondage and judgment, that a remnant for God's name and glory might be gathered out. Further, as in keeping with God's progressive revelation, a new era of divine activity is ushered in with a new group of miracles, as it was the case with the Exodus and the institution of Christianity.

Why Elisha resorted to the calming influences of music when he was about to prophesy is a matter beyond our human knowledge. The God who had called him to function as His prophet was surely able to impart the necessary inner peace and calm. As to the miracles he performed, they were domestic works rather than public, and were wrought to aid the poor and the distressed. Elijah's miracles were those of judgment, while Elisha's were those of mercy. While we have a somewhat full account of the mighty works of Elisha, we are told very little about the man himself. The sacred historian has given us not so much a biography as a series of miracles with few links of narrative. A consideration of these many miracles provides us with a conception of Elisha which is totally different from that of the prophet of judgment who preceded him.

The miracle at Jordan (II Kings 2:12-14)

The passing of Elijah greatly distressed Elisha. How poignant was his cry when the vision passed and he was left alone. "He saw Elijah no more." As a token of his extreme sorrow, Elisha rent his clothes in pieces (2:12; I Kings 11:30). There at his feet lay the mantle of his master whom he had seen taken up to heaven—the mantle that had been the token throughout Israel of the great work of Elijah, the prophet of Jehovah, the mantle Elijah himself had cast over the shoulders of Elisha as a sign that he was called to the same prophetic office. As Elijah ascended, his mantle fell off, indicating his work on earth was done. Now Elisha takes it up, as the symbol or badge that the prophetic office has been divinely transferred to him.

Returning to Jordan's banks, Elisha cried out, "Where is the Lord God of Elijah?" Did He leave the earth with His prophet? If not, then let Him now show His power. Elisha, seeking God as the only source of power, followed the action of Elijah and, taking his master's mantle, smote the waters and passed over on dry ground. Although God had raptured Elijah, He carried on His work through Elisha. "The spirit of Elijah doth rest on Elisha." Proof of continued power was in the repetition of the miracle. The miracle-working power lay not in the old mantle, nor in the man who handled it, but in God to whom power belongs. The sons of the prophets, watching from the heights, recognized in the miracle heaven's seal upon Elisha as Elijah's successor, and they reverenced him accordingly.

The miracle of the healed waters (2:19-22)

Elisha's mission was to "continue and carry out with more force than any other man of his time the work which Elijah had begun with new and wonderful power." In the exercise of such an honored task, Elisha lived "in the exercise of a constantly increasing influence" for a long period of fifty years. After the double miracle at Jordan, the rumor quickly circulated that the Spirit of power which Elijah had possessed was now with Elisha, and this accounts for the chief men of Jericho seeking his aid regarding the lack of the right kind of water for their city's need.

The evil effects of the lime-laden water from the mountain was of such a nature as to cause the trees to shed their fruit prematurely and the cattle, feeding off the herbage, to cast their young prematurely. The situation was such that a miracle was necessary to remedy the noxious quality of the water, which was unfit for drinking and injurious to the land. Calling for a new cruse and a supply of salt, Elisha went to the spring whence the waters issued and, casting in the salt as the symbol of grace, purification, and preservation, declared that the brackish waters were healed. On two occasions a great chemical change was wrought on water that was noxious. We have already seen that the bitter waters of Marah were sweetened by means of a tree cast into them (Exodus 15:25). Here the waters of Jericho were healed by salt, the symbol in Scripture of that which prevents corruption.

While the medium of salt was used, God alone could heal the waters. "Thus saith the Lord, *I* have healed these waters" (2:21). It was not by any power of Elisha, nor any natural virtues of the salt he used, that the spring was healed, but by the divine creative will. Elisha and the salt were simply the medium He used. After this miraculous interposition, the water was beneficial in harmony with the ordinary powers and properties of nature.

The miracle of judgment upon irreverence (2:23-25)

The miracle we have just considered was beneficial; the one before us was punitive. At the outset, let it be said that the destruction of the young lads was not an act of personal violence but an evidence of the sacredness of the prophet's office and judgment upon the sin of refusing the prophetic

channel of divine manifestation. On his way to visit Bethel, which since Jeroboam's time was one of the great seats of corruption, Elisha was met by a gang of teenagers bent on mischief. By the phrase, "little children," we are not to understand innocent children who had not reached the age of accountability, but rather young men. Very young children would not be able to use the biting sarcasm, nor sally forth in a body to insult the prophet as these Bethel youths did.

Meeting Elisha, the forty-two wanton, idolatrous, God-hating young men blatantly profaned all that the prophet stood for—and how their irreverence evidenced the lack of any good parental influence or restraint. They flung at the prophet the repeated contemptuous epithet—"Go up, thou bald head." *Go up* was a sneer at the report of Elijah's ascension. "Go on, up you go like Elijah." *Thou bald head* was a sarcastic taunt, either at Elisha's closely cropped hair, in contrast to Elijah's long hair, or at his premature baldness, which was conspicuous as a mark of leprosy (Leviticus 13:43). To be actually bald on the back of the head, which was the part the cowardly youth saw, was reckoned a blemish among the Israelites as well as among the Romans. Used by the youths, the epithet was a slight, not of Elisha as a man, but as a prophet, God's representative.

Justly angered at the insults, Elisha cursed the young men in the Lord's name. This was his only reply to the jeering crowd. He cursed them "to avenge the honor of Jehovah, violated in his person" (see Exodus 16:8; Acts 5:6). The result of such a curse was the attack by two she-bears out of the wood. Elisha had nothing to do with the attack. God, supreme in the animal kingdom, controlled the movements of those bears. Whether all the sneering youths were killed we are not told. The narrative says that the attacking she-bears *tare* them, which on the face of it implies fearful havoc and deserved punishment for their contempt of the prophet.

The miracle of the flooded ditches (3:1-22)

Elisha's services to king and country were numerous and significant. The first record of this was when God intervened to deliver the children of Israel from their enemies, the Moabites. Jehoram endeavored to resubjugate Moab, which had revolted under King Mesha. Combined hosts found themselves without water in the wilderness of Edom, and the situation was desperate. Jehoram appealed to Jehoshaphat and, learning that Elisha (who, because he had poured water on the hands of Elijah, was known as the one-time personal attendant of that greatest of prophets) was in the vicinity, was urged to help in such an extremity.

Elisha, who could be fiery in his indignation against apostate kings, refused to help Jehoram because of his idolatrous practices, but he offered to help for Jehoshaphat's sake. We cannot understand why the prophet had need to call for a minstrel to soothe his disturbed and ruffled spirit so that he could be in an equable and placid frame of mind to receive a divine communication. Certainly composure and serenity of soul were essential if Elisha was to hear the voice of God within, but as a God-fearing man he should not have had a perturbed spirit necessitating the natural means of music to calm him. Anyhow, as the minstrel played, the hand, or the Spirit, of the Lord came upon Elisha and he gave his command, "Make the valley full of ditches."

Without doubt, the miraculous was all worked here, for without *wind,* which in the East is the usual precursor of rain, and without *rain,* which supplies the earth with water (Elisha prophesied that the valleys would be filled with water, implying that its coming would be by the act and will of God. Digging the trenches before the water came was an act of faith which was honored with "a light thing" to God, namely, the country filled with water. Such necessary, God-supplied water served the double purpose of refreshing the host of Israel and frightening their enemies, who, seeing the water from a distance in the fiery glitter of the sun, mistook it for blood shed in the mutual slaughter of the confederate forces and exposed themselves to defeat and discomfiture. Thus God made use of the light and the laws of refraction to serve His purpose in the overthrow of the Moabites. After the meat offering, there came the water. God-given water to assuage our soul-thirst is ours as the result of the offering represented in Christ's death.

The miracle of the widow's oil (4:1-7)

The wondrous works of Elisha the prophet continues, and his ministry breathes "a spirit of gracious, soothing, holy beneficence." His miracles, as deeds of mercy,

suggest those of Jesus, the Prophet of Nazareth. In the beautiful cameo before us, we see Elisha multiplying the oil for a prophet's widow who found herself in dire extremity. We pass from the awful scene of blood and carnage in the defeat of the Moabites to a humble home in Israel, where a dear woman found herself unable to meet the demands of a creditor for payment of her husband's (Josephus identifies him as Obadiah) debts, which were not due in any way to profligate living. The creditor threatened to go to the utmost length of the law, claiming the right to hold the widow's two sons as bondmen (Leviticus 25:39-46. See Matthew 18:25). They would have had to remain in servitude until the Year of Jubilee.

In her dire need, the widow appealed to Elisha as the recognized head of the prophetic guild, and based her claim for help upon the ground of her godliness. The miracle that followed is not a fairy tale but a divine miracle showing God's ability to provide for His needy children. All that the woman had was a very small quantity of a coarse kind of oil, used for anointing the body after a bath, but "little is much if God is in it," and God multiplied the little for the benefit of the widow and of Elisha also. The little in the prophet's hand was enough to test and evidence faith. Elisha knew that this was a case warranting divine interposition, and he believed that his great God would undertake it.

Elisha commanded the widow to borrow all the vessels she could from her neighbors. "Not a few" means not a scanty supply. She had to secure all the vessels the neighbors were willing to lend. The more she had, the larger the supply of miraculous oil. Then Elisha requested her and her sons who had borrowed the vessels to retire to the privacy of their home for an act of faith. Pouring her own meager supply of oil, the borrowed vessels were filled to the brim, one by one. The action of shutting the doors also avoided publicity, undesirable in the case of such a miracle (see also Luke 8:51, 54). As the sons kept on placing the vessels before their mother, she kept on filling them. Her little pot of oil became a very fountain of oil as she continued pouring it into the empty vessels.

The miraculous flow only halted or stopped when there were no more vessels to fill. As the result of this supernatural provision, which no scientist can explain, the woman was able to pay off her creditor and live without any further fear on the price she secured from the surplus oil. "Only when there was no vessel left to fill was the miraculous supply of oil stayed," comments Fausset. "A type of prayer, with 'shut doors' (Matthew 6:6), which brings down supplies of grace so long as we and ours have hearts open to receive it (Psalm 81:10; Ephesians 3:20). Only when Abraham ceased to ask, did God cease to grant" (Genesis 18).

The miracle before us has also a spiritual significance. *Oil*, Habershon reminds us, is a fitting type of the Holy Spirit. The two miracles wrought upon oil by Elijah and Elisha give us two aspects of truth concerning the Spirit. The cruse that failed not and the pot that filled empty vessels illustrate John 4:14 and John 7:37-39—the well springing up and never running dry, the rivers overflowing. The woman was able to pay her debts by means of the miraculous provision—the Spirit's power is the only means whereby we can pay our debts when we feel, with Paul, that we are debtors to those who know not the Gospel.

The miracle of the Shunammite's son (4: 8-37)

How the supernatural abounds in the life of Elisha! In the restoration of the Shunammite's son to life, he performed one of his greatest miracles (4:8; 8:1). Perhaps, in all the Bible, there is no story so beautiful as that of the entertainment of the prophet in the hospitable home of the Shunammite. Her gracious hospitality and Elisha's practical manifestation of gratitude form a most charming picture. Although wealthy, the provision of the woman for Elisha was simple—a little chamber on the wall containing a bed, a table, a stool, and a candlestick—the four essentials in Oriental furnishing. When in conversation with the prophet, she stood in the doorway, recognizing thereby the sacredness of his office. Elisha's dignity is manifest in the attitude of people toward him. The widow of the previous miracle was in depressed circumstances—the Shunammite was affluent and well able to entertain.

Accustomed to accepting hospitality, Elisha so impressed "the great woman" and her husband with his sanctity that they made provision for the holy man of God that passed by continually. Grateful for the kindness of his hostess and host, Elisha asked if he could reward them in any way. Having influence at the court at that time, Elisha inquired if any boon was desired from the king. They sought no worldly reward from the prophet but were perfectly content with their condition in life. Gehazi, Elisha's servant, confided in his master that the woman was childless, and barrenness was at once a misfortune and reproach to an Israelitish wife (Genesis 30:23; Psalm 128:3, 4). Calling the Shunammite in, Elisha told her that as a reward for her kindness she would embrace a son, and in a year's time the promise was fulfilled and to her great joy she became a mother.

When old enough, the boy assisted his father in the fields and one day suffered a sunstroke and cried, "My head, my head." The father commanded a servant to carry the stricken boy into the house, and he expired in his mother's arms. Grief was not long in following gladness. Saddling an ass, the sorrow-stricken mother rode some fifteen miles to Carmel. Faith rose with the adversity and without delay she poured out her woe to Elisha. "Did I desire a son from my Lord?" Elisha sent Gehazi with his staff, which was laid on the boy's face without effect. A dead stick could not restore life. Such could only come from a living God through a living person, just as the law could not raise the dead in sins (Romans 8:3; Galatians 3:21); Jesus Himself must come and do *that*.

Receiving Gehazi's report of failure, Elisha hurried to the house of mourning, and realizing the full extent of the calamity, shut the door upon himself and the dead boy, stretched out on the bed, which the bereaved mother had provided for the prophet's use. Whether it was filling empty vessels or raising the dead, God worked behind shut doors. His sacred work was done in quiet, with no prying eyes looking on (Matthew 6:6). Elisha stretched himself twice on the child, mouth to mouth, eyes to eyes, and hands to hands (see Acts 20:10). Divine virtue by such personal contact passed the more readily from the living to the dead.

The Lord responded to the faith and prayer of His servant, and full vigor returned to the boy whose flesh "waxed warm." Life from God was miraculously imparted through Elisha to the lifeless body. The boy sneezed seven times, the repeated sneezing being a sign of restored respiration, and was delivered alive to his mother who, in deep veneration for God's prophet, bowed herself to the ground. Actually, the Shunammite woman experienced a double miracle. God removed her barrenness and then raised her young son from the dead. Both Elijah and Elisha proved the omnipotence of prayer to quicken the dead.

The miracle of the poisoned pottage (4:38-41)

There are some writers who do not look upon this deed of Elisha's as being a miracle in the modern sense of the term. But as Reuss observes, "By mistake a poisonous (not merely bitter) plant had been put into the pot, and the prophet neutralizes the poison by means of an antidote whose *natural* properties could never have had that effect."

During the famine foretold to the Shunammite, the sons of the prophets at Gilgal found it difficult to obtain supplies of food. They had to subsist on what they could find. One day, while out gathering for their repast, they secured, among other produce, some wild gourds or wild cucumber which they shredded into a pot of herbs. When they discovered the caustic, bitter taste of the pottage and suffered its violent, purgative effect, they cried out to Elisha, "There is death in the pot." By throwing in a quantity of wholesome, nutritive meal, a counteractive influence was produced, divesting the pottage of its noxious qualities. Now the hungry students could eat without fear of harm. The food in the pot was not wasted but miraculously purified of its deadly influence.

On one occasion harmless food was made harmful. In the miracle of the quails, the children of Israel devoured the quails so greedily that they were suddenly changed into deadly poison. Here, the pottage was harmful because of the presence of the wild gourds producing a deadly pot, but through the wonder-working meal it was transformed into a nourishing, health-giving pottage by God's power operating through Elisha. There are many death-dealing pots which Christ, as the Meal, can alone rid of their disastrous effects.

The miracle of multiplied food (4:42-44)

Here again is an incident robbed of its supernatural content by those who, rationalistic in their outlook, also deny that Elisha was responsible for any miraculous increase of food. They affirm that one hundred men were satisfied with the meager

offering brought and even had some to spare. The provisions were not insufficient for the number of men, they claim, and the emphasis of the narrative lies on Elisha's absolute confidence in God rather than on His wonder-working powers. Such an interpretation, however, is alien to the sacred historian's intention. While Elisha did not *perform* the miracle, he did *predict* it, and such predictive ability is supernatural.

During the same period of dearth, a person from Baal-shalisha brought the firstfruits of his harvest for the sons of the prophets—an evidence that the Lord was not forgotten even among the people of the Northern Kingdom. Twenty barley loaves and some full ears of corn, esteemed as a delicacy (Leviticus 2:14; 23:14), were apparently most inadequate for one hundred men in need of provision. But Elisha gladly received the offering to help an immediate need and ordered his servant to place the gifts before the sons of the prophets. To the servant the command seemed absurd, but Elisha assured the doubting man that the Lord would make the supply more than enough.

The supernatural effect was produced not by undoing an evil in the articles of food, as in the previous miracle, but by greatly extending their sustaining virtues. Just how the scanty provision was made sufficient, we do not know. Whether God secretly enlarged the cakes of bread, or rendered the little that was there to be supernaturally efficacious in relieving the hunger of the one hundred men, the Bible does not say. All Elisha did was to announce that there would be sufficient for one and all to eat.

The unselfish command of Elisha, "Give the people . . . to eat," typifies the bidding of One greater than Elisha. Christ's miracle of feeding more men with fewer loaves was preceded by a like want of faith on the disciples' part (Luke 9:13-17; John 6:9-13) and was followed by a like leaving of abundance after the crowd was fed. Elisha's feeding of one hundred men— a faint foreshadowing of our Lord's two miracles of feeding the hungry—symbolizes Christ, the Bread of heaven as being sufficient for all. He is the wonderful Bread of the Firstfruits (Leviticus 23:10, 11).

The miracle of Naaman's healing (5:1-19)

The record of Elisha's domestic miracles

is interrupted to give us in considerable detail the account of a miracle which made a great impression in Samaria and throughout the kingdom. Briefly told, the king of Syria had a captain of his host, Naaman, whom tradition identifies as the man who drew the bow at a venture and slew Ahab. Despite all his skill and bravery, position and prestige, Naaman was a leper. But in his household, attendant upon his wife, was a little maid captured and sold as a slave. Loving her kind and generous master, she was distressed over his loathsome, incurable disease and one day in her mistress's presence ventured to suggest that there was a prophet in Samaria who was able to perform miracles and that he might be able to help her afflicted husband. Finally the king came to learn of the miracle-working prophet and readily gave Naaman the necessary permission to journey to the prophet. Ultimately, after the unpleasant episode with Jehoram, king of Israel, Naaman's magnificent cavalcade came to the humble abode of God's representative.

Naaman naturally assumed that he would be treated according to his rank and that Elisha would appear and in some dramatic manner pronounce the cure for leprosy. How humiliated the mighty man of valor was when the servant Gehazi appeared to the waiting, anxious soldier and his rich retinue with the command that Naaman must go and wash in Jordan's muddy waters seven times, and that then his flesh would "come again" and he would be clean. This was a double insult, and in great indignation Naaman turned and left the city.

Why did Elisha treat Naaman with seeming scant courtesy? Why did he not come out to meet the great soldier? Was it out of any disrespect or fear of infection, or of becoming ceremonially unclean through touching a leper? No. Naaman had to learn that the God of Israel was not swayed by rank or riches, and that any cure would be wholly His work in response to faith. Pleading that the rivers of Damascus, Abanah and Pharpar, had purer waters to wash in, Naaman had also to learn that virtue was not in any waters, but in faith and obedience to God's word. Naaman's servants, distressed at the possibility of their master returning home uncured, pointed out to him with affectionate reverence that if Elisha had asked him to do some great thing he would have done

it. Then why refuse such a simple command as "Wash and be clean."

Persuaded by such reasoning, Naaman made his way to the despised Jordan, obeyed the injunction of Elisha, and came up out of the water the seventh time with flesh "like unto the flesh of a little child." The brave captain, accustomed to command, obeyed the prophet and realized that his cure was wholly due to the power of God. "The Syrians knew as well as the Israelites that the Jordan could not heal leprosy." As we shall see when we come to New Testament miracles, "Go wash" was also the command to a blind beggar (John 9:7). Keil says that Naaman went down seven times, "because *seven* was significant of the divine covenant with Israel, and the cure depended on that covenant; or to stamp the cure as a divine work, for *seven* is the signature of the works of God." Washing in Jordan can typify the spiritual healing of the leprosy of sin through washing in the "fountain opened for uncleanness" (Job 33:25; Zechariah 13:1; John 3:5).

Naaman returned to the prophet's house in a different mood from that in which he left it and was immediately ushered into Elisha's presence. He had come to express his gratitude and to confess that he now knew that there was "no God in all the earth but in Israel." This was Elisha's best reward, and not the royal gifts Naaman had brought to him. Politely he refused the proffered riches, for the cure of leprosy had not been by any power of his. Further, as a prophet of God, Elisha proved that he was not influenced by filthy lucre as evidently Naaman's master had supposed (Genesis 14:23; II Kings 5:5; I Timothy 3:3). Naaman was determined to worship no other god save Israel's God, even though he would have to accompany his king to the temple of the heathen god Rimmon. Appealing to Elisha to sanction the obeisance of his body before Rimmon, the prophet replied, "Go in peace." He knew that Naaman would only be engaging in an act due to his king and not in worship to a heathen deity. Elisha did not sanction Naaman's compromise. Tacitly he left his religious convictions to expand gradually.

The miracle of Gehazi's leprosy (5:26, 27)

Gehazi, who had served Elisha for many years, yielded to the temptation to covetousness and became the conspicuous trophy of such a sin in the Books of the Kings. Perhaps Gehazi had entertained the hope that one day he might succeed his master, as Elisha had succeeded Elijah. It may be that he was a little embittered because the passing years had brought no material reward for all his faithful service, and in a moment of temptation he yielded to the passion to possess wealth. In his covetousness, Gehazi stands in sad contrast to Elisha's disinterestedness, and he became as faithless as the heathen servants of Naaman were faithful. "The highly privileged often fall far below the practice of those with scarcely any spiritual privileges whatever."

Gehazi, whose true character is revealed by his avariciousness, ran after the returning, grateful Naaman and lied to gain two talents of silver and two changes of raiment. This tragic figure takes his place alongside of Judas and Ananias and Sapphira (see I Corinthians 7:29-31). But supernaturally aided, Elisha divined Gehazi's trick and, cognizant of his dark deed, justly reproved him. If Gehazi must have Naaman's money, he must also have his leprosy, and that forever. Elisha offered Gehazi no cure, for he was not able to effect a cure. This was God's work alone, and divine justice decreed that leprosy should plague the house of Gehazi.

The question may arise, was such an act of severity wholly deserved, or was the punishment imposed excessive? What we must bear in mind is that Elisha pronounced, inspired judgment upon the *sin* of Gehazi, and that covetousness and lying in the Bible are never spared. Gehazi's sin was committed under the cloak of religion. Not only so, his greed could have reduced Elisha and the God whose servant he was to the level of the Syrian priests and deities. So Gehazi's punishment was swift. "He who had sought and obtained the reward which Elisha had declined became himself a leper, white as snow."

The miracle of the axhead (6:1-7)

The history of Elisha's mighty deeds continue and we have in the above portion another miracle displaying God's power in the material world. The number of the sons of the prophets had increased and become too small to hold them. Their master's help was sought in the matter of enlarged accommodation. The students suggested that they should go to the well-wooded valley of Jordan and each fell a tree. Elisha not only allowed them to go and secure all the necessary wood but he went with them. But as one of the students was felling a tree the axhead came off the shaft and fell into the water.

It was useless to search for the lost head in the swift and muddy stream, so the young man cried to Elisha for help. What aggravated the loss was the fact that the axhead had been borrowed. Shown the place where it fell, Elisha cut down a stick and cast it into the water. The iron head came to the surface and was taken out by the young man. Such a miracle may seem contrary to our ideas and so out of proportion to the loss incurred. To discredit the miraculous in the story, it has been suggested that all Elisha did was to cut down a stick and, discovering the exact spot where the ax went in, stretched down the point of the stick into the hole for the handle and thus raised it to the surface. But whoever wrote the account of the incident understood it to be of a miraculous nature and worthy of a place among the "wonders" Elisha performed. Ellicott's comment is concise on Elisha causing the iron to float:

> Elisha's throwing in the stick was a symbolic act, intended to help the witnesses to realize that the coming up of the iron was not a natural, but a supernatural, event, brought about through the instrumentality of the prophet. As in the case of the salt thrown into the spring at Jericho, the symbol was appropriate to the occasion. It indicated that iron could be made to float *like wood* by the sovereign power of Jehovah. The properties of material substances depend on His will for their fixity, and may be suspended or modified at His pleasure. The moral of this little story is that God helps in small personal troubles as well as in the great ones of larger scope. His providence cares for the individual as well as the race.

The law of gravitation caused the iron to sink. Because iron is heavier than water or wood, the ax sank. Into the stick Elisha cast into the water a new force was introduced giving it a greater attractive power. Thus it became as strong as a magnet and overcame the attraction of gravitation and its hidden power brought the iron to the surface. Do we not have here another type of Christ? Was He not the "Branch" (Zechariah 3:8; 6:12) who was cut down and who, because He descended into the waters of death for us, is now able to raise us up into the air of heaven and restore us to our Owner for His use? This beautifully acted parable, says old Trapp, teaches us that "God can as easily make our hard, heavy hearts, sunk down in the world's mud, to float upon life's stream and see heaven again." The spiritual application has been fittingly expressed by John Newton in the lines:

> Not one concern of ours is small
> If we belong to Him:
> To teach us this, the Lord of all
> Once made the iron to swim.

Another application of the lost axhead is that the power of the Spirit for service may be lost by disobedience, lack of separation from the world, negligence of Bible reading, absence of prayer, and want of faith. Have you lost your axhead? Then you can find it where you lost it—there, and nowhere else. Once the sin responsible for loss is confessed, cleansed, and forgiven, the God of power is at hand to restore unto us both the joy and power of salvation.

The miracle of open and blinded eyes (6:8-23)

As a patriot as well as prophet, Elisha's life and ministry were very closely linked to the political and military history of his country. As a true worshiper of Jehovah, he hated the idolatrous practice of Israel's kings, but yet had hope that his people would reform, and thus stood by to help his nation religiously.

At this time Syria was a formidable adversary of Israel and, as Israel's power was at a very low ebb, she was unable to protect her borders against the plundering bands fostered by the king of Syria. As the *patriot,* Elisha warned the king of Israel about the necessity of carefully guarding those weak, border points so easily assaulted. Syrian plans were defeated and the king suspected treachery in his army. He came to know, however, of Elisha's divining powers—"the prophet that is in Israel, telleth the king of Israel the words that thou speakest in thy bedchamber" (6: 12)—a miracle of revelation. The Syrian king, learning of Elisha's part in the overthrow of his plans, sought to ambush the prophet. In some miraculous manner, Elisha was able to tell the king of Israel the very word the king of Syria spoke in his chamber when "he took counsel with his servants."

A fact overlooked by the king, however, was that the God who had instructed Elisha to save Israel was also able to shield His faithful servant against any plan of abduction. A trap had been set to catch Elisha. Horses and chariots and a large body of infantry surrounded the town during the night, the object being the seizure of Elisha. The prophet's servant or *minister*—not Gehazi who is never called Elisha's minister and who is usually mentioned by name—was alarmed over the safety of his master, for to him there seemed to be no way out of the difficulty.

But the prophet prayed, and three of his prayers, all of which had to do with sight and all of which were miraculously answered, are before us in this chapter. Elisha prayed:

That his servant's eyes might be opened;
That the Syrians' eyes might be blinded;
That the Syrians' eyes might be opened.

Being in the place of prayer, Elisha was able to help his friends and hinder his enemies. When we are controlled by the Lord, as Elisha was, we too can control the hand of the Lord. Prayer is the mightiest of all ministries.

Elisha assured his servant that a greater host was guarding them both. Elisha was conscious of those unseen forces not seen ordinarily by men and he prayed that his servant might share the vision of the invisible host, the heavenly retinue attending them (II Chronicles 32:7; Psalm 3:6; 4: 8; 34:7; Romans 8:11). How fascinated and awed the servant must have been when his eyes were opened and he saw the mountain full of the chariots and horses of Jehovah—visible impersonations to the spiritual eye of His might and guardianship. There was the inner, heavenly guard between Elisha and the Syrian army. Thus the eyes of the young man were opened by the Lord, just as Elisha's own eyes had been opened to see the like vision of unearthly glory when his master was taken away (2:10, 12; Numbers 22:31).

Again there was a vision of fire—the favorite symbol of God's visible presence and protection or destroying might from the days of early patriarchs onwards (Genesis 15:17; Exodus 3:2, etc.). Chariots and horses formed the strength of Israel's foes, and God caused Elisha's servant to see that He also had at His command chariots and horses—and that of *fire.* For one moment the veil of earthly existence was lifted so as to allow the servant a clear glimpse of the sovereignty of Jehovah. Conscious of divine protection, Elisha and his servant descended the hill to the Syrian encampment where God again displayed His power.

Elisha prayed that his enemies might be struck with mental blindness so that they could not recognize him as the man they wanted, nor realize that they were being led astray (Luke 24:16). The Syrians were dazed, bewildered. They had a confusion of mind amounting to illusion. "They saw, but knew not what they saw" (Genesis 19:11). Because of their confused state they were led off on a wrong way and marched into Samaria and found themselves at the mercy of the Israelites. Elisha pled for merciful treatment and prayed for the restored sight of the foe, and vengeance was stayed for a season. In this gracious act, Elisha anticipated the Spirit of the Saviour who urged His disciples to love their enemies (Luke 6:27; Romans 12:2). The purpose of the miracle of Elisha would have been frustrated if the Syrians, as prisoners of war, had been slain in cold blood. The purpose of the display of God's miraculous power was to force the Syrians and their king to acknowledge the might of the true God.

The miracle of the siege (6:24 - 31)

The next incident in the life of Elisha is a somewhat tragic one. Benhadad, king of Syria, manifested an utter disregard of gratitude over Elisha's merciful treatment of the Syrian host when he planned the siege of Samaria. The Israelites were encouraged to defend their capital to the last, but found themselves reduced to the last extremities of the famine—one of the fifteen sore famines in the Bible. The most fearful conditions prevailed—even to mothers cooking and eating their own children, thus fulfilling the curse (Leviticus 26:29; Deuteronomy 28:55-57). Such a famine was unparalleled in Israel's history until the Roman siege of Jerusalem in 70 A.D.

Jehoram, in horror and rage, vowed to take vengeance on Elisha who was made the scapegoat for Israel's calamity—eloquent proof of the prophet's political influence. The king used language identical to that of his mother's threat against Elijah (I Kings 19:2; II Kings 6:31) in his hasty order for Elisha's execution. Elisha, however, divined the king's murderous intention and anticipating his action, predicted an abundance of food on the morrow. But it seemed absolutely impossible to alter the situation unless windows in heaven could be opened and God rain down flour and barley upon the famine-stricken city —a contemptuous comment upon which Elisha pronounced an immediate penalty (7:2). Those who sneered at the prophet's prediction were about to experience that God would not allow Jehoram's perversity to stop the current of divine mercy.

That night panic seized the Syrian host. A thunderous noise was mistaken for the Hittites coming against them and they fled in headlong rout toward Jordan. Without the help of man, God wrought that same night, in the darkening twilight, a great deliverance for Israel. Everything came to pass according to the supernatural prediction of Elisha. Four roaming lepers discovered the deserted city—emptied by God's appointment—and at first hid their spoil (Matthew 13:44; 25:25). Later, fearing mischief from their selfishness (Proverbs 11:24), the leprous men could hold their peace no longer. Feeling it was a day of good tidings, they told it to the king's household.

The king sent a few men to confirm the report of the lepers and they found the camp deserted and treasures strewn everywhere. The Syrians had taken fright and fled, leaving all baggage and provisions behind. Everything had been forgotten save personal safety, and so the people in Samaria passed almost at once from the horrors of famine to the possession of plenty. Elisha's prediction of relief was speedily fulfilled, and his faith in God was thereby vindicated. As a man of God, Elisha rose in public estimation, even the king coming to regard him with profound respect. The recital of the great things he had accomplished became a source of inspiration (8:4). Jehoram and his people, however, while temporarily impressed by the miracles of Elisha, never renounced all their abominations for the pure worship and service of God. It was because of this that Elisha had to close his public career by calling into exercise the rod of divine vengeance, Hazael in Syria and Jehu in Israel being the instruments God employed.

The miracle of Elisha's bones (13:14-21)

After the siege of Samaria, Elisha went to Damascus and found Benhadad sick and diseased. Divinely instructed, the prophet told the king that although his disease would not be fatal, yet he would die (8:9, 10). Hazael, the king's captain, conveyed the news to the king about his recovery, and on the morrow, the fierce, ruthless captain smothered the king and took the throne (8:7-15).

Then we have the record of Jehu's vengeance upon the house of Ahab for its many sins. Baal was overthrown and an able king was brought to the throne. As we read the intervening chapters, we see how Elisha retained his fervent and patriotic spirit until the end of his career, his final act being in keeping with his long life of generous deeds and faithful patriotic service. While for nearly sixty years he was the great religious force in Israel, yet for more than forty years we have little record of his history.

The deathbed scene of Elisha is most impressive. The prophet is stricken in years and overtaken by a fatal sickness. King Joash, being told of Elisha's illness and hastening to the bedside of the old prophet, saw from his pale, shrunken face that the end was near. Before he passed from earth, God gave him another of those moments of rare insight. As Joash wept and cried, "My father, the chariots of Israel and the horsemen thereof," the dying prophet bade him take a bow and arrow and shoot eastward—an act symbolic of his victory over Syria. Even though dying, Elisha was capable of anger and he told the king that because he only smote the ground thrice instead of many times, he would only smite Syria thrice (13:14-19).

The last miracle in connection with Elisha occurs after his death when we have a post-mortem corroboration of his undying influence. Many of his miracles were manifestations of a life-power or "resurrection—energy overcoming the blight and down-drag of death," as Sidlow Baxter expresses it. Now, after his death, his bones continue and conclude Elisha's quickening ministry. The prophet died and they buried him (13:20, 21), where, we are not told. A dead body was cast hastily sideways into Elisha's grave and as it touched the prophet's bones the man revived and stood up on his feet. Tradition says that the unknown man thus restored to life only lived for an hour. Thus, as Bahr put it, "Elisha died and was buried like all other men, but even in death and in the grave he is avouched to be the prophet and servant of God." This last miracle in connection with Elisha was a sign to Israel that the

God of Elisha still lived and was ready to do wonders for them as before, if they would but seek and trust in Him. Typically the miracle suggest the vivifying power of Christ's death (Isaiah 26:19).

Hales remarks that this last miracle was the most extraordinary of all Elisha performed, and says:

This miracle was the immediate work of God, and concurred with the translation of Elijah to keep alive and confirm, in a degenerate and infidel age, the grand truth of a *bodily insurrection,* which the translation of Enoch was calculated to produce in the antediluvian world, and which the resurrection of Christ, in a glorified body fully illustrated.

17. The Miracle of Uzziah's Leprosy (II Chronicles 26:15-21; II Kings 15: 1-8)

Uzziah, also known as Azariah, is grouped among the good kings of Judah. He came to the throne at the age of sixteen, as the free choice of the people, and reigned for over fifty years. In foreign wars he was eminently successful in the subjugation of Judah's enemies, the Edomites, the Philistines, and the Arabians. Even the Ammonites paid tribute to Uzziah whose "name spread abroad even to the entrance to Egypt; for he waxed exceeding strong" (II Chronicles 26:8). This notable king also restored cities and ports and strengthened the defenses of his capital and country. He instituted military stations and provided cisterns for rain storage. His successes came rapidly, but in his fortieth year a great personal calamity overtook him.

A break in the prosperous career of this strong character is indicated by the words, "He was marvellously helped till he was strong." Uzziah failed to guard himself against the perils and danger of prosperity. When a man is constantly dependent upon God, he is ever independent of all else. The king, alas, came to feel himself independent of God and so courted disaster. In the earlier part of his reign, Uzziah had profited by the counsels of Zechariah, a man "who had understanding in the vision of God" (II Chronicles 26:5), and, during the lifetime of this godly seer Uzziah "set himself to seek God" and was marvelously helped of God. His heart, however, was lifted up in pride, which God abominates, and he trespassed against the One who had given him his success and strength. If only he had kept in mind the paradox that when we are *weak*, then are we strong (II Corinthians 12:9, 10; 13:4), how different Uzziah's end would have been (Proverbs 11:2).

Judah's king knew that among some of the great kingdoms of the East, the kings exercised priestly as well as royal functions and, elated with his God-given prosperity, Uzziah was tempted to imitate his royal neighbors. Possibly he thought that he was only exercising his royal prerogative in burning incense on the golden altar of the Temple. Thus, in an evil moment of pride, he entered the sanctuary and violated the ordinances of God concerning the offering of sacrifices. Azariah the high priest, with others associated with the sacred courts, offered stout remonstrance against such usurpation, but Uzziah was angry with such resistance and pressed forward with censer in hand to offer incense.

At the height of his wrath at the resistance of the priests, and as the king was about to scatter the incense on the coals, white spots of leprosy from God showed themselves upon his forehead—the seat of his conceit. Smitten in conscience and feeling it vain to resist the stroke of God, he hurriedly left the sanctuary a doomed man. Miriam was similarly punished for trying to appropriate Moses' prerogative (Numbers 12), but after seven days she was healed of her leprosy. Uzziah, however, remained a leper until he died. As a mark of power or judgment, leprosy was on several occasions sent by God. That this disease came upon the king is plainly implied (II Kings 15:5), although it is only in Chronicles that the occasion of his leprosy is recorded (II Chronicles 26).

Josephus, the Jewish historian, says that the great earthquake Amos mentioned (1:1) happened at the moment when Uzziah was threatening the opposing priests, and that a ray of sunshine falling upon the king's face, through the Temple roof, which was cloven by the shock, produced the leprosy. The Bible says, "The Lord smote him." That he lived the last part of his life a prisoner, isolated from his fellow men, is implied in his having to dwell in a separate, or *lazar*, house, since lepers were excluded from the sacred precincts and from the social relations and duties. Such

divine punishment offers a striking illustration of a principle from which God never departs, and which will be fully developed in the Day of Judgment, that "them that honor Him He will honor, and they that despise Him shall be lightly esteemed" (I Samuel 2:30). Uzziah was not buried in the royal tombs because a leper would have polluted them. It was the death of this leprous king that resulted in the glorious vision granted to Isaiah (6:1).

Uzziah, guilty of clerical pride, is a blazing warning against the spiritual pride resulting in presumption. Two of the chief snares of Satan for the servants of God today seem to be spiritual pride and fleshly lust. Another lesson to learn from Uzziah's record is that one great sin can blot an otherwise spotless character (II Chronicles 27:2; Ecclesiastes 10:1).

18. The Miracle of Assyrian Slaughter

(II Kings 18:13-37; 19; II Chronicles 32:21, 22; Isaiah 37:36)

Sennacherib, who succeeded his father Sargon as king of Assyria, was unrelenting in his revolt against, and invasion of, Judah. His greatest achievement was the creation of Nineveh as a metropolis of his empire. King Hezekiah was terrified by him and, yielding in panic, paid the enormous tribute exacted. Rabshakeh, King Sennacherib's zealous pleader, reckless of truth, looked upon God as one of the idols to be overthrown. In a letter to Hezekiah, he defied God and tauntingly insulted Hezekiah's faith in Him. But direct blasphemies against the name of God never go unpunished.

By Isaiah's oracle, or warrant of God, so lofty in thought and word, Hezekiah was encouraged to defy all insults. He spread the blasphemer's letter before the Lord and left the matter with Him. The predicted judgment upon the Assyrians was quick and final. The Almighty One, in response to Hezekiah's prayer, routed and destroyed the enemy of the Lord's people. The very night of the day when Hezekiah prayed over the threatening letter and Isaiah delivered his oracle, the Assyrian host of 185,000 men perished by a divine, terrible visitation. The destroying angel did his work in silence, suddenness, and secrecy, and Sennacherib's host perished in a single night. There was the other occasion when God, by His mighty power, destroyed a whole army (Exodus 14:28). No hint is given to the cause of death in Sennacherib's host. We only know that in the morning, instead of the dreaded invaders, there was an army of 185,000 corpses. "The Lord killeth and maketh alive" (I Samuel 2:6). It was God who brought such a catastrophe to pass (II Kings 19:25).

If our miracle-working God was able to destroy 185,000 with one angel, what is He able to do with a legion of angels? Josephus suggests that this secret and total destruction, an evidence of an invisible and irresistible power, was caused by a fatal, fast-working pestilence. Other writers suggest the agency of a storm with lightning, an earthquake, or a violent dust-laden wind. But as Ellicott comments, "a supernatural causation is involved not only in the immense number slain, and that in one night (Psalm 91:6), but in the coincidence of the event with the predictions of Isaiah, and with the crisis in the history of true religion." Perhaps Psalm 46 - 48 was composed by Isaiah to commemorate this great miracle.

Such a direct intervention of divine power resulting in great disaster to the Assyrians did not break the power of Sennacherib, who continued to reign for twenty years and waged many other victorious wars. Ultimately this great king was murdered by his own sons (II Kings 19:37).

19. The Miracle of Hezekiah's Healing

(II Kings 20:1-11; II Chronicles 32: 24; Isaiah 38)

Isaiah 37 ends with an account of the destruction of the Assyrian army by the direct act of God and the murder of Sennacherib at the hands of his sons. The next chapter gives us the story of Hezekiah's sickness, a sickness doubtlessly aggravated by the invasion of Sennacherib. Hezekiah's moment of triumph was to be a season of trial, for he fell sick, so sick that Isaiah told him to set his house in order for he was to die and not live. As the twelfth king of Judah, Hezekiah was the greatest in faith and faithfulness of all the kings. There was "none like him . . . he clave to the Lord" (II Kings 18:5,6), and he had the constant support of Isaiah in all his pious efforts.

It was in the fourteenth year of his reign that Hezekiah became sick, and fifteen years were added to his life after his sickness, making twenty-nine years the length of his entire reign. As to the nature of his deathly sickness, Fairbairn suggests that either the excitement of the contest with Sennacherib had proved too much for Hezekiah's frame and that a feverish attack ensued which prostrated his strength or that the pestilence which slew 185,000 Assyrians produced certain ravages polluting the camp of Israel and reaching even the king himself. Another writer suggests that Hezekiah's sickness was caused by an inflammatory carbuncle and abscess, and that having no heir, he shrank from death with a fear scarcely worthy of a believer.

Suddenly brought to the brink of the grave, Hezekiah turned his face to the wall and earnestly prayed. Grief instinctively seeks a hiding place. "Hezekiah deprecates an untimely death—the punishment of the wicked (Proverbs 10:27)—on account of his zeal for Jehovah and against idols. As Thenius remarks, there is nothing surprising in his apparent self-praise if we remember such passages as Psalm 7:8; 18:20; Nehemiah 13:14." As we are to see, in answer to his heart-felt prayer and by the intervention of Isaiah, Hezekiah was delivered from his sickness.

The sign of recovery given in answer to prayer has supplied us with an astronomical miracle. The shadow of the sun on the dial of Ahaz went ten degrees backward. Such a dial was in the center of the court, and the shadow of it could be seen by the sick king from his sick chamber. This receding of the sun's shadow could only have happened by a miraculous interposition. "A brief and partial direction of the sun's rays out of their natural inclination on that particular dial was all that was required for the occasion, and we reasonably conclude all that was actually produced." The Lord God who made the solar system could easily adjust the movements of earth and sun so that the sun could either stand still for a day or its shadow go back. The sign of the dial was obviously a token that Isaiah's word would come true. Ellicott observes:

> That the sign was granted, and that it was due to the direct agency of Him who ordereth all things according to His divine will, is certain. *How* it was effected the narrative does not in any way disclose.

The word "degrees" repeated six times in the record and five times in Isaiah's message are associated with Hezekiah's fifteen songs in Psalm 120 - 134. This addition of life reminds us that it is God who determines the length of life. Sickness and health are in His hand. The means used to cure Hezekiah's sickness, as well as its cause and course, is worthy of note. The king was instructed. Figs pressed into a cake had to be placed upon Hezekiah's boil. Evidently figs were supposed to have curative properties. But the plaster of figs was a sign or symbol of the cure, like the water in Naaman's healing (II Kings 5:10). God can make effective the simplest means. He can also heal without means.

God granted Hezekiah's earnest prayer, but three years later his son Manasseh was born. It was Manasseh who became the chief cause of God's wrath against Judah and of the overthrow of the kingdom (II Kings 23:26, 27; 24:3). "Our wishes, when

gratified, often prove curses." Hezekiah named his son *Manasseh,* which means "forgetting," and he was so named because God had made Hezekiah forget his troubles (see Genesis 41:51). What a sad name for him who became the worst of Judah's kings!

As a token of his gratitude for recovery from threatened death, Hezekiah composed a sacred hymn preserved for us, not in the historical books, but in Isaiah (38:9-20). It is a composition of a strictly personal character. In spite of the divine healing granted to the king, he was afterwards guilty of indiscretion. He manifested weakness during the Babylonians' visit by showing them all the treasures of his house. For this he was severely rebuked by Isaiah, who prophesied that the things they had seen, the visitors would ultimately take and carry away.

IV.

THE MIRACLES IN POST-CAPTIVITY BOOKS

(Ezra 7:27, 28; 9; Nehemiah 9: 6-33; Esther 6:1; 8:15-17)

There are six Old Testament books related to the return of the Jews back to Palestine after their long exile, namely, Ezra, Nehemiah, Esther, Haggai, Zechariah, and Malachi. The majority of the princes and people preferred to remain in Babylonia and Assyria and continue in their prosperity. These post-captivity books describe the yearnings of that feeble remnant which alone had a heart for God. The first three of these six books are the last three historical books of the Old Testament and form a united trinity in their one voice regarding God's almightiness. Strong and striking evidences of the supernatural are strewn over their pages.

EZRA

This first of the post-captivity books records the return of the Jewish remnant to Palestine under Zerubbabel by the decree of Cyrus in 536 B.C. Ezra's great task was the restoration of Jewish law and ritual, and manifold indications of divine sovereignty in the affairs of nations and men for the

reader to peruse are in the following passages:

(1) God's miraculous power in the realm of prophecy and in the control of a heathen king (1:1, 2; 7:23).

(2) God's guardianship, preservation, and also punishment of His own (5:5; 6:21, 22; 9:4, 6, 13; 10:9-11).

(3) God's supernatural strength and enablement imparted to Ezra for the accomplishment of his divine task (7:27, 28; 8:22).

NEHEMIAH

Some fourteen years after Ezra's return to Jerusalem, Nehemiah likewise returned with an additional company and restored the walls, gates, and the civil authority of the city. Both Ezra and Nehemiah were awed by the greatness of God, and are combined in revelation after a manner of which Moses and Aaron furnish the only parallel. "Ezra and Nehemiah, the spiritual and the civil rulers of the new constitution, have an equal dignity, and both are very subordinate characters in comparison with those first organs of divine revelation."

For an understanding of the moral state

of the Jews at this time, one must read the book of Malachi. Nehemiah gives us several rehearsals of the supernatural:

(1) There are instances of God's miraculous work in response to individual faith acting on the written Word (1:8, 9; 4:9; 5:13; 13:1. See II Timothy 2), and the putting forth of His great power to move the heart of a great king, and of His response to repentance and prayer (1:4, 10, 11; 2:4; 4:4-6, 9, 15; 10:31).

(2) God in a miraculous way can reveal His plans to His obedient servants. His secrets are for those who fear Him (2:12, 18, 20; 5:19; 6:9, 12; 7:5).

(3) God's supernatural care of His people during their wilderness experiences is rehearsed (9:6-38; 13:2, 3. See Judges 6:13).

ESTHER

Some may think it waste of time looking for evidences of the supernatural in a book in which no divine name occurs, nor any express reference to anything spiritual or miraculous, a distinction which the Song of Solomon shares with Esther. In the apocryphal additions of Esther preserved for us in the LXX Version, the name of God occurs frequently. But although the name of God is not to be found in Esther, no other book of the Bible is more eloquent regarding the truth of His providence and of His promise never to forsake His own.

The miracle of God's over-ruling providence

A unique feature of Esther is the secret care of God over His scattered people. While some critical thinkers object to the book's inclusion in the Bible, the Jews themselves esteem it next to the law of Moses. To them it is precious because of God's special providence toward them even though there is not one line respecting His presence and working, and because of the description Esther gives to the signal vengeance taken upon their enemies. The facts of Jewish history and unexampled train of events proclaim the special providence of God watching over His own people according to His promises that they who touched them touched the apple of His eyes (Isaiah 6:13; 65:8; Jeremiah 30:10, 11).

Who then can doubt that God was behind the sleepless night of Ahasuerus, which was a very important link in the chain of the defeat of Jewish enemies? "The God who never slumbers nor sleeps kept Ahasuerus from sleeping in order to illustrate how His providence makes use of the most trifling, and what to us might seem a most accidental circumstance to accomplish His will (6:1), and on the banks of the Asopus at Plataea, as well as for the preservation of the Jews in the provinces of Persia." The Feast of Purim is still observed by the Jews, at which time the whole book of Esther is read through in the synagogue service.

V.

THE MIRACLES IN THE POETICAL BOOKS

(Job 5:9; 9:10; 37:5; Psalm 78; Proverbs 8:22-34; Ecclesiastes 2:25, 26)

What is known as the poetical section of the Old Testament comprises the books of Job, the Psalms, Proverbs, Ecclesiastes, the Song of Solomon—a section rich in its devotional and instructional material. These five books are called "poetical" because they are wholly composed in Hebrew verse. As these books, with the exception of the non-religious book of the Song of Solomon, are God-saturated, it is not hard to trace in them declarations and displays of God's miraculous power. His sovereignty in creation, nature, and history dominates books like Job and the Psalms. These five poetical books are also known as the "Wisdom Books." Many of the wisdom sections are written in poetry so, in a general way, either term is applicable. As a whole, this group of books represents the spiritual thought of the golden age of Hebrew history.

JOB

Thomas Carlyle said of this remarkable book: "One of the grandest things ever written. . . . There is nothing written, I think, of equal literary merit." Victor Hugo's estimation is also worth recording: "The Book of Job is perhaps the greatest masterpiece of the human mind." Job himself is supposed to have lived before Moses and his book, as the oldest in the world, is supposed to contain the earliest record of patriarchal religion. It is not within the province of our study to attempt an exposition of the divine and human arguments comprising the book or "public debate, a poetic form on divine government." In keeping with one theme of the miraculous content of the Bible, we draw attention to the fact that Job is one of the outstanding books of the Bible when it comes to the setting forth of the supernatural.

Great phrases, like the following, are eloquent with the truth of God's almightiness:

"Who doeth great things and unsearchable, marvellous things without number" (5:9).

"Who doeth great things past finding out; yea, and wonders (miracles) without number" (9:10).

"Great things doeth He, which we cannot comprehend" (37:5).

"Touching the Almighty, we cannot find Him out: He is excellent in power" (37:23).

"I know that Thou canst do every thing, and that no thought can be withholden from Thee" (42:2).

How well these declarations and the whole tenor of the book remarkably display the providence of God and the plan of His moral government, and illustrate with unrivaled magnificence the glory of the divine attributes, particularly when the Almighty addresses Job! Attention is drawn to these aspects:

(1) The miraculous appears in God's dominion over Satan, who is only as a dog on a leash and cannot go any further than divine permission, even though there is the mystery of his access to the presence of God (1:6, 7; 2:1, 2, 6).

(2) The miraculous is indicated by God's supremacy in the realm of nature. As Creator, He can command any part of His creation to fulfill His supreme will (5:9; 9:4-17; 11:7-11; 12; 22:12-14; 26:7-14; 28; 36:4-33, 37-41; 38:7).

(3) The miraculous is attested to by God's power to impart life and to raise from the dead (19:25-27; 33:4; 35:10).

Such glorious displays of God's sovereignty in every realm should humble us and lead us to confess with Job, "Behold, I am vile . . . I abhor myself and repent in dust and ashes" (40:4; 42:6). Who are we but mere worms of the dust, utterly unworthy of the manifestations of God's miraculous power and provision on our behalf.

PSALMS

It would take a volume in itself to fully expound all facets of the supernatural to be found in this outstanding God-glorifying section of the Bible, of which W. E. Gladstone wrote, "All the wonders of the Greek civilization heaped together are less wonderful than those in the single book of Psalms." This book has been described as an epitome of the Bible, adapted to the purpose of devotion. This is why it is known as the "National Hymn Book of Israel," containing 150 poems, set to music for worship and called in the Hebrew, "The Book of Praises." The early Church Fathers assure us that the whole book was generally learned by heart, and that the Psalms were used at meals, at business, and also to enliven the social hour and soften the fatigues of life.

When one comes to indicate the expressions of praise and adoration, displaying the majesty, power, goodness, and other attributes of God, he finds himself embarrassed in the presence of so much spiritual wealth. Recognition and rehearsals of the supernatural are to be found on almost every page of the Psalms (50).

(1) For an insight into God's all-sovereign will concerning national and international affairs and the reign and rule of kings, read Psalm 2; 9; 21; 45-47; 46; 47; 67; 72; and 84.

(2) For a reminder of God's willingness to exercise miraculous power on behalf of His own, even to the supplying of food, raiment, and sleep, read Psalm 3; 23; 32; 34; 145.

(3) For a panorama of many of the transcendent attributes of God, all combined for the spiritual welfare of saints, read that majestic Psalm 139.

(4) For evidences of God's power and authority as Creator and His right to give or withold the benefits of nature in keeping

with His justice, read Psalm 8; 18; 19:
1-6; 24; 29; 65; 68; 74:12-17; 77: 18-20;
93; 95; 104; 147; 148.

(5) For the rehearsal of His miraculous
provision for and preservation of, His chosen people, read Psalm 78; 90; 91; 105 -
107; 114; 121; 124; 126.

Overwhelmed as we are at the greatness
and goodness, power and pardon of God
revealed in these majestic Psalms, what
else can we do but emulate the example of
the psalmist and ——

Praise God in the firmament of His power.
Praise Him for His mighty acts:
Praise Him according to His excellent
greatness (150:1, 2).

PROVERBS

"This collection of sententious sayings of
divine wisdom applied to the earthly conditions of the people of God" also contains manifestations of the supernatural.
Other parts of the Bible are like a rich
mine, where the precious ore runs along
in one continued vein. Proverbs, however,
is like a heap of pearls, which, though
they are loose and unstrung, are not therefore the less excellent and valuable. It
will be found that the reading of Proverbs
is most profitable when they are used to
illustrate their general truths by examples
from the historical characters of Old and
New Testament. "The folly of fools is
deceit" (14:8) is illustrated in Gehazi (II
Kings 5:20, 27), Daniel's accusers (Daniel 6:24), and Ananias and Sapphira (Acts
5:1-11).

Proverbs is not only "the best guide book
to success that a young man can follow,"
it is likewise a contribution to a revelation of our Almighty God, the Fount of all
true wisdom.

(1) For an insight into the habits and
ways of ants, birds, horses, serpents, and
men which God as their Creator endowed
them with, read 6:6-11; 26: 1, 2; 30:17-19.

(2) For a glimpse of Christ before
time commenced and of the marvels of
God's creative power, read 8:22-34. This
portion is a distinct adumbration of Christ
who came as the personification of the
attribute of divine wisdom. He was made
unto us *Wisdom* (I Corinthians 1:24; Colossians 1:15-17).

(3) For an assurance that God's sovereignty also takes within its sweep the
heart, tongue, and ear of man, read 16:14;

20:12. As to all the affairs concerning our
individual life, "The lot is cast into the
lap; but the whole disposing thereof is of
the Lord" (16:33). As our Redeemer He is
mighty to save and keep (23:11). It is His
glory to conceal His power and purpose
(25:2). In respect to so-called marvels of
modern science is the word of Solomon
true. Wonders visible today, like electricity,
telephone, radio, television and radar, were
invisible, or unknown half a century ago.
Yet God had concealed all these discoveries
in the universe when He created it. Scientists did not create them. They only revealed what God, in His glory, had hidden.

ECCLESIASTES

This part of Scripture, inspired of God
(II Timothy 3:16), is a record of man's
life "under the sun." His ideas and reasoning about life are set forth, yet divine con-
clusions are apparent. In this book Solomon
exposes the most fatal of all delusions,
namely, that the pursuit of happiness is
our chief good. True happiness can only
be found in fearing God and keeping His
commandments (12:13). Ecclesiastes is,
more or less, a penitential discourse, and
was probably written by Solomon a little
before his death, to warn others, by his
own sad experience, of the variety of all
created things, and of the misery of sin
both here and hereafter.

As one who knew something of the
greatness of God, Solomon adds further
evidence of God's majestic sovereignty in
every realm.

(1) Man is utterly dependent upon the
bounty of God's hand.

(2) Man can have no enjoyment except
as God is pleased to bestow it (2:25, 26;
5:18; 6:2).

(3) God has pre-ordained the times and
seasons of all human events, and supreme
happiness cannot be had except in conformity with His supreme will. Chapter
three extols the supremacy of God.

(4) In a marvelous way, God has
planted in man the certainty of immortality.
"He hath set eternity in their heart" (3:11
RV).

(5) Supernaturalness is seen in God's
ability to make straight things crooked and
crooked things straight (1:15; 7:13, 14).
God's supremacy as the Creator is to be
remembered, not only by the young, but

by all since He is to judge the secrets of all men (12:13, 14).

SONG OF SOLOMON

There is nothing of the supernatural in this non-religious book in which, from beginning to end, there is not a single word connecting it with religion. Yet it is included in Scripture and is reckoned a part of such a divine revelation, even though there is not one spiritual sentiment of any kind, nor the faintest allusion to any sacred rite or ordinance whatever. Its sole purpose is to express the sentiment of love.

If, as many expositors indicate, this idyl of love typifies the blissful relationship between Christ and His Church, then the spiritual mind can discern in the passionate language of the book something of the marvel and mystery of divine love. Such everlasting love will ever remain a miracle.

VI.

THE MIRACLES IN THE PROPHETICAL BOOKS

(Luke 24:25-27, 44; Acts 10:43; I Peter 1:10-12; II Peter 1:19-21)

This section of the Old Testament containing the prophetical books stretches from Isaiah to Malachi. These seventeen books are commonly divided into the five Major Prophets (Isaiah to Daniel) and the twelve Minor Prophets (Hosea to Malachi). The terms "major" and "minor" have nothing to do with contents of the books. They are only related to their size. *Isaiah*, for example, is made up of sixty-six chapters, while *Obadiah* has only twenty-one verses. Altogether, these seventeen books cover a period of about 400 years, beginning about 600 years after the giving of the law at Sinai, and ending about 400 years before the coming of Christ.

The miracle of prophecy

We cannot consider these prophetical books as a whole without being impressed with the abiding miracle of prophecy. The prophets themselves were *patriots* having a message for their own people and times; and, as revivalists, they stirred the heart and conscience of the nation. As *prophets*, they predicted divine purposes concerning the future of Israel and of those Gentile powers connected with Israel. Modern scholarship has endeavored to minimize predictive prophecy, yet it dominates Scripture, and without the prophetic key its treasures cannot be secured.

Briefly stated, the God of the Hebrew nation is to become the God of all nations. Such a prophecy is interwoven with every part of the Bible, from Genesis to Revelation. The portion we are presently considering is named "the Prophets" because, although history is slightly introduced (Isaiah 36-39), its leading subject is *prophecy*. For a full treatment of this fascinating aspect of Bible study, the reader is referred to the author's volume, *All the Kings and Queens of the Bible*.

The miracle of prophecy consists in the fact that Spirit-inspired prophets (I Peter 1:10-12; II Peter 1:19-21), were able centuries before the events occurred, to set forth predictions so numerous, varied, and minute as to preclude all possibility of chance. Truly we never cease to wonder at this literal fulfilment of prophecies. John Urquhart's *Wonders of Prophecy* should be in every Bible lover's hands. This unique volume provides us with solid ground for accepting the abiding miracle of prophecy.

(1) Predictions of the fate of Tyre and Sidon (Ezekiel 26:7-14).

(2) Predictions of Sidon, a neighboring and still more ancient city (Ezekiel 28:20-22; Isaiah 34:11; 47:1).

(3) Predictions about great and mighty Egypt (Ezekiel 30:14-16). The Old Testament contains many distinct predictions regarding Egypt generally, so that we may say they have written the history of its rise, its people, and its fall (Jeremiah 46:11; Ezekiel 29:14 15; 30:4, 6, 12, 13; Isaiah 14:17; 19:5, 6, 8-10, 15).

(4) Predictions regarding Idumea and the sea coast of Palestine (Numbers 20:14-27; Ezekiel 35:3-9).

(5) Predictions of the extinction of the Edomites (Isaiah 34:10; Jeremiah 47:5; Ezekiel 25:15, 16; 35:9, 15; Zephaniah 2:1, 5, 6).

(6) Predictions concerning Judea and Babylonia (Isaiah 6:11, 12; see Leviticus 26:27-34; Deuteronomy 29:28).

(7) Predictions as to the doom of Bethel (Amos 3:14, 15; 5:5).

(8) Predictions concerning Samaria (Micah 1:5, 6).

(9) Predictions relating to Jerusalem (Micah 3:12; Matthew 24:2).

(10) Predictive forecast of the world's history (Daniel 2:38-44; Matthew 21:42-44). See notes under *Daniel.*

(11) Predictions associated with Jewish history (Isaiah 2; 6:9-12; 49:4-7; Ezekiel 20:32, 37; Daniel 9:26; Hosea; Zechariah 11:1-6; Malachi 1:10, 11; Romans 11:25. See Deuteronomy 28; Leviticus 26:33). These are only a few passages relative to the miracle of the Jew. "That the history of the Jews was miraculous does not render it less constructive to us in this respect; for miracles do not alter principles upon which God acts; they only illustrate those principles in a more striking manner."

(12) Predictions of the Lord Jesus Christ (Isaiah 7:14-16; 9:6, 7; 11:1-5; 28:16; 32: 1, 2; 42:1-4; 52:13-53:12; 61:1-3; 63:1-6; Jeremiah 23:5, 6; 31:34; Ezekiel 34:23; 37: 24; Daniel 9:24-26; 8:13-15; Micah 4:3-5; 5:2 with Matthew 2:6; Haggai 2:7-9; Colossians 2:9; Zechariah 3:8; 6:12, 13; 9:9; 11:2; 12:10; 13:6, 7; 14:4; Malachi 3:1; 4:2).

1. The Five Major Prophets

ISAIAH

Although eminent as a prophet who prophesied during a period of fifty or sixty years, we know very little of Isaiah's personal history. There is a Jewish tradition that he was sawn asunder by Manasseh for his fidelity to God (Hebrews 11:37). It is not the purpose of the Bible to exalt man. Because *salvation* is one of the leading subjects of his book, Isaiah, whose name means *salvation of Jehovah,* is known as "The evangelical Prophet." That he had that mind which was in Christ Jesus (Luke 19:41) is seen in the following traits:

(1) He had a broken and contrite spirit (6:5; 56).

(2) He felt deep commiseration, not only

for the Jews, but for the Gentiles, his enemies, whose desolations he announced (16: 9; 21:3).

While there are no actual miracles in Isaiah, so heavy is its predictive element that there are many evidences and expressions of the exercise of God's miraculous power. Outstanding is the miracle vision of chapter 6. Isaiah and his children were for signs and wonders (8:18). For the student desiring an insight into Isaiah's witness to the supernatural, the following passages should be perused—12:5; 13; 19:21, 22; 25:8; 31:5; 37; 38; 40:25-31; 41; 42:5-7, 15-16; 43:1, 7; 45:1-4; 46:10, 11; 49:26; 50:2, 3; 54:11, 12, 17; 57:10; 58:12; 59: 1, 19, 20; 64:1-4; 65:17; 66:5. Such displays of God's supremacy in every sphere prompt one to exclaim, "How Great Thou Art!"

JEREMIAH

Because his tears over the sins of the people saturate the pages of his book—one of the longest in the Bible—Jeremiah is known as "The Weeping Prophet." Sensitive and intensely sympathetic, the prophet's hot tears fall as he declares the doom of his own nation. In him, sympathy and severity blend, and "his child-like tenderness adds force to the severity of his denunciations." His mission was a hard one, bringing him perpetual martyrdom. "He was rooted out, to pull down, to destroy, to throw down, to build up, to plant; he was to address a people who had forsaken God, burned incense to other gods, and worshiped the work of their own hands." For such a grim task he received a miracle vision, just as Isaiah had received (1:10-19; Isaiah 6). The mission of these two prophets differs in that Isaiah attempted the reformation of the Jews, but the awful nature of Jeremiah's message was to proclaim the near desolation of his own country, now hardened in impenitence.

Miracles are few in the prophetical books. It would seem as if the prophets themselves were God's *signs* or *wonders.* In this Church Age, God's redeemed people are His miracles, His signs and wonders to the world around. While Jeremiah performed no miracles, he experienced the miraculous effect of God's word in his own heart, and he was made the recipient of supernatural speech and strength to proclaim the burning message (20:9; 1:4-11).

The key word to Jeremiah's recognition of the supernatural can be found in the magnificent statement:

The great, the mighty God, the Lord of Hosts is His name . . . mighty in work (38:18, 19).

We herewith cite a brief outline of the prophet's reference to the miraculous for the reader to enlarge upon:

The miracles of God's creative works (4:23-28; 5:2; 8:7)

The miracle associated with natural forces (23:19)

The miracles of the Exodus (2:1-7; 32:19-25)

The miracle of bodily health (33:6)

The miracle of predictive prophecy (15-19; 30; 45-52).

A peculiar feature of many of these prophecies against several nations was the publicity Jeremiah gave them among those nations, for instance by sending bonds and yokes to their kings (27:3). In *Lamentations*, Jeremiah expresses with most pathetic tenderness his grief for the desolation of Jerusalem, the captivity of Judah, the miseries of famine, the cessation of all religious worship, and other calamities according to his inspired predictions. If deliverance is to come to his countrymen, it can only come from God in response to their repentance.

The third chapter is a declaration of divine supremacy. The key passage of this moving book is in verse 37 of the chapter:

"Who is he that saith, and it cometh to pass, when the Lord commanded it not?" (See also 1:15; 2:5).

EZEKIEL

Ezekiel, a priest and a prophet, was among the captives carried by Nebuchadnezzar to Babylon with Jehoiachin, king of Judah, and his ministry was to his captive countrymen, among whom he prophesied for about twenty-one years. Both his character and his prophecies are marked by a peculiar energy, of which his name is expressive—*Ezekiel*, meaning "the power of God girding with strength." Although stern and strong, he was not lacking in tenderness.

Briefly stated, the book of Ezekiel is made up of the glorious appearance of God to the prophet in connection with his office (1-3); denunciations against the Jews and predictions of the total destruction of the Temple and city of Jerusalem, desolation

and dispersion (4-24); prophecies against various neighboring nations, enemies and oppressors of the Jews (24-32); warnings, exhortations, and promises to the Jews of future and final deliverance and restoration (32-48).

The book is heavy with miracle content, even though this aspect is often passed over by expositors.

There are the miracle visions (1:28; 10; 47; 48:35)

The four living creatures with their separate faces and the four wheels with their complexity of movement represent certain aspects of the divine nature—God's sovereignty, majesty, glory, omniscience, omnipotence, and holiness. His absolute supremacy is in the fiat, "I will overturn, overturn, overturn" (21:27). These visions by which Ezekiel was arrested and inspired were visions of the essential glory of God which, by the Spirit, the prophet described in "terms of majestic suggestiveness which even to this day we read with great reverence and wonder." The effect of these visions of manifested glory was to leave Ezekiel prostrate. What saint is not overwhelmed by such supernatural revelations of the awfulness of God?

There is the miracle of the Spirit's control

Among the prophets, Ezekiel is conspicuous as a Spirit-possessed man. There are about twenty references to the Holy Spirit in the book. In several cases the phrase, "the hand of the Lord," is associated with Spirit-control. Ezekiel was possessed by the Spirit (2:2; 3:24), taken up by the Spirit (3:12; 11:24; 43:5), lifted up by Him (3:14; 8:3; 11:1), anointed by Him (11:5), carried out by Him (37:1). Judgment falls upon those who fail to prophesy by the Spirit; and an outpouring of the Spirit in latter times is promised.

There are miracles associated with speech (3:26, 27; 24:27)

There are miracles connected with Jewish history. These include the existence of the Jews (chapter 6) and the miracle of their resurrection or regathering as a nation (37).

There are miracles related to rivers and fish (29:4, 5; 47)

There are miracles connected with predicted judgments (37-38)—with natural forces being employed by God for the execution of His purpose (5). Life and death are in His hands (24:15-27).

There is the miracle of Ezekiel himself (12:6-11; 24:24, 27). The man himself was a sign to the people of the supernatural.

DANIEL

The miraculous events of this remarkable book prove before the world what Nebuchadnezzar and Darius were forced to acknowledge, that the God of Daniel and his three friends, Shadrach, Meshach, and Abed-nego, is the living God, the great King above all gods (3:28; 4:34; 6:26). Among the four captive young men especially named and set apart for their three years' preparation for court duties, Daniel is conspicuous. From the outset, he manifested strength of character and was raised to great rank and power in the courts of the Babylonian and the Persian princes (Proverbs 21:1).

Daniel's eminence for wisdom and piety, even in early life, was proverbial (Ezekiel 14:14-20; 28:3). He died at a very advanced age, having prophesied for the whole period of the seventy years' captivity. Amidst temptations of deepest adversity and most exalted prosperity, he preserved his godliness to the end of his days. From his book as a whole we learn:

(1) The relation between prayer and prophecy. Much can be learned by observing the occasions when Daniel's prophecies were received. For example, the glorious display of the great work of redemption was revealed to Daniel when, at prayer, he deeply bewailed his sin and the sin of the people (9:4, 21. See Isaiah 57:15).

(2) Prophecy is the harbinger of hope. Daniel wrote his book during the darkness of the most terrible captivity Israel ever suffered (Psalm 137). In such a tragic time, "The harp of prophecy was most inspired with hope, then the grandest revelations were made of the future glories of Israel and of the world, and of the providence of God controlling all events."

(3) The supremacy of God. The wisdom and power of God is overruling the punishment of the Jews to the spreading of the knowledge of Himself among Gentile nations is most striking. The book of Daniel affords unanswerable proof that "the world is God's world" (Psalm 75:7). God is Judge over all, and He exerts His authority in putting down one and setting up another. He also manifests His glory in the salvation of man (2:35; 9:24).

The right of God to perform the miraculous, not only in Daniel's age, but in any age, is summarized for us in the challenging statement:

He doeth according to His will in the army of heaven, and among the inhabitants of the earth: and none can stay His hand, or say unto Him, What doest Thou? (4:35)

The miracle of choice (1:2, 9, 17)

In dealing with the supernatural in the book of Daniel, it is usual to single out the fiery furnace and the lions as the only two miracles found in the book. But there are others. For instance, it was not by any chance that Daniel and his three companions were among the captives of Nebuchadnezzar when he took Jerusalem. Divine ordination was behind their captivity and then behind their choice as confidential servants of the King. "The Lord gave"; God had brought Daniel into favor"; "God gave them knowledge and skill." These pregnant phrases prove that the supernatural was at work in the preparation and position of Daniel, Shadrach, Meshach, and Abed-nego. Their advancement was of the Lord.

The miracles of visions (2-3:7; 4; 9-12)

The royal dreams, the failure of court magicians to interpret them, the God-given vision of Daniel when interpretations of God-caused dreams were granted unto the Spirit-possessed prophet, all testify to divine omnipotence in controlling the mind. When Nebuchadnezzar received the divine significance of his dreams, he recognized the God of heaven and praised Him whose works are true and whose ways are judgment. Much as we are tempted to digress and expound the prophecies regarding the world's entire history, we must adhere to the miraculous aspect of the various predictions respecting the great monarchies of Babylon, Persia, Greece, and Rome. Because God knows the end from the beginning, He was able to reveal beforehand to His honored servant Daniel the end of Christ, and the glorious millennial reign of Christ. The prophecies of this remarkable book extend from the first establishment of the Persian Empire more than 500 years before Christ, right on to the resurrection of the just and the unjust (12:2, 3). For a detailed study of the succeeding empires which Daniel describes, the reader is referred to our chapter dealing with this entrancing theme in *All the Kings and Queens of the Bible.*

The miracle of the fiery furnace (3:8-30)

There is a display of God's miraculous power, which from childhood days has never ceased to fascinate us! Although Nebuchadnezzar was convinced of God's supremacy when Daniel interpreted his dream, he was puffed up with pride and he set up in the plain of Dura a great golden image. To this image he commanded all peoples to bow down and worship. The dauntless three, Shadrach, Meshach, and Abed-nego, refused to bend their knee to a man-made image. Such obeisance on their part as God-fearing men would have been an act of idolatry (Exodus 20:4, 5). They were well aware of the price they would have to pay for their refusal, but with splendid heroism they cast themselves upon God. Little did they realize that they were to demonstrate, in a most dramatic manner before the assembled dignitaries of the far-flung empire, the almighty power of God over the boasted gods of Babylon.

Obedience to the higher law of the King of kings brought the three young men into the furnace. They reckoned not their lives dear unto them, and God vindicated their faith. Fully clothed and bound, they were cast into the burning furnace, and Nebuchadnezzar stood by to see the end of those who had dared to defy his edict. Would God abandon His servants to their fate? The king was over-awed by what he did see, for there were the happy trio walking around unhurt by the flames, no longer bound but free. The LXX Version adds a note that they were singing praises unto God. Jerome wrote of *The Song of the Three*. God could have prevented them going into the furnace, but it pleased Him to have His faithful servants cast into the flames, so that He could display His power by delivering them *in* the fiery furnace.

The miracle consisted in the divine suspension of natural laws. The human frame is naturally fuel for fire, as thousands of martyrs have proved when their bodies were reduced to ashes. For His glory, God arrested the normal processes of fire for His own, but allowed the intense heat to destroy the strong men who had cast the Hebrew youths into the flames. The terrible end they had designed for God's children overtook the executioners. The miracle is made more impressive by the fact that not "an hair of their head was singed, neither were their coats changed, nor the smell of fire had passed on them" (3:27). Not only did God arrest the action of the intense heat in the hour of trial, He condescended to become their Companion in the furnace, thereby fulfilling His promise, "When thou passest through the fire, thou shalt not be burned; neither shall the flame kindle upon thee" (Isaiah 43:2; Matthew 10:30; Hebrews 13:5).

The One Nebuchadnezzar saw had a form "like unto the Son of God." No mere angel accompanied and consoled the triumphant youths but One glorious in mien. Without doubt, this was one of Christ's theophanic appearances. "Thus the three were not merely delivered from bodily death, but they were saved with special marks of honor—were "more than conquerors." Such a supernatural deliverance so deeply impressed Nebuchadnezzar that he decreed that no word should be spoken against the God of Shadrach, Meshach, and Abed-nego, who were promoted to high honor in the province of Babylon.

Fausset's application of this miracle is suggestive. "The salvation God wrought therein is typified: the Son of God walking in the furnace of God's wrath by our sins; connected with the Church, yet bringing us forth without so much as 'the smell of fire' passing on us."

The miracle of the mystic hand (5)

King Belshazzar was not only a man of profligate habits, his was also an arrogant provocation of God and of all that was sacred because in the presence of his assembled lords, wives, and concubines, he was guilty of the heinous sin of using in drunken revelry the sacred vessels of the Temple of God. In such a carousal, Belshazzar's character was revealed, and in such a final manifestation of his sin, there came the strange and mysterious announcement of his doom. There appeared on the wall the miraculous handwriting of his end and that of his kingdom. As the hand of an unseen man etched out the message on the wall, the revellers were awed and Belshazzar stricken with fear. In desperation he sought for an interpretation of the message conveyed so miraculously. The king's wise men, like those in the reign of his father, were unable to interpret the meaning of the writing (see Exodus 32:16; Deuteronomy 10:4; John 8:6-11).

Daniel, who was not present at the profane feast and therefore knew nothing of the mystic handwriting, was sent for and, under God, interpreted the cryptic message. Full of dignity and heroic loyalty to God, Daniel declined the king's gift and then charged him with his terrible guilt. Says Dr. Campbell Morgan, "Daniel proclaimed God as seated high over the thrones of earth, and interpreted the writing as indicating God's knowledge of the kingdom, and His determination to end it and divide it among the Medes and the Persians." Belshazzar honored Daniel by making him the third ruler of the kingdom, which literally means that he shared with Nabonidus and his son Belshazzar the rulership of the empire. *The handwriting on the wall* has become a phrase applied to any omen of impending calamity or imminent doom.

The miracle of the lions' den (6)

Because of his conspicuous administrative ability, Daniel was suggested by Darius as the governor of the whole realm. This proposed prominence for Daniel naturally stirred up jealousy among the other presidents and satraps, who cunningly conceived Daniel's downfall and death. These Persian rulers charged Daniel with rebellion against Darius, just as for envy the Jews delivered Jesus to Pilate. Envy ever seeks opportunities for false accusation (Proverbs 27:2). Daniel's jealous foes knew that they had no case against one distinguished by an excellent spirit, sure in his relationship to God. They, therefore, induced King Darius to sign a decree that for thirty days no one should ask a petition of God or man, save of the king.

Such a subtle inducement was intended to flatter the weak, profligate sovereign and also to bring Daniel into discredit with him. Daniel, however, never swerved in his loyalty to God. Although his enemies knew only too well Daniel's habit of prayer, he nevertheless, in spite of the decree, kept his windows opened toward Jerusalem. Threat of death could not keep him from the continued observance of his seasons and acts of worship. Darius, unable to escape from his own decree which was engineered by his crafty counsellors, reluctantly committed Daniel to the den of lions. Although he escaped the fiery furnace, it seemed as if a similar fearful death was before him. But Daniel was willing to lose his life, and, in losing it, was to find it.

Actually, we have three displays of the supernatural in the episode before us. First, there was the sleepless night of King Darius, who had gone from the den to his palace to sleep. While a torn conscience contributed to his sleepless hours, God who is able to give or withhold sleep troubled the king over the casting of his principal officer into the lions' den. The high esteem for Daniel was evidenced by the night of mourning and fasting. Early the next morning the king hurried to the place of judgment and in tones of deep anxiety called to Daniel to know whether the God he trusted had delivered him from the lions. How amazed and relieved he was to hear Daniel's calm voice assuring the king that God had sent an angel to preserve him!

The *second* miracle is seen in the fact that Daniel remained alive and unhurt by the lions. By a supernatural interposition, the lions failed to act according to the instincts of their nature. As it is a law of the animal kingdom that beasts of the same kind always possess the same instincts, there must have been a higher law at work overruling the ordinary law in the den (Mark 1:13). The God who made the lions was able to suspend their natural ferociousness. Lions, kings of wild beasts, look to God for their food and never disobey their Creator (Psalm 104:21; I Kings 13: 24-28; 20:36). The same mighty God is able to deliver His own from another lion seeking to devour them (I Peter 5:8). Greatly honored and given high office in the Babylonian and Persian empires, Daniel, the excellent statesman who honored God, was honored by the lions. It has been suggested that Daniel had too much backbone for those lions to tackle!

The *third* miracle is just as stupendous, for the supremacy of God over all kings and councils of earth was not only manifested in God's supernatural deliverance of his faithful servant, but in the destruction of his foes. Darius was overjoyed as he heard Daniel's voice and realized that God had miraculously intervened and preserved His servant. Daniel came up out of the lions' den safe and serene, and the king commanded that all the accusers of Daniel, along with their wives and children, be cast into the den Daniel had just vacated. Immediately retribution overtook them. The divinely restrained appetite of the lions was released and their natural instinct to kill returned and they gorged themselves on the bodies of Daniel's foes. Because of this display of miraculous power Darius issued a proclamation that the God who had delivered Daniel was the only One able to work signs and wonders in the heavens and on the earth. Daniel had been among the lions but God preserved him and therefore He must be worshiped as the living God.

Before leaving the miracles in the book of Daniel, a word might be in season concerning the connection between prayer and faith and the display of the supernatural. Daniel was a very busy man and represented manifold responsibilities, yet he was never too busy to pray and God honored his believing prayers. In Hebrews (11:33), the miracle of Daniel's preservation is ascribed to his faith—"who through faith . . . stopped the mouths of lions." Daniel, however, told Darius that God sent His angel to shut the lions' mouths. There is no contradiction here. Faith caused God to work miracles on behalf of Daniel. When he had asked for time to interpret Nebuchadnezzar's dream, Daniel prayed, then went to sleep. He left the matter in God's hands and that was enough. When Daniel knew the seventy years' captivity was ending, he set his face to seek by prayer its promised accomplishments (9:2, 3). "Prayer itself is a part of a great miracle involving a wonderful exercise of God's power." If we study the great prayers of the Bible, we shall find that when God's servants poured out their hearts in supplication and intercession, they were evidently moved by the Spirit of God, who inspires intercession (Romans 8:26, 27). A full treatment of this entrancing theme can be found in *All the Prayers of the Bible*.

The miracle appearances

As there are frequent references in the book of Daniel to dreams, visions, and angelic appearances, a brief word is necessary regarding this realm of the supernatural. The reader will find the following references profitable to expand.

(1) "Nebuchadnezzer dreamed dreams" (2:1). The singular is used in verse three, "a dream," suggesting that the one dream consisted of several parts, hence the plural form in verse one. Dr. F. A. Tatford reminds us that in "a day of superstition, dreams and apparitions were always regarded as portentous, and the utmost importance was attached to their interpretation. That God speaks to individuals by the media of dreams is quite clear from Scripture (Numbers 12:6; Job 33:15, 16; Joel 2:28)." Nebuchadnezzar, although a heathen king, received two divine revelations

in dreams. His enchanters were unable to interpret the king's dream because he was not able to recall the dream. The impression of it remained, but its details had left his mind.

(2) "The secret revealed unto Daniel in a night vision" (2:19). The substance and interpretation of the king's dream were given to Daniel by God, not in a dream, but in a *vision* (Numbers 12:6). Just how the communication or the secret was revealed (2:28), we are not told. Such a revelation, however, was gratefully recognized by Daniel and he praised God for His almightiness in what was practically a psalm full of beauty.

(3) "I saw a dream which made me afraid" (4:5). This troubled dream came to the king in the midst of prosperity and pleasure in his palace, and again his enchanters were unable to interpret the dream. Nebuchadnezzar's confession of God's power to perform the miraculous is found in his exclamation, "How great are His signs! and how mighty are His wonders!" Daniel, Spirit-inspired (4:8, 18; 5:11), interpreted the dream as signifying that the king's heart was to be changed from a man's and become like a beast's, and a year later this miraculous transformation and tragedy took place.

(4) "The watchers . . . the holy ones" (4:17). Those who were to execute the decree were celestial beings, the angels who, as Pusey expresses it, "long that oppression should cease and join in the cry which for ever is going up from the oppressed to the throne of mercy and judgment, and pray for that chastisement which is to relieve the oppressed and convert the oppressor."

(5) "Daniel had a dream and visions of his head upon his bed" (7:1). These supernatural visions with their interpretations, beginning the second half of the book of Daniel, were granted to him through three reigns and constitute the prophetic light of each period. The final vision concerning the saints of the Most High greatly troubled Daniel, but he kept it in his heart. The action of "the four winds" and "the four beasts" reveal that all heavenly and earthly forces are under God's control and can only function by His permissive will.

(6) "The Ancient of days . . . thousands ministered unto Him, and ten thousands times ten thousand stood before Him" (7:9-12). In the vision of the setting of the

thrones there appeared the glory of One who overcame the beasts and received dominion, glory, and a kingdom. *Ancient,* applied to Deity, expresses the majesty of the Judge (Psalm 50:19; Deuteronomy 33: 27)—*white hair,* His purity and justice; *fiery flame,* his chastening and punitive righteousness; *wheels,* His omnipotent presence. The whole language of this vision suggests the omnipotence and omniscience of God, and a vast retinue attending Him to carry out His behests. Daniel was given a vision of Christ's millennial kingdom and reign (7:13, 14), for "the Ancient of Days" is "the Son of Man."

(7) "A vision appeared unto me, even unto Daniel" (8:1, 2). This further vision which came to Daniel in the third year of King Belshazzar's reign was supplementary to the one given in the previous chapter, and supplies various details respecting the second and third empires there omitted.

(8) "The appearance of a man . . . Gabriel" (8:16; 9:21; Luke 1:19, 26). In some mysterious fashion, either God or some high, angelic being assumed a human form and used a man's voice. This is the first time in the Bible where an angel is named. Evidently Gabriel's mission was to stand in the presence of God and act as His messenger on special occasions. Daniel fainted at the voice and message of Gabriel but was revived at the touch of the angel. Deep sleep was one of the effects of heavenly visions upon those who beheld them (8:18; Genesis 16:13; Exodus 33:20). Daniel alone understood the vision. When its fulfilment is at hand, then it will be generally understood (8:26, 27).

(9) "A certain Man . . . I Daniel alone saw the vision" (10:5-20). As we compare the appearance of this august Person, carefully distinguished from Gabriel (9:21), and from Michael (10:21), with John's vision (Revelation 1), there is no doubt whatever that the glorious Person appearing to Daniel by the side of the great river Hiddekel was the Lord Jesus Himself. Here we have one of His Old Testament preappearances. Such a radiant revelation reduced Daniel, as it did John (Revelation 1:17), to weakness, yet filled him with an overwhelming sense of awe. Daniel, prostrate in the dust, felt the touch of this most glorious One, who then told the prophet the history of his people in the latter days. Campbell Morgan has the suggestive comment:

There is a touch of mystic wonder about this story as this glorious One speaks with the kings of Persia, of being in conflict with principalities, having dominion over earthly kingdoms, and being helped by a prince Michael, evidently of spiritual nature rather than a material manifestation.

"Michael, one of the chief princes" (10: 13; 12:1, 5), The margin has it, "the first of the princes." Daniel speaks of him as "the great prince" (12:1) and Jude (9), as "the archangel." Only two good angels are named in the Bible, Gabriel and Michael. These head principalities of the unseen world appear as counterparts of governments of this world and as guardians of God's people. Michael appears to be the special angelic ruler for Israel (see also Jude 9 and Revelation 12:7). Some writers identify Michael as "the angel of the Lord." How little we know of the truth of invisible powers ruling and influencing nations! God's angelic host carry out God's purposes in the natural world (Exodus 12: 33), in the moral world (Luke 15:10), and in the political world. In Michael, Israel had a spiritual protector and champion (10:13). Daniel heard "the man clothed in linen" swear in mystic language that all that had been supernaturally revealed would be supernaturally accomplished. (See the writer's volume on *The Mystery and Ministry of Angels.*)

The miracle of resurrection (12:2)

That the Old and the New Testaments are one is seen in this advance glimpse of the resurrections of two distinct companies (Matthew 25:46; John 5:29). Here we have the eternal future of all souls. The Bible knows nothing of a general resurrection. There is the resurrection of the sleeping dead in Christ to eternal life (I Thessalonians 4:16) and resurrection of the wicked dead to eternal contempt (Revelation 20:11-15). May all wisdom be ours to turn many to righteousness so that they also will escape eternal shame and remorse!

2. The Twelve Minor Prophets

Although the only acted miracles in these twelve prophetical books are confined to the book of Jonah, each of the others adds its contribution to the Biblical revelation of God's almightiness. "To Him give *all* the prophets witness" (Acts 10:43). Our Lord could expound "in *all* the prophets" the things concerning Himself (Luke 24:27, 44). As we shall see, witness was given, not only to His sacrificial work and coming reign, but also to His miraculous power as Co-Creator (Colossians 1:16).

The burden of this last section of the Old Testament is *prophetical,* and as such offers a most direct proof of the divine authority of the Bible. Prophecy not only proves the Bible to be God's infallible Word, but is likewise an evidence of the miraculous. Bishop Horsley remarks:

> The evidence of prophecy lies in these two particulars; that events have been predicted which are not within human foresight; and that the accomplishment of predictions has been brought about which must surpass human power and contrivance; the prediction, therefore, was not from man's sagacity, nor the event from man's will and design. And then, the goodness of the design, and the intricacy of the contrivance, complete the proof that the whole is of God.

HOSEA

Hosea was contemporary with Isaiah and prophesied almost exclusively to the Ten Tribes. He addresses them under the title of Samaria, which was the capital of their kingdom, and also under the title of Ephraim, which was the most distinguished of the Ten Tribes and to whom Jeroboam II, their king, belonged. Hosea began his ministry in the reign of Jeroboam II when there was great prosperity and when iniquity was fast working the ruin of the nation. He labored for more than sixty years with very little success. Probably he lived to see his awful threatenings executed in the captivity of the Ten Tribes. Nicholls, says of Hosea that "he was a bright example, in the midst of an adulterous and sinful generation, of perceiving fidelity under the greatest discouragements." Against such a background, his references to the miraculous are impressive. Hosea's prophecy abounds in evidences of God's miraculous provision and patience toward His sinning people.

The miracles of divine judgment (2:6-23; 9:14-17; 13:7, 8)

The miracle of divine mercy (3:1-3; 14: 4-9)

God's sovereignty is seen in His power to make a people which are not His people so that they too shall confess, "Thou art my God!" To Hosea himself God was the

Most High (7:16). Israel forgot God as their Lord and Maker (8:14), yet forgiving grace was His.

The miracle of divine deliverance and preservation (13:4; 14:1)

The people were commanded never to forget the Lord their God, who not only brought them into being, but who also miraculously undertook for them from the days of their Egyptian bondage.

The miracle of victory over death (13: 14)

This sudden outburst of hope, along with Isaiah's declaration that death is to be swallowed up in victory (25:8), inspired Paul to write his tribute of praise for God's final victory over death (I Corinthians 15: 54-57).

JOEL

Joel, who addressed his prophecies to Judah, has been described as the "Prophet of the Holy Spirit," as Isaiah is emphatically the "Prophet of the Messiah." Briefly stated, Joel expounds with peculiar force the terrible judgments threatened against the people of Judah, exhorts them to repentance with fasting and prayer, and promises the favor of God to those who should be obedient.

The miracle of the plague of locusts (1: 15-20)

As we meditate upon the exhibition of God's power in the affairs of nations, we realize how true the comment of Dr. F. A. Tatford is that, "Divine interposition in earthly circumstances is not infrequent as might sometimes be concluded and the threads of power are still gathered up and held in the hands of the Supreme Ruler of the universe."

The miracle of final judgment (2:1-11; 3:1-16; Revelation 16:14)

The miracle of deliverance (2:18-27)

The miracle of the Spirit's effusion (2: 28-32; Acts 2:17, 21)

The miracle of the Second Advent (2: 30-32)

AMOS

Although Amos, as a herdsman and gatherer of sycamore fruit, had not the regular education of the schools of the prophets, nevertheless he was called of the Spirit to utter solemn judgments against the Ten Tribes and against Judah and against the kingdoms bordering on Palestine. The God who selects His servants from the tents of the shepherd as well as from the palace of a king knows how to qualify them for the service He calls them to (I Corinthians 1:27, 29). "No other prophets more magnificently described the deity, more gravely rebuked the luxurious, or reproved injustice and oppression with greater warmth or more generous indignation."

Phrases like "The Lord will roar" (1:2), "I will send fire" (1:4, 7, 10, 12, 14; 2:1, 5), "I will not turn away punishment" (1: 3, 9, 11, 13; 2:1, 4, 6), "I will turn mine hand against Ekron" (1:8; 2:3), and "I will break the bar of Damascus" (1:5) all affirm God to be the One who controls the destinies of nations. He has the right to judge them in any way He deems best. Because He is supreme, He can destroy their fruit from above and their roots from beneath (2:9; 6:14; 9:1-12).

The miracle of the wilderness journey (2: 10)

The miracle of divine revelation (3:7)

The miracle of the creation and the control of natural forces (4:6-13; 5:8; 7:1, 2; 8:9-11; 9:13-15)

OBADIAH

Obadiah who delivered his brief yet solemn prophecy soon after the destruction of Jerusalem by Nebuchadnezzar, denounced the descendants of Esau and predicted their judgment in spite of their fancied greatness and pride. Hating pride, God has His own way of humiliating those whose pride of heart has deceived them (2 - 4). Because of His almightiness, final sovereignty shall be the Lord's (21).

JONAH

There is no reason to doubt that Jonah himself wrote the book bearing his name. Its genuineness cannot be denied. The more one studies such a literary gem, the more convinced one is that the events took place as recorded. None but Jonah could have written or dictated the book, for here are details so peculiar that they could be known only to himself. The candor of the writer and the graphic style of the book harmonize with the resolute character of Jonah as seen in its pages. As Jonah was among the earliest of the proph-

ets who wrote, it is not difficult to accept him as the author of "this most wonderful story ever written."

Modernists reject the book as coming from Jonah. They affirm that it is a composition from various sources and that the historicity of Jonah is to be doubted—which affirmation casts a reflection upon the integrity of Jesus who spoke of Jonah as one who had actually lived. It is the fashion in scholarly (?) circles to treat Jonah as fiction, or as an imaginary hero, and his book merely as a symbolic narrative, "an anonymous Hebrew tract." Christ's testimony, however, proves the personal existence, miraculous fate, and prophetical offices of Jonah. To Him, Jonah was not a fictitious character, and his story was history, not allegory (Matthew 12:39-41).

All we know of Jonah is found in his book and in one other passage where he is spoken of as the son of Amittai, the prophet of Gath-hepher (II Kings 14:25). Jewish tradition identifies this Galilean with the widow's son at Zarephath, whom Elijah restored to life. Jonah himself was a prophet of the Northern Kingdom of Israel and a contemporary of Hosea and Amos. The formula opening the book, "The word of the Lord came unto Jonah," is that which introduced the prophecies of Jeremiah, Hosea, Joel, Micah, and Zephaniah and stamps the book as belonging to "the oracles of God" and therefore distinct from all other literature.

As to the interpretation of the book of Jonah, there are those, as we have already suggested, who treat it as being purely *mythical*—a legend that found its way into the Old Testament. Others deal with it as being *allegorical*—a tract written in the form of a story with a moral aimed at the exclusive attitude of the Jews, who regarded God as theirs and theirs only. Personally, we accept the *traditional* view of the book which affirms that Jonah was a real person and that the related events actually happened. Here we have a dramatic account of experiences that befell the prophet.

The miraculous or supernatural element characterizes the book as a whole. We seldom find so many and so great wonders accumulated in the compass of so brief a narrative. Those who deny the possibility of miracles offer a great variety of explanations for the presence of this book in the Bible. To the Christian mind, the actual history of Jonah rests upon the Lord's testimony as to Jonah's being an actual person whose death and resurrection was a sign of His own death and resurrection.

As to the object of the book, it teaches not only the nature and efficacy of true repentance—*individual* repentance in Jonah's case, and *national* repentance as in Nineveh. The book is also a protest against the grudging narrow-mindedness of Israel in denying the Gentile world and the grace and goodness of God. To the Jews, God was the God of Israel. Jonah shared the intolerance of his nation and needed to learn God's compassion for all men and nations. In His sight, none are outcasts, except by sin. Thus, as we are to see, the book is a remarkable demonstration of the sovereignty of God. Its miracles reveal Him as being supreme in any realm.

The observation of Charles Reade, in *Jonah*, is the most impressive we have encountered:

> The Book of Jonah is the most beautiful story ever written in so small a compass. In writing, it is condensation that declares the master; verbosity and garrulity have their day, but only hot-pressed narrative lives for ever. The Book of Jonah is in 48 verses, or 1,328 English words. Take our best current literature. Thirteen hundred and twenty-eight words—how far will they carry you? You get nothing at all but chatter, chatter, chatter. In Jonah, you hear a wealth of incident and all the dialogue needed to carry on the grand and varied action. You have also character, not stationary, but growing just as Jonah grew, and a plot that would bear volumes, yet worked out without haste or crudity in 1,328 words. In Jonah we have the perfect proportion of dialogue and narrative.

The miracle of the storm (1:1-16)

The book opens with Jonah's disobedience in refusing the divine commission to go to Nineveh and proclaim its doom. Jonah resolved to disobey, and because his disobedience was deliberate and wilful, he "fled unto Tarshish, from the presence of the Lord." Rather than obey so unwelcome a command, Jonah renounced his office as a prophet and supplied the reason of his flight (4:2; Deuteronomy 10:6). Knowing the loving-kindness of God, he anticipated that God would spare Nineveh on its repentence. Therefore he could not be a messenger of mercy to those people who had made war with his people.

Jonah fled, then, not because he was a coward, but because he knew that God would be merciful toward Nineveh. What he wanted was further respite and compassion for Israel, but swift and overwhelming judgment for Nineveh. The patriot within him was stronger than the prophet.

For a while everything seemed to favor Jonah's project. Reaching Joppa, he found a ship about to sail for Tarshish and, paying the fare, was accepted as a passenger. Runaway servants can usually find a convenient ship and misinterpret providences when the mind is set to disobey. Doubtless Jonah hailed the provision of the ship as a providential endorsement of his line of action, just as a backslider accepts favorable circumstances as an excuse or justification for sin. Punishment for the prophet's disobedience, however, came in the storm and its dire consequences.

As soon as Jonah decided on the effort he thought would be successful, God arrested His runaway servant by the judgment of a sudden and violent storm. A wild hurricane burst upon the ship. The narrative does not say that there arose a giant wind, but that "the Lord sent out a great wind into the sea, and there was a mighty tempest." Such a fierce storm is not attributed to the elements of nature, but to the direct action of the God of nature—to Him who is over all and *above* all. The Lawgiver is here found administering His laws (Psalm 107:23-31). How true it is that the winds and the waves obey His will! (Matthew 8:27).

God's controversy with His servant, and the intervening miracle, involved others in the danger of death, for the storm He sent forth not only pursued and punished Jonah, but brought peril to the others on the ship. The conduct of the heathen mariners, however, stands in striking and favorable contrast to that of God's prodigal prophet. They called upon their gods and exerted every effort to save the tempest-driven vessel. Jonah was moody, miserable, and weary with mental conflict and bodily fatigue and had to be roused from a deep sleep to consciousness and prayer by the reproaches of the heathen captain. What indignant surprise he expressed at the unreasonableness of Jonah's conduct (1:6)!

Jonah was never in greater peril than at that moment; yet he slept. "A quiet conscience is not always a good one." Our Lord, sleeping amidst the storm on the

lake, furnishes at once a comparison and a
contrast (Mark 4:38). The Mediterranean
storm ceased directly when Jonah was cast
out of the ship into the sea. The storm
ceased on the Galilean lake immediately
when the disciples received Jesus into the
ship. Although idolaters, the sailors, in the
danger and distress the divinely produced
storm had produced, recognized the supremacy of the God by whose providence
in the world is governed, and in whose
hands are the safety and life of all men
(1:6). They called upon their gods, then
urged Jonah to cry unto his God.

The casting of lots and the detection of
Jonah as the cause of the tempest, and
then his frank and full confession, are full
of instruction. Philo says, "One might see
in the scene a terrible tribunal! for the
ship was the court of justice, the judges
were the sailors, the executioners were the
winds, the prisoner at the bar was Jonah,
the house of correction and prison of safe
keeping was the whale, and the accuser
was the angry sea."

Realizing that Jonah was a worshiper of
the Most High and Almighty God and
that he should know how His anger could
be appeased, the sailors asked reproach-
fully, "Why hast thou done this? . . . What
shall we do unto thee?" In despair, Jonah
offered himself to death. He knew his
disobedience merited punishment. Whether
he conceived a hope of preservation and
in confidence rested on the grace of God is
not clear. Calvin remarks:

> Jonah goes forth to his death because he
> perceives and is assuredly persuaded that
> he is in a manner summoned by the open
> voice of God. And so there is no doubt
> that he patiently undergoes the judgment
> which the Lord has brought against him.

As Jonah was cast into the raging sea,
the sailors' vague fear of God vanishes and
they recognized the God of Jonah as Jehovah and paid their vows unto Him. To
them, it was evident that the whole thing
was of God, for immediately the wind
ceased its raging and the ship was saved.
The mariners recognized God's hand in
the sudden calm and experienced once
more peace of mind.

The miracle of the great fish (1:17 - 2)

Cast into the sea by the sailors at his
own request, Jonah is swallowed by a
large fish which the Lord prepared as a
tomb for His disobedient and now repentant prophet. The word "prepared," mean-

ing *assigned* or *appointed,* is the same word
and tense used of the gourd, the worm,
and the east wind (4:6-8). The word is
rendered "appointed" in Job 7:3; Daniel 1:
5, 10, and "set" in Daniel 1:11. Perowne
comments that "prepared" does not necessarily imply any previous or special *preparation,* much less the *creation* of these
various agents for the purpose to which
they were put, but merely that they were
appointed to it by Him, whom "all things
serve." God sent the fish there to do His
bidding. The inhabitants of the sea are
just as obedient to His control as other
creatures which He created.

Kalisch says, "By God's immediate direction [everything] was so arranged that the
very moment when Jonah was thrown into
the waves, the great fish was on the spot
to receive him: God charged the fish to
perform this function, as He afterwards
'spoke to' it (2:10) or commanded it to
vomit out the prophet on dry land." This
is the same God who prepared the rich
man's tomb in which Isaiah prophesied
Jesus would be buried (53:9). God spake
to the fish, and God's voice caused the
grave to open.

Personally, we believe that the miraculous in this transaction was not in Jonah's
preservation alive and conscious for three
days and three nights in a living prison,
but in his resurrection after having *died.*
We do not doubt for one moment that by
the working of Almighty God, he was
not able to keep Jonah alive and well in
the sea-monster's belly for the period mentioned. A comparison of Matthew 12:40;
16:4 with I Corinthians 15:4 shows that
the period of Jonah's stay in the fish was
divinely ordered to be a type of Christ's
being "three days and three nights in the
heart of the earth." In both cases we
affirm there was death and resurrection.

Dr. Hugh Martin in his volume on
Jonah says, "By the hand of God, Jonah
was in the judgment put to death and
brought to life again." How could one man
miraculously kept alive for three days in
his watery tomb be a fitting type of another Man dead and buried for three days?
Was not Jonah the chief type of our Lord's
death and resurrection and the only sign
granted to this generation? Of course it
would have been a miracle if Jonah had
retained his faculties for three days inside
the great fish and then escaped uninjured
in mind and body. But such a miraculous

preservation would not have been a type of physical death and resurrection.

Further, Jonah prayed "out of the belly of hell" (2:2), and the basic meaning of the word "hell" is *sheol*, the sphere of departed bodies (Psalm 18:5). Jonah considered the great fish his grave, and a grave is not for the living but for the dead. The whole of the prophet's prayer (he probably prayed before he lost consciousness, or out of hell as the rich man prayed (Luke 16) corroborates the conclusion that he actually died. Brought up from "corruption" (2:6) is a synonym of death. It was said of Lazarus, dead for four days, "he stinketh." Only of Christ is it said that He did not suffer "corruption" (Psalm 16:10). In Jonah's *Canticle*—"Salvation is of the Lord" (2:9), we have his praise for deliverance in its fullest sense, not only from his disobedience but from the death it deserved.

Would not his emergence *alive* from the fish greatly influence those Ninevites as Jonah intreated them to repent? It is said that the Florentines looked upon Dante as he passed through their streets with awe, and whispered to each other, "This is the man who has looked into hell." Jonah must have created a similar impression. Here was a prophet brought back from his peculiar grave to preach the message of divine grace, and as the apostles were so dynamic in their witness as they preached "Jesus and the Resurrection," so Jonah had added power in his preaching as one who had died and risen again. Not only forgiven but restored to life and to his office, Jonah is anew commissioned and is now ready to obey.

Preaching the shortest revival sermon on record—only eight words, "Yet forty days and Nineveh shall be overthrown," Jonah witnessed another miracle, namely, that of a city in sackcloth. The people, from the king down, repented of their sins and turned to God, and such national repentance was, in itself, a miracle of grace. Just as Jonah's message derived its authority with the Ninevites from his death and resurrection, so Christ's resurrection was the grand proof of His Messiahship and of His power and will to save. In each case, death and resurrection constituted the gate by which the Word of God passed from the Jewish world to the Gentile world. Both Jonah and the One greater than Jonah broke down the middle wall of partition (Ephesians 2:14. See Hosea 6:2 for a typical significance of Jonah's entombment).

The miracle of the gourd (4:6)

The clemency of God towards Nineveh because of its repentance greatly displeased Jonah, whose grief was not a selfish anger. The prophet was vexed and irritated over the largeness of God's mercy. It was the expectancy of such mercy that prompted Jonah's unwillingness to undertake the divine mission at the first. He preferred judgment to mercy. Now he is angry over the manifestation of divine grace and, returning from the city, waited to see if God would yet take vengeance upon the Ninevites.

While resting under the roof of a booth-like hut under which to watch for the fate of Nineveh, God caused a wide-spreading plant to spring up and cover Jonah's resting place with its refreshing shade. This particular plant, which because of its resemblance to the extended palm of the hand, gained for it the name of *Palma Christi* or *Palmchrist*, grows abundantly and to a great size in the neighborhood of the Tigris. Under favorable conditions, its rapid growth causes it to rise quickly to about eight feet in five or six months. In this instance, the naturally rapid growth of the plant was miraculously accelerated. As in many other miracles, the omnipotent God at once resembled nature and exceeded nature in the provision of a shadow for Jonah's head and in a means of deliverance from his grief. In this instance, God surpassed the course of nature.

Under the broad shadow of the gourd, Jonah was guilty of a gloomy and dissatisfied frame of mind—a sad feeling aggravated by the weariness and oppression of his spirit and also the heat and closeness of his booth, which was far from being impervious to the rays of the sun. Gradually the refreshing shade of the gourd gave Jonah bodily comfort and tended to calm and soothe his agitated mind. He was exceedingly glad of the gourd affording external comfort to turn such a single-minded man from his grief. Giving himself up to the delicious soothing of the cool shade, Jonah began to regain a brighter and healthier outlook and to rest his soul in God. How tender and tactful God is even when we give way to sullen moodiness.

The miracle of the worm (4:6)

Scarcely had Jonah begun to enjoy the

welcome shelter which the gourd afforded him from the burning rays of the sun, than God, in pursuit of His lesson, caused the plant to be attacked by insects which rapidly stripped it of its protecting leaves, causing it to wither. Gourds wither as rapidly as they grow, after a storm or injury to stems. Again, the Almighty God accommodated Himself to nature. While the destruction of the plant by the prepared worm may have been in the way of nature, God caused the worm at that precise moment to suddenly destroy the gourd. Ellicott observes that the word for "worm" can be taken collectively for a swarm of caterpillars as in Isaiah 14:11.

The sudden withering of the gourd taught Jonah another needed lesson. His joy over the gourd was short-lived, for the insignificant worm and the prepared sultry east wind exposed Jonah to the blazing sun and, giving way once more to despair, "he requested for himself that he might die." The life of the large, protective gourd was short-lived. Thus is it with many earthly confidences and joys (Psalm 30:7). The heart entwines around its gourds, or pleasing prospects, then in a moment one is stripped of all creature confidences.

The miracle of the vehement east wind (4:8-10)

The God who sent out that great wind to catch up with Jonah as he ran away from his task (1:4) now prepared a vehement east wind to rob him of his shelter. Both winds fulfilled His will. The occurrence of such a wind at sunrise is referred to by James as being usual. The same Greek word is used for "burning heat" as is used in the LXX Version (Jonah 4:8; James 1:11). The root meaning of "vehement" is *silent* and points to the "quiet sirocco," more overpowering than a more boisterous wind. When travelers encounter this sultry sirocco, they do not have energy enough to make a noise and "the very air is took weak and languid to stir the pendant-leaves of the tall poplars."

The hot sun accompanied by the hot wind proved too much for Jonah who fainted and desired to die. When fleeing from the wrath of Jezebel, Elijah expressed the same wish to die (I Kings 19:4). Perhaps Jonah had Elijah in mind when he gave vent to his request for death. The Hand that governs all things set in motion a series of events, large and small, to teach Jonah that God had a right to His own

way and a right to show pity on whom He would. In the raging storm, the prepared fish, the sheltering gourd, the destroying worms, and the wind, God taught His servant something of His power and grace.

Jonah's grief for the loss of the gourd was made by God the occasion of rebuking the prophet's want of pity for Nineveh, and of justifying His own merciful compassion in sparing that great city with its teeming population and much cattle (4:8-11). Were not men and women, innocent children, and very much cattle much better than a plant? Jonah had done nothing for the gourd. He had not planted, or trained, or watered it, yet he pitied it, and mourned for its decay with a yearning tenderness. All souls were fashioned by God, and His tender mercies are over all His works, and as the Lover of souls is ever compassionate. Thus God's pathetic and condescendingly touching appeal winds up this book of miracles. His tender accents are the last that reach the ear, the abruptness of the close making them the more impressive. "Thou hast had pity on the gourd, for which thou hast not laboured, neither madest it grow. . . . Should not I spare Nineveh?"

As we take leave of our meditation of "one of the deepest and grandest things ever written," we think of God as the All-Great who is the All-Loving too. He who can measure the waters in the hollow of His hand can also carry the lambs in His bosom. To Him belong both power and mercy. His power without the mercy would crush us; His mercy without His power would stagger and fail when it sought to deliver. We must have both in harmony and union, and the book of Jonah presents them thus. Divine omnipotence prevails in nature and over human impotence, and His gentleness makes us great.

MICAH

Here was a prophet, capable of deep sorrow over the calamities he was called to foretell, and also of tempering of his denunciations of severe judgment with promises of mercy (1:8; 7:13). One of his inspired predictions saved the life of Jeremiah (3:12; Jeremiah 26:18-24). The exaltation of the Divine Kingdom over all nations anticipates the glorious displays of divine might and mercy more fully revealed in the New Testament (4:2, 7 with Luke 1:33; 5:5

with Ephesians 2:14; 7:18, 19 with Luke 1:72, 73).

The miraculous power of the Divine Presence (1:3, 4; 3:11; 4:1; 5:10-15)

The miracle of the Spirit's power (2:7; 3:8)

The miracle of divine grace (6:8; 7:18, 19)

NAHUM

The book of Nahum should be read as a continuation or supplement of the book of Jonah, since both of them contain prophecies directed against Nineveh. Both books form connected parts of our moral history—*Jonah*, the remission of God's judgments—*Nahum*, the execution of these judgments. From the book of Nahum we learn the moral use of prophecy which contains not only anticipations of the future, but also confirmation of the faith of the true believer in present witness. Nahum's prophecy is one entire poem, opening with a sublime description of the justice and power of God, tempered with long-suffering (1:1-8).

The miracle of divine holiness (1:1-13)

The miracle of divine judgment (2:2, 13; 3:5)

HABAKKUK

Apart from the pronouncement of the destruction of the Chaldeans, who afflicted the Jews and completed the captivity of the remaining tribes, two noticeable features are observable. First the book of Habakkuk breathes the spirit of prayer. Expressing his holy indignation over the iniquity of his countrymen, he yet earnestly intercedes for their welfare. The concluding prayer, in which the prophet describes the wonders of God wrought for Israel in times past, inspired the godly among them with confidence as they faced their approaching calamity. The next feature is that the great principle characterizing the true servant of God in every age, namely, faith (2:3, 4—a passage quoted three times in the New Testament—Romans 1:17; Galatians 3:11; Hebrews 10:37, 38. See also Hebrews 11; Galatians 2:20). Such faith enables us to laugh at impossibilities and to joy even in tribulation (3:17-19; Romans 5:1-3).

The miracle of divine omnipotence—"O mighty God" (1:5, 14; Psalm 50:1).

The miracle vision (2:1-20). Because of His greatness and His power to interpose

His will, "let all the earth keep silence before Him" (2:20).

The miracle of divine glory (3:1-16). Is it not wonderful to realize that the Almighty One is our strength? (3:19)

ZEPHANIAH

Zephaniah, contemporary with Jeremiah, is another prophet of gloom who predicted the great day of distress, desolation, and darkness, and who declared that sin was the cause of such a fateful day (1:15). The prophet announces God's wrath against the nations persecuting His people; and foretells the dispersion and ultimate conversion of the Jews.

The miracle of divine judgment (1 - 2: 1-3; 3:8-13)

The miracle of divine might (3:17)

HAGGAI

Born in captivity and returning from Babylon with Zerubbabel (Ezra 2:2), Haggai was the first prophet who ministered among the Jews after their return to Jerusalem. He was raised up to exhort Zerubbabel and Joshua the high priest to resume the interrupted work of building the Temple (Ezra 5:1; 4:24), and his ministry was effective (Ezra 6:14).

The miracle of divine intervention (1:3-11; 2:6, 7) "I did blow upon it" suggests the defeat of the Spanish Armada when "God blew, and the ships were scattered."

The miracle of divine choice (2:23). All the chosen of the Lord form a miracle of His grace.

ZECHARIAH

Coming on to the scene about two months after Haggai, Zechariah seems to have had the same task to fulfill, namely, to encourage and urge the Jews to rebuild the Temple and to restore its public ordinances. Ezra tells us that the ministry of these two prophets was not in vain (Ezra 6: 14). Two objects of Zechariah's mission were, first of all, the symbolic presentation of the four great empires—Babylonia, Persia, Greece, Rome—and secondly, the foretelling of the future condition of the Jews after the destruction of the last empire, Rome. Zechariah had a fitting way of interspersing his prophecies with many moral instructions and admonitions. The second feature of the book of Zechariah is its most frequent and plain references to the advent, mission, and death of Christ. Next to Isaiah, Zechariah is outstanding in his prophecies of the coming Messiah, specifying some aspects not indicated by Isaiah. Both Advents of Christ are dwelt upon by the prophet (9:9 with Matthew 21:1-11 and Zechariah 14:3, 4).

The miracle of the ten visions (1 - 6)

The miracle of divine protection (2:5-13; 9:16)

The miracle of angelic appearances (3:1; 4:1)

The miracle of divine omniscience (4:10)

The miracle of divine accomplishment (8:6; 10:1, 5, 12; 12:1-10; 14:17, 18)

MALACHI

As the book of Malachi contains the last word from God before the silence of 400 years, it is important to observe the divine revelation preceding such a gap and also the new era to follow. Malachi exercised his ministry about the time of Nehemiah's administration and is the last of Old Testament prophets, as Nehemiah is the last of its historians. Nicholls says that Malachi's task as "a *minister* was to reprove the Jews for many great abuses which, even so soon after such judgments and such mercies as attended their captivity and return from Babylon, still prevailed among both priests and people."

Malachi was also among the prophets giving witness to Christ. Thus, "as a prophet he foretold the coming of our Lord, the Messenger of the Covenant, the Sun of Righteousness, and His forerunner, John the Baptist. As the spirit of prophecy was now to cease, the Messiah having been clearly and progressively made known to the Jews by a long succession of prophets more and more distinct in their predictions, Malachi, with peculiar solemnity concludes his mission, seals up the volume of prophecy by a description of a prophet which is applied in the New Testament to Him, with an account of whom the evangelists begin their Gospel history." Malachi was therefore the personal precursor of Christ and concludes the old dispensation with the Gospel of the new dispensation on his tongue.

It is Malachi who reminds us that God is "the great King, the Lord of Hosts" and that "His name is dreadful among the nations" (1:14)—that because of His supremacy He is able to curse our blessings (2:2); able to appear suddenly (3:1); able to bless (3:10, 11); and able to send, before the Day of the Lord, the miracle-working Elijah (4:5, 6).

While the purpose of our study is to cover the supernatural in Scripture, a paragraph or two may be in order regarding the spurious supernatural to be found in *The Apocrypha,* which was formerly printed between the Testaments in nearly all Protestant editions of the Bible. This collection of books, without divine inspiration, is simply an aggregate of human productions made up of fables and fiction, and was developed in the period between Malachi and Matthew. The term *Apocrypha* itself meant a material object hidden or concealed, then came to signify what was obscure, hard to understand unless one belonged to the initiated (Colossians 2:3). The term was applied by Clement of Alexandria and Tertullian to forged books which heretics put forward as belonging to Scripture, possessing *secret* esoteric knowledge.

The Apocrypha was never considered sacred by the Jews. Josephus, the Jewish historian who lived around Christ's time, rejected it, and our Lord and His apostles who endlessly quoted from the Old Testament, never once quoted *The Apocrypha.* The New Testament links itself immediately with the end of the Old Testament as if no inspired writing came between (Malachi 3:1; 4:5, 6; with Mark 1:2; Luke 1:16, 17). The Bible alone stands out in its sacredness before the world as God's only and final revelation to man.

Here are samples of the so-called miraculous both in *The Apocrypha* and in *Apocalyptic Writings.*

The historical romance of Judith in Nebuchadnezzar's time.

God's power in creation and the miraculous provision for Israel in the wilderness *Wisdom of Solomon* 11:17-20; 13:1-9; 16:20, 22; 17:18; 18:3, 12, etc.)

The laws of nature and their independence—cures by prayer (Ecclesiasticus 16:28; 38:1-14; 42:23-25; 43:11, 12, 27-32)

Bel and the Dragon, and other additions to the Book of Daniel

Revelations given to Enoch and Noah in the *Book of Enoch*

The Apocalyptic Writings, considered unreliable, is a form of literature in which the writer "assumed the name of some hero long since dead, and rewrote history in terms of prophecy."

PART TWO — THE NEW TESTAMENT

INTRODUCTION

The New Testament commences as if it were a continuation of the Old Testament, which, of course, it is. There is no recognized break. But, as we remarked at the end of our Old Testament study, there is a gap of some four hundred years between the two Testaments. Yet the record proceeds as the progressive revelation of God the Bible is.

The last word of the Old Testament is "curse" (Malachi 4:6), while the opening phrase of the New Testament is "the generation of Jesus Christ" (Matthew 1:1), which is as it should be. *Curse—Christ*. *Curse* summarizes the effect of man's disobedience of God's law in Old Testament Scriptures—"cursed is every one that continueth not in all things which are written in the book of the law to do them" (Galatians 3:10). As promised, Christ came to nullify that curse and deliver man from it (Genesis 3:15, 17; Deuteronomy 21:3). By His death and resurrection, Christ provided redemption from such a curse (Galatians 3:13).

The human, Jewish genealogy of Jesus, with which Matthew begins his gospel, is remarkable in that Jesus is traced back to Abraham and is thus associated with the history of His ancient people (Matthew 1:21). Yet although He came of "the tribe of Judah," He was distinct from it, for He came miraculously. The supernatural is also seen in the fact that from the first promise of Christ as the Seed (Genesis 3:15), the Devil sought to destroy that Seed, or the royal line, from which Jesus was to come from the human standpoint, and now and again he almost succeeded. But God, who is high over all, kept the line intact. Thus, miracle of miracles, Jesus came, born of a woman, born under the law. But as Dr. Campbell Morgan expresses it, "The Jewish system could not produce Him. He came to crown the system and transform it. So came the KING, but His name was called JESUS, for the kingdom had disintegrated and been devastated by sin, and He must begin by saving His people from their sins."

The fact of New Testament miracles

Agnostics and rationalists have tried to explain the miracles of the New Testament as natural phenomena. What cannot be denied, however, is the fact that the supernatural pervades the gospels. Modernists reject this miraculous element on the ground that no account embracing supernatural events can be accepted as historical. There has been a concerted effort to explain every miracle on the basis of natural causes. There are universal laws to which all phenomena, natural and spiritual, are subject; hence any interference with these laws is ruled out.

Before us in the gospels is a supernatural Person who is represented as having a supernatural birth, character, deeds, claims, and resurrection. There is the *miracle* of His miracles, the miracle both of His used and *unused* power. Modernists allow that this remarkable Man had the gift of healing, but all His cures were only "faith-cures," and not in any way supernatural. But all efforts to explain Christ's miracles as the product of the action of unknown natural laws break down in the presence of acts such as giving sight to the blind and raising the dead, which forcefully imply an exercise of creative power by One who transcends the ordinary powers of nature.

Christ came into the world, not only as God's personal representative on earth, but as God Himself manifest in flesh, and therefore appeared as a miracle in human form. But if one accepts the miracles of His birth, sinlessness, and resurrection, then any other miracle is possible. Further, the character and claims of Christ perfectly agree. His miraculous labors are bound up inseparably with His life; and labors and life harmonize completely. As the *Truth* (John 14:6), He proclaimed truth. His moral perfection and spiritual greatness make Him pre-eminent among the holiest of men. His was a sinless personality, a fact which in itself was a miracle and was only credible by a creative miracle of His origin.

Man is born in sin (Psalm 51:5; Romans 5:12), but Christ was born holy, harmless, undefiled, and separate from sinners (Luke 1:35; I Peter 2:22; Hebrews 7:26). Apart from the virgin birth, we cannot account for the miracle of

Christ's sinlessness, as we shall discover when we come to deal with His supernatural conception by the Holy Spirit. Conscious, then, of His sinless character—"Which of you convinceth Me of sin?" (John 8:46)—and therefore of His separation from sinners, He was likewise conscious of His God-given vocation to bless and relieve mankind in supernatural ways.

Because Christ was authoritative as a teacher (Matthew 7:28, 29) and sinless as a man, His miracles not only formed an integral part of His teaching but were proofs both of His authority as God's sent One and of His sinlessness. Because of who He was, He could not but perform miracles. Thus, as Fairbairn expresses it, "Christ's life and doctrine form one series of pillars, His miracles another, upon which the dome of the Christian Church is lifted towards heaven." Christ's miracles, then, implied an exercise of creative power as God and were His Father's way of authenticating the divinity of His Son's mission among men.

Another aspect of Christ's miracles is the way they mirrored His own character and naturally expressed His love and sympathy for suffering mankind. The activity of such loving sympathy is suggested by Luke's description of this Miracle-Worker as One who went about doing good, healing all that were oppressed by the Devil (Acts 10:38). Yet a study of His constant miracle ministry reveals that He never allowed His supernatural acts of love for man to interfere with His practice of private devotion (Mark 1:34, 35). Miracles were accompanied with prayer and with the giving of thanks (John 6:21; 11:41). In His humanity Christ depended not on His own power, but upon His almighty Father in heaven.

The features of New Testament miracles
Having already dwelt upon some of the comparisons and contrasts between miracles in the Old Testament and in the New Testament (see O. T. Introduction), all we need to add on this aspect is that for the most part Old Testament miracles were of an external nature, whereas in those of the New Testament, man's domestic life was the scene of most of Christ's mighty works. For other differences, attention can be drawn to Trench's chapter on the subject. Under the section before us, we are to trace some of the distinct features of Christ's miracles.

In the first place Christ's exercise of miraculous power was foretold (Isaiah 35: 5, 6; 42:7) and so was asked for by John the Baptist (Matthew 11:2-4), and it formed the basis by the people naming Him "The Son of Man" (Matthew 12:23; John 7:31).

Then the object of Christ's miracles was not merely to astonish those who witnessed them, because many were wrought on behalf of and in the sight of obscure people. When asked for a startling sign from heaven, Christ refused to oblige (Luke 11:16). He was no magician or conjuror, as Herod learned, who thought he could command Him to perform a miracle to satisfy his curiosity. But it is evident that some of His miracles did over-awe the beholders (John 7:45, 46; 18:6).

Another marked feature of Christ's supernatural ministry is that He never worked a miracle on His own behalf. Perhaps the finding of the coin in the fish's mouth is the only exception to His rule of using His supernatural power for His own need (Matthew 17:27). He wrought no miracle until He was thirty years of age and none after that to promote His own ease and comfort. Neither extreme hunger in the wilderness nor the intense suffering in Gethsemane or on the cross could drive Him to work a miracle for His own relief when the glory of God would not be promoted by it. A league of angels waited to obey His command, but He did not solicit their help (Matthew 4:2; 16:23). He provided ample food for the hungry that followed Him, yet would not transform stones into bread to satisfy His own hunger (Matthew 4:1-4; Mark 6:35, 41). As He was dying of extreme thirst, no water miraculously appeared to slake His thirst. He depended upon the compassion of the bystanders for a sponge full of vinegar to moisten His parched lips (Mark 15:36).

Further, Christ never paraded His supernatural power. His miracles were never wrought for display, or even to prove His claims. He rejected such use as a temptation and always refused to perform a miracle to satisfy the demands of unbelief (Matthew 4:6, 7; 16:4). When a miracle was necessary, He performed it. It took a miracle to raise Lazarus from the dead, but not to roll the stone away from his grave. That was something His disciples were well able to do. The gospels reveal an economy of divine strength. Christ never performed a miracle to create a sensation or to win adherents. There were occasions when He cured the diseased but strictly enjoined them *not* to go and publish the news of their healing abroad (Mark 1: 43; 44; 5:43; 9:9).

A study of our Lord's earthly ministry also makes it clear that He did not make *every* sick person well. While He refused none who sought His aid, many were not healed. He passed by a great multitude and selected only one for healing (John 5:3, 5). Both the Bible and experience prove that healing is not always the divine will. While we pray for the sick and desire their restoration to health, we must be subject to God's holy will and purpose. Some He heals. Others are ordained to suffer. Our first desire should be, not to be healed, but to know and do God's perfect will.

Another peculiarity distinguishing our Lord's miracles is the all-constraining motive behind them. His had a deep, unceasing sympathy for those afflicted with bodily and mental diseases. "Himself took our infirmities and bare our sicknesses" (Matthew 8:7). Twelve times we read that He was "moved with compassion" (Matthew 9:36, etc.) Thus, in all of His cures, there was no ulterior motive. They were all of a beneficent character, harmonious with His life and teaching. We cannot remove the miracles from the gospels without wrecking them, as the merciful works of Jesus were woven into the very texture of His character and claims.

Again, while Jesus did not highly esteem the faith produced by His miracles (John 4:48), healing was dependent upon the faith of those seeking aid, or the faith of those closely connected with the sufferers. Such personal or vicarious faith was always rewarded (Mark 5:25-34; 7:24-30; 10:46-52; Matthew 8:5-13). Unbelief prohibited the manifestation of Christ's miraculous power (Matthew 13:58; Mark 6: 5, 6).

Then our study of Bible miracles indicates that their performance did not always lead to repentance. Belshazzar, in spite of the warning received by the writing of the mysterious hand, maintained hardness of heart and died in his gross sin. That miracles do not always result in conviction of sin is proven in the story of the rich man and Lazarus (Luke 16:19-31). If one came from hell to warn men,

they would lock him up as a lunatic. One had come from heaven to warn men, but they crucified Him. Lazarus of Bethany was raised from the dead, but religious leaders would not accept the claims of the One who performed the miracle. They sought to put Him to death.

The methods Jesus employed in His miracles indicate that He could heal with or without external means. Sometimes He laid His hands on the needy or touched them. At other times, He healed without any contact with the sufferers. His word and will were sufficient. He could heal by remote control. There were those who touched His person or garments and were healed. Occasionally He used His spittal to cure.

The Godward aspect of the gospel miracles must likewise be considered. Our Lord reveals that in His works of healing He was guided in the exercise of such power by a regard for the glory of God. Relief of the afflicted was secondary (John 11:4). The gospel miracles have two great values. First of all, they are a revelation of the power and glory of God. Secondly, they reveal man's appalling need. Thus, the healing miracles represent the ruin caused by sin and God's power and will to repair such ruin. In several places miracles are also represented as having been wrought, not so much by Christ, as by God (Matthew 9:8; 15:31; Luke 7:16; 17:15; 18:43). Once Christ attributed a miracle to the power of the Holy Spirit, referring to Him as "the Finger of God" (Luke 11:20). So Christ was not only the Source but the Medium of the supernatural.

It is likewise evident that Christ's healing acts were never tentative. In the gospel narratives there is no trace of a failure or of a relapse of any one healed. How different this is to disillusioned souls which racketeer faith-healers profess to have healed! Then the range of Christ's activity proves Him to be supreme in every realm. One group of miracles shows His control over nature; another group His power over physical and mental diseases; another group, His ability to command the spirit world.

Another feature of Christ's miracles is that they were *signs*, not universal, but a testimony of His deity (Matthew 8:4). They were "the insignia of His God-Man-hood"—the evidence of His divine commission (John 3:2; 9:30, 33; Acts 2:22), just as the miracles of the Acts of the Apostles established the Church as a divine institution.

Christ's miracles were parables in deeds, just as His parables were miracles in words. The miracles were designed to symbolize His power to meet spiritual needs, as well as physical and material needs. They were "vehicles of instruction as well as signs of His divine commission," as Fausset expresses it. Says Westcott: "A Gospel without miracles would be, if I may use the image, like a church without sacraments. The outward pledge of the spiritual gift would be wanting."

In these days when physical and mental healing is in the foreground in religious circles, and alas! many quacks are trading upon the misery of the afflicted, these facts about miracles in the Gospels must be kept in mind:

(1) There is no evidence in Scripture that God meant the gift of healing to continue in the Church.

(2) Such a gift, if it existed, in order to be Scriptural, would have to conform to these distinctive features:

Every case contacted would be healed.

Sufferers would be healed *immediately*.

All would be healed *perfectly*—no trace of disease remaining.

Cures would include broken limbs and other organic troubles.

Permanency would characterize all cures —no recurrence following elation over cure.

No payment for attempts at healing. Many modern, professed faith-healers are extremely wealthy.

I.

THE MIRACLES IN THE GOSPELS

It is impossible to calculate how many miracles Christ performed. Most of them are referred to collectively, and those are greatly in excess of the number recorded in detail. Not all He said or accomplished is recorded, and the many references to unparticularized miracles indicate that those He relieved must have been considerable. (See Matthew 4:23, 24; 9:35; 11:21; Mark 6:53-56; Luke 4:40, 41; 5:15; 6:17-19; 7:21; John 2:23; 3:2; 4:45; 21:25; Acts 10:38). What a volume it would make if *all* the parables He uttered and *all* the miracles He performed could be traced! The miracles we do have on record were specially selected by the Holy Spirit for their spiritual value and teaching.

As to the specified miracles on record, it will be found that expositors in their writings differ as to the number. Fausset says, "The 40 miracles of Christ recorded are but samples out of a greater number." Scroggie says they are 35 in number. Trench, in his wellknown volume on *The Miracles* expounds 33 of Christ's miracles. It will be seen that what we have endeavored to do is to closely examine the four gospels and set forth *every* miracle and also every event of a supernatural character recorded by the evangelists—and such an arduous task was most revealing and rewarding. We have not only the miracles Christ Himself performed, but those performed for Him and those performed by, and for, others. Some writers have dealt with Christ's miracles according to their sphere—miracles of restored sight, miracles of resurrection, etc. What we have endeavored to do is to go through the gospels and deal with their miracles more or less chronologically.

1. The Miracle of Zacharias

(Luke 1)

The narrative dealing with the birth of John the Baptist, our Lord's forerunner, presents a series of initial miracles. First of all, there was the supernatural appearance and announcement as the blameless priest ministered before the Lord. When he was engaged in his priestly duties, an angel came to him on the right hand of the altar of incense and, quieting his fear, assured him that his prayer for the promised Messiah was heard, and that his wife Elizabeth and he would have a son who would prepare the Messiah's way.

As Zacharias and Elizabeth were "well stricken in years," meaning that Elizabeth was beyond the age of conceiving and bearing a son, the angelic announcement seemed impossible and called forth an expression of latent unbelief. Incredulously, Zacharias asked, "Whereby shall I know this?" for which the temporary judgment of dumbness was inflicted upon him. Shortly after this mark of divine displeasure was removed, the once silent lips magnified God, not only for the birth of John, but for the One to whom he would bear witness. Let us examine more particularly the miraculous in the narrative before us.

First of all, we have the appearance of the angel of high rank, Gabriel, whose privilege it was along with John the Baptist, (whose birth he came from before the presence of God to announce) to prepare the way for Christ's coming. As I have indicated in my volume on *The Mystery and Ministry of Angels*, Gabriel seems to be the angelic prophet, an interpreter of the prophetic Word and a revealer of the purposes of God. It was he who flew swiftly to Daniel and expounded to him the whole course of Gentile history and who also announced to Mary that she was to be the virgin mother of the Saviour of the world.

Then there was the penalty Zacharias suffered for his reaction to Gabriel's God-given revelation. The use of hand signs by the kindred of Zacharias, as well as the use of a writing tablet (1:62, 63), seem to suggest that the godly priest was deprived of the power of hearing as well as speech. His condition was that of a deaf-mute. The God who is able to make the dumb speak (Matthew 15:31) can cause men to be dumb (1:20, 64; Ezekiel 3:26, 27). In the dumbness of Zacharias, then in his restored speech, we have a double miracle.

In the conception of John the Baptist we have another miracle. Elizabeth had been barren all through her bearing years, and at the time of Gabriel's appearance she was, like Sarah of old, beyond the natural time of having a child. The Creator, however, not only removed the barrenness of Elizabeth but determined the sex of the child she was to bear—*a son*—and also announced his name before he was born—*John* (1:13, 63).

Another miracle, unobserved it may be, yet nevertheless real, is the way Elizabeth's unborn son leaped in her womb at the salutation of Mary (1:40-44). Not only did Elizabeth recognize that the Child which Mary was to bear would be the Son of the Highest, the long-expected Messiah, but also the babe in Elizabeth's womb came to life and by his lively movements indicated his recongition of Mary's unborn Son, One who would be greater than he. From that moment Mary was filled with the Spirit and gave utterance to her soul-stirring *Magnificat*. However, surrounded as he was by the supernatural, exercising as dynamic a ministry as he did, John the Baptist was not privileged to perform one miracle (John 10:41).

2. The Miracle of the Logos

(John 1:1-14)

John opens his gospel with a most amazing sentence—"In the beginning was the Word, and the Word was with God, and the Word was God." The "in the beginning" of Genesis 1:1 introduces us to the first creative act of the Godhead, but John's "in the beginning," going back beyond the starting point of time *Genesis*, begins with and asserts the pre-existence of the Creator. "Moses strikes the chord to descend the stream of time; John strikes it to look out on the expanse of eternity lying beyond created things, but in which the Word was already existing."

Chirst is presented to us as the *Word*— a designation of His eternal ministry. "His Name is called The Word of God" (Revelation 19:13). As the Word, He came as the revelation of the Father's mind (John 14:8, 9). As words make real our inner thoughts, so Christ as the Word made the mind of God audible and His will intelligible. Words express thoughts, and Christ came expressing the divine mind. As the Word, Christ was *with* God, meaning that He was ever in the bosom of the Father. From the dateless past, Father and Son had lived in unbroken communion. Then, as the Word Christ *was* God, which implies oneness of essence. "The Father and I are one" (John 10:30). For the assertion of this coequality, religious leaders tried to stone Him (John 5:18; Philippians 2:6).

Association with God in the marvelous work of Creation is emphasized in the declaration, "All things were made by Him and without Him was not any thing made, that was made" (1:3; Colossians 1:15, 16). *By Him* is actually *through Him,* and as Dr. F. B. Meyer observes, "The preposition *through* is always used of the office of our blessed Lord in the work of creation (I Corinthians 8:6; Colossians 1:16; Hebrews 1:2) and is full of meaning. It leaves God the Father as the Origin and Source of all things, so that the elders are justified in their perpetual ascription of worship before His throne (Revelation 4:11); but God the Son, our Lord, is the Organ through which the creative purpose moves. Through Him the infinite God utters Himself in His words."

Not any thing is inserted to make exceptions impossible. The Greek reads—*not a single thing.* Behind the miracle of creation was the miracle-working Christ whom the gospels present. He it was who created the world He was to inhabit, and man, who was fashioned in His image.

Christ, who called Himself "the Life" (John 14:6), was the One who called Life into existence in its varied forms—natural and physical, animal and intellectual, spiritual and religious. He also was "the Light." Hitherto, ineffable light was insufferable, but "Christ shed it forth on created vision, revealing yet tempering its beauty, passing it through the luminous and yet shrouding veil of His words." One of the miracles of the Incarnation was that *Life* became *Light.* True life is always luminous.

The miracle of miracles was this august Creator of life and light being made flesh and, living among men, manifested an eternal glory that could not be hid (1:14). writer, F. B. Meyer:

Christ was born of a woman; yet He made woman. He ate and hungered, drank and thirsted; yet He made the corn to grow on the mountains, and poured the rivers from his crystal chalice. He needed sleep; yet He slumbers not, and needs not to repair His wasted energy. He wept; yet He created the lachrymal duct. He died; yet He is the ever-living Jehovah, and made the tree of His cross. He inherited all things by death; yet they were His before by inherent right. What else can we do but bow in reverence before such a stupendous miracle!

3. The Miracle of the Virgin Birth

(Matthew 1:18-24; Luke 1; 2)

The Incarnation of Jesus Christ is both a mystery and a miracle. How great is this mystery of godliness—God manifested in flesh! If we try to explain His virgin birth, we lose our reason. If we discredit altogether this initial miracle of Christianity, we lose our soul, for no one is a Christian after the New Testament order who affirms that Jesus had a human father as well as a human mother. He is the only Babe the world has ever known who did not have a father after the flesh. Those who doubt Christ's miraculous conception affirm that it is all too common to exaggerate the doctrinal necessity of such a tenet. But if we reject the virgin birth, we also reject the inspiration of Scripture revealing the supernaturalness of such a birth. True faith rests on the declared fact that Christ was "conceived of the Holy Spirit and born of the Virgin Mary."

Job asks the question, "How can he be clean that is born of a woman?" (25:4). Christ was born of a woman (Galatians 4:4), and of a woman born in sin and shapen in iniquity like any other woman. That she realized her need of a personal Saviour is found in her *Magnificat,* "My spirit hath rejoiced in God *my* Saviour" (Luke 1:47). Job asks again, "Who can bring a clean thing out of an unclean? Not one" (14:4). But God was able to bring a clean Babe out of a woman tainted with inherited sin.

As we have already indicated, we cannot account for the sinlessness of Jesus if we reject His birth through a virgin by the Holy Spirit. As Mary was truly His mother, an additional miracle must have been necessary to prevent the transmission of the taint through her, and this subsidiary miracle took place within her womb. In the moment of conception, the Holy Spirit laid hold of that part of the Virgin's flesh out of which the body of Jesus was to be formed and purified it, as the alchemist purifies his metal, making possible the fulfilment of Gabriel's reference to "that Holy Thing that shall be born of thee" (Luke 1:35).

Another aspect of the supernatural in our Lord's birth was that in the moment of conception, the Holy Spirit took deity and humanity and, fusing them together, made possible the Lord Jesus, who came as the God-Man. The Spirit was the love-knot between our Lord's two natures. In such a miracle there was no violation of the laws of nature but the introduction of a new Agent. The Holy Spirit supplied the seed which Joseph would have if Mary and he had been man and wife.

Mary, like godly Simeon and Anna the prophetess, waited for the redemption of Israel. Having found favor with God, Mary was somewhat terrified at the announcment of Gabriel that she would conceive and bear a Son. How she would recall the words of the prophet Isaiah! (7: 14). What perplexed Mary was the reference to the conception and birth of a child with no mention of her approaching marriage to Joseph. Reverently, accepting the angel's words in faith, she sought to know the manner of such an accomplishment. Learning that the Holy Spirit, the Source of life in all creation (Psalm 104: 30), was to overshadow her, she willingly yielded her body to Him, saying, "Be it unto me according to Thy word," and in the fulness of time she brought forth her firstborn Son, the Dayspring from on high.

Divine intimations of Christ's birth were not only given to Mary and Joseph, but also to the lowly shepherds, the latter being privileged to hear the praise of a heavenly host over Christ's coming. There are one or two minor events, more or less of an unusual character, which may or may not have been necessarily miraculous. There was the appearance of the star in the East at the hour of the Saviour's birth. Halley says that this was "a distinct phenomenon, a supernatural light, which by direct revelation of God went before them and pointed out the exact spot; a supernatural announcement of a supernatural birth." This we do know, the wise men were students of Scripture and astronomy, and God used that with which they were familiar to guide them to the One born King of the Jews, and finding Him, they called the star, *His star*.

4. The Miracle at Jordan

(Matthew 3:16, 17; Mark 1:9-12;
Luke 3:21, 23; John 1)

While there was nothing miraculous in connection with the *act* of our Lord's immersion at Jordan, there were three super-

natural occurrences as He submitted to the rite of baptism. The question as to why He submitted to John's "baptism of repentance," since He was the sinless One, can be briefly dealt with. While it was probably the custom of candidates for John's baptism to either audibly or silently confess their sins, Jesus had none of His own to confess. Yet He may have a vicarious confession, confessing the sins of His people as He tarried at Jordan, the river of judgment.

Divinely pure, Jesus sought baptism on the ground of its *meetness*. It was "to fulfil all righteousness," and in submitting, He graciously identified Himself with the needs of the people and with their expectation of the Kingdom with its ethical demands. From now on He would be devoted in His life task of bringing in the Messianic salvation. What happened at Jordan marked His consecration to, and entrance upon, His Messianic career. John's reluctance at baptizing such a Holy One was overcome by our Lord's word of authority (Matthew 3:15), "Suffer it *now*"-at once.

While John was a cousin of Jesus and must have known of Him, did he receive a special revelation of the character of Him seeking baptism at His hands? When he said, "I knew Him not," did John mean that although he knew Him as his cousin, he did not as yet know Him as the Son of God or the One who would baptize with the Holy Spirit? Anyhow, John was given a sacred sign by which he should recognize Jesus as He offered Himself for baptism, and for this sign he had long waited. At last, as Jesus emerged from the waters, the long-expected sign was given. Then, radiant with victory, John could announce, "This is He of whom I spake . . . Behold the Lamb of God, which beareth away the sin of the world."

Three aspects of the sign are distinguishable—opened heavens, the descending Spirit, the Voice of heaven. While Jesus ascended from the water, still praying (Luke 3:21), the heavens opened or, to use Mark's more graphic statement, were "rent asunder." This forcible expression appears to be connected with the heavens stretched out as a curtain (Psalm 104:2; Isaiah 40:22). Opened heavens symbolized divine favor (Ezekiel 1:1; Acts 7:55, 56; Revelation 21:10, 11).

Out of the opened heavens came the

Holy Spirit and descended upon Christ. Twice over we are told that "He abode on Him." This was to be an abiding enduement—no transient experience. In some supernatural way, the Spirit came upon Christ in bodily shape as a dove. In Scripture, the dove is the symbol of peace (Genesis 8:11), and as a bird, it is noted for its remarkable quietness, tenderness, purity, and love—which qualities Jesus perfectly personified in the days of His flesh. Such a bestowal of the Spirit was a sign of God's satisfaction with the life of His beloved Son all through His thirty silent years in Nazareth, and also the symbol of all He was to accomplish as our Peace. The descent of the Spirit "as it were a dove in bodily form," implied the gift of supernatural power and wisdom necessary for the accomplishment of a God-given task. Thereafter, Jesus was full of this unction without measure (John 3:34).

Then there was the mysterious Voice speaking from heaven and uttering a benediction upon Jesus. By divine proclamation, God announced the presence of the King and set His seal upon the years He had lived. As Mary's Son, He had been misunderstood by some, rejected by others, but as God's Son, He had brought nothing but pleasure to His Father's heart. The mind of the Father rested with infinite content in the Son. Such an attestation also satisfied the human consciousness of Jesus as the Son of Man, who went forward to fulfil the Father's purpose. "The kingly character creates the kingly capacity."

Whether such a beatific vision was seen only by John and Jesus, we have no means of knowing. As it primarily concerned them, perhaps they alone saw the heavens opened and heard the divine Voice. The Baptist bore record that he had beheld these miraculous events at Jordan (John 1:33, 34). Legendary miracles have gathered around the simple narrative in the gospels. Justin adds, "a fire was kindled in Jordan." An Ebionite gospel says that "a great light shone around the place."

5. The Miracle in the Wilderness

(Matthew 4:1-10; Mark 1:12, 13;
Luke 4:1-13)

Matthew introduces his account of our Lord's temptation with the word "then." After the heavens opened, hell was opened.

After the dove, there came the Devil, and the two are never far apart. After any divine transaction, there comes a season of fierce antagonism. The temptation followed at once the Lord's baptism at Jordan. After such a remarkable experience, He wished to be alone. Endowed by the Spirit and commended by the Father, Jesus became conscious of the possession of new powers and sought the desert place for a period of what must have been intense self-concentration. It was then that the Devil came to Him. As the specific temptation came toward the close of the forty days, Jesus must have been undisturbed in His solitude.

We believe that the transactions between Christ and Satan are strictly historical. The temptation was not a mere vision Jesus had and which He afterwards described to His disciples. Neither was it a symbolical representation of what transpired in His inner consciousness, nor a myth embodying in historical form the idealizing faith—all of which are reasons adduced by those who discredit the truthfulness of the accounts of the temptation.

While a full exposition of the nature of the temptation is beyond the scope of our study, suffice it to say that before Jesus could deliver men and women from the shackles of Satan, He Himself needed to be victorious over the strength and subtlety of the foe. As Dr. Campbell Morgan so ably expresses it:

The King must not only be in perfect harmony with the order and beauty of the heavens, He must face all the disorder and ugliness of the abyss. Goodness at its highest He knows, and is; evil at its lowest He must face and overcome. And so in the wilderness He stands as humanity's representative between the two, responding to the one and refusing the other. How gloriously He won the battle and bruised the head of the serpent!

As to the three stages of temptation, they were directed to distrust, to presumption, and to worldly sovereignty, three phases Christ constantly faced—to spare Himself, to gratify Jewish sign-seekers, to gain power by sacrificing the right. Such temptations typify the whole round of satanic assault on man through body, soul and spirit (Luke 4:13; I John 2:16).

Coming to the miraculous element in our

Lord's temptation, we discern the following aspects:

First of all, Jesus had to decide whether or not to employ His newly acquired miraculous power for His own personal and private ends. Because He had been without natural food for forty days, would He satisfy the pangs of natural hunger in a supernatural way? The narrative implies that Jesus was continuously without food, eating nothing, as Luke reminds us, yet apparently He was not conscious of hunger till the end of the forty days. "Afterward hungered" suggests a return to the common life of sensation. Because of His humanity, the needs of the body made themselves felt.

We cannot explain away the miracle of our Lord's subsistence without food for almost a month and a half by saying that the complete absorption of the soul in higher realities and a higher degree of mental rapture made Him insensible to physical needs. No human frame under natural conditions can exist for more than a few days without food and liquid of some kind. Christ was miraculously sustained, just as Moses and Elijah were for a similar period (Exodus 34:28; I Kings 19:8). Further, our Lord resisted the temptation to convert the stones of the desert into bread to meet His need. Later on, He was to feed the hungry, but here He maintained the voluntarily assumed human position of absolute dependence on God. The same principle applies to the unwillingness of our Lord to fling Himself down from the pinnacle of the Temple (Matthew 4:5).

In the second place, there is the miracle of Satan's appearances and acts. It is clearly evident from the temptation narratives that the Devil did appear to Jesus in some visible shape, and he was permitted by God to transport Him from place to place as he saw fit. We must remember that the Devil, before he became the Devil, was Lucifer, the highest angelic being in heaven, one "perfect in beauty" (Ezekiel 28:12-15), and that Jesus, as the Eternal One was fully acquainted with him. Habershon says of the permission of Satan's strange and unexplained power:

One of the most stupendous and most inconceivable manifestations of Satan's power took place during the Lord's temptation in the wilderness, when the Lord permitted Himself to be carried by the Devil into the holy city and set on a pinnacle of the Temple; and again, when "the Devil taking Him up into an exceeding high mountain, showed unto Him all the kingdoms of the world, and the glory of them, in a moment of time" (Matthew 4:8; Luke 4:5). Here was a double miracle. Satan could have had no power at all except it had been given him of the Father, except the Son had permitted it, and the Spirit had thus led Him. Thus the whole Trinity allowed Satan to use his unexplained powers.

Our Lord's preservation from the wild beasts in such a wild, bleak, and desolate region affords another miracle (Mark 1:13). The presence, yells of hunger, ravening fierceness, and glaring eyes of these beasts, added to the terrors and loneliness of the wilderness, were enough to frighten a person. But not so the Lord, who was as safe there as Daniel was in the den of lions. Although He was with "the wild beasts," they harmed not their Creator. Had He not power over all the animals which He had made? (Job 12:7-10). In the Millenium, when Christ is to reign supreme, the very nature of wild beasts is to be transformed. Then no power to hurt or destroy will be theirs (Isaiah 11:6-9; 35:9; 65:25).

Last of all, we have the supernatural aid of angels (Matthew 4:11; Mark 1:13). Just how they came after the Devil had left Jesus and ministered unto Him, we are not told. The calm and beauty of their presence after that of the Tempter and the wild beasts must have consoled Jesus. Through the presence and provision of the angels, God fulfilled the promise of Psalm 91 in His own, not Satan's way. God charged His angels to care for His triumphant but now hungry Son (John 1:51).

6. The Miracle of Omniscience

(John 1:47-51; 2:24, 25; 4:29, 39; Mark 11:3)

One of the unnoticed miracles in the life of our Lord is the manifestation of His omniscience—a divine attribute He never surrendered when He took on humanity. Christ's foreknowledge of Nathanael greatly impressed this guileless man. The One before him was able to read to the very depths of his thought. Under the fig tree, Nathanael thought he was unseen by any eye, but he *was* seen by Him from whom nothing can be hid. Was not an actual Messianic presence in Nathanael's inmost thought?

The same evidence of omniscience can be found in John's declaration that "Jesus knew all men, and needed not that any should testify of man: for He knew what was in man." Then, as always, He read what was in man. "The eye which looked at, looked into, others, saw to the very depth of their hearts too, and knew all. It saw in that depth that the true inner man did not believe, did not commit itself to Him . . . He, on His part, did not commit Himself unto them" (see 8:31).

The woman at the well was likewise impressed with our Lord's omniscience. "Come, see a man, which told me all things that ever I did: is this not the Christ?" She felt that He must be a prophet since His words revealed her past life. This was a sign of Christ's Messiahship that the Samaritans could not question.

Then we have the incident of the ass and the colt at Bethphage (Matthew 21:1; Mark 11:1). Our Lord knew where the beasts were that He needed. Their owner obeyed the Lord's command without hesitation and the disciples found the ass and the colt as He had said. Other aspects of divine omniscience are indicated in the following miracles.

7. The Miracle at Cana

(John 2:1-11)

Having won a decisive victory over Satan in the wilderness, Jesus returned to Galilee in the power of the Spirit, and commenced His supernatural ministry (Luke 4:18, 19; 7:22; Matthew 11:5, 6). As to the scene of this miracle on behalf of others—Cana of Galilee—the reader is referred to the interesting *Appendix* Habershon has on the geographical setting of the miracles of the Bible. It was also in Cana that the nobleman's son was healed.

Entering upon a study of the miracle of the water being turned into wine, we first of all pause to note the significance of the phrase, "The beginning of miracles," by which is meant, absolutely Christ's first miracle. Although He had lived for thirty years, this was the first manifestation of the miraculous power He was to exercise. Such a fact nullifies the records of the miraculous in the Apocryphal gospels, universally excluded from Holy Scripture because of their mythic and spurious nature. Miracles

of Jesus' youth, descriptions of His personal appearance, His doing in the world of spirits, and miracles of the Virgin Mary are to be found in these Apocryphal gospels of which Bishop Westcott once wrote in his *Cambridge Essays:*

> Their mendacities, their absurdities, the barbarities of their style and the inconsequence of their narratives, have never been excused or condoned.

An impassable gulf separates these spurious gospels from the genuine gospels.

Here are samples of the unbridled imagination of those who wrote of the so-called miracles of the boy Jesus: When the holy family was threatened by a number of dragons emerging from a cave, Jesus leapt from His mother's lap and dispersed the dragons saying, "Fear not, for although I am only an infant, it must needs be that all the wild beasts should grow tame in My presence." Another miracle was that of the Child Jesus shortening a thirty day journey into one day, and as the family entered Egypt 355 idols in a heathen temple there fell prostrate on the ground. Then there is the weird story about Jesus making twelve sparrows out of mud, clapping His hands, and commanding them to fly. It is from these ridiculous fables that we turn to the first miracle Jesus actually performed, as He stood at the portal of His brief but dynamic ministry of some three years.

Leaving the wilderness, Jesus attended a wedding. Before entering His more public ministry, there was the more private unfolding of His glory to His disciples at the marriage feast. In Nazareth, there was the hiding of His power. Living in obscurity for thirty years and being subject to His parents, Jesus had worked no miracle. Now He breaks through the silence and performs His first miracle. As John is the only one who records this miracle, we might ponder how he came to know of it. Was he present as one of the guests, or did he hear all about the miracle from Mary when, after the death of Jesus, she went to John's home? If she was the one who narrated the miracle, she did not hide her own fault.

The occasion of the miracle was a wedding to which Jesus and His disciples had been invited. Possibly those who were to marry were relatives of Mary. Unlike John the Baptist, our Lord's forerunner and herald, Jesus was no ascetic (Luke 7:33, 34). "The Son of Man came eating and drinking," and He was the most accessible and gracious of men. Marriage is a divine institution, and our Lord's presence at the wedding signified His respect for the institution. The Church Marriage Order says that "Christ adorned marriage by His presence at the first miracle that He wrought in Cana of Galilee." It was fitting, therefore, that the Lord of life was at this joyous feast, since He came to sanctify all human life.

The presence of so many guests at a poor family's wedding party brought about a shortage of wine, and Mary, sensing the need and also the embarrassment such a shortage of wine would cause, appealed to Jesus saying, "They have no wine." Although Mary had never witnessed the performance of a miracle by her Son, cognizance of His divine mission was one of the things locked up in her heart that she had pondered over for many years. Jesus immediately rebuffed Mary. On two occasions do we find her intruding herself into the Lord's domain of service—here in John 2:3, 4 and in Matthew 12:46-50—and on each occasion Jesus set her aside.

The tone of our Lord's rebuke of His mother, "Woman, what have I to do with thee?" indicates that although intensely devoted to her as a son should be, He could not allow a merely natural relationship to influence Him. Mary's maternal authority was at an end. We must not read any harshness in the term "Woman" which was one of great respect at that time. This was the tender word He used when He addressed His mother from the cross, "Woman, behold thy Son."

The water pots in the feast chamber were empty, and at the command of Jesus the pots were filled with water. The preacher will find excellent expositional material in Spurgeon's four sermons on this first miracle, particularly at this point about the empty pots. Instantly, the water was transformed into wine of such excellent quality as to call forth high praise from the master of the feast, who called it "the best wine." He who would not work a miracle in the wilderness to meet His own need, here performed a miracle to supply a luxury for wedding guests. And how munificent was His provision!

Our Lord, it must be observed, did not touch one of the vessels. The servants poured water into them and then poured out wine, and such a real transmutation was effected by divine power and revealed our Lord's sway over the fruits of the earth. Actually, the miracle at Cana involved a speeding up process which required actual creative power. He was the One who ordained the fruitfulness of the vine and gave it power to drink in the rain and dew, assimilating the drops so as to form the juice of the grape. Now, in a moment, He willed the instant chemical changes whereby the water became like old wine mellowed with keeping.

The two-fold results of this first miracle are stated. First of all, it "manifested forth His glory." The miracle exhibited the fact that the exercise of creative power essentially belonged to deity. Here was illustrated the glory of His beneficent grace. Moses commenced his ministry in Egypt with a miracle of judgment—water was turned into blood, a curse was brought upon one of the common necessities of life. In Christ's first miracle, water was turned into wine—the addition of sweetness and joy to the common relationship of life. The Cana miracle then was symbolic, a sign, pointing to the contrast between the old dispensation and the new, and to the work of Christ as a transforming, enriching, and glorifying of the natural, through divine grace and power.

The other result of the miracle was that His disciples believed on Him. They were, of course, already believers. The demonstration of their Lord's power established faith in His deity. That first miracle proved to them His power to work every miracle. If He could turn water into wine by His will, then He could do anything and everything. Is it not interesting to notice the similarity between Christ's first miracle and the last one before His Ascension? Each were associated with a social meal—with *wine* and *bread*, suggestive of the remembrance feast which He Himself instituted and at which He is always present.

One could linger long on the lessons to be derived from Christ's first miracle in which He made all true delight, better and more sacred.

(1) Those who are truly His see His glory. "The servants knew." "His disciples believed" (2:9, 11).

(2) The world and sin give what they call their "good" first; afterwards that which is "worse." Jesus gives His best last (2:10).

(3) Satan turns good into bad and worse. The Saviour turns good into better and best.

(4) Our main business in life is to go through the world turning water into wine.

(5) As those water pots fulfilled the Lord's purpose, so He can use the poorest means. We are but poor earthen vessels, and somewhat cracked, yet He can use weak things to confound the mighty.

8. The Miracle of the New Birth

(John 3:1-16; I Peter 1:23; James 1:18)

In studying literature dealing with the miraculous element in the gospels, it is surprising to discover how writers omit any reference to regeneration as one of the evident miracles of God. But what a miracle it is for Him to take a poor, lost, hell-deserving sinner and make him a new creation—an heir of His and a joint-heir of His Son.

The opening words of this renowned third chapter of John, "There was a man," are linked to the last words of the previous chapter, "He knew what was in man." Because of our Lord's foreknowledge and omniscience, He knew what was in any particular man with whom He had anything to do. Nicodemus, one of the finest products of Judaism, thoroughly sincere and determined to investigate for himself the character and claims of Jesus, was another specimen of his race whom Jesus knew only too well. As a member of the Sanhedrin, Nicodemus had carefully scrutinized the credentials of John the Baptist, and now he seeks to examine the authority of this new Teacher whom he knew had come from God. This ruler of the Jews had an assured conviction of Christ's authority based upon the miracles already performed.

Nicodemus came to Jesus by night, not because he was cowardly, but because it was the most convenient time for both of them for an undisturbed and personal interview about spiritual matters. "Through humility and fearing to compromise his dignity, and possibly his safety, he came by night—when Jewish superstition would keep men at home." In the conversation that took place that night, we have our Lord's first instance of dealing with an inquirer, and it was to a man deeply religious and highly educated that Jesus re-

vealed the necessity and miracle of the new birth. He also revealed that His death and resurrection are the only way by which regeneration is possible. Redemption is the basis of regeneration (3:14-16).

First of all, Jesus reminded Nicodemus of the necessity of the new birth—"Ye must be born again." Such a fiat signifies the eternal necessity in the divine counsels. Man, born in sin, needs to be reborn. Thus, the nature of the human heart and the nature of heaven create the necessity. Unless heaven-born, we cannot be heaven-bound. F. B. Meyer says, "When Christ says *must*, it is time to wake up. He is so gentle, winsome, tender. He is always persuading, inviting, entreating. He so seldom used the imperative mood. When, therefore, He speaks thus, it becomes us to inquire into the matter on which He insists so earnestly."

The burden of our Lord's conversation is that "as there can be no entrance into the kingdom of the flesh-life save by natural birth, so there is no entrance into the spirit-life, save by spiritual birth." The wonder of such truth about a supernatural birth, gripped the mind of Nicodemus and is reflected in his double question to Jesus:

"How can a man be born when he is old?

"How can these things be?"

Christ had to rebuke Nicodemus for his lack of spiritual perception of the truth He expounded. But this thrice mentioned seeker (3:1; 7:50; 19:39) was, however, to experience that "with God all things are possible."

The miraculousness of the new birth is indicated by the words of our Lord, "That which is born of the Spirit is spirit. . . . The wind bloweth where it listeth, . . . so is everyone born of the Spirit." Jesus spoke of regeneration as a birth from above, or a new birth. Distinct from one's physical birth, it is a new birth and is from above, because the Holy Spirit from heaven makes it possible (I John 3:9; 4:7; 5:1, 4, 18). At first, Nicodemus was startled by the idea of a birth from heaven. Looking at the subject merely from the physical side, he said, "How can a man be born again when he is old? Surely he cannot enter the second time into his mother's womb." His *second time* was not the same as Jesus' *anew*. "He does not understand the difference between a *second* beginning and a *different* beginning."

A physical birth cannot be explained; neither can a spiritual birth. Physical life itself is dependent upon a birth, which is likewise true in the spiritual realm. While science can tell us much about life, the origin of life itself is still a mystery to man. Manifestations of life can be noted and classified, but life itself eludes the grasp and analysis of man. Thus is it with the new life the Spirit begets, whose action Christ symbolized by the free, irresistible, invisible wind. This Wind of heaven is not bound by any limitations of country, race, age, or sex. The God who created the winds and directs them is the only One who knows the workings of His Spirit in the hearts of men. We cannot see the all-pervasive wind, though we can feel it. As the Wind, the Spirit is "as viewless too." In the Greek, *wind* and *spirit* are identical. If the figure was suggested to Jesus as the wind of the night swept through the narrow street as Nicodemus and he discussed the marveled truths of regeneration and redemption, then Nicodemus must have come to see that the supernatural work of the Spirit was just as invisible as the wind, though its effects are evident to human vision (Ecclesiastes 1:6).

Although the formation of a new life in the womb is not visible but becomes so at birth, the begetting of a new life in Christ is the invisible action of the invisible, creative Spirit. But although regeneration is a miraculous work, it becomes visible in a transformed life in which old things have passed away and all things have become new. Marks of this washing by regeneration and renewing of the Spirit are given in Titus 3:5; Ephesians 5:26; I John 3:9, 14; 5:1, 4. "The work of grace and salvation, indeed, is all so far miraculous that it requires the influence upon our nature of a living power above that of nature" (H. Wace).

9. The Miracle of the Nobleman's Son

(John 4:46-54)

After healing a sin-sick soul in Samaria, where Jesus spent two happy, profitable days among those Samaritans who believed in Him and were deeply eager to hear His word, He found His way to Cana to heal the fever-stricken body of a nobleman's son. From "sympathetic Samaria He journeyed to unsympathetic Galilee." While this miracle was the second one to be performed in Galilee and is the first recorded particular healing miracle, Jesus had at Jerusalem accomplished some remarkable miracles which are not particularly recorded but which must have produced remarkable results. "Many believed in His name when they saw the miracles which He did" (2:23; 3:2).

Is there not a suggestive connection between the two miracles in Cana? The first was associated with a marriage, the second with an anxious home—the first with the joy of a wedding, the second with the sorrow of a family. At the first miracle, Christ added gladness to the feast; at the second, He banished sadness from the hearts of many. Returning to the place where He first manifested His glory, He knit Himself in closer union with the disciples He had made there. John's touch, "where He made the water wine," is characteristic of his manner to identify a place or person by some single circumstance conspicuous in the incident (see 7:50; 19:39; 21:20 etc.).

Further, John is the only one who records this miracle of the nobleman's son, which proves how particular he was in the selections of those incidents in the life and labors of the Lord he dearly loved. John felt that he should avoid what the first three evangelists had to say about Christ's ministry. The miracles and discourses John did choose were selected because of the deep and blessed lessons they suggested. Then, again, it was probably because of the many important and influential people in Galilee that John recorded this miracle at length.

News of Christ's miraculous ministry traveled fast, and among those attracted by the stir He had caused was the Capernaum nobleman, or courtier whom many have tried without success to identify. This distressed father, whose boy was at death's door, journeyed to Cana to solicit the help of the Miracle-Worker, whose fame was spreading. When he heard of Him, hope sprang to life in the heart of the nobleman, whose faith developed from a spark to a fierce flame.

First of all, there was the *quest* of faith. There must have been the germ of faith in this man's heart whose dire need drove him to Christ. He must have had the glimmer of faith to believe that if only he could attract the Healer to his home, his dying child would be restored. This first miracle of healing is important, then, because it emphasizes the link between miracle and faith. In dealing with this feature, Laidlaw remarks:

> In all these healing miracles Jesus takes the utmost pains to call out faith on the part of those to be healed, or (as in this case at Cana) those who scught healing for their dear ones. Notice the instructive variety which these narratives give us, of kinds and actions of faith. Sometimes Jesus is tenderly directing a weak faith. Again, by apparent refusal, He is drawing into view the strength of a strong faith. Another time, He is teaching that miracle is not the cause of faith so much as its reward; that bodily cures are chiefly of use to bring spiritual help; that belief in Him as a Healer is meant to lead men to faith in Him as a Saviour.

While the nobleman's sorrow was the birth-pang of faith, he revealed the *limit* of that faith when he limited the power of Christ to His local presence. He scarcely heard the rebuke of Christ, "Except ye see signs and wonders ye will not believe." With a foreboding sense of the loss of his son, he besought Christ, "Come down, ere my child die." He did not realize that the One whose aid he sought was able to heal just as easily from a distance as on the spot. He had faith to believe that where Jesus was present, disease would flee. He must "come down," if the son is to be cured. The desperate father was not prepared to believe the word of the psalmist, "He *sent* His word, and He healed them." Yet although the nobleman's faith was limited and feeble, it was nevertheless real. Our Lord detected with unerring accuracy the weak point of the anxious father's faith and nurtured it.

Faith in a wrong object, no matter how strong, never relieves; but faith in a right object, even although weak, will. It is not faith itself that relieves, but the power of the One in whom we believe. How prone man is to crave for the outward and physical manifestations of divine power! But, although Christ seemed to repel the request of the nobleman, His words were both *corrective* and *educative*.

We now come to the *reward* of faith. The nobleman never doubted the assurance of those majestic lips. Without any emotion whatever, without any sign or further word from Christ, the man believed the word

uttered and went his way. Evidently, experiencing the *rest* of faith (for it appears as if he made no particular haste to get back home), he accepted the declaration of Jesus that his son would be well. So, believing, he made no haste. The *spark* of faith which led him to Christ became a *flame* of faith as he left Him. On the way home, his servants greeted him with the happy information that his son was healed. Upon inquiry, the father found that the fever had left the boy at the very hour Christ had said, "Thy son liveth." Such a miracle had a double effect—the sick boy was healed of his fatal fever and the father was healed of his lack of full faith. Because of the miracle, the nobleman's whole household became believers in Christ. Nothing less than such a miracle could induce them to put their trust in Him. The lesson for our hearts from the miracle is that faith helps faith.

As to the nature of the miracle itself, Jesus healed the dying boy by "remote control." The distance between Capernaum and Cana was over twenty miles, yet by the exercise of His will, Jesus healed the boy by the word of His mouth. Through the march of modern science, a button pressed in one place releases the waters of a new mighty dam miles away. Christ had no set formula or regular plan. At times He commanded sick ones to be brought to Him (Matthew 17:17); yet He could heal without seeing the needy. He could heal by a word or a touch. Sometimes He used means; at other times healing was direct. The nobleman expected the cure of his son to be a gradual and progressive one, but the fever *left* him. Not gradually, but immediately, the stricken one was perfectly healed.

The healing of the nobleman's son in Capernaum was what the inhabitants of Nazareth had heard of and wanted Jesus to repeat in His own city (Luke 4:23). The Lord, however, wrought no miracles where He had lived for thirty years. There, the inhabitants had had the evidence of His holy life, and that was sufficient proof of His claims as the Mighty One.

Since the miracle of the nobleman's son and that of the centurion's servant are confused and sometimes made to appear as different versions of the same miracle, a brief concluding word might suffice as to the sharp distinctions between the two miracles, as Trench, Taylor, and others point out. Ellicott, we feel, gives the best summary of these distinctions:

(1) The nobleman pleads for his *son*—the centurion for his servant (Matthew 8:6; Luke 7:2).

(2) The nobleman pleaded in person—the elders of the Jews interceded for the centurion (Luke 7:3).

(3) The nobleman was a Jew—the centurion a Gentile (Luke 7:9).

(4) The nobleman heard the words of miracle in Cana—words to the centurion were spoken at Capernaum (Matthew 8:5; Luke 7:1).

(5) The nobleman's son had a fever—the centurion's servant a paralysis (Matthew 8:6).

(6) The nobleman wanted Christ to go down home with him—the centurion deprecated His going (Matthew 8:8; Luke 7:7).

(7) At Cana Jesus speaks the word only, and does not go down—at Capernaum He apparently did both (Matthew 8:13; Luke 7:7).

(8) At Cana, Jesus blames half-faith and the demanding of signs and wonders —at Capernaum He marvels at the fulness of faith (Matthew 8:10).

10. The Miracle of the Impotent Man

(John 5:1-9)

An important feature of the miracle we are now to consider is that it commenced that open conflict between Christ and the religious leaders which was to culminate in the cross. Because it was wrought on a Sabbath day, this miracle gave rise to the first outbreak of Christ's rejection. Speaking as One who claimed equality with authority, Jesus rebuked His foes for searching the Scriptures but failing to understand that they led to Him. Religious and careful about matters of the law, these rejectors of Christ's claims were destitute of compassion.

A year before this miracle at Bethesda, Jesus proved His Messianic claims by cleansing the Temple. Now He performs a miracle on the Sabbath for the deliberate purpose of destroying wrong ideas of such a holy day. By the miracle, the claims of His deity received the fullest possible publicity in the nation's capital, where He wrought few miracles because of unbelief. The explanation of His claims before the Sanhedrin only incited the leaders

with a desire to kill Him, a thing which they were the means of doing some two years later. Our Lord referred to the Bethesda miracle and to the determination of the Sanhedrin to kill some eighteen months later, when He called the attention of the rulers to their inconsistency in circumcising on the Sabbath while objecting to His healing ministry on such a day. It was for healing the man with the withered hand on the Sabbath that His foes planned to kill Him, as we shall see when we come to this miracle (Mark 3:6).

Altogether, there were seven Jesus healed on the Sabbath Day:

(1) The impotent man at Jerusalem (John 5:1-9)

(2) The man born blind (John 9:1-14)

(3) The demoniac in Capernaum (Mark 1:21-27)

(4) The mother-in-law of Peter (Mark 1:29-31)

(5) The man with the withered hand (Mark 3:1-6)

(6) The woman bowed together (Luke 13:10-17)

(7) The man with dropsy (Luke 14:1-6)

Bethesda, the scene of the miracle, means *house of mercy* or *compassion*. Our Lord found it *the house of misery* to many. It was situated on the east side of Jerusalem where there were, and still are, mineral springs. These were, and still are, intermittent and were resorted to by the needy in the East as medicinal springs are in the West. The traditional pool of Bethesda is now identified as *The Fountain of the Virgin*, where there is still an intermittent spring. The incident in the miracle of the descending angel is omitted in the most ancient Greek texts. Apart from the doubt of the baptismal angel, however, it is evident that God has His agencies, visible and invisible, fulfilling His will. It is John again who describes the activity of "the angel of the waters" (Revelation 16:5) accomplishing the divine purpose.

In some way or another when the waters of Bethesda moved, they had a peculiar power. Whether miraculously impregnated with medicinal virtue after an angel stirred the waters or permanently endued with healing virtue, we do not know. The narrative gives man's view of the beneficial pool was sufficient evidence that it was his around it. Ellicott's comment, quoted by Taylor, is the most satisfactory explanation we have met with:

The bubbling water moving as it were to life, and in its healing power seeming to convey new energy to blind and halt and lame, was to them as the presence of the living God. They knew not its constituent elements and could not trace the law of its action, but they knew the Source of all good, who gave intellect to man and healing influence to matter, effect to the remedy and skill to the physician, and they accepted the gift as direct from Him.

The five porches mentioned were provided to accommodate the invalids who desired to use the waters. Some of the early Church Fathers, who revelled in spiritualizing Scripture, saw in the five porches a type of the five books of Moses—the law. As Christ alone cured the needy, so grace alone can avail for the sinful. The law, in that it is weak, cannot deliver and save. As to the description of those who required healing, "impotent folk" means *sick*, or *people without strength*. The others were *blind, halt, withered*. The enumeration of four, when meant to be exhaustive, is frequent in Scripture (Ezekiel 14:21; Revelation 6:8; Matthew 15:31).

There is no question regarding the minute details of place and scene. Reaching the pool, Jesus was attracted to one poor sufferer who, for thirty-eight long years, had paid sin's penalty in some kind of physical disability. Our Lord's omniscience is emphasized in that He knew that the infirm man had been in such a predicament for a long time. Now at the pool, omnipotence met impotence. Have you not wondered at the superfluous question of Jesus, "Wilt thou be made whole?" The daily presence of the impotent man at the pool was sufficient evidence that it was his greatest desire to be made whole. Trench suggests that the question of Jesus had its purpose, since the man had been so often denied a cure and consequently hope was well nigh dead within him. It may have been that his heart had withered as well as his limbs. Jesus, pitying the man's hopeless case, assisted him to the faith which He was to demand of the man.

The helplessness of this infirm resident of the pool is suggested by his reply to Jesus' question, "Sir, I have no man, when the water is troubled, to put me into the pool." *Put* is literally "cast" and indicates "the hasty movement required to bring him to the water before its agitation should have ceased" (Mark 7:30; Luke 11:20).

The very face of this despairing creature bore the look of "hope deferred."

We now turn from the miserable patient to the Mighty Physician. Jesus said, "Rise, take up thy bed, and walk." The man waited for an angel to come his way, but that Sabbath, the Master of angels came and in infinite compassion healed the man. The command of Jesus was seemingly impossible, since the man could not rise on his own initiative, but this was the command of omnipotence, and His commands are His enablings. "Faithful is He who calleth you, *who also will do it*" (I Thessalonians 5:24). Thus, the power by which the man rose was not his own. As to the cure, it was instantaneous, immediate, perfect, and free—just like the spiritual restoration Christ supplies.

Then Jesus commanded the healed one to take up his bed, or his poor, rag pallet, and walk. There was no provision for a relapse. At the pool with his back on his bed, he now leaves with his bed on his back. Most likely he would have left the mass of rags he had been stretched out on behind, but Christ expressly told him to take his wretched bed with him for these reasons Laidlaw suggests:

(1) As a proof of his complete recovery, that he could not only walk, but carry his couch.

(2) As a mark of identity, to prove that he was the very man who had lain so long helpless at the pool.

(3) As a test of his faith in his Healer, and thankfulness to Him. Trusting Him, the man did exactly as he was commanded.

Although omnipotence prevailed over impotence, only one was singled out of the suffering, expectant multitude that Sabbath to become the recipient of Christ's supernatural power. Why did He not heal all at the pool that day? Trench says, "Christ healed one only, for He came not *now* to be the Healer of men's bodies, save only as He could annex to this healing the truer healing of their souls and spirits."

The Sanhedrists, the spiritual heads of the nation, had no joy in their cold hearts over the impotent man's relief. All they troubled themselves about was Christ's act of healing on the Sabbath. They forgot that God has no Sabbath where sin and misery are found. Then the cunning malice of His adversaries is seen in that they did not ask, "Who is he that healed thee?" but "Who bade thee take up thy bed?" But the healed man could not identify his gracious Benefactor. Jesus, John tells, "conveyed Himself away"—a word used nowhere else in the New Testament. How and where He went, we are not told. Is this an illustration of what we have called *the miracle of escape?*

Later on, the Healer and the one healed met in the Temple. The one impotent sufferer expressed his gratitude to the Omnipotence and bravely confessed the wonder of the miracle before Christ's foes. He was not able to wrangle about Sabbath-keeping or Sabbath-breaking. All this grateful soul knew was that the One who was able to work so great a cure had authority to say what should be and should not be done on the Sabbath.

That there is a vital connection between sin and suffering can be found in the solemn warning to the healed man—"Behold, thou art made whole: sin no more, lest a worse thing come unto thee." What the man's past grievous sin was we are not told. Christ, because of His omniscience, knew it—and the man was only too conscious of it. Cured of his bodily disease, he must be cured of his spiritual disease. "Rise up and walk"—"Sin no more." Power, then pardon, were granted. Whether "the worse thing" Jesus warned against would be in this life or the life beyond, we are not told. Doubtless the healed man who, in a moment, was reminded of "that biography of eight and thirty years long the sin which had been the prolific parent of all the sufferings he had endured for so long and so painful a period," went forth to be whole in soul as well as in body.

11. The Miracle of the First Draught of Fishes

(Luke 5:1-11; Matthew 4:18-22; Mark 1:16-20; John 1:35-43)

If experiences sanctify places, then Peter's ordinary boat became his most precious possession, because his Lord had made that boat His pulpit from which He uttered sublime truths and in which He displayed His glorious, supernatural power. That memorable morning, Peter was out on the same lake, in the same boat, handling the same nets as the fruitless night before, but what a mighty difference obedience to Christ produced! A bountiful harvest of the sea transformed everything for Peter.

Luke, with his more classical style than the other evangelists, is the only one to describe the Sea of Galilee as "the Lake of Gennesaret," and he alone records the striking miracle which led to the fuller discipleship of Peter and his partners. While the narratives cited above have many points in common, it has been questioned whether they all refer to the same event. In comparing the accounts of the call of Christ's first disciples, it would seem as if there are varying aspects of such a call. But as Trench puts it, "the same incident will present itself from different points of view to different witnesses. . . . We shall not wonder that two or three relators have brought out different moments, divers but not diverse, of one and the same event." We should be grateful that we can regard the acts of which is significant, from many sides.

Galilee had been prophesied by Isaiah as a chief scene of the beneficent activity of the Messiah (9:1, 2), and now that He had come, He taught the people who pressed upon Him to hear the Word of God, standing in a boat borrowed from Peter. Then He turned from the crowd and addressed Himself to the man who owned the boat, who was to learn much more from Christ's works than the people had from His words. Addressing the master of the little craft, Jesus said, "Launch out into the deep, and let down your nets for a draught."

Peter's reply was characteristic of the big fisherman—"Master, we have toiled all night, and have taken nothing." Luke, who wrote this record, is the only one and always the one to speak of Jesus as *Master*. He never uses *Rabbi*, as John does. After such a night of exhausting toil, Peter might have answered Jesus, "Now, Master, I am a fisherman and know all about the ways of fish. You are a carpenter. Night is the time to fish, not the morning hour when the sun is shining upon and piercing the water." But somehow the command of Jesus arrested Peter, who immediately replied, "Nevertheless at Thy word I will let down the net." You will note the passage from the plural to the singular. Jesus said *nets*. Peter replied *net*. It was as if he said to himself, "I'll obey His command, although I know the result will be as futile as the past night. I'll let down one net anyhow." Was this a matter of partial obedience? Was Peter ignorant of the power

of the Lord to command even the fish of
the sea when he said "at Thy word?" With
the word of such a King, there was power.

The result of the lowered net was staggering. There was such an immense draught
of fish straining the capacity of the net that
Peter had to seek the help of his fishing
partners in the other boat to help him
bring the haul to shore. The miracle here
consists in the shoal of fish being alongside
of Peter's boat at the precise moment Jesus
said, "Let down your nets." There is no
miracle in discovering a shoal of fish nor
in the periodic migrations of fish. Their
ways, as they pass through the paths of
the seas, may be marvelous, but are certainly not miraculous (Psalm 8:6, 8). The
inhabitants of the sea are just as obedient
to Christ's control as other creatures He
made. By His omniscience, He knew where
the fish were in Galilee, although Peter
could not catch them the night before,
and by His power He brought that heavy
shoal to that particular spot at that particular time. Thus, "the natural was lifted
into the domain of the miraculous by the
manner in which it was timed, and the end
which it was made to serve."

Christ is the true Sea-Lord, as well as
Land-Lord. He is the Lord of heaven, earth,
and sea (Psalm 8)—the sovereign Ruler of
all things. He could have brought 10,000
fish to the shore without them leaping into
a boat, but in this case He used means and
so directed the fish into a net. Such a
manifestation of the supernatural is beyond
what men call "natural laws" or "second
causes." Those fish did not happen to be
alongside of Peter's boat at that moment.
The fish obeyed a Higher Will. John records another miraculous draught of fishes
which we will deal with later on. At this
point we simply draw attention to the fact
that the first miracle of fish was at the
commencement of our Lord's ministry and
the second miracle at the consummation of
His ministry. Both miracles took place on
the Sea of Galilee after a night of fruitless
toil. Spurgeon has a most suggestive sermon on the contrasts and comparisons between the two miracles.

The miracle of *power* Peter witnessed
led to a miracle of *grace*. Such an exhibition of the supernatural gave him a striking
proof of Christ's omniscience and omnipotence and with such a revelation there
came the recognition of his own exceeding
sinfulness. "Depart from me; for I am a

sinful man, O Lord." It was a good thing
for Peter that Jesus did not take him at his
word and depart from him. In beholding
the Lord's glory, Peter saw his own evil
heart. Other saints had a similar experience
(Job 42:5, 6; Isaiah 6:5; Revelation 1:17).

Further, the miracle at Galilee gave
Jesus the opportunity He wanted of calling
Peter and the rest into the relationship of
discipleship. The miracle was designed by
Jesus to catch Peter in *His* net, which it
did. "Henceforth thou shalt catch men."
Bringing their boats to shore Peter, Andrew,
James, and John left them and their nets
and their homes and followed Jesus. What
happened to the remarkable haul of fish,
we are not told. This is evident that after
such an overwhelming display of power,
the fisherman knew that the One calling
them to full-time service was able to meet
their every need. The miracle had taught
them to have large expectations in Christ,
and how graciously He undertook for them
in the years that followed.

12. The Miracle of the Synagogue Demoniac

(Luke 4:33-36; Mark 1:23, 24)

This miracle was performed on a most
memorable Sabbath day. What a day of
intense activity and supernatural events it
was. In the earliest part of this holy day
Jesus, as His custom was, went to the synagogue where He read and taught in a most
impressive way, and the congregation
listened in astonishment. While He was
ministering, the service was suddenly disturbed by the outburst of a demon-possessed man, whom He delivered. Later on
in the day, while in Peter's home, He
raised his mother-in-law from her fevered
bed to perfect health. The same day, at
eventide, the whole town gathered round
the door of Peter's abode and Christ healed
all who were sick among them, revealing
thereby His unlimited resources. How
weary He must have been at the end of
such a day of wondrous activity! Jesus
was often weary *in* His work but never
weary *of* it (John 4:6). Alas, the deserved
rest of the night was brief, for we read
that He rose the next morning long before
daybreak and retired into the desert for
prayer.

On that memorable day, Jesus took
possession of both the Sabbath and the

synagogue, since He was Lord of both. The new matter and manner of His teaching, so authoritative and different from the dry recital of tradition by the scribes, turned that Sabbath into a new Lord's Day. While teaching with all majesty and force, His discourse was strangely interrupted. An extraordinary incident occurred, namely, the shriek of the demon-possessed man—an incident "transposed in Luke to bring into better contrast by juxtaposition Christ's rejection of the Sabbath before at Nazareth and His welcome Sabbath at Capernaum. Mark chronologically places the two cures *after* the miraculous draught, not *before*." The quiet of the sanctuary was disturbed by a wild cry and the Lord is revealed as the Master of the underworld of evil who had come to destroy the empire of Satan.

There is the question regarding the presence of a demoniac in the synagogue. How did he get there? Evidently, although possessed of an unclean spirit, he was not excluded from the public worship of God. Possibly it was not known that he was demon-possessed until the resident demon became conscious that he was in the presence of One stronger than the evil kingdom to which he belonged, and who with the instinct and consciousness of usurpation, cried out. It was the demon, and not the man he inhabited, who shrieked. Christ often meets demoniacs in the outside world, but that one should intrude into the very presence of God was extraordinary.

Have we anything today answering to the demon in the synagogue? Has history repeated itself? We think it has. When, in buildings erected for the preaching of the inspired, infallible Scriptures, preachers discredit the reliability of the Bible, repudiate the miracles, flout the virgin birth, the atoning blood, and the physical resurrection of Christ, what are they with all their education and polish but demons in the synagogue? As they do not represent the Spirit of truth, some other spirit must possess them. We are enjoined to have no fellowship with such unfruitful works of darkness, but rather reprove them (Ephesians 5:11). The distinguishable features of the demon in the miracle before us are as follows:

(1) It is described as being *unclean*.

This is the one case of demon-possession in which Luke adds such an epithet. "That the usurper is here called 'unclean' indicates the moral impurity by which he was characterized," says Taylor, "and so we are not surprised to find that he violently recoiled from the unsullied holiness which dwelt in Christ. With the higher intention of the spirit nature, he recognized the presence of that holiness, and was unable to endure it, so he cried out in fear."

(2) It was an incarnation.

This demon invaded the personality of the man and used it as the medium of expression. While such a possession may be inexplicable, it is a recorded fact. The Devil, as we know, is God's ape, and always tries to imitate Him. Thus when He became incarnate in His Son, it occurred to the Devil to become incarnate too. The demoniac in the synagogue was the Devil incarnate, or in human form. Judas was another who allowed himself to become Devil possessed (John 13:2, 27). In the case before us, there was the man's loss of conscious personality, so that he became identified with the demon whose mouthpiece he was (Mark 5:7).

(3) It recognized the claims of Christ as the Son of God.

Remembering that all demons, and the Devil, were once unfallen angelic beings, and as such dwelt in the presence of the glory of Christ in the dateless past, it is not surprising to find them owning His deity. The demon we are presently considering knew Christ and did not hesitate to confess Him as the Holy One, a title long before assigned to Him (Psalm 89:19). While Christ's teaching caused His listeners to marvel, the demon was disturbed by it and cried out, "What have we to do with Thee?" One wonders whether much of our modern preaching disturbs the evil forces of hell. Being destitute of the authority, power, and unction characterizing Christ's ministry, it never causes the least stir in the councils of hell.

(4) Its testimony of Christ was prohibited by Him.

Fausset suggests that Christ prohibited the demon to testify to Him so that the people's belief might not rest on such testimony, giving color to the Jews' slander (Matthew 12:24; Mark 1:34). Christ could not receive testimony from such a diabolical source just as Paul could not, when publicly witnessed to by a Pythoness in the streets of Philippi (Acts 16:16-18). Between Christ and the Devil there can be no affinity, but rather the deepest moral antagonism. "Woe unto you when all men speak well of thee." When the underlings of the Devil give testimony to a saint's worth, the only thing to do is to bid them hold their peace. Christ's refusal to accept the testimony of an evil spirit is not without its parallels (Matthew 8:29; Mark 1:34).

As to the cry of the demon, "What have we to do with Thee?" it is exactly the same as that of the Gadarene demoniac (Matthew 8:29). How those demons believed and trembled! (James 2:19). The shriek, "Let alone! Go away, Jesus of Nazareth! Art Thou come to destroy us?" revealed their knowledge of their deserved and determined doom. Such a hideous outcry was not the voice of supplication nor a prayer *for* mercy, but *against* mercy. "Let us alone!" What else can Christ do but let the Devil and his angels alone? Their evil character is fixed and their tragic judgment set. The plural *us* may refer to the possessed man and his evil possessor or to all demons. We hold it to be the latter. What have demons in common with Christ, at whom they shrieked in opposition and terror?

(5) It was expelled verbally by Christ. Christ rebuked not the man, but the demon possessing him, and said, "Hold thy peace," which actually means "Be gagged, or muzzled," and is the same word He uses when calming the winds and waves (Mark 4:39). He gave the evil spirit a short, direct order. Speaking sharply He said, "Silence! Come out." It was the harsh word such an unclean, tormenting demon deserved. Obedient to the command of silence, the demon did not *speak* any more, although it did cry with a loud voice, an inarticulate utterance of rage and pain. The demon had been the strong one in the man; now a stronger Man, superior in might to the prince of demons, destroys his works. The Devil, however, chafed over losing his hold on one he possessed, does all the harm he can; so in departing from the poor man his emissary threw him down and tore him with terrible convulsions. The victim was hurled with a convulsive leap into the midst of the astonished congregation and he was left prostrate but unhurt. There is no contradiction between Luke, who says that the evil spirt *hurt him not*, and Mark's description of the demon as having *torn* him. The man suffered no permanent injury, although cast

to the ground. "What the Devil cannot keep as his own, he will, if he can, destroy." Exorcisms, or casting out of demons, are common to the gospels, and were practiced by the Church for centuries. For a full study of this aspect of demonology, the reader is referred to the author's volume, *The Mystery and Ministry of Angels*. When we come to the Gadarene demoniac, we will deal with the problem of demon possession.

As the result of Christ's authority over unclean spirits, the people were all amazed. Such display of supernatural power was so new to them. Mark, who never missed an opportunity of recording the profound impression Christ's miracles made on those who witnessed them, tells us how overwhelmed the people were as He sounded the death knell of Satan's dominion.

13. The Miracle of Peter's Mother-in-Law

(Luke 4:38-40; Matthew 8:14-17; Mark 1:29-31)

Both Luke and Mark connect this miracle with the one just considered. On that same Sabbath, after Christ's exorcism of the unclean spirit, He, along with Andrew, entered the house of Simon Peter, where his wife's mother was bedridden with a fever. Doubtless, Christ retired to His disciple's home for rest and refreshment; but before He partook of the proffered entertainment, there was another work of mercy to perform. Having exercised His authority over evil, the Master is now revealed as having no difficulty in dealing with the result of evil in any form. He is supreme in every realm, especially in that of disease, as this early miracle of healing declares.

Our first observation of the cure of Peter's mother-in-law is that Peter had a wife. If, as the Roman Catholic Church claims, Peter was the first pope, then his marital life, which Jesus blessed by visiting his home, cuts clean across the enforced celibacy for popes and priests. As the Roman Church traffics in the dispensation of convenient marriage and divorces, it may be that Peter, as the alleged first holy father, had a special dispensation to remain married. How Peter must chuckle, if he has any knowledge of earthly matters in heaven, of all the Roman Church credits him with. It would seem as if Peter, his wife, and her mother (who was likely a widow) were happy together, and the family and friends were concerned over the distressed condition of the fever-stricken one. The household besought Christ for her, telling Him of her pressing need.

It is Luke who heightens the record by describing it as a "great" fever. This was the mark of the physician, ancient physicians distinguishing fever into *great* and *small*. Fevers, generated at the marshy land of Tabiga, were common at the spring time of the year when this miracle took place. Careful both as a physician and an historian, Luke recognized the necessity of close enquiry and of testing evidence in the setting forth of his material. Thus, his testimony to the miraculous power of Christ is of great importance. Trained as a physician, his description was that of a man of science in his use of a technical term for a violent fever. Their nature and healing of fevers were therefore well-known to him. This fact about Luke is especially valuable to remember when we come to the miraculous in the Acts (Luke 1:1-4; Acts 1:1-3).

Luke, with the graphic touch of his, tells us that Jesus, coming into the room where the elderly lady lay prostrate, "stood over her," and then adds a very arrestive phrase, *He rebuked her fever*, as if addressing the outbreak of some hostile power (see Isaiah 13:6). On another occasion, *He rebuked the winds and the sea*. Actually, a double miracle was performed that Sabbath afternoon. First of all, as Jesus took the woman by the hand and lifted her up, the fever left her. Here was a cure with a specific action, the touch or the laying on of His hand—a frequent action of Christ's which gave to the cures a sort of sacramental character. He even laid His hand upon *lepers*, though never, so far as we read, upon demoniacs. Through His hand there flowed that supernatural energy producing a direct and immediate cure. We can agree with E. R. Micklem in *Miracles and the New Psychology*, in spite of his somewhat rationalistic trend of mind, that probably Jesus also spoke to the woman and that His words were *therapeutic*. The factor of His personality displayed through His look and His bearing must also be taken into account. Doubtless news of the miracle Jesus had just performed in the synagogue encouraged the sick woman to believe that He would meet her need.

The second aspect of the miracle was the way Christ infused into the woman full strength, enabling her to minister to the household. Full health came into her wasted frame. She was not left in a condition of extreme weakness and exhaustion which such a fever as she had had ordinarily left a person and from which they slowly recovered. No convalescence was necessary in her case, for she immediately arose and ministered unto them. What appreciation there must have been over the meal she prepared! Trench reminds us that this is a pattern to all restored to spiritual health, that they should use this strength in ministering to Christ and His people.

Before we leave our study of this miracle, it is fitting to observe that it took place in a home. It was a natural and beautiful "home specimen" of Christ's healing power, as was the healing of the crowd at evening. His merciful acts began at home. How many homes of the sick and diseased do those modern "faith healers," who exploit the suffering for their own financial gain, visit? Home visitation to receive the needy would be too humdrum for them. They require the intense emotion of a large packed hall or tent, with all the paraphernalia of mass psychology to stage their so-called "miracles."

Further, all sickness is not the result of sin, as faith healing racketeers erroneously teach. It is wrong to assume that if a person suffers sickness or disease that they are suffering because of some special sin in their life. Peter was one of the most ardent and devoted followers of Christ, yet serious illness overtook his beloved mother-in-law, whose character was likewise commendable. Sickness is often permitted by God for His glory and that His Son might be glorified also (John 11:4). Even Jesus Himself was "made perfect through suffering" (Hebrews 2:10).

14. The Miracle of Mass Healing

(Luke 4:40, 41; Matthew 8:16, 17; Mark 1:32-34)

That historic Sabbath was to end with a still more glorious display of Christ's miraculous power. News of the synagogue miracle and that of the healing of Peter's mother-in-law quickly traveled, and at sunset it was like a hospital at the door of Peter's home. The miracle of the demoniac encouraged the people to bring all the demon-possessed they could, and Jesus healed them all, imposing upon them a vow of silence in regard to His identity as the Messiah. The instant and entire healing of the fever-stricken woman inspired friends to bring all the ailing persons of the town to Him so that, in the coolness of the evening with the setting sun registering the end of the Sabbath, Jesus could heal them. Tired though He must have been because of the limitations of His humanity, Jesus began His healing mission afresh, continuing far into the night His toilsome work, until He had "healed them all." His sympathy was individual, for Luke tells us that "He laid His hand on *every one* of them."

Jesus never saw a multitude without having compassion for all who formed it, and no sufferer ever made application for relief in vain. What a day that was for Capernaum as Jesus, in ceaseless energy, crowded the day with so many loving deeds! What a miracle He Himself was! Beholding the manifestation of His power, we wonder still more at the miracle of His unused power. The miracles on that Sabbath were looked upon as a fulfilment of the prophetic word, "Himself took our infirmities and bare our sicknesses" (Isaiah 53:4). He drew to Himself and absorbed the sufferings around Him. In Him, they all met, so that in Him they should all be done away. He bore sicknesses, "inasmuch as He bore that mortal suffering life, in which alone He could bring them to an end, and finally swallow up death, and all that led to death, in victory."

15. The Miracle of the Leper Cleansed
(Matthew 8:1-4; Mark 1:40-45; Luke 5:12-15)

It is not easy to harmonize the gospel narratives with any measure of certainty. Each record is independent of the other. Thus, there is no direct evidence of the exact order of events. Yet, taken together, the parallel narratives make any given record more vivid and complete. It would seem as if the cleansing of the leper took place after the Sermon on the Mount. Matthew disregarded the historical sequence in his presentation of the miracle, his object being to put in strong contrast the low faith of the Jewish leper with the strong faith of the Gentile centurion described in the verses immediately following. The King, descending the Mount, brings the kingdom nearer the people and bestows upon the needy His wonderful, kingly power. His miracles set the seal to the authority of His teaching, and vindicated His right to speak in the language of authority which He was wont to do (Matthew 7:29).

The lepers are cleansed. Such cleansing is mentioned as a specific part of our Lord's work of healing. Under the old dispensation, lepers were declared unclean, and no medical means were provided for their care. Therefore, this aspect of Christ's divine mission takes on a peculiar and added force. While doubtless many lepers were cleansed, individual cases, like the miracle before us, the ten lepers, and Simon the leper prove Christ to be the divine Healer. Such an aspect was also included in the apostles' commission.

As to *leprosy,* it was a loathsome and pitiful disease. Trench gives us the following description of it:

Leprosy was nothing short of a living death, a corruption of all the humors, a poisoning of the very springs of life; a dissolution little by little of the whole body, so that one limb after another actually decayed and fell away. The disease, moreover, was incurable by the art and skill of man—not that the leper might not return to health, for, however rare such cures might be, they are contemplated as possible in the Levitical law. But then the leprosy left the man, not in obedience to any skill of the physician, but purely and merely through the good will and mercy of God.

The Jews called leprosy "the finger of God," or "the stroke," indicating thereby that the disease was regarded as a direct punishment from God and absolutely incurable, except by the same divine power which permitted it. Luke, with the professional accuracy of a doctor, uses the precise term of the leper who came to Jesus as being "full of leprosy," a term frequently used by medical writers to describe an aggravated case. This sufferer, then, was in an advanced stage of leprosy. As a leper, he had to live apart from others, and wear on his brow the outward sign of separation, and cry out the words of warning, "Unclean! Unclean!" (Leviticus 13:45).

As to the miracle itself, Mark gives us more of the atmosphere of the event than Matthew and Luke. Mark writes of the leper as "falling on his knees." Luke describes him as "falling on his face"—the highest form of eastern homage. True reverence was his in the presence of the One he called "Lord." Acutely conscious of his need, the leper was to find cleansing at the feet of Him whose power is unlimited. When we accept the truth of His lordship, there is no difficulty in crediting Him with almightiness. The objection that miracles are inconsistent with natural laws is beside the mark, as we have shown in our Old Testament *Introduction.* As miracles are sovereign interpositions of the Lord, they are altogether apart from, and above, laws.

In the request of the leper and the reply of the Lord one can hear the chime of wedding bells, "Wilt Thou? . . . I will." Perhaps the leper had heard of Christ's work of healing or, having listened to His remarkable discourses, felt that He was able to act as well. The sufferer's request contained a singular mingling of faith and distrust. There was no doubt in his mind about Christ's power to heal his disease— "Thou canst make me clean." What the leper doubted was Christ's willingness to relieve him of his leprosy—"If Thou wilt." He wondered whether the divine Healer would stop and touch one so unclean. As he felt that his foul disease was the result of sin, would He pity and relieve?

It will be noticed that the leper sought cleansing, not *healing.* This was because of the notion that uncleanness was attached to the malady. "The Bible treats leprosy as an emblem of sin, in its aspect of pollution or defilement," says Laidlaw. "Thus, in its removal, it is never said to be *cured* or *healed,* but always *cleansed.*"

In our Lord's reply He employed the leper's own words and commanded him authoritatively to be cleansed. Mark tells us that as the Lord looked at the leper He was "moved with compassion." Others, meeting the leper, drew back in horror and evaded him. But the Lord was touched with feeling by the man's infirmity and compassion which led to *contact,* for He *touched* him. The first thing He did here was the last any other would have dreamed of doing (Leviticus 13:44-46). Under the Mosaic law, to *touch* a leper means defilement and social death. With the Lord of life and the Conqueror of death, however, it was different. As the Healer and Saviour of men, He stretched out His hand and touched the leper.

Had Jesus been a mere man, to have touched the leper would have been to defile Himself; but because He was the God-Man the touch did not defile Him. The sun shines on earth's pollution but remains unscathed in its own purity and splendor. The one He touched was cleansed. Through that supernatural touch health overcame sickness, purity overcame pollution and life, death. Trench quotes Theophylact as saying, "Christ touched the leper, showing that His sacred flesh imparted sanctification." Through Christ's hand, purity and power were communicated to the diseased one. Further, the putting forth of that divine hand was a proof of Christ's willingness, as well as power, to heal.

First the *contact,* then the *command,* and finally the *cure* was effected. Accompanying the deed with His kingly word, Jesus said, "I will," and the question of willingness was quickly settled and the element of doubt in the leper's mind vanished. The narrative says that the leper was *immediately* cleansed. Instantaneously, the leprosy disappeared and the skin was made whole. Sores were closed and the once foul flesh took on the tints and tones of robust health.

Christ imposed silence regarding the miracle on the cleansed man—"Tell no man!" Mark says that He "straitly charged" him, or vehemently urged him to say nothing about the cure. The healed man was bidden to show himself to the priest and offer a gift for a testimony. As this is the first instance of an Israelitish leper cleansed since the instructions given nearly 1,500 years before (Leviticus 13:34), the presence of a cleansed leper at the altar with his two birds would testify that God had come to His people and was meeting men's need altogether from priestly ministrations and religious ordinances. By showing himself to the priest, the healed leper fulfilled the requirement of the law as to his fitness to return to social life (Leviticus 13:14). Alas, however, this healed one had zeal without discretion! Elated over his new-found health, he disobeyed the Master's request and went out and blazed abroad the miracle, seriously retarding thereby the activities of the Healer. It would have been better for the man had he cherished his gratitude than wasted it in words. Jesus was forced to seek retirement in desert places, for if *all* lepers, hearing of the healed one, flocked to Him, His teaching ministry would have been hindered. Further, silence was imposed on the one-time leper lest the popular desire to make Jesus king should get beyond control. All unconsciously, disobedience to His request helped to hasten His end by those who were hostile to His claims.

As to the parable wrapped up in this miracle, He who is able to cure the disease which is a type of sin can cleanse sin itself. His healing miracles have a reference to Christ's Saviour works, for diseases are at once effects and emblems of sin. In the case of the leper, proof is given of the removal of *pollution* of sin; and in that of the paralytic, deliverance from the *power* or *bondage* of sin. The ugly, festering sores the leper bore in his body were the outward and visible tokens of sin in the soul, and in Christ's miracle of healing we have a symbol of His power to purify and save from sin. No matter how vile a sinner may be, "His touch has still its ancient power" to cleanse.

16. The Miracle of the Paralytic

(Luke 5:18-25; Matthew 9:2-7;
Mark 2:3-12)

The scene before us must have been a dramatic one. The vividness of the narrative makes it easy for us to picture what took place. The brightly colored crowds of interested peasants pressing in at the door, and within, either in a large upper room, or in the cool courtyard, was Christ the Teacher, proclaiming to Pharisees, the scribes, and the peasants the truths that seemed so new to them. Luke tells us that "the power of the Lord was present to heal them," which means that He was present to accomplish any work of healing. Four men arrived late that day with their poor, pitiful burden of the paralytic on his bed. Sizing up the situation, the bearers, in the invincible determination of love and hope, carried their burden upstairs to the roof and suddenly let down the bed before the Speaker, challenging thereby His attention and compassion.

It is interesting to note that this miracle took place in Capernaum, the city adopted by Jesus after He left Nazareth. Matthew speaks of Capernaum as "his own city." After His departure from Nazareth, the home of His childhood, Jesus never described it as *His own city*. Capernaum became His ordinary dwelling place (Matthew 17:24) after His rejection by the Nazarenes (Luke 4:30, 31). Chrysostom has the phrase, "Bethlehem bare Him, Nazareth nurtured Him, Capernaum had Him continuously as an inhabitant."

As to the malady of the man brought to Jesus, Luke uses a term in strict agreement with that of medical writers and says that he was *palsied*. The technical Greek word is used of pronounced paralysis from disease of some part of the nervous system. Jesus called the sufferer "son," or as it literally means, "child." Such a fatherly tone of love and pity suggests that the palsy-stricken one was comparatively young and completely disabled.

There are several aspects of this Capernaum incident to be distinguished. First of all, there were the four friends who were determined to bring their helpless friend into the circle of healing. Unable to get to Jesus in the ordinary way because of the crowd around and in the house (probably Peter's), the bearers took the palsied man to the roof. Their determination to place him at the feet of Jesus was an evidence of their faith that he would be healed. They realized only too well the problem of contact. Here they were with a helpless man on their hands, yet inside was the Teacher they were not able to reach who was able to restore their friend to full health. However, necessity being the mother of invention led to the resort of a novel way of getting the bedridden man to Jesus. Faith such as those four men had laughed at impossibilities, and so from an opening in the flat roof of the house, the pallet was let down by ropes.

One can imagine how the whole audience must have looked up in amazement at the bold action of the four men. The teaching of Jesus stopped; the people were agog with excitement; and the scribes and pharisees, suspicious at what might happen, were particularly watchful. Jesus, however, was not perturbed. The boldness of the act must have pleased Him. "He who never takes ill that faith which brings men to Him, but only the unbelief which keeps them from Him, is in nothing offended at this interruption." How quick He was to respond to it! He rewarded the faith of the four bearers. "Seeing their faith"—a faith penetrating through all obstacles to reach Him—Jesus miraculously undertook for the sick man. Faith was often the condition for which He waited before He could do any mighty work. Here He found it in the friends of the paralytic. It was *their* faith, rather than any faith the sufferer may have had, that Jesus honored. Pleased with the inventiveness and perseverance of their faith, Jesus responds to their desire.

We have then the double miracle, a miracle of grace, then a miracle of power. Forgiveness came before healing. How astonished the bearers and people alike must have been when they heard Jesus say, as the helpless man rested before Him, "Son, be of good cheer, thy sins are forgiven thee." Was that the act and word of healing that the friends and crowd breathlessly expected? What had forgiveness of sins to do with the palsy? But Jesus set the spiritual and temporal in their right relationship. By implication, sin was responsible for the man's paralyzed condition, so the cause is dealt with first before the effect. The bodily infirmity was not such an intolerable weight as the sin of the soul. So, as he lay there before God Incarnate, the paralytic's thought was not of his stiff limbs but of his wounded conscience. What is the use of all the physical healing in the world if there be no cure of the disease of sin?

Exercising His divine prerogative, Christ forgave the man his sins, fulfilling thereby the prophecy of old, "Who forgiveth all thy iniquities" (Psalm 103:3). In forgiving the man's sins, Jesus healed him radically. The command to rise and walk, as we shall see, was of the same piece. The murmuring enemies immediately cried, "What blasphemy! He professes to forgive sin, a right which belongs to God alone!" Rightly understanding the forgiveness of sins as a divine prerogative, those blind scribes failed to see in Jesus God manifest in flesh. Perhaps there is no other passage of Scripture which more unequivocally declares His deity than this.

Then we have an evidence of our Lord's omniscience in that "He perceived in His spirit that they so reasoned within themselves." His was the divine faculty to perceive the unspoken counsels and meditations of their hearts (John 6:61) and then to expose their malice. They had no need to give articulate expression to their thoughts—they were open as a scroll to Him who can read the hearts of all men. Having neither feared the frown nor courted the favor of the cavillers, Jesus gave them

a most decisive proof of His equality with God. He did not reply to their captious accusations by the ingenuity of argument but by the splendor of a healing miracle, giving an immediate and resistless proof of His divine authority and power. Through Christ's immediate act of intuition, the temper of those scribes was revealed, and all unconsciously they conceded to Him the divine dignity and equality He claimed.

Giving voice to the inner thoughts of the scribes, Jesus said, "Which is easier to *say* (not easier to *do*), what every rabbi or priest would, 'your sin is forgiven' or what none of them would care to say to a palsied man, 'Rise up and walk'?" *Pardon* was sealed by *power*. Immediately the pardoned one arose and took up his bed and walked. No wonder the people said, "We have seen strange things today." What an experience it was for the sinful paralytic— two miracles wrought on him by one act! The disease Jesus healed is one in which human skill is nearly unavailing, even in the present state of advanced science; yet Jesus healed the paralytic in a moment by a word. Although his couch was light, he lifted it up and carried it away. The sign of his sickness was now the sign of his cure. Bengel says, "The bed had borne the man, now the man was bearing the bed;" and the crowd once blocking up his path when he was carried to the house, now makes a way for him to walk out with a cleansed soul and a thoroughly healed body.

The result of the man's supernatural cure was instantaneous and remarkable. The people marveled, were afraid and overwhelmed, and ascribed glory to God who had given such power to a Man, even to Jesus, the true head and representative of the human race, so sin-stricken and disease-ridden. Alas! although this wonderful double miracle amazed the people, it only further irritated the blinded Pharisees, making them more determined to destroy this Man who made Himself equal with God.

One or two lessons can be gleaned from this miracle. First of all, palsy is a fit emblem of sin's paralyzing power and of the utter helplessness of the sinner to do anything for his own relief. Yet the cross made possible a merciful provision for a palsied race. "When we were yet without strength, in due time Christ died for the ungodly" (Romans 5:6).

Then the miracle presents Jesus as being able to *immediately* cancel the bondage of sin and raise the sinner from moral weakness. "He never leaves His pardoned ones under the paralyzing yoke of sin," says Laidlaw. "When He frees us from its guilt, He delivers us also from its service."

A further lesson is that while no moral paralytic can be saved by another's faith, yet that one can be brought by another to Him who alone can deliver. If you have a burden regarding a friend who is palsied by sin and is helpless and hopeless in his or her condition, then that one must be "borne of four"—your consecrated life, your compasisonate love, your prevailing intercession and your undaunted faith.

17. The Miracle of the Withered Hand

(Luke 6:6-10; Matthew 12:9-14; Mark 3:1-6)

As the two incidents of the plucking of the corn and the healing of the withered hand are placed together by Luke, it is somewhat necessary to understand the scene as a preliminary of the performance of the miracle mentioned in the three gospel narratives. Shortly after His return from Galilee, it would seem as if Jesus had become involved in fresh disputes with the Pharisees about the constant bone of contention between them, namely, Sabbath-keeping.

The first dispute was over His disciples plucking ears of corn and rubbing them in their hands and then eating them as they passed through the grainfields on a Sabbath day. Although the law permitted this liberty, Pharisaic interpretation of the law was loaded with trivial and vexatious rules, so much so that the Pharisees had converted the Sabbath into a day of wretched constraint. The accumulation of superstitious rites had exchanged the spiritual for mere ceremonial obedience. There was a sanctimonious use of the Sabbath without regard to human needs.

Jesus defended His disciples' action by reminding them of David and the show-bread (I Samuel 21:6), and then declared Himself to be greater than the Temple and also Lord over the Sabbath (Mark 2:27, 28). He emphasized that necessity overrides positive enactment and that the broad principles of the *design* of the Sabbath was made for man—for his highest physical, mental, moral, and spiritual well-being. John J. Maclaren, whose most comprehensive and concise summary of the life of Christ in *The International Standard Bible Encyclopaedia* from which we are drawing for the setting of the miracle, says that "The claims of mercy are paramount. The end is not to be sacrificed to the means."

Christ's second clash with the Pharisees was on another Sabbath in a synagogue (Luke 6:6) when there was present a man having a withered hand. His antagonists were present to entrap Him again on the question of healing on the Sabbath. They "watched" Him, or "kept watching," as the word implies. Their vigilance, suggests Ellicott, implies two facts:

(1) That the Pharisees expected our Lord to heal the man thus afflicted. They knew that commonly the mere sight of suffering of this kind called out His sympathy, and that the sympathy passed into action.

(2) That they had resolved, if He did so heal, to make it the ground of a definite accusation before the local tribunal, the "judgment" of Matthew 5:21. The casuistry of the rabbi allowed the healing art to be practiced on the Sabbath in cases of life and death, but "the withered hand," a permanent infirmity, did not come under that category.

In His masterly way, Jesus answered the traditionalists by citing their own practice in permitting the rescue of sheep that had fallen into a pit on a Sabbath day. Did they not engage in such an act of mercy because the need was paramount? Commanding the man who needed healing to stand forth, Jesus flung the question to the Pharisees: "Is it lawful on the Sabbath to do good, or to do harm—to save life or to kill?" Was the latter phrase, *to kill*, an allusion to the murderous intents of the Pharisees even on a Sabbath? When Jesus saw the man with his dried-up hand, His heart of compassion went out at once to him, and He knew that this was His opportunity of proving that a man was better than a sheep. Christ healed the man, and His religious watchers were angry because, according to their estimation of the Sabbath, He had discounted it.

The man Christ healed is said to have had "a withered hand." Luke is the only writer with professional accuracy telling us the specific hand—it was the right one. Ancient medical writers always stated whether the right or the left were affected. The hand was "withered" or "dried up," suggesting some form of paralysis. The arm was not withered. The condition must have been the result of an accident or disease and was called a "local atrophy," that is, a wasting or shrinking of one part of a limb. Luke's touch that it was the "right hand" lends color to the tradition that the man was a bricklayer who came and besought Jesus for a cure that he might be able to work for his bread. Disabled though he was, he was in the place of worship on the Sabbath and found there what he sorely needed. The One who healed this withered hand, withered the arm of another (1 Kings 13:4) as a miracle of judgment.

As Jesus came to heal the man in the synagogue, we read that He looked round about on His foes with anger, being grieved for the hardness of their hearts. Grief for these sinners went hand in hand with anger against their sin. This is the only recorded instance of His anger, except that we read that He was "moved with indignation" at His disciples trying to keep children from Him (Mark 10:14). "The anger that He felt at the sin resolved itself into pity and compasion towards the men that were guilty of it." Spurgeon's fine sermon on, "Jesus, Angry With Hard Hearts," should be read at this point. Because of His omniscient mind, Christ was able to read the thoughts and intents of their evil hearts.

Jesus uttered what seemed to be an impossible command, "Stretch forth thy hand." He was asked to do the very thing which had been impossible. But with the command there was power, for His commands are His enablings. The man was told to "stand forth," that is, he was ordered to come out into the view of all present so they could witness the miracle. The man obeyed and was instantly cured without even a touch of Christ's hand. He silently accomplished the cure by His own expressed will, and as the man raised his hand, it was no longer dried up, but perfectly restored and healthy like his other hand. There was positive proof to all that a miracle had been performed.

The effect of the miracle was immediate, for the Pharisees were "filled with madness," which implies a senseless rage as distinguished from the intelligent indignation such as Jesus manifested. Inflamed

with hate, the Pharisees, along with the Herodians, took counsel to destroy Jesus (Mark 3:6). Although the Pharisees could quibble over our Lord's healing on a Sabbath day, they had no qualms of conscience in plotting to kill on the same day. Such murderous intentions were the time and occasion of Christ's withdrawal to the solitary hills, where, away from the machinations of His enemies, He could commune with His Father and have time to choose the twelve apostles who should be His witnesses after His ascension. It is Mark alone who notes the eleven occasions when Jesus retired from His work in order to escape from His enemies or to pray in solitude, to rest, or to engage in private conference with His disciples (1:35; 3:7; 6:31, 46; 7:24, 31; 9:2; 10:1; 14:34).

The lessons to be gathered from this miracle are apparent. "By fulfilling its intention, the Lord of the Sabbath sacredly kept it in restoring this man to health and power." Then we have presented a forceful illustration of the character of faith. "Stand forth" tested the courage of the man's faith. It rose above human fear. The next bidding, "Stretch forth thy hand," tested the deeper quality of faith, namely, that of entirely trusting Jesus. He was healed in the act of obeying. The last lesson is that many of us are suffering from withered hands. Sin so paralyzed us so that we are not able to do much for Christ, whose pierced hands saved us. But withered hands can be healed and empowered to do great things for our Healer in the midst of a burdened and suffering creation.

18. The Miracle of the Centurion's Servant

(Matthew 8:5-13; Luke 7:1-10)

Having already dealt with the error of confusing this miracle with that of the nobleman's son, it can be pointed out that both miracles do agree in representing Christ as able to cure from a distance and in the absence of the sufferers through the medium of a word. As Matthew and Luke alone among the four evangelists record this miracle, it is interesting to note the way in which each describes it. There is no conflict in presentation. Each was guided by the Holy Spirit in his version of the incident. Here, then, are some points of contrast:

Matthew wrote with Israel especially in view, and thus affords our Lord's solemn warning to the nation about many coming from afar and being blessed with Abraham, Isaac, and Jacob. Such a warning was most necessary for a people building their hopes on religious associations and privileges to the neglect of personal faith.

Luke, as a Gentile, wrote for Gentiles and therefore omits the warning to Israel and introduced instead the aspect so instructive and encouraging to Gentiles, namely, that the centurion in the first instance persuaded the Jewish elders to plead for him with the Saviour. Matthew, by his warning, humbled Jewish pride. Luke, by his addition, sought to suppress Gentile conceit.

Luke tells us that the miracle was performed as Jesus came into Capernaum, and he gives us a closer glimpse of its details and circumstances.

Matthew's account reports the centurion as going to Jesus in person and relates the whole conversation as taking place between the Lord and himself.

Luke, with more circumstantial evidence, tells us that the centurion first of all employed his Jewish friends to intercede on his behalf. Matthew's more abbreviated record of the miracle relates what passed through others as if it had been directly transacted.

Matthew describes the centurion's servant malady as "palsy" and says that he was "grievously tormented," which implies a special kind of paralysis accompanied with excruciating pain.

Luke, tells us that the servant was "sick and ready to die." His medical approach forbade him expressing the precise nature of the man's fatal ailment.

The centurion himself was a courtier or commander of a hundred soldiers (Acts 21: 31). Judaism had made a deep impression upon his Gentile mind. In it, Ellicott reminds us, he found "a purity, reverence, simplicity, nobleness of life not found in any heathen religion." He loved the Jewish people and rebuilt, at his own expense, one of their synagogues in the town where he was stationed. He also knew all about Jesus as a Teacher endowed with supernatural power. The Jews around him knew his worth and were ready to support his prayers and efforts on behalf of his dying servant. In this centurion we have a promise of the breakdown of the barrier between Jew and

Gentile—a forecast of the spiritual brotherhood in Christ. This sincere soul was not far from the kingdom He was "a proselyte at the gate." Another centurion at the cross recognized the claims of Christ, and still another centurion was the first to be received into the Christian Church (Acts 10). There are at least four distinguishable traits in the character of the centurion which Matthew and Luke describe.

(1) There is his care and concern for his servant.

The word Luke used for "servant" is *slave*, yet he was not treated as a common, paltry, human chattel. He was more of a son than a slave. Luke also adds that this servant was *dear* or precious to his master. Although there was a bond of affection between the two, the dearness was of value, rather than of love. It was most unusual for wealthy Romans to deal thus with their slaves. Bishop Hall once wrote:

> Great variety of suitors resorted to Christ. One comes for his son, another for a daughter, a third for himself. I see none came for his servant, but this one centurion. Neither was he a better man than a master. His servant is sick, yet he doth not drive him out-of-doors, but lays him at home; neither doth he stand gazing at his bedside, but seeks forth, and he seeks forth not to witches and charmers, but to Christ. . . . Had the master been sick, the faithfulest servant could have done no more. He is unworthy to be well served that will not sometimes wait upon his followers.

The suffering of the valued servant touched the master's heart with pity. The centurion blended affection with authority. Accustomed to command, he was yet capable of concern for his sick slave.

(2) Another worthy trait of the centurion is his modesty and reticence in reckoning himself unworthy as a Gentile to approach Jesus, a Jew, whether personally or through the intercession of others. Luke expresses this humility more strongly than Matthew. This was no false humility. How proud some are of their humility! How offensive is a humility which is itself an affectation! Augustine's comment is fitting at this point. "He counted himself unworthy that Christ should enter his doors, he was counted worthy that Christ should enter his heart." The Lord has respect toward the humble. "The sense of unworthiness implied at once the consciousness of

his own sins," says Ellicott, "and the recognition of the surpassing holiness and the majesty of the Teacher he addressed."

(3) Then there was faith in Christ's ability to heal.

"Say in a word, and my servant shall be healed." What a conspicuous proof of the centurion's faith is here revealed! He knew there was no need of any magic influences operating by touch or charm. He did not ask, as Gideon did, for a sign of divine ability to perform a miracle. He did not ask for Jesus to come to his home, visit the sick servant, offer a prayer, and take him up by the hand. He felt that distance was nothing to Jesus, that His word at a mile's distance could cure as well as His actual presence and touch. His was a grand faith, desiring no visible sign. His spiritual eye could see the invisible and so his heart was fixed, trusting in the Lord. As Spurgeon expresses it, "The centurion's unstaggering faith required no clutch," and as we shall see, the Lord sent His word and healed the servant.

Further, it was this confidence in the efficacy of Christ's word to heal the dying man when He was personally absent that excited our Lord's commendation. Here was a man of authority believing that diseases had to obey Christ's bidding just as he had to obey his superior officers and those who were under him had to obey him. The uppermost idea in the centurion's mind was his profession, which supplied him with a conception of the grandeur of Him who is "the Autocrat of heaven and earth, the true Imperator, of whose authority Caesar was but an imperfect and poor shadow," as Cumming puts it. As a man of authority and under authority, personal presence was not necessary, for he could so delegate his soldiers or slaves to carry out his orders. So he argued that Christ, because of His sovereignty, could exercise His will through His word and that that would be sufficient.

(4) Last of all, there was the gracious reward of his great faith.

As soon as Christ heard of the plight of the slave and beheld the humility of the centurion, He said, "I will come and heal him." As He went on His errand of mercy, someone ran on in front to tell the centurion that his request was granted. "As thou hast believed, so be it done unto thee." Describing the cure, Luke says that the servant was made *whole*—a characteristic use of a technical medical term for a

healthy condition, or to be "in sound health." There was no slow abatement of the violence of the servant's disease, but a sudden departure of it altogether. As soon as the centurion believed and Christ uttered His all-commanding word, complete healing was experienced. "The healing word flowed from Jesus as naturally as the perfume from the flowers."

Such an instantaneous cure wrought on the patient from a distance is rare among the healing miracles of the Bible. This cure by remote control, or "distant healing" (see Matthew 15:21-28; Mark 7:24-30), baffles scientific psychologists who try to adduce parallels from modern orthodox psychotherapy. Fake faith healers seek to practice the healing of sickness by remote control through anointed handkerchiefs and other prayed-over (?) media.

In conclusion, Christ's commendation of the centurion's faith is worthy of a paragraph. That He should marvel at the magnitude of his faith is an evidence of His human consciousness. The act of faith which Jesus called "great" was so because the man asked for no sign but believed in Christ's conscious, supernatural ability and asked for nothing more. There are two instances of faith which were called "great faith" by Jesus, and both of those manifesting such faith were Gentiles—namely, the Roman centurion and the Syrophoenician woman (Matthew 15:28; Luke 4:26). The first begged for his servant—the second for her daughter. The miracle in both cases shows how the principle of faith is supreme over all privileges of race and birth. Laidlaw elaborates on the greatness of the faith Jesus so signally praised in these ways:

(1) It was great when we consider the man in whom it was found. As a Gentile, he had no claim in his own right to the mercy of Jesus. This Roman soldier was the morning star of western faith.

(2) It was great in its view of Christ's power. It was a faith that put the crown of the universe on His head and the scepter of universal dominion in His hand.

(3) It was great in its sole dependence upon Christ and His will. No personal contact nor external means were required. This man's faith was above all restrictions; it made nothing of difficulty or distance. By a silent act of His will, the cure was wrought.

(4) It was great in its self-forgetting humbleness. There was no vestige of desire for honor to himself, for consideration of his

standing, in the way the centurion preferred his request. This is faith's true mark—"None but Christ."

19. The Miracle of the Widow's Son
(Luke 7:11-18)

The day after the great miracle of the healing of the centurion's servant registered a far mightier and more wonderful miracle than Jesus had yet wrought. Luke, the only gospel narrator to give us this ressurection miracle, states that it took place after Jesus left Capernaum and came to "a city called Nain." If Luke had not witnessed the miracle, probably the account of it was received from "the devout women" (8:2, 3) in whose memories the circumstances of the miracle were still vivid. Twice over Luke uses the phrase "much people" to describe those who met just outside the cemetery. We have the "much people" made up of many disciples and interested followers of Jesus and the "much people" of all the mourners.

It was neither incidental nor accidental that these two companies met. Neither was the pause a mere natural one. Had Jesus and His company been a little late reaching the spot where the two companies met, the burial would have been over—not that that would have made any difference to the omnipotent One who later on was to raise Lazarus from his grave. That seemingly incidental meeting was deeply laid in the councils of divine providence. Says Spurgeon in his sermon on this miracle, "Carefully note the 'coincidences,' as sceptics call them, but as we call them, 'providences' of Scripture." This, then, was no accidental meeting but the prearrangement and determined providence of God. In His plan the two companies met, with God working in and through seemingly natural circumstances. "This is the great miracle of Providence," wrote Isaac Taylor, "that no miracles are needed for the accomplishment of its purposes."

The meeting of these two crowds outside the city of Nain must have been impressive, and as they met, life triumphed over death and sorrow was turned into joy. One procession was grief-stricken for it was being led by "the Pale Horse" to the grave with great exultation. The other procession was led by the living Lord, who only hath immortality, and as life and death met, the battle was short and decisive and death fled from the gates of the city.

While there may have been other resurrections from the dead (Luke 7:22), three specific records are chosen—a child, raised immediately after death; a young man raised at his funeral; and a full grown man who had been dead four days! At the raising of Jairus's daughter, Jesus was besought by her father; at the gate of Nain the miracle was unasked by the mother; at Bethany, the raising of Lazarus was unexpected by the sisters.

Two facts enhanced the bitterness of the woman's sorrow as the funeral cortege slowly proceeded according to eastern custom to the burying place outside the town. First, the dead youth was her only son. He had been the staff of her age, and the comfort of her loneliness—the support and pillar of the home. In the loss of her only son, the last remaining prop had been swept away. The Bible records no loss so severe and painful as the loss of an only son (Zechariah 12:10; Amos 8:10). "A Jewish wife felt it a calamity not to have a son, but it was the most terrible calamity when the only son, the stay and hope of the home, was removed by death. Then too, the weeping woman, who brought death into the world, widow understands the full sorrow of such a term. The sentence, 'She was a widow,' sounds like a knell. All that was left to her was dead and being borne to burial."

The designation "Lord," as used by Luke, suggests the profound reverence he had for Him. "When the Lord saw her," His quiet eye singled out the grief-stricken mother just behind the coffin. Edersheim in his *Jewish Social Life* says, "Had it been in Judea, the hired mourners and musicians would have *preceded* the bier; in Galilee they followed. First came the women; for, as an ancient Jewish commentary explains, women, who brought death into the world, ought to lead the way in the funeral procession."

Here, as in many other miracles (Matthew 20:34; Mark 1:41, etc.), "our Lord's works of wonder spring not from a distinct purpose to offer credentials of His mission, but from the outflow of His infinite sympathy with human suffering." What fulness of compassion was compressed into the simple, authoritative summons, "Weep not!" Yet this was not a mere request for the tearful mother to cheer up; it was an effectual glimpse and presage of His power. He was about to remove the cause of her tears and give to His own a glimpse of the time when

God shall wipe away *all* tears (Revelation 21:4).

As Jesus touched the bier, or coffin, the funeral procession stood still. Christ's compelling presence brought it to a halt. Jesus did not fear the ceremonial defilement of contact with the dead. How the mourners must have marveled that this great One, now known as the Teacher with authority, should touch the dead most Jewish rulers would have avoided as bringing pollution! Thus, "their sudden halt in the solemn march indicated, perhaps, both awe and faith, that the touch could not be unmeaning." We can imagine how Christ's followers, who had witnessed previous miracles, were wonder-struck with the mourners and thought, "What now! We have seen Him call men's lives across the line between sickness and health, weakness and strength, madness and sanity; but across this gulf will He ever dare or be able to call the departed back?"

Why should it be thought a thing incredible that God should raise the dead? (Acts 26:8). If He is supreme in the universe, then it is easy to believe in resurrection, however stupendous the miracle may be. Surely He who created man from dust is able to call him forth again from the domain of death if He should so please. As the *Life*, He was also the *Resurrection*, and in response to His majestic command, "*I say unto thee, Arise!*" death immediately yielded up its prey. With a calm certainty, He knew that as "the Prince of Life," His word would be obeyed. Are you not impressed with the potent brevity of Christ's words to the dead? "Young man . . . arise;" "Maid, arise!" "Lazarus, come forth."

As soon as Christ's command, so effective in the kingdom of death, was heard, the dead youth sat up and spoke. There was no doubt about him being dead. He was not in a swoon nor feigning death as some would claim, as Dr. C. Brewer indicates in his fascinating volume, *Dictionary of Miracles*. This youth was dead and was being carried out and was on the way to burial. Now, through supernatural interposition, he was alive again. "He that was dead sat up." There was no need of sorrowing friends to raise him up. Full vitality was his as Christ raised him from the bier, as easily as another from the bed.

Such a direct demonstration of our Lord's power brings us to the distinction previously mentioned between Himself and the prophets and apostles. Elijah, Elisha, Peter, and Paul raised persons from the dead but their power was delegated, for they had none of their own to wield. Elisha, with great effort and after partial failure, restored to life the Shunammite's child. Jesus simply said, "Come forth," and the dead arose (I Kings 17:20-22; II Kings 4:34; Matthew 10:8; Acts 9:40). Christ's power of resurrection proved Him to be God (II Corinthians 1:9). Divinely commissioned prophets and apostles were the media of resurrection, but with Christ it was different. All was done in His own name and in a direct and majestic manner. Power was not delegated to Him. All power *was* His.

As soon as the youth returned to life and sat up, he *spoke*. What he said, we are not told. We can imagine, however, how his once-silent lips were vocal with adoring praise of his divine Deliverer and with glad recognition of his dear mother. The silence of Scripture as to what the young man, or Jairus's daughter, or Lazarus expressed as they crossed "the great divide" is positively sublime. As far as we know, they did not lift the curtain on the after life. Christ delivered the raised youth to his mother. He sent him back to his own natural sphere of life. He was given back, for as Bengel remarks, "He had already ceased to belong to his mother." What a picture this is of the blissful reunion of the children of God at the coming of Christ (I Thessalonians 4:13-18)!

This miracle produced fear on all who witnessed it, but such fear, or terror, gave place to the still deeper and holier feeling of awe and reverence for the life-giving Lord. As the result of this crowning miracle of the period of His first Galilean ministry, the people acclaimed Him as the Great Prophet who should visit His people (Deuteronomy 18:15; Luke 1:68, 69, etc.) and who had vindicated His claims as the prophesied prophet by raising the dead. Quickly the fame of this Miracle-Worker spread, bringing deeper hostility on the part of the Jewish rulers who rejected the claims of Christ to absolute Godhead. The spiritual application of the miracle is not hard to make. Having power to raise the physically dead, Christ is well able, in virtue of His own death and resurrection, to raise to newness of life those who are dead in their sins and trespasses.

20. The Miracle of the Stilling of the Tempest

(Luke 8:22-25; Matthew 8:23-27;
Mark 4:35-41)

This miracle took place in the evening of that memorable day when Jesus taught the seven parables recorded in Matthew 13 (see Mark 4:35). By the phrase, "the same day," Mark fixes the precise time of the miracle. At this point Luke records the Parable of the Sower. Because of the great crowds still thronging Jesus, He commanded His disciples to take Him in their boat to the quieter region of Peraea on the other side of the lake. Before He left the multitudes, He uttered those three unique sayings to three who were part of the crowd (Matthew 8:19-22; See Luke 9:57-62) and then set sail. Examining the three records, we can distinguish these features of the miracle Christ performed that evening hour.

First of all, there was the weary Worker. How suggestive is Mark's phrase, "They took Him *even as He was* in the ship." How was He at that hour? It had been a most exhausting day of teaching and Jesus was weary and worn, both mentally and physically. Mark's description of His condition suggests extreme tiredness from the fatigue of His incessant labors. Seeing how exhausted He was, His disciples made haste to get Him away for a season of repose and freedom from interruptions and distractions. Thus, without any preparation for the sail to the other side of the lake, His followers rowed away.

Throwing Himself upon the pillow, or cushion, which was a usual part of the meager furnishing of the tiny craft, Jesus fell fast asleep. He who caused a deep sleep to fall upon others (see I Samuel 26:12) now enjoys one Himself. Never did a ship carry a more precious burden than that one. What a wonderful mingling of deity and humanity we have in this exhibition of supernatural power! Because of the limitations of His humanity, He, who now never slumbers nor sleeps, had need of the rest and refreshment of sleep. But as God, He arose from sleep and rebuked the storm. So deep was His much-needed sleep that the sudden storm which distressed His disciples did not disturb Him. To the fishermen, the danger was very real, and they were afraid for themselves and their divine Passenger. He, however, could sweetly sleep in the storm because His was a perfect trust in His heavenly Father's care and protection. Then was it not the God of the winds and seas Himself who lay asleep in the stern of that tempest-driven boat?

What a striking contrast there is between this ship and its sleeping Prophet and that other ship on the Mediterranean carrying a prophet who was fleeing from his God-given commission! The sleep of Jesus was undisturbed because it was a sleep of a pure and holy conscience. The sleep of Jonah in a storm was the opiate of a dead and benumbed conscience. Jonah was the cause of the storm he encountered—Jesus was the Queller of the storm. Jonah was a fugitive from God—Jesus was God's Messenger doing God's work in God's way for God's glory.

As to the storm itself, it was one of Gennesaret's sudden storms that burst upon the frail craft. It was a storm that literally "came down" from the heights surrounding the lake. Thomson, in his *Land and the Book*, writes of a storm wind from one of the deep ravines which "act like gigantic funnels to draw down the winds from the mountains." The tempest was "great," and the "storm of wind" filled the boat with water, so much so, that the disciples were in jeopardy. Mark, with minute detail, describes the waves beating into the boat. Vincent counsels us to "note the imperfects; *they were filling;* they *were beginning to be* in danger, contrasted with the instantaneous descent of the storm expressed by the words *came down.*"

Now let us take a look at the distressed crew who could not understand how Jesus could remain asleep in such a storm. Doubtless the disciples abstained from disturbing Jesus for a while, but now the need was desperate and so they aroused Him with the cry, "Lord, save us, we perish! Master, carest Thou not that we perish?" Fereday says that Mark, "with his customary observance of details, tells us the disciples roughly awoke their Lord with their cry. It is painful to transcribe the words; how cruelly they must have wounded the tender susceptibilities of the Saviour! . . . Yet, so gracious is He no word of censure escaped His lips for the heartlessness of their speech." Luke, in his characteristic way, is the only one in the New Testament to use the particular Greek word *epistates* for "Master" or "Rabbi." He also gives us the repetition, "Master, Master," which indicates the urgency of the cry.

We have then the awakening of Christ at the cry of His distraught disciples. As the Son of Man, He slept; now as the Son of God with power, He is awake and acts. He had no need of a rod like Moses or a mantle like Elijah to deal with water. His only instrument of power was His word. He spoke, and the wind ceased, and after a "great tempest" there was a "great calm." Is not this nature miracle related to the disharmony, disorder, and confusion of nature of which Christ alone is the Queller, and from which He alone will one day retrieve the world? He who was Co-Creator of the winds and waves knew how to control them. Long before He came, the psalmist wrote of Him, "Thou rulest the raging of the sea; when the waves thereof arise Thou stillest them" (Psalm 89:9). When He became man, He did not lay aside His omnipotence. That is why in the moment of sudden uproar on the lake, the forces of nature recognized His prerogative and yielded obedience to His word.

To *rebuke* was our Lord's favorite formula in the performance of some of His miracles—the fever, the frenzy of the demoniac, and here the tempest (Luke 4:39; 8:24; Mark 9:25). All were treated as if they were hostile and rebel forces under a dominating power that had to be restrained, and His word was sufficient to calm the sea in the world of nature, as previously the demons in the spirit world. Discords and disharmonies in the outward world are traced to their source in a person, as Trench suggests, "and this person can be no other than Satan, the author of all disorders alike in natural and spiritual world." Physical evils alike in nature and man are among those works of the Devil which Jesus was manifested to destroy.

When our Lord addressed the angry elements that night it would seem, from Mark's vivid word, that He spoke not to a mere force but to a figure in, and behind, the force. "Be still" means *be muzzled* or *gagged*, as though the storm was a maniac to be bound and gagged. Was there actually a sinister personality engineering that sudden, distressing storm for our Lord's destruction? George Pember in his arrestive volume, *Earth's Earliest Ages*, develops the idea that the waters of the earth are the dark prison of those evil spirits deposed from heaven when Satan rebelled.

We do know that there are two companies of those rebellious angelic beings.

There are the demons who are free and roam around and are associated with the miracles of demon-possession dealt with in this study. Then there is the other group which Jude (6) describes as being "reserved in everlasting chains under darkness." Pember's contention is that these bound evil spirits were cast into the seas and will remain within them until the "Great White Throne," when the sea must give up its dead (Revelation 20:13), which Pember affirms are not the wicked dead, since they are included "in the dead, small and great" (Revelation 20:12), but to the imprisoned evil spirits in the sea. These are to be raised and, along with the Devil and *all* his angels, judged and cast into the Lake of Fire. If we accept Pember's interpretation, then it is not difficult to associate the raging tempest with the Devil, whose avowed hatred of Jesus was behind every attempt to kill Him. Perhaps this murderer from the beginning felt that this was a most fitting opportunity to destroy Jesus, since He was fast asleep in the boat.

Turning from His rebuke of the storm, our Lord rebuked His disciples for the fearfulness and little faith. "Why were ye afraid? Where is your faith? Can any evil befall you while I am near?" Perhaps the reproof, "Why are ye fearful, O ye of little faith?" was uttered before the stilling of the storm, and then after it, "Where is your faith? How is it that ye have no faith?" "*Little* faith" was singularly appropriate. The disciples had not lost complete trust in their Master, but they had not learned the lesson of the centurion's faith, and were only at ease when they heard His voice and saw that He was watching over them. They had faith, as the weapon which a soldier has, but cannot lay hold of it, at the moment when he needs it most.

The disciples were not absolutely faithless, for believing in their unbelief, they cried, "Master, save us!" They knew, after what they had seen of His supernatural power, that He was able to calm the tempest. Where they failed was in not believing that sleeping or waking made no difference to Him. They should have remembered that no storm-tossed ship could possibly sink with Him on board. Was He not the One who ages before had shut up the sea with doors, saying, "Hitherto shalt thou come and no further; and here shall thy proud waves be stayed" (Job 38:8-11)? Christ's followers did not apply their faith fully. Fear, for the moment, paralyzed faith. Faith and fear can never exist together.

The result of the miracle is worth noting. Those awe-struck men received a new revelation of the majesty of their Master. It was not so much His power that impressed them, but the "manner" of the Man. The miracle brought them to His feet in a wonder not unmixed with dread. His simple mastery of nature's forces stirred their hearts. Here was a revelation of God in man. Elements seemingly beyond human control were yet subject to His sovereignty.

It only remains for us to adduce a few lessons from this dramatic miracle. As the Lord of Providence, Christ is ever at hand to defend His cause and people from danger. His perpetual presence in and with His Church, assures its protection and deliverance. The symbolic and prophetic aspect of this miracle, and all miracles for that matter, must not be lost sight of. Parables are wrapped up in the miracles. This is why there is a spiritual application of the stilling of the tempest which never ceases to be fresh. Combining the suggestions of Ellicott, Trench, and Taylor, we have these applications:

The *sea* is evermore in Scripture the symbol of the restless and sinful world (Daniel 7:2, 3; Revelation 13:1; Isaiah 57:20).

The *wind* is the blast of persecution, and the Lord of the Church seems as though He were asleep and heard not the cry of the sufferers, and the disciples are faint-hearted and afraid.

The tempest-driven *boat* is the Church of Christ, and it sails across the ocean of the world's history to the "other side" of the life beyond the grave. As Noah and his family, the kernel of the whole of humanity, were once contained in the Ark tossed on the waters of the deluge, so the kernel of the new humanity, of the new creation, Christ and His apostles in this little ship. The waves of the world rage against the Church, yet never prevail in overwhelming it—and this because Christ is in it (Psalm 46:1-3; 93:3, 4).

For the sinner rocked by the winds of sin and passion, there is hope if only he will cry, "Lord, save me; I perish." Immediately, He can give the storm-heaved spirit *peace*.

21. The Miracle of the Two Blind Men

(Matthew 9:27-31)

Matthew is the only writer to record this particular miracle and the one following it, namely, the dumb demoniac, both of which he records after the raising of Jairus' daughter. Matthew, for the most part, arranged the miracles of our Lord in groups, without regard to their chronological sequence. Because Matthew makes one miracle to run into the other, many expositors deal with them together. Because they are two distinct miracles, however, we are dealing with them separately, even though they may only be "minor miraculous incidents." The miracle of the blind men was probably wrought in Peter's home in which Jesus sojourned at Capernaum.

This miracle is the earliest in the notable group of similar miracles in the Gospels (Matthew 11:5; 12:22; 20:30; 21:14; Luke 7:21; John 9). These healings of the blind were a literal fulfilment of the prophetic word concerning the ministry of the Messiah—"The eyes of the blind shall be opened" (Isaiah 29:18; 35:5). Blindness was, and still is, a far more common calamity in the East than with us. The particular climate, soil, and customs of Eastern countries produce severe forms of ophthalmic inflamation resulting in blindness. Smith's *Dictionary* accounts for the prevalence and severity of eye troubles in those days in Palestine "by the quantities of dust and sand, pulverized by the intense heat of the sun; by the perpetual glare of the light; by the contrast between the heat and the cold sea air on the coast, by the dews at night while people sleep on the roofs, by smallpox."

The two men we are considering, who had lost their sight in consequence of some kind of eye disease, knew of Christ's supernatural power, since Matthew tells us that they followed Him from Jairus' house and were determined to take no silent denial. They proved the strength of their faith in Christ's ability to heal them. But in their importunity, and also in the acknowledgment of His Messiahship, they cried to Him, saying, "Thou Son of David," indicating thereby the popular belief that He was the expected Messiah as promised to Old Testament Jews. This royal title was also used by the woman of Canaan and by the blind at Jericho (Matthew 15:22; 20:30, 31; 21:9; Mark 10:47; Luke 1:32; 18:38, 39; see Ezekiel 34:23, 24).

Their first plea was for mercy, which carried with it the request for restoration of sight. Apparently, paying no heed to their cry, Jesus asked the pointed question, "Believe ye that I am able to do this?" Their faith in His Messiahship "must not stop short in this mere confession of Him; it must be further tried," hence His direct question. Then came their two-word answer, "Yes, Lord," and with such a reply He knew that they had faith to be healed and He gave them their sight. Our study of His miracles reveals that faith was the antecedent condition of a cure. "According to your faith be it unto you." This element of faith, which is belief in Christ's power, and its sufficiency for any particular need is fundamental. In his descriptive way, Trench tells us that such faith is "the conducting link between man's emptiness and God's fulness . . . the bucket let down into the fountain of God's grace without which the man could not draw up out of that fountain; the purse which does not itself make its owner rich, but which yet effectually enriches him by the treasure which it contains."

In the touching of the eyes of the blind men, we have the first recorded instance of the method Jesus seems always to have adopted in the case of the blind. Other sufferers, possessed of their sight, had their faith in Christ's ability to heal them by "the look of sympathy and conscious power which they saw in the face of the Healer." But from such an influence the blind men were shut out, and, "for them therefore its absence was supplied by acts which they would naturally connect with the purpose to heal them" (Matthew 20:34; John 9:6). Having proved and confessed their faith, Jesus, by touching their eyes, immediately and generously honored their faith with the inestimable gift of sight.

Christ's touch and other conductors of His power brings us to the matter of diversity of treatment in His miracles. At one time He used clay mingled with spittle—moisture of His mouth alone (Mark 8:23; John 9:6, 7), at another, a mere word (John 11:43). But we "nowhere read of His opening the blind eyes simply by His word, though this of course lay equally within the range of His power." What

those sightless eyes could not see, they felt, and sight became theirs.

The condition of silence was imposed upon the healed, for Jesus charged them saying, "See that no man know it." Such a prohibition followed the resurrection of Jairus' daughter, but not the healing of the Gadarene demoniac. These two men who had cried publicly after Christ were healed privately in the house and sent quietly away. "Notoriety of miraculous working among those who had already seen much of it, would only have fostered the false view of His Christhood which was rising," says Laidlaw. "His design was to prevent the people from being misled by the mere report of miracles." The prohibition was also rooted in Christ's regard for the spiritual welfare of those cured. Constant rehearsal of the miracle wrought on their behalf might tend to create and foster the spirit of Phariseeism, and lead them to think that they were better than others because of the manifestation of the supernatural on their behalf.

Alas! in spite of Christ's strong charge regarding silence, the men departed and spread abroad His fame which, no matter how Roman Catholic commentators applaud their action as being praiseworthy, was nothing short of gross disobedience. "To obey is better than sacrifice." Christ knew what was best for the cured men to do, and they should have respected His wish.

The spiritual application of this miracle needs little emphasis. Sin is constantly described as moral blindness and deliverance from sin as a removal of that blindness (Deuteronomy 28:29; Isaiah 59: 10; Ephesians 5:8; Matthew 15:14, etc.) Godward, a sinner is stone-blind. His blinded eyes cannot behold the perfections of Christ and the glories of heaven. But Christ is able to "open their eyes, and to turn them from darkness to light" (Acts 26:18). Would that multitudes all around, blinded by the god of this world, might come to experience the healing of Christ's touch!

22. The Miracle of the Dumb Demonic

(Matthew 9:32-35)

We have very little to go on in the three-verse record of this second miracle Jesus performed after His departure from the ruler's house. Probably the demoniac was brought to Jesus by those who knew him. Knowledge of His power to heal was becoming more widespread. Demon-possessed, this man was both deaf and dumb, as the one word used signifies. The demoniac element is here the ruling one. The mind had an organic defect. His condition was not the result of any local physical injury or disease, neither was it congenital. The man was dumb because he was possessed by a demon—not a devil. There is only one devil, but multitudes of demons.

Demoniacal possession, about which we shall have more to say when we come to the Gadarene demoniac, was not an ordinary physical disease. This demoniac's condition was not due to functional or organic disorder, so Jesus dealt not with the apparent malady, but with its root or cause by casting out the demon. We have no intimation of any action of Christ's part. The record simply says, "When the demon was cast out, the dumb spake," and such a work of healing restored the man to sanity rather than removed a bodily imperfection. One wonders what were the first words the restored man uttered. Doubtless it was a tribute of praise to his Healer.

The effect of this miracle was two-fold. First, "the multitudes marveled saying, 'It was never so seen in Israel.'" Beholding the cured man, they gave free expression to their natural wonder and saw in Jesus their predicated Deliverer. The proverb has it, "The saint who works no miracles has few pilgrims." The sinless Christ wrought many miracles which gathered an ever-increasing number of pilgrims. But what impressed the people only exasperated the enemies of Jesus, who said, "He casteth out demons through the prince of demons." They could not deny the reality of the miracle. As Jewish teachers, they professed to cast out evil spirits, but a deaf and dumb "possessed" was beyond their reach or the scope on any influence they could bring to bear on such an one. The same abhorrence reappears with the addition of the name "Beelzebub" as being the prince of demons (Matthew 12:24-30).

The divine Healer treats our spiritual disorders in the same way as He dealt with the demoniac. "Dealing with symptoms only will never please any good doctor, nor does it satisfy our Great Physician. A clean heart is what He promises first; then all thoughts, words, and actions will

be clean." Matthew concludes the record of the demoniac with the information that Jesus went on His way, teaching, preaching, and healing (9:33). Moved with compassion, He healed "every sickness and every disease among the people," meaning that He healed every variety of need coming His way, as faith on the part of the afflicted was manifested.

23. The Miracle of the Gadarene Demonic

(Luke 8:26, 27; Matthew 8:28-34; Mark 5:1-20)

Our Lord's visit to the Gadarenes or Gergasines across the lake is only one incident, but what a striking one it was. Although only in Gadara for a few hours, He found a demoniac and left behind a striking trophy of His power as a messenger to the people. There is no contradiction between the "two" demonics Mark and Luke refer to, and the "one" of Matthew's record. The natural explanation is that one was more prominent, more violent and fierce, more notable than the other. Since he acted as the spokesman, the other falls into the background. Matthew Henry's quaint remark on this seeming contradiction is that, "If there were two, there was one."

Fereday offers the explanation that because one case was more desperate than the other, Mark and Luke concentrate attention on one, but Matthew, who always wrote with Jewish leaders before his mind and who knew the weight two witnesses would have with such (Deuteronomy 17: 6; 19:15) was careful to record the fact that two men were blessed, even though he omits a crowd of other details. In Luke's raving maniac we have the manifold personality of the *one* untameable, wilderness inhabitant, guilty of self-mutilation with stones, naked, unclean, possessed of immense muscular, or supernatural strength, shrieking, yet ultimately delivered from demonic mastery.

Probably this is the best place in our study of the supernatural in Scripture to summarize the somewhat mysterious subject frequently mentioned in the gospels, namely, *demon possession*. At the outset it must be affirmed that we have no sympathy with the contention that our Lord accommodated Himself to prevalent ideas of His time. Any open-minded, honest reader of the Bible cannot escape the conclusion that our Lord believed in the Devil and in demons and also in their evil influence in, and over, human beings. Had He not believed in the dreadful powers of darkness He would not have spoken as earnestly, profoundly, and courageously about these hideous forces as He did. He openly declared the manifestation of evil in the bodies and souls of men as coming from an evil source.

The presence of demon possessions in the gospels is explained by attributing it to Babylonian and Persian beliefs or superstitions that had become part of the belief of the Jews, who applied physical and mental disorders to some sort of weird personality. Rejectors of the reality of demonic forces go on to say that Jesus accommodated His language to the idea, rife in those days, and that as a part of His divine mission He assumed the role of a corrector of popular beliefs by commanding the *supposed* spirits to come out of the possessed.

The clear, unmistakeable teaching of the Bible, however, is that the Devil and evil spirits are real beings, and that the Devil's power is exercised in a three-fold way— directly, by himself, by the demons who are subject to their prince, and through human beings whom he has influenced and possesses. Further, Scripture offers abundant evidence of the reality of demons—the former angelic beings who rebelled with Satan and who were expelled from heaven with their master. Man's subjection to this power of Satan is the fruit of the Fall and is a terrible reality not to be underrated.

What actually happens in demon possession is the invasion of the human personality by these denizens of hell. It is an intrusion into the physical and psychical domains with consequent discord and disharmony, as Trench shows in his valuable chapter on this subject. In the high places of the soul, the rightful Lord and Owner is cast from His seat and a usurper takes His place. Such demonic possession, however, cannot take place without the consent of the human will. Satan entered Judas (John 13:27. See also I Samuel 16:14; I Kings 22:21-23) because he had opened up the way for the evil intruder by his diabolical act of betraying his Master. "Judas first entertained a thought from Satan before Satan himself entered" (John 13:2). It is when men lose control over

themselves that evil spirits take the opportunity of effecting an entrance, and in these cases it is sudden. Moral depravity often precedes demon possession. Men give themselves up to the gratification of the lowest sensual desires of their nature and prepare themselves, thereby, for the incoming of evil spirits. Thereafter they become captives of the Devil and as his slaves they sink into as deep a degradation as the more conspicuous demonic. What debauchery and sensuality appear when men become devoted to their sinful appetites and lusts!

The Bible, then, recognizes that evil spirits do take possession of men's bodies —that sometimes men invited them to do so and became friendly with them. They are then called "familiar spirits" (Leviticus 19:31; 20:6, 27). Any who did so were put to death. Moral depravity might precede demon possession, but once the possession is effected, sensuality and violence become more marked. Once Satan enters, then surrender to his will is hard to resist. Physical and mental and spiritual disorders follow to which the evil spirits are more or less related.

That *all* disorders are not the result of demonic possession is clearly maintained in Scripture (Matthew 4:23, 24; 10:1; 11:5 etc.). Insanity, epilepsy, blindness, dumbness, fevers, etc., were frequent accompaniments and symptoms of demon possession (Matthew 12:22; 9:32; Mark 9:17, 25; Luke 11:14, 15, 16), but were not necessarily identified with it. Often, however, diseases were aggravated by these foreign powers. There were ancient beliefs that diseases were due to such a possession and that demons had to be expelled before the possessed could be healed.

That the demonic in the case before us was suffering from some mania or lunacy seems to be beyond doubt. The symptoms given are those cited by medical writers in connection with mania. But demon possession and lunacy are expressly distinguished (Matthew 4:24). It is, therefore, incorrect to say that demon possession is just another name for madness. With the Gadarene demonic, his disease was the result of his own wickedness, then was added to his madness the demonic element in its extremest form. Trench says, "It may well be a question, moreover, if an apostle, or one gifted with apostolic discernment of spirits, were to enter a madhouse now, he might not recognize some of the sufferers there as 'possessed.' Certainly in many cases of mania and epilepsy there is a condition very analogous to that of the demonics."

One wonders when he reads of the horrible, sadistic crimes of today whether those who commit them are not demon-inspired and possessed. This much is evident, that modern spiritism with its fearful consequences is a form of demon possession. Much of the so-called occult research practiced today is "an abomination unto the Lord." The horrible nightmares experienced by drunkards when in the D.T.'s may be a form of possession by evil spirits. Further, missionaries laboring for God amid the darkness of heathenism have no doubt about the superhuman power of the Devil and his angels. Paul speaks of the heathen as sacrificing to demons (I Corinthians 10:20 RV margin. See also Leviticus 17:7; II Chronicles 11:15; Psalm 106:37), and demon possession is still an undoubted fact in many parts of the regions beyond. Many missionaries have related their gruesome experiences with the demon possessed and tell how the peerless name of Jesus is still powerful in the casting out of demons. We must never lose sight of this cardinal fact, namely, that the Devil, as the prince of the power of the air, regulates the present course of things here, working in the children of disobedience (Ephesians 2:2). Yielding themselves to his authority, men become his slaves (Romans 6:16). With this necessary preamble in mind, we now come to examine the narratives dealing with the Gadarene manics.

While there are many references in the gospels to numerous miracles wrought on demoniacs (Matthew 4:24; 8:16; Mark 1:34; Luke 4:41; 8:2, etc.), only a few are particularized, like the two we are now to consider. In every case, however, an actual, literal, demonical possession is emphasized. The graphic description Mark and Luke give of the one demonic equally applies to his less prominent companion whom Matthew includes.

First of all, the demon possessing these men was an "unclean" one. Their inherent uncleanness through constant submission to evil became greatly accentuated by the presence of unclean spirits. Then we are told that Christ was met by one of these men coming "out of the tombs," which are still pointed out in the ravines

east of the lake. These tombs, hewn out of the rock, were shunned by the Jews as being unclean because of the dead men's bones they contained. To any ordinary Jew, tomb-dwelling was abhorrent, and to dwell in tombs was deemed a sign of insanity. How sin separates men from their fellow man!

Luke is the only one who mentions the fact that the demonic wore no clothes. As a physician, he takes pains to inquire whether this case of frenzied insanity was the same as other cases he had encountered. Sin makes men shameless and devoid of all modesty. The further from God they go, the more immodest they become. When bound with chains and fetters, his immense muscular or superhuman strength quickly broke them. "No man could bind him. . . . No man could tame him." What a creature of fierce passions the demons made this demented man! Attempts had been made to bind him, but without avail (for contrast see *Samson*). He was also "exceeding fierce," so much so that no traveler would pass that way. Sin destroys the finer qualities in man such as love, gentleness, and tenderness. Then he shrieked and cut himself with stones. Having yielded to sin, then to the evil spirits, he became his own worst enemy. What self-inflicted mutilations and misery were his! Sin is inevitably self-destructive. It is Luke alone who tells us that this man was "driven of the devil, or demon, into the wilderness." It was so with our blessed Lord, but because He came to destroy the works of the Devil, He emerged from the wilderness victorious.

The amazing feature is that when this more prominent of the two demonics saw Jesus afar off, he ran and worshiped Him. What a sight that must have been! No matter how blind men are to the personal glory of Christ, even though they may profess to be in the right mind, demons always recognize Him as Lord and trembled and cringed before Him. Those demons knew that Christ was no ordinary Man who had dared to set foot on his desolate domain. Conscious of the awful gulf that divided him from Christ and that in his degraded condition he could have nothing to do with Him, he yet recognized the deity of Christ. "Thou Son of the Most High God" (Mark 5:7). The time is coming when "every knee," whether saints, sinners, or satanic spirits must bow before Him. This is the first occurrence of such a divine designation of Christ in the New Testament, and it is a divine name going back to the patriarchal worship of the one supreme Deity (Genesis 14:18).

The demonic feared torment and he adjured Christ by God not to send him to his doom before the time. He knew that there was "a place of torment" (Luke 16: 28) and that the ministers of judgment are the "tormentors" (Matthew 18:34). The Devil and all evil spirits know that their doom is written large in Holy Writ and that with the ratification of the judgment at the Great White Throne, the Lake of Fire will be their eternal depository (Revelation 20:10; 21:8). No wonder the demons fear Christ when they know Him to be the dread Judge who will consign them to their doom! It is Matthew who adds the touch, "before the time." By his own confession, the demon-spokesman confirmed the entire victory of the kingdom of light over darkness and the final judgment of all hostile forces (I Corinthians 6:3; Jude 6; Revelation 20:10).

As Deliverer and demonic met, the unclean spirit was commanded to come out of the man—demons obey Him even if men don't. Yet the command of Christ was not immediately obeyed. The demons possessing the man remonstrated, being unwilling to abandon their prey. Trench has the enlightening comment:

No doubt He could have compelled them to this, had He pleased; but the man might have perished in the process (see Mark 9:26). Even that first bidding had induced a terrible paroxysm. It was then of Christ's own will, of the Physician wise and tender as He was strong, to proceed step by step.

First of all, Jesus asked, "What is thy name?" It is difficult to distinguish what belongs to the broken, incoherent consciousness of the man and to the evil spirits speaking through him. When Jesus asked His question, was He addressing the man himself, seeking to arouse the victim's shattered soul to some sense of his own individuality, or did He address the demons? The tenor of the reply to our Lord's question implies that the evil spirit within the man answered, although Trench suggests that the unhappy man, instead of giving Him his true name, used one describing the utter ruin of his whole moral and spiritual being, just as Mary Magdalene is spoken of as one out of whom seven demons were cast (Luke 8:2).

Whether it was the demon who spoke, or the man, or the demon making the man to reply, we do not know. "My name is *Legion,* for we are many." The irresistible might, the full array of the Roman legion with its six thousand soldiers, suggests Ellicott, seemed the one adequate symbol of the wild, uncontrollable impulses of passion and of dread sweeping through the soul of the demonic. Our Lord addressed him as if he was possessed by a single demon, but the answer said that the name of demons was *Legion.* Mark says that the swine which the demons entered were about two thousand (5:13). If this was the number of demons inhabiting the two demoniacs, each with a personality of his own, all under the power of one will, animated by one purpose and united in one mode of operation, as Taylor expresses it, then the plight of the two demoniacs must have been terrible in the extreme. The plural is used of these evil spirits. "The demons besought Him" (Matthew 8:31; Mark 5:12) "The unclean spirits" (Mark 5:13). "Demons long time. . . . many demons were entered into him. . . . they besought Him" (Luke 8:27-31).

These many demons presented a strange request to Christ. Before being cast out of the two men by Christ's power, the demons asked to be allowed to enter a herd of swine, and He said, "Go!" What glorious omnipotence was packed into that two-letter word! Because many Bible readers are perplexed over Christ's permission for the demons to possess the swine, with their resultant destruction, it may prove profitable to examine the matter. At the outset, let it be said that Christ did not *send* the demons into the swine. "He merely drove them out from the men; all beyond this was merely permissive." As Aquinas put it, "That the swine were driven into the sea was no work of the divine miracle, but was the work of the demons by divine permission."

The swine, panic-stricken as they became demon-possessed, lost control of themselves on the steep incline of the hillside, and once on the move, they could not stop. The swine preferred suicide to demon possession. Without doubt, there is the element of judgment here upon the owners of swine as an article of food. Though the Jews did not eat pork, Roman soldiers did, and the Jews had no compunction of conscience in providing forbidden meat for others. Thus the destruction of the swine was deserved punishment for the violation of God's law. Christ, therefore, had every right to deal with such illicit trading.

Another way of looking at the subject is to see in this destruction of the swine an answer to Christ's question, "How much better is a man than a sheep?" Two men had been delivered from Satanic bondage, but at the cost of 2,000 swine. Were two souls worth all those swine? The Gadarenes, in their blindness, thought not, but the Creator thought they were, so they besought Christ to depart from their coasts. They thought more of their property than the souls of men. The relaxation of the hold on the demonics was necessary for their permanent healing, and so the death of the swine was motive enough. Further, as all the beasts of the fields and the cattle on the hills are Christ's property, He has the right to do what He may choose with His own.

The Bible tells us of the powers of darkness entering into only two species of lower animals—the serpent and the swine—the first the symbol of intellectual cunning, and the latter the symbol of gross uncleanness. May we be delivered from sinning in either of these directions!

When the demons besought Christ not to command them to go out "into the deep," did they mean the deep waters of the Galilean lake? If so, then this is suggestive in the light of Pember's contention about the sea being the present abode of demons. The word "deep" means *abyss*, the bottomless pit (Revelation 9:1, 2, 11), and the demons asked for any doom but that. Their phrase about being tormented "before the time" is most remarkable in that they knew that the ultimate doom of everlasting woe would be theirs. Everlasting torment is to be theirs when they are in the place prepared for the Devil and his angels.

The Gadarenes, with the fatal short-sightedness and fear of the supernatural, entreated Jesus to depart out of their coasts. Doubtless many of them were filled with awe as they looked at this One who held sway over the occult and mysterious powers which ever haunt the dim recesses of human nature. City and country people, we are told, were afraid at the sight of the restored demoniacs. They had not prayed before; now they began "to pray Him" to depart, and Christ answered their

prayer to their own loss (Psalm 78:29-31). "God sometimes hears His enemies in anger (Numbers 22:20), even as he refuses to hear His friends in love" (II Corinthians 12:8, 9).

How graphic is the description of the delivered demonic—which goes for his companions as well—"sitting at the feet of Jesus, clothed and in his right mind. "The Gadarenes prayed Jesus to leave them—this man wanted to stay with Him and, as a learner, to sit at His feet (Luke 10:39). What a clinging attitude of faith this was! Did the man fear, as some writers suggest, that in the absence of his Deliverer the evil spirits might return and resume their dominion over him, and that his only safety was immediate nearness to Christ? We prefer to think that out of the gratitude of his heart, he wanted to be with the One who had transformed his life for him and to use him in His service.

By what means the demonics were cured we are not told. Stress is laid on the manner of their deliverance rather than its instrumentality. Vincent says that "the literal rendering of the imperfect brings out the *simultaneousness* of Christ's exorcism, the outbreak of demonic malice, and the cry "Torment me not." The change was evident. Instead of wild, terrifying restlessness, they were found sitting at Jesus' feet. They were clothed. Doubtless the disciples provided what was necessary to hide their shame. They were now in their right minds—Christ-possessed instead of demon-possessed. How all this illustrates the transformation Christ makes possible! Through Him, we are at His feet, clothed with the garments of salvation, and having His mind within.

Luke describes the one delivered man following Jesus to the boat after He was entreated to leave and praying that he might accompany Christ. But He saw that this was not the best discipline which was necessary for the man's spiritual progress. There was the better course of a more avowed discipleship, namely, that of proclaiming to his own family and people what Jesus had accomplished for him. We can imagine what a stirring evangelist he became to those around in Gadara and in Decapolis (Luke 8:39). "Shew what great things God hath done unto thee"—here is the true method of household missionary work. Jesus instructed the leper and the two blind men to say nothing about their cures (Matthew 8:4; 9:19). Here He told the cured demonic to go out and tell everybody about his deliverance. In Gadara, He was not as well known as in Galilee where popular movements to make Him a political king were almost out of hand.

"Go *home,* and proclaim," Jesus did not say, "Go into the synagogues of the land and proclaim the miracle of your cure," but, "Go *home!*" Often young converts, especially if saved from a conspicuous evil past, are thrust into the limelight and given public prominence. But Christ, in His wisdom and mercy alike, wanted this man to function as a memorial of His grace among his own friends and family, and to bring them to repentance. It was a hard command to obey, "Go to thy house unto thy friends," but he obeyed it resolutely and "went his way and began to publish in Decapolis how great things Jesus had done for him." A strong home testimony, tested by the surest discipline of reality is always effective. The Bible offers many powerful instances of the wisdom of such a course. Andrew's first work was done with his own brother, Simon Peter. Philip brought his friend Nathaniel to Christ, and Barnabas was not satisfied until he had preached the Gospel in his native, beloved Cyprus. It was thus that Jesus delivered the most terrible sufferer from infernal power in all the records of the gospels and fashioned him into a preacher of salvation to ten cities. Jesus went to Gadara and there found a demoniac, but He left behind an evangelist. What a miracle of power and of grace! The transformed Gadarene came to experience the sentiment expressed in a modern hymn.

There's a work for Jesus,
Only *you* can do.

24. The Miracle of Jairus' Daughter

(Matthew 9:18-26; Mark 5:22-43;
Luke 8:41-56)

The full narratives before us are among the most interesting in the gospels in that, taken together, they present a miracle wrapped up in a miracle. Jesus and the Twelve received a warm welcome on their return to Capernaum on the western side of the lake. The astounding miracle of the demoniacs was still fresh in the minds of the people, and as they gathered around the Master, a distressed father bowed before Him and presented a heart-felt plea for his dying daughter. In response to the man's request, Jesus immediately left for his home, but He was interrupted on His way. A woman with an issue of blood contacted Christ and was miraculously healed, and conversation with her occupied some time. So we have a miracle in a miracle. "Such overflowing grace is in Him, the Prince of life, that as He is hastening to accomplish one work of grace and power, He accomplishes another, as by the way." But let us separate the two miracles and deal with Jairus' daughter first.

Although Mark and Luke set the time of these two miracles after the Gadarene miracle, and Matthew places them after the curing of the paralytic, his own call, and some parables of our Lord's, there is no contradiction between the writers. Those who have endeavored to harmonize the gospel narratives favor Matthew's account, which is the briefest of the three. As these narratives complement each other, it is necessary to compare the record of each. Features of the miracle of the girl's resurrection are easily traced.

First of all, we have the distressed father, Jairus by name, who is described as one of the rulers, or princes, of the synagogue in Capernaum. His name is derived from one of the Israelite chiefs, *Jair,* who conquered and settled in Bashan (Numbers 32:41; Joshua 13:30), whose "name lingered down to the time of the Christian era, when, in the same region as that which he conquered, we find a ruler of the synagogue named Jair." Evidently he knew all about the remarkable teachings of Jesus and because of His miraculous ministry was convinced of His power and thus sought the gift of healing for his dying daughter. This ruler's reverent approach was a tribute to the honor in which Jesus was held by some of the Jewish rulers.

Intense earnestness was his, for he fell at Jesus' feet, worshiped Him, and besought Him greatly. By his recognition of Christ as the Miracle-Worker, Jairus revealed how deeply he felt the powerlessness of all ecclesiastical and legal machinery in the presence of death. The synagogue heirarchy could not help him, hence his request to the omnipotent Son of God. Although he expressed unhesitating faith in Christ's ability, his faith was not equal to the centurion's who believed the limit of space was no hindrance to limitless power. Jairus felt Christ's presence in the home of death was necessary and so pleaded for Him to come and lay His hand on the child. We are not told whether Jairus was a disciple previous to this contact with Christ. Doubtless the miracle in his home made him one.

As to the girl herself, whose need her father presented to Christ, Mark gives us an endearing touch peculiar to his style— "My *little* daughter." Luke, telling us that she was an only child, used the word meaning "only begotten." She was about twelve years of age. What her fatal malady was, we are not told. Matthew says that she was dead, but Mark and Luke record that she was at the point of death. There is no contradiction between these accounts. Such an apparent discrepancy is evidence that each evangelist wrote distinctly and separately from the other. There was no consultation to write the same account. As independent witnesses of facts they were independent records of the performance of those facts. Thus what appears to be discord is only a grand harmony when the independent witness is thoroughly understood.

The variation can be explained in this way. When Jairus left his little one, she was almost at her last gasp, and Matthew, feeling that life was ebbing away so fast, was confident that before her father could reach Jesus she would be dead, and so he wrote his version of the incident venturing a guess that she would not be alive when her father returned. As Jesus was on His way to the home, a friend came to Jairus with the sad news, "Thy daughter is dead." "Dead," in the Greek, is placed first for emphasis. "*Dead* is thy daughter." But, having met Christ, the sting in such a dread announcement had been removed for the sorrowful father.

This brings us a glimpse of Jesus as the divine Encourager. The cry of personal need brought forth the manifestation of His supernatural power. Unfailing readiness was His to help the afflicted. He never failed to respond to need. Though He refused to parade His power of the miraculous, He never turned aside from the call of suffering. Jesus overheard the message brought to the father. The language of "thy daughter is dead" precludes the idea of a swoon or a mere apparent death. Immediately He checked the rise of fear in the brokenhearted father. Is there not a gracious touch in the phrase "as soon?" Before the father's hope had a chance to perish, Jesus met the bearer's sad message with the encouraging word, "Fear not: believe only, and she shall be made whole." Unbelief did not have time to insinuate itself into the father's mind. Christ preoccupied the father with the word of hope, and with His usual tenderness and compassion He consoled him. His keen appreciation of the hour of greatest trial is revealed in His heartening message. Because of His omniscience, He knew the truth about the little girl, even before the bearer of sad news came, and as the omnipotent One, He was to raise the dead.

Reaching the home of sorrow, Jesus encountered a company of derisive mourners. It was nothing for a crowd of neighbors and the usual hired mourners to fill a house visited by death. Amid the confusion and noise, Jesus said, "Weep not, she is not dead, but sleepeth." For this, the crowd laughed Jesus to scorn, for they were ignorant of His use of the beautiful simile of "sleep" for death. Christ said the same of his dead friend Lazarus, "He sleepeth" (John 11:11). Death as a sleep is a simile common to all nations and was "the beautiful and prophetic color that Christ spread over the features of the dead, and was designed to intimate, that as sure as a morning comes to the sleeper on his couch, so sure an everlasting morning shall break upon the tenants of the tomb." Further, *sleep* is only used of the body of the dead —never of the soul. The Bible knows nothing of the soul-sleep theory which some erroneously teach.

Not wishing to cast His pearls before swine before raising the dead, Jesus expelled all the mourners except the parents of the girl. Then in the sacred privacy of the death chamber, we have the remarkable feature of quiet power and the calm of self-possession. Now the house is quiet and still, for those within it are in the presence of the dead, which was no place for boisterous and superfluous grief. One reason why Christ excluded the neighbors and townspeople was because they had seen enough of His mighty works; and, as we have already indicated, there was no prodigality about His miracles. They were never wrought to satisfy curiosity or merely to compel belief or overawe mankind. They were plentiful, however, when "the relief of human misery and the entrance of spiritual light were His objects." The studied privacy in the raising of Jairus' daughter is a contrast to the *public* raising of the Nain widow's son, each being dealt with as He saw best for them and for all His wise ends. On the clearing of the house of its derisive mourners, Bengel wrote, "Wonderful authority in the house of a stranger. He was really the Master of the house."

Jesus only took three of His disciples into the house, namely Peter, James, and John, doubtless because of their preparedness of spirit. These three disciples form an "election within the election," and were more than once withdrawn from the others to be with Christ. "The work on which Christ was now entering," says Trench, "was so strange and so mysterious that none but these, the flower and crown of the apostolic band, were its fitting witnesses."

In an atmosphere of faith, and not in the presence of curious onlookers, the mighty work was accomplished, for taking the frail corpse by the hand, Jesus said, "Maid, arise!" Mark gives us the expressive Aramaic, "Talitha Cumi," meaning the same thing. Probably Peter, having heard the very language Jesus used, told Mark what happened at the word and at the touch of the Master's hand. The Lord of life spoke a brief word and the little daughter of Jairus, "lying cold and voiceless and still in her white death robe," sprang to life. Two other commands to the dead were as brief— "Young man, arise!" "Lazarus, come forth." It is often so with the resurrection of those who were dead in sin—a verse of the Bible, an awaking providence, a seemingly trivial incident, or counsel of a friend is used by Christ to arrest the stedfast and pitiless march of death, and old things pass away and the believing soul begins to live.

Luke, with his medical precision, says that, "her spirit, or breath" returned, proving that this was a resurrection and no recovery from a death swoon. The spirit of the damsel returned from the unseen world and became reunited with her body. The Jews have an ancient legend that after death the soul of the departed hovers near the body for several days before it takes its final farewell. Paul, however, instructs us to believe that the moment we are freed from the body we are present with the Lord. How the miracle took place is a mystery. This we know, that no power but Christ's can raise the dead, and He knew not only the *when* of miracles but also the *why* and the *how*. It is thus with every spiritual resurrection—a divine act.

As soon as Jesus spoke and touched the girl, immediately she arose, and then came the delightful thoughtfulness of Jesus—"He commanded to give her meat." With His characteristic majestic sweetness and human sympathy, He thought of the girl's temporal need. He was mindful and thoughtful over every detail. His direction for nourishment indicated a weakened body and that restored life had to be strengthened, which proved that she was no ghost but had returned to the realities of a mortal existence—a fact that her parents in that ecstatic moment might easily have forgotten. Ellicott remarks: "The restored life was dependent, after the supernatural work had been completed, upon natural laws, and there was the risk of renewed exhaustion." How necessary, then, it was for the girl to eat, not to prove the reality of the miracle, but because after her fatal illness she was in need of nourishment, and because in the excitement of the moment, her parents should not forget the necessity of the commonplace. In advising a satisfying meal for the restored girl, Jesus acted as any kind and careful physician would have done in the circumstances.

A word is necessary about the desired silence, for although the fame of this miracle went abroad in all the land, Jesus charged that no man should know it or, as Luke says, He charged the astonished parents "that they should tell no man what was done." Our Lord knew that "it would not be good for the spiritual or the bodily life of the dear girl that she should be the object of the visits of an idle curiosity."

Does not this resurrection miracle predict the future in which there will be no more separation, when Christ will give us back our "unforgotten dearest dead," if they and we alike belong to Him? Have we not the assurance that the King of terrors will hold dominion over mine and me no more? "In the lovely day-dawn of eternity, the sea closed, the danger passed, I shall see my adversary slain on the shore." Yes, Christ has the right to speak the imperial word—"Arise!" The day is not far distant when all the "dead in Christ" will respond to that same quickening voice of His (John 5:28, 29; I Thessalonians 4:16).

Although we have yet to consider the resurrection of Lazarus, it may be profitable at this point to compare and contrast the three resurrections Christ wrought. While Jairus' daughter, the widow's son, and Lazarus all died, there were degrees of such a state. The little girl had been newly overcome and vanquished by the enemy;

the widow's son had been under the cold and tyrannous scepter of the adversary for a longer period; Lazarus in his Bethany grave was in the process of decay and corruption. Yet Jesus raised all three, proving that for each and for all there is "life through His name."

With the resurrection of the girl, there was ease and quietness, irresistibly suggesting the easy recall of her spirit from the unseen world. In the young man's case, Jesus laid His authoritative hand on the bier and called the dead youth to arise. In Lazarus' case, Jesus cried out with a loud voice, and His work at Bethany was a still mightier wonder than the resurrection of the young man on the way to burial. Then these three resurrections, probably chosen from many cases for specific record (Luke 7:22), are full of spiritual instruction for our hearts.

The death of Jairus' twelve-year-old girl reminds us that children die, and because they are born in sin, they require a Saviour. Just *when* the age of guilt and responsibility is may be difficult to decide. What we do know is that the youngest need to be quickened into new life. The young are not hardened by longstanding worldliness and indifference—they have not lain long under the shackles of trespass and sin, yet into their young and opening hearts the Tempter is instilling his poison and they need the quiet and gentle voice of Jesus to arrest the inroad of sin, and once saved they must be spiritually led and sustained.

The widow's son, a sturdy youth before death laid its cold hand upon him, speaks of the youth of today who have strayed far from God and who have forfeited thereby all spiritual vitality and vigor. Commendable in so many ways, as many are, yet blatantly defiant of God, as others are, the young must be called to remember their Creator in the days of their youth. Would that multitudes more of those who are "young and strong and free" might come to experience Christ's power to raise them from a grave of sin and lust!

Aging Lazarus, dead for four days, represents those who are hardened in sin, and who bear in their lives the sad traces of the presence and masterhood of evil. Yet no matter how many years have been spent in vanity and pride, Christ can utter the all commanding word, "Come forth." No matter how deep their sin or years of rejection, Christ is both able and willing to terminate the empire of sin and offer Himself as the Fountain of life.

"They laughed Him to scorn." The natural man is dead to an understanding of the things of God. The flesh can "make an ado and weep" one minute and "laugh to scorn" the next. The world may laugh at us as we declare that all have sinned and come short of God's Glory, but the Word declares that all sinners are dead in trespasses and sins, and that apart from Christ's quickening power they are both helpless and hopeless.

25. The Miracle of the Woman with an Issue of Blood

(Matthew 9:20-22; Mark 5:25-34; Luke 8:43-48)

We pointed out in our introduction to the previous miracle that the miracle we are now to consider was a miracle sandwiched in between two halves of another miracle and was a cure obtained without a word spoken beforehand. Coming as it does between another miracle, we can call this one a *parenthesis* miracle. On an errand of mercy for Jairus, Christ found another merciful work to do on the road to the house of mourning. The woman in question was probably a resident of Paneas or Caesarea Philippi who had wandered to Galilee seeking relief from her malady. In the apocryphal gospel of Nicodemus (5:26), she is called Veronica, whose legendary handkerchief is well-known. Ellicott tells us that Eusebius in his *Church History* states that the woman, in gratitude for her cure, set up two statues in bronze—one for herself in the attitude of supplication, and the other of our Lord standing erect and stretching forth His hand to her—and that these were shown in the historian's own day, in the early part of the fourth century.

Although it was most likely that the woman had never seen Jesus before, hers was not a forlorn hope as she sought the aid of the Galilean Healer. After all she had suffered and spent, she had a strong persuasion of His ability—a persuasion justified by facts for she had "heard the things concerning Jesus," which things must have included His miracles. It must have been with extreme difficulty that this woman contacted Jesus, since crowds of people thronged and pressed Him—language which means that the multitudes pressed around Him so as almost to suffocate Him. The pressure was so great that it was difficult for Him even to breathe. Actuated by mere curiosity, such a moving mass of humanity was eager to see the miracle Jesus was on His way to perform at Jairus' house. The three narratives recording these two miracles bear the marks of historical accuracy.

First of all, let us consider the disease of the woman lost and jostled in the crowd around Jesus. She suffered from "an issue of blood," which was a malady bringing with it ceremonial uncleanness and ostracism from male society. Mark called her complaint a "plague." Such a bodily discharge was probably something akin to hemorrhoids. Belcher describes it as "metrorrhagia, from organic disease of the uterus and its appendages." For twelve long years this woman had suffered from her plague. It was somewhat suggestive that the daughter of Jairus was twelve years of age. The rule's sorrow was sudden after twelve years of joyful hope; the woman's sickened hope was deferred through twelve years.

What happened as the woman touched Christ "throws a flood of light upon our Lord's character and His attitude to the law," says Micklem, "for the woman was virtually unclean, and, after she had touched Him, technically He was unclean, too" (Leviticus 15:25, 27). Perhaps it was this fact that accounts for the sense of shame which made her shrink from applying to the Healer openly and from confessing afterwards what she had done.

We are further told that during those twelve years, during which her life had been given over to the weary tragedy of an incurable disease, that all her money had gone in the fruitless search of a cure. Often when one's money goes, so do his friends. She had "spent all her substance on physicians, and was nothing bettered, but rather grew worse." With his usual professional pride and sensitiveness, Luke the physician omits "but rather grew worse." Her condition, then, was both painful and distressing. The nature of her malady, the length of its continuance, and the fruitlessness of her resort to physicians costing her all her means for costly remedies made her case a hopeless one.

Yet in her distress and despair there was determination. Working her way through the surging crowd, she said in her heart, "If I may touch but His clothes, I shall be whole." To quote Micklem again, "We obtain a glimpse on the one hand into her desperation of mind owing to her condition and failure to find a remedy, and on the other, into the faith which must have been hers to enable her to take the risk of the consequences of breaking a sacred convention and wilfully coming into contact with her fellow men." We need to remind ourselves of the enormity of the crime she had committed in coming through the crowd and touching Jesus. To her, in her desperate need, "necessity knew no law."

The faith of the woman bent on a cure had its strength yet weakness. She did not doubt for a moment her right to take healing if she could get it. So her confidence in Jesus to help her was strong and well founded. Her faith was fearless, prompt, and resolute, that before Jesus could utter a word, she believed, resolved, and acted. For *her* there was not a "more convenient season." She had come to the conclusion that although all other physicians had failed her, the Great Physician would not, and forming her resolution accordingly that touching Him would suffice for complete healing, she acted as she did. Marvelous faith!

Such real faith, however, had its defect. In her ignorance, the woman was blinded with superstition. She felt that healing depended upon some mode of contact or in the garments of Jesus as distinct from His person. She believed the virtue was in the fringe of His garment, the ribbon of blue to which so much importance was attached as a thing required by the law of Moses (Numbers 15:37-40; Deuteronomy 22:12). But power to heal was in Christ Himself. "She thought not of a will that seeks to bless and save, but of a physical effluence passing from the body to the garments, and from the garments to the hand that touched them." Hers was a material conception of Christ's healing power, a confidence that some magical influence flowed even from His garments.

Yet weak and defective though her faith was, Jesus did not despise the superstitions associated with her touch. He knew all that had taken place, and as we shall see, He did not "break the bruised reed or quench the smoking flax," but used what the woman manifested for something higher. He cured her by an act of His divine will and brought her to a more intelligent faith. Her faith, although imperfect, was in its essence most true and therefore effective, for as soon as she touched the hem of His garment, immediately "the fountain of her blood was dried up, and she felt in her body that she was healed of her plague." The thrill of a newly given life tingled through her frame. Within her there was that indescribable sensation which told her she had been healed of her long affliction.

We now come to our Lord's wise and tender reaction to what had happened in the body of the woman who might have carried away in secret the knowledge of the boon received. Divine omniscience is indicated by the fact that as soon as the border of His robe was touched, Jesus immediately perceived that virtue had gone out of Him. He who knew all about Nathaniel under the fig tree (John 1:48) was cognizant of the physical suffering of this woman and of the faith she had, which was the one channel of communication between Him and human need.

What was the "virtue" indwelling and emanating from Him? We are told that this word virtue is used in the old medical sense, the power of force which brings about a definite result. So men spoke of the soporific "virtue" of this or that drug. The term is used (Mark 5:30; Luke 5:17) with a like technical precision for the supernatural power that, as it were, flowed out at the touch of faith. Jesus was conscious of His power and knew that His power had gone forth. "Virtue" implies the same as "miracles" or "mighty works" and testifies to supernaturalness. A belief that outward things were endowed with "virtue" prevailed in Paul's time when "handkerchiefs and aprons" from his flesh became the means of healing (Acts 19:12).

Looking around the crowd for the woman who was hiding herself, Jeus asked, "Who touched Me?" He wanted to bring faith into clearness and purity by an open and conscious relation to Himself as the Healer. The woman must not be allowed to obtain healing by stealth, so she was brought to an open confession and was cheered by Christ's commendatory word. Even as He moved along with that Galilean crowd, He felt His solitariness, then suddenly His being was thrilled with that touch of faith, and He knew that in the multitude there was one with its secret need. And the hand which had in it "the appealing energy of faith reached and drew forth the answering energy of grace." So need and His great fulness met.

The disciples rebuked Jesus for thinking that anyone had touched Him in a particular way when such a crowd thronged Him, but He kept looking around until the woman met His loving gaze and came out "fearing and trembling, knowing what was done in her, and falling down before Him, told Him all the truth." How many throng Christ, are near to Him outwardly, yet never seem to touch Him! She learned, as Campbell Morgan puts it, that "contact that heals must always issue in confession that glorifies." Encouraged by the Healer's tenderness, she made her confession "before all the people," with the result that Jesus confirmed her cure as a permanent one and claimed Himself to be the knowing and willing Source of her healing. "Be whole of thy plague." Pestilence, or diseases, were regarded as a stroke of the divine hand. Reserve was the dear woman's fault —a wish to hide her cure, cheating herself thereby of the honor of confession, confirmation of her cure, and also withholding from her Healer His due honor.

After eliciting her frank confession of what had taken place, Jesus sent the woman home with comforting assurance, "Daughter, be of good comfort; thy faith hath made thee whole; go in peace." None was, and is, so gracious as He! A little girl's definition of a miracle was, "Something extraordinary that happens without any strings attached." Through the woman's touch, something extraordinary happened but there were no strings attached to this miracle, as there are in some others.

Thy faith hath made thee whole. There is no healing power in faith itself. It is the channel through which healing flows from the only Source of life. Faith is not itself the blessing, but the organ by which the blessing is received. It is so in our spiritual healing. "We believe that through the grace of our Lord Jesus Christ we shall be saved" (Acts 15:11). *Go in peace!* Actually, this phrase means "Go *into* peace." It was as if the Prince of Peace had said, "Take thankfully the cure which you have received for the body, but as you go away, enter into the peace which I came to impart to all those who trust in Me." It was a promise of peace in store.

The lesson to be learned from this miracle of healing is that the cure of *sin* is as thorough as that of the woman's plague.

Christ alone can grapple with our depraved state and by His death fully restore us. The woman's cure was also *immediate.* After twelve years of vainless search, she was instantaneously healed. Thus is it, the moment we are made conscious of our sin and believe in Christ, immediately salvation becomes ours. Then the woman's cure was *freely* provided. She had spent all her money on physicians without avail, and at last, "without money and without price," she received the precious boon of healing. Faith healers, who grow rich in their traffic with the suffering, ought to remember this fact of our Lord's miracles being performed *free.* Sinners cannot purchase the healing of their iniquity. No money, no tears, no penances can obtain salvation. It comes as God's free gift.

How forcefully and fully the old Sankey hymn summarizes the direct and spiritual aspects of the miracle of the woman with the issue of blood:

She only touched the hem of His garment
    As to His side she stole,
Amid the crowd that gathered around Him,
    And straightway she was whole.
Oh, touch the hem of His garment
    And thou, too, shalt be free!
His saving power this very hour
    Shall give new life to thee.

26. The Miracle of Feeding the 5,000

(Matthew 14:13-21; Mark 6:31-44;
Luke 9:10-17; John 6:1-14)

The importance of this outstanding miracle can be gathered from the fact that it is the only one of our Lord's miracles to be mentioned by all four gospels. This repeated miracle is also referred to a second time in Matthew and Mark, making in all six mentions in the gospels. In this prominent nature miracle, the lordship of Jesus over nature and providence is clearly seen. He is concerned about bodily needs, as well as spiritual, and is before us as the All-Sufficient One. Because of His sovereignty, He is capable of creative power exercised on behalf of the needy.

As to the background of the miracle, it is connected with the Lord's retirement to a desert place. The pressure of circumstances over the death of John the Baptist —a foreshadow of His own death in the following year—forced Him to retire privately for rest, not only for Himself but for His disciples, who had returned from their first mission. With them were the disciples of the Baptist who had brought the sad news of his murder. All needed a season of bodily and spiritual refreshment, for "familiarity with the crowd only produces hardening. Familiarity with God issues in a perpetual resensitizing of the heart, which prevents hardening."

This central miracle, then, is given the place of honor on account of its magnitude, and, as Ellicott comments, "no narrative of any other miracle offers so many marks of naturalness, both in the vividness of coloring with which it is told, and the coincidences, manifestly without design, which it presents to us. It is hardly possible to imagine four independent writers—independent, even if two of them were derived from a common source—reproducing in this way, a mere legend!"

The period of quietness which Christ sought, was however, short-lived, but He did not complain. As the Good Shepherd, the double need of the sheep without a shepherd was His first concern. The multitudes seeking Him seemed to grow like a rolling snowball, and He could not be hid. People found out where He was bound, and although they came the long way around by foot, while Jesus and His disciples made the journey by sea, the people *outwent* Him so that when He reached the north end of the lake, He found a large congregation to greet Him. He was not annoyed at being thwarted. Though denied the rest He sought, He was moved with compassion and embraced the opportunity of teaching the multitude and healing the sick among them. Few of us ever learn the art of adjusting one's self to what breaks our plans and to turning disappointment to good account. The heart of Jesus was ever ready to melt over the manifold needs of men. Sympathy prevailed over the quest for solitude. Others showed but little consideration to, or for Him, but in His perfect grace, He was ever ready to show the fullest consideration to them.

As the day wore on the disciples suggested to Jesus that the hungry multitude should be dispersed to seek necessary food in the nearest towns and villages. This He would not permit. He had already asked Philip how the people should be fed. In this testing of the measure of Philip's faith, we have a striking evidence of omniscience, for we read that He knew in Himself what He would do. Philip started to make an assessment of the total provisions the disciples had among them, failing to realize that what Elisha had done on a smaller scale, Jesus was able to accomplish on a larger scale. Bewildered, Philip said, "We have two hundred pennyworth of bread." But what could thirty-five dollars worth of bread do among the gathered thousands? There was no possibility of feeding the crowds with the meager supply of money on hand, but omnipotence was about to show that all things are possible. Man is made to feel his insufficiency and then when necessities are truly felt, a miracle is wrought, but only where a miracle is required.

Having drawn from Philip an admission of their inability to meet the need, Jesus said, "They need not depart." There was no excuse to send the hungry away. Faith must learn to draw on divine resources. Full of pity, Jesus was the personification of calmness. To Him, there was no such word as "impossibility." So there came the command "Give ye them to eat." With one mouth the disciples replied (perhaps a little sarcastically since the great outlay exceeded their meager means), "Shall we go and buy two hundred pennyworth of bread and give them to eat?" Not heeding what they said, Jesus proceeds, "How many loaves have you? Go and see." Andrew came forward with the information that there was a lad present with "five loaves and two small fishes," but what were they among so many? They had forgotten that they were speaking to the Creator of the universe, "who calleth those things which be not as though they were" (Romans 4:17). In their heartlessness and lack of faith, they would have driven the needy multitudes away. At hand, however, was the God who gave the manna and also the One who said, "I will satisfy the poor with bread" (Exodus 16; Psalm 132:15).

The lad with the slender stock of homeliest fare had no idea of the great possibilities of small opportunities and of how little is much if only God is in it. The loaves and fishes he carried were probably prepared by his mother for his father and himself for a day. The loaves were of "barley," the food of the very poor, while the small fishes were a sort of sardine, salted and used as a relish. Yet it was with this small package of food that the Lord was about to satisfy the multitude and prove to all that He was able to prepare a table even in the wilderness

(Psalm 78:19). The command was given for the people to sit down by companies upon the green grass. We have here two delightful touches. First of all, the early spring season made the grass an attractive resting place. Where the people sat was green grass tableland. John tells us that there was much grass in the place (6:10). Cumming remarks, "A mere writer of a story gotten up would never have thought of using that expression. It is so natural, so unartisticlike, that it is plainly the evidence of a story written upon the spot and describing facts that had been actually seen."

Then, that all things should be done decently and in order, Jesus commanded people to sit down in companies, by hundreds and fifties, proving that "order is heaven's first law." The disciples would have waited until there were sufficient victuals before getting the crowds to sit down. But the crowds were expectant and sat down circlelike around Jesus. What a prudent precaution it was to break the multitude up into orderly groups! Had the thousands not been broken up into manageable sections, there would have been confusion, with the stronger and ruder unduly aggressive, but the weaker, like the women and children, neglected. Such order is stamped upon all His ways whether in creation or grace. "God is not the author of confusion." Mark's description of the orderly grouping of the crowd is very graphic. He uses the plural of the word which signifies a garden plot or bed, portraying the people as reclining in ranks or divisions, so that the several separate companies resemble detached garden plots. In keeping with Eastern custom, the 5,000 men sat apart in the order indicated, and they alone are counted. How many women and children there were, we are not told. Their number, however, must have been considerable.

How dramatic it must have been as Jesus took the five loaves and the two fishes in His hands! We can imagine what hushed expectancy there was both among the disciples and the crowd. The first act of Jesus was to give thanks. What an exquisite instance this is of grace before eating! Trench says that "this eucharistic act Jesus accomplished as the Head of the household," and then goes on to cite the beautiful saying of the Talmud, "He that enjoys aught without thanksgiving is as though he robbed God." This public thanks for the food He was about to administer reveals the wonderful combination of human dependence and divine omnipotence in one Person. In taking bread and giving thanks, we have evidence of a creature. In making five loaves feed five thousand, we have the interposition of a God. Thanksgiving to God is the primary ingredient of that "elixir of life" which turns all it touches to gold.

Just as Jesus blessed, He brake. As Jewish loaves were thin cakes, a thumb's breadth in thickness, they were more easily broken than cut. In the miracle of the highest order, the process of multiplication is beyond our comprehension. Ellicott asks, "Did each loaf, in succession, supply a thousand with food, and then come to an end, its place taken by another? Was the structure of the fishes, bone and skin and head, reproduced in each portion that was given to the guests at that great feast?" The Bible does not say. All we do know is that it was "a stupendous act of creative power, no rationalizing of which can reduce it to natural dimensions." Every miracle is incomprehensible except to Him by whom it is wrought. The multiplication of those loaves afforded a striking proof of Christ's deity. By an act of His own creative power, with five loaves He ministered to the necessities of five thousand men. The reader is referred to the elaboration of the analogy between this "divinely hastened nature process," and the daily miracle of supplying food for the countless millions of humans, beasts, and birds. Trench says in his exposition of this miracle before us, "God's early day miracles grow cheap in man's sight by continual repetition."

The miracle that day was wrought by Christ's hands and mediated to the multitude by human hands, for He gave the blessed and miracle-produced loaves to His disciples, and they in turn gave them to the multitude. Why did Jesus send His gift of food by His disciples? Richard Glover in his commentary on Matthew suggests two reasons for Jesus employing His disciples:

(1) The people ate more freely.

Bread of miracle direct from the hand of Omnipotence, they might have feared to eat; but by going through the disciples' hands, the food became more homely.

(2) The disciples caught Christ's spirit by sharing in His work.

If they had been onlookers only, they would have been critics of the worth of the receivers and of the wisdom of the gift. In distributing the gift, they were able to catch Christ's generosity, see the need, behold the gratitude of men, and have at the close kindlier feelings and more love. Mutual ministry is the divine plan for the world. We receive in order to give.

It is interesting to observe the different tenses of *brake* and *gave*. The first implies the *instantaneous*, the second, the *continuous* act. He *brake*, and *kept giving* out. Farrow remarks that the multiplication of the loaves evidently took place in Christ's hands, between the acts of breaking and distributing. The record says that "they did *all* eat, and were *filled*." We do not know how the wonderbread was formed, but that it was is proved by the fact that there was enough and to spare. When the compassion of Christ, a lad's willing surrender of all he had, and the need of many meet, omnipotence has a three-fold reason for blessing, and does it bless. "Spare, and you have not enough for one; share, and you have enough for multitudes."

Further, there is nothing niggardly about the Lord's provision, which is ever abundant. After all the people were sufficiently fed, the disciples took up of the fragments of the loaves and fishes, twelve baskets full —one basket for each of the apostles. What generosity of the Supernatural! As waste is the enemy of such miraculous generosity, nothing had to be wasted. Care had to be exercised with the use of the leftovers. At the outset, what the lad gave to Jesus to multiply would not have filled one basket; now, after feeding thousands, there are twelve full baskets left. But nothing had to be lost. A most prodigal bounty and the exactest economy go hand in hand. What became of the fragments, or broken pieces, we are not told. Perhaps they were used later, or distributed among the poor in surrounding towns. We are left with the lessons that increasing goes along with scattering (II Kings 4:1-7; Proverbs 11:24), and that overabundance does not justify waste. "The marvellous display of creative power was not to supersede forethought, thrift, and economy in the use of the gifts it had bestowed."

What about the lad's reward for not withholding his frugal meal, but gladly surrendering all he had for the Master's use? What a thrill he must have had as he saw Jesus miraculously multiply the little he gave! Christ gave him good measure, pressed down and shaken together and running over, for he went home with a glad heart and with more food than he could carry for all his household. The Creator is no man's debtor.

The enthusiasm created by the miracle was intense. The people wanted to enthrone Jesus as king immediately and have Him lead them in a march to Jerusalem for the Passover. In the outburst of enthusiasm, the people felt that such a mighty ruler would be indeed a boon to long over-taxed men. But Jesus refused the kingdom. He knew it would be His, not at man's hands, but God's. In due time, He will establish a visible government in Jerusalem, and then social problems baffling the keenest sociologists of the present time will find a perfect solution.

The great lesson of the miracle is evident. Christ is the Bread of life to a perishing world, and as the Living Bread, must be passed on to others by the eaters themselves. The myriads around in their sin and indifference and the millions abroad in heathen darkness need not depart. In Christ, there is sufficient for each and for all. As Christ used what the lad gave Him and the disciples passed on the multiplied bread Christ gave them, so through our surrendered lives, Christ waits to make others the sharers of our knowledge and experience of His all-sufficiency.

27. The Miracle of Walking on the Water

(Matthew 14:22-36; Mark 6:45-54; John 6:15-21)

This fascinating miracle is referred to as an "appendix" of the previous miracle, since it took place on the eve of that momentous day. Our Lord's first act after the feeding of the 5,000 was to constrain His disciples to set out in their boat for the western shore of the Sea of Gennesaret. Care must be taken not to confuse this miracle with another when Jesus was asleep in a boat and was aroused to calm the angry deep. We here have a familiar story of exquisite beauty, about which there are few facts to be explained. The miracle seems to be associated with three aspects of the Miracle-Worker, namely, Jesus praying on the mountain, walking on the sea, worshiped in the ship.

After the miracle of the loaves and the enthusiasm created by such a wonder, Jesus constrained His disciples to go by boat to the other side of the lake. Why did He

constrain them to go? Because of their love and growing admiration of Him, were they reluctant to be separated from Him even for a moment? Knowing of the movement to make Jesus king, were they unwilling to leave Him at the moment of His approaching exaltation? To the disciples, no day had been so bright; now they must go before Him to the other side, and their bright day ended in a troubled night. They wanted to bask in the sun of the Master's popularity, but He knew that there was more danger in the favor of the crowd than from the fury of the storm. So Jesus sent them on, and the storm had the effect of saving them from wrong ambitions. They had to learn that the stormy night along with the bright day worked together for their good.

Another suggestion is that they had to learn that He who had fed His disciples miraculously with loaves and fishes was the same One who sent them to encounter the storms and waves of an angry, tempestuous sea. They had to learn that He never sends His own to a warfare at their own charges. Strength was theirs to suffer the trial ahead. Alas, however, as we shall shortly see, they forgot the miracles of the loaves!

As for Jesus, after the frenzy of the people to make Him king, He resorted to the mountain for rest, solace, and communion with God. He perceived that the people were seeking to take Him by force and make Him king. Here, at last, was the One powerful enough to deliver them from the tyranny and power of the Roman government. Thus He sought the solitude of the mountain, not only for calmness of heart, but to look at the clamor for His kingship in its right perspective. After those hours of prayer, He appeared the next day and preached a sermon in the synagogue that turned rejoicing into rejection so much so that almost all but His disciples left Him. The nearness to a path of earthly greatness would have led Him away from the cross, and in solitude on His knees the victory was won.

Going up to the mountain to pray also reminds us how deity and humanity were united in Jesus. On the afternoon of that day, we see Him as very God of very God, full of creative energy—at night we see Him a very Man of very Man, standing in the need of prayer. No one can explain this blending of deity and humanity, but there it is. As the Creator, we adore Him, and as the Man at prayer—solitary, continuous, and special prayer—He is our example and we must emulate such an example. We also have a picture here of what was soon to take place, namely, Jesus, at His Ascension, going up to God to enter His present ministry of intercession, leaving His Church to face the billows of this stormy world during His absence.

Out on the lake, the disciples were hard put, for one of the sudden furious storms common to the area gave the strong rowers hours of useless toil. Three hours after midnight they were still in the midst of the lake, about half way across, and, as the record says, "distressed in rowing" (Mark 6:48). What made the conquest with the storms more distressing was the fact that Jesus was not with them, as on the other sea-storm occasion. The disciples were tossed and tormented by the waves, for the winds were "contrary." These contrary winds are hard to face, yet when accepted in the right spirit, go to develop character and add to the joy of reaching the harbor.

What those weary, frustrated rowers did not know was that Jesus, in His prayer retreat on the mountain slope, saw them in the darkest hour of their extremity. In His solitude, the Eternal Being was watching the little specks of boats and was cognizant of the sore trouble of their toil. Buffeted by those contrary winds, the disciples were to learn of the Master's divine sympathy and of His willingness to enter the struggle. Thus it was that Jesus came to the distressed rowers in an unexpected way—walking on the sea, as if it had been a soft, smooth carpet. Here was a mode of progression unknown to the disciples. Every new experience of Jesus was an awe-filled surprise to them. He had seemed to neglect them, leaving them hour after hour wrestling with the storm, until they were almost exhausted. Once He calmed a storm for them, why not now? But the One who had been praying for them and watching them was now at hand, yet they knew Him not.

Jesus seemed to pass the disciples by. Alarmed, they cried, "It is a spirit." Because of the black night, the distressing storm, the somewhat frayed nerves, and the unexpectedness of Christ's presence, they deemed the One they saw to be some apparition come to welcome them to the abode of death. Among the Jews, there was a popular belief that the spirits of the dead visited their relatives long after death. Perhaps these men thought a spirit of some departed one had come to them. But they were to know that He who seemed to be a specter, terrible phantom of the night, was a Savior.

With infinite ease as Jesus moved naturally and majestically over the troubled waters, He sought to calm the cry of the fear of His own by the cheering call, "It is I—the great I Am—be not afraid." How assuring such an inspiring voice must have been! "The majesty of the approach was perfected in the tenderness of the address." Such a word at such a time begot peace, for it was as if Jesus had said, "It is all right. Don't be afraid. I am your Friend, your deliverer." So *Mr. Fearing* was comforted. Immediately their fears were rebuked and scattered as they, with others, were brought suddenly and in a most unusual way face to face with the Mighty One (see Genesis 16:11; Judges 6:13; Daniel 10:12, 19; Revelation 1:17, etc). Commenting on the impression the incident made on the minds of the disciples, Ellicott says:

> To hear the familiar tones and the cheering words was enough, even amid the howling of the winds and the dashing of the waves, to give them confidence and hope. We can scarcely doubt that in after years that moment came back to their recollection, invested for them, as it has been since for the Church at large, with something of a symbolic character. . . . He was coming to them through the storm. "Be of good cheer" became the watchword of their lives.

As the heart of the miracle was that of Jesus walking on the sea, we must give some consideration to such a direct act of control over natural law. How are we to explain this seeming contradiction of the known law of gravity? Actually, there was no contradiction nor suspension of the universal law of gravity, but the exercise of a stronger power. The law of gravity is not set aside when the magnet collects the iron filings; it is only that the superior force of magnetism has overcome gravitation. So what happened that stormy night was the exercise of Christ's omnipotence, as He, the Creator of seas and winds, revealed His authority over them, and they being His, He could use them as He desired. It was His *will* which bore Him triumphant above those waters. Such a supernatural feat was a further evidence of His sovereignty, and also a foregleam of the time when, in His spiritual and glorified human body, He would be able to counteract ordinary natural laws, like that of passing through closed doors (John 20:19).

When the human mind contemplates the works and ways of God, the question arises, "How can these things be?" Such a query, however, is of unbelief, not of faith. No wonder should stagger the heart that has learned to trust God and believe in His word. With Him, all things are possible. As the Man, Jesus prayed for His disciples; now as God, He walks the sea for their deliverance. Though He would not fling Himself from the Temple pinnacle for self-glory, He flung Himself on the waves to reassure His own that He was near.

Convinced that the One who trod the waves was indeed the Christ, lovable, impetuous Peter, ever the spokesman of the apostolic band, said, "Lord, *if* it be Thou, bid me come unto Thee on the water." He wanted a sign that the suspected apparition was the Master and that he too must walk upon the waters. Jesus replied, "Come!" The "unto Me" disappeared from His answer. This was a permissive *Come*, containing an implicit pledge that Peter should not be swallowed up by the raging waters. Peter took to the waters and at first his faith sustained him as he "walked on the water," a sharer with his Master in that "intensity of spiritual life which suspended the action of natural laws by one which is supernatural."

Although the faith of ardent, impulsive Peter was deficient in depth—not a pure, courageous faith, but a carnal over-boldness, it was nevertheless a faith enabling him to attempt the seemingly impossible for a mere man. Jesus in His gracious rebuke did not say, "Wherefore didst thou come?" but, "Wherefore didst thou doubt?" As Bengel put it, "He was not blamed because he came out of the ship, but because he did not remain in the firmness of faith." It was as if Peter had said, "Since it is indeed Thyself, let me be sharer with Thee in the calm repose which can move thus, unaffected by the storm around Thee and unsubmerged by the waves beneath Thee."

The difference between the impulse of faith and the test of reality, however, was quickly manifest, for looking at the turbulent waves, Peter became afraid and cried out, "Lord, save me!" In the conflict between sight and faith, faith went out and fear came in. The delegated supernatural power left him, and although as a fisherman he was a strong swimmer, the waters began to engulf him. Peter turned his eye from the Master and focused them on the surging waves, and because he feared, he fell, but did not drown. When he began to sink, Jesus saved him, for He never leaves His own to sink. Poor Peter, he saw something else beside Jesus that night, and taking counsel of flesh and blood, revealed his weakness and lack of true faith. After making a show of courage transcending the rest of the disciples, Peter must have been humiliated.

Christ's rebuke was most tender, "Wherefore didst thou doubt?" With Peter He entered the ship and immediately the winds *ceased*—a word meaning, it grew weary, sank away like one who is weary. The rough elements spent themselves of their raging as the Master of the universe displayed His power, and immediately the shore was reached. As soon as Jesus entered the ship, the rest of the voyage was supernaturally accelerated.

The astonishment of the disciples is indicated by Mark—whose eye for detail is characteristic of his gospel—"They were sore amazed in themselves beyond measure and wondered." But there was no need for their amazement, even though Jesus, after coming to them when it was dark, walked on the sea to their aid. They should have remembered the great miracle of the loaves and fishes wrought earlier in the day. They should have reasoned from the multiplying of the loaves to the stilling of the sea. "Had they understood all the divine energy which the miracle of the loaves involved, nothing afterwards, not even the walking on the waves, or the lulling of the storm, would have seemed startling to them." The miracle of the loaves should have eclipsed the new marvel of Christ's mastery of the elements.

Once Jesus was settled in the boat and all was calm, the disciples had a fresh glimpse of His greatness. They worshiped Him, saying, "Of a truth thou art the Son of God." This should ever be the attitude of those delivered by Christ's power. He accepted their confession of His deity as "the Son of God" and permitted their worship of Him. The record of the miracle ends with the display of Christ's miraculous power on all the diseased brought to Him by interested friends. Emulating the action of the woman with the issue of blood, the sick touched the hem of His garment, and all who touched it were made perfectly whole, that is, were completely restored.

The precious lesson of the miracle is instructive and comforting. Faith is tested by the storms of life, but struggling homeward "midst wind and rain and storm," He is ever near. Tossed to and fro on the waves of a troublesome world, it may seem as though He has forgotten, but His eye is ever upon us, and suddenly in our extremity He undertakes for us in marvelous ways. Peter began to sink in *familiar* waters, and on a *permitted* path, but his Saviour was not far away. If the darkness of the night and the fury of the storms are upon us and we are beginning to sink into despair and doubt, may our cry be, "Lord, save me"—and He will! (Psalm 46:1-3).

28. The Miracle of the Syro-Phoenician Woman's Daughter

(Matthew 15:21-28; Mark 7:24-30)

It would seem as if, in order of time, this miracle was performed shortly after the miracle of the feeding of the five thousand. The first feature of the miracle before us is "the change, at this point, in the scene and the circumstances of our Lord's miracles, says Laidlaw. "The *year of success* was ended, the *year of opposition* was now begun. His labors consist henceforth of a succession of tours and journeys." It was a time of peril for Jesus, for Herod was suspicious of Him and the Pharisees could not conceal their excited hostility and hatred toward Him. The people, hitherto enthusiastic over His dynamic teaching and marvelous works, were now taking deep offense at some of His words. Feeling, then, the need of retirement and the need of further instructing the Twelve, Jesus sought the seclusion of a friend's home, and would have no one know of it, but as we read, "He could not be hid." Concealment for Him was impossible. The more He tried to conceal Himself, the more He became known. Who can hide the glory of the sun? As Light, Jesus could not be buried in a world of darkness. So great a Physician could not go unnoticed in a world of suffering. As the fragrance of flowers cannot be hid, how could He, whose name is as ointment poured forth, be hid? "The ointment betrayeth itself."

Although Jesus departed for the borders of Tyre and Sidon, we are not told that He actually entered this half-heathen territory. Trench says that, "We have no reason to think that at any time during His earthly ministry our Lord had passed beyond the borders of the Holy Land." A short time before He had held up Tyre and Sidon as places specially hardened (Matthew 11:21), but a woman from this heathen area—a pagan outside of the Covenant—was to refresh His distressed spirit. His ministry kept Him within the limits of the land of Israel; yet here He goes to the borders of Tyre and Sidon for a single deed of mercy toward one outside of the Holy Land. In sending out the Twelve, His precept was, "Go not into the way of the Gentiles;" yet here He is headed in that direction. The time was not ripe to go out into all the world.

As to the miracle itself, Campbell Morgan calls it "one of the sweetest stories of them all—the mother's heart carrying the need of her daughter with unswerving faith to Him who had created the love of the mother." It seems to revolve around the Syro-Phoenician's race, religion, reason, reception, resourcefulness, and reward. Actually there were two Syro-Phoenician women who were recipients of the supernatural—the one we are considering and the other in the Old Testament whom the prophet helped when he was sent to Sarepta, a city of Sidon (I Kings 17:24; Luke 4:26). Both are called Syro-Phoenicians, for Phoenicia was then regarded as a part of Syria.

In the reference to the Syro-Phoenician who came to Jesus, she is spoken of as a woman of *Canaan,* meaning that, as a descendant of the original inhabitants of Canaan, she was a Gentile of the Gentiles. The nation she represented was marked by divine judgments, and its guilt had risen up to God and cried out for vengeance, and retribution fell upon it. She came of the "accursed race once doomed of God to excision root and branch (Deuteronomy 7: 2), but of which some branches had been spared that should have destroyed all" (Judges 2:2, 3). As a Phoenician, she worshiped the great mother-goddess, "Ashtoreth," or "Astarte," or "Queen of heaven," giver of all life in plant, animal, and man. This goddess was supposed to give her devotees everything good and was indulgent as to permit them to do almost everything evil. Yet it was one from a country stained with infamy and sin that this woman came to Jesus, conscious of her own deep sense of personal demerit, seeking divine mercy both for herself and for her demon-possessed daughter.

She is also referred to as a *Greek,* which means "Gentile," and as such was without the Jewish covenant. She was a pagan and is perhaps the only example of a heathen being blessed by our Lord Himself in the flesh. Another Gentile, the Capernaum centurion, was helped by Jesus, but it is obvious that he was a convert to the Jewish faith when he encountered Him for his sick servant. The Syro-Phoenician woman was as a flower in the untrodden desert attracted to Jesus by the sweetness of His character and the supernaturalness of His work.

The reason for her approach to Jesus was the plight of her demon-possessed daughter, who was, as Matthew expresses it, "grievously vexed with a devil" (demon). The language used implies that she was "badly demonized." Nothing is said of any bodily sickness, or epilepsy, or other physical and mental disturbances common to demon possession in which there are degrees of misery. One of the Devil's fallen spirits had entered and taken possession of the girl, resulting in total disability—a condition in which her anxious mother was utterly unable to do anything for her relief. Meeting the divine Healer, she presented her request, "Have mercy on me, O Lord, Thou son of David; my daughter is grievously vexed with a devil."

Probably this distressed mother was a widow and therefore all the more desperate to help her child. Addressing Jesus as "Lord," she revealed her respect for Him as a great and superior Being. In calling Him "the Son of David," she recognized in this Prophet of Nazareth, one who would travel beyond the limits of Galilee. This pivot-phrase in her importunate cry called upon Jesus, as Israel's Messiah, to help her. In her heart-felt pleas, she revealed her affection for her dear, distressed daughter. But it will be noted that she seeks mercy, first for herself, then for her daughter. Was it possible that her sin had brought this judgment upon her child, or was she just identifying herself with her daughter's need, implying that deliverance for one would mean mercy for the other? This is evident that her "help *me*" was associated with her "help *her*" and was a fulfilment of the royal law of bearing one another's burden. Here she was making her child's misery her own. It was as if there was only one soul and one interest between them. The two were fondly bound together. Jesus was the One able to bless both mother and daughter alike.

But what a seemingly chilly reception from Jesus she received as she came to Him in her dire need. "He answered her not a word." Could this be the gracious Helper and Healer she had heard so much about, who though He anticipated the needs of others (John 5:6), was withdrawing from her? How this attitude of the ever-merciful One must have startled her. This strange reception was far from the infinite beneficence she had heard of and the miracles of power she had probably witnessed. "The Word" had no word for her aching heart. He was deaf to her appeal, but not to that of others who had come from Tyre and Sidon (Luke 6:17). Could it be that Christ was like her old Canaanitish deity, not regarding human woe? Where was His help now as "the Husband of the Widow, and the Father of the fatherless"? Usually, His patients and suppliants were healed at the first word, or led up to their cure by some statement or question—why His absolute silence in her case? Ah, she was to learn that—

> Behind a frowning countenance,
> He hides a smiling face.

Because of His omniscience, He knew all about the woman from Canaan and what had brought her to Him, just as He knew all about His disciples "toiling in rowing," although He was not with them. Like a skilful physician, He adapted Himself to each person's peculiarity. He knew all about Abraham's faith before He sorely tried him, and He was likewise cognizant of the tenacity of this woman's faith before He tried *it* on the shore of Canaan. It would seem as if, after treating the woman's plea with silence, Jesus arose and left the house. If this was so, then she was not to be shaken off, for she followed Him with her entreaties, so much so that the disciples were annoyed with her importunity. The more she was repulsed, the closer she crept to Him, and kept knocking at His door.

The appeal of the Twelve to be rid of the woman reveals how weary they were with the persistent entreaties as she cried after them. "Send her away"—give her what she wants and dismiss her because of her persistence. She is a nuisance and is interfering with our retirement. But Jesus did not answer His disciples according to their wish, any more than He did the woman's according to hers. "He delays the answer with a divine 'much more' of mercy and abounding grace in which He means to bless her." What Jesus did say seems to set the seal of hopelessness upon the woman's plea. "I am not sent unto the lost sheep of the house of Israel" (see Matthew 10: 5, 6), which was indeed His mission at that time, as a true "Minister of the circumcision for the truth of God to confirm the promise made unto the father" (Romans 15:8). So, as a Gentile, the woman had no claim upon Jesus whatever.

At first there seems to be a contradiction here, since He came as the promised Seed in whom, not one nation, but all nations should be blessed (Psalm 72:11; Luke 2: 32; Romans 15:9-12). Then was there not His own declaration that other sheep, not of the Jewish fold, must be brought to Him (John 10:16)? Did He not come and die as the Saviour of the world? There must have been a purpose therefore in the restriction of His ministry almost exclusively to Judea. Augustine says, "We understand then by this, that it behoved Him to manifest His bodily presence, His truth, the exhibition of His miracles, and the power of His resurrection among that people—Israel." Jerome put it, "He was reserving the perfect salvation of the Gentiles for His passion and resurrection." Thus His mission was local that it might become universal. The ultimate design of His Gospel, we learn from His last commission, was for His followers to go into *all* the world and preach that Gospel which His death and resurrection made possible. For great, wise, and righteous ends then, His personal ministry was confined to Judea where the majority of His miracles were wrought and His precious discourses delivered, and the scattered instances of Gentiles tasting of His goodness were forerunners of the great future when the Spirit would be poured out alike upon Jew and Gentile. Since Pentecost, the mystic fabric known as "the Church of the living God" is composed of both Jews and Gentiles regenerated by His power. Cornelius and the Syro-Phoenician woman foreshadowed the present dispensation of grace (Romans 11:11). They were "the first drops of that gracious shower

which should one day water the whole earth" (John 12:30-32).

The next phase of the story is most impressive. Hearing what Jesus said to His disciples about His exclusive ministry and that the children—the Jews—must first be filled, the woman drew close to Jesus and worshiped Him saying, "Lord, help me." With the renewal of her passionate entreaty, there was the act of prostrate homage. Up to now, He had spoken to His disciples; now He speaks to the woman in words that meant, "You are not of Israel, and to them am I sent. It is the children's bread I have come to give, and you are outside the family circle." Perhaps a word is necessary about our Lord's usage of "children" and "dogs." By "children," of course, He meant the Jews, "the children of the kingdom" (Matthew 8:2), while "dogs" were the symbol of Gentiles, as sunk in impurity, and was a proverbial expression used by the Jews to denote a sense of their national superiority over other nations. Jesus did not call the Gentiles "dogs." He only applied the aphorism of His time to the case on hand. Gentiles were called "dogs" by the Jews. "Is thy servant a dog that he should do such a thing?" (II Kings 8:13).

It is interesting to note that the word Jesus used for "dogs" was a soft one, meaning "little dogs," or "puppies." Laidlaw suggests that the word did not denote the large, wild dogs which prowled about Eastern cities, but those which the Roman had introduced—those treated as domestic animals. It was a diminutive word Jesus used in His description of a family around the table at mealtime with house pets wailing for their morsel. Jesus did not call the woman a "dog." He only echoed what was in His disciples' mind.

The woman, however, was not discouraged by Christ's words. With perfect logic, she drew the sweetest meaning out of their seeming bitterness. Christ's reply was enough to daunt anyone else but this woman whose faith in Christ was so strong, and whose love for her demon-possessed child was so strong that she turned the repulse of Jesus into a reason for approaching Him more closely and confidentially. She changed "a dissuasive into a persuasive."

In her reply there was not only resourcefulness, but a clear insight into the heart of Jesus, who probably gave her the occasion —meaningly and lovingly—to turn a seeming refusal into an implicit assent. Here are the words, "Truth, Lord: yet the dogs eat of the crumbs which fall from their masters' tables." She did not turn away from the divine answer in a rage, as Naaman did, but she catches at the form which had softened the usual word of scorn and presses the privilege it implied. She owned that she and her people were "dogs," outsiders altogether, and therefore had no claim. Her sense of unworthiness was very deep, but even dogs get scraps, and what she sought would not impoverish others, yet it would enrich herself. She did not ask that the children should be deprived of any fragment of their rightful portion, but taking her place contentedly among the "dogs," she could claim Jesus as her Master and ask for the "crumbs" of His mercy. She used the same diminutive word as He did, a *little crumb* for her little daughter was all she sought. She also spoke in the plural *masters'*, because of the dogs, each of which had its own master.

Somehow her ear and her heart, heard an undertone of "yea" in the loud-spoken accents that breathed only "nay," and she did not enter into controversy with Jesus. She wanted no alteration of His desires. Accepting His point of view, she admitted that she was a Gentile and therefore should be called a "dog," but as such should not be excluded from having food, but rather receive it. She never asked for a child's place. Taking a dog's place, all she asked for was dogs' food, namely, the crumbs. Counting herself a "dog," she *by faith* was counted by God His *child* (Galatians 3: 26). Her argument was perfect and prevailed. Although outside the elect family of Israel, she had confidence that such was the goodness of the divine heart that there was blessing in it for even the meanest of His creatures. Micklem suggests that Jesus at length gave way to the woman, not only because of her great faith but also because He was delighted with her ready wit. "She entangles Christ in His own words, seizes, and takes Him. The argument He had used against her, she gently retorts upon Himself."

The pleader's reward was two-fold; she was commended for her great faith, and she received a cure for her child. Christ's reply approved the woman's boldness and honored her faith, which, along with her persistency and humility, won her request. "True prayers never come weeping home." She knocked and knocked at the door until it was opened unto her. If her attitude teaches us anything, it is perseverance in prayer. Let us look at Christ's gracious commendation of her faith. As in the case of the centurion, He found a faith greater than He had met with in Israel.

Although at first it seemed as if hers was to be the denial of the smallest boon, now there is opened to her the full treasure house of divine grace. Through taking the lowest place, her faith in Christ won her the highest praise from Him. Says Spurgeon, "He tried her faith by His silence and by His discouraging replies, that He might see its strength; but He was all the while delighting in it, and secretly sustaining it, and when He had sufficiently tried it, He brought it forth as gold, and set His own royal mark upon it in these memorable words, 'O woman, great is thy faith; be it unto thee even as thou wilt.' " All her faith had to rest upon was what she had heard of Christ, and probably seen of His power, yet such was sufficient, although she was a heathen woman, to seek a cure from Christ. Her unparalleled faith in Christ proved that it is not blood, proving the true Abraham lineage, but faith, and, tried by that test, she was a spiritual daughter of Abraham. "If she is a Gentile in nationality, she is an Israelite in disposition, and as such she has been blessed." The strength of her faith is seen in that she overcame, not physical obstruction as in the case of the paralytic or in the case of Bartimeus whose faith enabled him to overcome hostile obstructions, but obstructions apparently in Christ Himself.

As to the display of the supernatural on behalf of her afflicted daughter, Jesus said, "Be it unto thee even as thou wilt"—which is always His last word. It was as if He, the Lord of glory, "surrendered at discretion to the conquering arms of a woman's faith." Mary, responding to the announcement of Gabriel, said, "Be it unto me according to thy word." We are not told the method of the miracle. The patient was not in sight of the Healer when she was cured. It was another remote control miracle. Christ willed the girl's healing, and it was done. Micklem says that "the cure may have been performed previously, when the woman first made her request, and unbeknown by her, Jesus kept her in conversation because He was interested in her and enjoyed her repartee." This much is clearly evident, that the woman believed that nearness or distance made no difference to His power to heal her daughter, and so went home in perfect confidence, there to find her loved one healed and at rest after the tumult that had so long raged within her. Says Trench, "She had offered in her faith a channel of communication between her distant child and Christ. With one hand of that faith she laid hold on Him in whom all healing grace was stored, with the other on her suffering daughter—herself a living conductor by which the power of Christ might run, like an electric flash, from Him to the object of her love."

The Syro-Phoenician woman was another of the "other sheep" not of the Jewish fold which Jesus said He would bring. Probably she was His first convert from heathenism. This we do know, that with the demon cast out of her daughter, the Spirit of God more largely entered her heart. Coming as a suppliant, she went back to her people a missionary and the church which began at Tyre grew to large dimensions afterwards. Briefly, the lessons taught by the miracle are these:

The secret of blessing is lying low at the feet of Him from whom we deserve nothing. Born of a sinful stock and individually guilty of sin, we have no claim on God except for judgment. But if we humbly acknowledge our guilt and need in virtue of all He accomplished on our behalf, He will abundantly pardon.

Another lesson is that of the reward for persistent faith—the faith that changes despair into the full assurance of hope—the faith that overcame all obstacles like silence, exclusion, and apparent reproach—the faith in Christ's willingness and ability to undertake for us. "This is the victory that overcometh the world, even our faith."

29. The Miracle of the Deaf and Dumb Man of Decapolis

(Mark 7:31-37)

Mark, who is the only one of the evangelists to record this miracle, tells us that Jesus, after His special journey to the borders of Tyre and Sidon for the healing of the Syro-Phoenician woman's daughter, made a circuit of the Decapolis district, which consisted of ten cities which had been granted special privileges by the Roman conquerors about a century earlier. Here, as everywhere else, Jesus found abundant

need for the exercise of His divine might and mercy. Matthew tells us that when Jesus returned from Tyre and Sidon, multitudes came bringing their sick to be healed —the lame, blind, dumb, maimed, and many others, and He healed them (15:30). Mark selects the one sufferer we are now to consider probably because of incidents associated with the miracle which had not occured on any other like occasion.

As to the malady of the man in question, we are told that he "was deaf, and had an impediment in his speech." If not wholly a deaf-mute, at least he was incapable of uttering articulate sounds. First of all, the man was deaf—and what a sore affliction deafness is! Bishop Horsley says, "Of all natural imperfections, deafness seems the most deplorable, as it is that which excludes the unhappy sufferer from society." Although he had his sight, the deaf man Mark describes was altogether isolated in company, for in that far-off day they never had the powerful hearing aids the deaf can use in our modern age. Evidently the man had not been born deaf. If he had, he would not have been able to speak at all. How he lost his hearing, the Bible does not say. Probably some disease or accident was responsible for his solitary silence—a stillness unbroken.

Then he is also described as having an impediment in his speech. It is not said that he was completely dumb. After Christ's touch, he was able to speak "plain." Evidently the afflicted man was unable to utter articulate and intelligible sounds. Trench says that, "his case differs, apparently, from that of the dumb man mentioned in Matthew 9:32; for while that man's evil is traced up distinctly and directly to a spiritual source, nothing of the kind is intimated here." The word Mark uses for "impediment" stands for *dumb* in the Greek version of Isaiah 35:6, which prophecy he may have had in mind. The tongue of a dumb person was considered in ancient popular belief to have been bound by a demon.

What a picture is here presented of the sinner's moral and spiritual condition as the fruit of the Fall! God lost man's ear in the garden, and since that fatal day he will listen to anyone else rather than God. "Oh, that My people had hearkened unto Me" (Psalm 81:13; Hebrews 2:1-3). The tongue of the unsaved person is as estranged from God as his ear. Even the most cultured and educated sinner betrays an impediment in his speech as soon as spiritual truths are introduced.

The methods the Master used for the healing of this "deaf stammerer" were unique. They were not so much means by which He conveyed healing, but signs intended to explain to the sufferer's mind how healing was to come. The graphic touches Mark gives us reveal the variations marking Christ's miracles. There was nothing stereotyped about His methods. Some were healed in a crowd, others in solitude. Others were healed by a word, or by a touch, or by spittle or by clay. There were those healed at a distance and others when present. One method of healing was instantaneous, while another was healed gradually. Because of His wisdom and omnipotence, He works in ways He deems best.

In this case Jesus took the man aside from the multitude. Probably there was the desire, not only for privacy, but to prevent excitement and also to obviate any profane imitations of His curative act (7:33). Away from the tumult and interruptions of the crowd, in solitude and silence, the sufferer's receptiveness would be more deep and impressive. Jesus wanted to awaken in the man himself a more confident hope, with an assured faith that he was to be healed. Then, of course, by withdrawing from the crowd He rebuked the disposition of many who were constantly seeking after a sign, and "who allowed the external miracle to eclipse the better and more glorious miracle of grace which it was the chief glory and happiness of Christ to perform." For our own hearts the application is apparent. It is good for us to be alone in the divine presence, away from the busy hum and din of a noisy world which is never conducive to spiritual reflection. It is only in the hush of God's presence that we learn of our sin and guilt and of our deep need of sovereign grace.

Isolating the man from the multitude, the first thing Jesus did was to put His fingers in the ears of the deaf man. Such a symbolic action was a mode of speech to the deaf and would awaken his faith and stir up in him the lively expectation of healing. As he could not hear, if he was to be encouraged at all, it had to be by a touch, and Christ's fingers were "put into the ears as to pierce through the obstacles which hindered sounds from the seat of hearing." Trench also remarks, "This was the fountain-evil; the man did not *speak* plainly, because he

did not *hear;* this defect, therefore, is first removed."

The text then says, "He spit." There was a popular thought that saliva had medicinal properties. This case and that of the blind man at Bethsaida (Mark 8:22-26) are the only instances in the first three gospels where we are given a picture of Jesus employing popular medical remedies in the curing of disease. Warneck, writing on beliefs and practices among the Battaks says: "Saliva is medicinal, because it contains soul power, and is frequently spread upon the sick. Those who offer sacrifices spit upon the offering to add to it a part of themselves. Expectorated saliva must not be allowed to fall into the hands of an enemy."

With the spittle of His own mouth upon His finger, Jesus then touched the tongue which He alone was able to release from the bands that held it fast (see John 9:6). Jesus used His saliva, not for any medicinal virtue it contained, but as an apt symbol of the supernatural residing within, and emanating from, Himself. Micklem observes that these actions of Christ are "a valuable reminder of how human and non-magical the actual scene was."

Next, Jesus is spoken of as "looking up to heaven," which upward look was a sign to the deaf man whence His power to heal came. Such a heavenward look was also an acknowledgement of His oneness with the Father, and that He did only those things which He saw His Father do (Matthew 14:19; John 5:19, 20; 11:41, 42). Perhaps there is also the suggestion that He prayed for the necessary miracle to be performed (John 11:41). With His glance there was also a groan, for "He sighed." Such a "sigh" has its counterpart in the "groans" and "tears" John speaks of (11:33, 35, 38). Sadness of sympathy was His at the sight of suffering. As the Man of sorrows and of loneliness, the poor, helpless creature before Him who was a "living proof of the malice of the Devil in deforming the fair creatures of God's original creation, wrung that groan from His heart." The scene sets before us the solitary Saviour in the presence of sins and sufferings of a lost race, and of how His deep sympathy sprang from His lofty communion with God.

One of the characteristic peculiarities of Mark as an historian is seen in the record of the very word in the Aramaic vernacular Jesus used to give vent to His emotion— *Ephphatha,* meaning "be opened." Mark was not only an eye witness of the miracle, but an ear witness as well, and so gives us some of the actual words Christ used (see 5:41). A look to heaven, a groan, a word, and the miracle is wrought. This was the divine work of power, for immediately the man heard and spoke distinctly. First of all, the organs of hearing were restored, then "the string of his tongue was loosed, and he spake plain." The "string" was the "bond" which confined and hampered speech. The Jews around would feel that demoniac fetters were broken and a work of Satan undone.

The order of the cure is somewhat significant—right speech returned directly when the ear was opened. Laidlaw observes that this is the order of nature. "The receiving of articulate sounds by the ear and their action in the brain and mind awakens and educates functions of speech. It is only when we consider this relation between sound and speech in the mechanism of the senses and the brain that we can appreciate the truly stupendous nature of the miracle. The entire process of establishing communication between the centers of hearing and speech was bridged in a moment." In the spiritual realm it is the same, for the ear must be opened to receive divine instruction before the tongue is able to speak forth God's praise. "We believe, and therefore we speak" (Romans 10:17; II Corinthians 4: 13). Receiving by way of the ear the Gospel of redeeming love and grace into the heart, we delight to speak of the marvels of divine grace to all around.

As to the result of the miracle, Jesus charged those who came to know about it to tell no man. But "the more He charged them, so much the more a great deal they published it." Jesus was back in the region where the people had tried to make Him king and so He cautioned the people to be quiet and avoid publicity. But the request not to blazon abroad the miracle was disregarded, for the desire of Jesus to suppress any popular excitement based on mere wonder was counteracted by an honest enthusiasm on the part of the friends of the newly healed man. Jesus never desired any cheap popularity.

The astonished crowd who knew that Jesus had made the deaf to hear and the dumb to speak exclaimed, "He hath done all things well"—or "beautiful" as the last word means. If Christ's "Be opened" reminds us of the Creator's *fiat*, the exclama-

tion of the people, "He hath done all things well" recalls creation's praise (Genesis 1:31). Matthew, in his general description of what happened at this juncture of our Lord's ministry says that "they glorified the God of Israel." Many of those in the half-heathen regions of Decapolis witnessing the supernatural work of Jesus, were heathens, who, as they beheld His miraculous power, confessed that He who had chosen Israel for His own possession was God above all gods.

30. The Miracle of the Feeding of the 4,000

(Matthew 15:30-38; Mark 8:1-9)

Here is another illustration of what Habershon calls "the double miracle," and much that we have written in connection with the feeding of the 5,000, which probably took place not far from the same scene as the miracle before us, is common to the feeding of the 4,000. The latter miracle is only found in Matthew and Mark, while the former is recorded in all four gospels. Because of the obvious resemblances in the two miracles, modernists treat them as differing versions of the same incident, or, as they say, legend. But while there are echoes of the similar miracle of the 5,000 in the one of the 4,000, there are yet many contrasts to be observed. Before we consider the miracle itself, let us indicate the various points of difference, proving that there were two different miracles.

First of all, the occasion and motives in the two miracles were different. Also in the miracle of the 5,000, the disciples spoke first, while in that of the 4,000 Jesus takes the initiative. Then the location was different. The 5,000 were fed at the head of the lake, near the entrance of Jordan into it and in the district of Bethsaida—the 4,000 were fed on the eastern shore of the lake in the region of Decapolis. Then the circumstances of each were different. In the narrative of the 5,000, Jesus had crossed the lake for rest, but was followed by the multitudes. After the miracle, Jesus sent His disciples away in a boat; and then there came the miracle of walking on the sea. Here in the miracle of the 4,000, Jesus came from the region of Tyre and Sidon, and there is no hint of any storm.

Other differences are evident—for instance, with the 5,000 Jesus was only one day in their company—in the 4,000 He was with them for three days. Then the 5,000 came from the immediate neighborhood, while the many of the 4,000 came "from far." When the 5,000 were before Jesus, He put no testing questions to His disciples, as with the 4,000, but simply declared His compassion for the people's need and His intention of supplying it. The number of people miraculously fed differed—5,000 beside women and children; 4,000 beside women and children. The 5,000 were fed with five loaves and two fishes, the 4,000, a smaller company, had a larger provision, seven loaves and a few little fishes—not enough for one meal for the Twelve, but apparently quite enough for the Master's purpose. With the 5,000, the multitudes were commanded to sit down in orderly fashion upon the green grass. Then it was the time of flowers. Several weeks later, the 4,000 sat on the ground, because the grass would be burned up. Doubtless the same orderly precision was observed as with the 5,000, namely, the men grouped by hundreds and by fifties, and the women and children grouped apart from the men.

Further, the word used for "basket" is different. In the miracle of the 5,000 the word for "basket" is one from which "coffins" comes, the Greek being *cophinus*, so named because of their coffin shape. These were small hand-baskets, specially provided for the Jews to carry levitically clean food while traveling in Samaria or other heathen districts. The word used in the miracle of the 4,000 means a *large provision basket* or *hamper*, of the kind used for letting Paul down over the wall at Damascus (Acts 9: 25). Twelve of the smaller baskets were needed for the fragments of the 5,000—seven of the larger baskets for the fragments of the 4,000. In both cases there had to be no waste, even though the need was supplied miraculously. "Fragment-gathering is one of the great secrets of *manufacturers*, of joy, of wealth, of usefulness. While the foregoing considerations are of themselves sufficient to prove that the two miracles are entirely different, all possible doubt regarding the matter is removed by the fact that our Lord recognized two distinct miracles, and that He connected each with a word specially appropriate to it (read and compare Matthew 16:9, 10; Mark 8:19-21)." Some writers make the repetition of the miracle symbolic or prophetic, namely, that Christ showed Himself as the Bread of life twice—to the Jew first, and also to the Gen-

tile. It is better, however, to see in the reduplication of the miracle and the recounting of both a double enforcement of the duty of remembering the Lord's mercies. "Do ye not understand, neither remember?" (Matthew 16:9).

Proceeding to a more particular consideration of the miracle of feeding the 4,000, we note the following aspects: A great multitude of Gentiles from the region of Decapolis followed Jesus into a desert place and, attracted by His unique and marvelous teaching, they remained with Him for three days. On the third day, Jesus, proposing to send the people to their homes, was concerned about the lack of provision for their physical needs. Any food they had brought with them was exhausted, and they had nothing to sustain them on their return journey. Knowing that the people were on the borders of exhaustion, Jesus knew that He must act, and so He said to His disciples, "I have compassion on the multitude, because they continue with Me now three days, and have nothing to eat; and I will not send them away fasting, lest they faint by the way." What a revelation this is of divine compassion and considerateness!

Such an instinctive, spontaneous compassion is one of the great glories of the Godhead, and so unlike the cold philosophy which only chills men's hearts. *Lest they faint.* How fatherly is the heart of Christ in which compassion rises spontaneously! Ellicott says that "it is significant that there, as so often before, the display of miraculous power in its highest form originates not in answer to a challenge, or as being offered as a proof of a Divine mission, but simply from compassion."

The answer of the disciples to Christ's decision to feed the hungry was a confession of the insufficiency of their own resources to cope with the need. They had no supply for such an emergency. "Whence should we have so much bread in the wilderness to satisfy so great a multitude?" Why was it that the former miracle of the 5,000 was not fresh in their memories, or if they remembered such a mighty interposition of Christ, did they doubt whether He would choose a second time to exercise His creative might? As before, He knew in Himself "what He would do" (John 6:6), so He asked what supplies were available and was told, "Seven loaves, and a few little fishes"—not enough for one meal even for the twelve disciples! Jesus commanded the multitude to be seated in orderly fashion and then gave thanks. Matthew says that after He had taken the loaves and fishes, Jesus gave thanks—Mark tells us that first He gave thanks for the bread, and afterwards blessed the fishes. Either way, His gratitude to God for temporal mercies is emphasized. "According to the Jewish ordinance," Vincent tells us, "the head of the house was to speak the blessing only if he himself shared in the meal; yet if they who sat down to it were not merely guests, but his children or household, then he might speak it, even if he himself did not partake."

The breaking of the bread and loaves, the distribution of the multiplied food to the seated companies through the mediation of the disciples, and the gathering up of the fragments when the repast was finished closely resemble the former occasion. Once the people were entirely satisfied with the meal miraculously provided, Jesus sent them home—"not left them. There is a courtesy which acts as the host, and will not leave till the guests have gone with a benediction." Thereafter, Jesus and His disciples took ship and came into the coasts of Magdala, and a postscript to the miracle is the Master's rebuke of His own for their forgetfulness. They had forgotten to take some of the fragments for the journey and they took the Master's warning to "beware of the leaven of the Pharisees" as an allusion to their carelessness. In His unique way, Jesus made use of their strange blunder, and by rebuking them caused them to repeat the details of the two miracles of the loaves and fishes (Matthew 16:1-12). "His questions are a sweet reminder that it is unimportant whether any loaves at all, leavened or unleavened, are forthcoming," comments Richard Glover in his *Matthew* commentary, "since He can supply all their need, as He has abundantly proved; so that His warning is of something deeper than the loaves of bread."

As to the lessons of the miracle, Scripture numerals are significant of spiritual truths and we can discern in the *seven* loaves and *four* thousand people an application for all time. *Seven*, twice repeated in the record, is the number of perfection, while *four* is the world number from which we learn symbolically that when the Lord opens His hand to remedy the woes of men, there is perfection of blessing, not merely for Israel, but for the whole world.

Then there is the truth that Jesus is "the

Bread of life for hungry hearts." Spiritually, we have nothing of ourselves which can quicken and support our souls, but in Christ there is true sustenance which all can appropriate by faith.

The thoughtful kindness of Jesus in refusing to send the multitude away exhausted and hungry and miraculously supplying their need teaches us that He is our kind, considerate, ever-watchful Provider, able to undertake for us no matter what necessities or circumstances may arise.

There is the further lesson of blessing for those with large hearts. The disciples had to give all the provisions they had on hand: no doubt some of them wondered why because, although in the miracle we have an illusion of the working of the supernatural in relation to the natural, by a positive creative act Jesus could have provided food for the hungry *without* the surrendered loaves and fishes. But what they gave was multiplied. The more they gave, the more there was for others.

Last of all, we must not forget the lesson of gratitude. Jesus "gave thanks" and "blessed" the food, turning thereby, the poor materials into a royal feast. The giving of thanks is a blessing upon our daily food. A grateful heart will bless, and in a sense, multiply our bread. Jesus was not ashamed to offer public thanks for temporal mercies —are we?

31. The Miracle of the Bethsaida Blind Man

(Mark 8:22-26)

It is Mark alone who records this miracle wrought at Bethsaida, not far distant from the scene of the miracle of the feeding of the 5,000. While some of the details of the miracle of the blind man closely resemble that of the deaf stammerer of Decapolis, the two miracles are, of course, different. Interested friends brought the blind man from his home into contact with the great Healer, just as the deaf man had not come on his own accord but was brought by others who desired his relief. Micklem says that, "Apparently those who brought him thought it was only necessary for Jesus to touch him in order to regain his sight (8: 22). But Jesus was not a miraculous theraputic machine: He dealt with individuals individually and personally and not in a mechanical way."

Jesus, meeting the man, gave His time and attention to him. Taking him by the hand, He led him to some distant place in order to avoid public excitement or idle curiosity on the part of the crowd, and performed a miracle different in operation than any of His other miracles which were all wrought instantaneously. Here is the only miracle brought about by a gradual process, for as we are to see it was wrought in two stages. The adaptation of the method of healing was similar to that of the recovery of the deaf man.

The first stage of the miracle was the application of moisture from our Lord's mouth to the eyes of the blind man. Here, as J. N. Darby puts it, "He uses that which was of Himself, that which possessed the efficacy of His own Person to perform the cure." Then Darby gives us this footnote: "Spittle, in connection with the sanctity of the rabbins, was highly esteemed by the Jews in this respect; but here its efficacy is connected with the Person of Him who used it!" This strange act "brought Jesus under ordained but despicable means," says Spurgeon. Pliny mentions that the use of spittle was a common human remedy in vogue at that time and that *saliva jejuna* was reckoned to be a remedy for blindness.

Christ's variety of methods in His healings proves that He was not bound to any one particular method of healing and that the outward operation was nothing of itself. Because of His sovereign will, He could change the outward *modus operandi*, or manner of working. When He used means, as here with His spittle or in bidding His disciples to anoint with oil (Mark 6:13. See James 5:14), He was only clothing the supernatural in the form of the natural. As the omnipotent One, He could heal with or without means, because He Himself was the true Source of healing and life.

Christ's question to the man, "Dost thou see ought?" indicates that the first visual movement is naturally towards the source of light. The man looked up and said, "I see men as trees walking," and this ability to describe what he saw reveals that he had not been born blind. Although he knew they were men he saw, he could not discern the shape and magnitude of the objects before him. Many have tried to explain this gradual cure in the imperfection of this blind man's faith. Did Jesus awaken in him a longing for complete restoration of sight by His first touch of his eyes? Without doubt, this

gradual work was a testimony of the free-ness of divine grace, "which is linked to no single way of manifestation, but works in divers manners, sometimes accomplishing only little by little what at other times it brings about in a moment." Our Lord's method certainly illustrates the progressive step in our spiritual enlightenment. At first, we do not see clearly; much of the old blindness remains; but with fuller faith and complete obedience, clarity of vision comes from Him who is not only the *Author* of our faith but also its Finisher.

Touching the man's eyes again, Jesus bade him look up, and this time complete sight was his, for he saw every man clearly. His vision was no longer blurred. Eye-surgeons of our day know what it is to heal defective sight by degrees. At first, a glimmer of light is allowed, for the optic nerve must grow accustomed to light before the eyeballs can stand the full light of day. The double benedictions of the hands of Jesus was effective, for the man saw clearly. If, in His spittle, Jesus gave the man a part of Himself, did virtue also stream from His person through His hands as He touched the man twice over? Trench gives us this quotation from Chemnitz, "He lays on His hands to show that His flesh is the instrument through which and with which the Eternal Word Himself accomplishes all His life-giving works." Anyhow, the fully restored sight proves that Jesus never leaves His work unfinished. "He saw" means *he looked stedfastly*, denoting the first exercise of his restored sight. Spurgeon, in his unique, suggestive way, supposes that after the divine touch and the man's eyes were fully opened, "the first person he saw was Jesus, for he had been taken away from the crowd, and could only see men at a distance. Blessed vision, to drink in the sight of that face, to perceive the beauties of that matchless Lover of souls."

The request of Jesus was explicit—the man was to go home, avoiding the town on the way so as not to publish the fact of the miracle. There was, of course, no need for the man to speak of this miracle to those who knew of his former blindness. The fact that he came home seeing was a silent proof of the miracle. The prescription of quietude was good for the man's spiritual discipline. It would save him from any hasty utterance of excitement over the restored boon of sight. Whether the man respected the request of Jesus any better than others who were blessed of Him, we are not told (Matthew 9:31; Mark 1:45; 7:36). It is to be hoped that in his gratitude, he did respect the wishes of Jesus, realizing that because of His divine wisdom He knew what was best, and also because "to obey was better than sacrifice, and to hearken than the fat of lambs" (I Samuel 15:22). Faith and obedience are what He asks of us. It is essential to follow His will, asking no questions and offering no objection.

Lessons of the miracle are obvious for, along with other miracles, this one has a symbolic aspect—it was an acted parable. One expositor suggests that it took two miracles of feeding to fully open the eyes of the disciples to the full glory of their Lord. We are not fully sanctified and enlightened all at once by some magical transformation without process or pain. While here below in the flesh, imperfect spiritual vision will be ours, even though we have been brought out of darkness into His most marvelous light. Cataracts form over the eyes of the soul, which in all His skill and tenderness He is able to remove. Once we enter the pearly gates of the Holy City and see Him face to face, then undimmed, eternal vision will be ours. Presently, our daily prayer should be that the Spirit might open the eyes of our understanding to discern more fully the divine will for life.

32. The Miracle of the Transfiguration

(Matthew 17:1-13; Mark 9:1-13; Luke 9:28-36; II Peter 1:16-18)

It is to be regretted that the majority of books covering the miracles of the gospels do not include a study of the miraculous associated with the Mount of Transfiguration, where God revealed how He had placed His treasure in an earthen vessel. On that "holy mount" we have many facets of the supernatural. This remarkable interlude in the life of our Lord is recorded in much the same language in the first three gospels, and all represent it as taking place about six to eight days after His first distinct announcement of His approaching death and resurrection. Matthew has *six days*, Luke *eight*. The one account excludes from, and the other includes in, his reckoning the day of the last event and the day of this event. Matthew says, "After six

days"—days of silence for we have no record of what transpired. Doubtless they were days of gloom for the disciples, for the strange declaration of the cross must have crushed their hearts. What happened on the mount occurred shortly before Christ's final departure from Galilee and between four to six days before His death (Luke 9:51). How we need special grace to approach and apprehend the foretaste of heaven described by the evangelists! Here we have "Christ's brief land of Beulah, with its delectable mountains." It may be found profitable to deal with the august theme before us in the three-fold way, *The transfigured Christ, the two heavenly visitors, the three awe-struck disciples.*

The transfigured Christ

Luke tells us that Jesus went up into an high mountain, probably Hermon, to pray. *Apart—to pray.* How true it is that although "He had not where to lay His head, He had always somewhere to pray." The night and the mountain were available to Jesus and He made good use of them. Although the shadows were thickening around Him, His refuge was in prayer, and if *He* found prayer the secret of His strength, how essential it is for us humans to make time and place for prayer. Further, it was while He was in the act of praying that a sudden blaze of glory enveloped Him so that the fashion of His countenance was altered and His raiment became white and glistening, or as Mark puts it, "white as snow, so as no fuller (or dyer) on earth could make them."

Everything about the night on that holy mount was supernatural. First of all, let us think of the transfiguration of Jesus Himself. As He prayed, He was "transfigured before them." The word for "transfigured" means not only an outward change of clothes or acts as fashion may dictate, but an inner, essential change. "The fashion of this world passeth away" (I Corinthians 7:31). Paul wants us not to be conformed to such a fleeting fashion but to be "transformed" or "transfigured," the change taking place by the renewing of the *mind* (Romans 8:29; 12:2; II Corinthians 3:18, etc.). As Vincent in his *Word Studies* points out, the description of the transfigured Saviour not only describes a change in His outward appearance, but an outflashing of His inner, essential divine nature. His transfiguration was prophetic of His revelation "as He is," in the glory which He had with the Father before the world was (John 17:5; I John 3:2). Deity shows through the glorified face and shining raiment of Christ. Such radiance was the revelation of His incarnate deity.

"His face did shine as the sun," or as Luke expresses it, "The fashion of His countenance became other than it had been." In full communion with His Father, divine glory flowed out into visible brightness. Such a transcendent manifestation was experienced in a lower degree by Moses whose face shone as he came down from the mount, and by Stephen whose face became "as the face of an angel" (Exodus 34:29; Acts 6:15). Ellicott writes of "the metamorphic power of prayer which invests features that have no form or comeliness with the rapture of devout ecstacy." William Pennefather, a saint of a past decade, was known as the man with "the glory face." Vincent says that the word "shining" or "glistering" is used of "a gleam from polished surfaces—arms, sleek horses, water in motion, the twinkling of the stars, lightning."

His veiled glory (John 1:14) also suffused His garments, changing them into a dazzling brightness. They became "white as the light," or as "snow"—a figure of speech which may have been suggested to Mark's vivid imagination by the surrounding snows of Hermon. Then there was the "bright cloud overshadowing" all upon the mount as Jesus conversed with Moses and Elijah. This was the *Shekinah* wrapping Him around—the same Shekinah glory which appeared above the Tabernacle Moses reared. God, now flesh and tabernacling with men in human form, has His Tabernacle covered with the same glory (Exodus 33:9; I Kings 8:10). To the Jews, this Shekinah represented the abiding presence of Jehovah, the symbol that He was with His people. The appearance at this moment on the mount witnessed to the fact that no tabernacle made by hands was now needed since Christ was the true Tabernacle of God. In Him the tabernacle of God was with men. "We beheld His glory," says Peter, in his reference to the Transfiguration. When Jesus turned aside from the Father's abode and took upon Himself the likeness of our flesh, He did not leave His glory behind but brought it with Him. Thus, what we have upon the

mount is the out-flashing of that inherent glory.

Adding to the supernaturalness of the occasion was the voice of the Father speaking out of the bright cloud, and saying, "This is My beloved Son in whom I am well pleased; hear ye Him." A similar commendation was heard at our Lord's baptism (Matthew 3:17). Then the divine Voice assured Christ, as the Son of Man, of the greatness of His Being. Now the same awesome Voice approves the Saviour's consecration in showing Himself obedient unto death. Amid His increasing sufferings and coming sacrifice, He was "satisfying" His Father's "good pleasure" as the one perfect sacrifice. This was the grand, climactic witness direct from heaven that Jesus was the One in whom the Old Testament prophecies emerged and found their fulfilment. Such a manifestation of glory confirmed Peter's previous confession, "Thou art the Christ, the Son of the living God." Here, where God called His Son *beloved*, He used a word meaning "most dearworthy."

A fact we must not forget as we meditate upon our Lord's transfiguration is that it actually represents His great refusal, for had He wished, He could have stepped into heaven from the mount. As Campbell Morgan expresses it in *Crises of the Christ*, He was "perfect in creation, perfect in probation, and was now ready to be perfected in glory." But He turned aside from the glory, came down to a valley of need, and set His face stedfastly toward Jerusalem where He died upon the cross so that countless myriads might share glory with Him (Hebrews 2:10). The glory of the mount was a counterpoise to the announcement of His death.

No wonder the disciples were awestruck by what Matthew calls a "vision," and in after days, as they looked back on the scene, they were to say, "We were eyewitnesses of His majesty." Such a supernatural vision confirmed their faith in His deity against the shock of troublous days ahead. The privileged three never got over such a blaze of glory. It gave them a sense of security as they came to face their own martyrdom for His sake (II Peter 1:14-18).

The two heavenly visitors

The miraculous is also indicated by the two heavenly visitors, Moses and Elijah who, although in glorified form, were recognizable by Peter even though he had never seen them in the flesh. Whether he recognized them by intuition or revelation does not alter the fact that these two Old Testament saints retained their identity. The sole theme of conversation between the transfigured Christ and the two glorified saints was Calvary. "They spake of His decease—His exodus (same word used in II Peter 1:15)—which He should accomplish at Jerusalem." What a spectacle that must have been as "pure and spotless humanity stands in the glory of unsullied light and holds familiar conversation with the spirits of just men!" In the best sense, Moses and Elijah were yet to be the heroic comforters of Christ, for they had known the sorrows of saviors. Peter had urged Christ not to speak of His death, but Moses and Elijah came all the way from heaven to talk about nothing else, and they discoursed about it with rapture. Did not He come into the world to die for sin, and to put away sin, by the sacrifice of Himself? (Hebrews 9:26). We were born to live— Jesus was born to die.

Why were these two Old Testament warriors chosen from among the myriads of saints in heaven to come to the mount and do homage to the Son of God? Both were chosen because of their relation to each other and because they were the proper representatives of the old dispensation about to end with the death and resurrection of Christ. Moses was the great representative of the law he brought from God to Israel from another mount, and under such a law the people lived from Moses to Christ. Elijah was the fitting representative of the goodly fellowship of the prophets and of prophecy. What a strenuous advocate of the law he was! He was also the ardent reformer of the people when they drifted from that law, and the giant wrestler who hazarded his life to defeat the corrupters of the law and preserve for posterity its heritage of blessing. Moses and Elijah appeared, therefore, to witness to the passing of the old order, and to hail the incoming of the new. Together they represented law and prophecy which, in Christ, are happily combined.

The three awe-stricken disciples

Although Christ had twelve disciples, He only took three with Him to the mount, indicating that the rest were not fit to bear such a supernatural vision. Was He helped by the presence of sympathetic souls? By choosing Peter, James, and John, Jesus confirmed these three as primates among the Twelve so that they might not lose faith because of his foretold sufferings (Matthew 16:21, 27, 28). Such a glorious experience was intended to confirm their faith in Christ's divine sonship and glory and also to prepare them for the dark days ahead, which already were overshadowing them.

Luke says that they were "heavy with sleep," and when "fully awake they saw His glory" (9:32). It would seem, however, from Matthew's account that they were not in slumber when the heavenly radiance of Christ was being manifested but that they were completely dazzled by such a blinding sight. They were "sore afraid," or "aghast by dread," over such a revelation of deity, but when touched by the divine hand, they opened their eyes and saw *Jesus*—Jesus as they had seen Him before His transfiguration, and they were comforted.

Overwhelmed by such glory and the presence of the glorified saints on the mount, Peter made one mistake—He wanted to fix the transient and to sacrifice the future for the present. He wanted the rapture to continue; but he was not permitted to build the three tabernacles, for earth is not heaven. It might have been consideration on Peter's part to build those booths out of brushwood lying near so that, because it was night, the heavenly visitors might retire after their interview, but heaven was a more delightful abode to them. As for Jesus, such a rough hut was a poor sort of dwelling for One who inhabits eternity, yet longs to dwell in the contrite heart. Peter forgot, as we are apt to, that "glimpses of heavenly glory are given, not to wean us from duty on earth, but to prepare us for the trials connected therewith," as the consideration of the next miracle will clearly show.

As we have seen, Paul teaches us that the experience of "the holy mount" is for the servant as well as for the Master. For all in Christ, there has come a transfiguration of standing and position, of character and life, of outlook and hope. One happy day we shall "behold His face in righteousness" and find ourselves completely satisfied when we "awake with His likeness."

33. The Miracle of the Demonic Boy

(Matthew 17:14-21; Mark 9:14-29; Luke 9:37-43)

What a striking study in contrast the previous miracle and this one offer! Jesus came from communion with His Father to contact with the Devil! The contrast is so marked, for the summit all is sublime but in the valley all is confused and deplorable. He descended from the harmony of fellowship with Moses and Elijah for some of the wildest and harshest discords of earth: from the Father's honor and glory, He now comes to face the hatred and murderous intents of the religious leaders, thirsting for His blood. On the mount we see the King in His supernatural splendor; below we have His disciples baffled and beaten. Heavenly beings above, demons and unbelieving disciples below. The mission of the mount, however, was for the valley of need. The same compassion that brought Jesus down from heaven to earth now brings Him down from the mount of rapture to the vale of suffering and service. There are too many who, like Peter, want to build their tabernacles away from all earth's sin and suffering. But if we are to rescue the perishing, we must be found where they are. Our Lord's first miracle after His transfiguration then, was the cure of the demoniac boy, the features of which are the distressed father, the demented son, the omnipotent Christ, the impotent disciples.

The distressed father

Comparing the three accounts of the miracle before us, we notice that Mark, as usual, supplies us with greater fulness of detail. The distressed father approached Jesus with all true humility and reverence. "He kneeled down to Him." As one of the multitude, he came forward to make a plea on behalf of the miserable case of his child, his only one. He certainly came in the right attitude to receive a blessing from the Healer, and his plea was accompanied with his tears. What a heartache must have been his! Love for, and anguish over, his lunatic boy made him bold. So while the scribes were nonplussed by Christ's appearing and the disciples depressed over their failure, a distressed father revealed an intense solicitude to secure Christ's help. While he could not hide a fear that perhaps his boy's case was too

hopeless to be healed, yet his plea in its weakness was linked to omnipotence.

The despairing father turned to Jesus Himself because he had been disappointed by the disciples, who should have been able to make potent use of the Saviour's name. "I spake to Thy disciples that they should cast it out, and they were not able." Challenged with the father's request, the disciples—the nine who were left below while the other three were on the mount —found themselves baffled. This new experience perplexed them, and they were humiliated and put to shame before the onlookers, specially the scribes who would likely sneer at the disciples because they could not cure the boy. So the anxious father, eager and desperate, turned to Jesus and said, "If Thou canst do anything, have compassion on us, and help us." What an approach to the Lord of all! How out of place were the *if* and *canst* in the appeal to Him who created the universe, and all that is therein, and who already had revealed His power over the Devil and his angels.

Christ's reply shifted the *canst* to the right quarter. "Bring him hither to me. . . . If thou *canst* believe. . . ." What little faith the man had quickened under Christ's reply. "I believe; help thou my unbelief," and he soon realized that "all things are to him that believeth."

The demented boy

In order to understand the greatness of Christ's cure, let us gather together what the gospels record of the boy's terrible symptoms—severe convulsions, foaming at the mouth, grinding of the teeth, and general rigidity of body. Because of sudden unexpected attacks, he often fell into the fire and into the water. Another symptom overtaking the boy because of the evil possession was deafness and dumbness, the dumbness being only in respect of articulate sounds. It was not a natural defect, nor were the needful organs for speech wanting. All of these calamities came as the consequence of his unhappy condition and they left him so emaciated that he seemed as one whose very springs of life were dried up.

The word *lunatic* used to describe his condition means, "moonstruck," *luna* being the Latin word for "moon." Epilepsy, from which the boy suffered, was regarded as a disgraceful disease and was supposed to have been inflicted on persons who had sinned against the *moon,* and it was believed that changes in the moon governed the period of epileptic seizures. It was also looked upon as a "sacred" or "divine" disease, as being a direct supernatural infliction. That the boy's fits were sudden and lasted remarkably long is indicated by the phrase that the evil "hardly departeth from him." The demoniac's paroxysm became more violent when before Jesus, for he fell on the ground, rolled about and foamed at the mouth, as Mark in special detail tells us. The convulsion came on when the demoniac saw the Lord—*"When he saw him,"* etc. What a sore trial this demented child, the only child, must have been to that heart-broken father! For a fuller understanding of the implications of demon possession, the reader is referred to our study on the Gadarene and also to the chapter on the subject in the author's volume, *All About Angels in the Bible.*

The omnipotent Christ

No case, however, no matter how depraved or demon-ridden, is too hard for Christ to whom all power was given. After rebuking the faithless and perverse generation, which rebuke was obviously addressed both to the scribes and the disciples, Jesus rebuked the devil, or demon, possessing the boy, and he departed out of him, and "the child was cured from that very hour." After inquiring about the boy's condition from his father, Jesus with solemn adjuration, ordered the foul spirit out of the boy and forbade it to return. The result was that, after shrieking and being violently convulsed, the patient became like a corpse, and onlookers thought he was dead. "I charge thee," and the demon dared not disobey that order. Then any return into the boy was barred—"Enter no more into him."

In his chapter on this miracle, Canon Guy King, whose rich expositions should be more widely known, summarized it thus:

> The boy was mad.
> The father was sad.
> But the devil was mad
> And the crowd was glad.

The dear father had witnessed so many relapses that Christ's complete and permanent cure must have thrilled his heart. Taking the boy's hand, Jesus raised him up and delivered him to his father, thus crowning His work of healing grace. "Calm-

ness and peace and self-possession were seen instead of the convulsive agony. The spiritual power of the Healer had overcome the force, whether morbid or demoniac, which was the cause of the boy's sufferings."

Is it not wonderful and assuring to know that there is no impotence in Christ, that every woe of the human heart yields to His control? Demons and men recognize His sway.

The impotent disciples

Before we conclude this meditation, there are two aspects of the miracle we must dwell upon, namely, the amazement of the multitude and the shamefacedness of the disciples. When the multitude saw Him, they were "greatly amazed." Some writers suggest that this amazement was caused because Christ's face and person were still glistening. Something of the glory which had radiated from it on the mount still remained and, as with Moses, the skin of His face still shone. Yet, as Trench points out to us, the effect of the shining face was different. When Moses came down from the mount, the people were "afraid to come nigh him," for the glory on his face was "a threatening glory, the awful and intolerable brightness of the Law. But the glory of God shining in the face of Jesus, though awful too, is an *attractive* glory, full of grace and beauty; it draws men to Him, does not drive them from Him."

As to the disciples, we have first of all their question, "Why could not we cast him out?" This question from the disciples left below when Jesus went apart with Peter, James and John suggests that they could not see any reason for this failure. Christ's reply was direct and emphatic. "Because of your unbelief . . . this kind goeth not out but by prayer and fasting." Here He emphasized the necessity and power of faith, and the need of intercession and self-denial. Their great lack was that of faith—not lack of intellectual assent to all Christ stood for, but the lack of that living faith in divine omnipotence. Wherever there is such faith, even though small as a grain of mustard seed, the mountains become plains.

"They could not"—what a pathetic phrase, one that carries a sting with it. "It is still a pain and a wound to Christ to see His Church stand impotent and depressed amidst the woes she might cure, if only she could stir up the power that is in her." It was somewhat interesting to observe, as this study was being prepared, a report in the daily press of a conference of the House of Laity of the Church of England which met in the Church House, Westminster, London, the day before. One of the speakers, Arthur Macmillan, brother of the British prime minister, Harold Macmillan, declared his belief in demons and evil spirits. He is reported to have said,

"First, evil spirits or demons do exist that do, in certain cases, affect human beings.

Second, that the casting out of evil spirits is part of our Lord's commission to His Church."

Mr. Macmillan disagreed with the modern churchmen who explain Bible references to possession by evil spirits as another expression of psychiatric disorders. Then he urged a consideration of exorcism, and his resolution was carried by a large majority of the bishops present. Are we failing to appropriate by faith all the power the Lord has in Himself, and of which He is willing to make us the recipients?

As for abiding lessons of the miracle, one is that of the vicarious, as well as the victorious, power of faith. "The success of the father for his child is typical of a whole class of our Lord's acts of mercy," says Laidlaw. "One half of the detailed healings in the gospel history were wrought at the prayer of friends. This father remains a monument of faith, timid yet true, because his love for his boy made him that. His 'Have compassion on *us*, and help *us*,' like the heathen mother's 'Have mercy on *me*,' was highly honored by Jesus." Is such a faith for the relief of the distressed ours?

Then, as with all the Lord's miracles of healing, this one has also a spiritual parable. Sinners are in bondage to Satan, deaf to God's truth, dumb in utterance to His praise, and no human power can emancipate them from their depravity. When, however, they are stirred to realize their appalling need and pray, "Lord, I believe," then the miracle of grace takes place in their heart.

34. The Miracle of the Coin in the Fish's Mouth

(Matthew 17:27)

Abiding in Capernaum, probably in the home of Peter, Jesus spent His time in-

structing His disciples in His coming death and resurrection. He wanted His sayings to sink down into their hearts. Although they were not to look upon His death as a mere foreboding of disaster, nevertheless they were "exceeding sorry," for as yet they did not fully understand all that Jesus was to accomplish by His passion. How mistaken was their sorrow! Was not the death they feared to be the cure of all sorrow and the fount of all joys? What triumph would have been theirs had the Master's "He shall be raised again" really gripped their hearts!

The miracle before us is not only remarkable in itself, but also in the fact that Matthew, the onetime taxgatherer, alone records it. Further, his gospel is that of the King and His kingdom. Why, therefore, should the King's Son and King of the Temple be subject to any tax? Coming to Capernaum, the tax collector met Peter with the question, "Doth not your Master pay tribute?" The word for *tribute* here is not the same used in verse 25, where it represents a poll-tax. The word in verse 24 is *didrachma* and means "half-shekel" —about 35 cents. It was the temple rate paid by every male Israelite above the age of 20 (Exodus 30:11-16; II Chronicles 24: 9). The *toll* was duty on goods—the *tribute* upon individuals. This rate or atonement money was collected from Jews in foreign countries and paid into the Temple treasury and used to defray Temple services. The collection of this religious rate was not regarded with the hatred and contempt which the publicans who gathered taxes for the Romans received.

Those responsible for the collection of the shekels for the service of the Temple came to Peter and asked if his Master paid the *didrachma*. Perhaps those collectors had an idea that the Prophet of Nazareth had evaded, or disclaimed, the necessity of such a payment, or they may have felt that He was only an itinerant preacher, and therefore liable for the impost as well as others. These foes of Christ, ever active in trying to trap Christ, were eager to know if He had transgressed the law in this respect. Their question as to whether Christ had paid the half-shekel was asked in a mild manner. Had the taxgatherer been asking about the tribute payable to Caesar, they would have adopted a harsher attitude.

Peter erred in answering the inquiry in

the affirmative. Anxious that his Master should be esteemed a good Jew, and without consulting Him, he said "Yes," acnowledging thereby His liability to pay a fitting tax as if He were a mere son of Jacob. Peter's reply implied that Jesus had paid the tax and would continue to do so as every devout Jew should. Now it was the turn of Jesus to ask a question, which He did as Peter came into the house after answering the question of the taxgatherers. "What thinkest thou, Simon? of whom do the kings of the earth take custom or tribute? of these our children, or of strangers?" We have the phrase, "Jesus prevented him." The word *prevented* means "anticipated," meaning that Jesus did not wait for Peter to tell Him the question of the taxgatherer. He anticipated Peter in speaking about it. He knew all about the question and its answer, revealing thereby His omniscience, which is an attribute of deity. Christ proved to Peter His divine knowledge of that which took place at a distance from Himself. The blundering apostle answered Christ's question in the only possible way— "of strangers." Then Jesus said to him, "Then are the children free."

He spoke of Peter and Himself as both children of the King of the Temple, and as such, free from the tribute, but rather than cause any offense, Jesus arranges for the money to be found in a most miraculous way. "Lest we should stumble them." The considerate Christ "would rather pay any figure, however unjust or objectionable, than endanger the testimony of God by provoking invidious comments from the unregenerate. How little has His example been heeded by Christians when smarting under a sense of wrong!" We are thus brought to the miracle of the coin in the fish's mouth, of which several interpretations have been given.

There are those, like Laidlaw, who affirm that the story Matthew gives us is not strictly a miracle narration at all, for the miracle is not actually told. It does not say whether Peter succeeded in finding the piece of money. The uses of the narrative, says Laidlaw, are two-fold: *doctrinal*, for what is taught is the place of Jesus in the kingdom of heaven—His own place of sonship by right of nature—and *ethical*. The moral enforced is that greatness in the kingdom is best proved by service and humility. "Lest we cause them to stumble" provides a lesson of meekness and wisdom.

Then the rationalists, who would exhaust the incident of its miraculous element, offer the absurd explanation that the Lord bade Peter go and catch as many fish as would sell for the required sum to pay the tax. We also reject this purely allegorical interpretation of the miracle. The command of Jesus to Peter to go and catch a fish bristles with the miracle of divine foreknowledge and planning. Peter went to the sea and cast a hook—the only time in the New Testament when a hook is used in connection with fishing. Only a single fish was caught, and never before or after had Peter caught a fish like that one. Catching the fish, Peter found in its mouth the piece of money which Jesus said he would find there. We have no need to intensify the miraculous by affirming, without warrant, that that piece of silver was *created* for the occasion. It is the nature of most fish to catch at anything bright, hence the various records of articles of precious metal being found in fishes.

The miracle before us did not consist only in our Lord's foreknowledge—a second sight He possessed to an eminent degree —that the fish would yield the necessary money, but also in the fact that the first fish that came to Peter's hook contained the precise sum that had been indicated. It was the purpose of Christ's will—a will to which all creation was obedient—that guided that single fish out of myriads in the lake, to the hook of Peter. The psalmist reminds us that the Lord controls all things, even "the fish of the sea." Further, because "the silver and the gold are his," He was able that day to bring the fish and the coin together. So, He not only *knows* all things but can *do* all things. "All things were made *by* Him, and *for* Him." It was therefore through the exercise of His deity that Jesus made a fish produce sufficient money to pay the temple dues.

Incidentally, the failure to meet those dues without a miracle indicates the self-imposed poverty Jesus endured. The small amount needed—one shekel, about 70 cents —was not on hand. Creation had, therefore, to supply the small sum at His command. Jesus and His disciples returned from their journeys, occupying some three or four weeks, and were penniless with not so much as a *stater*—a shekel—between them. "Rich—yet for our sakes He became poor." Richard Glover gives us the application that—"He who became penniless that we may be rich will find money for His needs in strangest ways." We must not, however, affirm that Christ resorted to a miracle because of His poverty. Such a way of paying the assessment would have meant working a miracle for His own advantage which, as we have previously pointed out, was contrary to His supernatural acts. The Temple tax was paid by a miracle to keep before the minds of His disciples the glorious fact that He was the Son of God with power—and He paid it in a way to show that He had supreme dominion over the whole creation.

The piece of money found in the fish's mouth was, as the Greek expresses it, a *stater*, or a full shekel, two didrachmas —half a shekel for Christ, half a shekel for Peter—"for Me and thee." Just enough was found, adequate to the present necessity—no more, no less. Jesus put Himself alongside of Peter as sharing His position and relationship. How astounding is His grace! No longer servants, but sons through the Son of God (Galatians 3:26). Jesus takes common part with His own, not by a necessity of nature but because of His condescending grace. Ransomer and ransomed are one. "I ascend unto *My* Father and *your* Father, and to *My* God, and *your* God" (John 20:17).

The tax was paid in such a way that payment of it was an act of condescension by, and on the part of, the King's Son. As Fausset puts it, "As son of the Temple's King, He might claim exemption from the Temple tribute, but His dignity shone only brighter by His submission." Thus the motive of the miracle was to avoid giving needless offense and leaves us with the lesson of obeying the apostolic injunction, "If it be possible, as much as lieth in you, live peaceable with all men" (Romans 12:18).

35. The Miracle of the Man Born Blind

(John 9)

This miracle, which John alone records, has a somewhat striking setting. It was an illustration of the remarkable utterance on the previous day of Jesus as "the Light of the world" (8:12). The light of divine salvation in His face was to overcome the darkness of man's moral, and physical blindness. Thus, as the Light, He was to give a blind man sight. Trench, in his opening remarks on this miracle, says that it was "most probable that this work of grace and power crowned the day of long debate with Jewish adversaries, which, beginning at John 7:34, reaches to the end of chapter 10—the history of the woman taken in adultery being only an interruption and an intercalation easily betraying itself as such."

The last verse of the previous chapter says that His foes took up stones to stone Him, but that He passed through the midst of those who sought to kill Him. Those stones "were the last argument of his foes." Did Jesus disappear miraculously? Although He had to escape for His life because of the fury of His enemies, Jesus was entirely self-possessed and composed, so much so that He took note of the misery and need of the blind beggar on the roadside, and stopping with deliberation, leisurely healed him. Twice over in the context we have the phrase "passed by" (8:59; 9:1). In a supernatural way, "Jesus passed by" in defiance of those who sought to stone Him, then "He passed by" the blind man, and taking note of the man's misery and need, He tarried to heal him without any requests on his part. Our Lord knew that, in spite of the murderous animosity of His enemies, He was immortal until His work was finished. "I must work the works of Him that sent Me"—and the Devil, demons, or evil men were not able to frustrate that holy task. None could hurt him or "penetrate with word and stone the encasing envelope of the presence of God. Secure in that protection, He was able to go and come, fearless and unharmed, serene and quiet, restful and peaceful, blessing and blessed."

This Sabbath miracle, which irritated the Jewish leaders because of their distorted views of the Sabbath, can be divided into these sections: The plight of the blind man, the question of the disciples, the answer of Jesus, the cure of the blind beggar, the division among the Pharisees.

The plight of the blind man

First of all, then, we have the sad, hopeless plight of the man John describes. He was *born* blind, the only blind person in the gospels referred to this way. It was this fact that gave the case its special feature because "since the world began, was it not heard that any man opened the eyes of one that was born blind' (9:32). Further, it was because of this calamity that he had to beg for a living. "Sitting and begging denotes the customary position, causing him to be well-known to wayside crowds as he appealed for alms. Probably, it was near the Temple that this man sat and begged, for beggars were found near its gates to ask alms (Acts 3:2).

The question of the disciples

The sight of the beggar and the knowledge that he had been born blind prompted the question of the disciples, "Who did sin, this man, or his parents, that he was born blind?" With the suffering of the man, they connect the idea of sin which in some way was responsible for his affliction—that his special suffering was the result of special sin (Luke 13:1-4). The disciples felt that one of two reasons accounted for the man's plight—either he himself had sinned or his parents had. The questioners, however, must have felt the self-contradiction involved in the first part of their question for the fact that the blind man's affliction reached back to his birth at once excluded and condemned the uncharitable suspicion that personal sin was responsible for his blindness. There was also prevalent among the Jews the idea of a previous existence, some kind of transmigration of souls, and because of that the disciples may have implied, "Did this man so sin in some former state of existence as to come into this world blind?"

As any former sin was impossible, the next part of the question is not difficult to understand—"or his parents." It was a common Jewish belief that the merits or demerits of parents would appear in their children and that the thoughts of a mother might affect the moral state of her unborn offspring. It is common knowledge that certain diseases are entailed upon children by the iniquity of their parents. The second commandment speaks of iniquities of fathers being inflicted upon the children. But while it is the general law under the government of God that suffering is the result of sin, Jesus revealed that there are exceptions to such a law.

The answer of Jesus

The answer of Jesus was explicit that in this case neither the man himself nor his parents had sinned. By such a reply our Lord did not imply that either the blind man or his parents were absolutely sinless. All He said was that the chastisement of blindness had not been inflicted on him because of sin (Exodus 20:5). Nor did He

deny that infirmities often *are* the punishment of sin (Deuteronomy 28:22; I Corinthians 11:30; James 5:15). He emphatically affirmed the real reason for the beggar's blindness, namely, that "the works of God should be made manifest by him." Mysterious as this may appear, our Lord declared by such an answer that not *all* the suffering existing in the world is the result of sin. God permitted the man to be born blind that through his blindness His power in Christ might be manifested to others in its removal. The man was born blind that by divine power *on,* and *in,* him, he might be made to see, not only physically, but spiritually. "He was born blind for the sake of his own spiritual and eternal good that he might be led to the perception and acceptance of Jesus as the Son of God and, in turn, because of his experience, become a channel of divine grace to others." When we come to Lazarus we shall see that his sickness was not the result of any sin but was permitted that "the Son of God may be glorified thereby." We may not be able to read the meaning of our tears on this side of heaven, but once with Him, who never causes any child of His one unnecessary tear, we shall understand His wise and good reasons for permitted trials. Then we shall—

> Bless the hand that guided,
> And the heart that planned.

This man's blindness, then, was traced back to the divine counsel, and although allowed by God, was yet overruled by Him, for His own glory and for the sufferer's highest good. (See John 11:6; Romans 5:20; 8:28; 9:17; 11:25, 32, 33).

The care of the blind beggar

The details given of the relief of the blind man suggest that they are stated by an eyewitness of the miracle. First of all, Jesus spat on the ground and made clay of the spittle. Physicians of that time had applied such means to cases of post-natal blindness, but congenital blindness had always been regarded as incurable. As we have already indicated, no instance of the contrary had ever been heard of. A marked feature of this man's case is that he never requested a cure, nor was he brought by others to Jesus to heal, as in the case of the blind man of Bethsaida. In his total blindness and evidently unacquainted with the healing ministry of Jesus, how surprised the blind beggar must have been when Jesus began to cure him of his blindness!

As to what has been said about the remedial properties of old-time saliva, there can be added the accounts Vincent gives us of its peculiar virtue, not only as a remedy for diseases of the eye, but generally as a charm, so that it was employed in incantations. *Persius,* describing an old crone handling an infant, says, "She takes the babe from the cradle, and with her middle finger moistens its forehead and lip with spittle to keep away the evil eye." *Pliny* says, "We are to believe that by continually anointing each morning with fasting saliva, that is, before eating, inflammation of the eyes are prevented."

It would seem as if the action of covering the eyes of the blind man with spittle-clay was better calculated to make a seeing man blind than to make a blind man see. We would have thought that such a mixture would have sealed the eyes more firmly. What then was the design of the application of the plaster of moistened clay? Some expositors see in the use of the clay a symbolism to be traced back to creation, when man was formed of the dust of the earth, the thought being that our Lord will here "exercise the same creative power as that which made man, and will complete, by the gift of sight, the man, who had hitherto been maimed and without the chief organ of sense."

The primary reason of placement of the spittle-clay upon the man's eye sockets was to evoke hope and expectation in him. The latent power of faith had to be stirred, and the sufferer made conscious of the fact that it was Jesus, whom he could not see but could feel, who was the Healer. So the divine hand touched the sightless eyes, leading the blind man to expect a cure, hence his prompt obedience to the Lord's command. Another reason for the application of the moist clay may have been the conviction of those that stood by that virtue was not so much in the use of means, but in the Healer Himself. While He used natural remedies as conductors or channels to convey His grace (II Kings 4:41; Isaiah 38:21), He was yet able to manifest His divine power without means, as in other cases of blindness (Matthew 9:27-30; 20:30-34). That Sabbath day, then, both the blind man and all who stood by were made conscious of the fact that, although He

used the medium of clay, the actual power to heal was in Him alone. By using ordinary means, He taught men that the healing powers of nature are His gracious gift, and that they are increased at the Giver's will.

The command to go and wash in the pool of Siloam further encouraged the man, who could not see the compassionate look in the eyes of Jesus, but felt that through the applied plaster, and now the commanding word his ear heard, that He was the One to help him. Such a command was a still further test of the man's faith, to confirm and strengthen it. Habershon remarks: "It seemed useless for a man who had been born blind to do such a simple thing as this in order to obtain his sight; but, having obeyed, he was cured. . . . The blessing still comes by the way of obedience." It was so with Naaman. The blind man, without delay or reluctance, obeyed the divine command, and went, and washed, and saw. How commendable is the promptitude of his obedience!

Healing resulted immediately, and the wonder the cured man must have felt is expressed in that one phrase of simple majesty: "He washed, and came seeing." The washing was necessary to remove the clay from his eyes. Usually, in the recovery of sight, seeing is a thing which needs to be learned, and that slowly. But the "acquired perceptions of sight" were not necessary here, for Jesus gave the man perfect sight so that he could see clearly as soon as his eyes were opened. Expositors have dwelt upon the symbolic character of the means used by Christ for the man's recovery of sight. The clay, for example, symbolizes our Lord's humanity and the water of the pool, the ministry of the Holy Spirit. "Thus when a man apprehends by the Spirit's aid the momentous fact that the mighty God became human for his salvation, and that He who walked here abased was indeed the 'Sent' One of the Father, his spiritual blindness is dispelled for ever." Trench says that, "The waters of Siloam, in which the blind man washed and was illuminated, may well have been to John a type of the waters of baptism (I Peter 3:21), or indeed of all the operations of grace by which the spiritually blind eyes are opened; the very name of the pool had therefore for him a presaging fitness, which by this notice he would stamp as more than accidental."

The division among the Pharisees

The impact of the miracle on others was of an opposite nature as a study of the question and friendly discussion of the neighbors and the division among the Pharisees reveals. The questions of the chapter make a profitable study.

"*How* were thine eyes opened?" (10)

"*Who* is He?" (36)

"*What* did He to thee?" (26)

"*Where* is He?" (12)

"*What* sayeth thou of Him?" (17)

"*Dost* thou believe on the Son of God?" (35)

"*Are* we blind also?" (40)

We have in the examination of the healed man one of the most striking instances of opposition to Christ shown by the Jewish authorities, with the contrast between the "we know" of the Pharisees (24) and the "I know" of the man (25). It would take a chapter in itself to discourse upon the official pride, the utter formalism, the deliberate bias, and the absolute falsehood on the part of those who were determined to reject Christ. The Pharisees were divided into two camps, "some reasoning that Jesus could not be of God because He had broken the Sabbath—the old charge; others, Nicodemus-like, standing on the fact that a man who was a sinner could not do such things."

Amid all the wrangling, however, is the healed man applying the logic of common sense: "If this Man were not of God, He could do nothing." Disowned by his parents and cast out of the synagogue by the Pharisees, the man had the benediction of Him who Himself knew the weariness and pain of excommunication. It is interesting to note the man's progress of knowledge respecting his Healer. He speaks of Him as a Man (11), a Prophet (17), from God (33), Son of God. Is ours an ever-deepening knowledge of Him? Is ours the confession, "Whereas I was blind, now I see?" This man believed, confessed and worshiped. How commendable are the man's implicit faith, his fearless confession of his healing to his neighbors and the hostile Pharisees, his utter disregard of consequences because of his expulsion from the synagogue, his brave confession, his simplicity in confounding the wise, his belief in, and worship of, the Son of God! May grace be ours to emulate such traits!

36. The Miracle of the Infirm Woman

(Luke 13:10-17)

This narrative, peculiar to Luke, who does not state the time and place of the miracle, simply tells us that it was wrought in one of the synagogues on a Sabbath day. His description indicates that it is the report of a trained observer, which Luke, as a physician and gifted historian, was. The writer does not tell us the exact synagogue where the miracle took place. Synagogues were in every place and in these, on every Sabbath, prayers were offered and the Old Testament read and expounded (4:16, 17; Acts 13:14, 15; 15:21).

On no day of the week was our Lord so closely watched by His adversaries as the Sabbath, in the hope that they might trap Him in some breach of the law concerning it. What those blind leaders of the blind did not understand in their unbelief and perverseness was that they were condemning the very One who gave the law from the fiery mount. Their sin was heightened by the fact that they were supposed to be the religious leaders of God's chosen people. Another aspect of the comparative prominence and frequency of the Master's Sabbath day cures is that by the working of so many miracles on this day, He consecrated it to the purposes of His Gospel. The salient features of the miracle we are now to consider are the crippled woman, the healing Christ, the cavilling ruler, the grateful crowd.

The crippled woman

The physical condition of the woman was pitiable in the extreme. For eighteen long years she had endured her deformity, described first of all as "a spirit of infirmity" which does not mean that she was of a weak and infirm spirit. The phrase denotes one of those mysterious derangements of the nervous system, having their rise in the mind rather than in the body. Her physical curvature was the consequence of mental obliquity, making her melancholy. Thus her strange malady was partly physical and partly mental. She was "bowed together, and could in no wise lift up herself." "Bowed together" is a phrase found nowhere else in the New Testament, and it indicates a dislocation of the vertebrae of the spine. What an expressive picture this is of every man's spiritual condition through sin—bowed down, unable to look up into the face of his God, and without strength to remedy his evil plight (Psalm 40:12; Romans 5:6). Then Christ's description, "whom Satan hath bound," does imply that she was a case of diabolical possession. Paul speaks of his thorn in the flesh as being a messenger of Satan to buffet him (II Corinthians 12:7). "True to its principle of contrast, this book (Luke) gives Satan a prominent place." Such a phrase, of course, shows that the woman's calamity had a deeper root than a physical.

Then Jesus spoke of this suffering woman as "a daughter of Abraham," who was better in His eyes than the ox or ass about which He chided the Pharisees. Her given title suggests that she was one of the inner circle of pious Israelites "waiting for the consolation of Israel" (2:25; 19:9). As a "daughter of Abraham," she was possessed of Abraham's faith and such faith had not to tarry for healing because it was the Sabbath day. Faith, not works of ceremonial observance, is the standing principle of blessing from God (Romans 4:5-16). This inheritress of Abraham was in the right place to be healed. Her terrible crippled state could not keep her from the house of God. In the synagogue, as her habitual custom was, she was present that day when Jesus attended to worship. Had she been absent that day, what a blessing she would have lost! "What good cheer is in this story for those who, amid bodily infirmities, mental oppression, or household burdens and afflictions, find their way statedly to God's house."

The healing Christ

The condition of the woman appealed to the sensitive spirit of Jesus who noticed her bent form and called to her and said, "Woman, thou art loosed from thine infirmity." We are not told whether she had known of Jesus, far less that she knew that the divine Healer would be in the synagogue that Sabbath day. She did not apply to Him for healing; neither did He wait to be asked. Jesus saw her, and her plight singled her out as special object of His mercy. As Laidlaw expresses it:

Her bent form and furrowed face were to Him as a book in which He read the story of her eighteen years' bondage and patient struggle to sustain her infirmity. Her faithful attendance at divine worship, and perhaps other features to which we have

no clue, showed Him her genuine religious and spiritual character.

Her habitual devotion, and therefore her faith, make her worthy and receptive of the healing power of Jesus. Trench suggests that her presence in the synagogue was "a tacit seeking of that aid."

Jesus laid His hand on the woman and immediately she was made straight. Such bodily contact was a help to the woman's faith (See Matthew 9:29). Chrysostom says, He lays also His hands on her, that we may learn that the holy body possessed the power and energy of the Word of God." "Thou art loosed"—this is the only passage in the New Testament where this word is used of disease. "Medical writers use it of releasing from disease, relaxing tendons, and taking off bandages." Accompanying the Master's word of power was a current of new life entering the woman, so that her bonds, spiritual and physical, were loosened. "She was made straight." The word used here to describe her immediate erectness after eighteen years is also employed in connection with the *setting up* of the tabernacle of David, and of *lifting up* the hands which hang down (Acts 15:16; Hebrews 12:12). Hobart says of the miracle:

In addition to the medical words used in describing it, there are traces of medical writing. After mentioning the length of time the woman labored under the infirmity, Luke states the several stages of the process of recovery—first the relaxing of the contracted muscles of the chest; and as this of itself would not have been sufficient to give her an erect posture, on account of the stiffening of the muscles through many years, the second part of the operation is described by the removal of the curvature, and the strength to stand erect.

For this immediate, unasked-for act of divine power, there was immediate gratitude, for the woman "glorified God." She poured forth her joy in a continuous strain of praise, as the phrase implies. Doubtless others in the synagogue, friends of the healed woman, also glorified God (Matthew 9:8; 15:31), but her grateful piety broke forth into an irrepressible thanksgiving to the gracious Author of her cure which became a voluntary act of praise before all the people.

The cavilling ruler

But what a different effect the miracle had on the ruler of the synagogue (see Matthew 21:15, 16). The blessed woman poured adoration upon her Healer, but the ruler poured his anger upon Him. The ruler "answered with indignation" that there were six other days in the week in which to work without profaning the Sabbath. Had there been a spark of spiritual discernment in the narrow mind of the offended presiding elder, he would have recalled the ancient psalm which calls upon men to bless the Lord "who healeth all thy diseases" (Psalm 103). But instead he blazed forth his indignation and raised a question which Ellicott explains in this way:

> The traditional law for the work of the Jewish physician was that he might act in his calling in cases of emergency, life and death cases, but not in chronic diseases, such as this. This law the ruler of the synagogue wished to impose as a check upon the work of the Healer here. . . . We can scarcely fail to think of "the beloved physician" as practicing his art for the good of men, his brothers, on the Sabbath, as on other days. . . . For such a one it would be a comfort unspeakable to be able to point to our Lord's words and acts as sanctioning his own practice.

Our Lord answered His adversary with such unusual severity as to shame him into silence. Not daring to attack either the Lord Himself, or even the woman, in a covert and cowardly manner he spoke to the crowd (13:14). But Jesus answered him in a well-merited manner which silenced all His adversaries and won the admiration of His hearers. "Thou hypocrite!" The Pharisees themselves did not hesitate to loosen their oxen and asses from the stalls and lead them to watering on a Sabbath, so why criticize Christ for unloosing a Jewess, a possessor of Abraham's faith and therefore better than an ox or ass, of her terrible burden? Every word of Christ's answer told as He laid bare the hypocrisy of those Pharisees. When God prescribed the Sabbath for man, forbidding him to work therein, He did not thereby bind His own hands and make it improper for Himself to work, mercifully, on that day. As the Lord of the Sabbath, nothing, not even such a day, can stay Him in His ministry of grace and power.

The grateful crowd

While His adversaries attacked Him and then were ashamed, the people around "rejoiced for all the glorious things that were done by Him." The phrase "were done" actually means "are being done" and denotes the "things" being then in progress. Such a benediction must have gladdened the Healer's heart and at the same time shrivelled up the ungrateful hearts of His critics.

What is the lesson to be drawn from this miracle? Why, there are many spirits bound with infirmity! Sin has made them crooked, and they look downward to the earth rather than upward to the skies. They are in dire need of the loosening of the fetters of their iniquity, and Christ alone can perform the miracle of majesty and mercy whereby they can walk straight before Him and before man. If the woman's condition appealed to the heart of Jesus, how moved He must be by the countless millions bound by Satan! The question is, Do we share His vision and compassion, and are we striving to bring the sin-bound to Him, whose "truth has still its ancient power?"

37. The Miracle of the Dropsical Man

(Luke 14:1-6)

This last Sabbath healing of Christ's follows more or less the pattern of the miracle just considered. Here we have another Sabbath day incident, not in a synagogue this time, but in the house of one of Israel's chief ecclesiastics who occupied a high position in the organization of Phariseeism. Have you ever wondered why the Pharisees invited Jesus to this Sabbath feast? Was their motive an hostile one? We read that as the guests were eating that they "watched" Jesus. Because of this suspicious attitude nothing more need be said concerning such an attitude of the host and his friends towards their Guest. They were sitting at the table with God manifested in flesh, and they "watched" Him, yet they were so blind that they knew Him not. Jesus had accepted the invitation in love, even though it had not been given in good faith, for their close and more accurate watching of Him was to discover an accusation against Him.

Some expositors suggest that the dropsical man was brought to the feast purposely—though unconsciously on his part. Knowing of Christ's compassion, His malignant adversaries laid a snare for Him. When He saw the afflicted man, would He again profane the Sabbath by one of His healings? The result of such a plot, the dropsical man himself was no party to, must have astonished the company. Whether He was invited out of respect (7: 36), or idle curiosity, or in craft, He used the occasion for the shame of His foes.

Those Sabbath feasts were an integral part of the social life of the Jews, the day being one for festal entertainment. Plutarch said of these feasts, "The Hebrews honor the Sabbath day chiefly by inviting each other to drinking and intoxication." Religious though they were, the Pharisees did not practice a rigorous austerity of the Sabbath, but turned it into a day of riot and excess. They had no compunction of conscience about feasting on such a day, but to heal the sick was unforgiveable (Mark 3:1-6). Because Jesus came eating and drinking with publicans and sinners, He accepted invitations to feasts (15:1, 2), knowing full well that He could use them as platforms upon which to display His grace and power.

The unnamed man Jesus saw at the feast "had the dropsy," which was the usual way of marking such a sufferer in medical language. He is the only dropsical case referred to in the gospels. Whether he was present as an invited guest, invited by one of the richer Pharisees in order to parade his hospitality, or came in order to be healed, we are not told. The term Luke used to describe the man's condition was a strictly technical one. Luke's training as a physician influenced his style and language in his gospel and the Acts, both which abound in technical phraseology. This is why he, more than any other writers, made specific inquiries as to the diseases Jesus healed. As to "dropsy" itself, the same was and is generally considered to be a symptom of an organic disease—usually disease of the heart or of the kidneys. Micklem reckons that the man Jesus healed suffered from some kind of an "hysterical" affection. What we call "dropsy" manifests itself in edema or swelling of various parts of the body.

Jesus took the man, "healed him, and let him go." Healing was effected by actual contact. At His touch, the disease fled and the healed man was allowed to leave the feast before Jesus resumed His conversation with His cavilling critics. The cure was unasked for but graciously given, and through its performance Christ enforced His teaching, for He appealed to His critics' acts of humanity of their animals on the Sabbath. The arguments He used were almost similar in substance as those He used in other cases (6:6-9; Matthew 12:9-14; Mark 3:1-6).

Here Jesus took the initiative in the controversy. He asked the questions first, not the Pharisees, and because His questions were so clear and rightly stated, His adversaries found them unanswerable. "They held their peace." "They could not answer Him—or were powerless to answer Him," as the original implies. But such a public silencing only irritated them and stiffened their determined antagonism to Christ. They held their peace and bided their time (Matthew 12:14). The approach He made was forthright, for He went straight to the mark, opened the topic Himself, anticipated the objections of His watchers, and then "appealed to their conscience, charity, and religion—not loaded with senseless human additions, but as it stood in the intent of the Lawgiver" (14:3). In the former miracle, "He compared the loosing of an ox or ass from the stall—and the loosing of a believing woman from her eighteen years' curvature. Here, an animal fallen into a pit was the appropriate parallel to a man in danger of death from dropsy, the 'much more' being equally cogent in both cases." Grotias expressed it, "The man with a dropsy He compared to a beast drowning, the crooked woman, to a beast bound." By healing the dropsical man, Jesus proved that it was merciful to heal on a Sabbath day and by His illustration of the ass or ox, He exposed their lack of consistency. How such reasoning closed the mouths of those whose hearts were destitute of mercy towards suffering humanity!

There are two ways of applying this last miracle of the seven miracles Christ performed on Sabbath days. By these Sabbath healings He emphasized "the humane element in the original institution as a day of rest, rescuing it from the exaggeration of Pharisaism. Also He gave it the sanction of His observance as a day of public worship. By these deeds of healing He honored it specially as a day of showing mercy. The Lord's Day is consecrated by His Spirit for the service of man, as well as for the worship of God.

The other application of the miracle is that Christ's constant compassion for human suffering is a mirror of His compassionate heart for sinners. He lived to relieve the afflicted and oppressed—He died to emancipate men and women from a worse disease than that of any physical nature. By His shed blood, He can take the sinner by the hand and heal and let him go out to walk in newness of life.

38. The Miracle of Lazarus

(John 11:1-46)

To fully expound all the aspects of the great miracle of resurrection found in this story, told with matchless simplicity and fulness by the evangelist himself, would require a book in itself. "The circumstantiality of this beautiful narrative speaks irrestibly for its historical truth, and the objections raised by critical writers center really in their aversion to the miraculous as such." It was about a month before His own death and resurrection that Jesus visited Bethany and wrought His third miracle of resurrection—the most remarkable of all His mighty works, and which foreshadowed His own resurrection and also made a profound impression in Jerusalem but brought the Sanhedrin to its final decision to seek the death of Christ. After the miracle, Jesus retired to the wilderness of Ephraim to await in quietness with the Twelve, the Passover and His final hours. This was the last of seven miracles recorded by John. Cognizant of all the other miracles recorded by Matthew, Mark, and Luke, John realized that there were many other miracles of which there was no account. He knew it was impossible to give a complete list of Christ's miracles, but rather he chose typical ones and gives the apostolic recognition of the extent of His miracle ministry in these words:

Many other signs (miracles) therefore did Jesus in the presence of His disciples, which are not written in this book. . . . There are also many other things which Jesus did, the which, if they should be written every one, I suppose that even the world itself could not contain the book that should be written (20:30; 21:25).

While we do not know how often Jesus visited the Bethany home of Mary, Martha, and Lazarus, we do know that it was ever a sweet spot and one of the few places on earth where He was loved and understood and where His wounded spirit found rest. Probably their parents were dead, and Lazarus and his sisters constituted a delightful home circle. These three loved each other, each one had faith in the despised and rejected Messiah, and in turn each was equally loved by Him. Previous visits to such a loving home are recorded by the other evangelists (Matthew 21:17; Mark 11:11, 19; Luke 10:41, 42). Now sickness invades the home and the sisters turn in their need to Jesus. They were to learn, however, that the wisdom of divine love does not always shield its objects from suffering, sorrow, and death. United in the tenderest bonds of affection and honored by Christ's peculiar friendship, the family was yet permitted to experience sickness and anguish. There are few passages in Scripture more touching and impressive than that which records the most striking miracle performed by Christ—one which was a sublime prelude to the stupendous proof of His supernatural power, soon afterwards to be displayed in His own resurrection from the dead.

We are not told the nature of the sickness of Lazarus. Evidently it was serious enough for the sisters to request the aid of the Healer Friend who loved the favored trio, each of which felt that disease would fleet at His presence. The fact of the illness was couched in words of touching simplicity. The anxious sisters felt that the sad message required no addition, and that there was no necessity for a prayer to help. "Weakness, conscious of strength which loves, needs but to utter itself" (11:21). Bengel puts it, "They do not say *come*. He who loves needs but know." The information the sisters sent is expressed in the line, "Lord, behold, he whom thou lovest is sick."

Before we proceed, a word might be said about the particular love of Jesus. He "loved Martha, and her sister, and Lazarus." This love of chosen friendship proves that He loves differing personalities. He loved *Martha*, the active, practical keeper of the home, intent on looking after the material comfort of her guests. Evidently she was a strong, robust woman with more strength than pathos. *Mary* was different from the somewhat anxious and restless temperament of her sister. She was of a contemplative cast, spiritual, "gifted with all a woman's delicacy of insight and tender sympathy." *Lazarus* was a man of few words, quiet and unobtrusive. All three were devoted to the Master and appreciated Him in their own way. As Dr. Griffith Thomas observes: "To Lazarus He was the mighty Lord. To Martha the eternal Life. To Mary the incarnate Love." Thus He dealt with each according to temperament, in His kind, wise, sufficient, discriminating, and satisfying affection.

When Jesus received the news about the sickness of Lazarus—because of His omniscience He already knew about it—He said to the messengers and to His disciples that such a sickness would not have death as its *final* result but was being permitted for two things—namely, the furtherance and accomplishment of the purpose and glory of God, and also that Jesus Himself might be glorified thereby. What must have been hard to understand was the delay of Jesus. Although He loved Lazarus, He not only permitted his sickness but allowed it to continued and end in death. Yet those two distressed sisters were to learn that His delays are not denials. How often love permits pain. There are qualities which unrelieved suffering alone can perfect. Jesus Himself "learned obedience by the things that He suffered."

Mary and Martha were sure Jesus would come. But just because He loved them, "*therefore* He abode two days in the place where He was," and in those two days His friend died. Can we wonder that these sisters, with minds so perplexed over His strange delay said, when He came at last, "Lord, if Thou hadst been here my brother had not died?" How they were to learn that there was no neglect, only a purpose of love in the bewildering delay! It must have been painful even to our Lord's natural feelings to wound those of Mary and Martha whom He loved by allowing Lazarus to die. But He wanted to reveal to them, and also to us, that whatever our power to help our friends or inclination to do so, we must be guided in the exercise of that power by a regard to God's glory and their spiritual welfare, rather than the gratification of their present feelings.

As Jesus left for the sorrowing home at Bethany, He gave those around Him a beautiful description of death. He knew Lazarus had died and He said, "Our friend Lazarus sleepeth; but I go, that I may awake him out of sleep." His disciples thought He was referring to natural sleep and that Lazarus, after a good sleep, would recover from his sickness. Then Jesus said plainly, "Lazarus is dead." Christians must learn to see death with Christ's eyes. What sleeps is the body, not the spirit within the body. Absent from the body but present with the Lord is a blissful, conscious state. But the body sleeps in the dust, awaiting the resurrection.

When Jesus ultimately arrived at Bethany, Lazarus had been in his grave four days. It was a common Jewish idea that the soul hovered about the body until the third day, when corruption began, and then it took its flight. Martha said to Jesus, "Lord, by this time he stinketh." Corruption had set in, but a memorable miracle was about to be performed. A deed, fragrant with divine power, stayed and reversed the process of the ravages of decay. Jesus was raised from the dead before the fourth day, for it had been prophesied that He should not see corruption (Psalm 16:10).

How assuring the message must have been, "Thy brother shall rise again," and the assertion that Jesus was "the Resurrection, and the Life." It was Martha who confessed faith in His Messiahship, "Yea, Lord, I belive that Thou art the Christ, the Son of God, which could come into the world," and believing, she knew that He was able to recall her brother to life. Mary, who after the manner of mourners sat in the house, came quickly, in response to Martha's entreaty, to meet Jesus. But Mary's greeting of Christ with the words, "Lord, if thou hadst been here, my brother had not died," caused Jesus to groan in His spirit and become troubled. The groaning means that He was moved with indignation of spirit and troubled Himself, that is, there was the outward manifestation of His strong feeling, not only over the hypocritical mourning of the Jews, but over the temporary triumph of Satan, who had the power of death.

We now come to the shortest sweetest verse in the Bible, "Jesus wept." The tears of the suffering sisters touched His heart and, not only that, but in Lazarus He had lost a friend He loved. "The sympathy with human sorrow is not less part of His nature than the union with divine strength." As Jesus moved along towards the grave of His friend, His tears flowed, causing the bystanders to say, "Behold how He loved him." The sorrow of the sisters drew out His sympathy, and He was borne along with the high tide of grief and did not seek to resist it. What a gospel there is in those warm tears of His! We think of their source and origin, their wide range and power and issue. On Olivet, He wept for a great city doomed to death and He mourned over its sins, but those tears issued in the atoning death of the cross. On Olivet He had shed His tears for the sins of Jerusalem—on Calvary, He shed His blood for those sins. Here He weeps for a friend loved and lost, for one He could not bear to lose, but those blessed tears resulted in new life for Lazarus. As Doone put it, "The tears of our text are as a spring, a well, belonging to one household, the sisters of Lazarus. The tears over Jerusalem are as a river, belonging to a whole country. The tears upon the cross are as the sea, belonging to the whole world." (See also Hebrews 5:7).

All through this chapter we have a valuable testimony to the naturalness of Jesus' human emotions. How amazed we are at the miracle of His humanity—He loved, He needed the comfort of a home, He could be glad, He groaned, He wept, He had need of prayer. Yet deity and humanity are combined in this miracle. As the Man, He wept—as God, He cried, "Lazarus come forth." As the Man, He sympathizes with us in our sorrows and separations, and as the God, He can banish them. Pagan gods are not touched with the feeling of human infirmity. Being mythical, they are beyond all touch of grief or care.

As the miracle He was about to perform was one of His Father's works, Jesus prayed and blessed God for the answer He knew would follow. The sphere of human instrumentality is also present in the miracle, for Jesus said to His disciples, "Take ye away the stone" and "Loose Him, and let Him go." These actions required no miracle. With the exercise of His will, without a word, He could have caused the stone to remove from its socket, and the raised man to come forth without his graveclothes. But Jesus never wasted His power; He never performed a miracle unless such was necessary. The study of the miraculous convinces us of the economy of divine strength. After speaking to God, Jesus cried to Lazarus with a strong voice, and as "the *Resurrection* of the dead," and as the

Life of the living," He not only provided resurrection, He *is* the Resurrection. He not only gives life, He *is* the Life.

He who "vanquished death and all its powers" caused His voice to echo through the chamber of death and "without any interval between the call and the life," Lazarus came forth. He had life but needed liberty from his grave clothes, so Jesus called upon those near at hand to "loose him, and let him go." All Jesus did was to repeat the dead man's name and add two commanding words. One old divine has suggested that Jesus had to call Lazarus by name. Had He not, all the sleeping saints would have risen from the dead. That authoritative voice of His pierced the deep stillness of the sepulcher and was instantly obeyed, and Lazarus was given back to those who loved him. Is not that same "loud voice" an earnest of the trump of the archangel when he comes to announce the resurrection of all the dead in Christ?

We have no record of the secrets Lazarus brought back from the world beyond. There have been those who have made vain guesses as to what he revealed. There is an old legend to the effect that the first question asked by Lazarus after his resurrection was whether he should be required to die a second time, and that on being answered in the affirmative, he never smiled again. How expressive are these lines of Tennyson:

"Where wert thou, brother, these four
    days?"
  There lives no record of reply,
  Which, telling what it is to die,
Had surely added praise to praise.

From every house the neighbors met;
  The streets were filled with joyful sound;
  A solemn gladness even crowned
The purple brow of Olivet.

Behold a man raised up by Christ!
  The rest remaineth unrevealed;
  He told it not, or something sealed
The lips of that evangelist.

This miracle had diverse results as the conclusion of the chapter shows. As the result of Christ's resurrection power, many Jews believed on Him, but this miracle and all other miracles only angered the Pharisees and made them more determined about His death. Caiaphas, the high priest, a creature of Rome and a Sadducee—one who did not believe in resurrection—suggested to the Council that it would be better to kill Jesus than to lose their position. The works of Jesus, as well as His words, divided light from darkness, the believing from the unbelieving, and it is still true that there is "a division because of Him."

As the word John used for "miracles" in his gospel represents "wonders," "portents," or "signs," and not "mighty works," a fuller explanation of this characteristic word than that given in our Old Testament *Introduction* is necessary. The term John uses thirteen times (2:11, 23; 3:2; 4: 54; 6:2,14,26; 7:31; 9:16; 10:41; 11:47; 12:18, 37), and again in Revelation, as we shall see when we reach the miracles of this book, means, to quote Bullinger:

A signal, and ensign, a standard, a sign by which any thing is designated, distinguished or known; *hence,* used of the miracles of Christ, as being the signs by which it might be known that He was the Christ of God, a sign authenticating Christ's mission; a sign with reference to what it demonstrates.

Thus, John speaks of the miracles as "signs," the word the RV gives all through, and implied that they were symbols, proofs, messages, object lessons of spiritual truth embodied in the wonders themselves. They were living parables of Christ's action, embodiment of the truth in deed. To John, the miracles of the Master "were not merely signs of supernatural power, but expressive intimation of the *aim* of His ministry and of *His own* all-loving character; the spiritual restoration, which was His main end, being shadowed forth in the visible works of power and mercy." In this connection it is interesting to note that in John's gospel the miracles are introduced for a didactic purpose. They are usually followed by some lesson, discussion, or discourse.

The lesson of the stupendous miracle is evident. Christ is the Quickener of the dead, spiritually and physically. He is able to quicken the souls of those who are dead in their trespasses and sins. As He brought the body of Lazarus back from corruption, so He is able and willing to deliver men from their loathsome sins, His life-giving miracle of grace is as truly remarkable as His quickening miracle of power. Then at the appointed hour He will raise all those redeemed by His blood for glory with Himself in the Father's home, and at the final

dissolution of all things He will raise all His foes for the resurrection of judgment.

For our own hearts there is the assurance that, if Jesus does not return in our lifetime and we have to go home by the way of a grave, He will be closer to us than flesh or world or friends in our last hour re-echoing the comforting word of the psalmist, "Yea, though I walk through the valley of the shadow of death, I will fear no evil, for *Thou* art with me."

39. The Miracle of the Ten Lepers

(Luke 17:11-19)

On His last pilgrimage to Jerusalem where He was to die outside the city wall, Jesus passed through Samaria and Galilee, areas He knew so well and in which He had displayed His power. Normally, when the Jews went to Jerusalem they took the longer route across Jordan in order to avoid the unhospitable land of the Samaritans, with whom the Jews had no dealings (John 4:9), but petty differences between people were unrecognized by Him who came as the Saviour of the world. He never practiced any *apartheid.*

The miracle before us has its own peculiarities. Ten lepers bound together in a common misery forgot their national differences. Although one was a Samaritan and the other nine Jews, they were poor outcasts with one common need (II Kings 7:3). Together they formed "a piteous group, with clothes rent, heads bowed, and hair dishevelled, a cloth bound strangely on the lower face and upper lip." A common disease put them all on one level, and they were only too conscious of their need. The great leveller of all is sin, of which leprosy, as we have seen, is in Scripture an expressive type. "There is no difference, for *all* have sinned" (Romans 3:23).

In the miracle of the one leper Jesus cleansed (Matthew 8:1-4), we discussed the nature of the loathsome disease of leprosy. Here we pause to note the number Jesus cleansed on this occasion—ten. Ten is the figure suggesting the completion of God's order, as can be seen in the Ten Commandments. Here, *ten* came signifying the sum of human need and hopelessness. The lepers *stood afar off.* They did not run and fall at the feet of Jesus but observed the legal distance of 100 paces. They dare not approach clean people with such a measured distance as the law commanded (Leviticus 13; 46; Numbers 5:2; II Kings 5:5). The distance was not only necessary because of contagion, it also typified the great separation sin makes.

Out of a deep sense of their misery and with the hope that the Healer would hear their cry and help, the lepers lifted up their voices and cried from a distance, "Lord, have mercy on us." They expressed their desire for a cure in the word "mercy." "There is skill in the cure of disease, and there may be attention, for all of which we are to be thankful; but in the cure of every disease there is also mercy,—mercy to forgive the sin which is the root of suffering; and it is the end of mercy to heal the diseases which are only the expression and product of that sin." Probably knowledge of earlier instances of lepers being healed encouraged them to call to Jesus (Matthew 8:2; 11:5). Commenting on the voices of the lepers, Trench says:

All who have studied this terrible disease tell us that an almost total failure of voice is one of the symptoms which accompany it. It is not then for nothing that we are presently told of one who had been restored to health that he returned *with a loud voice* glorifying God; it is here the earnestness with which the boon was sought is sufficiently indicated by the fact that they *lifted up their voices,* found such an utterance as it might have seemed beforehand the disease would have denied them.

The attitude and treatment of the compassionate Healer are impressive. He never touched them as He did the single leper we have just referred to. When He saw and heard the ten lepers, He simply said "Go shew yourselves to the priests," and, as they went, "they were cleansed." No healing word was spoken, yet such was the assurance of the lepers that when Christ said "Go," the command meant healing, that they immediately went to the priests. Christ gave them no pledge or outward means of healing. As yet, they felt no change in their diseased bodies, but as they went steadily on together in all their rags, wretchedness, and uncleanness, in some supernatural way what they yearned for happened. Can we not imagine the cry of joy breaking from one and another and another as new life shot into their wasted frames and all the ten saw in each other the wonderful trans-

formation? Their cure, however, did not take place till they had proved their faith by obedience. Then, whether suddenly or by degrees, the taint disappeared and their flesh became as it had been in the days of their previous health.

By sending them to the priests, Jesus showed that He had not come to destroy the law, but to fulfil it. The priests could not cleanse leprosy; they could only pronounce lepers clean. How interesting it is to note how Jesus varied His treatment according to the varying needs of sufferers! Theirs was a keen trial of faith to go to the priests as the law demanded (Leviticus 14: 3, 4), without any sign of restoration. Says Spurgeon:

Before they began to feel their foul blood cleansed, before the horrible dryness of leprosy had yielded to healthy perspiration, they were to go towards the house in which the priest lived to be examined by him and to be pronounced clean.

What a world of significance is in the phrase, "As they went, they were cleansed." Do we not have here an unmistakeable evidence of Christ's deity? As the lepers went, somehow and somewhere, on the road, "the air they breathed became the vehicle of divine power; the distance, as it lengthened between the lepers and Jesus, was spanned by His almighty goodness; His mercy followed its objects, and neither missed them in its transit, nor misapprehended them in its application." Is He not the same miracle-working Lord today? His power was not parted with by His ascension; nor is it in the least spent in its daily passage to the earth, but operates in miracles still.

The result of the miracle has its bright, yet dark, side. Only one out of the ten returned to thank the Giver for His gift, and the stress in the miracle is on the one who returned to give thanks. The language implies that the work of healing was not accomplished till the company was out of sight of the Master and that the one leper, as soon as he was healed, did not continue his journey to the priest but swung right round to bless the Great High Priest for his cure. Vocal powers were restored, for with a loud voice he glorified God, and falling down before Jesus expressed the gratitude of his heart. The other nine went on their way to the first priest they could find.

Gratitude came to Jesus from the most unlikely quarter, for the cleansed leper who returned was a "Samaritan," a "stranger." The other nine were Jews and probably separated themselves from the Samaritan as soon as they were cleansed. "Men want more than the 'misery' which our common proverb associates with 'strange' companions, before they learn the lesson of brotherhood in its fulness." None returned "save this stranger"—sometimes we receive more generous treatment from strangers than from our own friends and relatives. To quote Spurgeon again:

> Poor and feeble as their voices had become through disease, yet they lifted them up in prayer, and united in crying, "Jesus, Master, have mercy on us!" They all joined in the litany, "Lord, have mercy upon us! Christ, have mercy upon us!" But when they came to the *Te Deum* magnifying and praising God, only one of them took up the note.

Is there not a tinge of sad disappointment in our Lord's question, "Were there not ten cleansed, but where are the nine?" Why was He robbed of the worship and gratitude of these healed men? By failing to return, they indicated that they thought more of themselves than of their Healer—a fitting type of multitudes who externally profit by the mercies of Christ. What we must not forget is that although Christ addressed His question to the one leper who did return, yet he was silent about the other nine. He had no censure against those cruel, thankless nine; he was too much occupied with his own cure and personal adoration for same.

The other nine had faith to be healed, but their faith failed to show itself further in gratitude and love. Why did they push on their way unmindful and ungrateful? Calvin suggests that "they slipped away to banish the memory of their disease." Bernard puts it, "Importunate to receive, restless till they receive, ungrateful when they have received."

Perhaps the nine failed to return because they knew the danger of committing themselves to Jesus, because there were His foes who deemed it an offense to receive a cure from Him. It may be they were afraid that now the Healer would have a claim upon them and would begin to press His claim. Having given them new life, He might demand their loyalty. Probably they thought that they had only got what was their due, for leprosy was an injustice and a grievance, and health was their right, so why be grate-

ful? Alas! by their lack of appreciation they indicated that their Benefactor was no longer necessary to them. Urgent want was past. They had all they asked for and the disappearance of their need made a vast difference. Let us intreat God to save us from the dark sin of ingratitude.

As for the one who did not forget his benefit, he received another blessing from the Lord. "Arise, go thy way: thy faith hath made thee whole." His cure was confirmed by Jesus and to it was added the moral cure—a pronounced salvation. "The nine had had sufficient faith for the restoration of the health of their body," says Ellicott; "his had gone further, and had given a new and purer life to his soul."

If we have received the absolving word of mercy and know that our old sins have been purged (II Peter 1:9), may we never lose the sense of wonder regarding our spiritual healing. May our gratitude for the Lord's saving grace and power be expressed, not only in words, but in a life of devotion to Him! Yes, and since He loads us daily with His benefits, material, physical and spiritual, may our praises ever ascend to Him from whom all blessings flow.

40. The Miracle of Blind Bartimaeus

(Matthew 20:29-34; Mark 10:46-52; Luke 18:35-43)

As we compare the narratives containing the account of this miracle, we encounter the same apparent contradiction we met with in the miracle of the Gadarene demoniac (refer to it). Matthew says that there were two blind men and that the miracle was wrought as Jesus departed from Jericho. Mark and Luke say that there was only one blind man. Luke says the miracle took place as Jesus drew near to Jericho, and Mark is the only writer naming one of the blind men. Luke was not an eyewitness of the occasion. As there were many blind beggars on the wayside, perhaps there were two healings. Adversity finds some relief in fellowship. Bengel suggests that one man cried to the Lord as He drew near to Jericho yet He did not cure him then, but on the next day, as He went out of the city, He cured him together with the other man to whom in the meanwhile he had joined himself. This is the third instance in Matthew in which he notes two sufferers where the other gospels speak only of one.

Fausset's explanation is, "The distinction between the *new* and the *old* towns may solve the seeming discrepancy between Matthew, who makes the miracle of the blind to be when Jesus was *leaving* Jericho; and Luke, who says it was when Jesus was come nigh to Jericho." We are in hearty agreement with Taylor when he says that if we were in possession of all the facts as they really occurred, it is quite likely that we should see at once how all three accounts are consistent with truth, and with each other.

As Mark names one of the men, Bartimaeus, it may be that he was more conspicuous and better known than the other. Probably he was more active and vocal in seeking mercy which, when bestowed, included both men. It is for this reason that we take Bartimaeus by himself, whose healing illustrated what Jesus had been teaching, namely, that He came into the world not to be ministered to, but to minister, and to give His life as a ransom for many. Accompanied by His disciples and a large number of people forming an orderly procession, Jesus was journeying to Jerusalem for the last time. In less than a week His sorrows would be over. Death, with its agony and shame, would be forever past. Although His sensitive spirit felt the weight of all that was before Him, yet such a burden was not permitted to stay His beneficent hand. Human misery and need aroused the tenderness of His compassionate heart.

He left Jericho after being a guest of Zacchaeus (Luke 19). The fact that this city had lain under a curse for ages was no barrier to Him who was about to die, and through death, remove the curse of sin. Thus we come to the story before us. As Jesus moved along, a blind beggar heard the tramp of a crowd and inquired the reason for such commotion. He was told that Jesus of Nazareth was passing by. Mark, as usual, is particular about names and tells us that the conspicuous beggar was Bartimaeus, the son of Timaeus. In some of the older MSS. he is spoken of as "*the* blind man," as though he was well-known by name and prominent because of his occupancy of the same place on the wayside, as a customary object of charity. Being blind, he could only beg.

Although he could not *see*, he could *hear*, and that acutely, and was thus desirous of knowing the reason for the unusual excitement around him. Having to depend on his hearing, Bartimaeus perceived that there was something unusual going on, and speaking not only for himself but for his blind companion who drops out of the narration in Luke and Mark, he asked the bystanders what all the commotion was about and was told that Jesus of Nazareth was passing by on His way to Jerusalem. Bartimaeus had heard the gossip of the town as to Christ's gracious words and wonderful works and shared with others the romantic expectation of the long-promised Son of David coming to advance His claim to the kingdom. When he heard that Jesus was near, he seized the opportunity of calling upon Him. This was his first and last opportunity of securing from Jesus what he sorely needed, and he made good use of it. Lifting up his voice he cried, "Jesus, Thou Son of David, have mercy on me."

Ordinarily, as a beggar, Bartimaeus would have sought to make capital out of the crowd. More passers-by meant more money in his box. But as sight was more important to him than money, he deliberately sacrificed financial advantage for eyesight. He would have been a fool had he acted otherwise. Would that many today who are too busy making money to think about their soul's salvation would realize what a treasure they are sacrificing.

In his cry, Bartimaeus combined deity and humanity for he called Jesus the Man of Nazareth and also "the Son of David." Such a manner of address signified acknowledgement of His Messiahship, the future King of Israel. "Son of David" was the popular designation of the great expected Prophet (Ezekiel 34:23-24; Matthew 9:27; Luke 1:32). Here was the One, promised of old, at whose coming the eyes of the blind would be opened (Isaiah 29:18; 35:5), and Bartimaeus had faith in His person and in His power. The difference between Christ and himself did not concern Bartimaeus, and he received no rebuff from Jesus for addressing Him by His august title. Born of the stock of Israel, he was justified in calling upon the King of David's line to grant him sight. Misery, too, had the prerogative to beg for divine help, and his description of Jesus anticipated the cry of the palm-bearing multitude as He was escorted to Zion, His capital, as David's Heir.

The crowd following our Lord rebuked Bartimaeus and his companion for crying out to Jesus. Such an eager supplication was looked upon as being somewhat intrusive. Was not the great Prophet on His way to claim His promised kingdom? Then why delay Him? Perhaps the crowd tried to smother the cry of the blind because they supposed it beneath the dignity of the Son of David to parley with beggars; or probably, it might have been that the religious leaders in the crowd could not bear to hear the blind give Jesus the august titles of honor which they themselves were not willing to accord Him. Hilary says: "Lastly the crowd rebukes them, because it was bitter to it to hear from the blind men the assertion which it denied, that the Lord was the Son of David."

But the beggars could not thus be silenced. Their appeal was to Jesus, not to the crowd, and no answer would be taken, except from Him, who never refuses need. Bartimaeus, the crier for the two, cried "the more a great deal, Thou Son of David have mercy on me," and such a cry of need could not be stifled. The rebuke of the crowd only made the blind men more desperate. We owe more than we realize to opposition. Out of the unsilenced cry, "Have mercy upon us, O Lord," the Church fashioned its famous *Litany*. "Lord, have mercy upon us."

The cry for mercy, quickened by the urgency of despair immediately reached the heart of mercy, and ignoring the effort of the crowd to deter the beggar, Jesus stood still and bade, or commanded, them to be called. This was a sudden pause in the hurrying footsteps and a change in voices. Mark, with more graphic fulness, gives us the words of the Master's message, "Be of good cheer, arise, He calleth thee," and Bartimaeus, leaping up, flung off his outer garment used for protection from the weather, and with an instinct of faith as sure as sight, came to Jesus. At last the tension was over, as Bartimaeus' intensified sense of hearing detected relief in the compassionate voice of Jesus. Multitudes today need to cast away the garments of self-righteousness they are wrapped in, if they would find themselves at Jesus' feet (Romans 10:3). Those whom He calls must lay aside every weight and besetting sin (Matthew 13:44-46; Philippians 3:7; Hebrews 12:1-3). Luke tells us that the blind were "brought unto" Jesus, and used a phrase peculiar to him in the sense of bringing the sick to Him. Vincent

says that Luke used "the compound verb which was a common medical term for bringing the sick to a physician both in that and in other senses." (See 9:41; Acts 16:20; 27:24).

Our Lord's question is somewhat intriguing. As the omniscient One, He knew what they needed. Did not these sightless eyes provide sufficient cause for the cry of the blind? Jesus often asked questions of those desiring healing. He likes the needy to express their need and faith in words. For some of His questions see Matthew 9: 28: John 5:6; 21:15. "What will ye that I shall do unto you?" Jesus wanted the blind men to say what they wanted that in the fuller exercise of faith they might be prepared to receive the desired blessing. Trench says that the Lord's question was in part "an expression of His readiness to aid, a comment in act upon His own words, spoken but a little while before, "The Son of Man came not to be ministered unto, but to minister" (Matthew 20:28); it was in part intended to evoke into livelier exercise the faith of the petitioners (Matthew 9:28).

There was no faltering, or trepidation, or suspense in their reply, for the men knew what they wanted and with a definiteness born of earnestness uttered their seven-word prayer, "Lord, that our eyes may be opened." Such prayer was music to His ears and expressed faith, His delight. How the attitude of the men touched His heart! No wonder He had "compassion on them." He shrank from the popular demand for the display of His miraculous power, but compassion drew from Him the exercise of the supernatural which otherwise He would have shrunk from here. Where there is divine compassion, there is power to bless, and such compassion is always creative and saving. How calm, strong, and rich in mercy was Jesus—"He healed them!"

Just how the miracle of restoration happened, we do not know. Matthew says, "He touched their eyes, and immediately their eyes received sight." Mark says that Jesus told him "to go thy way and immediately he received his sight." Luke's version is that Jesus said, "Receive thy sight." No matter how the restoration was effected, whether by a touch or by the authorative word, or both, the cure was instant and perfect. There was no gradual process as in the case of the other blind man who saw "men as trees walking." "The pertinacious vitality of faith proved itself in this instance, and met with an instant and full reward." There was the outburst of gratitude for the cure received for they glorified God (Luke 10:17; 17:15). Jesus did not say, "My power hath saved thee," but *"Thy faith* hath saved thee." It was true that the miracle had been wrought through the exercise of divine power, but Christ impressed on the healed the value of the disposition of faith.

The word "saved," while primarily associated with the miracle of restored sight, may have carried with it as Ellicott suggests, the salvation, or "healthiness of spiritual vision, of which the restoration of bodily sight was at once the type and the earnest" (Luke 7:50). Gratitude for the cure is seen in the willingness of the healed to "follow Him." They made good use of their healing to accompany the Healer, who did not bid them be silent about the miracle as when He healed the two blind men some time before (Matthew 9:30). Christ was about to present Himself publicly in Jerusalem as Israel's long-expected King, and it was well that such a testimony as the restoration of sight should be rendered at this juncture to His person and His power. Thus it came about that the blind, formerly obliged to stay in one spot, were now able to see and they used their new-found faculty of freedom of motion to swell the crowd going to Jerusalem. In the Apocryphal *Gospel of Nicodemus,* Bartimaeus appears as one of the witnesses for the defense at our Lord's trial. "All the people," Luke adds, "when they saw it, gave praise to God." Those who had witnessed the miracle burst forth in praise to God (Luke 13:17; 18:43; Acts 3:8-10).

Little needs to be said about the lesson of this miracle, which is a readiness and power to act. Lang says, "The story is past in time, but it is eternal in truth. Bartimaeus is the soul of humanity struggling for the Light. Jesus of Nazareth is the Light of the world—the shining forth of God who is Light, and in whom is no darkness at all." Blindness, as a simile of man's ignorance and darkness, is common in Scripture (Isaiah 42:7, 18; Matthew 23:26; Romans 11:25; II Corinthians 4:4; Ephesians 4:18 RV; Revelation 3:17). The effect of blindness in a man reveals itself in many ways:

In not seeing whither he is going (I John 2:11),

In getting in the way of others and leading others wrong (Luke 6:39),

In missing all the beauty of light and walking in darkness (John 8:12),

In knowing nothing of the glorious things above and around (II Kings 6:17).

Bartimaeus knew what begging was, and he applied it to his greatest need. When sinners take their place as beggars and plead for mercy, they find it, and their blind eyes are made to see that Jesus is the Light and Deliverer.

41. The Miracle of the Withered Fig Tree

(Matthew 21:17-22; Mark 11:12-14, 20-24)

This further miracle Jesus wrought before His death is peculiar and distinctive in that it is His only miracle of judgment. Every miracle performed by Him on earth was an act of goodness and mercy with the exception of this one which stands alone as being destitute of a merciful or beneficent character. There are those who affirm that "it was a symbol or prediction of judgment, hardly falling within the class of miracles. It was an acted parable." Yet, as we shall see, it is both a miracle and a parable. He who came "not to destroy," is apparently contradicted in the miracle which, although only wrought on a tree, is still a miracle of destruction.

The setting of the miracle is appealing. Jesus found consolation, rest, and peace in the home of those at Bethany who were dear to Him, which was something He could not find in the crowded city. In His accepted poverty for our sakes, Jesus became dependent upon others. He was born in another man's stable, dined at another's table, slept in a borrowed bed, was buried in another's grave. In Jerusalem He found hatred and plots to slay Him, although He yearned to save them, but in Bethany He found love, gratitude, and peace. Can we say that our heart is His Bethany in which He rests, while around us there is a world hating Him? For ourselves, it is blessed to have some quiet Bethany, where we can rest and pray, even in days of conflict and strain.

This miracle also furnishes us with a striking evidence of our Lord's two natures —divine and human. As God, He blasted the tree—as Man, He needed the sleep the Bethany home afforded and also food of the tree to sustain Him. This is why we read "He hungered." Evidently He had started early that Monday morning for Jerusalem without eating. Glover remarks, "Rapt up in the contemplation of sins He had to censure and judgments He had to predict, all Mary's importunity was unavailing to make Him eat." But as Jesus journeyed on, the walk permitted hunger to assert itself and appetite for food arose, and with a noble fig tree ahead, He saw a way of relieving His hunger.

Remarkable, is it not, that He who had miraculously fed thousands would not perform a miracle to satisfy His own physical need? Already, in the *Introduction* of this study, we have dwelt upon the self-restraint in the use of the supernatural by Jesus. Latham has a chapter on, "The Laws of the Working of Signs" in his *Pastor Pastorium* in which he lists five:

(1) Our Lord will not provide by miracle what could be provided by human endeavor or human foresight.

(2) Our Lord will not use His special powers to provide for His personal wants or for those of His immediate followers.

(3) No miracle is to be worked for miracle's sake, apart from an end of benevolence or instruction.

(4) No miracle is to be worked to supplement human policy or force.

(5) No miracle is to be worked which should be overwhelming in point of awefulness so as to terrify men into acceptance, or which should be unanswerably certain, leaving no loophole for unbelief.

Bruce, in *The Miraculous Element in the Gospels,* develops similar points.

If hunger, however, brought Jesus to the fig tree, the sight of it made Him soon forget the hunger, for at once He saw in the barren tree a figure that pretentious profession and utter barrenness of the city He had wept over and was now to die in. "Pity moved Him to give a prophecy in action—a parable in fact." There are one or two aspects of our Lord's disappointment calling for consideration. He came to the tree "if haply He might find fruit thereon." With this particular tree, the leaves came *after* the fruit. In early spring before the leaves appeared, the Palestinian fig tree produced green fruit relished by the peasants. If there were no green figs on the tree when the leaves opened in the spring,

there would be no harvest in the late summer (Song of Solomon 2:13; Luke 21:29, 30). The tree in leaf was a silent proclamation that it had fruit, since that appeared before the foliage, but Jesus, seeking green figs, found nothing but leaves. These fig trees were often planted by the wayside because of the idea that the dust suited them.

An apparent difficulty arises when we remember that our Lord was omniscient and therefore must have known before He came near the tree that it would be fruitless. Why, then, as the omniscient One and as the absolute Lord of truth, did He expect to find figs when He must have known the tree contained none? Both Trench and Cumming offer the following explanation of the difficulty:

The Lord approached the tree, appearing to expect fruit upon it, and yet knowing that He should find none, deceiving thereby those who were with Him. It is sufficient to observe that a similar charge might be made against all figurative teachings, whether by word or by deed, for in all such there is a worshiping of the truth in the spirit and not in the letter. A parable is told *as* true; and though the incidents are feigned, and the persons imagined, it is true, because of the moral or spiritual truth which sustains the outward framework of the story. Even so a symbolic action, although not meaning the thing which it professes to mean, is no deception, since it means something infinitely higher and deeper, of which the lower action is a type, and in which the lower is lost. What was it, for instance, here, if Christ did not intend really to look for fruit on that tree, being aware that it had none? Yet He did not intend to show how it would fare with a man or with a nation, when God came looking for the fruits of righteousness, and found nothing but the abundant leaves of a boastful yet empty profession.

Trench gives a long quotation from Augustine along similar lines and cites this phrase from Fuller, "He who spake many, here *wrought* a parable."

Finding no fruit on the tree, Jesus caused it to wither up and doomed it to barrenness. Why did He curse the tree? (and remember, it was *only a tree* which He doomed.) Was He justified in dealing thus with a tree at all, since it was incapable of good or evil and therefore not a fit object of ruin or reward? Such an action was *not* unjust even though the tree was just a thing, because it was lawfully used as a means for ends lying beyond itself. "Christ did not attribute moral responsibilities to the tree when He smote it because of its unfruitfulness: but He did attribute to it a fitness for representing moral qualities. All our language concerning trees, a *good* tree, a *bad* tree, a tree which *ought* to bear, is the same continual transfer to them of moral qualities, and a witness for the national fitness of the Lord's language."

The vine is used in the Bible to represent what is beautiful and good, but the fig tree is rarely used except as a symbol of what seems bad. There is a Jewish legend to the effect that the tree of knowledge of good and evil was a fig tree. The Greeks called a bad man, a fig tree man. Thus the word *sycophant* (a flatterer, a man who acts dishonestly), when literally translated, means a man that shows figs.

Some people see a difficulty in the words Mark gives us, "The time of figs was not yet." Do these words acquit the tree even of any figurative guilt? Is not the symbol defeated and put in contradiction with itself? Are we perplexed that Christ should look for figs when they *could no*t be found and be indignant over such a lack? One answer is that at that period of the year, March—April, neither leaves nor fruit were naturally expected but this tree, by putting forth leaves made pretension to be something more than others, to have fruit upon it, since fruit appears before leaves. The tree, therefore, was "punished not for being without fruit, but for proclaiming by the voice of those leaves that it had fruit; not for being barren, but for being false. This was the guilt of Israel, a guilt so much deeper than the guilt of the nations." (See Ezekiel 17:24; Romans 3:17-24; 10:3, 4, 21; 11:7, 10).

Certainly the destruction of a fig tree beside the road (Matthew 21:19)–hence no one's private property—was just an object lesson to the disciples that they would never forget. They would not think of our Lord as treating the tree as a moral agent, or that the blighting of the tree was a wanton destruction of property, utterly unwarranted and unjustifiable. They saw in the miracle God's abhorrence of hypocrisy. The cursing of the fig tree which boasted of having fruit that was not there is seen later in the sudden death of Ananias and Sapphira (Acts 5:1-11). There is apt to be

most profession where there is least performance.

Further, Christ had perfect right to make use of what He chose in the operation of His power to teach His truths. His right is not questioned. "It is the Lord, let Him do what seemeth Him good" (I Samuel 3:18). As Habershon expresses it, "When the Lord cursed the barren fig tree, and decreed that it should never again yield figs, He was but exercising the power which He had so often put forth before. Trees, which had once been fruitful, ceased to bear; or if the fruit began to ripen, the trees dropped their fruit at His command." Fruit was destroyed at His bidding (Deuteronomy 28:38, 40-42). Jesus had already prepared His disciples for understanding and interpreting His act, and the Old Testament use of this very symbol of the tree would be in their minds (Hosea 9:10; Joel 1:7. See Romans 11). Thus, "the parable of the fruitless fig tree explains the meaning which underlies the cursing of the tree on the Bethany road. In both parable and miracle the judgment fell on the fig tree. In the miracle it was cursed; in the parable it was to be cut down after its further season of opportunity (Matthew 21:19, 34; Luke 16: 6-9).

Christ's solemn word of doom, "Let no fruit grow on this henceforth for ever," proves that divine providence only spares that which is useful. Where there is only profession, there is judgment. Jesus vainly sought figs to allay His hunger—emblem of the early privileged profession but spiritually barren people of God now doomed (Hebrews 4:16; 6:7, 8). The stroke of judgment was swift, for *immediately* the tree dried up from its roots. Sudden destruction came to undue pretension—a striking symbol of the outwardly religious but spiritually destitute community of Israel. That withered tree stood in the sight of all who passed, as Israel stands, the open scorn of the world—"Judaism, a dead and fruitless religion; a monument of divine judgment."

The miracle of the fig tree is actually an appendix to the barren tree dug about and dunged (Luke 13:6-9), and it is a parable, a prophecy, and a miracle all in one. The cursing of the fig tree was a symbolic action; for the tree represented Israel under the old covenant, soon to be utterly rejected as hopelessly unfruitful to God. When God does gather fruit for His ancient people, it will be from a new generation under the covenant of grace in the Millennial Kingdom.

The doom, "Let no man eat fruit of thee hereafter for ever," does not imply eternal barrenness. "For ever" here means "until the age" or "until the dispensation." The Jewish fig tree blasted by curse shall not be blasted eternally but until the dispensation that is to come which Paul describes for us in his Roman epistle (Romans 11). As the Gentile age ends, the fig tree is to put forth its branch, and from the Lord, its fruit will be found (Hosea 14:8; Matthew 24:32, 33).

The moral of the miracle can be found in our Lord's use of the occasion to stress the omnipotence of faith and in His added counsels or prayer. Mark, who alone names Peter as the speaker, adds "Have faith in God," or "Have the faith of God." As they passed the spot the morning after the miracle, Peter drew the Master's attention to the withered-up condition of the tree. This resulted in His homily. There is not contradiction in linking judgment with prayer and faith. The only judgment the disciples could inflict must be a judgment whose root is love. The withering of that tree was a result of Christ's faith in God, and if the disciples exercised a similar faith, power would be given to accomplish greater things (Matthew 21:21, 22). If they had faith in God, whatsoever things they desired when they prayed, they would deceive—receive them already at the inspiration of the wish. What they asked had to be in harmony with God's will and laws (Matthew 7:7).

The removal of mountains symbolizes the removal of obstacles. The Jewish rabbis, because of their ability to deal with difficulties, were known as "mountain movers." Faith can remove substantial obstacles in the path of mercy. There is no such word as "impossible" in the vocabulary of those who can lay hold on God. Trust leaves its desires with God in confidence, knowing they will be fulfilled in His way and time.

> Faith laughs at impossibilities,
> And cries, "It shall be done."

There are one or two lessons of the miracle we can mention as we close this study. Does not the cursing of the fig tree have a message for Christendom today, as well as for Israel, whose history is a mirror in which men everywhere may see their own reflection? The Christendom of today is as unreal and as unfruitful for God as Israel of the past. There are plenty of leaves of religious activities and performances, but so little of the fruit redounding to God's glory. The Lord still comes down to earth looking for practical fruits, even the fruit of the Spirit (Galatians 5:22). Nothing else will satisfy His hunger.

For our individual hearts the solemn message is that the failure to improve privilege entails the removal of the privilege itself. If the branch fails to bear fruit, it is taken away (John 15:2-6). The lamp which fails to shine is taken out of its place (Revelation 2:5). Trees that do not bear fruit are hewn down and burned (Matthew 7:19). What the Lord of the harvest desires is performance as well as profession—fruit as well as leaves.

42. The Miracle of Malchus' Ear

(Matthew 26:51-56; Mark 14:46, 47; Luke 22:50, 51; John 18:10, 11)

This last miracle of healing Jesus wrought before His death has a sad setting. It happened on the eve of the Saviour's last woe. The cross was looming before Him with all its anguish and shame. He had just emerged from Gethsemane with its great agony, distressful prayer, and bloody sweat. Is there not material here for a meditation on *The Miracle of Gethsemane?* There was the supernatural strength imparted by an angel, and our Lord's use of such imparted physical strength only to agonize in prayer, even to blooddrops falling to the ground. The lack of human ministry on the part of His disciples had to be supplied angelically as He endured the conflict, bereft of human sympathy and alone. While the three disciples slept, there was His threefold wrestling with God until victory was attained and calm restored, and He could say to His own, "Arise, let us be going."

As Jesus emerged from Gethsemane, He was met by a great multitude with swords and staves who had come from the chief priest to take Him prisoner. How ludicrous the scene must have been—a multitude strongly armed to take one defenseless Man! The kiss of the traitor had signalled to them the One they sought. As His foes advanced, He calmly asked, "Whom seek ye?" They answered, "Jesus, the Nazarene," and He replied, "I am He." For Him, there was no peril as He chose to yield Himself to the malice of His captors.

Overcome by the sound of His majestic voice, His quiet dignity of demeanor, and the outflashing of His power, they went backward and fell to the ground. Was this not a minor miracle? Knowing, as they did, that Jesus was equipped with altogether superior powers, perhaps they wondered what miracle He might perform to escape capture. Impressed with His obvious calmness and lack of fear, and with conspicuous regal dignity, they were temporarily overcome and could not lay hands on Him. One of the aspects of Christ's use of the miraculous we have dealt with is that of His refusal to use His power to relieve Himself. Here is another illustration of this fact. Nothing would have been easier for Him than to walk away, had it so pleased Him. But having been born to die as an atoning sacrifice, He meekly submitted Himself to His foes.

Further, He wished no defense on His behalf, for His settled principle was that when He suffered, He "threatened not," but willingly drank the cup His Father permitted. The narrative tells us that He could have had "twelve legions of angels" to protect Him had He asked for them. He desired, however, not the assistance of angels, but the fulfilment of God's plan. Around Him were *twelve* weak *men*, one a traitor, one who was to deny Him, and the rest equally timorous, yet He refused *twelve* legions of the armies of the Lord. What a miracle of miracles He was—and is!

Although the incident of the healed ear is found in all four gospels, it is John alone who gives us the name of the servant who lost his ear, namely, *Malchus*. John knew the high priest and was familiar with the composition of his household. Malchus is called specially *the* servant of the high priest, and so was probably his personal attendant who would be constantly addressed by his name by all about the palace. Thus it was natural for John to introduce him by name. John, also, is the only writer naming Peter as the one who cut off the ear of Malchus. Doubtless the other three evangelists also knew whose hand it was that struck the blow. Luke the physician, is the only one of the four writers recording the healing of the ear. A unique feature of the miracle is that it is the only one of its kind among our Lord's works in which a wound inflicted by violence was miraculously healed.

In regard to Peter's defense of his Master, while we applaud the right kind of enthusiasm, we must guard ourselves against the danger of mere impulse. Peter never waited for an answer to the question, "Lord, shall we smite with the sword?" As a Galilean, he was pugnacious and aimed a blow at the high priest's servant for daring to lay his profane hands upon his Lord. As Trench puts it: "*Word*-bearer for the rest of the apostles, he proves that when occasion arises, he can be *sword*-bearer also; and his act shows him the prompter and more daring in action than them all." Peter "drew his sword." There were only two swords among the twelve disciples (Luke 22:38), and one of these was in the possession of Peter, as the leader of the whole band.

The blow struck by Peter was the act of an ardent, indignant man. Aiming at the head of Malchus, Peter aimed hard. Fortunately for Malchus, the blow missed the target, and only his ear was cut off. It may appear brave on Peter's part to act as he did, since a multitude with swords and staves surrounded him. Had this impulsive disciple only paused for a moment, he might have realized how hopeless it was for eleven men with only two swords among them to protect Jesus against a well-armed contingent. But not accustomed to looking before he leaped, Peter struck the servant, and the deed was done almost before he knew. Perhaps Peter remembered his proud, empty boast about dying for his Lord if need be, and now he starts to fulfil his boast. No matter how we look at the action, it was a mistaken one. Peter was guilty of unholy zeal. His Master was wonderfully submissive, but Peter manifested an outburst of fleshly activity. An hour or two later when Jesus was before the high priest confessing a good confession, Peter was denying Him in the presence of the servants with oaths and curses (Luke 22:54-62; I Timothy 6:13). Where was his vaunted courage when, in the presence of a servant girl, he was ashamed to own his Lord?

We now come to our Lord's rebuke of Peter for impetuosity of temperament and for the use of carnal weapons to defend the spiritual. If this miracle proves anything, it is that as the personification of peace, Jesus is against violence and bloodshed. Gentleness, mercy, and benignity are

His powerful, victorious weapons. Alas! Peter at that time had an imperfect knowledge of the nature of Christ's Kingdom. Eagerness to use a sword also evidenced his slowness to appreciate the spiritual nature of the conflict ahead of him.

Jesus had said, "I came not to send peace on earth, but a sword," and failing to understand the symbolism and spirit of His words, the disciples said, "Here are two swords," and He dismissed the conversation with the reply, "It is enough." By such a reply He did not imply that two swords would be sufficient for the need. What He implied was, as Godet suggests: "Yes, for the use which you shall have to make of arms of that kind, those two swords are enough." When in His rebuke of His own, He said, "Suffer ye thus far," He virtually meant, "Hold now; ye have gone thus far in resistance; but let this suffice."

As to the cure wrought by the half-manacled hand of Jesus, Luke, as a physician, had a special interest in all such cures and is the only one telling us of our Lord's extraordinary display of healing grace. Asking for a free hand for a moment, our Lord touched and healed the smitten ear—His last miracle before the cross where He was to heal the sin-wound of a lost world. Ellicott remarks that it is characteristic of Luke's technical, professional accuracy that he uses the diminutive form of "ear" as if part only were cut off. In Deuteronomy 15:17 it seems to be applied specially to the fleshly lobe of the ear.

Although we are not informed just how the ear of Malchus was healed, we do know that this was one of the few miracles Jesus performed without any formal expression of desire, or exercise of faith, on the part of him for whom it was wrought. This aspect, then, must not be lost sight of. Jesus had come to lay down His life for sinners, and in the art of healing the wound of Malchus, He embodied His own precept about loving our enemies. This final miracle before He died was wrought upon an enemy. What amazing grace! Truly, there is no limit to it. An open antagonist healed and blessed! Is this not the essence of the gospel which Paul loved to preach (Colossians 1:21; I Timothy 1:12-15)? All His ways are ways of matchless grace. It is to be hoped that through his experience of Christ's healing power, Malchus was led to the perception of His true character and Messianic dignity and became a true follower of His. The crowd must have wondered at His gracious healing act. As for Peter and his companions, after a brief flush of carnal courage, they forsook Jesus and left Him to face His bitter death—alone.

As for any lessons to be gleaned from the miracle, what else can our Lord's words about putting the sword back in its sheath, for "they who take the sword shall perish with the sword," mean but the only proper place for a sword is *in* the sheath. Is He not here disavowing *force, policy, and anger* as rude methods of opposing wrong? His method of conquering force was by submission; violence, by meekness; sin, by the cross. He wins His victories, not by a sword, but by His scars.

Further, the miracle shows us that in whatever other cause it may be lawful to use carnal weapons, it is not right to draw the sword for Christ and His truth (II Corinthians 10:4). The sword should never be used for the extension or the regression of any purely religious opinions, or for the propagation of what is believed to be the truth. The Crusaders made the mistake of defending a religious cause with carnal weapons. They sought to fight the devil in others with swords, without being ready to fight the devil in their own hearts with self-denial. "All violence used in religion by inquisitors, or by men impatient to enthrone the right, is an example of Peter's mistake. All *hatred* of those doing wrong, all vituperation of them is as Peter's sword."

Jesus calls men to bear His cross, not draw swords for Him. Violent ways fail, but "love never faileth." Taylor says that "Christianity saves men, not by the spilling of *their* blood, but by the shedding *of its own*." Church history provides us with the record of those who were willing to perish by the sword rather than defend themselves with it, and who have ever been the Church's noblest saints. How true it is that "the blood of the martyrs is the seed of the Church."

43. The Miracles En Masse

(John 20:20; 21:25; Acts 10:38)

Having considered all the actual recorded miracles Jesus performed in the days of His flesh, we desire in this section to prove that the many we have considered by no means exhaust the list. Comparatively few of our Lord's miracles are recorded. What we do have serve as samples of the large body of signs Jesus wrought in the presence of His disciples. A full list of *all* He wrought would fill volumes, as John reminds us. We append the following secondary list of partially described miracles for reasons which are apparent. Such a generalization proves how great was our Lord's power.

"Healing *all* manner of sickness and *all* manner of disease" (Matthew 4:23).

"*All* the sick . . . possessed with devils . . . lunatic . . . palsy . . . He healed them" (Matthew 4:24).

"Healed all their sick" (Matthew 8:16).

"Great multitudes followed Him, and He healed them *all*" (Matthew 12:15).

"Healing *every* sickness and *every* disease among the people" (Matthew 9:35).

"These mighty works" (Matthew 13:54, 58).

"He healed their sick . . . They brought unto Him *all* that were diseased" (Matthew 14:14, 35).

"Great multitudes followed Him; and He healed *them* there" (Matthew 19:2).

"The blind and the lame came to Him . . . He healed them" (Matthew 21:14).

"*All* that were diseased . . . He healed *many*" (Mark 1:32-34, 39).

"He healed *many*" (Mark 3:10, 11).

"*Many* mighty works are wrought by His hands" (Mark 6:2, 5).

"As *many* as touched Him were made whole" (Mark 6:55, 56).

"He laid His hands on *every* one of them, and healed them" (Luke 4:40, 41).

"To be healed of their diseases . . . they were healed" (Luke 6:17-19).

"He cured *many*" (Luke 7:21, 22).

"Certain women—healed of evil spirits and infirmities" (Luke 8:2).

"He healed them that had need of healing" (Luke 9:11).

"They saw the miracles which He did" (John 2:23).

"They saw His miracles which He did on them that were diseased" (John 6:2).

There was nothing niggardly in the dispensation of His blessings—He healed them all. Whenever and wherever He met need, He exercised His divine and chosen vocation as the Healer of a disease-stricken humanity.

O. E. Davis, in his evidential study of *The Miracles of Jesus,* has a chapter dealing

with the corroborative evidence in support of the credibility of the Master's miracles that can be adapted for the benefit of the reader. There are a large number of indirect references to miraculous action on the part of Jesus. In the gospels there are forty-two such references. The majority of them are to be found in one gospel only; some are found in two of the gospels and some in three. Nineteen indirect references are found in John's gospel. Here is a rough classification of these references.

Jesus. There are fourteen indirect references by Jesus Himself—Matthew 11:5, 20-24; 16:9, 10; Mark 11:29, 33; Luke 4:22, 25-27; 10:13, 23, 24; 13:32; 20:8; John 4:48; 5:20, 21, 26; 6:26; 7:21; 10:25, 32; 14:10-12; 15:24.

The evangelists. The evangelists report remarks made by others containing references to Christ's miraculous action. In nearly all cases, they explain the conduct of others by a reference to the miracles of Christ. There are many references of this nature. Mark 3:8, 10-12; 5:27; 6:52; Luke 5:15; 7:3, 18; John 4:45; 6:2; 12:1, 9, 17, 18, 37; 20:20, 31.

Nicodemus, John 3:2.

The people. Six indirect references to the miracles of Jesus attributed to the people. Matthew 13:54; Mark 6:2; Luke 19:37; John 7:31; 10:21, 41; 11:37.

Priests. References belonging to this class can be found in Matthew 21:23; 27:42; Mark 3:22; 11:28; 15:31, 32; Luke 20:2; 23:35; John 11:47.

Herod, Matthew 14:1, 2; Luke 9:7-9; Mark 6:14.

Requested miracles, Matthew 12:38; 16:1-4; Mark 8:11, 12; Luke 11:16; John 2:18; 6:30, 31; 7:3.

Insistence on silence with respect to miracles, Matthew 8:4; 12; 16; Mark 1:34, 43, 44; 3:12; 5:43; 7:36; 8:26; Luke 5:14; 8:56.

References to Old Testament miracles. We know how the New Testament is immersed with Old Testament Scriptures. Attention is drawn, and use made of: Elijah, Luke 4:24-26; Moses, John 3:14; manna, John 6:31, 49; Lot's wife, Luke 17:32; Jonah, Luke 11:29-32, etc.

Miracles performed by apostles in the gospels, Matthew 28:18; Mark 3:15; 6:7; 16:17-20; Luke 9:1, 2; 10:9, 17, 19. We shall have more to say about their delegated supernatural power when we come to the Acts.

44. The Miracles at Calvary

(Read each gospel account)

The supernatural surrounds the cross, even as the darkness did, as Jesus died upon it. The miraculous piles up as we study the gospel narratives of the Crucifixion. Arnold of Rugby, in one of his sermons to his "boys," in speaking of the evidence of our Lord's death and resurrection, referred to the many times he had weighed and examined those who had written on these cardinal truths of the Christian faith, and how he himself came to this conclusion:

> I know of no one fact in the history of mankind which is proved by better and fuller evidence of every sort, to the understanding of a fair inquirer, than the great signs (or miracles) which God hath given us that Christ died and rose again from the dead.

There are miracles *through* the cross, miracles *from* the cross, miracles *at* the cross.

As to miracles through the cross, it would take volumes to demonstrate these. The greatest miracles as the result of that "old rugged cross" was the accomplishment of a perfect salvation for a sinful and sinning race. "It took a miracle of grace" to provide redemption for "a world of sinners lost and ruined by the Fall," and at Calvary we behold the spectacle of such a miracle. The purpose of the tremendous miracle of the Incarnation was to work the equally great miracle of man's emancipation from sin's penalty and power. All the miracles He performed while in the flesh were but mirrors, each reflecting its own angle, of His great mediatorial and redemptive work. The creation of the world only cost Him His breath; its redemption cost His blood.

> 'Twas great to call a world from naught,
> 'Twas greater to redeem.

Calvary, or the Hebrew, *Golgotha*, meaning, "the place of a skull," was a fit place for Jesus to die. In death's stronghold the Lord of life gave death His deathblow through. By "dying, death He slew" (Hebrews 2:14). Death on a cross was confined to slaves and malefactors of the worst class. Those thus condemned were usually scourged and stripped. Yet the miracle is that the cross, being in itself the most vile and repulsive of objects, has become in the minds of believers the symbol of all that is holy and precious. The early Christians looked upon His cross as the emblem of victory and hope. Apart from the miracle of salvation accomplished through the cross, in itself it remains what it ever was—a base, contemptible thing, utterly incapable of imparting either life or blessing. But Christ by His death on a cross transformed its vileness into victory.

Dr. G. Campbell Morgan says that "the story of the cross is best read in reverent quietness and meditation. We see all the forces of evil as represented in the Jewish priests and as Pilate joining hands to secure the murder of Jesus. Dr. Alexander Maclaren has remarked that there is something impressive in the unbroken continuity of the clauses in Luke's narrative which follow one another, linked by a simple 'and,' like the waves of the Dead Sea which roll heavily in dreary succession. It is for us to stand on the margin of that sea of unutterable anguish, and to remember that His submerging was for our deliverance."

There are multitudes in heaven and on earth who are rejoicing the marvel of divine grace exhibited at Calvary. Spurgeon could say that his theology could be condensed into four simple words—*He died for me*. How blessed and safe we are if, with John Bunyan, we too can exclaim:

> Blest cross! Blest sepulcher!
> Blest rather be, the Man that there
>   was put to shame for me!

Aside from rejoicing in the miracle of salvation through Christ's finished work, another fascinating aspect of the cross is the miracles associated with it as it stood out silhouetted against the darkening sky. In this connection, reference can be made to that literary treasure by Bishop Nicolson *The Miracles of Calvary*. We commence with the strange, supernatural dream Pilate's wife had as the destruction of Jesus was sought. A common dream, one knows to be common, but this was no common dream. It was light from heaven declaring the innocence of the One about to be crucified. God has His own way of conveying intimation of His will directly, even to heathens like Pilate and his wife, (legend affirms that the latter became a convert to Judaism). That troubled dream was not the mere reflection of the day-thoughts of a sensitive and devout woman—but a divine warning intended to save her husband, who also believed in Christ's innocence, from the guilt into which he was on the point of plunging.

The next miracle wrought at the cross was that of the miracle of prophecy, fulfilled in the parting of and the gambling for Christ's garments. The manifold coincidences of the language of the psalmist (Psalm 22:18) with the facts of the Passion are impressive (Matthew 27:35; John 19:24). Scripture was again fulfilled when Jesus cried, "I thirst" (Psalm 69:21; John 19:28). He had refused the usual stupefying drink at the moment of crucifixion. His holy mind was clear as it offered Himself as the substitute for sin. But when all was accomplished and the moment of His release from death was at hand, He seeks relief from the physical agony of the thirst caused by His wounds. Even in all the cruel events of that day, His mind was on the prophetic word. In God's law He had meditated day and night, and now that law comforts His broken heart.

Other evidences of the miracle of prophecy are seen in Christ being numbered with His transgressors (Isaiah 53:12; Mark 15:28). This is one of the few instances in which Mark draws attention to the fulfilment of prophecy. Then we have the prophecy about His bones being spared from being broken (Exodus 12:46; Numbers 9:12; Psalm 34:20; John 19:36). The leg-breaking, a detail John alone records, consisted in striking the legs with a heavy mallet in order to expedite death. It was sometimes inflicted as a punishment upon slaves. Christ, being dead, was spared this grim treatment, and prophecy was thereby fulfilled. Another Scripture was fulfilled as those around the cross gazed upon its Victim. "They shall look on Him whom they have pierced" (Zechariah 12:10). All alike, Jewish rulers, Roman soldiers, relatives and friends of Jesus, and mere onlookers stood and gazed at that cross and, as Ellicott comments:

That scene is typical. He shall draw all men unto Him, and the moral power over the heart of humanity will be the heart of love, which loves and therefore saves him that has pierced it through and through. "While we were yet sinners Christ died for us."

A further miracle at Calvary was the darkness that covered the land from noon until three in the afternoon. Christ's crucifiers had taken from Him His clothes—the last remnant of His earthly possessions, and the sun refused to shine on its naked Creator writhing in agony and in deeper anguish of soul. Such unusual darkness was nature's sympathy with her suffering Lord, and also another possible fulfilment of prophecy (Amos 8:9).

Through the gloom of Calvary fell the gladsome sunshine of heaven's forgiveness, for this miracle was a further attestation by God to the superlative character of the work His Son was accomplishing by His death. At His birth the darkness of night was turned into the brightest glory; now the brightness of the day is supernaturally turned to night by a pall of darkness, the degree and nature of which is not defined. Halley suggests that "inanimate nature hid her face in shame at the unspeakable wickedness of man, and was, perhaps, trying to express her sympathy with the Son of God in His final grapple with the dark powers of hell. God may have meant the darkness to be creation's symbolic mourning for Jesus while He was suffering the expiatory pains of the lost." It is evident that that outward darkness checked and ended the jests and pleasures of wicked men. Such darkening of the sun was an earnest of "the great and terrible day of the Lord" (Joel 2:31, 32).

The outward darkness, however, but symbolized the inner darkness Jesus was experiencing through the withdrawal of His Father's presence. None of us will ever know what He endured that dark night which He passed through as He died as the Substitute for sinners. What "dumb darkness wrapt His soul apace" as He cried, "My God, my God, why hast Thou forsaken Me?" But this "horror of a great darkness" was but a passing shadow (Genesis 15:12). "In the horror of darkness and distance, the Son of God was enduring the birthpangs of redemption and being cut off in the midst of His days," says Neil Fraser in his volume *The Grandeur of Golgotha.*

According to John Milton, when Adam ate of the forbidden fruit:

Earth trembled from her entrails, as again
In pangs, nature gave a second groan
Sky lour'd, and, muttering thunder, some
    sad drop
Wept at completing of the mortal sin
Original.

We now come to the miracle of the rend-
ing of the veil as the Great High Priest
was about to enter with the blood of His
propitiation into the Temple not made with
hands. The significant feature here is that
the veil was rent "from the top," not *from
the bottom*, meaning, of course, that it was
rent by God, not man. This veil was reckoned to be a hand-breadth in thickness and
woven of seventy-two twisted plaits, each
plait consisting of twenty-four threads. It
was sixty feet long and thirty wide. Two
of them were made every year, and 400
priests were needed to manipulate a veil.
Thus it would have been a herculean task
for a man to rend the veil. What a deep,
spiritual truth is herewith emphasized! The
barrier between God and man was destroyed. The Temple and the old ceremonial
form of worship were no longer needed. A
new and living way was opened into the
presence of God. From that moment, the
cross became that which admitted to,/or
excluded from, the Holy Place, according to
the relation men bore to Christ (Hebrews
9:8; 10:19-31). Ambrose, in an ancient
hymn, expressed it, "When Thou hadst
overcome the sharpness of death Thou didst
open the kingdom of heaven to all believers."

Another supernatural salute to the conquering Saviour was the earthquake and
the rent rocks. Although the area around
Calvary was not supposed to be volcanic,
underground forces were available if the
God of creation should choose to use them,
as He did. When He commands an earthquake, the earth opens at the very spot He
indicates and in no other (Psalm 18:7; 104:
32; Matthew 27:52). In studying Biblical
earthquakes, it is necessary to distinguish
between actual earthquakes and those associated with divine manifestations of power.
For references to the latter, see Matthew
24:7; 27:51, 54; Mark 13:8; Luke 21:11
and earthquakes in the book of Revelation.
In spite of the earthquake at Calvary, the
cross stood.

Accompanying the miracle of the earthquake was another miracle. Graves were
opened and many bodies of the saints which
slept arose. Not *all* the saints arose. The
term "saint" was applied almost from the
very first of the collective body of disciples
(Acts 9:13, 32, 41), and as used by Matthew implies that those believing in Jesus
during His ministry and who had died before His death were those raised at this
time. Jesus, in entering the grave, burst it,
and that opening of graves and visitations
of the glorified were the first fruits, slight
intimations of what is to be, a snowdrop
peering about the wintry ground—the pledge
and promise of the resurrection of all the
dead in Christ.

Then we have the miracle of the blood
and water flowing from the pierced side of
Jesus. John relates this incident with the
solemn affirmation and of the authority of
an eyewitness. If His heart was ruptured,
the blood would have separated out in the
pericardium, that is, the bag enclosing the
heart—into clot and water-looking serum.
This was no more natural phenomenon, the
result of a rupture of the heart, but something entirely unexpected and marvelous.
Christ literally died of a heart broken over
the sin of the world. *Blood and water!* Here
we have symbolized "the double cure." His
death has blood to atone, water to cleanse
(I John 5:6).

Legend has it that as Jesus died, a tidal
wave of immense volume swept around the
world and rose high up in the rivers and
estuaries. If this be true, how symbolic it
is of the abounding grace which on that day
Jesus died rose high above the mighty obstacles of human sin and is destined to lift
the entire universe nearer God, who through
the cross will reconcile all things to Himself, whether in heaven or on earth.

We now come to examine some of the
miracles Jesus accomplished as He died
upon the cross, for He exercised the prerogatives of deity in the very agonies of death.
There was the miracle of self-abnegation,
for He not only died for sin—He died to
self. "Himself He cannot save." He could
have saved Himself from the agonies of
death, but because He was the Son of God,
He did not save Himself. Had He done so,
there would have been no salvation for us.
We cannot save ourselves and others at the
same time. It is only as we lose life that
we find it. Jesus was urged to come down
from the cross, and by such an exercise of
power prove that He was God, but it was
ordained that deity should die. As the Redeemer, He had to drain the cup of its
bitter dregs.

We could tarry and profitably meditate
upon the miracle and mystery of Christ's
God-forsakenness, and think of the depth
of His despair in that moment of terrible
aloneness; "God forsaken of God," as Martin Luther expressed it. Then there was the

miracle of His great sympathy for His dear mother, whose welfare He considered, even though He was experiencing such deep physical anguish. He wrought no miracle for her future support, because that could be better accomplished by ordinary means. Further, there was the manifestation of His divine power in the pardon of the dying thief, who was to be the first trophy of the efficacy of His shed blood. In the moment of His greatest weakness He was able to save to the uttermost the repentant soul turning to Him for forgiveness.

As we close this particular chapter, we desire to draw attention to the tremendous miracle Jesus wrought when He dismissed His own spirit. Augustine says: "He gave up His life *because* He willed it, *when* He willed it, and *as* He willed it." His life was not *taken*, it was *given*. He Himself said that He had power to lay down His life, and to take it away; and both His death and resurrection were at His own command. He knew that all things were now accomplished—an evidence of His omniscience—and so resigned His commission on earth to assume a new one above. It is because of the committal of His spirit to God (Psalm 31:5) that grace can be ours to resign our spirits also in the hope of our final exodus. May ours be the death of the righteous!

> In peace let me resign my breath
> And Thy salvation see;
> My sins deserved eternal death,
> But Jesus died for me!

The multiplication of so many miracles had an overwhelming effect upon the Roman centurion, who confessed that the Man who had died on that middle cross was indeed a supernatural Person—"Truly this was the Son of God" (Matthew 27:54). Pagan though he was, he yet described Him as One worthy to be worshiped and obeyed. While the disciples were silent, this heathen soldier, who apparently had not restrained his men in the cruel mockings of the Saviour, now rises up to witness to, and for, Him. How true it is that His cross draws *all* men unto Him. The phrase "glorified God," used of the centurion, is peculiar to Luke. Then the solemn majesty of such an awful death resulted in many of the people smiting their breasts. Great grief was theirs over such a spectacle.

45. The Miracle of His Resurrection

(Matthew 28:1-10; Mark 16:1-11;
Luke 24:1-12; John 20:1-18;
I Corinthians 15:4-8)

While the resurrection of our Lord Jesus Christ was the crowning miracle of His earthly sojourn, there are one or two minor miracles associated with this cardinal truth of Christianity which demand attention as an introduction to the great miracle itself.

First of all, there was the accompanying great earthquake. The earth shook as Jesus entered the grave (Matthew 27:51); now it quakes again as he leaves it. But just as the first earthquake did not disturb the position of the cross, so this second one did not dislodge the massive stone at His tomb. Nature, in her omnipotence, honored the victorious Christ. To those around the tomb, this further earthquake was another reminder of God's control of all natural forces.

In the second place, we have the appearance, action, and announcement of the august angel of the Lord. Each gospel writer emphasizes different particulars of the Resurrection. Matthew, for instance, only mentions one angel, whose appearance was as lightning. Mark refers to him as "the young man inside the tomb . . . sitting on the right side arrayed in a white robe." Luke speaks of "two men in dazzling apparel;" and John says that there were "two angels in white sitting one at the head and one at the feet where the body of Jesus had lain." This duplication of phenomena was noticed in our studies of the demoniacs (Matthew 8:28) and the blind men at Jericho (20:30). At such a time of intense emotionalism, terror and astonishment, perception and memory are not always very definite about details. It is the appearance of the angelic visitor or visitors we are attracted by—"countenance was like lightning . . . raiment white as snow." The latter phrase has its counterpart in the record of the Transfiguration and the vision of the Ancient of Days (Mark 9:3; Daniel 7:9). Such a supernatural appearance and the stainless robe of white prostrated the soldiers. Through fear of the angelic being, the "keepers did shake and became as dead men." So the feeble women at the tomb found allies in angels. Unexpected help came from unexpected quarters.

How mighty was the ministry of the

angel, or angels! The great, massive stone, "weighing at least fifteen hundredweight, possibly a ton, and probably needing the strength of two or three men for its removal," had been rolled away as easily as if it had been a very small stone. Such a ponderous stone appeared to the disciples as being the object sufficient to entomb the precious body of their Master forever. But this mighty, heavy stone was not only rolled out of its socket, lo! such an obstacle became the seat of the angel. Incidentally, as our Lord in His resurrection body passed through closed doors, He could have easily passed through that solid slab blocking the entrance to the tomb. The rolling away of the stone was not necessary for the departure of Jesus. It was the evidence of the defeat of Rome's power by which the tomb had been sealed, and the assurance that the grave was empty.

Then we have the glorious, angelic announcement, "He is not here: for He is risen, as He said. Come, see the place where the Lord lay"—not where it was, but had been. With comforting tones the angel assured the woman who had come to mourn a dead Christ that He was alive forevermore, and in a moment their whole world was changed. Death was not able to keep its prey. Faith rose from the grave and resumed its trust in God. Hope and consolation also rose from the grave. He lives!

Another minor miracle is that of the peculiar position of Christ's graveclothes. They were "wrapped together," or neatly rolled up, suggesting an orderly arrangement of everything in the tomb, marking the absence of haste and precipitation in the awakening and rising from the dead. It is John who gives us a considerable amount of detail in connection with the graveclothes which are mentioned no fewer than three times, as though some peculiar significance was attached to them. "The napkin that was upon His head" was rolled or coiled up in "a place by itself." The very fact that the napkin was folded did not escape John's eye, nor fade from his memory. Why all this meticulous description of the mere cerements in which the body of Jesus had been wrapped? Had His body been stolen, the valuable clothes saturated with costly spices would not have been left behind. Thieves would not have been at pains to fold up the garments so carefully. Had the clothes been scattered out

in a disorderly fashion, the disciples might well have concluded that the tomb had been disturbed by lawless men.

The miracle here is seen in the fact that on that first Easter morning those graveclothes were found to be in precisely the same position in which they had been left the night before. Not a fold had been displaced. Our Lord's body, in possession now of altogether new powers, had simply passed through the clothes which still retained the shape of His body. The very form of those clothes, and of the napkin carefully folded, convinced the disciples that something wonderful and unprecedented had occurred during the still night watches within the precincts of that new tomb. Their Master had gone, and had left behind these apparently trivial relics associated with death.

In approaching the Resurrection itself, it will be understood that because of the limit of space we cannot fully develop every aspect of such a stupendous miracle. For these, the reader is advised to study the excellent summary to be found in Fairbairn's *Bible Encyclopedia*, which tells us that:

> It is impossible to over-estimate the importance of the resurrection of our Lord, either in itself or in its bearing on the Christian life; nor is it too much to say that a firm conviction of the truth of this one event would dispel almost every difficulty connected with the supernatural origin of our faith, afford conclusive testimony to the claims of the New Testament revelation, and impart to all the followers of Jesus a far larger amount of Christian privilege, and a far loftier standard of Christian living, than is commonly exhibited by them."

Nothing is more explicit in the New Testament than the resurrection of Christ which, with resurrection in general, is mentioned almost 150 times. Christ in the totality of His person came back to this world. His spirit left Paradise and again took possession of His body and was raised from the grave. There are three facts recorded with the utmost clarity and simplicity which no honest mind can deny, namely, Christ died on the cross, was buried in Joseph's tomb, and three days later had risen from the grave. These three facts constituted the gospel which Paul was never ashamed to preach (I Corinthians 15:1-3).

When we accept God in all His almightiness, then anything is possible. "Why should it be thought a thing incredible that God should raise the dead?" (Acts 26:8). The three Persons of the Trinity were united in that resurrection. "God . . . raised Him from the dead" (Colossians 2:12). Jesus said, "I lay down My life that I may take it again" (John 10:17 RV). Then we read that "the Spirit raised Him from the dead" (Romans 8:11; I Peter 3:18).

The resurrection of our Lord is the foundation and one of the central truths of Christianity. "It is inextricably woven into the fabric of the New Testament, and the threads are in both warp and woof of that fabric. To tear it hence would be to destroy the whole." Christ Himself predicted His resurrection (John 2:19 RV), and His empty tomb demonstrated the fulfilment of that prediction. Of no other great religious leader has it ever been said, "He is risen." The body of Guadama, the founder of Buddhism, was duly burnt after his death; that of Mahomet was buried in Mecca; that of Confucius, in his family village. No affirmation of resurrection is associated with any of these three founders of great religions. History turned over a new leaf when Jesus arose triumphant from His grave.

It was on the Resurrection that New Testament writers chiefly rested Christ's claim to be the Son of God (Romans 1:4) and consequently their own claim for inspiration; for if He had not risen, then their preaching was vain (I Corinthians 15:14). The apostles preached the Resurrection on the very spot where it happened and before the very men who had crucified Jesus, and who were aware that He would rise again (Matthew 27:62, 63). The Church was born as the result of the Resurrection. On the day of Pentecost, 3,000, many of whom had assisted in Christ's death, became His disciples, thus giving fresh proof of the power of His resurrection (Acts 2: 36). Later on, other thousands more were added to the Church (4; 21:20). The conversion of Paul is, in itself, an unanswerable proof of the miracle of the Resurrection. In turn, the apostle gave up the *Magna Charta* of the Resurrection, Christ's and ours, as found in I Corinthians 15. Paul also uses the resurrection as a parable of the beginning, the manifestation, and the goal of the new life in Christ (Romans 6:4). Paul likewise reminds us that the King of Glory, who sweetened death by entering the grave, "abolished death" (II Timothy 1:10). The regenerating power of the message he preached authenticated the Resurrection. How he experienced in his fruitful ministry "the power of His resurrection!"

In spite of all the intimations of His Resurrection which Christ gave His disciples, they did not believe them. Had they believed He would rise again, they would not have expended money and effort on the embalmment of His body. One of the most striking evidences, therefore, of the Resurrection is the transformation of the state of mind and conduct of His relatives and friends. Before His death, His own forsook Him and fled. They were abandoned in their despair and hardened in unbelief, in spite of all prophecies they had received (Mark 10:34; Luke 9:22; John 2:19, 21; 10:17). Even when some of the dear women told them of the vision of angels who declared that Jesus was alive, "their words seemed to them as idle tales, and they believed them not" (Luke 24:11, 23). The mournful chant describes their attitude:

Now He is dead! Far hence He lies
  In the lorn Syrian town;
And on His grave, with shining eyes,
  The Syrian stars look down.

But what a different song they sang, one throbbing with confidence and joy, once they were convinced of the reality of the resurrection of their Master. Mark the contrast of their conduct as they testified of the Resurrection, and observe the glow of holy joy they manifested even in the midst of their bitterest sufferings which showed them to be more than conquerors (Acts 4: 13; 5:41, etc.) Read Peter's epistles, knowing that he was the one who had denied his Master with oaths and cursing, who also knew that if Christianity was true, he should die by crucifixion (John 21:18, 19); then ask yourself whence he could have attained his utter devotion to Christ, his hopes and joy, apart from "the resurrection of Jesus Christ from the dead" (I Peter 1: 3). To Peter and the rest of the apostles that Resurrection became the pledge and seat of Christ's acceptance with the Father, and likewise the pledge and seal of a completed redemption; and as they preached this truth, multitudes were saved as they believed that Jesus rose from the dead (Romans 10:9, 10).

It is, therefore, inconceivable that that

scattered and disheartened remnant at the cross could have found "a rallying point and a gospel in the memory of one who had been put to death as a criminal, if they had not believed that God had owned Him and accredited His mission in raising Him up from the dead." We likewise rejoice in the fact that His resurrection is the pledge and earnest of our own. Through Him we, too, have the power of an endless life. "Christ, the first-fruits, afterwards they that are Christ's at His coming." If, in His providence, we go home by the way of a grave, ours is the hope that "this corruption shall have put on incorruption, and this mortal have been clothed with immortality." Alexander Smellie, writing about those who deem Christ's resurrection to be "a baseless dread," says: "If Jesus be not risen, the God of my trust will have played me false. But there let me stop. I cannot bear to go further with the cheerless supposition. And there is no need, for Jesus is risen, and all is well with me, His little one, now and through the everlasting years." (See Luke 20:27, 28; John 5:28, 29).

46. The Miracle of the Second Draught of Fishes

(John 21:1-13)

After several resurrection appearances among His disciples, Jesus manifested Himself to several of them at the Sea of Tiberias. He had requested them to go on before and to meet Him in Galilee (Matthew 28:16), and that is where they are found as the chapter opens. This last chapter of John is regarded as an appendix to the main treatise of his gospel with which it is incorporated. Trench says, "If we regard John 1:1-14 as the prologue, this (21:1-13) we might style the epilogue of his gospel. As here is set forth what the Son of God was before He came from the Father, even so this, in mystical and prophetic guise, how He should rule in the world after He had returned to His Father."

The miracle we are now to consider was the last to be wrought by Jesus before His ascension and closes the series of symbolic acts of power by which Jesus on earth sealed His ministry. While His disciples, who had witnessed so many of those miracles, needed no further proof to convince them of His Godhead, they did need proof that He was really risen from the dead, and

in this miracle He proved in a striking way that it was their own much-loved Jesus who was alive forevermore. He addressed Himself to their memory and their faith, doing again exactly as He had done before on the same lake, the works no other man could do. His highest kind of proof for His identity drew from His disciples the heartfelt confession, "It *is* the Lord."

While Peter and the rest waited for Jesus to come, they felt the time must not be wasted. They must not loiter around; so, finding a boat, the disciples went fishing, as if to suggest, "When He does come, He'll find us among the fish tackle." They simply wished to fill up the time with some kind of occupation. They were only following "the wise rule of the Jewish rabbis, who were ever wont to have some manual trade or occupation on which to fall back in time of need." Paul's skill in making tents came in handy when he was not engaged in his missionary work (II Thessalonians 3:8). So we are not to understand the phrase, "I go a fishing," as if Peter was surrendering his high position as an apostle or that he had any doubt about Jesus not fulfilling His word about meeting him in Galilee. In no way had Peter, or the rest, given up the old Messianic hope and were returning permanently to their previous occupations. When Jesus did finally appear, He had no rebuke for His disciples when He found them fishing.

That night's fishing, however, was futile, for the disciples caught nothing. The word "caught" is slightly different from that used in the first miraculous draught of fishes (Luke 5:5). This particular word appears in no other gospel but is a favorite word of John's (7:30, 32, 44; 8:20; 10:39; 11: 57; 21:3, 10. See Revelation 19:20), one which he used to describe the seizure of Christ by the authorities. The same term is used of apprehending Peter and Paul (Acts 12:4; II Corinthians 11:32)—of the taking by the hand (Acts 3:7)—of the taking of the Beast (Revelation 19:20).

Why were the disciples unsuccessful in their quest for necessary fish to eat? F. B. Meyer answers such a question in his own unique, devotional way: "That night was the most favorable time! These men knew the lake well and were experienced in their craft. They did their best but caught nothing! Why was this? Was it a chance? No, it was a providence; it was carefully arranged, disappointing and vexing though it was, by One who was too wise to err, too good to be unkind, and who was preparing to teach them a lesson which should enrich them and the whole Church forever."

The failure put an arrest on their temporal pursuits. Had they been successful that night, it would have been very much harder for them to renounce the craft forever; but their non-success made them more willing to give it up and to turn their thoughts to the evangelization of the world.

When they returned in the early morning without a catch, Jesus stood on the shore, but in the dimness of the twilight the disciples failed to recognize Him (20:14). He gave no indication of His presence, and when and how He came we are not told. In His resurrection body He was not bound by the limitations of human locomotion. "His body after the resurrection was only visible by a distinct act of His will." Christ was able to appear and disappear with mysterious suddenness, for He was no "longer subject to the laws of the material order to which his earthly life had been previously conformed." Bishop Westcott says: "The continuity, the intimacy, the simple familiarity of former intercourse is gone. He is seen and recognized only as He wills, and when He wills." Further, an indication of a mysterious change in Christ's appearance when He was seen is in the question the disciples asked openly: "Who are thou?" Such a supernatural change in the manifestation of His presence was to change everything for His own.

Our Lord's question, "Children, have you any meat?" failed to reveal His identity. The term "children" is not one expressing affectionate tenderness as previously used (13:33). It means *sirs*, or *lads*, implying His plan to conceal His identity a little longer. The disciples probably felt that the questioner was a stranger passing by who wanted to buy some fish, and they had to answer, somewhat dismally, "No." Fish dealers usually went to greet fishermen on their return from the night's toil, in order to buy up the fish. Some writers see in this answer a picture of the present barrenness of Israel. "The question was indeed asked to draw forth this acknowledgement from their lips: for it is well that the confessions of man's poverty should go before the incomings of the riches of God's bounty and grace" (see John 5:6; 6:7-9).

The eyes of the disciples were still temporarily veiled, and the identity of the stranger still undetected. When He said, "Cast the net on the right side of the ship, and ye shall find," they thought that perhaps this Man had seen fish on the right side which they had not noticed. But they obeyed and had a tremendous haul of fish. The Almighty One knew where the fish were located and could direct them into the net. Since He was the Creator of the fish, they obeyed His call (Psalm 8). Such a display of omniscience and power revealed to John, whom Jesus loved, the identity of the One who made the great haul of fish possible. With keen insight, he exclaimed to Peter, "It is the Lord!" The net had to be cast on the right side of the ship—the right was the hand of good omen and value. There is only one way of working with the Lord—the *right* way.

As soon as Peter heard that it was the Lord, he put on his outer fisher's coat and, impetuously, plunged into the sea, swam to the shore—the first to do homage at the feet of Jesus. John was the seer, the man of faith; Peter was the doer, the man of action. Then the ship came in, dragging the net full of fishes, but what a pleasant surprise awaited them that early morning on the shore. Breakfast of fish and bread was all ready for them—and the cook and host, JESUS!

How was that morning meal prepared? Was the fish and bread secured and the fire kindled in a natural way, or did Jesus in some miraculous way produce the fire and the food, as in some Old Testament miracles? The Bible does not say. Habershon remarks that "to those who believe that the One who stood that morning on the shore of the lake was indeed the Son of God, the wonder of the scene is not the net full of fishes, but the fire of coals and the fish upon it. The Creator could easily summon the creatures He had, but we marvel that He should stoop to light a fire. We are not told how He did it. Did the nail-pierced hands collect the wood and lay the fire, or did He at a word cause the fire to appear? We know not, nor could we say which were the greater marvel." Jesus requested His disciples to bring to the fire side the fish they had caught. He could have created fish enough to feed the hungry men, but that was unnecessary since 153 great fishes were at hand. "Christ is willing to deal lavishly in miracles so long as needed, but not a pinch beyond. He is frugal of the miraculous."

As to the exact number of the great fishes caught (153 altogether), some prove that it was no ordinary catch. Being large, the fishes were easily counted. The 153 indicate the number of the species of fish found in the Sea of Galilee. One of every known kind was in the net. Spurgeon comments on Peter's reasoning for counting the fishes. "I think I know why the Lord made him do it. It was to show us that though in outward instrumentality of gathering the people into the Church the number of the saved is to us a matter of which we know nothing definitely, yet secretly and invisibly the Lord has counted them even to the odd one. He knoweth well how many the Gospel net shall bring in. . . . How many are in the *invisible* Church? He has counted them, foreordained their number, fixed them, and settled them. The number 153 seems to represent a large, definite number." Many of the early Church Fathers had mystical interpretations of the 153. Some suggested that the number expresses symbolically the name of Simon Peter.

What a sweet invitation the disciples received from their Master! "Come and dine." With so much fish to eat, what a breakfast they must have had! There was enough and to spare in such a catch. Bengel says, "By the Lord's gift they had caught them: and yet, He courteously says, that *they* have caught them." We are not told whether Jesus Himself partook of the meal. In His resurrection body, the material was no longer necessary. The richest feature of the simple repast was the presence of their Lord, yet, so filled with awe and reverence at the sight of Him who had risen from the dead, they did not dare question His identity; they knew it was Jesus. As He took the bread and fish and blessed them, those scars were visible in His hands. "None durst ask Him, Who are Thou?" All of them knew that it was the Lord. This early meal was a kind of resumption of the Last Supper. There was something mysterious and majestic about His form—rather felt than seen.

That meal of the Lord's own preparing and dispensing—*upon the shore*—is surely a symbol of the great festival in heaven which He is preparing for His own. That lake shore is a foregleam of the time when, after His return for His toiling servants, He will "make them to sit down to meat, and will come forth and serve them." What

a day that will be when we hear His musical voice say, "Come and dine."

> Christ shall the banquet spread,
> With His own royal hand,
> And raise His faithful servant's head,
> Amid the angelic band.

Before we leave this final miracle of Christ's before His ascension on high, it may be profitable to compare and contrast the two miraculous draughts of fish. For a rich and rewarding study of this aspect, the reader is referred to Spurgeon's unique exposition on *The Two Draughts of Fishes*. The first draught was at the beginning of our Lord's ministry (Luke 5:4-7)—the second draught, at the end of His sojourn on earth. While both took place on the shore of Galilee after a night of fruitless toil and brought Peter to the feet of his Master, at the first miracle he was commissioned to be a fisher of men—at the second miracle, a shepherd of the sheep. The first miracle convicted him of the lack of holiness, the second, of the lack of love. At the first miracle Christ manifested His glory, and His disciples—not others—believed on Him. In this, His last miracle, He *manifested Himself*, He *was manifested*, according to His pleasure; and faith apprehended Him.

Further meanings of the two miracles are as follows: The first miraculous draught was as much a parable as a miracle. It qualified the disciples for service as they continued with the Lord. It also represents the visible Church containing good and bad. Often the net breaks and many escape. The second miraculous draught was a symbol of the disciples' future work they were to render after Christ had left them— a witness to be maintained by the Spirit's presence and power. This miracle symbolizes God's elect foreknown by Him. All in this net are good and will be brought to shore with the net unbroken (John 17:11-13).

Would not the disciples feel in their deepest hearts the true significance of this repeated sign from their risen Lord and gracious Host? Did they not discern that in His closing hours with them He was preparing them to carry out His commission about going into all the world to preach the redeeming Gospel which He made possible by His death and resurrection? Henceforth they were to cast the net on the right side of the ship and great success in missionary enterprise was to be theirs, and to this end they left their boats, nets, and fishing forever.

In the conversation following the significant meal, of which Trench says that "it was sacramental in character, and had nothing to do with the stilling of their present hunger," Jesus asked Peter the threefold question about love. When He said, "Lovest thou Me more than *these?*" (whether He meant by *these* the other disciples, or the fishes, boats and nets), Peter who had thrice denied his Lord, now thrice declares his love for Him, and is thrice entrusted with service for Him. With the commission Peter received, there also came a prophecy of his death, and out he went to serve his Lord most faithfully until he sealed his testimony with his blood.

47. The Miracle of Post-Resurrection Appearances

Associated with and affording incontestable proofs of the resurrection of Christ, are His many appearances to His disciples before His ascension. These were "infallible proofs," says Luke, that He was alive (Acts 1). How He appeared, or in what form, whether with radiance surrounding Him, as on the Mount of Transfiguration (Matthew 17:1-13), we cannot say. Fausset says, "The Transfiguration before His passion shows how His resurrection body could be the same body, yet altered so it will be more or less recognizable to beholders. The progress of its progressive glorification probably began from His resurrection, and culminated at His ascension.'" His body, lacerated and broken, was placed in a tomb; yet on the third day it was revived into a body of flesh and blood, capable of being handled and of recovering food and drink. His appearances were no apparitions of a spiritualistic kind, neither was His a normal life in the body. Somehow His face and form were different, and He could suddenly appear, and just as suddenly vanish (Luke 24:31; John 20:26).

It is clearly evident, as Graham Scroggie suggests, that "there was nothing 'docetic' about Jesus' body, yet there was something supernatural." While among men, He exhibited a unique power somewhat strange to us. He could pass through the midst of His enemies and go on His way, or hide Himself as He chose (Luke 4:30; John 5:13; 8:59). Swete reminds us that "before the Passion the Lord's sinless human will possessed a power over His body which is wholly beyond our experience or comprehension." Such power was accentuated after His resurrection.

We now come to an examination of His supernatural appearances, all of which bear evidence to His defeat of death (Luke 24:15; John 20:20; Acts 10:41). "For Him now, physical limitations, as regards time and space, do not exist, and this freedom from temporal conditions resulted in a life which transcended ordinary experience." The places and number and variety of these appearances can be tabulated in this order:

Our Lord appeared—

(1) To certain women—the "other Mary," Salome, Joanna, and others—as they returned from the sepulcher after having seen the angel who told them that the crucified, buried Saviour had risen. These women were the first heralds of the miracle of His resurrection. Of this appearance Matthew alone gives us the full account (28:1-10), but some details of the company and of the visit which Matthew omits are found in Mark 16:1-8 and Luke 24:1-11.

(2) To Mary Magdalene at the sepulcher, in all probability upon her second visit to it that morning, and after she had run to tell Peter and John the glorious news that the grave was empty. This appearance, recorded at length by John (20:11-18), is also attended to by Mark (16:9-11). This appearance raises the question as to what Jesus wore, since He left all His burial clothes behind in the grave. Through her tear-filled eyes, Mary failed to recognize her Lord, yet there He was, figure, features, and clothing. Since she supposed Him to be the gardener, did He assume such a human guise so as not to frighten her? He spoke to her in her own language, yet she did not recognize His voice, but when He mentioned her name there was something about the tone of that much-loved voice that revealed the identity of the speaker. Her name brought back all the old associations and crying, "Master!" she fell at His feet to embrace Him. But such a customary reverential embrace was not permitted. Mary wanted to cling to His visible presence. She had to learn, however, that He had not returned to earth to abide permanently with His disciples, but that it was expedient for Him to go away that the *Paraclete* might come.

(3) To the Apostle Peter, under circumstances of which we have no particular account. It would seem as if this appearance took place on the first day of the Resurrection, and before evening (Luke 24: 23; I Corinthians 15:5). How Peter would remember his declaration of love as he saw his Lord, the vision of whom must have intensified that love.

(4) To the two disciples on the Emmaus road, toward evening of the first day of the Resurrection (Luke 24: 13-15; Mark 16:12, 13). We read that "He was manifested in another form" to these two men. What is meant by "a different form" is hard to determine. Some old writers take it to refer to Jesus' dress, and since He was mistaken as a stranger to those parts, was this another guise He adopted? The reason given for the non-recognition is that "their eyes were holden." Their senses were under supernatural control so that they knew Him not. His garb and tone suggested that He was only a man of like passions with themselves.

(5) To the ten apostles, Thomas being absent, and "others with them" whose names are not given (Luke 24:33). These disciples were assembled together on the evening of the first day of the Resurrection (Mark 16:14-18; Luke 24:33-36, 49; John 20:19-23; I Corinthians 15:5). After this visit, a week passed with no appearance of the risen Saviour. The following Sunday, however, His appearances continued.

(6) To the eleven disciples, Thomas now being present, when Jesus permitted him to handle the nail prints and drew from him the confession, "My Lord and my God." This appearance also took place at Jerusalem, and most probably in the same apartment when Jesus came to the ten apostles.

In connection with this supernatural appearance, there is another of those minor miracles we cannot afford to neglect. We read that for fear of the Jews, the disciples shut and bolted the doors of the apartment. They never meant to bar the doors against Jesus. As yet, they had not been baptized into the heroism of Pentecost. The spirit of fearlessness was not theirs. At any moment the staves of Jewish enemies might beat upon the door, and they were afraid. But although the doors were shut, Jesus, without giving any secret knock for admission, passed through those fast-closed doors

and stood in their midst. How He entered we do not know. Already He belonged to another realm.

Scientist John Best gives us an interesting and possible explanation of the miracle. A liquid can pass through a solid, as when water passes through a sponge or a filter, and a solid can pass through a liquid as well as one falls to the bottom of a pond, but how can a solid pass through a solid? Jesus could pass through obstacles more or less impervious to nature, as through winding sheets, stone barriers, and closed doors. Paul speaks about "the spiritual body" (I Corinthians 15:35-45; II Corinthians 5:1-4), a frame which is not made with hands, but is eternal, and one in which he longed to be clothed. What is this "spiritual," or "ethereal" body? Is it a body composed possibly of some still finer substance at present unknown to us, but in any case a physical body, possessed of extension and presumably of a number of inter-related parts?

If this is admitted, then Jesus had a "spiritual body," only with this one great difference—that in virtue of His superior powers, He could at any moment and in any place "materialize" and afterwards "dematerialize" Himself whenever He willed to do so. Best goes on to say that when Jesus appeared to His disciples in the upper chamber on the evening of that first Easter day, not only did its closed doors offer no obstacle to His spiritual body passing through them but He could immediately afterwards by "materialization" present Himself to them in His well-beloved familiar form.

Another manifestation of the miraculous at this appearance was the strange blending of the natural and supernatural. His natural features and nail prints were visible. Then there was His question about having anything to eat. How He could be independent of food, yet partake of it, and also become visible or invisible at will, are matters beyond our present knowledge.

(7) To several disciples, of whom at least four, and probably the rest, were apostles, at the Sea of Galilee when they were fishing. John is the sole recorder of this appearance when Jesus prepared a breakfast for the weary fishermen.

(8) To the apostles and more than 500 brethren at once, upon an appointed mountain in Galilee. Both Matthew (28:16-20),

and Paul (I Corinthians 15:6) refer to this appearance.

(9) To James, under circumstances of which we have no record. (I Corinthians 15:7). Whatever the occasion, this valiant witness must have been inspired to serve his Lord more devotedly.

(10) To the apostles at Jerusalem immediately before the Ascension, when they accompanied Jesus from Jerusalem to Mount Olivet, where they witnessed His glorious ascent to heaven, till a cloud received Him out of their sight (Mark 16: 19; Luke 24:50-52; Acts 1:3-9).

(11) To the Apostle Paul on his way to Damascus to slay the Lord's people. Without doubt, this was a special manifestation of Jesus after His ascension, and was one resulting in the conversion of Christ's outstanding trophy of grace (Acts 9:3-9, 17; I Corinthians 9:1; 15:8).

While we have indicated eleven different occasions upon which, after His resurrection, Jesus manifested Himself to His disciples, we have no means of knowing whether these were the only occasions. From Luke's declaration that Jesus "showed Himself alive after His passion, by many infallible proofs, being seen of them forty days, and speaking of things pertaining to the kingdom of God" (Acts 1:2, 3), it would seem as if there may have been other occasions when the apostles at least had the opportunity of beholding and conversing with the Master they all dearly loved. This we do know, that the evidence of so many who saw Him is sufficient proof for the stupendous nature of the miracle of the Resurrection. How apt are the lines of Dr. Harkness:

I know not how the miracle was wrought,
The story says the stone was rolled away;
That angels sat within as Mary sought
Her risen Lord; that linen grave clothes lay.
That Jesus stood there speaking words of cheer
And walked with two along the Emmaus road.
That when eleven were gathered, sick with fear,
They felt His presence, saw the wounds He showed.
"How can it be?" I hear men say in doubt,
Like Thomas, who must see the nails' imprint,
I know not how these things could come about.

48. The Miracle of the Ascension

(Mark 16:19, 20; Luke 24:50-52; Acts 1:4-11)

The glorious ascension of our blessed Lord only ratified and presented in a final form the lessons of the forty days in which it is included. What a blessed consummation this was to His mission on earth! *He ascended into heaven.* Christ's resurrection and ascension join with His life and death to assure Him of immortal honor and worship. Faith has no doubt regarding His visible ascension into heaven. "The incidents of the forty days between the Resurrection and the Ascension are so full of new wonders," says Habershon, "and so clearly prove that in His resurrection body the Lord put forth new powers, that we can believe the story of the Ascension without attempting to explain how it was possible from a human standpoint. The witnesses of the Ascension were as reliable as those of the Resurrection; and their testimony is corroborated by the fact that the Lord Himself was seen in like glory by Stephen, by Paul, and by John."

After Christ's promise that His disciples should be His witnesses from Jerusalem to the uttermost parts of the earth, their last glimpse was of Him in the act of blessing them, even as His Sermon on the Mount began with blessing them (Luke 24:51; Acts 3:26). This sacramental benediction was symbolic of the continuous ministry He was entering upon in heaven, where He ever liveth to make intercession for us. The high priest bestowed his benedictions upon the people as he emerged from the Temple at important festivals (Psalm 110; Hebrews 7 - 9). How assuring it is to know that His priestly hands are ever uplifted on our behalf.

The mention of the miracle

Both Old and New Testament references to the Ascension require our close study, and their teaching must be carefully observed. While this great event is omitted by Matthew, and may appear to be treated somewhat scantily in Mark and Luke, yet there are sufficient certain anticipations of it that cannot be ignored. Hastings *Dictionary of the Bible* remarks that —

The Resurrection is itself the strongest witness to the reality of the Ascension, as the virgin birth, nor would either in the nature of the case have been capable of winning its way to acceptance apart from the central faith that Jesus actually rose from the dead.

The Ascension and exaltation of Christ were foretold by the psalmist (Psalm 68: 18; 110:1, 5).

During the course of His earthly ministry, Christ alluded to His coming enthronement in glory. The event was constantly before Him and was also eagerly anticipated. While, as Hort observes, "The Ascension did not lie within the proper scope of the gospels . . . its true place was at the head of the Acts," nevertheless the gospels give sufficient evidence of the reality of the event. As to gospel references to the Ascension, the following should be looked up and their language closely observed—Mark 16:19; Luke 9:51; 24:26, 50, 51; John 3:13; 6:62; 7:33, 34; 12:32; 13:3; 14:2-4, 12, 28; 16:5, 7, 10, 16-19, 28; 17:11; 20:17. Then we have the testimony in the rest of the New Testament—of Luke in Acts 1:9-11; of Peter in Acts 2:32-34; 3:15, 20, 21; 5:30, 31; I Peter 3:21, 22; of Paul in Romans 8:34; Ephesians 1:20, 21; 2:6; 4:8; Colossians 3:1; I Timothy 3:16; Hebrews 1:3; 4:14; 8:1; 9:24; 10:12; 12:2; of Stephen in Acts 7:55, 56; of John in Revelation 1:1, 10-20; 5:5-13; 6:9-17; 14:1-5.

A study of these passages clearly reveal that the living Christ who is in heaven is active on behalf of His Church and will be until His return for her. Summarizing the teaching of the foregoing references, we agree with Griffith Thomas that "the Ascension is regarded as the point of contact between the Christ of the gospels and of the epistles. The gift of the Spirit is said to have come from the ascended Christ. The Ascension is the culminating point of Christ's glorification after His resurrection and is regarded as necessary for His heavenly exaltation. The Ascension was proved and demanded by the Resurrection, though there was no need to preach it as part of the evangelistic message. Like the virgin birth, the Ascension involves doctrine for Christians rather than non-Christians. It is the culmination of the Incarnation, the reward of Christ's redemptive work, and the entrance upon a wider sphere of work in His glorified condition, as the Lord and Priest of His Church" (John 7:39; 16:7).

The miracle of the miracle

No fewer than thirteen words are used to describe Christ's departure from earth to heaven, and taken together they reflect shades of meaning of such a stupendous event. He is described as being "taken up," "received up," "borne up," "raised up," and "carried up," phrases indicating the mode of His ascension, a transition from one locality to another, as well as from one condition to another. While none of His disciples saw Jesus rise from the dead, all of them did witness His ascent into heaven. It was necessary that they should see Him ascend in order to be sure that He had ascended. While such a miraculous event may be beyond scientific scrutiny, the fact is plain that He who came into this world went from it, and never since has been physically in it. There is no greater difficulty in accepting the Ascension than there is in accepting the Incarnation or the Resurrection. The laws of nature were divinely superseded in all three events. In some supernatural way the human, glorified body of Jesus was uplifted till it disappeared. As the Lord of nature, He is beyond all physical laws or atmospheric pressure, presently making it impossible for us to rise from the ground. The Ascension was Christ's final de-materialization, or disappearance into the spiritual world. The same miracle will take place for all the Lord's people when they are "caught up" to meet the Lord in the air. Then, like Him, we too shall withdraw from "a world of limitations to that higher existence where God is." Without concern about any scientific explanation of ascending bodies, we accept the essential fact that Jesus departed and disappeared and that we too shall follow His ascent into heaven.

The meaning of the miracle

The true significance of the Ascension is excellently summarized by Dr. W. Griffith Thomas in The International Standard Bible Encyclopaedia. "The Ascension is not only a great fact of the New Testament, but a great factor in the life of Christ and Christians, and no complete view of Jesus Christ is possible unless the Ascension and its consequences are included. It is the consummation of His redemptive work. The Christ of the gospels is the Christ of history, the Christ of the past, but the full New Testament picture of Christ is that of a living Christ, the Christ of heaven, the Christ of experience, the Christ of the present and the future."

The inner message of the Ascension is that He who from the beginning had dwelt in divine glory with the Father now returns to Him in a human yet glorified form; and that His ascension was to Him, the final proof that He was indeed the Christ, the Son of God, and at the same time the Almighty God with power to fulfill His promises. His exaltation to the right hand of God therefore meant that such a glorious event was:

(1) The proof of victory (Ephesians 4:8, 11; Psalm 68:18).
(2) The position of honor (Psalm 110:1; Philippians 2:9-11).
(3) The place of power (Acts 2:33; I Peter 3:22).
(4) The place of happiness (Psalm 16:11).
(5) The place of rest (Hebrews 1:3, "seated").
(6) The place of permanence—"Forever" (Hebrews 10:12).
(7) The place of prevailing prayer (Romans 8:33, 34; Hebrews 7:24, 25).

Christ's ascent to heaven is the point of contact between the Man Jesus Christ as seen and known in the gospels and the glorified Christ of the epistles, and it "preserves the historical character of the former and the universality of the latter in true continuity. It enabled the disciples to identify the gift of Pentecost with the promise of the Holy Spirit, which had been specially connected with the withdrawal of Jesus from bodily sight and return to His Father." As the result of His being "carried up," provision was made for His universal presence in the Church which His death, resurrection and ascension brought into being.

As Jesus entered heaven, two men left there and came to the spot in Bethany He had just left. They assured the men of Galilee whose eyes were still strained upward that the One who just left them would return in the same manner as He had gone into heaven, which, of course, is the truth Paul elaborated (I Thessalonians 4:13-18). Bishop Hall, that spiritually-minded expositor of a bygone age, left us this illuminating paragraph and prayer:

> There are three bodily inhabitants of heaven, Enoch, Elijah, and our Saviour Christ: the first before the law; the second under the law; and the third under the Gospel, all three in a several form of translation. Our blessed Saviour raised Himself to, and above, the heavens by His own immediate power. He ascended as the Son, they as servants; He as God, they as creatures. Elijah ascended by the visible ministry of angels, Enoch sensibly.

Then follows the dear Bishop's prayer:

> Wherefore, O God, hast Thou done this, but to give us a taste of what shall be; to let us see that heaven was never shut to the faithful; to give us an assurance of the future glorification of this mortal and corruptible part? Even thus, O Saviour, when Thou shalt descend from heaven with a shout, with the voice of the archangel, and the trump of God, we that are alive and remain shall be caught up, together with the raised bodies of Thy saints, into the clouds, to meet Thee in the air, to dwell with Thee in glory. Amen!

II.

THE MIRACLES IN THE ACTS

The fifth book of the New Testament presents some of the most graphic writing to be found in the whole Bible, or in the entire realm of literature, for that matter. It is a book saturated with the supernatural. Take away the miracles out of the Acts of the Apostles and there is little left, as our study of its miraculous content will show. The majority of the book's miracles were wrought by Peter and Paul, the two outstanding personalities in apostolic history.

Actually, the title is not altogether in keeping with the contents of the book, for what it records is not so much the acts of some of the apostles, as the acts of the Holy Spirit through the apostles.

It is because the manifold ministry of the Holy Spirit—mentioned by name some sixty times—dominates the book that it has been called *The Acts of the Holy Spirit Through the Apostles*. Everywhere there is a manifestation of His power. In dealing with the work of the Spirit, a distinction must be made between His *miraculous* and *ordinary* influences. In the book before us, the former are most prominent. Chrysostom called Acts, "The Gospel of the Holy Spirit."

The book itself was written by Luke, the "beloved physician, an eyewitness of all recorded therein. In his Prologue (Luke 1:3), Luke tells us that, "It seemed good to me also, having had perfect understanding of all things from the very first, to write unto thee, most excellent Theophilus." The phrase *from the very first* is elsewhere translated *from above* (John 3:31; 19:11; James 1:17; 3:15, 17), and seems to indicate that Luke's perfect understanding of all things was the result of divine inspiration, and not merely the outcome of his own carefully calculated order of events.

Further, Luke narrates that Acts concerns those things which "Jesus *began* to do and teach." Thus the book is a continuation of the miraculous and teaching ministry of Jesus. Rotherham has this note in his valuable *Emphasized Bible*, "The *first* narrative (Luke's gospel) told of all which Jesus, while on earth, *began* to do and to teach; this *second* narrative (Luke's Acts) tells of all things which Jesus, from heaven, *went on* to do and to teach. This emphatic implication is a key to the following story." Jesus said that He would build His Church (Matthew 16:16), and His death and resurrection were the foundation of that Church. "With His own blood He bought her." At Pentecost, through the coming of the Spirit, the disciples, existing as units, were fused into the mystic fabric known as the Church of the living God. As the divine commission was fulfilled, the Church grew most rapidly through the ministry of the apostles. Thus, the story of the Acts can be briefly stated—the Lord going up; the Spirit coming down; and the Church going out; and as she went out in the name and power of her risen Lord, great and mighty things happened.

The gospels close with a prophetic allusion to several facts recorded in the Acts, with a promise of the Holy Spirit, of which this book gives the fulfilment (Mark 16:17; Luke 24:27-29; John 14:12-17). The epistles also plainly suppose that those facts had actually occurred which the Acts relates, hence the importance of the latter, as a kind of postscript to the gospels, and as an introduction to the epistles, is designed for the enlightenment of Christians concerning the historic origins of Christianity. It is the first church history, in which is described the establishment of the Church in Jerusalem and her expansion to Samaria and all over the Roman Empire.

Coming to the miraculous content of the Acts, it is obvious that in such a dynamic, dramatic book God made abundant use of the supernatural in giving Christianity a start in the world. The reader will recall what we have already indicated about groups of miracles being associated with particular crises or epochs. In approaching a study of the particular miracles in the Acts, attention must be drawn to the fact that the supernatural work in the Bible may be divided into two classes, as Habershon points out:

(1) Those in which God put forth His power and, working alone, did something which seemed above nature—works with which men were unfamiliar (Isaiah 44:24). This type of miracle has not altogether ceased.

(2) Those in which He worked by means of a visible agent. In this type of miracle, we have delegated power—power passing through a human agent. Most of these miracles were evidential miracles, given as credentials of God's messengers at the beginning of a new dispensation. For instance, Christ's deity as God's Son was authenticated by His miracles. Miracles of this type ceased with the apostles. The Acts relate both kinds of miracles—direct and indirect.

1. The Miracle of Christ's Resurrection

(1:3)

Because of the prominence given to the resurrection of our Lord in apostolic preaching, this miracle book of the Acts has been called, "The Gospel of the Resurrection." It was the emphasis of this cardinal truth of Christianity that made the apostles so dynamic and successful in their ministry. Having dealt with the victory over the grave, we simply pause for a moment to draw attention to the word "infallible" which Luke uses to describe the incontestable proofs of the Resurrection. No other writer in the Bible uses this word for which, Ellicott says, "there is no adjective in the Greek answering to it." The noun, however, "is one used by writers on rhetoric for proofs that carried certainty of conviction with them, as contrasted with those that were only probable or circumstantial." Plato and Aristotle employ the Greek for "infallible," to denote "the strongest proof of which a subject is susceptible."

Faith in the Resurrection, then, rests not on *fallible* hopes but on *infallible* proofs; not on pious expectations, but on demonstrative evidence. Luke limits the proofs to the ministry of Jesus between His resurrection and His ascension, "being seen of them forty days." Such a period had its counterpart in the forty days of the Temptation (Luke 4:2), and in the experiences of two Old Testament prophets (Exodus 24:18; I Kings 19:8). Ellicott comments that "There was a certain symbolic fitness in the time of triumph on the earth coinciding with that of special conflict. If we ask what was the character, if one may so speak, of our Lord's risen life between His manifestation to the disciples, the history of the earlier forty days in part suggests the answer. Then, as before, the life was, we believe, one of solitude and communion with the Father, no longer tried and tempted, as it had then been, by contact with the power of evil—a life of intercession such as that which uttered itself in the great prayer of John 17."

2. The Miracle of the Ascension

(1:9-11)

As this notable event has also been previously considered, only a passing word is necessary as we meet with it in this miracle book. It was from His much-loved Bethany that Jesus was taken up from His disciples. "A cloud received Him out of their sight." How baffled we are as we try to understand the process of His glorious ascension! Here we are in a region of thought in which it is not easy to move freely. To quote Ellicott again:

With our thoughts of the relations of the earth to space and the surrounding orbs, we find it hard to follow that motion upward and to ask what was its direction and when it terminated. We cannot get beyond the cloud: that that cloud was the token of the glory of the Eternal Presence, as the Shekinah that of old filled the Temple (I Kings 8:10, 11; Isaiah 6:1-4), and it is enough for us to know that where God

is, there also is Christ, in the glory of the Father, retaining still, though under new conditions and laws, the human nature which made Him like unto His brethren.

3. The Miracle of the Second Advent

(1:10, 11. See I Thessalonians 4:13-18; Revelation 22)

It is interesting to note that our Lord uses the same word of our coming ascension as Luke here uses to describe Christ's ascension. "A cloud received Him"—He is to "receive" us unto Himself (John 14:3) which, of course, is equivalent to meeting Him in the air (I Thessalonians 4:16, 17). Later on, when we come to the epistles, we shall deal more fully with the theme of our Lord's return. Here, we tarry for a moment to point out what exactly happened at this moment. As soon as Jesus left earth and entered heaven, two men in white apparel left heaven for earth to assure the awe-struck disciples that the Christ who had just left them would return "in like manner" as He went away.

First of all, the message of these two men, who were likely Moses and Elijah, confirmed the declaration of Jesus concerning His return (John 14:3). "I will come again"—"shall so come." Then the phrase "in like manner" suggests that His descension is to correspond to his ascension. If we realize how He went away, then we know His return will correspond. Well, Jesus went away in the presence of His own — personally — visibly — suddenly — in a cloud, and His second advent will follow the same pattern, as the heavenly visitants affirmed.

4. The Miracles at Pentecost

(2:1-47)

Obedient to divine instruction, the disciples tarried at Jerusalem, there to await the coming of the Holy Spirit (1:4, 5), when He came in all the plentitude of His power. It must be borne in mind that He came, not because the disciples tarried, but because He had been promised by the Father and the Son (Luke 24:49). The waiting period, however, prepared the disciples spiritually to receive the Spirit when He came to inaugurate the Church. Pentecost has been referred to as "the birthday of the Church"—which it was, historically.

Everything about that memorable day was supernatural. Had it not been divinely chosen as the day on which the disciples were to receive the promised Spirit, in whose power they were to fulfil the divine commission of witnessing unto the Lord (Matthew 28:18-20; Acts 1:8)? As to the various aspects of the miraculous, we have, first of all, the history and symbolic fitness of the Feast of Pentecost. There were three great, yearly feasts when all the males· in Israel were required to go up to Jerusalem, namely, the Passover, or Feast of Unleavened Bread; Pentecost, or Feast of Weeks, Feast of the First Fruits, Feast of the Harvest, because the first-fruits of the harvest were then presented to God; and the Feast of Tabernacles.

Pentecost, signifying "fiftieth" (Leviticus 23:15-17), began on the morrow after the Passover Sabbath, when the sheaf of the first fruits of the harvest were waved before the Lord (as a type of Christ the First Fruits). From that, the Jews numbered seven Sabbaths complete, and then came the Feast of Pentecost. At this feast, the people were required to bring out of their homes two wave loaves baked with leaven; "they are the first fruits unto the Lord." Thereafter, through all the generations succeeding Moses such a feast strikingly symbolized the miracle before us, for those two loaves represented the two divisions of the human family, Jew and Gentile. Peter became the apostle to the Jews, and Paul, the apostle to the Gentiles, and through the ministry of these two prominent evangelists in the Acts, thousands of Jews and Gentiles were saved and formed the foundation of the Church of God.

After the ten days of waiting, the Holy Spirit came upon those gathered together with one accord in one place, and that momentous day dated a new history of the world, God's new creation, His Church. Suddenly, a new dispensation was wonderfully inaugurated, and since then the world has been living in the age of grace, during which God is gathering out of the world a people for His name. The Church was established by a miracle, and her continuance through the centuries is miraculous, and her consummation at the Rapture will be just as miraculous. As Pentecost commemorated the promulgation of

the law at Sinai, it is fitting that the Church was inaugurated when the day of Pentecost was fully come, for through her there was to be the promulgation of the Gospel, and the gathering of a harvest of souls for the Redeemer.

The peculiar circumstances of the miracle of Pentecost afford striking evidences of the wisdom and mercy of Him in whose hands are the times and seasons and Who ordereth all things in heaven and on earth. The time and place at which this miracle was wrought were precisely calculated to give immediate publicity to the advent of the Spirit, whose instantaneousness and wonderful ministry was of a nature to produce irresistible conviction.

First of all, there was the sudden sound from heaven as of "a rushing mighty wind." Having created the winds, God understands their nature and can command them to obey His will (Job 28:23-28). Wind, or "breath" (the word is the same), is one of the Bible similes of the Holy Spirit (Ezekiel 37; John 3:8). As in the *time* of the working of the miracle we see types fulfilled, so in the *working* of the miracle we see similes or emblems illustrated. Eyes and ears that great day recognized in the tempest of wind the inexplicable, yet effectual operation of the Spirit of God on the minds of men. That "great and strong wind" that rent the mountains on Horeb (I Kings 19:11), is now felt and heard as the Spirit, who moved upon the face of the waters and produced creation (Genesis 1:2), now brings in a new creation, namely, the Church which He inhabits (Ephesians 2:20-22).

Jesus prepared His disciples for the supernatural inbreathing of the Spirit when He "breathed on them and said, 'Receive ye the Holy Spirit'" (John 20:22). Now it becomes a mighty tempest filling all the house where the disciples were sitting—typical of the supernatural effusion of the Spirit extending to the whole Church, the house of God (I Timothy 3:15). The story of the Acts proves how those Spirit-possessed disciples were borne along by His energizing, irresistible power.

The next manifestation of the Spirit's presence and power is seen in the cloven tongues like as of fire, sitting upon each of the disciples, of whom there were some 120 (Acts 1:15). In our consideration of Old Testament miracles, we observed that fire is symbolic of divine power. Among the properties of fire are illumination, warmth, and purification. Such were the effects of the outpoured Spirit who inflamed the disciples with love to their Lord and transformed them into His image. The Spirit also empowered them to communicate light and understanding to the world. The fire was a miraculous, visible demonstration of His presence and power. In them, the prophecy was fulfilled, for they were baptized with the Holy Spirit and *with fire* (Matthew 3:11). The tongues of fire were cloven, or parted, and a tongue rested on each disciple, symbolizing that their own tongues would glow with the message of a risen, ascended, interceding, and returning Saviour.

The wind and fire were outward signs of a still greater spiritual miracle. The Holy Spirit filled the disciples—that is, He "pervaded the inner depths of personality, stimulating every faculty and feeling to a new intensity of life." They became God-intoxicated men. Theirs was a state of rapturous ecstasy and joy, so much so that those around said, "These men are full of new wine." Under this mighty impact of the Spirit, the disciples "began to speak with other tongues" (2:4; 10:46; 19:6). It is not our purpose to deal with every phase of the difficult and mysterious subject of speaking in tongues. If the reader has access to Ellicott's *Commentary on the Bible*—the finest commentary of its kind—attention is drawn to the most enlightening summary on "Tongues" given at this portion we are considering.

The tongues, or languages, used by the disciples were tongues different from their own native tongue and also different tongues spoken by different apostles (Acts 2:4). The tongues were not some ecstatic, non-recognizable gibberish common to the "tongues movement" today. It was the use of the languages of the nations represented at Jerusalem, and which they clearly understood. *Utterance* is a word used only by Luke, and here in the narrative Vincent tells us that it is a peculiar word and was purposely chosen to denote the *clear, loud* utterance under the miraculous impulse.

What a great miracle the Spirit wrought that day! Here was a miracle of hearing on the part of the hearers as well as of speech on the part of the speakers. Think of the many dialects represented by the audience, yet all heard in their own

tongue—"Parthians, and Medes, and Elamites, and the dwellers in Mesopotamia, and in Judea, and Cappadocia, in Pontus, and Asia, Phrygia, and Pamphylia, in Egypt . . . Libya, and . . . Rome." Commenting on this exceptional phenomena, Ellicott says:

> We cannot honestly interpret Luke's records without assuming either that the disciples spoke in the languages which are named, or that, speaking in their own Galilean tongue, their words came to the ears of those who listened as if spoken in the language with which each was familiar. The first is at once the more natural interpretation, the language by the historian, and, if we may use such a word of what is in itself supernatural and mysterious, the more conceivable of the two.

Brewer, in his *Dictionary of Miracles*, cites the supposed experience of Saint Bernardine, 1380-1444, who on one occasion had to preach to the Greeks, but not knowing the Greek language, preached in his native Italian and was understood as well as if he had spoken in Greek the wonderful words of God. . . . We believe, however, that God, in order to confirm and establish Christianity, was pleased to invest the apostles with supernatural powers, and by signs and wonders, so that the foreigners could hear the message of Grace "every man in his own tongue." As the result of this linguistic miracle, the foreigners were amazed and marveled, as they heard in their own tongues the wonderful works of God.

At Babel, "God confounded their language, so that they could not understand one another." Before that there had been no confusion of language, for all were "of one language and one speech." Because of this confusion of language, the knowledge of the true God was lost. At Pentecost, there was not a restoration of the unity of language among the nations, but a miraculous display whereby God's chosen servants were enabled to address all the people in their native tongue. Was it not a stupendous miracle which enabled a number of illiterate fishermen to address foreigners of different nations, whose languages they had probably never heard before? Without doubt, they proclaimed the message with as much ease, fluency, and propriety as if they were using their own language. Those "tongues," then, were typical, manifesting "the universality of the Christian dispensation designed for every tongue, so counterworking the division of man through the confusion of the tongues at Babel."

There is no evidence that this power to speak in other tongues was permanent. "It came and went with the special outpouring of the Spirit, and lasted only while that lasted in its full intensity." Paul distinctly declared that where there were tongues, they would cease (I Corinthians 13). The operations of the Spirit are no longer audible in sounds or visible in tongues of fire. Today, missionaries do not address themselves to foreigners without previous study of the vernacular of the people among whom they desire to labor. Societies translating the Scriptures into the languages and dialects of men are still continuing the aim of Pentecost, namely, to give "every man in his own tongue . . . the wonderful works of God."

The continuing amazement of the people over the miracle prepared them for Peter's remarkable Pentecostal sermon, in which he started out by quoting from the prophet Joel (2:28), whose prophecy was not exhausted by the Spirit's effusion at Pentecost. Such a miracle was a mere beginning, or type of a far more imposing display of divine power still in the future (Daniel 12:1; Zechariah 14:2; Matthew 24:15-31). As to the content of Peter's sermon, the apostle charged his hearers, not with sins in general, but with the sin of all sins in rejecting and murdering Jesus who had exhibited His divine credentials in vain. The effect of such a Christ-honoring sermon was overwhelming. As unmistakable evidence of the resurrection of Jesus and of the preaching of it was that about 3,000 were convicted of their sin, repented, and were baptized and added to the Church. What a glorious display of mass evangelism that was!

The historical account of the Pentecostal miracle closes with a beautiful cameo of the exceptional unity of the new society formed that day. All who were saved continued *stedfastly* in the apostles' doctrine and fellowship, and in breaking of bread, and in prayer. Believers loved each other and were so happy in Christ that the world was nothing to them. Earthly possessions were of little value in their esteem except to serve the need of poorer brethren. Praise filled their hearts, and having favor with all people, the Lord added to the Church daily those who were being saved. The fellowship of those days had these predominant notes—"a wholesome fear, a powerful service, a mutual ministry, constant worship, a great gladness, a gracious influence, and perpetual growth." Would that these features characterized the Church of today!

While we may not live in a miraculous dispensation such as Pentecost represents and no longer receive miraculous gifts from the Spirit, yet the same silent and powerful Spirit Himself is still with us, and our obligation is to co-operate with Him as He seeks, through the established Gospel, to bring men of all nations to a knowledge of Christ, who alone can save.

5. The Miracle of the Lame Man

(3:1-26)

As we come to an enumeration and examination of the miracles the apostles performed, perhaps this is a fitting point to consider their miraculous ministry in general. Their power, like those of the prophets, was delegated. Peter, in the miracle of the lame man, declared that he had no power of his own in contrast to his Master who never hesitated to act in His own name and receive praise accordingly. If the *gospels* present the life of Jesus in the flesh and *Acts*, His life in the Spirit, such a life was conveyed to others through the media of Spirit-empowered men. While Jesus was among His disciples, He made them the recipients of the power to perform miracles (Luke 9; 10:9, 17-20; Mark 6:13; Matthew 10:8), and He promised them a continuation of delegated power after His ascension (Matthew 28:18; Mark 16:20), which power is so manifest throughout the Acts (1:1; 2:43; 5:12, etc), in which their commission is attested to by many "signs and wonders" (2:43; 5:12-16, etc.). It must not be lost sight of, however, that while miracles authenticated a divine commission (I Kings 17:24), they were not, in themselves, an evidence of true discipleship (Matthew 7:22, 23. See John 10:41).

Luke give us a most vivid account of a miracle of a very remarkable kind, for the man was born lame and was more than 40 years old when the cure was effected (3:2; 4:22). We often say that "we know not what a day or an hour may bring forth," and nothing was further from the expectations of this poor cripple or of the friends who brought him that morning to his accustomed stance at the Temple gate, than that a miracle would take place with far-reaching results. Perhaps all the lame beggar expected that day was a generous response in alms from passers-by. A perfect cure of his condition, with all attendant benefits of it for his body and soul, was far from his thoughts. Peter and John also, as they approached the Temple, had no thoughts of conferring such a benefit upon the lame man till God by His Spirit inspired them to act and speak as they did. What a profound impression this first miracle of the apostles produced!

The association of Peter and John in the miracle emphasizes the friendship and fellowship continuing between them after the ascension of their Master. We find them often mentioned together in the gospels (Luke 5:10; 8:51; John 18:15; 20:2, etc.), and there they are together going to the Temple at the hour of prayer. "Blest be the tie that binds."

"The Beautiful Gate," where the cripple was usually seen, was the outer gate of Herod's Temple. It was made of Corinthian brass and surpassed in costliness the nine others of the outer court which were covered with gold and silver. This outer gate was so heavy that twenty men were required to close it. The doorway consisted of lintel, threshold, and sideports (Exodus 12:7, 22). Josephus tells us that this massive gate was found open unexpectedly shortly before the destruction of Jerusalem under Titus. The approaches to the Temple were commonly thronged with sufferers of all kinds (John 9:8). Thus it was that as Peter and John came to the gate, they saw the cripple and "fastened" their eyes upon him. This same characteristic word is used elsewhere (1:10; Luke 4:20), and is a word indicating the gaze which read character in the expression of the cripple's face, and discerned thereon, faith to be healed (3:16). The cripple, in turn, "looked on them that he might read in their pitying looks, not only the wish to heal, but the consciousness of power to carry the will into effect."

First of all, let us think of the man's condition—lame from birth. Mephibosheth's lameness was due to an accident in infancy which evidently produced some form of bone disease necessitating constant dressing (II Samuel 4:4; 19:24). Jacob's lameness was divinely caused (Genesis 32:31). Lameness was a disqualification for the priesthood (Leviticus 21:18). Christ healed many lame people (Matthew 21:14), and here is another man born lame and having his affliction for 40 years, who was to receive from the apostles something greater than alms, which they did not possess to give the needy beggar because of their accepted poverty. "Silver and gold have I none" (see Matthew 10:9).

The needy man was found in the right place, namely, at the House of prayer, which, says Dr. Campbell Morgan, illustrates this constant fact—"Approximation to God is a habit of humanity in its need. Mendicants are not often found at the doors where an infidel lecture has been delivered." In speaking to the man, Peter revealed the essential meaning of Christianity. He was not able to minister to the man in material things so far as silver and gold were concerned. He was, however, able to communicate to him something which would make him master of his disability.

As to the man's cure, it was unsolicited, sudden, and complete. In a moment, he leaped up, stood, and walked, and by such a change showed forth the wonderful works of God (3:8, 9). Does not this miracle illustrate God's "*overt* answers to prayer"? Instead of coins, the cripple received a cure. God gave him more than he could have asked or thought. Mercy, which he had no thought of seeking, was conferred upon him unsought. No natural means could have effected his cure so instantaneously, and although he was a cripple for 40 years, the cure did not leave behind any weakness or stiffness of limbs. At once he showed himself as strong and vigorous as if he had never been crippled at all.

What exactly happened when Peter, after having looked fixedly upon the cripple, took him by the right hand and with a firm grasp raised him up? First, his ankle bones received strength. This is purely technical phraseology which Luke alone uses and in medical language applied to bones in particular. The words "established" and "stedfastness" (Acts 16:5; Colossians 2:3) are associated with "received strength." "Leaping up" is also another medical term. It is only used here in the New Testament and implies "the sudden starting of a bone from the socket, of starting from sleep, or of the sudden pound of the pulse." Then the healed man began to walk, testing his newly acquired power. Here, then, are the progressive steps of the recovery—leaped up, stood, and walked. First of all, we have the man's poverty, then power, then praise. Leaping as a hart (Isaiah 35:6), the healed man, full of exuberant joy over his new consciousness of power, entered the court of the Temple, where worshipers at the evening sacrifice were filled with amazement as they saw the well-known crippled beggar walking so vigorously. Gone forever were any crutches he had used.

It is a noteworthy fact that again and again Peter emphasized that the cure had not been effected by any power he had, but only by that of Jesus Christ (3:6, 12, 16; 4:9-12. See 9:34). "In the name of Jesus of Nazareth rise up and walk." It must have been a test of faith on the part of the lame man to rise and walk in the name of the despised Nazarene, but as the *name* represented all Jesus was and is, in Himself, power accompanied His person. For Peter himself this miracle was a continuation of the exercise of like powers (Mark 6:13; 16:18). All through the Acts much is said of the *name*. Faith in this *name*, above every name, was the avenue through which God wrought many wonders. That the peerless, precious name of Jesus had lost nothing of its power by His visible absence from earth is proven by the miracle before us.

Humbly, Peter disavowed his own power to perform. He pointed to Christ as the Source of all power. No glory must accrue to man for divine works. No glory was due to the man who was healed, since his faith was not brought into play at all. (3:13). As to the effect of this divine miracle, the people who had seen the man at the gate as he begged there through the years were filled with wonder and awe. Then the miracle gave Peter and John a great opportunity of preaching a mighty sermon before the Sanhedrin, as chapters 3 and 4 describe. The way was opened for faithful testimony to the Jewish rulers whose hatred for Christ and His disciples was only incensed and resulted in a persecution that burst like a cloud upon the disciples.

What a change this event reveals in Peter! Not long before he was afraid of the taunt of a servant-maid. Now he boldly confronted the whole Sanhedrin and charged them all with the murder of their Messiah. Later on, Peter could write about giving a reason of the hope within us with *meekness and fear* (I Peter 3:15). Here, he had no unworthy fear. He was not afraid to vindicate the cause of his Master. No wonder the people marveled when they saw the boldness of Peter—they remembered his denial.

As to the lesson of the miracle: The Beautiful Gate of the Temple and all its ritual could do the lame man no good, but the name of Christ gave him instant strength and joy. That poor cripple exhibited a just view of every man born into the world. Says Charles Simeon: "He from the very womb was incapable of those exertions for which the limbs were originally designed. And so it is with fallen men, in reference to the powers of his soul. He cannot walk before God as Adam did in Paradise, nor as God's saints and servants do even in their fallen state. But, by the name of Jesus Christ, who is there that may not be healed? Who is there, however deplorable his state, whom the power of divine grace cannot renovate, so as to make him altogether a new creature?"

Multitudes of cripples, cripples in morals, in will power, in the energies of the soul; cripples through the sin of others, and through their own, surround our churches, whose doors stand open. Alas! however, so few of these cripples are healed. The great mass of impotent men and women remain impotent. Why? The Church has her educated and cultured preachers and priests, her rubrics and ritual, her ornate buildings and manifold activities, her prestige and wealth; but she is sadly destitute of power to say to a world crippled by sin, unrest, and dread of war, "In the name of Jesus of Nazareth rise up and walk." Would that a mighty revival could bring her back to her power in the Acts, when she was to be dreaded as "an army with banners."

6. The Miracle of a Second Pentecost

(4:31-33)

This fourth chapter of the Acts is a continuation of the previous chapter. No attention should be paid to the division here, for the division of the Bible into chapters and verses is of human origin and often unwisely made. Peter is still before the Sanhedrin charging the Jewish rulers with the crimes of setting at naught, while pretending to be builders, the only Stone that could brace the whole structure of salvation together. In no other name but Christ's was their salvation. Astonished at the boldness of Peter and John, the rulers, perceiving that they were illiterate persons of the vulgar herd, took knowledge of them that they had been with Jesus. This confession did not simply mean that they recognized them as men whom they had formerly seen with Jesus. The language implies that Christ was still with these men and was working through them. To those proud ecclesiastics, Jesus could be heard in the stones of the voices of Peter and John and was revealed in the defiant flash of their eyes. Here were two men who, although uneducated and despised fishermen, were far superior to their critics, and whose whole bearing was in the power of the Spirit.

After the questioning, the rulers dismissed Peter and John, forbidding them to speak at all or teach in the name of Jesus. They were determined, however, to obey God rather than men, and on their dismissal "they went to their own company," that is, the rest of the disciples, to whom they reported the proceedings in the Sanhedrin. Then there came the mighty prayer of the apostles in which they praised God for the signs and wonders accomplished by the name of God's holy child, Jesus. No wonder such a prayer resulted in another supernatural visitation. While there is only one Pentecost, this shaking of the place was a renewal of that day without its symbols of wind and fire. The Holy Spirit confirmed the inward, spiritual consciousness of the apostles, and in turn they preached the commissioned word with boldness. With the apostles filled with the Spirit, no room was left for the flesh to manifest its presence. Such is still the secret of power. (Acts 1:8; John 7:38, 39; 15:7). That "second Pentecost," as it has been called, was an outer proof of inner power. No wonder it was "with great power they gave witness of the resurrection of the Lord Jesus: and great grace was upon them all."

The chapter closes with a beautiful picture of brotherly love and unity in that first Christian community. The disciples were of one heart and of one mind, happy in the conscious possession of Christ. Earthly possessions were of little value in their esteem, except as they could minister to the needs of saints, so they had all things in common. How the Church has strayed from this early conception of Christian unity and brotherhood!

7. The Miracle of Ananias and Sapphira

(5:1-11)

Satan acts quickly to mar the wonderful works of God. It was so at creation when, as the serpent, he beguiled our first parents and sin entered to deface the handiwork of God. At the Incarnation, Satan was the instigator in the wholesale murder of the innocents, hoping that the infant Jesus would be included in such cruel butchery. Here the peaceful atmosphere pervading early Church life is soon disturbed and its unity impaired. The grievous sin of Ananias and Sapphira must be read in the light of what goes before. Disciples having lands or houses sold them, and the money secured by their sale was put into one common treasury and used as needed. Barnabas is singled out as having sold all his possessions and surrendering the money received to the common fund. Because of this self-chosen poverty, Barnabas afterwards worked, as Paul did, for his livelihood (I Corinthians 9:6). Evidently Barnabas gained praise and prestige by his self-sacrifice, and Ananias had an idea that he could get the same result more cheaply. But the generous, sincere, and spontaneous gift of Barnabas and the others sets forth in dark relief the calculated deceit of Ananias and Sapphira. "The brighter the light, the darker the shadow."

Ananias was a disciple, a saved man, and sincere up to a point for he had cast in his lot with the despised "Nazarenes," but he desired to gain as high a name as Barnabas by seeming to have surrendered to the common treasury all he had gained by the sale of his possessions. He was not *obliged* to throw in all he received into the one Christian fund. He could have kept any part of his own money. "After it was sold, was it not in thine own power?" His terrible sin consisted in *professing* to have given all into the common fund, when knowingly he kept part of the price. Satan entered his heart and suggested a compromise between love of Christian praise and worldliness. He was guilty of double-mindedness. His was an acted lie. Thus, although it was the Pentecost season when the first-fruits were presented unto the Lord, evil was there as typified in the two loaves baked with leaven (Leviticus 23:17).

If, as Bagster suggests, the name *Ananias* means, "the cloud of the Lord," he certainly brought a dark cloud over the peaceful atmosphere of that first Christian community. He was the "Achan" in the camp, and if his sin of deceit had not been instantly detected and judged, its effects would have been as disastrous as the iniquity brought upon Israel by the frown of the Lord (Joshua 7). Ananias had a heart exercised with covetous practice; he secretly clung to his cherished possessions, and this, coupled with his desire for popularity, led him to sacrifice truth. But he learned to his tragic loss that "a lying tongue is but for a moment" (Proverbs 12:19).

Sapphira was in full accord with her husband in his hypocrisy. Peter implies that their souls were attuned to each other in respect to their decision. They "agreed together to tempt the Spirit of the Lord" (5:9). Husband and wife agreed to tell a lie about the amount received for their property, little thinking that there was One who would expose their falsehood and who would punish them, to tell a tale of solemn warning in all subsequent time. The pair were guilty of "the hidden things of dishonesty," and they suffered accordingly. Deceit in word and deed is so common today that it may be said to be the habit of the world. The Christian, however, should shun hypocrisy or deceit in any form. Pretending to be or do what we have no real intention of being or doing is sin. May that "simplicity and godly sincerity" which God ever blesses be ours.

The question arises, How was Peter able to immediately detect the hypocrisy of Ananias and Sapphira? Evidently their secret pact was unknown to the other disciples who, therefore, were not able to convey knowledge of the deceit to Peter. The only answer to this question is that the Holy Spirit, who had become so real to Peter and who is the omniscient Spirit, knew all about the acted lie and revealed to Peter the truth of the matter (see I Kings 14:5).

Another prominent aspect of this miracle is the emphasis given to the personality, deity, and power of the Holy Spirit. In lying to Him, they had lied to God (5:3, 4). One cannot lie against a mere impersonal influence. Peter knew that the Spirit came at Pentecost, not simply to manifest miraculous gifts, but as a permanent endowment resting upon and within the disciples and investing the Church, to the end of her sojourn on earth, with power. "Ye shall receive power, the Holy Spirit coming upon you" (1:8). In the incident before us, the presence and presidency of the Spirit in the Church is evident as it is throughout the Acts.

The sin of Ananias and Sapphira was therefore that of dishonest dealing with the Holy Spirit, and the judgment was swift and terrible. Peter stigmatized their act as lying to the Spirit who was in the apostles and whom they thought they could elude. Actually the sin was one against the omniscience of the Spirit. Simeon has the paragraph: "Peter calls their sin 'a lying unto,' and 'a tempting of the Holy Spirit,' for it was an attempt to deceive the apostles, whom the Holy Ghost had invested with miraculous gifts, and it tempted the Holy Ghost to show whether He were an omniscient, holy, and just Being, or not."

The Searcher of all hearts, from whom nothing is hid, quickly revealed not only His omniscience but also His power. As soon as Peter pronounced the intensity of the guilt, Ananias dropped down dead. What a solemn display of divine judgment upon hypocrisy that was! The severity of such judgment can be justified by the consideration that the united act of Ananias and Sapphira was "the first open venture of deliberate wickedness within the Church." The sudden, tragic punishment was therefore "an awe-inspiring act of divine church discipline."

It should be noted that Peter never pronounced the doom of Ananias, as he did that of Sapphira some three hours later. Peter did not consciously will such a fatal death. He was not the deliberate agent of judgment, even though his exposure of hypocrisy was the occasion of it. Neither did Ananias suddenly expire as the result of the natural excitement over the sudden exposure of his sin by Peter. Doubtless "the shame and agony of detection, the horror of conscience not yet dead, were enough to paralyze the powers of life." Sentence of death was immediately executed by God in whose hands are life and death (I Samuel 2:6). "The visitation of God" was the cause of death. Peter was only the instrument of justice. At any moment, He is able to recall the breath He had given. It was thus that He smote Nabal, Jeroboam, and Herod (I Samuel 25:38; II Chronicles 13:20; Acts 12:23). The phrase, "gave up the ghost," is rare, a medical one used only by Luke. The young men of the Church wound up Ananias' body in a shroud and buried him. Quick burials were necessitated by the hot climate and also because of ceremonial uncleanness caused by contact with a corpse (Numbers 19:11-16).

What a shock Sapphira must have had when she heard the news of her husband's death and burial which took place within three hours! She had no knowledge of what had transpired. Bengel says, "The woman whose entrance into the assembly of the saints was like a speech." Peter's question to the woman gave her an opening for repentance for her share in the acted lie, but, as Ellicott comments, "It had been in her power to save her husband by a word of warning protest. It was now in her to clear her own conscience by confession. She misses the one opportunity as she had misused the other. The lie which they had agreed upon comes glibly from her lips, and the irrevocable word is spoken."

In the case of Sapphira, Peter pronounced her doom. Immediately she fell down dead, and the young men who had just returned from the burial of Ananias carried Sapphira out and buried her beside her husband. As far as we know, these were the first deaths in that early Christian community—and what tragic deaths they were! As the result of this display of divine power, great fear came upon the Church, whose leaders had been clothed with supernatural powers. Such judgment came at the beginning of the Church's course as an awful example to guard her in guileless sincerity from the world's corruptions. Ananias and Sapphira, although they lost their lives, did not lose their souls, because they were believers.

The lesson for our own hearts from this terrible episode is clearly evident. God is never mocked, and because He desires truth in the inward parts, He bids us beware of the sin of covetousness. Our one path of safety is true heart sincerity. What a mercy it is that God does not act today as He did with Ananias and Sapphira! If He struck church people dead because of religious hypocrisy, there would be those falling down dead in our churches all the time. How merciful He is! Yet let us not trade upon His mercy. He is patient and long-suffering with our make-believe and our covetousness, but in the end, if unrepented of, they bring their own deserved judgment.

8. The Miracle of Peter's Shadow

(5:12-16)

How reminiscent this paragraph is of the miraculous ministry of the Lord, who was "approved of God among the disciples by miracles and wonders and signs, which God did by Him" (Acts 2:22). Here we have a continuation of His supernatural work, for "by the hands of the apostles were many signs and wonders wrought among the people." The three synonyms express different aspects of the same facts—

Miracles —the power displayed in the act

Wonders—the marvel of the act as a portent

Signs —its character as a token or note of something beyond itself.

The supernatural works of the apostles made the people realize what a solemn matter it was to be part of that Church which the mighty Spirit had brought into being. This is why we read that many of the people dared not join the disciples, even though they magnified them. The salutary effect of their miracles was seen in the people's fear of joining the new community. Unbelievers were deterred by the fate of Ananias and Sapphira from uniting themselves to the Church under false pretences. To "join himself" implies a forced, unnatural, or unexpected union, the sense of which comes out clearly in I Corinthians 6:16. Notwithstanding the tragedy overtaking the Church, the work went forward and the tide of blessing flowed on, for multitudes more were added not merely to the Church, but to the Lord (5:14). Prompt discipline in putting down manifested evil in the Church resulted in revival.

Solomon's Porch, scene of the apostles' marvelous works, was a large portico of one of the Temple buildings. It is mentioned three times in the New Testament. It was there that Jesus declared the eternal security of His own (John 10:22-28); it was there the first Gospel discourse was delivered after Pentecost in explanation of the

first miracle of the new dispensation (3:
11); and it is here as the common meeting
place of believers and the rallying place of
the needy. What a sight that must have
been with every street around crowded with
beds and couches carrying the sick and
demon-possessed, that at least the healing
shadow of Peter as he passed by might fall
on them!

The continuing tense Luke uses implies
that for days and weeks the sick were laid
along the streets, and that the apostles
were successful in healing the sick and ex-
pelling demons, just as if Christ had been
with them as in the old days (Matthew 17:
14-21; Mark 9:18, 19; Luke 9:40, 41).
Through their developed faith, Christ
was nearer to the apostles now than He
was when visibly with them. Then it must
be noticed that they "healed every one."
Modern fake healers practice a selective
process before their healing (?) session, and
choose those with no organic diseases but
principally the neurotic whom they can
masterfully command.

As to the healing "shadow" of Peter,
there is nothing here to suggest any contradiction of the laws governing the supernatural. Christ could heal directly, without
contact of any kind, or through material
media, such as the hem of His garment or
clay. The shadow of Peter accomplished
what the "handkerchiefs and aprons" from
Paul's skin could do, or what the use of oil
could accomplish. "The medium employed
which had in itself a healing power, with
which the prayer of faith was to co-operate." We never read of any sick being
brought into the streets that the shadow
of Jesus might fall upon them. Bless Him,
He is always as good as His word, and
better than our fears.

9. The Miracle of Opened Prison Doors

(5:17-42)

The apostles knew what it was to "advance through storm." After the storm of
the Sanhedrin, there was advance (4:13-
37). Then the storm occasioned by the de-
fection and death of Ananias and Sapphira
was followed by another advance (5:1-16).
We now come to another storm of opposition from the Jewish authorities as the result of the apostles' wide-spread healing
ministry, which opposition only resulted in
further progress (5:40-42).

Envious over the growing popularity of
the apostles, the Sadducees, the ancient
materialists among the Jews, put the apostles
in the common prison. But bolts and bars
are nothing to Him who rolled back the
stone from the sepulcher and raised up
Jesus from the dead. "An angel of the Lord
by night opened the prison doors, and
brought them forth, and said, Go, stand
and speak in the temple to the people all
the words of this life." It was not the function of the angel to preach, for God's
treasure is in earthen vessels (II Corinthians
4:7). When morning came the prison doors
were found shut, but the prisoners were
gone. Later on, as we shall see, prison
doors were miraculously opened, but the
godly prisoners were still in prison (Acts
16:28). Those men were not delivered from
the vile companionship to which they had
been condemned.

Those who reject any supernatural interposition for the relief of the godly affirm
that the "angel" Luke refers to was likely
some zealous and courageous disciple, and
that the apostle, in the darkness of the
night and the excitement of his liberation,
ascribed his rescue to the intervention of
an angel. But a mere disciple would not
have commanded the apostles to go to the
Temple and proclaim an authoritative message. The Jewish council had no doubt as
to the miraculous in the escape of the
prisoners, and such a deliverance was a
sign, not without its influence, on the subsequent decision of that council and on
the courage of the two apostles.

Releasing the apostles, the council commanded them not to teach in the name of
Christ. Those priests were conscience-
stricken over their crime of His crucifixion.
The apostles, however, declared that God
must be obeyed, and in holy defiance they
continued their dynamic, Christ-honoring
ministry. They felt they were privileged to
suffer shame for His dear name, and in
spite of all opposition, they ceased not, in
God's house and the houses of the people,
to teach and preach Jesus Christ (5:41,
42), and the number of the disciples was
multiplied (6:1).

10. The Miracles of Stephen

(6:1-15)

As the history of the Church continued,
it seemed to alternate between the opposi-

tion of the outside crowd and the condition of the Church in its own borders; yet in spite of everything, "the word of God increased." The disciples who were Greek-speaking Jews (distinguished from the Hebrews, who were natives of the Holy Land), complained about an unjust discrimination against the widows of the foreigners in the distribution of the charities of the Church. Seven men of honest report, full of the Holy Spirit and wisdom, were appointed to care for this secular piece of work. The seven chosen were all, as their names indicate, of Grecian origin or associations, proving both the wisdom and the grace that controlled the disciples in their selection.

Among the seven was Stephen, a man full of faith and therefore of power, who did great wonders and miracles among the people. Scripture is silent about the type and number of these miracles of Stephen. This we do know, that as the result of them the rage of the Devil was aroused, and Stephen was arrested on a charge of blasphemy. Witnesses were obtained to testify against Stephen who, as he sat before the council, had a face shining with angelic glory. The wrongly accused was holding such high and holy fellowship with his Lord that nothing could disturb his inner peace, and, consequently, his very countenance, like Moses before him, shone with the radiance of heavenly glory (Exodus 34:29).

What a stirring chapter this is! The accused suddenly became the accuser; the prisoner at the bar appeared as a stern and terrible judge. Stephen read from Old Testament scriptures a long and tremendous indictment of the Jewish nation, and infuriated by the condemning testimony, the Jewish leaders gnashed with their teeth, and Stephen realized that it only remained for him to seal his testimony with his blood and to gain the honor of being the Abel of the Christian dispensation.

Everything about the brutal death of Stephen is supernatural—his stedfast heavenly gaze and the vision of heaven's hand reaching out across the border to welcome him home. Our Lord after His ascension is always depicted as sitting (Hebrews 1:3; 10:12; Ephesians 1:20, 21; Colossians 3:1). Here, He stands! Can this mean that out of honor to Stephen who was faithful unto death, Jesus rose to bid His first martyr welcome home? As he was being stoned to death, there was no trace of resentment toward his contemptible murderers. He prayed to Christ to receive his spirit, thereby imitating the Master as He died (Luke 23:41), and as he died, he fell asleep. Does this not provide us an inspiring picture of Christ's reception of us when we leave the conflict here below for the mansions above?

Stephen's victorious death was not in vain, for a young man witnessed his death and heard his cry for the forgiveness of his murderers and even though that blood-stained yet angelic face of Stephen only made young Saul's hatred of Christ more intense, such an unforgettable sight left its mark. Stephen's dying message lodged deep in the soul of Saul and paved the way for the Damascus vision. Stephen's martyrdom was the price paid for Saul's soul—and what a trophy of grace he was to become!

11. The Miracles of Philip

(8:5-8, 13)

Saul, in his anger, made havoc of the Church as he "persecuted *this way* unto death" (22:4). As Christ is "the Way," it was actually against Him that Saul strove, as we shall see when we come to his miraculous conversion. Those were dark days for the infant Church, yet the overruling hand of God is seen in that as the saints were scattered abroad, their number increased. Thus it was that Philip, one of the recently chosen deacons, went down to Samaria, thereby fulfilling his part of the divine commission (1:8)—"in Samaria." There God wonderfully used His servant. The people with one accord gave heed to Philip as he preached the glad tidings of the Word.

Supernatural power was also his, for he accomplished miracles. The demon-possessed were delivered; the palsied and lame were healed. Simon the sorcerer was converted as the result of the miracles and signs Philip wrought. It will be observed that many of the Samaritans "believed without any other sign than the person and the teaching of the Lord Jesus. Miracles came not as the foundation, but for the strengthening, of their faith; perhaps also as a corrective to the adverse influences of Simon the sorcerer," who bewitched the Samaritans.

The apostles in Jerusalem, learning of the

great revival in Samaria, visited the scene of Philip's mighty work and prayed for them that they might receive the Holy Spirit and from Him the gift of power that had been bestowed upon the apostles on the Day of Pentecost. Hands were laid upon those baptized believers—an act at once the symbol and the channel of the communication of spiritual gifts and offices, as seen in the appointment of the seven deacons (6:6).

Before we take leave of Philip, there is another evidence of the supernatural in his ministry to which we must draw attention. When Peter and John returned to Jerusalem, Philip gave himself anew to his great work, and one day he was visited by the angel of the Lord who commanded him to leave the revival in the city and go to a desert place some 30 miles away to speak to an individual about the saving grace of Christ. Acting under divine guidance, Philip went to the desert and brought the truth to the first of the dark-skinned of Africa, and, if legend be true, the Ethiopian returned to his country and not only led Queen Candace to Christ, but became the bishop of the first Christian Church in Africa. What a miracle of grace!

The phrase we find somewhat intriguing is "Philip was found at Azotus" (8:40). Was the evangelist miraculously transported, and that suddenly, from one place to another, as Elijah was supernaturally energized to run very swiftly, or to be transferred suddenly from one place to another? (I Kings 18:12). As space is no hindrance to God, He can instantaneously transfer things or persons from one place to another as He wills (John 6:21). As great a miracle will take place when the saints are suddenly caught up from earth to heaven.

12. The Miracles of Simon the Sorcerer

(8:9-24)

Although Philip, like Stephen, was not an apostle, yet the many signs of an apostle were his. As Philip preached the Gospel and wrought many miracles in Samaria, (the same city Jesus had to go through in order to give salvation unasked for by a fallen and unhappy woman there—(John 4), a renowned inhabitant of the city appeared to be greatly influenced by Philip's message and miraculous ministry. He was a man called *Simon*. While *Magus* is not applied to his name in the Bible, such a usual description, from which the word "magic" is derived, indicates his profession, namely, that of a magician or sorcerer. Simon "appears as a type of a class but too common at the time, that of Jews trading on the mysterious *prestige* of their race and the credulity of the heathen, claiming supernatural power exercised through charms and incantations."

Simon Magus is referred to in different ways. First of all, he used *sorcery*, bewitching thereby the people of Samaria. The word "sorcery" occurs only here in the New Testament and implies one who practiced upon the credulity of the people by conjuring, juggling, and soothsaying, or who was a caster of lots for the purposes of divination. Jannes and Jambres (II Timothy 3:8) were of the same class. Legendary forms of Simon's sorcery are touched on at the conclusion of this study. Because of his magic, Simon "bewitched" the people, which literally means that he threw them into a state of trance or ecstasy.

Beside themselves, the entranced people declared Simon to be "some great one," and "the great power of God," which designations echoed his own boast. He was deemed to be an impersonation of divine power, the highest of powers, and was so called "the Great." He aped the incarnate One, "the Power of God" (Luke 22:69). Legend says that the multitude accepted him as "the Great Power of God," bowed themselves in awe before him, and kissed his garments. Justin Martyr, who mentions Simon, speaks of him as visiting Rome where he was honored for his magical impostures with a statue bearing the inscription, "To Simon the Holy God." Justin Martyr further mentions that "almost all the Samaritans, and even a few of other nations, worshiped him as 'First God.'"

Luke tells us the Samaritans from "the least to the greatest" gave heed to this charlatan whom they highly regarded. This conspicuous sorcerer appears as the earliest type of those who were to come with lying signs and wonders so as to deceive, if it were possible, even the elect (Matthew 24:24; II Thessalonians 2:9). It was natural for a supposed miracle-worker like Simon to succumb to the influence of the divine miracles wrought by Philip. In fact, so great was the impact of Philip's preaching and performances—performances far greater than anything he himself practised—upon Simon that he believed and was baptized.

Was Simon a true believer? The fact that Peter told him that he was still in "the gall of bitterness and the bond of iniquity" seems to imply that Simon was not truly converted. His belief was only head-work. He recognized in Philip a power far greater than his own, which power, so different from his own, "amazed" him. After having amazed the people by his own tricks, he "wondered," or was "bewitched"—same word used of the effect of his art—at Philip's miracles and signs, and yielded to a spell mightier than his own. Thus, in the Presence of a Power above his own, Simon accepted Philip's message and believed. His faith, however, rested on outward miracles, and the difference between this Samaritan and the believing Samaritans was that to the latter, miracles only served to confirm a faith which rested on the "prophetic word" spoken by the Son of Man (John 4: 42). Simon was merely overwhelmed by evidence that appealed to his intellect.

After his baptism, Simon accompanied Philip and was regarded as a new disciple, but the hypocrisy of heart was soon discovered and it was seen that in spite of his pretensions to conversion and grace, he was still, as much as ever, in a state of nature. As there was a Judas among the apostles, so there was a Simon Magus among Philip's converts. Simon's exposure came as the result of the visit of Peter and John to Samaria. Having heard of Philip's great work, the two apostles came to pray for the Samaritans that they might participate in Pentecost's gift of the Spirit and receive through the laying on of hands the spiritual gifts of the Spirit.

While doubtless Simon, upon embracing the Christian message, ceased from the practice of his magic arts, nevertheless his desire of gain and his love of man's applause were not altogether mortified. The gift of the mighty Spirit to the believing Samaritans opened up a prospect of self-aggrandisement to Simon, and so he offered to buy from Peter a conferment of the Holy Spirit. "He offered Peter and John money." Peter instantly rebuked Simon for his bold and ungodly request in language of such sternness as to cause him to plead with Peter that the threatened judgment might not fall upon him for his sin. Peter could discern that Simon wanted the gift and gifts of the Spirit, not to honor God or to benefit the saints, but for the advance of his own reputation and interest.

When Peter said, "Thy money perish with thee," he literally meant, "Thy money be together with thee, for perdition," the last word being the equivalent of "the son of perdition" (John 17:12; Hebrews 10: 39), and hardly the language to describe a truly born-again person. "Thou hast neither part nor lot in this matter: for thy heart is not right in the sight of God." Because of ulterior motives, Simon could have no inheritance in the spiritual gifts nor in the spiritual offices of the Church. Power attached to apostleship or true discipleship was not a thing for traffic. The heinousness of Simon's sin is seen in the employment of his name to indicate the crime of buying or selling a spiritual office for a price in money—*simony*.

Peter called upon Simon to repent of his wickedness, for the apostle's stern words were meant to save, not slay. The door of mercy was opened for the adventurer, who had traded on the credulous superstition of the people, that he might truly repent of his sin, which came very near that "sin against the Holy Spirit which hath never forgiveness" (Matthew 12:31). Peter knew that God alone, and not he, could absolve Simon's sin. When the apostle told Simon that he was "in the gall of bitterness, and in the bond of iniquity," he used most expressive language. "In the gall" means "thou hast fallen *into* and continuest in." *Gall* is used only here and in Matthew 27:34. *Gall of bitterness* is bitter enmity against the Gospel. As to "the bond of iniquity," such a phrase implies that the iniquity of Simon had bound him as with the iron chains of a habit from which he could not free himself. The word "bond" denotes a *close, firm* bond, and is used of the bond of Christian peace (Ephesians 4:3); of the close compacting of the Church represented as a body (Colossians 2:19); and of love as the *bond* of perfectness (Colossians 3:14. See Isaiah 58:6).

In his request for Peter's intercession, Simon still blundered, for he sought, not deliverance from his present bond of iniquity, but only from the vague terror of future punishment for his sin. Then Simon turned "not, as Peter had bidden him, to the Lord who was ready to forgive, but to a human mediator. Peter must pray for him who had not faith to pray for himself." Whether Simon truly repented and became a sincere disciple, we are not told. At this point, he disappears from the Bible. Perhaps the Spirit who inspired Scripture left Simon standing before God in purposed obscurity, that those who profess to be Christians may carefully avoid the more distant approach to his sin (Matthew 5:13; 12:31, 32; Colossians 1:23; II Peter 2:20, 21).

Later traditions of Simon's history indicate that Simon, like a sow, went back to his wallowing in the mire and became "the hero of the romance of heresy." Irenaeus, who has much to say about Simon, says that Simon Magus was the originator of *gnosticism,* and that his followers became known as "gnostics," a Greek word signifying "knowledge," on account of the superior knowledge of God to which they laid claim. Simon's followers were also known as *the Simoniani,* an eclectic sect whose belief was a mixture of paganism, Judaism, and asceticism. On the many legends of Simon Magus, it is not our purpose to elaborate. The reader is referred to the list of traditions given in Brewer's *Dictionary of Miracles.* One of these legends affirms that Simon met his death at Rome after an encounter with the Apostle Peter. During this final controversy with Peter, Simon had raised himself in the air by the help of evil spirits, and in answer to the prayer of Peter and Paul, he was dashed to the ground and killed. Previously, Simon ordered his disciples to bury him in a grave, promising that he would rise again on the third day. His wish was carried out, but there was no resurrection.

Among those consigned to "the Lake of Fire" are *sorcerers* (Revelation 21:8; 22:15).

13. The Miracle of Saul's Conversion

(9:1-22)

The book of Acts, which is the handbook on salvation, contains no greater token of God's saving grace and power than that of Saul of Tarsus, the persecutor of the Church, who became its most illustrious apostle. While Philip was active in his revival work in Samaria, building up the Church, Saul was as active in his determination to destroy the Church. He gloried in his association with the tribe of Benjamin (Philippians 3:5) and bore the name

of its great hero-king, and is seen at the opening of this chapter before us exhibiting a characteristic feature of the tribe, "devour the prey, and at night divide the spoil" (Genesis 49:27). With the high priest, Saul formed a coalition to obliterate all the disciples of the Lord he could find. Although Saul's threat was to slaughter Christians, he was providentially saved from shedding innocent blood. It was while he was on his purposed mission of destruction of those who followed Christ as "the Way" that Saul came near to Damascus, one of the oldest cities in the world. As he approached the city, its renowned beauty met "the bodily eye of the fanatic persecutor," but a more dazzling spectacle was to meet his inward gaze.

The first mention of the young man Saul is at the stoning of Stephen, a brutal death to which he consented (Acts 22:20). Now on his way to martyr more believers, Saul was miraculously converted, which is the great event in his life we want to concentrate upon in this study. Briefly stated, Saul's history, given principally by himself, is as follows: He was a Jew of Tarsus, a city of Cilicea; a free-born Roman citizen; a Pharisee, the son of a Pharisee; a Hebrew of the Hebrews; brought up at the feet of Gamaliel; taught according to the perfect manner of the law of his fathers; conversant not only with Jewish but Greek literature; a member of the Sanhedrin; had a married sister in Jerusalem; was a persecutor, a blasphemer, and injurious; miraculously converted and ordained and instructed by the Lord; his name was changed to Paul, a chosen vessel to bear His name before the Jews, but more particularly before the Gentiles; became the possessor of many supernatural gifts such as the gift of prophecy, visions, and revelations, signs of an apostle, power to work miracles, the exercise of discipline in the Church; suffered all kinds of hardships and dangers. Saul, thus distinguished from the rest of the apostles as a man of education and learning, continued laboring for thirty years till, as is generally believed, he was beheaded by order of Nero at Rome, about A.D. 60.

As nothing, however, in Paul's life is comparable in importance as that of his conversion, let us now gather together its miraculous elements. The message and martyrdom of Stephen left a deeper mark on Paul's mind than he knew, and although after the cruel death he had witnessed he became distinctly hostile to Christ and His followers, "the struggle against his course was in the subconscious mind. There a volcano had gathered, ready to burst out"—and burst out it did.

We have, of course, no sympathy with those who, trying to explain the supernatural in Paul's conversion, explain it on naturalistic grounds by saying that "he had an epileptic fit, that he had a sunstroke, that he fell off his horse to the ground, that he had a nightmare, that he was blinded by a flash of lightning, that he imagined that he saw Jesus as the result of his highly wrought nervous state, that he deliberately renounced Judaism because of the growing convictions that the disciples were right." Such prejudice against the supernatural appears ludicrous alongside the unvarnished accounts of such a remarkable conversion as given by the careful historian, Luke.

There are three accounts of what took place on that Damascus road. The one Luke narrates in chapter 9 contains Paul's personal rehearsal to the historian of what took place. Then there is Paul's recital of the events of his conversion before the Sanhedrin (22:6-11). and the repetition before Agrippa (26:13-18). While there are slight variations in these accounts, they mutually supplement one another and must be studied together. Their united testimony is that God is able to make the wrath of man to praise Him.

The first supernatural aspect of Paul's supernatural change of life was the sudden blaze of heavenly light that shone round about him as "the brightness of the sun" (26:13). This was not a sudden thunderstorm, as some critics suggest. Had it been, "the gathering gloom, the dark rolling clouds, would have prepared the traveler for the lightning flash." What Paul experienced was an instantaneous supernatural manifestation. Above the brightness of the noonday sun in that eastern clime, Paul, along with those who were with him, fell to the earth overpowered by the dazzling glory of heaven and became speechless (9:7; 26:14). Was this the out-flashing of the glory of the One appearing to Paul? In all visible manifestations of deity recorded in the Old Testament—the burning at Horeb, the pillar of fire in the wilderness, the Holy of Holies—*light* was the magnificent symbol selected for the awful purpose, and most appropriate of Him who dwells in light unapproachable.

Then was heard the majestic voice of Jesus saying, "Saul, Saul, why persecutest thou Me?" Impressed with the deepest awe at the acknowledged symbol of the presence of the Holy One of Israel, Saul now hears the voice of Him before whom the pillars of the earth tremble. Amidst the ineffable glory, the Voice says, "I am Jesus, whom thou persecutest; it is hard for thee to kick against the pricks." One accounts says that Paul's companions "heard a voice, but saw no man," while another account has it, "they heard not the voice of him that spake" (9:7; 22:9). Both statements are strictly true. They heard the voice, but they did not hear its articulate utterances that reached the heart of Paul. They heard a voice, but not the words spoken; they heard a sound, but did not understand the meaning of it. Israel beheld Joseph's sons, yet we are told that Israel's eyes were dim so that he could not see—that is, he could see, but not distinctly—could not distinguish the features unless they came near (Genesis 48:8, 10. See also John 12:28, 29). Habershon's comment on this feature of Saul's conversion is apt:

> The mysteries of sound are as great as those of light; and several incidents in the Bible show us that not only does God fix the laws, but He can make use of sound as He will. . . . Not only can God cause miraculous sounds to be heard, but He can so arrange them that they are heard only by those for whom they are intended. On the road to Damascus, Saul alone heard the voice of the Lord Jesus; for though in one account we read that his companions heard the voice, in the other we read, "they heard not the voice of Him that spake to me." They heard a sound, but could not understand it.

Further, it cannot be too strongly emphasized that this was no vision, but the actual manifestation of Jesus to Paul, as he himself makes clear in his great *resurrection manifesto*—"Last of all, He was seen of me also." While Paul refers to subsequent visions and ecstatic experiences (I Corinthians 14:1-19; II Corinthians 12:1-11; Galatians 4:13, 14), what he experienced that noonday was no vision, but the real, visible presence of Jesus. Certainly, he refers to this experience as a "heavenly vision" (26:19), but he claims most emphatically that he had seen the Lord (I

Corinthians 9:1; 15:8). Paul had listened to Stephen's dying words, "I see the heavens opened, and the Son of Man standing at the right hand of God;" now the persecutor himself sees Him and experiences the transforming power of a personal vision of Christ.

Paul's question, "Who art Thou?" received the answer, "I am Jesus whom thou persecutest." In a moment the persecutor realized that his intense hatred was not against defenseless Christians but against the Christ they served. Christ deigned to express His intimate sympathy in the woes and sufferings of His people; and to declare that although in heaven, He maintains with the Church militant on earth that indissoluble union which alone can give that Church the strength, vigor and life she needs. Christ and His Church are one (John 17; Matthew 10:40). Every stroke given to the weakest member of Christ's body reaches the living Head, and every wrong inflicted upon the little ones that believe on Him is an injury to Himself (I Corinthians 8:12; Ephesians 5:30; Mark 9: 41). Then He reminded Paul that it was hard for him to kick against the pricks, meaning that to resist a power altogether superior to one's own is a profitless and perilous experiment. "The goad did but prick more sharply the more the ox struggled against it."

Those "pricks" against which Paul, as Saul, "kicked" were the conversions of the friend and companion of his youth, Barnabas (4:36), the warning counsel of Gamaliel, in whose school Paul studied (5:34-39), the angelic face of Stephen and his dying prayer (6:15; 7:60), and the daily spectacle of those who were ready to go to prison and even die rather than renounce the Lord they loved. There had been a wilful resistance to light and knowledge, but immediately Paul's chains fell off and a free, although undeserved, forgiveness becomes his (I Timothy 1:12, 13).

There is still another supernatural element to be considered, namely, the blindness that afflicted Paul. "He saw no man." For three days and nights he continued in this blind state and at the expiration of this period, "there fell, as it were, scales from his eyes." As Jesus had lain three days in the darkness of the grave, Paul was blinded for three days in order to learn the full meaning of death itself and the law and all in which he trusted. During this period of seclusion, he was cut off from the visible world, conditions of outward life were suspended, and he became dependent on others to lead him around. Such blindness was not only the natural result of the vision of supernatural glory; it was divinely arranged and doubtless held for Paul a spiritual significance. It was emblematic of the blindness of his state by nature and of the light into which he was now to be brought. He had boasted of his light and of the fact that he was as a "guide of the blind" (Romans 2:19). Now, with his temporary blindness, there came outward light shining upon him and inward light. In spite of his knowledge of Scripture as a Jew, he was blind to their glorious truths. Now, the eyes of his understanding were to be opened. Although he never saw the sun for a season (13:11), Paul saw the Sun of Righteousness and became His devoted slave. Shut in with Him in spiritual communion with the invisible, Paul's whole life was brought into tune with the Infinite.

The first to help Paul on his changed course was Ananias, a disciple of Damascus, to whom the Lord told in a vision the facts about Paul and where and how he could be found. Two visions are to be noted here. The one Ananias had of Paul (9:10) and the other Paul had of God's purpose with Ananias (9:12). How commendable it is that the three-day-old convert was found praying! Instead of breathing out slaughter, he is now breathing out praise to the Lord for His mighty deliverance. Ananias' timidity to visit Paul because of all he had heard about him was quickly overcome when he was assured by the Lord that He had saved and called Paul to be a chosen vessel. How comforting to Paul's heart must the salutation of Ananias have been when as he met him he said, "*Brother* Saul." The *blasphemer* is now a brother. The stranger is now one of the family. Ananias pronounced a double reception—that of sight and of the Spirit's infilling for the service and suffering ahead.

Scales fell from Paul's eyes. While he does not mention blindness in his testimony before Agrippa, he does refer to both the blindness and the recovery of sight when before the Sanhedrin. It was characteristic of Luke as a physician to use the language which medical writers employed of the falling scales from the skin and of particles from diseased parts of the body. Ellicott says that "the description suggests the thought that the blindness was caused by an incrustation, caused by acute inflammation, covering the pupil of the eye, or closing up the eyelids." Now Paul can see for "the glory of that light" (22:11), but spiritually the god of this world could blind him no longer. He had seen "the light of the knowledge of the glory of God in the face of Jesus Christ" (II Corinthians 4:6), and everything else had lost its charm for Paul. His surrender to Christ was instantaneous and complete. "Lord, what wilt Thou have me to do?" Unreservedly, he gave himself to his newly found Lord and was ready to become His "minister and witness."

It was Paul's energetic faith, founded on irresistible conviction, that produced the generous surrender of self and transformed the relentless persecutor into the "very chiefest of the apostles." Running all through his after-ministry was his own experience of grace. As Dr. James Stalker puts it, "Paul's whole theology is nothing but the explanation of his own conversion." His changed life brought its testings, for the persecutor became the persecuted. As the result of his miraculous conversion, the Church had rest from persecution, but Paul was to experience what it was to suffer for His name (9:24). When ultimately he came to Jerusalem, some of the disciples were afraid of him, but Ananias and Barnabas stood by him and encouraged him as he endeavored to become the chosen vessel to propagate the faith which he had labored so hard to destroy.

14. The Miracle of Aeneas

(9:32-35)

While there is no record of Peter meeting Paul in Jerusalem after Barnabas's introduction of the new convert to the apostles, it is almost certain that they had contact with each other and that Peter was thrilled over the conversion of such a renowned Pharisee, as well as an enemy of the faith. As Paul was in Jerusalem, coming in and going out witnessing boldly in the name of the Lord Jesus (9:28, 29), Peter must have rejoiced over such a notable addition to the growing number of saints. Because of the remarkable conversion of Paul, the pressure of persecution of Christians was some-

what eased and Peter was able to move more freely in his evangelistic and teaching ministry.

Christianity was now spreading into the regions beyond Jerusalem, and Peter's journeys "here and there," indicated a progressive approach of the spread of the Gospel by the apostles at the Jerusalem center. As the Acts proceeds, the circumference widens. It was thus that Peter came to Lydda, the territory so successfully evangelized by Philip, hence the number of saints at Lydda whom Peter visited and encouraged. The term "saints," which appears for the first time as a designation of the disciples in verse 13 and then here in verse 32, came into being to describe those who had consecrated themselves to Christ and who, by His Spirit, covenanted to live a holy, devout life. It would appear as if Aeneas was of the saints in Lydda having been brought to Christ through the labors of Philip. Ellicott suggests that because of his Greek name, Aeneas belonged to the Hellenistic section of the Church.

A distinctive feature of the various kinds of miracles in the Acts is the naming of those who were the recipients of the supernatural—Ananias and Sapphira, Simon Magus, Elymas, Aeneas, Dorcas, Eutychus, Publius. Another striking feature, as Habershon points out, is the way the majority of the miracles go in pairs.

Miracles of judgment—Ananias and Sapphira (by Peter), death; lied to the Spirit. Elymas (by Paul), blindness; tried to buy the Spirit's power.

Raising the dead—Dorcas (by Peter); Eutychus (by Paul).

Healing of the lame—Man at the gate (by Peter); cripple at Lystra (by Paul).

Curing of the sick—Aeneas (by Peter); father of Publius (by Paul).

Special miracles—Shadow of Peter; handkerchief and aprons from Paul.

Deliverances from prison—Jerusalem, Peter, by an angel; death to jailers; Philippi, Paul, by an earthquake; life to jailer.

The notice of the duration of the malady of Aeneas, and the fact that he had been bedridden for eight years, are characteristic of a physician's thoroughness in recording medical facts (3:7; 9:18; 28:3). The word used here for the *bed* of the paralytic is that used of the couches or pallets of the lower class and "suggests the thought that poverty also was added to his sufferings." There is a somewhat striking similarity between the description of this case and that of the Capernaum paralytic. Luke takes only four verses—surely the briefest record of a miracle—to tell us all there is to know about Aeneas.

Peter's message to the paralytic about his cure—a cure unasked for—is likewise a model of brevity. Only five words were needed to end the eight long years of helplessness—"Jesus Christ maketh thee whole." Surely this was glad tidings of great joy in a nutshell. The poet describes such short sentences as,

> Jewels five words long,
> That on the strech'd forefinger of all time
> Sparkles forever.

Peter gives us one of the five-word jewels that will sparkle for ever. Is there not a wealth of meaning in each of these five healing words?

JESUS. To Paul, newly converted, came the announcement "I am Jesus." This was His favorite name, His human designation, linking Him on to the humanity He became part of and which He came to save. It was also the name with which He was associated in His great healing work in the days of His flesh. This is why this name above every other name is sweet in a believer's ear, for it tells him that Jesus became a partaker of his nature, as his Kinsman—Redeemer, the Man of Sorrows, who understands his grief so thoroughly.

CHRIST. He is not only "Christos," the Anointed One, but "Chrestos," the One most gracious (I Peter 2:3). His fitness as the Miracle-Worker was guaranteed by the fact that He came as the Anointed of the Father, the commissioned Mediator. All power was, and is, His as "Christ, the Son of the living God," as Peter once called Him.

MAKETH. Peter used the continuous tense to describe the unsought gift of healing for this paralytic, and the force of this present tense must be noted. How impressive is the comment of Alexander Smellie on this fact!

O blessed continuousnes and perpetuity of His redeeming activity and grace! Though He has gone up on high, though my eyes do not see Him, He has lost none of His ancient power. He lives, He works, He heals, He reigns. He is the same today as He was yesterday. What He did for palsied Aeneas at Lydda when the Church was young, He does for me in the late autumn of the Church's circling year.

THEE. That personal pronoun would remind him that although he was a suffering saint, through the years of his physical disability the Lord had not forgotten him. He knew all about the condition of Aeneas and the stance where his bed could be found, and He directed Peter to it. *Thee.* Do we not bless Him for the personal address and singular number? He separates *you* from all around you. He knows all about *you.* "The Son of God who loveth *me*," Paul could write (Galatians 2:20). So He knows *your* need and can complete *your* cure. He has a care for *you* in the separateness of *your* temperament, in the plague of *your* heart, in the possibilities of *your* life.

WHOLE. The cure provided was perfect and complete. It was not a progressive healing. Immediately Aeneas rose from his bed and made it. "Arise, and make thy bed. And he arose immediately." For eight years this helpless man had been so dependent upon others, even to the making up of his bed. Now all is changed, for he now does for himself what other had done for him. Making his own bed was an evidence of restoration; it had been a symbol of his weakness. Is not Peter's command reminiscent of the manner in which Jesus wrought His work of healing in similar bedridden cases? (Matthew 9:6; John 5:8). This wholeness, Peter ascribed to Jesus Christ and not to any power or holiness he possessed (3:12). Peter was only the channel of healing. The same power instantly gives eternal life to the helpless sinner that believes.

Is this wholeness ours in the spiritual realm? Christ gives soundness, wholesomeness, holiness, health. He chases the last relics of sin away, and gives us power as well as pardon. He perfects that which concerns us and continues His perfect work until we share His own glorious likeness.

The healing of Aeneas caused the whole region where he lived to embrace his divine Healer. "*All* that dwelt at Lydda and Saron saw him, and turned to the Lord." Is the impact of our saved and sanctified life producing the same result? Are those around us where we live and labor more interested in the Lord because of the way we exhibit Him in character and conduct? Many Jews, seeing Lazarus raised from the dead, "went away, and believed in Jesus" (John 12:11).

15. The Miracle of Dorcas

(9:36-42)

From Lydda, Peter hastened on to neighboring Joppa at the earnest request of two disciples who were distressed over the death of a much valued female disciple. Peter's miraculous cure of Aeneas at Lydda led Tabitha's believing friends to send for the apostle in the hope that, under God, he could resurrect the dead woman before interment. Here again, in this seaport town, we can see the work of Philip the evangelist who was the probable founder of the infant church there.

The double name of the widow who sickened and died, and who apparently headed up a sisterhood of mercy, calls for a brief explanation. *Tabitha*, her Aramaic name, means "gazelle," which in the East was a favorite type of beauty (Song of Solomon 2:9, 17; 4:5; 7:3). *Dorcas* was the Greek equivalent of the former name. It was the custom at this period for Jews to have two names, one Hebrew and the other Greek or Latin. As Joppa was both a Gentile and Jewish town, it was usual for people to have two names. Both names of the deceased woman also implies some points of connection with both the Hebrew and Hellenistic sections of the Church. Doubtless this female disciple was well-known by both names.

Attention can also be drawn to the fact that she is spoken of as a "disciple," before a woman "full of good works and almsdeeds." Without faith in Christ as Saviour, the best of works are dead works. On the other hand, all profession of religion unaccompanied with maturity in good works is vain (Matthew 7:21; James 2:13-17). Luke, describing the reputation of Dorcas, says that she was "full of good works," the word "full" describing the physician-historian's "favorite formula for conveying the thought of a quality being possessed in the highest degree possible." So we have Luke's "full of leprosy" (5:12), "full of grace" and "full of faith" (Acts 6:5, 8. See 13:10; 19:28). Her "good works" consisted in making under-coats and outer-garments for the widows and needy (see Job 31:19, 20).

As to her material status, we have no knowledge. Perhaps she was in a middle state, between poverty and riches. Of the use she made of her substance and time we are fully informed. She employed herself in administering to the necessities of the poor, who were continually before her eyes. How she emulated the example of her Master who "went about doing good" as she diffused good will all around her! She not only did good *works*, but was full of *cheer* and made her exercises of benevolence her habitual *practice*, as the real force of the Greek implies. See I John 3:9, where the original conveys the same idea. Her example provoked others to the same good works. Probably she put more sewing circles in business than any other person in history, and Luccock says of Dorcas that she was "the founder of an international ladies garments workers' union, one of the greatest labor unions of all time, with branches in all lands."

Although renowned for her piety, diligence, and self-denial, Dorcas was not exempt from sickness and death. A conspicuous saint, she was yet called upon to suffer a sickness resulting in her death, and at the loss of her all the church at Joppa mourned. Hearing of Peter, who had healed by a word a man who had been confined to his bed for eight years, two of the disciples were appointed to hurry to him, some six miles away, and request his immediate interposition with God on behalf of Dorcas. Arriving at the house of mourning, Peter was met with the grief of friends, expressed in a most affecting manner. The widows stood weeping. Evidently these godly widows, who became the object of a special provision (see 6:1), formed an organization of charity. These widows displayed before Peter fruits of the industry and benevolence which must have touched the apostle. How Dorcas illustrates the ancient proverb, "The memory of the just is blessed" (Proverbs 10:7).

Peter dismissed all the mourners from the room where the body of Dorcas lay. He did not want to be interrupted in his supplications to Him who alone could raise the dead. Probably Peter remembered the same action of the Master in the raising of Jairus' daughter (Matthew 9:23-25). Peter had no power of his own to bring Dorcas back to life. In the silence and solitude of communion with God, he must learn the divine will concerning Dorcas and exercise the power of the prayer of faith. Peter "kneeled down, and prayed." Christ prayed but never kneeled down, to perform His mightiest miracles. While the miracle was wrought in the name of the Lord, and by the word of the Spirit, it was also accomplished in answer to believing prayer.

Having prayed, Peter turned to the corpse and uttered the word of power, "Tabitha, arise"—a call similar to *Talitha cumi* (Mark 5:41). The utterance of the words implied the internal assurance that prayer in silence has been answered. Opening her eyes, Dorcas saw Peter and sat up. Then Peter took her by the hand and lifted her up from her bed of death, and calling the disciples and widows into the room, presented her alive. Dorcas thus became one of the seven resurrections, apart from Christ's, mentioned in the Bible. As with others brought back to life, Dorcas gave no indication of her experiences after death. We can imagine how she returned to her former habits of life, with the same disposition to enjoy the society of those who loved her and to abound in every good work. As the result of her restoration to life, many "believed in the Lord." Here the word "believe" is obviously used definitely for the Lord Jesus as the Object of their faith.

This notable chapter with its miracles ends with a reference to a miracle that took place in the thinking of Peter. He tarried many days in Joppa with one, *Simon a tanner*. The profession of the "tanner" was absolutely repugnant to the Jew, because it brought one into contact with the carcases and hides of dead beasts, risking thereby ceremonial defilement. But the fact that Peter was willing to live in Simon's house was a sign in spirit that Peter was already learning the lesson of how mere national exclusiveness was at an end in the economy of Christ. Peter was discovering, if only partially, the lesson Jesus taught as to that which alone can bring with it real defilement (Mark 7:17-23). Fuller illumination came to Peter, as our next miracle proves.

16. The Miracle of Peter's Trance

(10:1-48)

Significantly enough, the events of this remarkable chapter took place in the home of Simon, the curer of pigs' hides—an illegitimate craft from a Jewish standpoint. Peter's sojourn in this hospitable home was an evidence that old, exclusive prejudices were beginning to disappear. It was also in this home that Peter was to face one of the most decisive experiences of his life. Further, Joppa, the scene of the events before

us, was the place where, 800 years before, God had to reveal His purpose to Jonah about blessing a Gentile nation, as well as the Jewish nation Jonah was a part of.

This most notable chapter in the Acts is conspicuous for its display of the supernatural both in heavenly manifestations, and in the furtherance of God's plan to bless all men, irrespective of nationality. By a vision, God drew Cornelius, a Gentile, toward His glorious Evangel, and by another vision He prepared Peter, a Jew, to proclaim that Evangel. The miraculous nature of these respective visions is seen in the way that the two visions mutually support each other. Their complete agreement proves that they were of God.

First of all, there was the vision granted to Cornelius at the season cf prayer in the Temple, during the offering up of the evening sacrifice. As he was a *centurion* (that is, a commander of a small part of the Roman army), it is interesting to observe that all the centurions mentioned in the New Testament stand in good light. There was the one who earned Christ's commendation for his great faith and the one who witnessed Christ's death and was moved to confess His deity. In the Acts, "the centurions appear in good circumstances, and Cornelius fits this patterns." Cornelius, although a rough Roman soldier was yet a man of religious refinement. Devout and pious, he is a striking instance of the need all have of the full knowledge of Christ and of being brought into contact with the preached Word. Although he had renounced his heathenism and engaged constantly and devoutly in the worship of the true God, and is described as having known *of* Christ as He was preached to Israel, he did not realize that He was for the Gentiles also.

It was to this devout man, who with his dear ones, soldiers, and slaves, feared the Lord, who was generous in his gifts to the needy, who prayed to God alway, that God granted a definite manifestation in response to his prayers, fastings, and good works. Cornelius was the recipient of a vision—not a dream (Matthew 1:20; 2:13), or a trance (Acts 10:16; 22:17), but the appearance of a messenger from heaven, who is described as "an angel of God," "an holy angel," and as "a man in bright clothing" (10:3, 22, 30)—language used to describe the raiment of the angels and of the Bride of the Lamb (Revelation

15:6 19:8). The content of this supernatural manifestation was a direct communication regarding Peter as being ordained of God to be the instructor of Cornelius in the way of life. Peter was to be God's ambassador to his soul. In his supernatural message, the angel revealed how heaven has an intimate knowledge of human life, for he told Cornelius the full name of Peter and where and with whom, he lodged. How gracious of God it was to prepare a human heart for the reception of Christ and His salvation! Beforehand, then, the soul of Cornelius was ready for the divine blessing already provided for it.

Acting upon the supernatural manifestation and message, Cornelius called two of his slaves and also a devout soldier, who was likewise a convert to the faith of Israel, to go to Joppa, a distance of some 30 Roman miles, and interview Peter. As they journeyed to Joppa, God prepared Peter for their reception. Thus we come to Peter's supernatural visitation and revelation. During a period of prayer and fasting, he fell into a "trance," a word from which *ecstasy* springs. This was a condition in which the normal action of the senses was suspended, as in the cases of Balaam and of Paul (Numbers 24:4; II Corinthians 12:3). Vine explains the word as meaning "a state in which ordinary consciousness and the perception of natural circumstances were withheld and the soul susceptible only to the vision imparted by God." In the vision, Peter received in symbolic form a revelation of the divine will and purpose.

The vision consisted of the great sheet holding all manner of four-footed beasts, wild beasts, and fowls of the air. Three times over Peter heard the divine Voice requesting him to rise and eat *all* beasts, clean and unclean. But Peter's exclusiveness comes out in his reply, "Not so, Lord; for I have never eaten anything that is common or unclean." Back came the divine rebuke, "What God hath cleansed, that call not thou common." Farrar says of this incident, "with that simple and audacious self-confidence which in Peter's character was so singularly mingled with fits of timidity and depression, he boldly corrects the voice which orders him, and reminds the divine Interlocutor that He must, so to speak, have made an oversight."

Being let down from heaven, clean and unclean beasts were in the same class, and Peter seems to have forgotten God's purpose to gather *unclean* Gentiles as well as *clean* Jews into His fold (Genesis 25:1; 41: 4, 5; Isaiah 11:9 etc.). Now he was to learn that God is no respecter of persons, that his Jewish prejudice must go, and the keys entrusted to him open the door both to Jews and Gentiles. Thus, as God gave Cornelius a particular revelation of *deeper* fellowship, He also gave to Peter a revelation of *inclusive* fellowship. The three-fold repetition of the divine Voice was meant to assure Peter of the complete ratification of the old-time prophecy that "in thee [Abraham] and in thy seed shall *all* the nations of the earth be blessed" (Genesis 12:1-3).

Returning to normality, Peter wondered about the full significance of his supernatural visitation and was again the recipient of a heavenly Messenger. This time it was the Holy Spirit (10:19) who told Peter of the messengers from Joppa whom the Spirit Himself had sent. Hearing of their errand, Peter left Joppa for Caesarea and met Cornelius and all those under his command. Cornelius reported his vision to Peter, and then there came his great speech with its far-reaching scope. Great themes like peace through Jesus Christ, His life, miracles, death, and resurrection, were dealt with, as well as the witness of all the prophets to the great doctrine of remission of sins through faith in Christ's name (10:43). As the result of the preaching of these great facts of the Gospel, a large company of Gentiles were baptized with the Holy Spirit, their share of the gift of Pentecost. After this, and as a sign of the essential divine baptism, they were baptized with water. An evidence of the transaction was the gift to speak in tongues, and by them magnify God.

In the miracle before us the action of the Holy Spirit must be noted. He not only came upon the Gentiles, but did so without the laying on of apostolic hands. "In this case, the gift of the Holy Spirit preceded baptism, to convince Peter and the rest clearly that they were accepted of God. . . . The lesson is obvious; the work of the Spirit is independent of confession or baptism (a fact all who teach baptismal regeneration should note); nor need there be an interval of time between the acceptance of Christ and the reception of His Spirit in all the fulness of His power." Those Gentiles became Christians first and were baptized afterwards. "The work of grace preceded the sign of it. The fact that these persons became members of the *invisible* Church before being joined to the *visible* Church proves beyond question that the sacrament of baptism is an evangelical, rather than absolute, necessity."

What remarkable supernatural events, then, are unfolded with minuteness in the chapter we have considered? Great though the heavenly visitations were, the greatest event that happened that day was the miracle of grace in which Spirit-filled Christians entered the Church of Jesus Christ without going through the narrow gate of Judaism (11:1-18). At last it was settled. Christ came to save sinners, whether Jews or Gentiles. Christianity was freed from the swaddling bands of Judaism, and the Christian Church was not to be treated as an appendix to the synagogue. She was to be God's new creation composed of regenerated Jews and Gentiles (Ephesians 2).

17. The Miracle of Peter's Deliverance from Prison

(12:1-19)

The miracles of grace in Antioch as the result of God's purpose in granting repentance of life unto the Gentiles, and the Spirit-inspired prophecy of Agabus regarding a wide-spread famine, occupy the eleventh chapter of the Acts. We now come to the persecution fomented by the Jewish rulers because of the new society of Jews and Gentiles the Church represented. King Herod became the instrument of the jealousy of the rulers and set about curbing the activities of the apostles, who were now realizing what it meant to be baptized with His baptism (Matthew 20:23). James, the brother of John, became the second martyr among the disciples. While the martyrdom of Stephen is described at length, that of James, the first martyr among the apostles, is related in two words "the sword." *This* James was one of the three inner circle friends of Jesus. Then, because Herod knew it would please the Jews, he apprehended Peter and put him in prison and intended to behead him after the seven days of the Feast of Unleavened Bread were over.

Are we not confronted with the mystery of God's selective purpose as we think of the death of one apostle and the deliverance of another? Discussing this very point,

Campbell Morgan says, "It may remain to us a perplexing question why James was slain and Peter delivered. There is no explanation. Nevertheless, the revelation of the facts is assuring. That God delivered Peter proves His power to have delivered James. That He did not deliver James proves that the death of James was within the compass of His will, and we know that in the great unveiling all will be seen to have been right."

Knowing of Peter's previous escape from prison, the authorities were determined to take all precautions to prevent any escape from this his second imprisonment. A round-the-clock guard was installed. Four quarternions of soldiers were assigned to keep him safe until the feast was over. This meant that Peter was chained to two soldiers—one on either wrist—and guarded by sixteen, four of them at a time. What hope was there of his escape this time, with guards within his cell and sentinels at the door? Although Peter's friends were numerous, what power had they to rescue him? This was his last night before the execution and there were none even in Herod's court to plead for him. It seemed as if he must die, even as James had.

We come, however, to one of those blessed *buts* of the Bible. "*But* prayer was made without ceasing." From human interference there was no hope; but the poor, trembling disciples did not yield to despair. Constant contact with the miraculous had taught them to believe that what was impossible with man is possible with God. So the Church gave themselves to continued, intense, and earnest prayer. With redoubled importunity, Peter's friends addressed themselves to God. Had his guards known of those prayers, they would have deemed them foolish means of delivering Peter from Herod's decree of death. But more things are wrought by omnipotent prayer than this world dreams of. Those praying men and women had read and knew that believing prayer had opened and shut heavens, vanquished armies, saved kingdoms, and raised the dead; so on through the hours they prayed.

As the saints prayed, Peter slept, undisturbed by the fear of coming martyrdom. Here we have a picture of calm repose as of one to whom God had given the sleep of His beloved (Psalm 127:2). Even the extraordinary, heaven-produced light flooding the cell did not interrupt his slumbers. In fact, so deep was Peter's sleep that he did not awake until the angel smote him. But heaven quickly responded to that continuous church prayer meeting, for the great iron gates of the prison were set moving of their own accord and Peter's angelic deliverer led him out of the dungeon. The angel came not only to the prison, but to the very cell where Peter was confined.

The various aspects of this miracle are obvious. There was the unusual light of which Peter became conscious, but not the guards who had become in some miraculous way unconscious of what was transpiring and therefore were unable to resist. Remember that Peter was bound to two of the soldiers, yet the chains fell off. The Roman Church professes to have these chains as relics. Then the angel bade Peter to put on his sandals and cloak and led him from his inner cell through two courtyards to the great iron gate at the prison's entrance, which opened on its own accord. How remarkable was God's interposition on behalf of His faithful witness! No one and nothing can stop Him in the fulfilment of His purpose.

The yielding of that iron gate is perhaps the most notable instance in the Bible of heavy objects being quietly set in motion in obedience to an unspoken command, and it is an example of how easy it is for God to exercise His power over inanimate matter in any shape or form. His power pervades all particles of matter because He created them. Peter, aroused suddenly out of sleep and hurried out of prison, found himself free and out in the open street. As this happened, he thought he saw a vision, but soon came to realize that it was no dream but a repetition of a previous experience (5:19).

Coming to himself, after awaking from a dazed condition produced by being suddenly aroused from sleep and from being confronted with a supernatural appearance, Peter, now conscious of his freedom as he stood in the street, knew he must go somewhere, and where better than the home of Mary, where he was sure to find friends and where, unknown to him, the prayer meeting for his release was still in progress. Knocking at the door, the female slave, Rhoda, came to open it. Peter must have spoken. Probably he said, "It's me, Peter. Open the door." Rhoda knew his

voice but did not open the door for gladness. Instead she ran to the praying friends and, interrupting them, said that Peter was standing outside. Answer to prayer had overpowered the dear child's presence of mind.

As for the disciples who had prayed long for Peter's deliverance, they lacked faith that God would answer their earnest petitions, for they told Rhoda she was crazy, or perhaps she had seen Peter's "angel"— the guardian angel in human form which Jews believed every true Israelite had assigned to him. But—another *but*—Peter continued knocking, and the rest within came to the door and were astonished to see the answer to their prayers standing before them. Once inside the house, Peter rehearsed the miracle the Lord performed on his behalf. Back in the prison, there was a different story. The soldiers who had guarded Peter were dumbfounded, and because they could not account for his release, they were put to death.

The lessons of this miracle are evident. "Is there anything too hard for the Lord?" There is no adverse situation out of which the Lord is not able to deliver His faithful children. Then, it is not enough to pray even long and earnestly. Prayer to God must be accompanied by faith that He can answer any prayer in accordance with His will. Further if a prayer period is interrupted, do not be disturbed. Interruption may be the answer to your prayer.

18. The Miracle of Herod's Tragic Death

(12:20-25)

This member of the Herodian family is known as *Herod Agrippa I*, who ruled with great munificence and who was very tactful in his dealings with the Jews. When he was forced to take sides in the grim struggle between Judaism and the rapidly growing Christian Church, he never hesitated to persecute the latter. It was in the role of the Church's bitterest persecutor that he slew James the apostle. With this Herod, Herodian power had virtually run its course. While he lived, Judaism had its "Indian summer." Even the Pharisees, sworn foes of Christ and of Christianity, thought well of him. When he was at the Imperial Court in Rome, he lived as one who knew Rome well, but when he came to Jerusalem, "he wore his Judaism as a garment made to order. . . . But the pagan streak in him was sure, sooner or later, to come to light," as we are now to see.

Herod, a New Testament pharaoh, still baffled and angry over the miraculous escape of Peter, went to Caesarea, and a popular demonstration was staged to proclaim him a god. The narrative informs us that he was greatly offended with the people of Tyre and Sidon and contemplated war against them, but through the intercession of his own chamberlain, Blastus, he forgave them. We now come to the two aspects of Herod's career as given by Luke, namely, his pride and his punishment.

In the great theater in Caesarea, built by Herod the Great, Herod appeared in royal apparel and sat upon his throne. Josephus, the Jewish historian, tells us that Herod was arrayed in a robe of silver tissue which glittered with a dazzling brightness under the rays of the morning sun. Seated, Herod made a speech, his oration probably being on the subject of his clemency toward Tyre and Sidon. Struck with the splendor of his appearance and the force of his eloquence, and desiring to conciliate him by flattery, his courtiers, in the Roman fashion of honoring kings and emperors, hailed Herod as a god, and prayed him, as such, to bless them. While Herod did not *claim* the honor accorded him, nevertheless, he was *pleased* with it and acquiesced to the blasphemous acclamation of his admirers, instead of reproving it. When Paul and Barnabas were offered divine honors, they rent their clothes and condemned their admirers in the strongest terms (14:9-15).

Pride, the sin God hates, was one of Herod's conspicuous sins. This was why the flattering unction of human applause greatly pleased him. He failed to hate "that solemn vice of greatness, *pride*." But Herod was to learn the truth of the lines of Thomas Gray—

> How vain the ardor of the crowd,
> How low, how little are the proud,
> How indigent the great!

Pride, above all things, provokes "a jealous God," who will not give His glory to another, and His whole creation stands ready to vindicate the honor of His injured majesty.

Herod's punishment for pride was supernatural, sudden, and severe. Immediately, "the angel of the Lord smote him." The an-

gel who had delivered Peter from his persecutor now deals dramatically with the persecutor himself for his act of impiety. The reason for the angelic stroke is given— "because he gave not God the glory." Herod had paraded himself before a servile multitude as if he were a little Caesar, a god on earth; but an angel swiftly ended his vaunted deity by a disease in his bowels so acute and terrible that, as Josephus tells us, Herod was constrained to acknowledge before the assembly in the theatre that God had punished him for not rejecting with abhorrence their impious acclamations, so they were to witness the end of their *god*.

The Bible tells us that Herod was "eaten of worms" and "gave up the ghost," and thus his degradation was as manifest as his pride had been presumptuous. As in the plagues of Egypt when God commanded frogs and lice to inflict punishment on Pharaoh, the hardened monarch, so now He assembled a large number of worms to avenge His quarrel against Herod, who must have died in great agony—died, not from natural causes, but suddenly in divine judgment.

Luke's description of the disease resulting in Herod's quick death is characteristic of his medical precision. The form of the disease, because of its exceptionally loathsome character, had always been regarded as a method of divine chastisement. Herodotus says of Pheretima, queen of Cyrene, renowned for her cruelties, that after taking vengeance on the people of Barea, a most horrid death overtook her. "Her body swarmed with worms, which ate her flesh while she was still alive." Antiochus Epiphanes, the great enemy of the Jews, died a similar death.

Josephus tells us that as judgment was about to overtake Herod, the monarch looked up and saw an owl perched on a rope behind him, which was an omen to him of his imminent death and that such an omen fulfilled a prediction which had been made to Herod by a fellow-prisoner during his confinement at Rome. After great agony, he died five days later. But notice carefully the statement following the Bible account of Herod's terrible death. It commences with another *but*, which suggests a wonderful contrast: "*But* the Word of God grew and multiplied." It has been so through succeeding centuries. Sooner or later, enemies of Christ have been swept away, but the march of His triumphant Word has never ceased for a moment.

The lesson from the sin and death of Herod for our own heart is this: Beware of flattery, which, although pleasant to the carnal mind, is disastrous to the Christian's inner peace and progress in his spiritual walk. How easy it is to be lifted up with pride and to fall into the condemnation of the devil! Pride of flesh is an ordeal few can bear, and he who makes use of it, "spreads a net for his brother's feet" (Proverbs 27:1; 29:5).

19. The Miracle of Elymas the Sorcerer

(13:4-10)

In the section from this chapter through the rest of the Acts, we have an account of the rapid spread of Christianity among the idolatrous Gentiles, together with its further progress among the Jews and Gentile proselytes. For the first time Saul is named Paul, a Roman name falling in with his coming witness to Christ in the imperial city. It was purely accident that his new name *Paul* was like the name of the man converted by his instrumentality. To suggest, as some writers do, that Paul adopted his name out of respect to Paulus, or as a memorial of his conversion, would have had "an element of vulgarity impossible to Paul." From now on, Paul is prominent. Hitherto, Peter, the converted Jew, functioned as the apostle to the Jews and also opened the door of the Church to the Gentiles. Now Paul, another converted Jew, becomes the apostle to the Gentiles and establishes churches in so many parts.

Both Sergius Paulus and Bar-Jesus—the Jewish name of Elymas the sorcerer—had heard about the teaching and miracles of the apostles which aroused the curiosity of Sergius, but the fear of Elymas. When Barnabas, John Mark, and Paul came to Paphos after having preached the Word of God at Salamis, Sergius called for the apostles and desired to hear from them the new and startling message they were preaching. Sergius is described as a prudent man. As "deputy" of his country, he had manifested intelligence and discernment, and so recognized in the apostles men of high character. Associated with this proconsul of Cyprus was Elymas who sought to check the interest of Sergius in the Chris-

tian message. Evidently this charlatan feared the loss of the influence he had previously exercised over the mind of Sergius.

Elymas withstood the apostles because he could see that Sergius was passing from the false to the true, from doubt to faith. Farrar says, "The position of soothsayer to a Roman proconsul, even though it could only last a year, was too distinguished and too lucrative to abandon without a struggle." Paul sensed the evil in Elymas and was under no bad impression when he spoke and cursed him as he did. He was filled with the Spirit as he addressed the sorcerer, and speaking so scathingly did not violate in any degree the decorum, or love, his office as an apostle required. Through a supernatural inflow of the Spirit, Paul had a swift insight into the character of Elymas, and exposing his evil, he pronounced his judgment. As a renegade Jew, Elymas brought forward all the arguments he could muster against Christianity, but he found more than his match in the Spirit-filled apostle. The peculiar malignity of Elymas' character justified the severity of Paul's message. Such a phony prophet and impostor merited the announced judgment.

Because Elymas was full of all subtlety and trickery, Paul did not hesitate to call him a "child of the devil." He was full of deceit, not of wisdom. *Bar-Jesus*, meaning "Son of Jesus," had become a "son of the devil." Unceasingly he had perverted "the right ways of the Lord." The word for *right* is "straight," an allusion to the crookedness of Elymas, who was a crooked man who seemed to be beyond straightening (Isaiah 40:4).

As to the miracle of blindness overtaking Elymas, Paul, like Moses, began his public ministry combatting a false magician. Moses confined his miraculous activity to external nature, whereas Paul turned on Elymas himself, smiting him with blindness. Inspired by the Spirit of power, Paul worked a wonder on the false wonder-worker, thus revealing to Sergius, who had been previously swayed by Elymas, the divine power delegated to the apostles. The display of such power was not an act of Paul, but of God. This first miracle of his—one of judgment—corresponds to the first public miracle of Peter which was also a judgment-miracle (5:5, 10). Gloag, quoted by Vincent, says that, "The first miracle which Paul performed was the infliction of a judgment; and that judgment the same which befell himself when arrested on his way to Damascus." Because of His almightiness, God can instantly open blind eyes (John 9:32) and just as instantly can blind seeing eyes. Grace was mingled with judgment, for the sudden blindness was "for a season," suggesting that it was designed to be remedial and not simply retributive. God was desirous of delivering Elymas from "the blackness of darkness for ever" (Jude 11, 13). That opportunity was to be his to repent so that he could "recover himself out of the snare of the devil."

Luke, with the precision of the trained physician, adds the touch that Elymas sought the help of others "to lead him by the hand." Ellicott comments that, having used his knowledge to guide others to his own advantage, Elymas now seeks for others to guide his own steps. This expositor also suggests that "the tense of the Greek verb—'he was seeking,' seems to imply that Elymas sought and did not find. He had no friends to help him and was left to his fate unpitied." Such blindness remained a terrible emblem of the blindness of his soul.

The result of this miracle of judgment was the conversion of the deputy. Astonished as he looked upon blinded Elymas, he believed the doctrine of Christ which Paul preached. Disregarding the efforts of Elymas to pervert such teaching, Sergius became an avowed disciple of Christ. Had he put off his convictions, as Felix did, he would probably have been left to perish in his sins. But grace prevailed, and the physical blindness of one led to the spiritual sight of the other.

For a lesson of the miracle, we turn to old Charles Simeon, who says: "Let those then who will not embrace the Gospel, beware how they labor to pervert the faith of others: if they must perish, they had better perish alone, than under the guilt of destroying the souls of others."

20. The Miracle of the Cripple at Lystra

(14:1-18)

After the miracle of Elymas, Paul and his company found their way to Antioch in Pisidia where, in the synagogue, Paul gave a rehearsal of Jewish history and magnified God for His miracles on behalf of His people. In his discourse, the apostle also emphasized the reality of Christ's resurrection, and so powerful was the impact of his message that the Gentile element persuaded Paul and Barnabas to preach again the following Sabbath. When the Sabbath arrived, the apostles had to face fierce opposition from the Jewish element who were hostile to the truth. There were the despisers to whom Paul said, "Wonder, and perish." These envious Jews in rejecting Paul's message forced him to reject them and turn to the Gentiles who were yearning for the light. Paul and Barnabas left the coasts of Antioch, and in obedience to Christ's command, shook the dust off their feet (Matthew 10:14) and came to Iconium. No opposition, however, could daunt these men who were willing to hazard their lives for Christ's sake. They were "filled with joy, and with the Holy Ghost."

In Iconium, the reception was also mixed. Many Jews and Gentiles believed, but the unbelieving Jews stirred up animosity against the apostles, who not only testified "to the word of His grace," but who also received power to work miracles, as the confirmation of faith (14:3). Stoned out of Iconium, Paul and Barnabas came to Lystra, where they were to have a most unique experience. Such, then, is the background of the miracle we are now to consider. Lystra itself was a garrison town and a center of Roman culture. Because there was no synagogue, the Gentiles whom Paul and Barnabas dealt with were pagan—their paganism being evidenced by their attempt to worship Paul and Barnabas as deities, and by the effort to stone Paul because he refused to be worshiped. Paul visited Lystra four times (14:6, 21; 16:1; 18:23) and addressed it in his Galatian letter. Timothy was a native of this area.

The needy man Paul encountered at Lystra was impotent in his feet, meaning, they were weak and unusable. The word for *weak* is found here and in Romans 15:1. He was crippled from his mother's womb, indicating some physical disturbance during pregnancy. Micklem suggests that the man's severe organic affliction was due to *infantile paralysis*. The phrase, "who never had walked," is the physician's touch accentuating the duration of the cripple's malady and also his utter helplessness. Friends had to convey him around.

Two verses, however, are sufficient to relate the supernaturalness of the cripple's care. This unfortunate man had heard Paul speak. He was among the apostle's hearers as he preached the Gospel of a crucified, risen Christ and how sufficient He was to meet every need. As "faith cometh by hearing," the cripple believed as Paul preached that Christ was able to undertake for him in his helplessness. Paul evidently was impressed by the man's rapt attention, for he "stedfastly beheld" the cripple with the fixed gaze of one having strong powers of sight (13:9), and with such an inner look, there came the perception that the man had faith to be healed. His earnest, upward look convinced Paul that the man was ready to receive what he had never possessed— power to walk. "Here, as so often as if it were general, though not the universal, law of miraculous working, faith is pre-supposed as the condition" (Mark 10:23).

Five words (another "jewel five words long") were sufficient to cure the man. Paul commanded in a loud voice: "Stand upright on thy feet." It is interesting to compare the method of operation here with that of similar miracles (Matthew 9:6; John 5:11; Acts 3:3). With the apostle's command, there was power to obey. What God commands, He makes possible. Ellicott remarks that, "The command, which would have seemed a mockery to one who did not rise beyond the limits of experience, is obeyed by the will that had been inspired by the new power of faith."

The cure was instantaneous and complete for the man born a cripple "leaped and walked," a double action similar to the cripple Peter was the means of curing (3:8). Expositors point out the differing sense of these two verbs. "Leaped" was a sudden, simple act. With a single bound, he was out of bed and standing upright on his feet, something he had never been able to do. Then he "walked," denoting a continuous action. "Leaped" implies a *crisis*—"walked," a *process*. The spontaneous affect of this cure was remarkable. Evidently many people of Lystra witnessed the miracle, and they declared, "the gods are come down to us in likeness of men."

Paul had been speaking in Greek, but the Lycaonians shouted their adulation of the apostles in their own tongue, which explains why the apostles did not interfere when they saw the preparations for sacrifice. Not understanding the Lycaonian tongue, Paul and Barnabas were not aware of what the people were saying about their divine character. The exclamation about the apostles being gods in the likeness of men reveals the pagan belief that gods visited the earth in human form.

Paul was called *Mercury*, or *Hermes*, the Greek name of the deity. As the herald of the gods, Mercury was the god of skill in the use of speech and of eloquence in general. As the Lystrans listened to Paul, they were impressed with his gift of eloquence. Barnabas was named *Jupiter*, or *Zeus*, the tutelary diety of Lystra who was commonly represented as accompanying Mercury on his visits to the earth. Probably the taller stature and more stately presence of Barnabas, whose personal appearance was different from the weak, bodily presence of Paul (II Corinthians 10:1, 10), suggested to the people the likeness of Barnabas to the imposing stature of Jupiter, who was reckoned as the lord of the air, dispensing thunder, lightning, rain, hail, rivers, and tempests.

It was only when the heathen priest of Jupiter brought garlands to grace the necks of the apostles and oxen for a sacrifice to the gods, that Paul and Barnabas realized what the people were about to do as the result of the miracle they had performed. The apostles immediately protested against any recognition of supposed deity. Stopping the sacrificial procession, they rent their clothes in an expression of horror over such acted blasphemy, and they assured the pagan crowd that they were only men of like nature to themselves. Even Paul's impressive speech about the omnipotence of God scarcely restrained the people. But the miracle wrought on the cripple was all of God, and He must have all the glory.

21. The Miracle of Paul's Recovery from Stoning

(14:19-28)

Although the citizens of Lystra hailed Paul and Barnabas as gods, they quickly changed their minds when rebuked for ascribing deity to the apostles. Honor turned to hate, and a sacrifice to stoning. How fickle were the plaudits of the mob as it turned so quickly from praise to persecution at the instigation of the angered Jews from Antioch and Iconium. So rapid was the transition from one extreme to another that those who had been stirred up were willing to stone as an impostor the one they had just worshiped as a god. There was only a step between the deification and destruction of Paul. In this respect, he was following the footsteps of his Master who received the hosannas of the multitudes but who, three days later, heard them cry, "Crucify Him!" (Matthew 21:9; 27:22). As we shall see, Paul encountered a like sudden change at Melita (28:6).

The stoning of Paul, planned and executed by the Jews, indicated that they believed they were inflicting punishment upon a blasphemer. If Paul and Barnabas were not "gods in the likeness of men," then they must be sorcerers or evil demons. The Jews themselves attributed signs and wonders to Beelzebub, the prince of demons (Matthew 9:34; 12:24). As the blinding, stunning blows fell upon Paul—nothing is said about any persecution of Barnabas—the apostle must have thought of Stephen as he was stoned to death—a death Paul had had a share in. But now, "the martyr expiated the guilt of the persecutor." Paul's stoning was the one instance of such suffering (II Corinthians 11:25). All he endured here at Lystra "stands out, at the close of his life in the vista of past years with a marvelous distinctness" (II Timothy 3:11).

The question arises, Was Paul stoned to death and immediately raised again? The people guilty of such cruel treatment supposed him to be dead, and the disciples powerless to help Paul as he was being stoned, waited around, and when all was over stole out with the purpose of giving the blood-spattered body a decent burial. Was the beloved apostle dead, or only stunned? Habershon says, "We cannot tell whether Paul was really dead and was raised to life; probably he did not know himself, for it has been thought that he referred to this time when he wrote, 'Whether in the body, or out of the body I cannot tell: God knoweth.' As his body lay there in the midst of the sorrowing disciples, his spirit probably had been caught up into Paradise, where he heard unspeakable words that he was not permitted to utter."

Whether Paul died or not a great miracle was wrought for and upon him, for after being stoned and left for dead, he rose up and returned to the city. He was so suddenly and completely cured that he traveled the following day to Derbe, and at once began preaching, and that without any apparent pain and fatigue such as his terrible suffering would have resulted in. Paul practiced what he preached (Acts 15:25, 26). Returning to Lystra, Iconium, and Antioch to encourage and exhort the disciples, he told them that it was only through much tribulation that they could enter the kingdom of God (14:22). Later on, he was to write, "All that will live godly in Christ Jesus shall suffer persecution" (II Timothy 3:12).

Can it be that young Timothy, who evidently witnessed the apostle's afflictions, was influenced by them? As Paul calls him his "beloved son," he must have led him to Christ, and as he is before us in the Acts as a Christian (16:1), it may be that Paul's holy courage under suffering when he might have had adoration instead by compromise of principle led this young man with a godly mother to embrace the Christ who could do so much through, and for, Paul (II Timothy 3:10, 11).

22. The Miracle Vision at Troas

(16:6-15)

Supernatural interruptions of Paul's plans are seen in the Holy Spirit's forbidding him to preach the word in Asia and in His refusal to let Paul go to Bithynia. The control of Paul's activities by the Spirit resulted in his coming to Troas, and in prayer he knew where he must next preach the glad tidings of Christ. In a vision, he had the divine explanation of the varied promptings and drawbacks of his journey. A greater door of opportunity was open before him, for the Gospel was to pass from Asia to Europe. The Macedonian call was to result in the Gospel covering the whole western world. In obedience to the vision of a man of Macedonia, Paul went and preached in this first European country to hear the message of a Saviour's love and grace.

These visions in Acts (9:10-16, 12; 10:3, 17-19; 11:5; 16:9, 10; 22:18-21; 27:23, 24) brought much solace and stay with them. Their recipients were assured by them that there were "chariots of fire and horses of fire" round about them. The vision of the Lord and of "troops of beautiful, tall angels" sent to "enshield them from all wrong" greatly encouraged the apostles. They felt that heavenly squadrons encircled them and that invisible and most mighty hands were holding them up.

The vision itself, of which there are several in the Acts, was not a mere dream but a supernatural revelation of God's purpose to the receptive mind of Paul. Such a vision allowed no delay and must be immediately obeyed. Paul, therefore, took a boat and came to Philippi, where he found that the man of Macedonia "turned out to be a woman," as one writer puts it. In a military town like Philippi, there was possibly no synagogue, so Paul went to the riverside "where an oratory was established." Here he found a few women—no men—and ministered the Word to them. Amid degraded paganism, a bright light was to shine forth. Lydia, a seller of purple, of Thyatira, who was one of the higher types of Gentiles (Acts 17:12) drawn to Judaism, came to the riverside Bible reading, listened eagerly to Paul, and became the first Gentile convert in Europe.

The conversion of Lydia was miraculous, for the Lord not only knocked upon the door of her heart, but He opened it. Although religiously inclined, her once-pagan heart was closed to the truth of the Gospel and needed to be opened for its reception. She was subdued to obedience of faith, believed, and was baptized. Her household immediately followed her in surrender to the Lord's claims. An evidence of Lydia's miraculous change of heart is seen in her large-hearted hospitality, which the apostles gratefully accepted and afterwards enjoyed (16:40).

23. The Miracle of the Female Soothsayer

(16:16-24)

What a chapter of miracles this is—miracles of grace and power! How it extols God's saving power! He can save the young, like Timothy (16:1); a cultured, religious person, like Lydia; a degraded woman like the one in this portion; a hard-hearted, coarse, and brutal pagan like the jailor. God's power can transform all classes and conditions. Lydia was at the top of the social ladder, the degraded woman at the bottom of it. But God can save the best and the worst.

The unfortunate woman before us was a victim of benighted heathenism and was possessed both by the devil and by evil men, the devil's instruments. As a female ventriloquist, she uttered soothsayings inspired by evil spirits, and her masters traded upon her supposed inspiration to give people oracular guidance in the perplexities of their lives. This woman's art was not a conspiracy between her and her masters to deceive the world by juggery and imposture. She was possessed by an evil spirit from whom she received powers, different from any that are common to the rest of mankind.

On their way to the riverside for prayer and teaching, the apostles were accosted by this enslaved woman, who recognized them as servants of the most high God. As demons recognized the deity and authority of Jesus, so here the evil spirit in the woman was cognizant of the power and authority of the Spirit-possessed apostles. In her confession that they were able to show the way of salvation, was there the expressed desire for deliverance, peace, and calm her inner heart yearned for? Did she see in these men those who were unlike the men who traded on her maddened misery?

The constant cries of the woman hindered Paul's work as he tried, above their din, to teach those who had gathered at the riverside. Why did Paul allow her to plague him for several days? Why did he wait to release her from her evil bondage? Perhaps he did not know until an exact moment of divine revelation that he was to be given grace to release the girl, or perhaps he wondered whether it was right for him to do as his Master had done with demoniacs (Matthew 8:28-34) and "restore the woman to her true self, by teaching her to distinguish between her longing for deliverance and the wild passions that hindered her from attaining it."

Paul was grieved both because she was obstructing his ministry and because of her enslavement. Endued with the power of working miracles, Paul commanded the evil spirit to come out of the woman and the demon obeyed the Christ that Paul represented. Instantly, the woman was liberated from her sore bondage and there her history ends. We can rest assured that divine grace prevented her from drifting back into ignorance and unbelief. Doubtless the women who labored with the apostle (Philippians 4:2) cared for her, and probably her gift of gratitude for such an emancipation from the thraldom of evil was included in the

gifts sent to the apostles from this area
(Philippians 4:15).

The business of the converted woman's
one-time masters and the spirit of divination passed away together. "When the demon *went out*, the men's hope of gain *went
out*—same form of verb is used in verses 18
and 19." With their tainted source of support gone, the exploiters were determined
to take vengeance on Paul for liberating
the girl and breaking up their illegitimate
traffic. They incited the Roman rulers
against the apostles. Luke and Timothy,
being less conspicuous, escaped, but Paul
and Silas were thrown into prison. Bad
works usually are the cause of a prison
sentence. Paul and Silas were in prison for
their good works.

24. The Miracle of the Great Earthquake

(16:19-40)

As a Roman citizen, Paul could have
claimed exemption from the beating with
rods. He could not, however, assert *his*
right and let Silas be scourged, so Paul
suffered with him. Altogether this brave,
early missionary was thrice beaten (II
Corinthians 11:25). But suffering as they
did from bleeding backs and their feet in
stocks, at midnight Paul and Silas prayed
and sang praises unto God. They say that
when the larks suffer, they sing. Well, the
apostles were given songs in their night of
adversity. I once heard General William
Booth, founder of the Salvation Army, say
that "God was so well-pleased with the
prayers and praises of Paul and Silas, that
He said *Amen!* with a mighty earthquake."
The prisoners heard those prayers and
praises—so did God!

How varied are the methods of God to
bring sinners to Himself. Lydia required no
fear or terror to incline her heart heavenward. It opened as silently as a bud to the
morning sun. With the savage mind of the
jailor, more drastic measures were necessary
to make him sensible of his guilt and peril;
so, as he treated God's servants in a brutal
way, God was about to shew His power
and transform a brute into a believer. God
sent the earthquake, His servants were supernaturally delivered, and the jailor was
supernaturally saved. Peter was delivered
from prison by an angel, but Paul and Silas
were set free by an earthquake. No angel
visited their common prison.

The apostles experienced that dark midnight hour the truth of the psalmist's words:
"He looketh on the earth, and it trembleth"
(104:32), and He, who can make the wrath
of nature, no less than that of man, to praise
Him, opened the prison doors by His power
and then opened the jailor's heart. That
earthquake aroused the keeper of the prison
from sleep, and also awakened him to see
his need of salvation. God restricted the
power of the earthquake. The prison was
not destroyed, although its foundations were
shaken. The purpose of the display of divine
power was to open the securely fastened
doors and unfetter the prisoners.

The supernatural calmness and courage
of Paul and Silas stand out in the incident.
The jailor, thinking the prisoners had escaped, started to commit suicide. In a few,
simple words, Paul calmed the distracted
man who, made conscious by the manifestation of divine power of his need as a sinner, asked how he could be saved, not from
the darkness of the cell, but the inner darkness of his soul. The convicted sinner received Christ as his personal Saviour, and
almost immediately he led his whole household to Him. An evidence of his repentance
and conversion comes out in his changed
disposition. Before the earthquake, he was
so brutal that he could lash prisoners and
never turn a hair as he watched their backs
oozing with blood. Now, as soon as he was
saved, he takes water and washes the very
stripes he had inflicted. He himself had
been cleansed from wounds worse and more
perilous than those he had inflicted by his
rods. The least he could do was to wash
the blood stripes of the prisoners. He then
set food before Paul and Silas, and what
a meal that must have been! No wonder
they all rejoiced.

25. The Miracle Vision of Encouragement

(18:7-11)

That there were conspicuous converts to
Christianity is proven by the mention of
Justus who was a devout worshiper, and of
Crispus, the chief ruler of the synagogue,
whom Paul baptized (I Corinthians 1:14).
A great ministry faced Paul in Corinth.
Great opportunities and also opposition were
to be his, and he needed to be fortified
against the eighteen months of teaching
and trial. The many visions mentioned in

the Acts come within the region of the supernatural because they were distinct revelations of the divine mind to man's mind. It is thus that we have the recurrence of these visions at each great crisis in the life of Paul (9:4-6; 22:17). In this, a night vision, "when deep sleep falleth upon men," Paul passed from "the strife of tongues into the presence of his divine Friend."

As we read the chapter before us, we can see how necessary it was for Paul to have that divine "Be not afraid." There were those hostile Jews who were to make insurrection against him and bring him to the Roman judgment seat. Then there was Ephesus and the stupendous tasks awaiting the apostle in that great center. If he was given to fear and depression and felt keenly the trial of seeming failure and comparative isolation, Paul needed divine encouragement. That he went forth girded with divine boldness is evident from what he wrote to Timothy, one of his Lystra converts, "God hath not given us the Spirit of fear; but of power, and of love, and of a sound mind" (II Timothy 1:7).

The divine command, "Speak, and hold not thy peace," was explicitly obeyed. If, because of his manifold trials and apparent failure, Paul was tempted to be silent concerning Christ, this message from Him would hearten the apostle. Similar experiences befell Elijah and Jeremiah (I Kings 9:4-14; Jeremiah 1:6-8; 15:15-21). Then there was the Lord's promise following His command, "I am with thee and no man shall set on thee to hurt thee: for I have much people in this city." After being stoned and left as dead, the assurance that no man could now hurt him must have cheered Paul's heart. When He deems fit, no weapons formed against us can prosper. Elijah thought he was alone in his witness, yet there were 7,000 in Israel who loved God even as the prophet did. Paul, feeling somewhat isolated in his dynamic witness, was to discover that "even in the sinful streets of Corinth, among those plunged deepest into its sin (I Corinthians 5:10, 11), there were souls yearning for deliverance, in whom conscience was not dead, and who were waiting only for the call of repentance."

The year and a half Paul spent in Corinth gave him time to win many for the Lord who came to him in the vision, and to establish a church there in His name. "The unimpeded progress of this period came to him as an abundant fulfilment of the Lord's promise, and prepared him for the next persecution when it came."

26. The Miracles at Ephesus

(19:1-20)

It was in Ephesus, the metropolis of Asia, an important and magnificent city, that Paul accomplished "the most marvelous work in all his marvelous life." Here the promise of the previous vision was fully realized. For three years, he taught in the city synagogues and for two years in the renowned school of Tyrannus, the philosopher. Ephesus was also the great center of heathen worship, and multitudes of Diana worshipers became Christians, enabling Paul to found churches in communities for a hundred miles around. Because of the manifestation of divine power in grace, Ephesus became the hub of the Christian world. It was here that many of the epistles were written and where John resided in his old age.

Because of the vast importance of the establishment of the Gospel in Ephesus, where the great throngs attending its heathen festivals gave Paul remarkable opportunities to "speak, and hold not his peace" (19:8), God gave the apostle power to perform special miracles. For example, there were those Ephesians ("about twelve" [19: 7]) who, repenting and believing, were baptized and who then received a supernatural gift. Through the laying on of Paul's hands, the men received the gift of the Spirit, and then from Him a special gift, namely, that of "tongues." Such a gift was used for praise and preaching. It was the natural expression of their new enthusiasm and intensity of spiritual joy. That such a supernatural gift was only temporary, given for the establishment of the Church as a divine institution, is evident from Paul's letter to the Corinthians that tongues would cease (I Corinthians 13: 8).

While Paul was in Ephesus, God wrought special miracles through him. Periodically, Paul exercised such delegated power. No miracles are on record as being wrought at Damascus, Jerusalem, Tarsus, Antioch, Pisidia, Derbe, Athens, or Rome. We have only Cyprus, Iconium, Lystra, Philippi, Corinth, Ephesus, and Melita as the places where the Lord permitted Paul to use super-natural power.

The miracles in Ephesus were no common works of power. Luke, who recorded the incident at this point, used the technical language of the physician for healing powers of a special kind. This is why he dwells on the various phenomena used by the supernatural gift of healing God granted Paul. "From his body was brought unto the sick handkerchiefs or aprons, and the diseases departed from them, and the evil spirits went out of them" (19:11, 12). There was no virtue whatever in the handkerchiefs and short aprons Paul gave to the diseased and demon-possessed, even though the cured may have retained them as precious relics. They were only the *media* of the supernatural gift of healing Paul exercised at that time. Ellicott says that "The efficacy of such *media* stands obviously on the same footing as that of the hem of our Lord's garment (Matthew 9:20, 21), and the shadow of Peter (Acts 5:15), and of the clay in the healing of the blind" (John 9:6). *Media* were not imperative, for God, through His Son and the apostles, wrought miracles with and without means.

In a heathen city like Ephesus where, because of the worship of Diana and the professed healing charms of the small silver models of the heathen goddess, Paul's miracles were adapted for the attraction of the heathen mind given over to the superstitious. "It was something for the Ephesians to learn that the prayer of faith and the handkerchief that had touched the apostle's skin had a greater power to heal than the charms in which they had previously trusted." Faith brought the sufferers to Paul for relief, and from him came power from on high to heal their diseases and deliver them from the evil spirits. The aping of the healing handkerchief by modern fake healers is to be deplored. Handkerchiefs and other articles, supposedly prayed over by a self-styled healer, are reckoned to have power to convey healing to those who are deluded into sending money for such worthless rags. Strange, is it not, that although Paul had power to heal so many at this time, he could not heal his own beloved friend and co-worker? (II Timothy 4:20). In His sovereign will, God bestows or withholds supernatural gifts.

27. The Miracle of the Seven False Exorcists

(19:13-20)

Another Ephesus miracle with far-reaching results was that of seven vagabond Jews who professed to have divine power to expel demons. Exorcism was their profession, and they pretended with their charms and spells to relieve those who were demon-possessed. These seven who applied themselves to such a practice were the sons of Sceva, the only Jewish person in the Bible to bear this name. He is spoken of as a high or chief priest—on what ground is not explained. His seven sons were guilty of the folly of believing that, as the spectators of our Lord's miracle of casting out demons ascribed His power to a confederacy with Satan, and as the apostles were thought by some to cast out evil spirits in the Lord's name by means of magical incantations, so they thought that by using the name of Jesus, they could produce the same results.

On this particular occasion, knowing something of the power of the Christ Paul preached about and manifested, the seven exorcists undertook to expel a demon from the possessed man. They adjured the evil spirit in the name of Christ to come out of him. The spirit acknowledged his inability to withstand the command of Christ Himself when uttered by an apostle duly authorized to use such a name, but he would not obey counterfeits. The man identified with the demon, on whom the seven tried to perform, guided supernaturally, said, "Jesus I know, and Paul I know; but who are ye?" They stood condemned as usurpers of divine power.

The evil spirit, using the man he indwelt, leaped on the seven men with great vehemence. "Demoniacal possession brought with it, as is the case of the Gadarene, the preternatural strength of fiends," and the cowardly imposters were driven from the possessed man, naked and wounded, and were happy to escape with their lives. We cannot but believe that afterwards Paul came into contact with the demon-possessed man and that he was one of those out of whom the evil spirits went (19:12). This great testimony to the power of Christ and to the authority of Paul carried conviction to the minds of multitudes. The circumstances turned to favorable account for the spread of the Gospel and increased the desire to hear Paul preach it.

As the result of Paul's miracles and the incident of Sceva's sons, a revival swept through Ephesus. Jews and Gentiles were stricken with fear, and the name of Christ was magnified. Many believed and confessed their heathenism and, as evidence of their change of heart, made a huge bonfire of their curious arts and books. Those charms, incantations, books of divination and of interpreting dreams represented a sum of over 5,000 dollars. Their owners did not convert their wares into money and use it for beneficent purposes. They showed a disregard for worldly honor and worldly interests and honored God by destroying what was hateful to Him. As the tense of the verb Luke uses implies the present form, it would seem as if the burning was an oft-repeated act, or one that lasted for some hours.

We cannot wonder that as the result of the miracles of healing power and the miracle of grace that "mightily grew the Word of God and prevailed," and that as Ellicott puts it, "In this complete renunciation of the old, evil past, we may probably see the secret of the capacity for a higher knowledge which Paul recognized as belonging to Ephesus more than to most other churches." From his epistle to the Ephesians we learn how quickly the saints passed from heathenism to deep spiritual understanding. Later on, the church was upbraided for leaving its first love (Revelation 2:4).

28. The Miracle of Eutychus' Resurrection

(20:1-12)

Back at Troas, Paul had a full gathering to receive him and to listen to his message. At the evening breaking of bread on the Lord's Day, the hunger of the people for the truth encouraged Paul to preach on and on until the midnight hour. As the lights burned in that upper chamber, greater spiritual illumination came to those who drank in the blessed words of life. The drowsiness of Eutychus as the result of the heat and smell arising from the numerous lamps in the crowded stuffy chamber, the length of the discourse, and the lateness of the hour, are characteristic of a physician's narrative (see Luke 22:45).

Eutychus, who found a seat on the win-

dowsill, was overcome by sleep and fell to the ground and died from a broken neck or concussion, as the result of his three story fall. Abruptly ending his long sermon, Paul came down and embraced the dead youth, as Elijah and Elisha had embraced the dead (I Kings 17:21; II Kings 4:34), and by divine power he raised him to life. Without doubt, there was a miraculous resuscitation. When it said that "his life is in him," the implied sense is the same as when Christ said, "The damsel is not dead, but sleepeth." The resurrection of the young man brought comfort to the disciples who took up their fellowship with Paul till the break of day, when he departed to continue his missionary journeyings. Dr. John H. Gerstner, in his studies on the Acts in *The Biblical Expositor*, says somewhat humorously, "While many lesser men than Paul, in less time, have been able to put their Eutychuses to sleep, they have not always so successfully roused them."

29. The Miracle of Paul's Deliverance from Conspiracy

(23:1-24)

What trials and tribulations beset Paul as he tirelessly traveled on, scattering the good seed all along the way, and glorying even in his infirmities! A double bondage was his. He was "bound in the Spirit," meaning, not the higher element of his own nature, but the constraint of God's Spirit, and Paul could obey no other will but God's. Necessity was laid upon him to follow divine direction (I Corinthians 9: 16). Then came physical bondage prophesied by Agabus (21:11), which brings us to the murderous plot in the chapter before us. As the result of the tumult in the Temple, Paul was beaten then bound with chains (21:33), and carried into the castle, from the stairs of which he rehearsed the account of his miraculous conversion.

The impatient audience demanded the death of Paul. The people said that he was not fit to live. Their craving for blood demanded immediate execution without a trial. The chief captain of the castle brought Paul into the castle, scourged him, then bound him with thongs. The apostle, however, claimed his rights as a Roman citizen and was liberated and brought before the Jewish Council. In the council, an uproar took place resulting in Paul's further imprisonment in which he received a visit from the Lord for whose cause he was suffering.

What miraculous preservation was granted Paul! He wanted to go to Rome but wondered whether he would ever get away from Jerusalem alive (Romans 15:30-32). But the Lord's eye was upon His great servant who, like his Lord, had set his face as a flint to go forward. Paul, although he knew little of the *via dolorosa* stretched before him, was reminded of it at each step—Miletus (20:15), Tyre (21:4), Caesarea (21:11, 12). Now in the castle dungeon, Jesus comes to assure His courageous servant that he will see Rome.

Paul had no fear of suffering or death. He was troubled lest his great task should be cut short. Would he fall a victim to the Jews and thus be frustrated in his long-cherished desire to preach the Gospel in Rome, the renowned capital of the emperor (Romans 1:13; 15:23)? After an exhausting day before the council, back in his cell he found comfort in prayer, which was answered by a "vision and apocalypse of the Lord," who did not send an angel to console and strengthen His servant but appeared Himself to cheer the apostle's troubled heart.

The message, "Be of good cheer," coming from the lips of the Lord, must have thrilled the soul of Paul. Further delay, suffering, and trial would be his, but the goal was certain, for the divine Consoler and Protector woud see to it that Paul reached Rome. "To him, tossed on these waves and billows of the soul, as once before to the twelve tossing on the troubled waters of the Sea of Galilee (Matthew 14:27), there came the same words, full of comfort and hope."

The conspiracy to take Paul from the castle and lynch him was divinely overruled through the intervention of the apostle's nephew, and another effort failed to prevent his journey to Rome. Reaching Caesarea, Paul testified with great power before Felix, Tertullus, and Festus. Appealing, as a Roman citizen, to appear before Agrippa, Paul found himself before this king to whom he told the story of his supernatural transformation. Agrippa could find nothing about Paul's case worthy of bonds or death and would have set him free had he not appealed to Caesar.

30. The Miracles at Melita
(28:1-10)

The background of Paul's remarkable experience at Melita is, of course, his perilous sea voyage during which he and his fellow travelers were miraculously preserved. Altogether Paul sailed in three ships—on one from Caesarea to Myra; on another from Myra to Melita; on the third from Melita to Puteoli. On the second voyage taken at a very risky time, there were 276 on board, and when the ship encountered stormy weather, Paul proved himself to be a master of navigation and a leader of men. The story of his shipwreck makes classic reading, and Paul's sound sense and faith in God in adversity inspire the soul.

The apostle found the sea to be as tumultuous as the hostile Jews he had encountered all the way along, but by a supernatural revelation he knew that the ship would be wrecked but all passengers would be saved. As the hurricane lashed the sea into fury, causing the ship to be tossed about as a cork, Paul, the only calm man on board, exhorted the terror-stricken around him to be of good cheer. As the Master had come to him in an hour of need and said, "Be of good cheer," so now, in his Master's name and by His power, he tells the rest not to be afraid. What a scene that must have been! One of the prisoners, so calm and confident amid misery and dejection, infusing courage into the panic-stricken all around him. The source of courage, strength, and presence of mind Paul manifested was supernatural, as the others detected.

Paul, as the captain in such a perilous situation, gave the orders, even to some of the soldiers who tried to escape. During the hearty meal after long fasting, with Paul making the feast a sacramental one, soldiers and prisoners, 276 souls, bade farewell to all despair and were all of good cheer. The undaunted spirit of their leader communicated itself "as by a kind of electric sympathy" to his fellow travelers.

The apostle's miraculous handling of the ship until it ran aground stood him in good stead. When the ship grounded and broke to pieces, the soldiers, fearing the prisoners would escape, wanted to kill them all. The centurion, however, who admired Paul for his fine courage and his conduct of ship and passengers during the storm and was eager to save him, spared the prisoners, all of whom escaped safely to land.

The island they escaped to was Melita, the modern Malta, where the people, although barbarous at that time, showed the shipwrecked company "no little kindness," meaning, unusual hospitality. A fire was kindled because of the rain and the cold, Paul himself helping to gather sticks to feed the fire. A viper, however, was concealed in the shrubs in Paul's hand, and as it felt the heat, it seized hold of his hand, gripping it with its teeth. Paul betrayed no fear. He held up his hand for a moment with great composure and then shook off the venomous creature into the fire. The stranded passengers, amazed at Paul during the shipwreck, are now more amazed over the further manifestation of supernatural protection.

At first, the populace of Melita, looking for Paul's hand to swell and then for him to drop down dead, felt he was a murderer and that this was divine vengeance upon him for his crime. But when they saw no harm came to him, they changed their minds and called him a "god." Such a miracle was not only a further authentication of Paul's apostleship, it was the means of recommending the Gospel to those who needed it. The lesson for our hearts is that although we are not to expect visible and miraculous interpositions on our behalf in time of need, yet as those redeemed by the blood of Christ, we have the assurance that He will take care of us. Paul's experiences can be summed up in the lines—

> With joy exultant, Lord, we see
>   Events attest Thy Word;
> The viper fails; the devils flee;
> The sick are healed; the bond are free;
>   The dead to life restored.

31. The Miracle of Publius' Father

(28:7-10)

The chief of the island, Publius, was kind to Paul and Luke and gave them lodging for three days. During this brief period, the father of Publius took sick of a fever and of a bloody flux. *Fever* is actually "fevers," a peculiar word used by Luke the physician to denote successive and varying attacks of fever. By "a bloody flux," a phrase used only here in the New Testament, we are to understand a condition comparable to our word *dysentery*. All Luke's terms of diagnosis are medically exact and can be vouched for from medical literature. Evidently the stricken father lived with his son. Paul entered into the room, prayed over the man, laid hands on him, and healed him. As the result of this miracle, the apostles were kindly treated by the inhabitants. The honors they received were those provisions, clothing, and the like, so necessary for the sea voyage ahead. The word Luke uses for "honors" is *honorarium*, or fee, paid to the physician, and its use here is accordingly characteristic of Luke's profession as a doctor.

The kind and generous friends of Melita saw Paul off, and when he arrived in Puteoli, some 150 miles from Rome, friends met him there, and still others came out to greet him all along the way (28:11-16). "On seeing them, Paul thanked God and took courage." Paul's foes had driven him to Rome, but the love and affection of friends made the journey a blessed one. The long and tedious voyage over, many of the saints met Paul outside of Rome, and soon he was in the capital to begin his wonderful ministry. Four sentences cover Paul's movements and ministry:

"I must also see Rome" (19:21)
"So must thou bear witness also at Rome" (23:11)
"Unto Caesar shalt thou go" (25:12)
"So we came to Rome" (28:14).

As the result of Paul's witness in Rome, a great and glorious day dawned for the Gentile world. Dwelling in his own hired house, none forbad him as he preached the message of redeeming love and grace. "The overruling Lord made a prisoner in the imperial city for two years an apostle of the King and City yet to be manifested." Our absorbing study has revealed how our miracle-working Lord delegated supernatural power to the prophets and the apostles (Mark 6:7-13; 9:36-40; Luke 10:17, etc). But in referring to His own miracles, Jesus said, "Greater works than these shall ye do, because I go to My Father" (John 14:12). Greater works than *miracles!* What could be more supernatural than a miracle? The spiritual conquests of the Church are these "greater works.' The majority of the miracles we have considered were local, temporary, and temporal: "greater works" are spiritual miracles, are universal and eternal. The physically dead who were raised, died again. The spiritually dead, quickened by the Spirit, live forever-more.

There are diseases, worse and deeper than bodily diseases—stings of conscience, dead-ness of heart, blindness to divine truth, paralysis of energy to serve God, hideous inner leprosy. Do those of us who are the Lord's not need supernatural power if we are to lay hands on the sin-sick and bring recovery to them? Through us His restor-ing efficacy can still flow to the needy. He waits and longs to do His *greater works* through our lives, and *signs* are bound to follow faith in His power to bless.

"In His name, I should *cast out devils,*" says Alexander Smellie, "the demons of sin, the selfishness of pride, of worldliness—from my own heart and from the hearts of others. Jesus in me ought to bruise Satan under His feet today.

"In His name, I should *speak with new tongues*—voices of testimony, whispers of comfort, messages of instruction, accents of warming, assurances of hope. Jesus in me ought to publish His good tidings still.

"In His name, I should *take up serpents, and, if I drink any deadly thing, it ought not to hurt me.* For Christ's servant is un-dying until his work is done. He moves through fear and pain, and receives no harm thereby.

"In His name, I should *lay hands on the sick, and they should recover.* Those quiet, cooling, rest-giving healing hands—how I covet them as mine! But, instead, my touch is feverish and I only inflame and intensify the malady I seek to cure."

While God is still the same wonder-working God in His own universe, this is the age of spiritual miracles and all things are possible to him that believeth. May grace be ours to adopt William Carey's in-spiring motto:

Expect great things from God.
Attempt great things for God.

III.

THE MIRACLES IN THE EPISTLES

Altogether there are 21 epistles which are usually divided into two sections. There are the *Pauline,* from Romans through He-brews, 14 books in all. While there is doubt about Paul having written Hebrews, we have no hesitation in giving it to him, be-cause so much of its thought and language is Pauline. Then there are the *general epistles,* from James through Jude, 7 books from different writers—James, Peter, John, and Jude.

All of these epistles or letters, which they really are, were written by Christians for Christians, and contain Christian truth in written form. The majority of the letters were intended for the churches. One or two of them were addressed to individuals. The churches founded by the apostles "bristled with problems induced by the high ethical demands of the new faith," and these letters were necessary to build up the faith of converts and to guide young churches in matters of policy and doctrine.

In the gospels, we have the "facts" of Christ. They give us the historical accounts of His words and works. These four books reveal God the Son, just as the Old Testa-ment reveals God the Father.

In the epistles, the same Figure domi-nating the gospels is central, but not as the seen One on earth. In the gospels, Christ Himself is the principal Speaker; in the epistles, He is the principal One spoken of. These books are dominated by God the Holy Spirit, who takes of the things of Christ as Lord and Head of the Church and reveals them to the saints. The gospels set forth the "facts" of Christ; the Acts, His "fruits;" and the epistles, His "fulness." Paul's favorite key phrase, "in Christ," speaks of all we have in and through Him.

The Church, which is prophesied in the gospels (Matthew 16:18; 18:17) and in-stituted in the Acts, is established in the epistles, for in the latter we are shown how the Holy Spirit molds together Jews and Gentiles into one new man in Christ and creates the Church as His Body, and as its Head fills it and directs its life and activities by the Spirit. The epistles, then, are the books of the Trinity in unity, while the Revelation is the book of the unity in the Trinity—the name *Jehovah* reappearing in its elemental grandeur (1:4).

The epistles, as a whole, seem to have a two-fold purpose:

(1) To enunciate and lay bare the great cardinal principles of divine action which underlie the Gospel facts.

(2) To apply these principles of God's dealings with us experimentally to man's conscience and need.

With such a brief introduction in mind, we now approach the study concerning us, namely, the revelation of the supernatural in the epistles, which can be brought under the four heads—the miracles of creation, the miracles of history, the miracles of providence, the miracles of grace.

1. The Miracles of Creation

The display of God's miraculous power in His created works runs like a golden strand through the section of the New Testament we are presently considering.

God's visible creation bears the stamp of omnipotence and deity.

His invisible attributes are His eternal power and Godhead (Romans 1:19, 20).

All things proceed from God, were made by Him, exist for His glory and the fulfilment of His purposes (Romans 11: 36; Colossians 1:16, 17; James 5:7).

The creation of man and woman, and their interdependence and divine ownership (I Corinthians 11:8-12).

The creation of the body and its functions (I Corinthians 12:14-26).

The creation of fishes and birds, sun and moon and stars (I Corinthians 15:39, 40).

The creation of an eternal body (II Corinthians 5:1-4; Philippians 3:21).

The subtility of Satan in serpent form (II Corinthians 11:3; I Timothy 2:13, 14).

The transformation of Satan into an angel of light (II Corinthians 11:14).

The great immortal Potentate, King and Lord of All (I Timothy 6:15, 16).

The creative activity of God the Son (Hebrews 1:3; 1:10-12; 2:7, 8, 10; Colossians 1:16, 17).

The finished creation of God (Hebrews 4:3, 4; 11:3).

The new and eternal creation (II Peter 3:12, 13).

It will be seen that no attempt is being made to expound the various aspects of the supernatural touched upon in the epistles. Already, the majority have been fully dealt with in their original setting. For the guidance of the reader, we are attempting a simple classification of the miraculous as referred to by the apostolic writers.

2. The Miracles in History

As Jews, the New Testament writers were conversant with Old Testament history. Our Lord, however, had to rebuke some of His Jewish disciples for being slow of heart to believe all the prophets had written (Luke 24:25). Historical references abound in the epistles, as the following list proves:

The incarnation, miraculous ministry, and resurrection of Christ, the Son of God (Romans 1:4; 4:24, 25; 6:4, 9; 8:11; 14:9; I Corinthians 15; I Peter 1:21; II Corinthians 4:14; 13:4; Ephesians 1:20; Philippians 2:6-11; 3:10).

The miracle of Abraham and Sarah (Romans 4:18-21; 9:9; Hebrews 11:11).

The miracle of the believer's resurrection (Romans 8:23; I Corinthians 6:11; 15: 13; I Thessalonians 4:13-18; Titus 2: 13).

The miracles in Pharaoh's time (Romans 9:17).

The miracles of the Apostle Paul (Romans 15:18, 19; I Corinthians 2:4; II Corinthians 12:9; Galatians 3:5; Hebrews 2:4).

The supernatural revelation of the Spirit (I Corinthians 2:10, 11; Galatians 1: 12; 2:2).

The miracle of the Red Sea (I Corinthians 10:2; Hebrews 11:29).

The miracle provision of the wilderness (I Corinthians 10:3, 4; Hebrews 3:9).

The miracle destruction by serpents (I Corinthians 10:5-11).

The miracle gifts of the Spirit (I Corinthians 12:1-31; 13:8; 14:22; Ephesians 4:8).

The miracle of the human body (I Corinthians 12:14-26).

The miracle of Moses' shining face (II Corinthians 3:13, 18. See Jude 9).

The miracles of Paul's preservation and revelations (II Corinthians 11:23-26; 12:1-6, 9; II Timothy 4:17).

The supernatural power of evil forces (Ephesians 2:2; II Thessalonians 2: 8-10; I Timothy 4:1; II Timothy 3:8).

The supernatural judgment of the lost (II Thessalonians 1:7-11).

The miracle of Christ's manifestation and Ascension (I Timothy 3:16; Hebrews 1:3; 9:24; II Peter 1:18, 19).

The miracle of Enoch's translation (Hebrews 11:5; Jude 14).

The miracles of the flood (Hebrews 11: 7; I Peter 3:20; II Peter 2:5; 3:6, 7); of Isaac (Hebrews 11:15, 19); of Moses (11:23-27); of Jericho (11:30); of prophets, kings, martyrs (11:32-40); of the dumb ass (II Peter 2:16; Jude 11).

The miracles at Mount Sinai (Hebrews 12:18, 21).

The miracles of Elijah (James 5:17, 18).

The miracle of Sodom and Gomorrah (II Peter 2:7-9; Jude 7).

The miracle of earth's dissolution (II Peter 3:10-13).

3. The Miracles of Providence

Divine Providence is manifested in a two-fold direction. First of all, in God's power to order or intervene in the affairs of nations and men for His own glory and man's good. Having omniscience with regard to the future, He can rule and over-rule. He preserves and governs all things and has absolute control over what man calls "the vast empire of chance, as borne out in the experiences of Joseph and Rebekah (Genesis 24:7, 12-15; 37:25). God's government over the minds, wills, passions, counsels, and actions of bad men, as well as over all the evil machinations of the Devil and his agents, is amply proved in the Bible (Genesis 1:20; Acts 4:28; Romans 8:32, etc.).

Another aspect of divine providence is the benevolent care, goodness, and guidance of God. Knowing the end from the beginning, God is able to foresee what needs will be ours, and in His love, He provides accordingly. We cannot read the future, but He can, and as we repose trust and confidence in Him, He daily loads us with His benefits. How the early saints loved to dwell upon their all-provident God!

He is able to arrange prosperous journeys (Romans 1:10, 11; 15:32; I Corinthians 4:19; Philemon 22; James 4:13-15; III John 2).

His goodness is spiritual, and temporal mercies should lead us to repentance (Romans 2:4; 11:22).

He has the power to cause *all* things to work together for our good (Romans 8:28).

He is ever for us, no matter who may be against us (Romans 8:31, 38, 39; I John 5:15).

He is supreme over all rulers and powers (Romans 13:1-3).

He should be glorified in the use of what He provides (I Corinthians 10:31; Hebrews 13:5, 6).

He is able to comfort our hearts (II Corinthians 1:3-5; 7:6, 7; I Peter 5:7).

He can meet our every need, and giving never impoverishes Him (II Corinthians 9:7-9; 12:9; Ephesians 3:20; Philippians 4:6, 11, 19; I Thessalonians 5:12; I Timothy 4:4; 6:8).

He is able to succour and relieve the tested (Hebrews 2:18; 4:16; 12:6; 13:8).

4. The Miracles of Grace

The matchless, marvelous grace of God as personified in His Son and manifested through all His ways, words, and works, permeates the epistles, particularly those Paul wrote. His so-called "prison epistles" (Galatians, Ephesians, Philippians, and Colossians) are the heart of the New Testament.

Grace represents unmerited favor and is made to refer to different aspects of such a general theme. It is applied to God's mercy in the pardon of sin, bestowed without any merit in us—"Being justified freely by His grace" (Romans 3:24). It is made to refer to the Gospel as a whole—"The grace of God that bringeth salvation, hath appeared unto all men" (Titus 2:11). It is associated with holiness, as an effect of God's grace, since we are His workmanship, created in Christ Jesus unto good works: "Grow in grace" (II Peter 3:18). Not grow *into* grace, but once in it, grow *in* it. To quote all the passages relating to the supernaturalness of divine grace would be to set forth the best part of the 21 epistles. How one is embarrassed by spiritual riches when handling such a glorious doctrine as grace! Here are a few aspects to muse upon:

This Gospel is the power of God unto salvation (Romans 1:16; 5:1, 2).

Grace is provided for all sinners whether Jew or Gentile (Romans 3:23-25, 29; Titus 2:11).

Recipients of this mighty grace are blessed (Romans 4:7; 5:20, 21; 8:17).

Such a provision covers our future, as well as our past and present (Romans 8:23; I Corinthians 6:11; II Corinthians 4:16, 17; I Peter 1:3; I John 3:2).

The source of this amazing grace is Christ (II Corinthians 8:9; Galatians 2:20; Ephesians 1:4).

Through grace we are more than conquerors (Ephesians 6:10-18; Colossians 1:11, 13); and are made recipients of high privileges (I Peter 2:9, 10).

God grace becomes ours as we repent and believe (I John 1:9).

IV.

THE MIRACLES IN THE APOCALYPSE

This remarkable climactic book of the Bible is permeated with the supernatural. No other New Testament book can equal the dignity and sublimity of composition as the book of Revelation. Here, some of the secret things belonging to God are revealed for our enlightenment and edification. For those who would trifle with the prophetic portion dominating the book, the weighty words of Sir Isaac Newton should be solemnly considered:

God gave this (Revelation) and the prophecies of the Old Testament, not to gratify men's curiosity, by enabling them to foreknow things, but that, after they were fulfilled, they might be interpreted by the event and His own providence, not the interpreter's by then manifested thereby to the world.

Already we have discoursed upon the miracle of prophecy, and the prophecies of the Apocalypse are essential for the full consummation of the great scheme of the Gospel, when God shall finally prevail over all the corruptions of the world, and His prophetic plan shall be fully realized. In this mysterious yet marvelous book before us, the omniscient God, almost 2,000 years ago, gave the Church His blueprint of the future. What folly and darkness are ours if we fail to understand this divine panorama of coming events! Tempted as we are to give an exposition of the Revelation as a whole, all that concerns us in our general study of the supernatural in Scripture is the miraculous as found in this closing book of Holy Writ.

1. The Miracles of the Book Itself

(1:1-3)

Looked at from any point of view, the book of Revelation is a supernatural product—supernatural not only in its contents, as we are to find, but also in its conception, communication, and composition. While to the average reader the book appears to be a great mystery, consisting of strange fantastic symbols and predictions, yet to those who seek the aid of the Spirit who inspired John to write it, the book unfolds itself as one of the most remarkable ever written.

In our approach to Revelation there are one or two facts which, if borne in mind, will greatly help us in the understanding of it. First of all, it is the only wholly prophetic book in the New Testament, and it contains the only divine, full, and accurate account of future events. Then, it is not a sealed book. Although symbolic, as Scripture is compared with Scriptures, the key to all the symbols becomes apparent. Further, simple faith in all its statements is necessary in the preparation of mind for the study of the book. This is the only book in the Bible to which a special blessing is given to its readers and hearers (1:3). As it is addressed to all the Lord's servants, their lives are enriched as its inner truths are discovered. The book is also peculiarly important because it closes God's sacred volume. In this respect it must be compared with Genesis, the Book of Beginnings. The Bible opens in a garden and ends in one.

The communication of the contents of the book was supernatural. It is spoken of as the "Revelation," not "Revelations," as it is sometimes called. There are not *several* revelations in the book, only one, namely, that of Jesus Christ, who is revealed in various ways. The word "Revelation" is from the Greek "apocalupisis," from which we have "Apocalypse," meaning to "uncover," or "unveil." The idea behind the term is that of the taking away of a veil, as when a covered statue is unveiled to view. Here, then, is the unveiling of the majestic person of Christ and the uncovering of those events preceding and accompanying His return to the earth.

Such a revelation was conceived by God, given by Him to His beloved Son, then given by the Son to "His angel." Who this selected angel is we are not told. Basing this contention on 22:8, 9, some writers suggest that he was likely one of the Old Testament prophets raised for the purpose. Then this "angel" gave the revelation to John, who was simply the writer of it, since God Himself was the Author of it, and John gave it to the Lord's servants, or to His Church. Such a mode of communication was not as direct as many others throughout the Bible (II Kings 5:26; 6:32; 8:10, etc.). This revelation which John received at Patmos is embodied in the visions he beheld, and the single term gives unity to the many and diversified communications, whether in word or vision, contained in the book.

Interpretations of the aim of the book differ. There are those known as the *preterist school,* who assert that all within it was fulfilled in the struggles of the Jews and the early Christians during the terrible conquests of Greece and Rome, particularly the latter. Then there is the *historical school,* which claims that the prophecies of the book are being progressively fulfilled and that the great part of these prophecies have been fulfilled. The *spiritual school* neglect the prophetic aspect and hold that Revelation depicts in symbolic form the spiritual conflict between Christ and Satan, between light and darkness. The *futural school,* however, believe that the most logical interpretation of the book is that the bulk of it will be fulfilled after the Rapture of the Church. Those of this school hold that the only satisfying interpretation of the book lies in the three-fold natural division revealed to John by Jesus (1:19).

(1) "Write the things which thou *hast* seen"—*past.* This aspect refers to the vision John had before he began to write of Christ as the central Object in the midst of the seven candlesticks (1:10-18, 20).

(2) "Write the things . . . which *are*"—*present.*

These "things" are the seven letters constituting chapters 2 and 3; where the professing Church is traced through contemporary and successive stages of the history from Pentecost to the Rapture.

(3) "Write the things . . . which shall be *hereafter*"—*future.*

This division covers chapters 4 through 22:14, and is essentially the prophetic portion of the book. These three sections correspond to Him who *was—is—*and *is to come* (1:8).

Who but God could have conceived such a supernatural book made up as it is of a group of seven sevens, which are easily traceable!

(1) The seven churches (1:9-20; 2:3).
(2) The seven seals (4 - 8:2).
(3) The seven trumpets (8:2 - 11:19).
(4) The seven mystical Personages (12 - 14).
(5) The seven last plagues (15 - 16).
(6) The seven great events after Babylon (19:11 - 20:15).
(7) The seven new things (21:1 - 22:5).

Truly the *words* and *works* of Revelation are miraculous! The omniscient God Himself is the only One who could have given us such a book remarkable for its unity and consistency of prophetic outline associated with the Church, Israel, the nations, the world, eternity. "The method is apocalyptic; the movements of the great drama unfold on a scale of unrivaled grandeur. The earth staggers under the shock of battle and the strokes of judgment. The abyss with its unending horrors, and heaven with its felicities, are opened to view." Genesis gives us *Paradise Lost,* Revelation, *Paradise Regained.*

What book is that, which brings before our view
The fair creation ere he defiled it with his
Trail, that speaks of Paradise that
Had no sorrow till he entered in,
Of human bliss enjoyed so briefly there?

What book is that, which shows all
Evil overcome, Satan, defeated, bound,
Destroyed with all his works, our
Paradise regained, and bliss eternal gloriously received?

2. The Miracles Wrought by Heavenly Forces

All heaven is united in the final overthrow of hellish forces. Here God the Father, God the Son, God the Spirit, and the unfallen angelic host are bound together in the conquest of evil and powers and in the inauguration of a new and perfect order. With such a heavenly force, great and glorious events are bound to happen. While the person and prerogatives of Jesus Christ dominate the book, God, to whom power belongeth, is revealed, not only as the Source of such a revelation (1:1), but also one of its Subjects. His miracle-working power is never lost sight of. His creation and judicial work and almightiness are dealt with (2:3; 3:12, 14; 4:8; 5:10; 7:2, 10, 11, 15, 17; 9:4; 11:4). He unfolds His mystery to His servants (10:7); is the Author of life (11:11); the righteous Judge (14:10, 19); the Remover of earth's sorrows (21:4).

That the Son is in full harmony with the Father is evident from all that is said of His divine titles and judicial deeds. It would take a volume in itself to set forth and expound the significance of all the designations used of Christ from the first as "the faithful and true witness" (1:5), right on until the last, "the root and the offspring of David, and the bright and morning star" (22:16). The same Lord who was the medium of supernatural works in the days of His flesh, is here seen traveling in the greatness of His strength. When we come to examine the miracles of the book, we shall see that He is supreme in every realm.

That the Persons of the Trinity are in unity throughout the book is seen in the way the Holy Spirit shared in every aspect of its recorded events. It was while under the Spirit's control that John received this marvelous Revelation (1:10; 4:2). For the time being, the apostle lost the consciousness of his surroundings and found himself in another state of being. John was held by, and was absolutely subservient to, the Spirit, and thus he became the recipient of all we have in his book. Then the supernaturalness of the Spirit is to be found in His description as "the seven Spirits of God" (1:4; 5:6). There are not seven "Holy Spirits," only One, but He has a sevenfold manifestation and operation (Isaiah 11:1-3). As One having "seven horns," He shares the omnipotence of God, and of Christ. "Horn" is the symbol of power—"Seven," the number suggesting perfection. His, then, is the perfection of power. The last glimpse of the Spirit in the book is where He is found joining with the Church in the advent prayer, "Come Thou" (22:17).

Allied with the Trinity is the angelic host above. Angels, as the executors of divine judgment, dominate the book. In some cases "angel" represents a "human" messenger, rather than a "heavenly" one (2:1, etc.). If the reader follows all references to "angels," he will find that they are before us as the *media* of revelation, authority, and judgment; that their host is unnumbered; must not be worshiped; will witness the torment of the wicked (see author's volume *All About Angels in the Bible*.)

3. The Miracles Wrought by Hellish Forces

(13:13, 14; 19:20)

Over against the Trinity of heaven—Father, Son, and Spirit—we have the Trinity of hell—the Dragon, the Beast and the False Prophet. Trench points out that side by side with divine miracles "runs another line of wonders, the counter-workings of Satan, who is the imitator of the Most High; who has still his caricatures of the Holiest." While the Bible attributes Satan with supernatural works, true miracles are rigidly defined and shut in by the power of God. He alone can perform miracles beside the whole order of nature. "God alone doeth great wonders" (Psalm 136:4). "What God is there in heaven or in earth that can do according to Thy works, and according to Thy might?" (Deuteronomy 3:24). Satan's instruments, like Pharaoh's sorcerers and Elymas, may do lesser wonders, but God, and God only, can perform mighty wonders.

God has reserved to Himself the power of miracles as a prerogative. Satan cannot hasten nature or hinder nature, antedate nature or post-date nature, bring things to pass sooner or retard them, as God can. "False miracles are distinguished from true by their efficacy, their usefulness, the manner of their working, their end, their worker, and the occasion whereon they were wrought." In dealing with Old Testament miracles, we referred to Satan's power in the realm of the supernatural. His wonders however, are "lying" ones (II Thessalonians 2:9), not because in themselves they are mere illusion and jugglery, but because they are wrought to sustain his kingdom of lies.

Our Lord predicted the spectacular displays of unusual power by satanic forces in the end time period of world history (Matthew 24:21). About our Lord's time, there were many false christs professing and promising the miraculous. The Egyptian whom the Roman tribune supposed that he saw in Paul (Acts 21:38) and of whom Josephus gives us a fuller account, led a tumultuous crowd to the Mount of Olives, promising to show them from hence how, as a second and greater Joshua, he would cause the walls, not of Jericho, but of Jerusalem, to fall to the ground at his bidding.

During the Great Tribulation, the Antichrist, inspired by Satan, will attempt the miraculous, as Paul predicted (II Thessalonians 2:9). One of the hardest trials of the elect will be that of distinguishing between heavenly and hellish works of power. In the realm of the supernatural, it would seem as if the Antichrist is to have all the stage to himself. Multitudes are to be deceived by the number of mighty signs and miracles performed by the Beast (13:4-8). The display of these supposedly supernatural powers will win for him great adoration and worship.

As the Holy Spirit uses signs and wonders in testifying of Christ, even so the evil spirit in the second beast uses all powers and signs and lying wonder in testifying of the Antichrist. As the Spirit of truth formed the Church, the image of the First-born, the witness of Christ on earth; even so, the False Prophet makes an image of the Beast and causes it to testify on his behalf. As the mission of the Spirit through His servants is to make disciples of all nations, even so the work of the False Prophet is to make the earth worship the Beast and receive his name. The Lord's followers are sealed by the Spirit until the day of redemption; even so, the followers of the Beast are sealed by the False Prophet until the day of perdition. No wonder this dread period represents the *mystery of iniquity!*

The double miracle to be performed consists of making fire come down from heaven and causing the image to speak. The descent of fire will be the counterpart of Elijah's miracle. That Satan, who will energize the False Prophet, can do this is proved by the divine permission he received to bring down fire from heaven and burn up all Job's possessions (1:16). In this evil miracle-worker's power to make the image speak, we have another attempt to ape God, the Source of life. Science is able to make a dead robot speak. But these false miracle-workers are to endure terrible retribution for the working of their miracles (19:20; 20:9, 10; 21:8).

Thus the opposing moral forces are set, and there is no doubt as to the final outcome of the conflict between light and darkness depicted in vivid colors throughout the book. Much of the conflict centers in the Person of Christ as the Lamb slain. Whatever vicissitudes mark its progress, the issue is certain. The rivalry of the powers of darkness is illustrated by a series of contrasts. It is the Bride *versus* the harlot; the Lamb slain and alive again *versus* the Beast whose head receives a deadly wound but lives again; the worship of Jehovah *versus* the worship of Antichrist; but victory is the Lord's as all persons and things are brought into subjection to Himself. At long last, Satan is paid back in his own coin. He cast some into prison (2:10), but is ultimately bound in the abyss (20:3, 7). The Saviour's sepulcher was sealed (Matthew 27:66); now an angel seals Satan's place of imprisonment. How glorious and triumphant is the conclusion of this miraculous book! "I am Alpha and Omega, the beginning and the end, the first and the last." *Hallelujah!*

4. The Miracles Associated with Natural Forces

In examining the miracles to be wrought after the Rapture of the Church, we discover the majority of them to be replicas of Old Testament miracles. The Great Tribulation will experience a repetition of the supernatural plagues of ancient days. It is to be hoped that the following classification will prove helpful for those who desire to pursue this fascinating aspect of such a theme more fully.

Resurrection (1:18; 11:8-11; 20:5, 6)

While hardly within the province of natural forces, resurrection from the dead is yet a triumph over many such forces resulting in death. Christ who is "the Life" yet became dead, but is now alive forevermore. There are two miracles here: "The living One became dead, and the dead One is alive forevermore."

The supernatural surrounds the presence of the two witnesses whom some writers suppose will be Moses and Elijah because of the similarity of their acts to those of the witnesses. The wonder here is that whoever they are, they are brought to earth and given human bodies in which they serve and suffer. These witnesses are murdered by the Beast near the spot where their Lord was crucified, and after three and a half days, their bodies are raised. Life from God re-enters those dead bodies and the witnesses rise in power and stand upon their feet. Then, with eternal life which death cannot touch, they are taken up to heaven.

Further, there is the resurrection of the Beast who received a deadly wound and whose return to life wins him the wonder and worship of the world (13:1-4). How dreadful will be this human figure endowed with satanic energy, openly defying God and invested with the royal power and world-wide authority of Satan! The world has had many cruel dictators, but the resurrected Beast will be unparalleled in the history of the race.

Then there is the miracle of the resurrection of the martyred saints. Walter Scott suggests that during the Great Tribulation no saint will die a natural death. He either lives through the period or is martyred. Probably these resurrected martyrs are those who are slain under the fifth seal (6:9-11).

Ascension (4:1; 11:12)

John's experience of being caught up to heaven is a prophecy of the Church supernaturally translated to be with the Lord. The "door opened in Heaven" and enabled John to pass in. "Heaven opened" is for saints to pass out on divine missions (19: 11).

The triumphant ascension of the two witnesses is graphically described by John. Their enemies witnessed such a miraculous translation from the scene of service and suffering. Up the witnesses went from earth's scorn, reproach, and murder. All was accomplished in a moment, as it will be when the true Church is caught up (I Corinthians 15:52).

Lightnings and thunderings (4:5; 6:1; 8:5; 10:3-5; 11:9; 14:2; 16:18)

What convulsions of nature the earth is to experience when God sends forth "the artillery of heaven" to accomplish His purposes! Lightnings and thunderings, precursors of coming judgment, issue out of the throne, the seat of royal authority. God is about to assert Himself in power. From these signs of judicial dealings (Psalm 29: 3-5), there will be no escape. The most approved class of preservatives against lightning were thought to be the eagle—Jupiter's choice; the sea-calf—the choice of Augustus Caesar; the laurel—Tiberius' favorite. But man has no preservative when God strikes in judgment.

In the first seal, as the living creature speaks with "the voice of thunder," he introduces the first prophetic event. Prophecy opens with such a loud summons that none can fail to hear. Later (8:5), an angel's act is accompanied by symbolic signs of God's almightiness. Four terms are used as harbingers of coming successive outbursts of divine wrath in the earth—*voices, thunder, lightnings, earthquake.* "These terms compose a *formula of catastrophe;* and the fourfold character here denotes the universality of the catastrophe in respect of the thing affected."

The seven thunders, indicate the perfection of God's intervention in judgment, a judgment from which none can escape. Bodies scathed and persons struck dead during a thunderstorm were said to be incorruptible and anyone so distinguished was held by the ancients in great honor. How different it will be with those who suffer death when God releases the destructive forces of nature! The Revelation is saturated with Old Testament quotations, and "thunder" is God's voice in judgment, the expression of His authority and power therein (I Samuel 7:10; Psalm 18:13; Job 26:14).

With "the seventh bowl" of wrath, the symbols of almighty power in judgment are accompanied by "voices," intimating that the execution of judgment will be intelligently directed and that these signs and tokens of God's wrath will strike terror to the hearts of men.

Earthquakes (11:13; 16:18)

God, having created the earth, controls it, and when He looks upon it, it trembles and shakes (Psalm 104:32). Under the sixth seal in which we have the complete subversion of all governmental and civil authority, "a great earthquake" describes a violent description of the organized state of things. Here the earthquake, along with other signs, is a public intimation of coming wrath. It is called *great*, as its effects upon men amply testify. What fear and terror are to be theirs! (6:17).

In God's public vindication of the slain witnesses there is mention of an earthquake slaying 7,000 men (11:13). The earthquake appears again in God's remembrance of Israel (11:19). In the seventh bowl of wrath, we have an earthquake of a most unusual kind spoken of as "a great earthquake . . . such an earthquake so great." The world has experienced very disastrous earthquakes, but in magnitude and dire results, this one John describes is to surpass all previous ones. While there will be physical earthquakes in many places (Mark 13:8), the "great earthquake" will result in a vast, unparalleled upheaval. Here we have symbolized a most violent disruption and collapse of all earthly government and authority. One of the distastrous effects of this mighty earthquake will be the overthrow of Satan's gigantic confederation.

Hail (8:7, 9; 16:21)

Hail forms another part of God's artillery (Job 38:22). The seventh plague upon Egypt was marked by terrific hail, accompanied by fire running along the ground (Exodus 9:24). With hail, God killed the five allied kings of Palestine, the foes of His people (Joshua 10:11). To the "hail and fire" under the first trumpet, a third element is added, "mingled with blood" (see Joel 2:30). The blood is not a separate, devastating agency but is allied with the first two. This singular combination of a trinity of forces is entirely outside the domain of nature. Here we have a judgment of a peculiar and superhuman character, a judgment ruinous and widespread. The third part of the sea will become as blood, recalling another Egyptian plague (Exodus 7:20, 21).

Hail signifies in Scripture a sudden, sharp and overwhelming judgment from heaven, with God as the Executor of it (Isaiah 28:17; Revelation 11:19; 16:21). The "great hail" under the seventh bowl of wrath represents a general horror intensified by a hurricane of divine judgment, descending upon the godless with irresistible and crushing force. The hail stones are to be of "a talent weight"—about 125 pounds. These hailstones, the most disastrous ever experienced, will signal the crowning act of divine judgment. Such severe judgment, however, will not result

in crushing hearts, for the moral effect is given in the plainest terms, "Men blaspheme God," just as Pharaoh hardened his heart as the plagues became more intense.

Fire (8:5, 7; 9:18; 11:5; 13:13; 14:10, 11; 15:2; 19:12, 20; 20:9, 10, 14, 15; 21:8; 22:5)

This fearsome force of nature is mentioned more often than any other in the Revelation. Fire, the symbol of divine holiness and divine hatred of sin, is another force God uses to fulfil His will and word (Psalm 148:8). Christ is depicted as having eyes "like unto a flame of fire" (2:18; 19:12), symbolizing His divine omniscience and power to search the hearts of men (2:22). "His feet are pillars of fire" (10:1) indicates stability and firmness, the unbending holiness of His judicial action. No one and nothing can escape His searching glance. Under the first trumpet, "fire" is the expression of God's wrath. "Thorough, unsparing, agonizing judgment is denoted by fire." Under the sixth trumpet, or second woe, the riders of horses are spoken of as having "breastplates of fire." Walter Scott says that "the combination of fire, jacinth, and brimstone has been well termed the *breastplate of hell*." Fire and brimstone are judicially inflicted (Genesis 19:24) and are symbols of everlasting torment (14:9-12) and of unutterable anguish (Revelation 19:20; 20:9, 10-15; 21:8).

Fire out of the mouth of the witnesses testifies to their miraculous power. This sign of a supernatural kind accredits their mission as God's representatives (see Psalm 68:18). "The glass sea, mingled with fire" intimates the fiery persecution under the Beast, a trial far exceeding in its combination of suffering anything hitherto experienced (Mark 13:19). There will be nothing to equal the horrors of the Great Tribulation. How grateful we are that through grace we shall be delivered from experiencing them!

Winds (6:13; 7:1)

Created by God, the winds fulfill His word. We have already seen how He controls and commands them (Genesis 8:1; Exodus 10:13; Matthew 8:24-27). The four angels holding fast the four winds, that no wind might blow upon the earth nor upon any tree until God's bondmen are sealed, reveals how these natural forces can be restrained. *Four*, the number of the earth, marks the completeness and the universality of Divine action. In a footnote, Walter Scott draws attention to the fact that in Scripture, political and other troubles are expressed in the term "winds of the earth" (Job 1:19; Jeremiah 49:36; Daniel 7:2). "Winds of the *heaven*" and "winds of *earth*" are to be distinguished. The former expression points to the providential agencies employed by God to execute His purposes, whereas the latter denotes attention to the guilty sphere of these judgments and calamities, namely, the earth.

The plagues (15:1, 6; 18:8; 21:9, 10; 22:18, 19)

A general word about *plagues* is necessary before we come to the particular plagues cited by John. Seven angels are mentioned as "having seven plagues, the last." The first plagues were those that fell upon the Egyptians; here we have the last providential judgments of God. With the outpouring of the seven vials, the pent-up and concentrated wrath of God is fully expressed. Further strokes of divine vengeance are to be inflicted, but these represent the wrath of the Lamb (Revelation 19; Matthew 25:31-46).

The final warning of the Revelation is a most solemn protest against those handling rashly or deceitfully any part of God's infallible Word, particularly its last book. To those who add to, or take from, the sacred volume there is plague and punishment (Deuteronomy 4:2; 12:32). To tamper with the words of the prophecy of Revelation is to bring oneself under the divine lash. Adding to these words will bring added retribution. Taking from them will result in the forfeit of the tree of life. How fatal it is to trifle with God's supernatural Word (II Timothy 3:7).

> Light accepted bringeth light;
> Light rejected bringeth night;
> Who will give me power to choose
> If the love of light I lose?

Famine (6:6-8)

God, from whom all blessings flow, can provide food or withhold it. As we saw in Old Testament miracles, famine was often a visitation from God for sin (II Kings 8:1; Psalm 105:16; Ruth 1:1; Genesis 41:25-36; 42; Jeremiah 4:28). Under the third seal, we have a description of a sore famine. The two main cereals, wheat and barley, constituting the staff of life, are to be doled out by weight and sold at famine prices—

a marked sign of scarcity (Leviticus 26:26; Ezekiel 4:10-17). In the dreadful days the seer depicts, death will be a happy release from the agonies of hunger.

Locusts (9:3-11)

The armies of locusts obey the command of Him who made them (Exodus 10:13, 19). Myriads of these creatures execute God's vengeance upon the rebellious (Exodus 8:19). The locust army John wrote about is a symbolic representation of judgment of a superhuman kind. The sting of the scorpion, a creature shunning the light, causes dreadful suffering. It constantly shakes its tail to strike, and the torment of the sting is very grievous. The language John uses suggests a defined and limited scourge, a scourge under control and covering five months—the time of natural locust life. This specified time points to a brief and determinate period of woe, not necessarily one of five literal months. The king of this locust army is Satan. That keen observer of nature, King Solomon, wrote that "the locusts have no king" (Proverbs 30:27). Satan, however, is to be the leader of the hosts of evil in the grim contest yet to come. Whatever this plague may be, God's children are assured of preservation (Luke 10:19). Nothing will hurt those who have the seal of God in their foreheads. The marvelous description given of the locusts sent forth to torment men has no reference to the anatomical features of the natural locusts.

Sores (16:2)

Out of the first bowl of wrath, there is to come "an evil and grievous sore," afflicting those who bear the mark of the Beast and who worship his image. This supernatural judgment is comparable to the sixth Egyptian plague, which was the first of those plagues attacking the bodies of the Egyptians, including the magicians (Exodus 9:10, 11). These painful boils were a disgusting and loathsome disease (Deuteronomy 28:27-35). Lazarus, the beggar, was covered with these generally incurable sores. Sufferers under the first bowl are to endure unhealthy humors, discharging in a highly offensive form. Physical, mental, and moral anguish are identified with the "evil and grievous *sore*"—the word literally meaning "a bad ulcer."

Sea as blood (16:3, 4; 18:21)

Under the second bowl and the third bowl of wrath, rivers and fountains are to be turned into blood—a plague reminding us of Exodus 7:17-25. Angels have been set over the winds (7:1) and over the fire (14:18), and here we have the angel of the waters (16:5). The first Egyptian plague resulted in the waters being turned into blood, literally and actually. Here John, in these two bowls or vials, depicts a scene of moral death and complete alienation from God, the Source of life. *Waters* signify peoples (Isaiah 17:12, 13), and the *sea* suggests commotion and unrest among the peoples (Isaiah 57:20; Daniel 7:3). The martyred saints are spoken of as drinking blood, for they are worthy. To them blood, freely and wantonly poured out by foes, is the witness of death.

Darkness (16:10, 11)

Actually, "night's cloak," as Shakespeare describes "darkness," is a negative quantity. Literal darkness is the absence of transmitted light from the luminaries above. By removing light, God caused darkness that could be felt to cover Egypt (Exodus 10:21-23; 20:21); and likewise to cover the shame of His beloved Son as He died upon the cross. Here, under the fifth bowl of wrath, the Beast's kingdom is darkened. As of old, we can expect God's people then on earth to be spared such utter darkness with its horror (Exodus 10:23).

With the ancient plague of darkness, the kingdom boasting itself so full of light became darkened; and the much vaunted empire of the Beast, with all its light and learning, will be plunged into a darkness accompanied with great terror (Isaiah 2: 12-22; Revelation 6:12-17). Alas! even the failure of light will not work repentance, for the subjects of the darkened kingdom are to "gnaw their tongues with pain." Such a phrase, indicating the most intense and excruciating agony, is not found anywhere else in the Bible. Loving darkness and its evil deeds, the Beast and his subjects are to blaspheme the God of heaven and remain unrepentant. Is not this darkness a forerunner of the more terrible blackness of darkness for ever? (Matthew 25:30). How different is the angel "having great power, and the earth was lightened with his glory" (18:1), and the eternal abode of the redeemed in which "there shall be no night" (22:5)! Presently, our consolation is that "darkness and light are both alike to Thee." God has His abode in the thick darkness, as well as in the light (I Kings 8:12; I Timothy 6:16).

Sun, Moon, Stars (6:12-17; 8:10-12; 9:2; 12:4; 16:8; 22:5)

These supernatural creations are conspicuous in the Bible's last book. Because they are the sources of earth's light, it is interesting to trace the part they play, literally and symbolically, in God's prophetic plan. Having created all of the universe, He is able to control any phase of it for the accomplishment of His just and beneficent purposes. "The heavens declare the glory of God" (Psalms 8:3; 19:1; 147:4; Isaiah 40:26; 44:24). In past studies, we have dealt with miraculous events which we can call astronomical miracles which "the great Work-Master of the universe" wrought. Now, in this closing book, we have further evidences of His supreme power in creation.

The state of things described under the sixth seal is fearful in the extreme. "The darkening of the heavenly bodies is an awful calamity in the physical world, and hence the aptness of the figure" used by John. The *sun* symbolizes the supreme governing authority (Genesis 37:9; Revelation 21:1), Walter Scott says, and "black as hair sackcloth" denotes the darkening power of Satan and points to the supreme authority of earth—on which all were dependent—in a condition of utter collapse (Isaiah 50:3; Ezekiel 7:18).

The *moon* in the heavens is a secondary planet because it has no light of its own. It simply reflects what it receives from the sun. As used here, the moon symbolizes derivative authority in the moral realm, and becoming as "blood" indicates the moral death and apostacy of every subordinate authority. "Blood" is a universal figure of death. (Revelation 11:6; 19:2, 13).

The *stars* are reckoned as lesser luminaries, although some of them are larger than the moon. When the stroke of divine judgment falls, lesser authorities, as individual rulers, civil and ecclesiastical, morally fall from their exalted position. As the wintry winds of God's wrath sweep over the scene, then those who are not His, however exalted their position, must suffer punishment (Isaiah 34:4). Under the third and fourth trumpets, the sun, moon, and stars are again used collectively to symbolize the whole governing body from the supreme head down to all lesser authorities—a complete system of government in all its parts. Some writers regard the great fallen star as denoting the personal Antichrist (9:2).

Satan, as a "great red dragon," is to draw the third part of the stars of heaven (12:4), meaning, his soul-destroying influence permeating the western part of the Roman earth. What intolerable agony will be experienced when the fourth bowl of wrath is poured on the sun, and men are burnt (16:8, 9)! In God's New Jerusalem there will be no need of sun, moon, and stars. No created or artificial light will be required for all who bask in the undimmed glory of the Lord (22:3-5).

Under the sixth bowl of wrath (16:12-16), the great river Euphrates is dried up, suggesting the removal of a barrier by an act of judgment, so that the Eastern nations can the more readily pour their armies into Canaan. The appearance of "frogs" reminds us of the Egyptian plague (Exodus 8:1-14). Allusion to copious rains from heaven (11:6) takes us back to Elijah's supernatural power to close the skies (I Kings 17:1). Another miracle already considered, and appearing in the apocalypse, is the supernatural transference from one place to another. Space presents no barrier to God (I Kings 18:12; Acts 8:39). The woman's flight into the wilderness affords another illustration of the miraculous, rapid motion God alone can provide (12:13-17), just as John's movement in the Spirit likewise indicate (1:10; 4:1, 2).

Words may tell of that transhuman change

. . .

Thou know'st, who by Thy light didst
bear me up.

Speech (13:5, 6)
Another miracle is that related to man's speech. Men may say, "Our lips are our own: who is lord over us" (Psalm 12:4), but God makes it clear that He has power over speech and language, as we saw in the miracles of Babel and of Pentecost. In the portion before us, the Beast was given

"a mouth speaking great things and blasphemies," and as he opened his mouth, it was to blaspheme God, His Name, His Tabernacle, and them that dwell in heaven. Power also was his over "tongues." Liberty to speak was *given* unto the Beast. He had no power beyond what was given; "behind his reckless and apparently irresistible power there stands the veiled but real power of God." Did not Jesus say to Pilate, "Thou couldest have no power against Me, except it were given thee from above"?

After reviewing the fascinating displays of divine power in every realm throughout the Bible, what else can we do but join in the glorious Song of Moses, and the Song of the Lamb, saying,

Great and marvellous are Thy works,
Lord God Almighty.
Just and true are Thy ways,
Thou King of the nations.

Who will not fear, O Lord, and glorify
Thy name?
Because Thou only art holy.

Because all the nations shall come and
worship
In Thy presence:
Because Thy judgments were manifested.

God's miracle Book closes with a benediction for mind and heart and life—"The grace of our Lord Jesus Christ be with you all" (22:21). This, too, is the prayer of my heart, as the writer of this volume, for all those who may read it. An old bookmark I have bears the adage—"To open a good book is to unlock the gate of a new world." I would fain believe that to the best of my ability and under divine direction, I have produced a book of value and that it will unlock the gate of a new world of the power of Him who is great and greatly to be praised.

BIBLIOGRAPHY

When this work on *All the Miracles of the Bible* was decided upon by the publishers and myself, the first effort was to seek out those writers who had dealt with such a field of Bible study. It was somewhat revealing *and* disappointing to discover that there are hardly any books extant covering Bible miracles as a whole. Volumes were found dealing with selected miracles. Reliable and exhaustive commentators touch upon the miracles as they occur in the Bible. The majority of published works, however, only expound the miracles recorded in the four gospels, and particularly those associated with the life and labors of our Lord, as the following list reveals.

Best, John H. *The Miracles of Christ.* London: Society for Promoting Christian Knowledge, 1937.

Boulton, A. H. *The Place of Miracles in Modern Thought and Knowledge.* London: Victoria Institute, 1950.

Brewer, Cobham. E. *A Dictionary of Miracles.* London: Chatto and Windus, 1901.

Bruce, A. B. *The Miraculous Element in the Gospels.* Edinburgh: T. and T. Clark, 1900.

Burns, Jabez. *Sermons on the Parables and Miracles of Christ.* Grand Rapids: Zondervan Publishing House, 1954.

Colett, Sidney. *The Scripture of Truth.* London: Partridge & Co., 1904.

Cumming, John. *Lectures on Our Lord's Miracles.* London: Arthur Hall, Co., 1854.

Davies, Lt. Col. Merson. *The Bible and Modern Science.* London: Marshall, Morgan and Scott.

Davies, O. E. *The Miracles of Jesus.* London: Hodder and Stoughton, 1913.

Fereday, M. W. *Our Lord's Miracles.* Kilmarnock, Scotland, 1940.

Fraser, Neil, *The Grandeur of Golgotha.* London: Pickering and Inglis, 1959.

Habershon, A. R. *The Study of Miracles.*

Grand Rapids: Kregel Publications, 1957.

Laidlaw, J. *The Miracles of Our Lord.* London: Hodder and Stoughton, 1897.

Lang, Cosmo Gordon. *The Miracles of Jesus.* London: Isaac Pitman & Sons, 1906.

Le Bas, C. W. *Considerations on Miracles.* London: W. Blackwood, 1828.

———. *Lectures on New Testament Miracles.* London: W. Blackwood, 1927.

Lias, J. J. *Are Miracles Credible?* London: Hodder and Stoughton, 1928.

London Minister, A. *Miracles and Parables of the Old Testament.* Grand Rapids: Baker Book House, 1959.

Macintyre, R. S. *Bible Types and Parables.* Wheaton, Illinois: Van Kampen Press, 1940.

Micklem, E. R. *Miracles and the New Psychology.* London: Oxford University Press, 1922.

Morgan, G. Campbell. *Crises of the Christ.* London: Hodder and Stoughton, 1910.

Pember, George. *Earth's Earliest Ages.* London: Pickering and Inglis, 1900.

Spurgeon, C. H. *The Miracles of Our Lord.* London: Marshall, Morgan and Scott, 1959.

Taylor, William U. *The Gospel Miracles.* London: Hamilton, Adams Co., 1880.

———. *The Miracles of Our Saviour.* London: Hamilton, Adams Co., 1827.

Thomas, W. H. Griffith. *The Apostle John.* Grand Rapids: Wm. B. Eerdmans, 1948.

Thomson, W. D. *The Christian Miracles.* Edinburgh: T. and T. Clark, 1950.

Thomson. *Land and the Book.* New York: T. Nelson, 1891.

Thorne, Henry. *Readings in Genesis.* Sterling, Scotland: Drummonds Tract Depot.

Trench, C. R. *The Miracles of Our Lord.* London: Kegan Paul, Trench Co., 1889. Abbreviated volume by Baker Book House, Grand Rapids, Michigan, U.S.A.

Webster, T. S. *Jonah.* London: Marshall, Morgan and Scott, 1906.

Wood, Nathan. *The Secret of the Universe.* London: Perry Jackman, 1957.

For an examination of words and phrases, use was made of two valuable study books:

Vincent, Marvin R. *Word Studies in the New Testament.* 4 vols. New York: Charles Scribner, 1906.

Vine, W. E. *Expository Dictionary of New Testament Words.* London: Oliphants Ltd., 1940.

Grateful and liberal use was made of the following commentaries and Bible study books:

Baxter, J. Sidlow. *Explore the Book.* 6 vols. Grand Rapids: Zondervan Publishing House, 1960.

Bullinger, E. *Companion Bible.* London: The Lamp Press, 1957.

Edersheim, Alfred. *The Life and Times of Jesus the Messiah.* 2 vols. Grand Rapids: Wm. B. Eerdmans, 1959.

Ellicott, C. J. *Commentary on the Whole Bible.* 8 vols. Grand Rapids: Zondervan Publishing House. 1954.

Fairbairn, Patrick. *Fairbairn's Imperial Standard Bible Encyclopedia.* 6 vols. Grand Rapids: Zondervan Publishing House, 1957.

Fausset, A. R. *Fausset's Bible Dictionary.* Grand Rapids: Zondervan Publishing House, 1956.

Glover, Richard. *A Teacher's Commentary on the Gospel of Matthew.* Grand Rapids: Zondervan Publishing House, 1956.

Halley, H. H. *Halley's Bible Handbook.* Grand Rapids: Zondervan Publishing House, 1960.

Hastings, James. *Dictionary of the Bible.* Edinburgh: T. and T. Clark, 1949.

Henry, Carl F. H. *The Bible Expositor.* 3 vols. London: Pickering and Inglis, 1960.

Hottel, S. W. *Through the Bible Book by Book.* 9 vols. Cleveland, Ohio: Union Gospel Press, 1950.

Jamieson, Fausset and Brown. *Commentary on the Whole Bible.* Grand Rapids: Zondervan Publishing House.

Josephus. *Complete Works.* Translated by William Winston. Grand Rapids: Kregel Publications, 1960.

Morgan, G. Campbell. *An Exposition of the Whole Bible.* London: Pickering and Inglis, 1960.

Scroggie, W. Graham. *A Guide to the Gospels.* London: Pickering and Inglis, 1948.

Simeon, Charles. *Expository Outlines on the Whole Bible.* 21 vols. Grand Rapids: Zondervan Publishing House, 1956.

The International Standard Bible Encyclopedia. Ed. by James Orr, and others. Chicago: The Howard-Severance Company, 1957. 6 vols.

SUBJECT INDEX

A

SCRIPTURE INDEX